Lecture Notes in Computer Scier

Stefano Spaccapietra (Ed.)

Journal on Data Semantics VII

Springer

Volume Editor

Stefano Spaccapietra
Database Laboratory, EPFL
1015 Lausanne, Switzerland
E-mail: stefano.spaccapietra@epfl.ch

Library of Congress Control Number: 2006935770

CR Subject Classification (1998): H.2, H.3, I.2, H.4, C.2

LNCS Sublibrary: SL 3 – Information Systems and Application, incl. Internet/Web and HCI

ISSN 0302-9743
ISBN-10 3-540-46329-1 Springer Berlin Heidelberg New York
ISBN-13 978-3-540-46329-0 Springer Berlin Heidelberg New York

Springer is a part of Springer Science+Business Media

springer.com

Typesetting: Camera-ready by author, data conversion by Scientific Publishing Services, Chennai, India
Printed on acid-free paper SPIN: 11890591 06/3142 5 4 3 2 1 0

The LNCS Journal on Data Semantics

Computerized information handling has changed its focus from centralized data management systems to decentralized data exchange facilities. Modern distribution channels, such as high-speed Internet networks and wireless communication infrastructure, provide reliable technical support for data distribution and data access, materializing the new, popular idea that data may be available to anybody, anywhere, anytime. However, providing huge amounts of data on request often turns into a counterproductive service, making the data useless because of poor relevance or inappropriate level of detail. Semantic knowledge is the essential missing piece that allows the delivery of information that matches user requirements. Semantic agreement, in particular, is essential to meaningful data exchange.

Semantic issues have long been open issues in data and knowledge management. However, the boom in semantically poor technologies, such as the Web and XML, has boosted renewed interest in semantics. Conferences on the Semantic Web, for instance, attract crowds of participants, while ontologies on their own have become a hot and popular topic in the database and artificial intelligence communities.

Springer's LNCS *Journal on Data Semantics* aims at providing a highly visible dissemination channel for most remarkable work that in one way or another addresses research and development on issues related to the semantics of data. The target domain ranges from theories supporting the formal definition of semantic content to innovative domain-specific application of semantic knowledge. This publication channel should be of the highest interest to researchers and advanced practitioners working on the Semantic Web, interoperability, mobile information services, data warehousing, knowledge representation and reasoning, conceptual database modeling, ontologies, and artificial intelligence.

Topics of relevance to this journal include:

- Semantic interoperability, semantic mediators
- Ontologies
- Ontology, schema and data integration, reconciliation and alignment
- Multiple representations, alternative representations
- Knowledge representation and reasoning
- Conceptualization and representation
- Multi-model and multi-paradigm approaches
- Mappings, transformations, reverse engineering
- Metadata
- Conceptual data modeling
- Integrity description and handling
- Evolution and change
- Web semantics and semi-structured data
- Semantic caching

- Data warehousing and semantic data mining
- Spatial, temporal, multimedia and multimodal semantics
- Semantics in data visualization
- Semantic services for mobile users
- Supporting tools
- Applications of semantic-driven approaches

These topics are to be understood as specifically related to semantic issues. Contributions submitted to the journal and dealing with semantics of data will be considered even if they are not within the topics in the list.

While the physical appearance of the journal issues looks like the books from the well-known Springer LNCS series, the mode of operation is that of a journal. Contributions can be freely submitted by authors and are reviewed by the Editorial Board. Contributions may also be invited, and nevertheless carefully reviewed, as in the case for issues that contain extended versions of best papers from major conferences addressing data semantics issues. Special issues, focusing on a specific topic, are coordinated by guest editors once the proposal for a special issue is accepted by the Editorial Board. Finally, it is also possible that a journal issue be devoted to a single text.

The journal published its first volume in 2003 (LNCS 2800). That initial volume, as well as volumes II (LNCS 3360), III (LNCS 3534), V (LNCS 3870), and coming volume VIII represent the annual occurrence of a special issue devoted to publication of selected extended versions of best conference papers from previous year conferences. Volumes III and VI are annual special issues on a dedicated topic. Volume III, coordinated by guest editor Esteban Zimányi, addressed Semantic-based Geographical Information Systems, while volume VI, coordinated by guest editors Karl Aberer and Philippe Cudre-Mauroux, addressed Emergent Semantics. The fourth volume was the first "normal" volume, built from spontaneous submissions on any of the topics of interest to the Journal. This volume VII is the second of this type.

The Editorial Board comprises one Editor-in-Chief (with overall responsibility), a co-editor-in-chief, and several members. The Editor-in-Chief has a four-year mandate. Members of the board have a three-year mandate. Mandates are renewable. New members may be elected anytime.

We are happy to welcome you to our readership and authorship, and hope we will share this privileged contact for a long time.

Stefano Spaccapietra
Editor-in-Chief
http://lbdwww.epfl.ch/e/Springer/

JoDS Volume VII – Preface

This JoDS volume results from a rigorous selection among 35 abstract/paper submissions received in response to a call for contributions issued July 2005.

After two rounds of reviews, nine papers, spanning a wide variety of topics, were eventually accepted for publication. They are listed in the table of contents herein.

We would like to thank authors of all submitted papers as well as all reviewers who contributed to improving the papers through their detailed comments.

Forthcoming volume VIII will contain extended versions of best papers from 2005 conferences covering semantics aspects. Its publication is expected towards the end of 2006.

We hope you'll enjoy reading this volume.

Stefano Spaccapietra
Editor-in-Chief

Reviewers

We are very grateful to the external reviewers listed below who helped the editorial board in the reviewing task:

Daniele Barone, Università Milano Bicocca, Italy
Stefano Borgo, Laboratory for Applied Ontology (ISTC-CNR), Italy
Federico Cabitza, Università Milano Bicocca, Italy
Flavio De Paoli, Università Milano Bicocca, Italy
Denise de Vries, Flinders University, Australia
Ying Ding, University of Innsbruck, Austria
Gillian Dobbie, University of Auckland, New Zealand
Fabrice Estiévenart, University of Namur, Belgium
Silvia Gabrielli, Università di Roma 1 "La Sapienza," Italy
Birte Glimm, The University of Manchester, UK
Giancarlo Guizzardi, Laboratory for Applied Ontology (ISTC-CNR), Italy
Benjamin Habegger, Università di Roma 1 "La Sapienza," Italy
Markus Kirchberg, Massey University, New Zealand
Jacek Kopecký, DERI Innsbruck, Austria
Changqing Li, National University of Singapore, Singapore
Sebastian Link, Massey University, New Zealand
Andrea Maurino, Università Milano Bicocca, Italy
Jean-Roch Meurisse, University of Namur, Belgium
Diego Milano, Università di Roma 1 "La Sapienza," Italy
Wei Nei, National University of Singapore, Singapore
Fabio Porto, EPFL, Switzerland
Saurav Sahay, Georgia Institute of Technology, USA
Christelle Vangenot, EPFL, Switzerland
Evgeny Zolin, The University of Manchester, UK

JoDS Editorial Board

Table of Contents

Discovering the Semantics of Relational Tables Through Mappings *

Yuan An[1], Alex Borgida[2], and John Mylopoulos[1]

[1] Department of Computer Science, University of Toronto, Canada
{yuana, jm}@cs.toronto.edu
[2] Department of Computer Science, Rutgers University, USA
borgida@cs.rutgers.edu

Abstract. Many problems in Information and Data Management require a semantic account of a database schema. At its best, such an account consists of formulas expressing the relationship ("mapping") between the schema and a formal conceptual model or ontology (CM) of the domain. In this paper we describe the underlying principles, algorithms, and a prototype tool that finds such semantic mappings from relational tables to ontologies, when given as input *simple correspondences* from columns of the tables to datatype properties of classes in an ontology. Although the algorithm presented is necessarily heuristic, we offer formal results showing that the answers returned by the tool are "correct" for relational schemas designed according to standard Entity-Relationship techniques. To evaluate its usefulness and effectiveness, we have applied the tool to a number of public domain schemas and ontologies. Our experience shows that significant effort is saved when using it to build semantic mappings from relational tables to ontologies.

Keywords: Semantics, ontologies, mappings, semantic interoperability.

1 Introduction and Motivation

A number of important database problems have been shown to have improved solutions by using a conceptual model or an ontology (CM) to provide *precise semantics* for a database schema. These[1] include federated databases, data warehousing [2], and information integration through mediated schemas [13,8]. Since much information on the web is generated from databases (the "deep web"), the recent call for a Semantic Web, which requires a connection between web content and ontologies, provides additional motivation for the problem of associating semantics with database-resident data (e.g., [10]). In almost all of these cases, semantics of the data is captured by some kind of *semantic mapping* between the database schema and the CM. Although sometimes the mapping is just a *simple* association from terms to terms, in other cases what is required is a *complex* formula, often expressed in logic or a query language [14].

For example, in both the Information Manifold data integration system presented in [13] and the DWQ data warehousing system [2], formulas of the form $T(\overline{X})$:- $\Phi(\overline{X}, \overline{Y})$

* This is an expanded and refined version of a research paper presented at ODBASE'05 [1].

[1] For a survey, see [23].

S. Spaccapietra (Ed.): Journal on Data Semantics VII, LNCS 4244, pp. 1–32, 2006.

are used to connect a relational data source to a CM expressed in terms of a Description Logic, where $T(\overline{X})$ is a single predicate representing a table in the relational data source, and $\Phi(\overline{X},\overline{Y})$ is a conjunctive formula over the predicates representing the concepts and relationships in the CM. In the literature, such a formalism is called local-as-view (LAV), in contrast to global-as-view (GAV), where atomic ontology concepts and properties are specified by queries over the database [14].

In all previous work it has been assumed that *humans* specify the mapping formulas – a difficult, time-consuming and error-prone task, especially since the specifier must be familiar with both the semantics of the database schema and the contents of the ontology. As the size and complexity of ontologies increase, it becomes desirable to have some kind of computer tool to assist people in the task. Note that the problem of semantic mapping discovery is superficially similar to that of database schema mapping, however the goal of the later is finding queries/rules for integrating/translating/exchanging the underlying data. Mapping schemas to ontologies, on the other hand, is aimed at understanding the semantics of a schema expressed in terms of a given semantic model. This requires paying special attentions to various semantic constructs in both schema and ontology languages.

We have proposed in [1] a tool that assists users in discovering mapping formulas between relational database schemas and ontologies, and presented the algorithms and the formal results. In this paper, we provide, in addition to what appears in [1], more detailed examples for explaining the algorithms, and we also present proofs to the formal results. Moreover, we show how to handle GAV formulas that are often useful for many practical data integration systems. The heuristics that underlie the discovery process are based on a careful study of standard design process relating the constructs of the relational model with those of conceptual modeling languages. In order to improve the effectiveness of our tool, we assume some user input in addition to the database schema and the ontology. Specifically, inspired by the Clio project [17], we expect the tool user to provide *simple correspondences* between atomic elements used in the database schema (e.g., column names of tables) and those in the ontology (e.g., attribute/"data type property" names of concepts). Given the set of correspondences, the tool is expected to reason about the database schema and the ontology, and to generate a list of candidate formulas for each table in the relational database. Ideally, one of the formulas is the correct one — capturing user intention underlying given correspondences. The claim is that, compared to composing logical formulas representing semantic mappings, it is much easier for users to (i) draw simple correspondences/arrows from column names of tables in the database to datatype properties of classes in the ontology[2] and then (ii) evaluate proposed formulas returned by the tool. The following example illustrates the input/output behavior of the tool proposed.

Example 1.1. An ontology contains concepts (classes), attributes of concepts (datatype properties of classes), relationships between concepts (associations), and cardinality constraints on occurrences of the participating concepts in a relationship. Graphically, we use the UML notations to represent the above information. Figure 1 is an enterprise ontology containing some basic concepts and relationships. (Recall that cardinality

[2] In fact, there exist already tools used in schema matching which help perform such tasks using linguistic, structural, and statistical information (e.g., [4,21]).

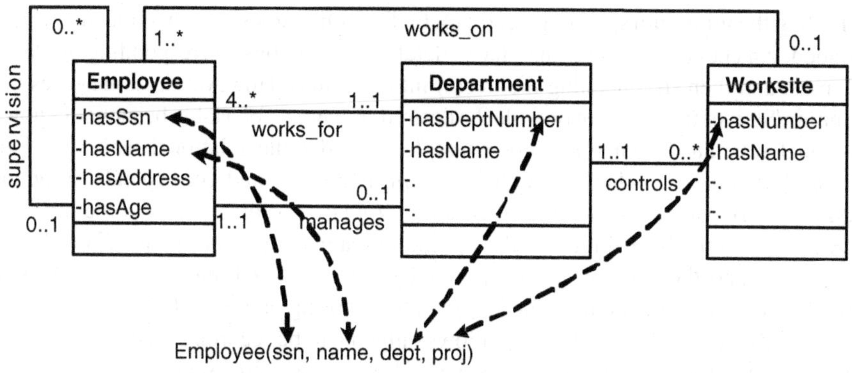

Fig. 1. Relational table, Ontology, and Correspondences

constraints in UML are written at the opposite end of the association: a Department has at least 4 Employees working for it, and an Employee works in one Department.) Suppose we wish to discover the semantics of a relational table $Employee(\underline{ssn}, name, dept, proj)$ with key ssn in terms of the enterprise ontology. Suppose that by looking at column names of the table and the ontology graph, the user draws the simple correspondences shown as dashed arrows in Figure 1. This indicates, for example, that the ssn column corresponds to the $hasSsn$ property of the $Employee$ concept. Using prefixes $\mathcal{T}$ and $\mathcal{O}$ to distinguish tables in the relational schema and concepts in the ontology (both of which will eventually be thought of as predicates), we represent the correspondences as follows:

$\mathcal{T} : Employee.ssn \leftrightsquigarrow \mathcal{O} : Employee.hasSsn$

$\mathcal{T} : Employee.name \leftrightsquigarrow \mathcal{O} : Employee.hasName$

$\mathcal{T} : Employee.dept \leftrightsquigarrow \mathcal{O} : Department.hasDeptNumber$

$\mathcal{T} : Employee.proj \leftrightsquigarrow \mathcal{O} : Worksite.hasNumber$

Given the above inputs, the tool is expected to produce a list of plausible mapping formulas, which would hopefully include the following formula, expressing a possible semantics for the table:

$\mathcal{T}$:Employee($ssn, name, dept, proj$) :-
 $\mathcal{O}$:Employee(x_1), $\mathcal{O}$:hasSsn(x_1,ssn), $\mathcal{O}$:hasName(x_1,$name$), $\mathcal{O}$:Department(x_2),
 $\mathcal{O}$:works_for(x_1,x_2), $\mathcal{O}$:hasDeptNumber(x_2,$dept$), $\mathcal{O}$:Worksite(x_3), $\mathcal{O}$:works_on(x_1,x_3),
 $\mathcal{O}$:hasNumber(x_3,$proj$).

Note that, as explained in [14], the above, admittedly confusing notation in the literature, should really be interpreted as the First Order Logic formula

$(\forall ssn, name, dept, proj)\ \mathcal{T}$:Employee$(ssn, name, dept, proj) \Rightarrow$
$(\exists x_1, x_2, x_3)\ \mathcal{O}$:Employee$(x_1) \wedge \ldots$

because the ontology *explains* what is in the table (i.e., every tuple corresponds to an employee), rather than guaranteeing that the table satisfies the closed world assumption (i.e., for every employee there is a tuple in the table). ■

An intuitive (but somewhat naive) solution, inspired by early work of Quillian [20], is based on finding the *shortest* connections between concepts. Technically, this involves

(i) finding the minimum spanning tree(s) (actually Steiner trees[3]) connecting the "corresponded concepts" — those that have datatype properties corresponding to table columns, and then (ii) encoding the tree(s) into formulas. However, in some cases the spanning/Steiner tree may not provide the desired semantics for a table because of known relational schema design rules. For example, consider the relational table $Project$ ($\underline{name}$, $supervisor$), where the column $name$ is the key and corresponds to the attribute $\mathcal{O}$:$Worksite.hasName$, and column $supervisor$ corresponds to the attribute $\mathcal{O}$:$Employee.hasSsn$ in Figure 1. The minimum spanning tree consisting of $Worksite$, $Employee$, and the edge $works\_on$ probably does not match the semantics of table $Project$ because there are multiple $Employee$s working on a $Worksite$ according to the ontology cardinality, yet the table allows only one to be recorded, since $supervisor$ is functionally dependent on $name$, the key. Therefore we must seek a functional connection from $Worksite$ to $Employee$, and the connection will be the manager of the department controlling the worksite. In this paper, we use ideas of standard relational schema design from ER diagrams in order to craft heuristics that systematically uncover the connections between the constructs of relational schemas and those of ontologies. We propose a tool to generate "reasonable" trees connecting the set of corresponded concepts in an ontology. In contrast to the graph theoretic results which show that there may be too many minimum spanning/Steiner trees among the ontology nodes (for example, there are already 5 minimum spanning trees connecting $Employee$, $Department$, and $Worksite$ in the very simple graph in Figure 1), we expect the tool to generate only a small number of "reasonable" trees. These expectations are born out by our experimental results, in Section 6.

As mentioned earlier, our approach is directly inspired by the Clio project [17,18], which developed a successful tool that infers mappings from one set of relational tables and/or XML schemas to another, given just a set of correspondences between their respective attributes. Without going into further details at this point, we summarize the contributions of this work:

- We identify a new version of the data mapping problem: that of *inferring* complex formulas expressing the semantic mapping between relational database schemas and ontologies from simple correspondences.
- We propose an algorithm to find "reasonable" tree connection(s) in the ontology graph. The algorithm is enhanced to take into account information about the schema (key and foreign key structure), the ontology (cardinality restrictions), and standard database schema design guidelines.
- To gain theoretical confidence, we give formal results for a limited class of schemas. We show that if the schema was designed from a CM using techniques well-known in the Entity Relationship literature (which provide a natural semantic mapping and correspondences for each table), then the tool will recover essentially all and only the appropriate semantics. This shows that our heuristics are not just shots in the dark: in the case when the ontology has no extraneous material, and when a table's scheme has not been denormalized, the algorithm will produce good results.

[3] A Steiner tree for a set M of nodes in graph G is a minimum spanning tree of M that may contain nodes of G which are not in M.

- To test the effectiveness and usefulness of the algorithm in practice, we implemented the algorithm in a prototype tool and applied it to a variety of database schemas and ontologies drawn from a number of domains. We ensured that the schemas and the ontologies were developed independently; and the schemas might or might not be derived from a CM using the standard techniques. Our experience has shown that the user effort in specifying complex mappings by using the tool is significantly less than that by manually writing formulas from scratch.

The rest of the paper is structured as follows. We contrast our approach with related work in Section 2, and in Section 3 we present the technical background and notation. Section 4 describes an intuitive progression of ideas underlying our approach, while Section 5 provides the mapping inference algorithm. In Section 6 we report on the prototype implementation of these ideas and experiments with the prototype. Section 7 shows how to filter out unsatisfied mapping formulas by ontology reasoning. Section 8 discusses the issues of generating GAV mapping formulas. Finally, Section 9 concludes and discusses future work.

2 Related Work

The Clio tool [17,18] discovers formal queries describing how target schemas can be populated with data from source schemas. To compare with it, we could view the present work as extending Clio to the case when the source schema is a relational database while the target is an ontology. For example, in Example 1.1, if one viewed the ontology as a relational schema made of unary tables (such as $Employee(x_1)$), binary tables (such as $hasSsn(x_1, ssn)$) and the obvious foreign key constraints from binary to unary tables, then one could in fact try to apply directly the Clio algorithm to the problem. The desired mapping formula from Example 1.1 would not be produced for several reasons: (i) Clio [18] works by taking each table and using a chase-like algorithm to repeatedly extend it with columns that appear as foreign keys referencing other tables. Such "logical relations" in the source and target are then connected by queries. In this particular case, this would lead to logical relations such as $works\_for \bowtie Employee \bowtie Department$, but none that join, through some intermediary, $hasSsn(x_1, ssn)$ and $hasDeptNumber(x_2, dept)$, which is part of the desired formula in this case. (ii) The fact that ssn is a key in the table T:$Employee$, leads us to prefer (see Section 4) a many-to-one relationship, such as $works\_for$, over some many-to-many relationship which could have been part of the ontology (e.g., $\mathcal{O}$:$previouslyWorkedFor$); Clio does not differentiate the two. So the work to be presented here analyzes the key structure of the tables and the semantics of relationships (cardinality, IsA) to eliminate/downgrade *unreasonable* options that arise in mappings to ontologies.

Other potentially relevant work includes *data reverse engineering*, which aims to extract a CM, such as an ER diagram, from a database schema. Sophisticated algorithms and approaches to this have appeared in the literature over the years (e.g., [15,9]). The major difference between data reverse engineering and our work is that we are given an existing ontology, and want to interpret a legacy relational schema in terms of it, whereas data reverse engineering aims to construct a new ontology.

Schema matching (e.g., [4,21]) identifies semantic relations between schema elements based on their names, data types, constraints, and schema structures. The primary goal is to find the one-to-one simple correspondences which are part of the input for our mapping inference algorithms.

3 Formal Preliminaries

We do not restrict ourselves to any particular language for describing ontologies in this paper. Instead, we use a generic conceptual modeling language (CML), which contains *common* aspects of most semantic data models, UML, ontology languages such as OWL, and description logics. In the sequel, we use CM to denote an ontology prescribed by the generic CML. Specifically, the language allows the representation of *classes/concepts* (unary predicates over individuals), *object properties/relationships* (binary predicates relating individuals), and *datatype properties/attributes* (binary predicates relating individuals with values such as integers and strings); attributes are single valued in this paper. Concepts are organized in the familiar **is-a** hierarchy. Object properties, and their inverses (which are always present), are subject to constraints such as specification of domain and range, plus cardinality constraints, which here allow 1 as lower bounds (called *total* relationships), and 1 as upper bounds (called *functional* relationships).

We shall represent a given CM using a labeled directed graph, called an *ontology graph*. We construct the ontology graph from a CM as follows: We create a concept node labeled with C for each concept C, and an edge labeled with p from the concept node C_1 to the concept node C_2 for each object property p with domain C_1 and range C_2; for each such p, there is also an edge in the opposite direction for its inverse, referred to as p^-. For each attribute f of concept C, we create a separate attribute node denoted as $N_{f,C}$, whose label is f, and add an edge labeled f from node C to $N_{f,C}$.[4] For each **is-a** edge from a subconcept C_1 to a superconcept C_2, we create an edge labeled with *is-a* from concept node C_1 to concept node C_2. For the sake of succinctness, we sometimes use UML notations, as in Figure 1, to represent the ontology graph. Note that in such a diagram, instead of drawing separate attribute nodes, we place the attributes inside the rectangle nodes; and relationships and their inverses are represented by a single undirected edge. The presence of such an undirected edge, labeled p, between concepts C and D will be written in text as `[C] ---p--- [D]`. If the relationship p is functional from C to D, we write `[C] ---p->-- [D]`. For expressive CMLs such as OWL, we may also connect C to D by p if we find an existential restriction stating that each instance of C is related to *some* instance or *only* instances of D by p.

For relational databases, we assume the reader is familiar with standard notions as presented in [22], for example. We will use the notation $T(\underline{K}, Y)$ to represent a relational table T with columns KY, and key K. If necessary, we will refer to the individual columns in Y using $Y[1], Y[2], \ldots$, and use XY as concatenation of columns. Our notational convention is that single column names are either indexed or appear in lower-case. Given a table such as T above, we use the notation key(T), nonkey(T) and columns(T) to refer to K, Y and KY respectively. (Note that we use the terms "table" and "column" when talking about relational schemas, reserving "relation(ship)" and

[4] Unless ambiguity arises, we say "node C", when we mean "concept node labeled C".

"attribute" for aspects of the CM.) A foreign key (abbreviated as *f.k.* henceforth) in T is a set of columns F that *references* the key of table T', and imposes a constraint that the projection of T on F is a subset of the projection of T' on $\mathsf{key}(T')$.

In this paper, a *correspondence* $T.c \leftrightsquigarrow D.f$ relates column c of table T to attribute f of concept D. Since our algorithms deal with ontology graphs, formally a correspondence L will be a mathematical relation $L(T, c, D, f, N_{f,D})$, where the first two arguments determine unique values for the last three. This means that we only treat the case when a table column corresponds to single attribute of a concept, and leave to future work dealing with complex correspondences, which may represent unions, concatenations, etc.

Finally, for LAV-like mapping, we use Horn-clauses in the form $T(X)$:- $\Phi(X, Y)$, as described in Section 1, to represent *semantic mappings*, where T is a table with columns X (which become arguments to its predicate), and Φ is a conjunctive formula over predicates representing the CM, with Y existentially quantified, as usual.

4 Principles of Mapping Inference

Given a table T, and correspondences L to an ontology provided by a person or a tool, let the set $\mathcal{C}_T$ consist of those concept nodes which have at least one attribute corresponding to some column of T (i.e., D such that there is at least one tuple $L(\_, \_, D, \_, \_)$). Our task is to find semantic connections between concepts in $\mathcal{C}_T$, because attributes can then be connected to the result using the correspondence relation: for any node D, one can imagine having edges f to M, for every entry $L(\_, \_, D, f, M)$. The primary principle of our mapping inference algorithm is to look for *smallest* "reasonable" trees connecting nodes in $\mathcal{C}_T$. We will call such a tree a *semantic tree*.

As mentioned before, the naive solution of finding minimum spanning trees or Steiner trees does not give good results, because it must also be "reasonable". We aim to describe more precisely this notion of "reasonableness".

Consider the case when $T(\underline{c}, b)$ is a table with key c, corresponding to an attribute f on concept C, and b is a foreign key corresponding to an attribute e on concept B. Then for each value of c (and hence instance of C), T associates at most one value of b (instance of B). Hence the semantic mapping for T should be some formula that acts as a function from its first to its second argument. The semantic trees for such formulas look like functional edges in the ontology, and hence are more reasonable. For example, given table $Dep(\underline{dept}, ssn, \ldots)$, and correspondences
$T{:}Dep.dept \leftrightsquigarrow O{:}Department.hasDeptNumber$
$T{:}Dep.ssn \leftrightsquigarrow O{:}Employee.hasSsn$
from the table columns to attributes of the ontology in Figure 1, the proper semantic tree uses `manages`$^-$ (i.e., `hasManager`) rather than `works_for`$^-$ (i.e., `hasWorkers`).

Conversely, for table $T'(\underline{c, b})$, where c and b are as above, an edge that is functional from C to B, or from B to C, is likely not to reflect a proper semantics since it would mean that the key chosen for T' is actually a super-key – an unlikely error. (In our example, consider a table $T(\underline{ssn, dept})$, where both columns are foreign keys.)

To deal with such problems, our algorithm works in two stages: first connects the concepts corresponding to key columns into a *skeleton tree*, then connects the rest of the corresponded nodes to the skeleton by functional edges (whenever possible).

We must however also deal with the assumption that the relational schema and the CM were developed independently, which implies that not all parts of the CM are reflected in the database schema. This complicates things, since in building the semantic tree we may need to go through additional nodes, which end up not corresponding to columns of the relational table. For example, consider again the table $Project(\underline{name}, supervisor)$ and its correspondences mentioned in Section 1. Because of the key structure of this table, based on the above arguments we will prefer the functional *path*[5] `controls⁻.manages⁻` (i.e., `controlledBy` followed by `hasManager`), passing through node *Department*, over the shorter path consisting of edge `works_on`, which is not functional. Similar situations arise when the CM contains detailed *aggregation* hierarchies (e.g., $city$ part-of $township$ part-of $county$ part-of $state$), which are abstracted in the database (e.g., a table with columns for $city$ and $state$ only).

We have chosen to flesh out the above principles in a systematic manner by considering the behavior of our proposed algorithm on relational schemas designed from Entity Relationship diagrams — a technique widely covered in undergraduate database courses [22]. (We refer to this er2rel *schema design*.) One benefit of this approach is that it allows us to prove that our algorithm, though heuristic in general, is in some sense "correct" for a certain class of schemas. Of course, in practice such schemas may be "denormalized" in order to improve efficiency, and, as we mentioned, only parts of the CM may be realized in the database. Our algorithm uses the general principles enunciated above even in such cases, with relatively good results in practice. Also note that the assumption that a given relational schema was designed from some ER conceptual model does not mean that given ontology is this ER model, or is even expressed in the ER notation. In fact, our heuristics have to cope with the fact that it is missing essential information, such as keys for weak entities.

To reduce the complexity of the algorithms, which essentially enumerate all trees, and to reduce the size of the answer set, we modify an ontology graph by collapsing multiple edges between nodes E and F, labeled $p_1, p_2, \ldots$ say, into at most three edges, each labeled by a string of the form $'p_{j_1}; p_{j_2}; \ldots'$: one of the edges has the names of all functions from E to F; the other all functions from F to E; and the remaining labels on the third edge. (Edges with empty labels are dropped.) Note that there is no way that our algorithm can distinguish between semantics of the labels on one kind of edge, so the tool offers all of them. It is up to the user to choose between alternative labels, though the system may offer suggestions, based on additional information such as heuristics concerning the identifiers labeling tables and columns, and their relationship to property names.

5 Semantic Mapping Inference Algorithms

As mentioned, our algorithm is based in part on the relational database schema design methodology from ER models. We introduce the details of the algorithm iteratively, by incrementally adding features of an ER model that appear as part of the CM. We assume

[5] One consisting of a sequence of edges, each of which represents a function from its source to its target.

that the reader is familiar with basics of ER modeling and database design [22], though we summarize the ideas.

5.1 ER_0: An Initial Subset of ER Notions

We start with a subset, ER_0, of ER that supports entity sets E (called just "entity" here), with attributes (referred to by $\mathsf{attribs}(E)$), and binary relationship sets. In order to facilitate the statement of correspondences and theorems, we assume in this section that attributes in the CM have globally unique names. (Our implemented tool does not make this assumption.) An entity is represented as a concept/class in our CM. A binary relationship set corresponds to two properties in our CM, one for each direction. Such a relationship is called *many-many* if neither it nor its inverse is functional. A *strong entity* S has some attributes that act as identifier. We shall refer to these using $\mathsf{unique}(S)$ when describing the rules of schema design. A *weak entity* W has instead $\mathsf{localUnique}(W)$ attributes, plus a functional total binary relationship p (denoted as $\mathsf{idRel}(W)$) to an identifying owner entity (denoted as $\mathsf{idOwn}(W)$).

Example 5.1. An ER_0 diagram is shown in Figure 2, which has a weak entity *Dependent* and three strong entities: $Employee$, $Department$, and $Project$. The owner entity of *Dependent* is *Employee* and the identifying relationship is $dependents\_of$. Using the notation we introduced, this means that
$\mathsf{localUnique}(Dependent) = deName$, $\mathsf{idRel}(Dependent) = dependents\_of$, $\mathsf{idOwn}(Dependent) = Employee$. For the owner entity $Employee$, $\mathsf{unique}(Employee) = hasSsn$. ■

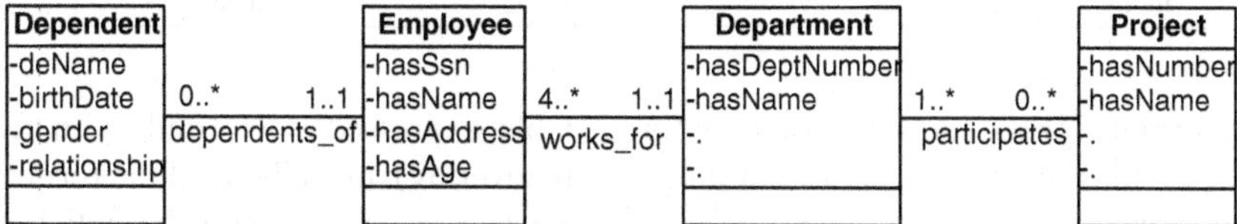

Fig. 2. An ER_0 Example

Note that information about multi-attribute keys cannot be represented formally in even highly expressive ontology languages such as OWL. So functions like unique are only used while describing the er2rel mapping, and are not assumed to be available during semantic inference. The er2rel design methodology (we follow mostly [15,22]) is defined by two components. To begin with, Table 1 specifies a mapping $\tau(O)$ returning a relational table scheme for every CM component O, where O is either a concept/entity or a binary relationship. (For each relationship exactly one of the directions will be stored in a table.)

In addition to the schema (columns, key, f.k.'s), Table 1 also associates with a relational table $T(V)$ a number of additional notions:

- an *anchor*, which is the central object in the CM from which T is derived, and which is useful in explaining our algorithm (it will be the root of the semantic tree);

Table 1. er2rel Design Mapping

ER Model object O	Relational Table τ(O)	
Strong Entity S	*columns:*	X
	primary key:	K
Let X=attribs(S)	*f.k.'s:*	none
Let K=unique(S)	*anchor:*	S
	semantics:	$T(X)$:- $S(y)$,hasAttribs(y, X).
	identifier:	identify$_S(y, K)$:- $S(y)$,hasAttribs(y, K).
Weak Entity W	*columns:*	ZX
let	*primary key:*	UX
E = idOwn(W)	*f.k.'s:*	X
P = idrel(W)	*anchor:*	W
Z=attribs(W)	*semantics:*	$T(X, U, V)$:- $W(y)$, hasAttribs(y, Z), $E(w)$,$P(y, w)$,
X = key($\tau(E)$)		identify$_E(w, X)$.
U =localUnique(W)	*identifier:*	identify$_W(y, UX)$:- $W(y)$,$E(w)$, $P(y, w)$, hasAttribs(y, U),
$V = Z - U$		identify$_E(w, X)$.
Functional	*columns:*	X_1X_2
Relationship F	*primary key:*	X_1
E_1 --F->- E_2	*f.k.'s:*	X_i references $\tau(E_i)$,
let X_i = key($\tau(E_i)$)	*anchor:*	E_1
for $i = 1, 2$	*semantics:*	$T(X_1, X_2)$:- $E_1(y_1)$,identify$_{E_1}(y_1, X_1)$, $F(y_1, y_2)$, $E_2(y_2)$,
		identify$_{E_2}(y2, X_2)$.
Many-many	*columns:*	X_1X_2
Relationship M	*primary key:*	X_1X_2
E_1 --M-- E_2	*f.k.'s:*	X_i references $\tau(E_i)$,
let X_i = key($\tau(E_i)$)	*semantics:*	$T(X_1, X_2)$:- $E_1(y_1)$,identify$_{E_1}(y_1, X_1)$, $M(y_1, y_2)$,$E_2(y_2)$,
for $i = 1, 2$		identify$_{E_2}(y2, X_2)$.

– a formula for the semantic mapping for the table, expressed as a formula with head $T(V)$ (this is what our algorithm should be recovering); in the body of the formula, the function hasAttribs(x, Y) returns conjuncts $attr_j(x, Y[j])$ for the individual columns $Y[1], Y[2], \ldots$ in Y, where $attr_j$ is the attribute name corresponded by column $Y[j]$.
– the formula for a predicate identify$_C(x, Y)$, showing how object x in (strong or weak) entity C can be identified by values in Y[6].

Note that τ is defined recursively, and will only terminate if there are no "cycles" in the CM (see [15] for definition of cycles in ER).

Example 5.2. When τ is applied to concept *Employee* in Figure 2, we get the table T:*Employee*(<u>*hasSsn*</u>, *hasName*, *hasAddress*, *hasAge*), with the anchor *Employee*, and the semantics expressed by the mapping:

T:Employee($hasSsn$, $hasName$, $hasAddress$, $hasAge$) :-
  $\mathcal{O}$:Employee(y), $\mathcal{O}$:hasSsn(y, $hasSsn$), $\mathcal{O}$:hasName(y, $hasName$),
  $\mathcal{O}$:hasAddress(y, $hasAddress$), $\mathcal{O}$:hasAge(y, $hasAge$).

[6] This is needed in addition to hasAttribs, because weak entities have identifying values spread over several concepts.

Its identifier is represented by
$\mathsf{identify}_{Employee}(y, hasSsn)$:- $\mathcal{O}$:Employee(y), $\mathcal{O}$:hasSsn($y, hasSsn$).

In turn, $\tau(Dependent)$ produces the table $\mathcal{T}$:$Dependent(\underline{deName, hasSsn}, birthDate,...)$, whose anchor is $Dependent$. Note that the $hasSsn$ column is a foreign key referencing the $hasSsn$ column in the $\mathcal{T}$:$Employee$ table. Accordingly, its semantics is represented as:

$\mathcal{T}$:Dependent($deName, hasSsn, birthDate, ...$) :-
  $\mathcal{O}$:Dependent(y), $\mathcal{O}$:Employee(w), $\mathcal{O}$:dependents_of(y, w),
  $\mathsf{identify}_{Employee}(w, hasSsn)$, $\mathcal{O}$:deName($y, deName$),
  $\mathcal{O}$:birthDate($y, birthDate$) ...

and its identifier is represented as:

$\mathsf{identify}_{Dependent}(y, deName, hasSsn)$:-
  $\mathcal{O}$:Dependent(y), $\mathcal{O}$:Employee(w), $\mathcal{O}$:dependents_of(y, w),
  $\mathsf{identify}_{Employee}(w, hasSsn)$, $\mathcal{O}$:deName($y, deName$).

τ can be applied similarly to the other objects in Figure 2. $\tau(works\_for)$ produces the table $works\_for(\underline{hasSsn}, hasDeptNumber)$. $\tau(participates)$ generates the table $participates(\underline{hasNumber, hasDeptNumber})$. Please note that the anchor of the table generated by $\tau(works\_for)$ is $Employee$, while no single anchor is assigned to the table generated by $\tau(participates)$. ■

The second step of the er2rel schema design methodology suggests that the schema generated using τ can be modified by (repeatedly) *merging* into the table T_0 of an entity E the table T_1 of some functional relationship involving the same entity E (which has a foreign key reference to T_0). If the semantics of T_0 is $T_0(K, V)$:- $\phi(K, V)$, and of T_1 is $T_1(K, W)$:- $\psi(K, W)$, then the semantics of table T=merge(T_0,T_1) is, to a first approximation, $T(K, V, W)$:- $\phi(K, V), \psi(K, W)$. And the anchor of T is the entity E. (We defer the description of the treatment of null values which can arise in the non-key columns of T_1 appearing in T.) For example, we could merge the table $\tau(Employee)$ with the table $\tau(works\_for)$ in Example 5.2 to form a new table $\mathcal{T}$:$Employee2$ ($\underline{hasSsn}$, $hasName$, $hasAddress$, $hasAge$, $hasDeptNumber$), where the column $hasDeptNumber$ is an f.k. referencing $\tau(Department)$. The semantics of the table is:

$\mathcal{T}$:Employee2($hasSsn, hasName, hasAddress, hasAge, hasDeptNumber$):-
  $\mathcal{O}$:Employee(y), $\mathcal{O}$:hasSsn($y, hasSsn$), $\mathcal{O}$:hasName($y, hasName$),
  $\mathcal{O}$:hasAddress($y, hasAddress$), $\mathcal{O}$:hasAge($y, hasAge$),
  $\mathcal{O}$:Department(w), $\mathcal{O}$:works_for(y, w), $\mathcal{O}$:hasDeptNumber($w, hasDeptNumber$).

Please note that one conceptual model may result in several different relational schemas, since there are choices in which direction a one-to-one relationship is encoded (which entity acts as a key), and how tables are merged. Note also that the resulting schema is in Boyce-Codd Normal Form, if we assume that the only functional dependencies are those that can be deduced from the ER schema (as expressed in FOL).

In this subsection, we assume that the CM has no so-called "recursive" relationships relating an entity to itself, and no attribute of an entity corresponds to multiple columns of any table generated from the CM. (We deal with these in Section 5.3.) Note that by the latter assumption, we rule out for now the case when there are several relationships between a weak entity and its owner entity, such as $hasMet$ connecting $Dependent$ and $Employee$, because in this case $\tau(hasMet)$ will need columns $deName, ssn1$, $ssn2$, with $ssn1$ helping to identify the dependent, and $ssn2$ identifying the (other) employee they met.

Now we turn to the algorithm for finding the semantics of a table in terms of a given CM. It amounts to finding the semantic trees between nodes in the set $\mathcal{C}_T$ singled out by the correspondences from columns of the table T to attributes in the CM. As mentioned previously, the algorithm works in several steps:

1. Determine a skeleton tree connecting the concepts corresponding to key columns; also determine, if possible, a unique anchor for this tree.
2. Link the concepts corresponding to non-key columns using shortest functional paths to the skeleton/anchor tree.
3. Link any unaccounted-for concepts corresponding to other columns by arbitrary shortest paths to the tree.

To flesh out the above steps, we begin with the tables created by the standard design process. If a table is derived by the er2rel methodology from an ER_0 diagram, then Table 1 provides substantial knowledge about how to determine the skeleton tree. However, care must be taken when weak entities are involved. The following example describes the right process to discover the skeleton and the anchor of a weak entity table.

Example 5.3. Consider table $\mathcal{T}$:*Dept*($\underline{number, univ}$, $dean$), with foreign key (f.k.) $univ$ referencing table $\mathcal{T}$:$Univ$($\underline{name}$, $address$) and correspondences shown in Figure 3. We can tell that $\mathcal{T}$:*Dept* represents a weak entity since its key has one f.k. as a subset (referring to the strong entity on which *Department* depends). To find the skeleton and anchor of the table $\mathcal{T}$:*Dept*, we first need to find the skeleton and anchor of the table referenced by the f.k. $univ$. The answer is $University$. Next, we should look for a total functional edge (path) from the correspondent of $number$, which is concept *Department*, to the anchor, $University$. As a result, the link `Department ---belongsTo-->- University` is returned as the skeleton, and *Department* is returned as the anchor. Finally, we can correctly identify the $dean$ relationship as the remainder of the connection, rather than the $president$ relationship, which would have seemed a superficially plausible alternative to begin with.

Furthermore, suppose we need to interpret the table $\mathcal{T}$:*Portal*($\underline{dept, univ}$, $address$) with the following correspondences:

$T : Portal.dept \rightsquigarrow \mathcal{O} : Department.hasDeptNumber$

$T : Portal.univ \rightsquigarrow \mathcal{O} : University.hasUnivName$

$T : Portal.address \rightsquigarrow \mathcal{O} : Host.hostName$,

where not only is $\{dept, univ\}$ the key but also an f.k. referencing the key of table $\mathcal{T}$:*Dept*. To find the anchor and skeleton of table $\mathcal{T}$:*Portal*, the algorithm first recursively works on the referenced table. This is also needed when the owner entity of a weak entity is itself a weak entity. ■

The following is the function getSkeleton which returns a set of (skeleton, anchor)-pairs, when given a table T and a set of correspondences L from key(T). The function is essentially a recursive algorithm attempting to reverse the function τ in Table 1.

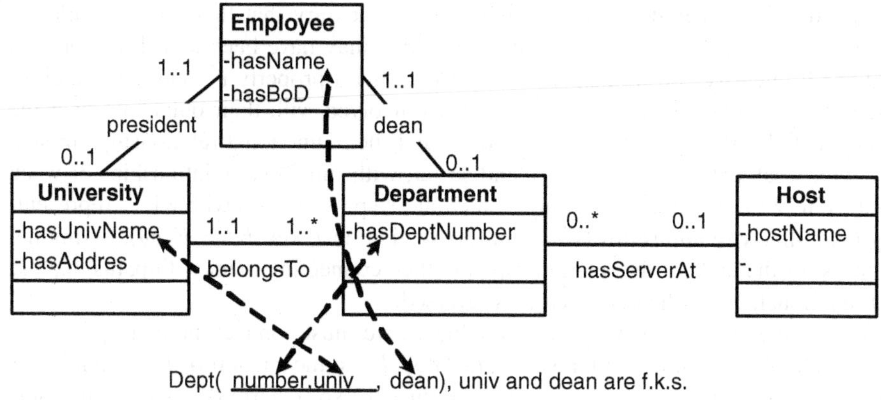

Fig. 3. Finding Correct Skeleton Trees and Anchors

In order to accommodate tables not designed according to er2rel, the algorithm has branches for finding minimum spanning/Steiner trees as skeletons.

Function getSkeleton(T,L)
input: table T, correspondences L for key(T)
output: a set of (skeleton tree, anchor) pairs
steps:
Suppose key(T) contains f.k.s $F_1,\ldots,F_n$ referencing tables $T_1(K_1),..,T_n(K_n)$;

1. If $n \leq 1$ and onc(key(T))[7] is just a singleton set $\{C\}$, then return $(C, \{C\})$.[8]/**T is likely about a strong entity: base case.**/
2. Else, let L_i=$\{T_i.K_i \leftrightsquigarrow L(T, F_i)\}$/**translate corresp's thru f.k. reference.**/; compute (Ss_i, Anc_i) = getSkeleton(T_i, L_i), for $i = 1, .., n$.
   (a) If key(T) $= F_1$, then return (Ss_1, Anc_1). /**T looks like the table for the functional relationship of a weak entity, other than its identifying relationship.**/
   (b) If key(T)=F_1A, where columns A are not part of an f.k. then /**T is possibly a weak entity**/
   if $Anc_1 = \{N_1\}$ and onc(A) $= \{N\}$ such that there is a (shortest) total functional path π from N to N_1, then return (combine[9](π, Ss_1), $\{N\}$). /**N is a weak entity. cf. Example 5.3.**/
   (c) Else suppose key(T) has non-f.k. columns $A[1], \ldots A[m]$, $(m \geq 0)$; let N_s=$\{Anc_i, i = 1, .., n\} \cup \{onc(A[j]), j = 1, .., m\}$; find skeleton tree S' connecting the nodes in N_s where any pair of nodes in N_s is connected by a (shortest) non-functional path; return (combine(S', $\{Ss_j\}$), N_s). /**Deal with many-to-many binary relationships; also the default action for non-standard cases, such as when not finding identifying relationship from a weak entity to the supposed owner entity. In this case no unique anchor exists.**/

---

[7] onc(X) is the function which gets the set M of concepts corresponded by the columns X.
[8] Both here and elsewhere, when a concept C is added to a tree, so are edges and nodes for C's attributes that appear in L.
[9] Function combine merges edges of trees into a larger tree.

In order for getSkeleton to terminate, it is necessary that there be no cycles in f.k. references in the schema. Such cycles (which may have been added to represent additional integrity constraints, such as the fact that a property is total) can be eliminated from a schema by replacing the tables involved with their outer join over the key. getSkeleton deals with strong entities and their functional relationships in step (1), with weak entities in step (2.b), and so far, with functional relationships of weak entities in (2.a). In addition to being a catch-all, step (2.c) deals with tables representing many-many relationships (which in this section have key $K = F_1F_2$), by finding anchors for the ends of the relationship, and then connecting them with paths that are not functional, even when every edge is reversed.

To find the entire semantic tree of a table T, we must connect the concepts corresponded by the rest of the columns, i.e., nonkey(T), to the anchor(s). The connections should be (shortest) functional edges (paths), since the key determines at most one value for them; however, if such a path cannot be found, we use an arbitrary shortest path. The following function, getTree, achieves the goal.

Function getTree(T,L)
input: table T, correspondences L for columns(T)
output: set of semantic trees [10]
steps:

1. Let L_k be the subset of L containing correspondences from key(T); compute (S', Anc')=getSkeleton(T,L_k).
2. If onc(nonkey(T)) – onc(key(T)) is empty, then return (S', Anc'). */*if all columns correspond to the same set of concepts as the key does, then return the skeleton tree.*/*
3. For each f.k. F_i in nonkey(T) referencing $T_i(K_i)$: let $L_k^i = \{T_i.K_i \leftrightsquigarrow L(T, F_i)\}$, and compute (Ss_i'', Anc_i'')= getSkeleton(T_i,L_k^i). */*recall that the function $L(T, F_i)$ is derived from a correspondence $L(T, F_i, D, f, N_{f,D})$ such that it gives a concept D and its attribute f ($N_{f,D}$ is the attribute node in the ontology graph.)*/* find π_i=shortest functional path from Anc' to Anc_i''; let S = combine$(S', \pi_i, \{Ss_i''\})$.
4. For each column c in nonkey(T) that is not part of an f.k., let N = onc(c); find π=shortest functional path from Anc' to N; update $S :=$ combine(S, π). */*cf. Example 5.4.*/*
5. In all cases above asking for functional paths, use a shortest path if a functional one does not exist.
6. Return S.

The following example illustrates the use of getTree when seeking to interpret a table using a different CM than the one from which it was originally derived.

Example 5.4. In Figure 4, the table T:$Assignment$(<u>emp, $proj$</u>, $site$) was originally derived from a CM with the entity $Assignment$ shown on the right-hand side of the vertical dashed line. To interpret it by the CM on the left-hand side, the function getSkeleton, in Step 2.c, returns `Employee` `---assignedTo---` `Project` as the skeleton, and no single anchor exists. The set $\{Employee, Project\}$ accompanying the skeleton is

[10] To make the description simpler, at times we will not explicitly account for the possibility of multiple answers. Every function is extended to set arguments by element-wise application of the function to set members.

returned. Subsequently, the function getTree seeks for the shortest functional link from elements in $\{Employee, Project\}$ to $Worksite$ at Step 4. Consequently, it connects $Worksite$ to $Employee$ via $works\_on$ to build the final semantic tree. ■

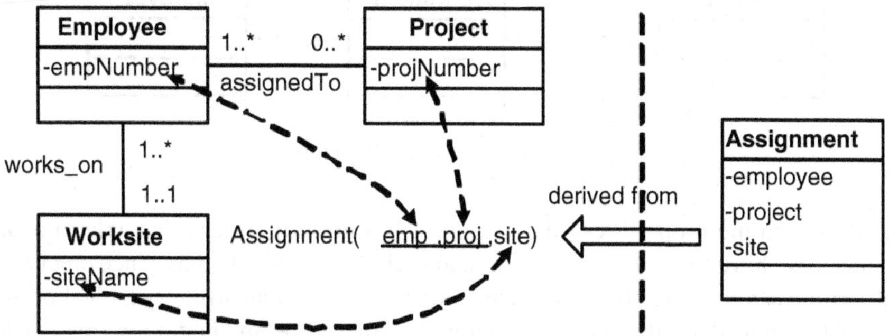

Fig. 4. Independently Developed Table and CM

To get the logic formula from a tree based on correspondence L, we provide the procedure encodeTree(S, L) below, which basically assigns variables to nodes, and connects them using edge labels as predicates.

Function encodeTree(S,L)
input: subtree S of ontology graph, correspondences L from table columns to attributes of concept nodes in S.
output: variable name generated for root of S, and conjunctive formula for the tree.
steps: Suppose N is the root of S. Let $\Psi = true.$
1. if N is an attribute node with label f
   find d such that $L(\_, d, \_, f, N) = true$;
   return$(d, true)$. */*for leaves of the tree, which are attribute nodes, return the corresponding column name as the variable and the formula true.*/*
2. if N is a concept node with label C, then introduce new variable x; add conjunct $C(x)$ to Ψ;
   for each edge p_i from N to N_i */*recursively get the subformulas.*/*
      let S_i be the subtree rooted at N_i,
      let $(v_i, \phi_i(Z_i))$=encodeTree(S_i, L),
      add conjuncts $p_i(x, v_i) \wedge \phi_i(Z_i)$ to Ψ;
3. return (x, Ψ).

Example 5.5. Figure 5 is the fully specified semantic tree returned by the algorithm for the T:*Dept(number, univ, dean)* table in Example 5.3. Taking *Department* as the root of the tree, function encodeTree generates the following formula:

Department(x), hasDeptNumber(x, $number$), belongsTo(x, v_1), University(v_1),
hasUnivName(v_1, $univ$), dean(x, v_2), Employee(v_2), hasName(v_2, $dean$).

As expected, the formula is the semantics the table T:*Dept* as assigned by the er2rel design τ. ■

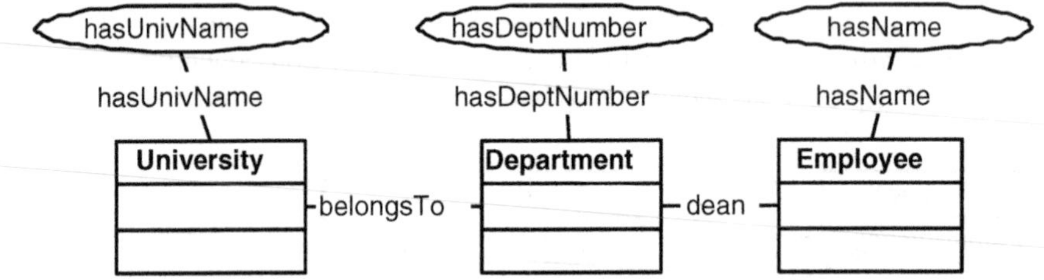

Fig. 5. Semantic Tree For *Dept* Table

Now we turn to the properties of the mapping algorithm. In order to be able to make guarantees, we have to limit ourselves to "standard" relational schemas, since otherwise the algorithm cannot possibly guess the intended meaning of an arbitrary table. For this reason, let us consider only schemas generated by the er2rel methodology from a CM encoding an ER diagram. We are interested in two properties: (1) A sense of "completeness": the algorithm finds the correct semantics (as specified in Table 1). (2) A sense of "soundness": if for such a table there are multiple semantic trees returned by the algorithm, then each of the trees would produce an indistinguishable relational table according to the er2rel mapping. (Note that multiple semantic trees are bound to arise when there are several relationships between 2 entities which cannot be distinguished semantically in a way which is apparent in the table (e.g., 2 or more functional properties from A to B). To formally specify the properties, we have the following definitions.

A *homomorphism* h from the columns of a table T_1 to the columns of a table T_2 is a one-to-one mapping h: $\mathsf{columns}(T_1) \rightarrow \mathsf{columns}(T_2)$, such that (i) $h(c) \in \mathsf{key}(T_2)$ for every $c \in \mathsf{key}(T_1)$; (ii) by convention, for a set of columns F, $h(F[1]F[2]\ldots)$ is $h(F[1])h(F[2])\ldots$; (iii) $h(Y)$ is an f.k. of T_2 for every Y which is an f.k. of T_1; and (iv) if Y is an f.k. of T_1, then there is a homomorphism from the $\mathsf{key}(T_1')$ of T_1' referenced by Y to the $\mathsf{key}(T_2')$ of T_2' referenced by $h(Y)$ in T_2.

Definition 1. *A relational table T_1 is isomorphic to another relational table T_2, if there is a homomorphism from* columns(T_1) *to* columns(T_2) *and vice versa.*

Informally, two tables are isomorphic if there is a bijection between their columns which preserves recursively the key and foreign key structures. These structures have direct connections with the structures of the ER diagrams from which the tables were derived. Since the er2rel mapping τ may generate the "same" table when applied to different ER diagrams (considering attribute/column names have been handled by correspondences), a mapping discovery algorithm with "good" properties should report all and only those ER diagrams.

To specify the properties of the algorithm, suppose that the correspondence L_{id} is the identity mapping from table columns to attribute names, as set up in Table 1. The following lemma states the interesting property of getSkeleton.

Lemma 1. *Let ontology graph $\mathcal{G}$ encode an ER$_0$ diagram $\mathcal{E}$. Let $T = \tau(C)$ be a relational table derived from an object C in $\mathcal{E}$ according to the* er2rel *rules in Table 1. Given L_{id} from T to $\mathcal{G}$, and L' = the restriction of L_{id} to* key(T)*, then* getSkeleton(T, L') *returns (S, Anc) such that,*

- *Anc is the* anchor *of T (*anchor(T)*).*
- *If C corresponds to a (strong or weak) entity, then* encodeTree(S, L') *is logically equivalent to* identify$_C$.

Proof The lemma is proven by using induction on the number of applications of the function getSkeleton resulting from a single call on the table T.

At the base case, step 1 of getSkeleton indicates that key(T) links to a single concept in $\mathcal{G}$. According to the er2rel design, table T is derived either from a strong entity or a functional relationship from a strong entity. For either case, anchor(T) is the strong entity, and encodeTree(S, L') is logically equivalent to identify$_E$, where E is the strong entity.

For the induction hypothesis, we assume that the lemma holds for each table that is referenced by a foreign key in T.

On the induction steps, step 2.(a) identifies that table T is derived from a functional relationship from a weak entity. By the induction hypothesis, the lemma holds for the weak entity. So does it for the relationship.

Step 2.(b) identifies that T is a table representing a weak entity W with an owner entity E. Since there is only one total functional relationship from a weak entity to its owner entity, getSkeleton correctly returns the identifying relationship. By the induction hypothesis, we prove that encodeTree(S, L') is logically equivalent to identify$_W$. ■

We now state the desirable properties of the mapping discovery algorithm. First, getTree finds the desired semantic mapping, in the sense that

Theorem 1. *Let ontology graph $\mathcal{G}$ encode an ER$_0$ diagram $\mathcal{E}$. Let table T be part of a relational schema obtained by* er2rel *derivation from $\mathcal{E}$. Given L_{id} from T to $\mathcal{G}$, then some tree S returned by* getTree(T, L_{id}) *has the property that the formula generated by* encodeTree(S, L_{id}) *is logically equivalent to the semantics assigned to T by the* er2rel *design.*

Proof. Suppose T is obtained by merging the table for a entity E with tables representing functional relationships $f_1, \ldots, f_n$, $n \geq 0$, involving the same entity.

When $n = 0$, all columns will come from E, if it is a strong entity, or from E and its owner entiti(es), whose attributes appear in key(T). In either case, step 2 of getTree will apply, returning the skeleton S. encodeTree then uses the full original correspondence to generate a formula where the attributes of E corresponding to non-key columns generate conjuncts that are added to formula identify$_E$. Following Lemma 1, it is easy to show by induction on the number of such attributes that the result is correct.

When $n > 0$, step 1 of getTree constructs a skeleton tree, which represents E by Lemma 1. Step 3 adds edges $f_1, \ldots, f_n$ from E to other entity nodes $E_1, \ldots, E_n$ returned respectively as roots of skeletons for the other foreign keys of T. Lemma 1 also shows that these translate correctly. Steps 4 and 5 cannot apply to tables generated according to er2rel design. So it only remains to note that encodeTree creates the formula for the final tree, by generating conjuncts for $f_1, \ldots, f_n$ and for the non-key attributes of E, and adding these to the formulas generated for the skeleton subtrees at $E_1, \ldots, E_n$.

This leaves tables generated from relationships in ER_0 — the cases covered in the last two rows of Table 1 — and these can be dealt with using Lemma 1. ■

Note that this result is non-trivial, since, as explained earlier, it would not be satisfied by the current Clio algorithm [18], if applied blindly to $\mathcal{E}$ viewed as a relational schema with unary and binary tables. Since getTree may return multiple answers, the following converse "soundness" result is significant.

Theorem 2. *If S' is any tree returned by* getTree(T, L_{id}), *with T, L_{id}, and $\mathcal{E}$ as above in Theorem 1, then the formula returned by* encodeTree(S', L_{id}) *represents the semantics of* some *table T' derivable by* er2rel *design from $\mathcal{E}$, where T' is isomorphic to T.*

Proof. The theorem is proven by showing that each tree returned by getTree will result in table T' isomorphic to T.

For the four cases in Table 1, getTree will return a single semantic tree for a table derived from an entity (strong or weak), and possibly multiple semantic trees for a (functional) relationship table. Each of the semantic trees returned for a relationship table is identical to the original ER diagram in terms of the shape and the cardinality constraints. As a result, applying τ to the semantic tree generates a table isomorphic to T.

Now suppose T is a table obtained by merging the table for entity E with n tables representing functional relationships $f_1, \ldots, f_n$ from E to some n other entities. The recursive calls getTree in step 3 will return semantic trees, each of which represent functional relationships from E. As above, these would result in tables that are isomorphic to the tables derived from the original functional relationships $f_i, i = 1...n$. By the definition of the merge operation, the result of merging these will also result in a table T' which is isomorphic to T. ■

We wish to emphasize that the above algorithms has been designed to deal even with schemas not derived using er2rel from some ER diagram. An application of this was illustrated already in Example 5.4. Another application of this is the use of functional paths instead of just functional edges. The following example illustrates an interesting scenario in which we obtained the right result.

Example 5.6. Consider the following relational table

$T(\underline{personName}, cityName, countryName)$,

where the columns correspond to, respectively, attributes $pname$, $cname$, and $ctrname$ of concepts $Person, City$ and $Country$ in a CM. If the CM contains a path such that `Person -- bornIn ->- City -- locatedIn ->- Country`, then the above table, which is not in 3NF and was not obtained using er2rel design (which would have required a table for $City$), would still get the proper semantics:

T($personName, cityName, countryName$) :-

Person(x_1), City(x_2),Country(x_3), bornIn(x_1,x_2), locatedIn(x_2,x_3),
pname(x_1,$personName$), cname(x_2,$cityName$),ctrname(x_3,$countryName$).

If, on the other hand, there was a shorter functional path from $Person$ to $Country$, say an edge labeled `citizenOf`, then the mapping suggested would have been:

T($personName, cityName, countryName$) :-

Person(x_1), City(x_2), Country(x_3), bornIn (x_1,x_2),citizenOf(x_1,x_3), ...

which corresponds to the er2rel design. Moreover, had `citizenOf` not been functional, then once again the semantics produced by the algorithm would correspond to the non-3NF interpretation, which is reasonable since the table, having only $personName$ as key, could not store multiple country names for a person. ■

5.2 $\mathbf{ER_1}$: Reified Relationships

It is desirable to also have n-ary relationship sets connecting entities, and to allow relationship sets to have attributes in an ER model; we label the language allowing us to model such aspects by ER_1. Unfortunately, these features are not directly supported in most CMLs, such as OWL, which only have binary relationships. Such notions must instead be represented by *"reified relationships"* [3] (we use an annotation * to indicate the reified relationships in a diagram): concepts whose instances represent tuples, connected by so-called "roles" to the tuple elements. So, if $Buys$ relates $Person$, $Shop$ and $Product$, through roles $buyer$, $source$ and $object$, then these are explicitly represented as (functional) binary associations, as in Figure 6. And a relationship attribute, such as when the buying occurred, becomes an attribute of the $Buys$ concept, such as $whenBought$.

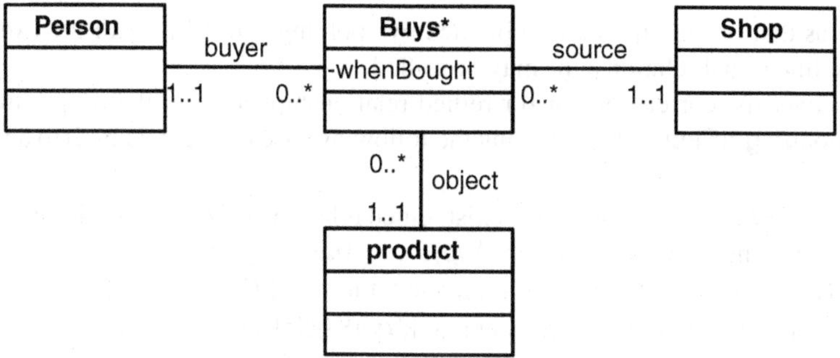

Fig. 6. N-ary Relationship Reified

Unfortunately, reified relationships cannot be distinguished reliably from ordinary entities in normal CMLs based on purely formal, syntactic grounds, yet they need to be treated in special ways during semantic recovery. For this reason we assume that they can be distinguished on *ontological grounds*. For example, in Dolce [7], they are subclasses of top-level concepts $Quality$ and $Perdurant/Event$. For a reified relationship R, we use functions roles(R) and attribs(R) to retrieve the appropriate (binary) properties.

The er2rel design τ of relational tables for reified relationships is an extension of the treatment of binary relationships, and is shown in Table 2. As with entity keys, we are unable to capture in CM situations where some subset of more than one roles uniquely identifies the relationship. The er2rel design τ on ER_1 also admits the merge operation on tables generated by τ. Merging applies to an entity table with other tables of some functional relationships involving the same entity. In this case, the merged semantics is

Table 2. er2rel Design for Reified Relationship

ER model object O	Relational Table $\tau(O)$	
Reified Relationship R	*columns:*	$ZX_1 \ldots X_n$
if there is a functional	*primary key:*	X_1
role r_1 for R	*f.k.'s:*	$X_1, \ldots, X_n$
E1 --<- r1 ->-- R	*anchor:*	R
--- rj ->-- Ej	*semantics:*	$T(ZX_1 \ldots X_n)$:- $R(y)$,$E_i(w_i)$, hasAttribs(y, Z), $r_i(y, w_i)$,
let Z=attribs(R)		identify$_{E_i}(w_i, X_i), \ldots$
X_i=key($\tau(E_i)$)	*identifier:*	identify$_R(y, X_1)$:- $R(y)$, $E_1(w)$, $r_1(y, w)$,
where E_i fills role r_i		identify$_{E_1}(w, X_1)$.
Reified Relationship R	*columns:*	$ZX_1 \ldots X_n$
if $r_1, \ldots, r_n$ are roles of R	*primary key:*	$X_1 \ldots X_n$
let Z=attribs(R)	*f.k.'s:*	$X_1, \ldots, X_n$
X_i=key($\tau(E_i)$)	*anchor:*	R
where E_i fills role r_i	*semantics:*	$T(ZX_1 \ldots X_n)$:- $R(y)$,$E_i(w_i)$, hasAttribs(y, Z), $r_i(y, w_i)$,
		identify$_{E_i}(w_i, X_i), \ldots$
	identifier:	identify$_R(y, \ldots X_i \ldots)$:- $R(y), \ldots E_i(w_i)$, $r_i(y, w_i)$,
		identify$_{E_i}(w_i, X_i)$,...

the same as that of merging tables obtained by applying τ to ER_0, with the exception that some functional relationships may be reified.

To discover the correct anchor for reified relationships and get the proper tree, we need to modify getSkeleton, by adding the following case between steps 2(b) and 2(c):

- If key(T)=$F_1F_2 \ldots F_n$ and there exist reified relationship R with n roles $r_1, \ldots, r_n$ pointing at the singleton nodes in $Anc_1, \ldots, Anc_n$ respectively, then let S = combine($\{r_j\}, \{Ss_j\}$), and return $(S, \{R\})$.

getTree should compensate for the fact that if getSkeleton finds a *reified* version of a many-many binary relationship, it will no longer look for an unreified one in step 2c. So after step 1. we add

- if key(T) is the concatenation of two foreign keys F_1F_2, and nonkey(T) is empty, compute (Ss_1,Anc_1) and (Ss_2, Anc_2) as in step 2. of getSkeleton; then find ρ=shortest many-many path connecting Anc_1 to Anc_2; return $(S') \cup$ (combine(ρ, Ss_1, Ss_2))

In addition, when traversing the ontology graph for finding shortest paths in both functions, we need to recalculate the lengths of paths when reified relationship nodes are present. Specifically, a path of length 2 passing through a reified relationship node should be counted as a path of length 1, because a reified binary relationship could have been eliminated, leaving a single edge.[11] Note that a semantic tree that includes a reified relationship node is valid only if all roles of the reified relationship have been included in the tree. Moreover, if the reified relation had attributes of its own, they would show up as columns in the table that are not part of any foreign key. Therefore, a filter is required at the last stage of the algorithm:

[11] A different way of "normalizing" things would have been to reify even binary associations.

– If a reified relationship R appears in the final semantic tree, then so must all its role edges. And if one such R has as attributes the columns of the table which do not appear in foreign keys or the key, then all other candidate semantics need to be eliminated.

The previous version of getTree was set up so that with these modifications, roles and attributes to reified relationships will be found properly.

If we continue to assume that no more than one column corresponds to the same entity attribute, the previous theorems hold for ER_1 as well. To see this, consider the following two points. First, the tree identified for any table generated from a reified relationship is isomorphic to the one from which it was generated, since the foreign keys of the table identify exactly the participants in the relationship, so the only ambiguity possible is the reified relationship (root) itself. Second, if an entity E has a set of (binary) functional relationships connecting to a set of entities $E_1,\ldots,E_n$, then merging the corresponding tables with $\tau(E)$ results in a table that is isomorphic to a reified relationship table, where the reified relationship has a single functional role with filler E and all other role fillers are the set of entities $E_1,\ldots,E_n$.

5.3 Replication

We next deal with the equivalent of the full ER_1 model, by allowing recursive relationships, where a single entity plays multiple roles, and the merging of tables for different functional relationships connecting the same pair of entity sets (e.g., `works_for` and `manages`). In such cases, the mapping described in Table 1 is not quite correct because column names would be repeated in the multiple occurrences of the foreign key. In our presentation, we will distinguish these (again, for ease of presentation) by adding superscripts as needed. For example, if entity set $Person$, with key ssn, is connected to itself by the $likes$ property, then the table for $likes$ will have schema $T[\underline{ssn^1, ssn^2}]$.

During mapping discovery, such situations are signaled by the presence of multiple columns c and d of table T corresponding to the same attribute f of concept C. In such situations, we modify the algorithm to first make a copy C_{copy} of node C, as well as its attributes, in the ontology graph. Furthermore, C_{copy} participates in all the object relations C did, so edges for this must also be added. After replication, we can set $\text{onc}(c) = C$ and $\text{onc}(d) = C_{copy}$, or $\text{onc}(d) = C$ and $\text{onc}(c) = C_{copy}$ (recall that $\text{onc}(c)$ retrieves the concept corresponded to by column c in the algorithm). This ambiguity is actually required: given a CM with $Person$ and $likes$ as above, a table $T[\underline{ssn^1, ssn^2}]$ could have two possible semantics: $likes(ssn^1, ssn^2)$ and $likes(ssn^2, ssn^1)$, the second one representing the inverse relationship, $likedBy$. The problem arises not just with recursive relationships, as illustrated by the case of a table $T[\underline{ssn}, addr^1, addr^2]$, where $Person$ is connected by two relationships, $home$ and $office$, to concept $Building$, which has an $address$ attribute.

The main modification needed to the getSkeleton and getTree algorithms is that no tree should contain two or more functional edges of the form `[D] --- p ->-- [C]` and its replicate `[D] --- p ->-- [`C_{copy}`]`, because a function p has a single value, and hence the different columns of a tuple corresponding to it will end up having identical values: a clearly poor schema.

As far as our previous theorems, one can prove that by making copies of an entity E (say E and E_{copy}), and also replicating its attributes and participating relationships, one obtains an ER diagram from which one can generate isomorphic tables with identical semantics, according to the er2rel mapping. This will hold true as long as the predicate used for **both** E and E_{copy} is $E(\_)$; similarly, we need to use the same predicate for the copies of the attributes and associations in which E and E_{copy} participate.

Even in this case, the second theorem may be in jeopardy if there are multiple possible "identifying relationships" for a weak entity, as illustrated by the following example.

Example 5.7. An educational department in a provincial government records the transfers of students between universities in its databases. A student is a weak entity depending for identification on the university in which the student is currently registered. A transfered student must have registered in another university before transferring. The table T:$Transferred(\underline{sno, univ}, sname)$ records who are the transferred students, and their name. The table T:$previous(\underline{sno, univ}, pUniv)$ stores the information about the $previousUniv$ relationship. A CM is depicted in Figure 7. To discover the seman-

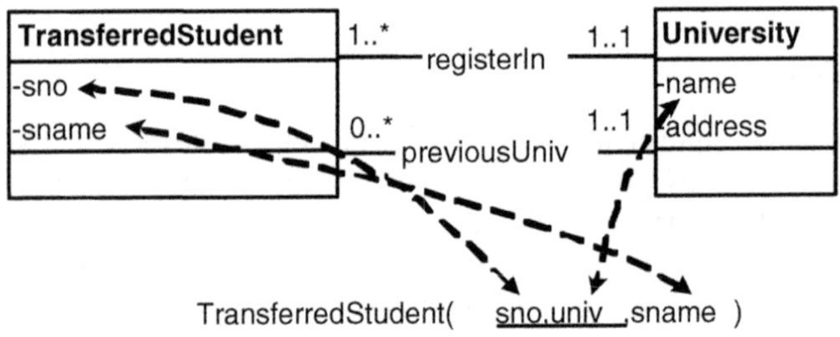

Fig. 7. A Weak Entity and Its Owner Entity

tics of table T:$Transferred$, we link the columns to the attributes in the CM as shown in Figure 7. One of the skeletons returned by the algorithm for the T:$Transferred$ will be `TransferredStudent --- previousUniv ->-- University`. But the design resulting from this according to the er2rel mapping is not isomorphic to key($Transferred$), since $previousUniv$ is not the identifying relationship of the weak entity $TransferredStudent$. ■

From above example, we can see that the problem is the inability of CMLs such as UML and OWL to fully capture notions like "weak entity" (specifically the notion of identifying relationship), which play a crucial role in ER-based design. We expect such cases to be quite rare though – we certainly have not encountered any in our example databases.

5.4 Extended ER: Adding Class Specialization

The ability to represent subclass hierarchies, such as the one in Figure 8 is a hallmark of CMLs and modern so-called Extended ER (EER) modeling.

Almost all textbooks (e.g., [22]) describe several techniques for designing relational schemas in the presence of class hierarchies

1. Map each concept/entity into a separate table following the standard er2rel rules. This approach requires two adjustments: First, subclasses must inherit identifying attributes from a single super-class, in order to be able to generate keys for their tables. Second, in the table created for an immediate subclass C' of class C, its key $\mathsf{key}(\tau(C'))$ should also be set to reference as a foreign key $\tau(C)$, as a way of maintaining inclusion constraints dictated by the is-a relationship.
2. Expand inheritance, so that *all* attributes and relations involving a class C appear on all its subclasses C'. Then generate tables as usual for the subclasses C', though not for C itself. This approach is used only when the subclasses cover the superclass.
3. Some researchers also suggest a third possibility: "Collapse up" the information about subclasses into the table for the superclass. This can be viewed as the result of $\mathsf{merge}(T_C, T_{C'})$, where $T_C(K, A)$ and $T_{C'}(K, B)$ are the tables generated for C and its subclass C' according to technique (1.) above. In order for this design to be "correct", [15] requires that $T_{C'}$ not be the target of any foreign key references (hence not have any relationships mapped to tables), and that B be non-null (so that instances of C' can be distinguished from those of C).

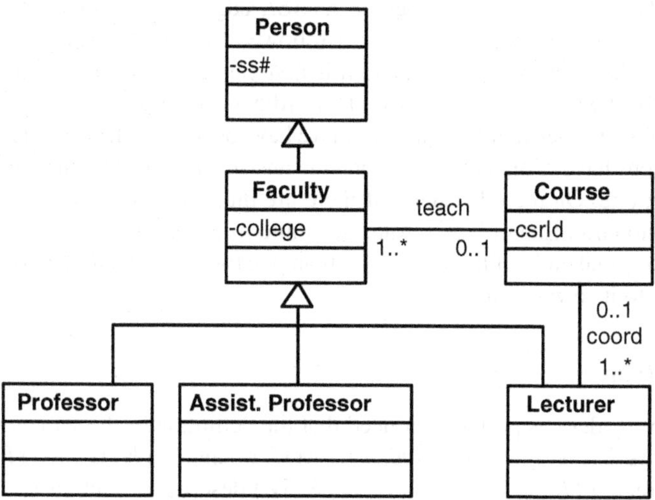

Fig. 8. Specialization Hierarchy

The use of the key for the root class, together with inheritance and the use of foreign keys to also check inclusion constraints, make many tables highly ambiguous. For example, according to the above, table $T(\underline{ss\#}, crsId)$, with $ss\#$ as the key and a foreign key referencing T', could represent at least
(a) $Faculty$ teach $Course$
(b) $Lecturer$ teach $Course$
(c) $Lecturer$ coord $Course$.
This is made combinatorially worse by the presence of multiple and deep hierarchies (e.g., imagine a parallel $Course$ hierarchy), and the fact that not all ontology concepts

are realized in the database schema, according to our scenario. For this reason, we have chosen to deal with some of the ambiguity by relying on users, during the establishment of correspondences. Specifically, the user is supposed to provide a correspondence from column c to attribute f *on the lowest class whose instances provide data appearing in the column*. Therefore, in the above example of table $T(\underline{ss\#}, crsId)$, $ss\#$ should be set to correspond to ssn on $Faculty$ in case (a), while in cases (b) and (c) it should correspond to $ss\#$ on $Lecturer$. This decision was also prompted by the CM manipulation tool that we are using, which automatically expands inheritance, so that $ss\#$ appears on all subclasses.

Under these circumstances, in order to deal appropriately with designs (1.) and (2.) above, we do not need to modify our earlier algorithm in any way, as long as we first expand inheritance in the graph. So the graph would show `Lecturer -- teaches; coord ->- Course` in the above example, and $Lecturer$ would have all the attributes of $Faculty$.

To handle design (3.), we add to the graph an actual edge for the inverse of the **is-a** relation: a functional edge labeled $alsoA$, with lower-bound 0; e.g., `Faculty --- alsoA ->-- Lecturer`. It is then sufficient to allow in getTree for functional paths between concepts to include `alsoA` edges; e.g., $Faculty$ can now be connected to $Course$ through path `alsoA` followed by `coord`. The `alsoA` edge is translated into the identity predicate, and it is assigned cost zero in evaluating a functional path mixed with `alsoA` edge and other ordinary functional edges.[12]

In terms of the properties of the algorithm we have been considering so far, the above three paragraphs have explained that among the answers returned by the algorithm will be the correct one. On the other hand, if there are multiple results returned by the algorithm, as shown in Example 5.7, some semantic trees may not result in isomorphic tables to the original table, if there are more than one total functional relationships from a weak entity to its owner entity.

5.5 Outer Joins

The observant reader has probably noticed that the definition of the semantic mapping for $T = \text{merge}(T_E, T_p)$, where $T_E(K, V)$:- $\phi(K, V)$ and $T_p(K, W)$:- $\psi(K, W)$, was not quite correct: $T(\underline{K}, V, W)$:-$\phi(K, V)$,ψ (K, W) describes a join on K, rather than a left-outer join, which is what is required if p is a non-total relationship. In order to specify the equivalent of outer joins in a perspicuous manner, we will use conjuncts of the form $\lceil \mu(X, Y) \rceil^Y$, which will stand for the formula $\mu(X, Y) \vee (Y = null \wedge \neg\exists Z.\mu(X, Z))$, indicating that null should be used if there are no satisfying values for the variables Y. With this notation, the proper semantics for merge is $T(\underline{K}, V, W)$: $-\phi(K, V), \lceil \psi(K, W) \rceil^W$.

In order to obtain the correct formulas from trees, encodeTree needs to be modified so that when traversing a non-total edge p_i that is not part of the skeleton, in the second-to-last line of the algorithm we must allow for the possibility of v_i not existing.

[12] It seems evident that if B is-a C, and B is associated with A via p, then this is a stronger semantic connection between C and A than if C is associated to D via a q_1, and D is associated to A via q_2.

6 Implementation and Experimentation

So far, we have developed the mapping inference algorithm by investigating the connections between the semantic constraints in relational models and that in ontologies. The theoretical results show that our algorithm will report the "right" semantics for most schemas designed following the widely accepted design methodology. Nonetheless, it is crucial to test the algorithm in real-world schemas and ontologies to see its overall performance. To do this, we have implemented the mapping inference algorithm in our prototype system MAPONTO, and have applied it on a set of real-world schemas and ontologies. In this section, we describe the implementation and provide some evidence for the effectiveness and usefulness of the prototype tool by discussing the set of experiments and our experience.

Implementation. We have implemented the MAPONTO tool as a third-party plugin of the well-known KBMS Protégé[13] which is an open platform for ontology modeling and knowledge acquisition. As OWL becomes the official ontology language of the W3C, intended for use with Semantic Web initiatives, we use OWL as the CML in the tool. This is also facilitated by the Protégé's OWL plugin [12], which can be used to edit OWL ontologies, to access reasoners for them, and to acquire instances for semantic markup. The MAPONTO plugin is implemented as a full-size user interface tab that takes advantage of the views of Protégé user interface. As shown in Figure 9, users can choose database schemas and ontologies, create and manipulate correspondences, generate and edit candidate mapping formulas and graphical connections, and produce and save the final mappings into designated files. In addition, there is a library of other Protégé plugins that visualize ontologies graphically and manage ontology versions. Those plugins sustain our goal of providing an interactively intelligent tool to database administrators so that they may establish semantic mappings from the database to ontologies more effectively.

Schemas and Ontologies. Our test data were obtained from various sources, and we have ensured that the databases and ontologies were developed independently. The test data are listed in Table 3. They include the following databases: the Department of Computer Science database in the University of Toronto; the VLDB conference database; the DBLP computer science bibliography database; the COUNTRY database appearing in one of reverse engineering papers [11] (Although the *country* schema is not a real-world database, it appears as a complex experimental example in [11], and has some reified relationship tables, so we chose it to test this aspect of our algorithm); and the test schemas in OBSERVER [16] project. For the ontologies, our test data include: the academic department ontology in the DAML library; the academic conference ontology from the SchemaWeb ontology repository; the bibliography ontology in the library of the Stanford's Ontolingua server; and the CIA factbook ontology. Ontologies are described in OWL. For each ontology, the number of links indicates the number of edges in the multi-graph resulted from object properties. We have made all these schemas and ontologies available on our web page: www.cs.toronto.edu/ ~yuana/research /maponto/relational/testData.html.

[13] http://protege.stanford.edu

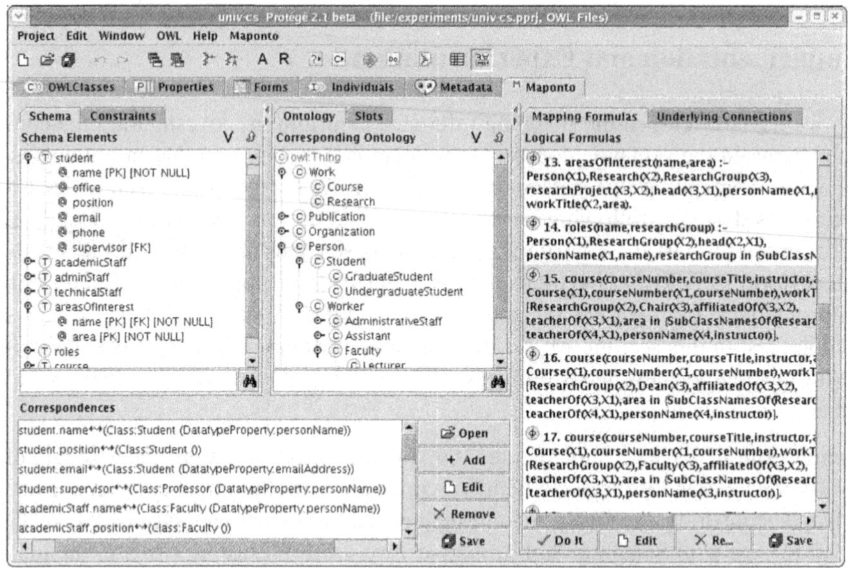

Fig. 9. MAPONTO Plugin of Protege

Table 3. Characteristics of Schemas and Ontologies for the Experiments

Database Schema	Number of Tables	Number of Columns	Ontology	Number of Nodes	Number of Links
UTCS Department	8	32	Academic Department	62	1913
VLDB Conference	9	38	Academic Conference	27	143
DBLP Bibliography	5	27	Bibliographic Data	75	1178
OBSERVER Project	8	115	Bibliographic Data	75	1178
Country	6	18	CIA factbook	52	125

Results and Experience. To evaluate our tool, we sought to understand whether the tool could produce the intended mapping formula if the simple correspondences were given. We were especially concerned with the number of formulas presented by the tool for users to sift through. Further, we wanted to know whether the tool was still useful if the correct formula was not generated. In this case, we expected that a user could more easily debug a generated formula to reach the correct one instead of creating it from scratch. A summary of the experimental results are listed in Table 4 which shows the average size of each relational table schema in each database, the average number of candidates generated, and the average time for generating the candidates. Notice that the number of candidates is the number of semantic trees obtained by the algorithm. Also, a single edge of an semantic tree may represent the multiple edges between two nodes, collapsed using our $p; q$ abbreviation. If there are m edges in a semantic tree and each edge has n_i $(i = 1, .., m)$ original edges collapsed, then there are $\prod_i^m n_i$ original semantic trees. We show below a formula generated from such a collapsed semantic tree:TaAssignment($courseName, studentName$) :-

Course(x_1), GraduateStudent(x_2), **[hasTAs;takenBy]**(x_1,x_2),
workTitle(x_1,$courseName$), personName(x_2,$studentName$).

where, in the semantic tree, the node $Course$ and the node $GraduateStudent$ are connected by a single edge with label **hasTAs;takenBy**, which represents two separate edges, $hasTAs$ and $takenBy$.

Table 4. Performance Summary for Generating Mappings from Relational Tables to Ontologies

Database Schema	Avg. Number of Cols/per table	Avg. Number of Candidates generated	Avg. Execution time(ms)
UTCS Department	4	4	279
VLDB Conference	5	1	54
DBLP Bibliography	6	3	113
OBSERVER Project	15	2	183
Country	3	1	36

Table 4 indicates that MAPONTO only presents a few mapping formulas for users to examine. This is due in part to our compact representation of parallel edges between two nodes shown above. To measure the overall performance, we manually created the mapping formulas for all the 36 tables and compared them to the formulas generated by the tool. We observed that the tool produced correct formulas for 31 tables. This demonstrates that the tool is able to infer the semantics of many relational tables occurring in practice in terms of an independently developed ontology.

We were also interested in the usefulness of the tool in those cases where the formulas generated were not the intended ones. For each such formula, we compared it to the manually generated correct one, and we used a very coarse measurement to record how much effort it would take to "debug" the generated formula: the number of changes of predicate names in a formula. For example, the tool generated the following formula for the table $Student(name, office, position, email, phone, supervisor)$:

Student(x_1), emailAddress(x_1,$email$), personName(x_1,$name$), Professor(x_2),
Department(x_3), head(x_3,x_2), affiliatedOf(x_3,x_1),
personName(x_2, $supervisor$)... (1)

If the intended semantics for the above table columns is:

Student(x_1), emailAddress(x_1,$email$), personName(x_1,$name$), Professor(x_2),
ResearchGroup(x_3), head(x_3,x_2), affiliatedOf(x_3,x_1),
personName(x_2, $supervisor$)... (2)

then one can change the predicate *Department($x3$)* to *ResearchGroup(x_3)* in formula (1) instead of writing the entire formula (2) from scratch. Our experience working with the data sets shows that at average only about 30% predicates in a single incorrect formula returned by the MAPONTO tool needed to be modified to reach the correct formula. This is a significant saving in terms of human labors.

Tables 4 indicate that execution times were not significant, since, as predicted, the search for subtrees and paths took place in a relatively small neighborhood.

We believe it is instructive to consider the various categories of problematic schemas and mappings, and the kind of future work they suggest.

(i) *Absence of tables which should be present according to* er2rel. For example, we expect the connection `Person` -- `researchInterest` --- `Research` to be returned for the table $AreaOfInterest(\underline{name}, \underline{area})$. However, MAPONTO returned `Person` -<- `headOf` --- `ResearchGroup` -<- `researchProject` --- `Research`, because there was no table for the concept *Research* in the schema, and so MAPONTO treated it as a weak entity table. Such problems are caused, among others, by the elimination of tables that represent finite enumerations, or ones that can be recovered by projection from tables representing total many-to-many relationships. These pose an important open problem for now.

(ii) *Mapping formula requiring selection.* The table $European(\underline{country}, gnp)$ means countries which are located in Europe. From the database point of view, this selects tuples representing European countries. Currently, MAPONTO is incapable of generating formulas involving the equivalent to relational selection. This particular case is an instance of the need to express "higher-order" correspondences, such as between table/column names and ontology values. A similar example appears in [17].

(iii) *Non-standard design.* One of the bibliography tables had columns for $author$ and $otherAuthors$ for each document. MAPONTO found a formula that was close to the desired one, with conjuncts $hasAuthor(d, author)$, $hasAuthor(d, otherAuthors)$, but not surprisingly, could not add the requirement that $otherAuthors$ is really the concatenation of all but the first author.

7 Filtering Mappings Through Ontology Reasoning

Rich ontologies provide a new opportunity for eliminating "unreasonable" mappings. For example, suppose the ontology specifies that in a library, once a book is reserved for an event, it cannot be borrowed by a person. In this case, a candidate semantic formula such as

$$\text{Book}(x), \text{borrow}(x, y), \text{Person}(y), \text{reservedFor}(x, z), \text{Event}(z)$$

can be eliminated, since no objects x can satisfy it[14].

When ontologies, which include constraints such as the one about $borrowing$ and $reservedFor$, are expressed in OWL, one can use OWL reasoning to detect these problems. To do so, one first translates the semantic tree into an OWL concept, and then checks it for (un)satisfiability in the context of the ontology axioms, using the standard reasoning algorithms for Description Logics.

[14] Maybe a relationship like $contactAuthor(x, y)$, different from $borrow(x, y)$, needs to be used.

For example, the above formula is equivalent to the OWL concept:

```
<owl:intersectionOf>
    <owl:Class rdf:about="#Book"/>
    <owl:Restriction>
       <owl:onProperty rdf:resource=#borrow/>
       <owl:someValuesFrom rdf:resource="#Person"/>
    </owl:Restriction>
    <owl:Restriction>
       <owl:onProperty rdf:resource=#reservedFor/>
       <owl:someValuesFrom rdf:resource="#Event"/>
    </owl:Restriction>
</owl:intersectionOf>
```

The algorithm for performing this translation in general, encodeTreeAsConcept(S), is almost identical to encodeTree, except that the recursive calls return OWL concepts C_i, which lead to conjuncts of the form restriction(p_i, someValuesFrom(C_i)):

Function encodeTreeAsConcept(S)
input: subtree S of ontology graph
output: abstract syntax of OWL concept logically equivalent to the FOL formula encodeTree(S, L)
steps: Suppose N is the root of S.
1. if N is an attribute node with label f
return restriction(f,minCardinality(1)). */*for leaves of the tree, which are attribute nodes, just ensure that the attribute is present.*/*
2. if N is a concept node with label C, then initialize Ψ to be intersectionOf(C);
for each edge p_i from N to N_i */*recursively get the restrictions */*
let S_i be the subtree rooted at N_i;
let ϕ_i=encodeTreeAsConcept(S_i);
add to Ψ a someValuesFrom(ϕ_i) restriction on p_i.
3. return Ψ.

The ontologies we have found so far are unfortunately not sufficiently rich to demonstrate the usefulness of this idea.

8 Finding GAV Mappings

Arguments have been made that the proper way to connect ontologies and databases for the purpose of information integration is to show how concepts and properties in the ontology can be expressed as queries over the database – the so-called GAV approach.

To illustrate the idea, consider Example 1.1, from Section 1, where the semantic mapping we proposed was
$\mathcal{T}$:Employee($ssn, name, dept, proj$) :-
$\mathcal{O}$:Employee(x_1), $\mathcal{O}$:hasSsn(x_1,ssn), $\mathcal{O}$:hasName(x_1,$name$), $\mathcal{O}$:Department(x_2), $\mathcal{O}$:works_for(x_1,x_2), $\mathcal{O}$:hasDeptNumber(x_2,$dept$), $\mathcal{O}$:Worksite(x_3), $\mathcal{O}$:works_on(x_1,x_3), $\mathcal{O}$:hasNumber(x_3,$proj$).

In this case, we are looking for formulas which express $\mathcal{O}$:*Department*, $\mathcal{O}$:*works_on*, etc. in terms of $\mathcal{T}$:*Employee*, etc., as illustrated below.

We note that a strong motivation for mappings between ontologies and databases expressed in this way is that they can be used to populate the ontology with instances from the database – a task that is expected to be important for the Semantic Web.

An essential initial step is dealing with the fact that in the ontology (as in object oriented databases), objects have intrinsic identity, which is lost in the relational data model, where this notion is replaced by external identifiers/keys. For this purpose, the standard approach is to introduce special Skolem functions that generate these identifiers from the appropriate keys, as in:

$\mathcal{O}$:Employee($\mathsf{ff}(ssn)$) :- $\mathcal{T}$:Employee(ssn,_,_,_).

One then needs to express the external identifiers using axioms that relate these Skolem functions with the appropriate ontology attributes:

$\mathcal{O}$:hasSsn($\mathsf{ff}(ssn)$,ssn) :- $\mathcal{T}$:Employee(ssn,_,_,_).

Finally, one can express the associations by using the above identifiers:

$\mathcal{O}$:works_on($\mathsf{ff}(ssn)$,$\mathsf{gg}(dept)$) :- $\mathcal{T}$:Employee(ssn,_,$dept$,_).

The following less ad-hoc approach leads to almost identical results, but relies on the logical translation of the original mapping, found by the algorithms presented earlier in this paper. For example, the actual semantics of table $\mathcal{T}$:*Employee* is expressed by the formula

$(\forall ssn, name, dept, proj)$ $\mathcal{T}$:Employee$(ssn, name, dept, proj) \Rightarrow$
$(\exists x, y, z)$ $\mathcal{O}$:Employee$(x) \wedge$ $\mathcal{O}$:hasSsn$(x,ssn) \wedge$ $\mathcal{O}$:hasName$(x,name) \wedge$
$\mathcal{O}$:Department$(y) \wedge$ $\mathcal{O}$:hasDeptNumber$(y,dept) \wedge$ $\mathcal{O}$:works_for$(x,y) \wedge$
$\mathcal{O}$:Worksite$(z) \wedge$ $\mathcal{O}$:works_on$(x,z) \wedge$ $\mathcal{O}$:hasNumber$(z,proj)$.

The above formula can be Skolemized to eliminate the existential quantifiers to yield[15]:

$(\forall ssn, name, dept)$ $\mathcal{T}$:Employee$(ssn, name, dept) \Rightarrow$
$\mathcal{O}$:Employee$(\mathsf{f}(ssn, name, dept)) \wedge$ $\mathcal{O}$:hasSsn$(\mathsf{f}(ssn, name, dept),ssn) \wedge$
$\mathcal{O}$:hasName$(\mathsf{f}(ssn, name, dept),name) \wedge$ $\mathcal{O}$:Department$(\mathsf{g}(ssn, name, dept)) \wedge$
$\mathcal{O}$:hasDeptNumber$(\mathsf{g}(ssn, name, dept),dept) \wedge$
$\mathcal{O}$:works_for$(\mathsf{f}(ssn, name, dept),\mathsf{g}(ssn, name, dept))$.

This implies logically a collection of formulas, including

$(\forall ssn, name, dept)$ $\mathcal{O}$:Employee$(\mathsf{f}(ssn, name, dept)) \Leftarrow$ $\mathcal{T}$:Employee$(ssn, name, dept)$.
$(\forall ssn, name, dept)$ $\mathcal{O}$:hasSsn$(\mathsf{f}(ssn, name, dept),ssn) \Leftarrow$ $\mathcal{T}$:Employee$(ssn, name, dept)$.
$(\forall ssn, name, dept)$ $\mathcal{O}$:works_for$(\mathsf{f}(ssn, name, dept),\mathsf{g}(ssn, name, dept)) \Leftarrow$
$\mathcal{T}$:Employee$(ssn, name, dept)$.

Note however that different tables, such as $\mathcal{T}$:*manages*($\underline{ssn, dept}$) say, introduce different Skolem functions, as in :

$\mathcal{O}$:Employee$(\mathsf{h}(ssn, dept)) \Leftarrow$ $\mathcal{T}$:manages$(ssn, dept)$.
$\mathcal{O}$:hasSsn$(\mathsf{h}(ssn, dept),ssn) \Leftarrow$ $\mathcal{T}$:manages$(ssn, dept)$.

Unfortunately, this appears to leave open the problem of connecting the ontology individuals obtained from $\mathcal{T}$:*manages* and $\mathcal{T}$:*Employee*. The answer is provided by the fact that $\mathcal{O}$:*hasSsn* is inverse functional (ssn is a key), which means that there should be an ontology axiom

$(\forall u, v, ssn)$ $\mathcal{O}$:hasSsn$(u, ssn) \wedge$ $\mathcal{O}$:hasSsn$(v, ssn) \Rightarrow u = v$

[15] For simplicity, we eliminate henceforth the part dealing with projects.

This implies, among others, that
$(\forall ssn, name, dept)\ \mathsf{f}(ssn, name, dept) = \mathsf{h}(ssn, dept)$.
So we need to answer queries over the ontology using all such axioms.

A final, important connection to make in this case is with the research on answering queries using views [6]: The semantic mappings found by the earlier algorithms in this paper can be regarded as view definitions for each relational tables, using conjunctive queries over ontology predicates ("tables"). What we are seeking in this section is answers to queries phrased in terms of the ontology predicates, but rephrased in terms of relational tables, where the data instances reside — which is exactly the problem of query answering using views. The kind of rules we proposed earlier in this section are known as "inverse rules" [19], and in fact Duschka and Levy [5] even deal (implicitly) with the alias problem we mentioned above by their solution to the query answering problem in the presence of functional dependencies: keys functionally determine the rest of the columns in the table.

The one difference in our case worth noting is that we are willing to countenance answers which contain Skolem functions (since this is how we generate object id's in the ontology).

9 Conclusion and Future Work

We have proposed a heuristic algorithm for inferring semantic mapping formulas between relational tables and ontologies starting from simple correspondences. Our algorithm relies on information from the database schema (key and foreign key structure) and the ontology (cardinality restrictions, **is-a** hierarchies). Theoretically, our algorithm infers all and only the relevant semantics if a relational schema was generated using standard database design principles. In practice, our experience working with independently developed schemas and ontologies has shown that significant effort can be saved in specifying the LAV mapping formulas.

Numerous additional sources of knowledge, including richer ontologies, actual data stored in the tables, linguistic and semantic relationships between identifiers in tables and the ontology, can be used to refine the suggestions of MAPONTO, including providing a rank ordering for them. As in the original Clio system, more complex correspondences (e.g., from columns to sets of attribute names or class names), should also be investigated in order to generate the full range of mappings encountered in practice.

Acknowledgments. We are most grateful to Renée Miller and Yannis Velegrakis for their clarifications concerning Clio, comments on our results, and encouragement. Remaining errors are, of course, our own. We also deeply appreciate the reviewers' careful readings and constructive comments.

References

1. Y. An, A. Borgida, and J. Mylopoulos Inferring Complex Semantic Mappings between Relational Tables and Ontologies from Simple Correspondences. In *ODBASE'05*, pages 1152-1169, 2005.

2. D. Calvanese, G. D. Giacomo, M. Lenzerini, D. Nardi, and R. Rosati. Data Integration in Data Warehousing. *J. of Coop. Info. Sys.*, 10(3):237–271, 2001.
3. M. Dahchour and A. Pirotte. The Semantics of Reifying n-ary Relationships as Classes. In *ICEIS'02*, pages 580–586, 2002.
4. R. Dhamankar, Y. Lee, A. Doan, A. Halevy, and P. Domingos. iMAP: Discovering Complex Semantic Matches between Database Schemas. In *SIGMOD'04*, pages 383–394, 2004.
5. O. M. Duschka and A. Y. Levy. Recursive Plans for Information Gathering. In *IJCAI'97*, pages 778-784, 1997.
6. A. Y. Halevy. Answering queries using views: A survey. *VLDB Journal*, 10(4):270-294, 2001.
7. A. Gangemi, N. Guarino, C. Masolo, A. Oltramari, and L. Schneider. Sweetening Ontologies with DOLCE. In *EKAW'02*, pages 166–181, 2002.
8. F. Goasdoue et al. Answering queries using views: A KRDB perspective for the semantic web. *ACM TOIT*, 4(3), 2004.
9. J.-L. Hainaut. *Database Reverse Engineering*. http:// citeseer.ist.psu.edu/ article/ hainaut98database.html, 1998.
10. S. Handschuh, S. Staab, and R. Volz. On Deep Annotation. In *Proc. WWW'03*, 2003.
11. P. Johannesson. A method for transforming relational schemas into conceptual schemas. In *ICDE*, pages 190–201, 1994.
12. H. Knublauch, R. W. Fergerson, N. F. Noy, and M. A. Musen. The Protege OWL Plugin: An Open Development Environment for Semantic Web Applications. In *ISWC2004*, Nov. 2004.
13. A. Y. Levy, D. Srivastava, and T. Kirk. Data Model and Query Evaluation in Global Information Systems. *J. of Intelligent Info. Sys.*, 5(2):121–143, Dec 1996.
14. A. Y. Levy. Logic-Based Techniques in Data Integration. In Jack Minker (ed), *Logic Based Artificial Intelligence.*, Kluwer Publishers, 2000
15. V. M. Markowitz and J. A. Makowsky. Identifying Extended Entity-Relationship Object Structures in Relational Schemas. *IEEE TSE*, 16(8):777–790, August 1990.
16. E. Mena, V. Kashyap, A. Sheth, and A. Illarramendi. OBSERVER: An Approach for Query Processing in Global Information Systems Based on Interoperation Across Preexisting Ontologies. In *CoopIS'96*, pages 14–25, 1996.
17. R. Miller, L. M. Haas, and M. A. Hernandez. Schema Mapping as Query Discovery. In *VLDB'00*, pages 77–88, 2000.
18. L. Popa, Y. Velegrakis, R. J. Miller, M. Hernandes, and R. Fagin. Translating Web Data. In *VLDB'02*, pages 598–609, 2002.
19. Xiaolei Qian. Query Folding. In *Proc. ICDE*, 48-55, 1996.
20. M. R. Quillian. Semantic Memory. In *Semantic Information Processing*. Marvin Minsky (editor). 227-270. The MIT Press. 1968.
21. E. Rahm and P. A. Bernstein. A Survey of Approaches to Automatic Schema Matching. *VLDB Journal*, 10:334–350, 2001.
22. R. Ramakrishnan and M. Gehrke. *Database Management Systems (3rd ed.)*. McGraw Hill, 2002.
23. H. Wache, T. Vogele, U. Visser, H. Stuckenschmidt, G. Schuster, H. Neumann, and S. Hubner. Ontology-Based Integration of Information - A Survey of Existing Approaches. In *IJCAI'01 Workshop. on Ontologies and Information Sharing*, 2001.

Specifying the Semantics of Operation Contracts in Conceptual Modeling

Anna Queralt and Ernest Teniente

Universitat Politècnica de Catalunya
Dept. de Llenguatges i Sistemes Informàtics
c/ Jordi Girona 1-3, 08034 Barcelona (Catalonia, Spain)
{aqueralt, teniente}@lsi.upc.edu

Abstract. This paper presents an experiment to recognize early hypoxia based on EEG analyses. A chaotic neural network, the KIII model, initially designed to model olfactory neural systems is utilized for pattern classification. The experimental results show that the EEG pattern can be detected remarkably at an early stage of hypoxia for individuals.

Keywords: Chaotic neural network; Hypoxia; EEG.

1 Introduction

According to the hypoxia at the 25th minute, both NE test and EEG give response (T-test on NE results shows $p<0.05$ and the mean correction rate by EEG is 92%). At the 16th minute, NE test makes no response to the hypoxia, However, By KIII network, normal and hypoxia EEGs in this moment can be distinguished remarkably (the mean correction rate is 97%). It provides the possibility to measure the subtle hypoxia quantitatively while other traditional method does not work.

The correction rate at the 16th minute is higher than the one at the 25th minute. It may attribute to adaption of human. Although NE results indicate that the moment, in which the hypoxia pattern comes into being, is the 25th minute, actually, the time is the 16th minute by EEG. Between the 16th and 25th minute, human can adapt to hypoxia, step by step. So, the response to hypoxia at the 16th minute is more intensive than that at the 25th minute. At the 7th minute, the mean correction rate is 51%. The results imply that the time is so early that the hypoxia pattern in EEG has not appeared clearly. Even KIII network, which is sensitive to pattern transition in EEG, can not work well.

The KIII model has good capability for pattern recognition as a form of the biological intelligence. It needs much fewer learning trials when solving problems of pattern recognition. In our study, it is extremely time consuming to use a digital computer to solve the numerous differential equations within KIII model. This problem restricts the application of the KIII network in real time. The implementation

S. Spaccapietra (Ed.): Journal on Data Semantics VII, LNCS 4244, pp. 33 – 56, 2006.

of the KIII in analog VLSI [11] is surely a promising research for building more intelligent and powerful artificial neural network.

By providing feature vectors for classification, the EEG might be made to serve as a quantitative indicator of the subtle hypoxia in real time, which might significantly improve the safety of those who work in high altitude.

According to the hypoxia at the 25th minute, both NE test and EEG give response (T-test on NE results shows p<0.05 and the mean correction rate by EEG is 92%). At the 16th minute, NE test makes no response to the hypoxia, However, By KIII network, normal and hypoxia EEGs in this moment can be distinguished remarkably (the mean correction rate is 97%). It provides the possibility to measure the subtle hypoxia quantitatively while other traditional method does not work.

The correction rate at the 16th minute is higher than the one at the 25th minute. It may attribute to adaption of human. Although NE results indicate that the moment, in which the hypoxia pattern comes into being, is the 25th minute, actually, the time is the 16th minute by EEG. Between the 16th and 25th minute, human can adapt to hypoxia, step by step. So, the response to hypoxia at the 16th minute is more intensive than that at the 25th minute. At the 7th minute, the mean correction rate is 51%. The results imply that the time is so early that the hypoxia pattern in EEG has not appeared clearly. Even KIII network, which is sensitive to pattern transition in EEG, can not work well.

The KIII model has good capability for pattern recognition as a form of the biological intelligence. It needs much fewer learning trials when solving problems of pattern recognition. In our study, it is extremely time consuming to use a digital computer to solve the numerous differential equations within KIII model. This problem restricts the application of the KIII network in real time. The implementation of the KIII in analog VLSI [11] is surely a promising research for building more intelligent and powerful artificial neural network.

By providing feature vectors for classification, the EEG might be made to serve as a quantitative indicator of the subtle hypoxia in real time, which might significantly improve the safety of those who work in high altitude.

According to the hypoxia at the 25th minute, both NE test and EEG give response (T-test on NE results shows p<0.05 and the mean correction rate by EEG is 92%). At the 16th minute, NE test makes no response to the hypoxia, However, By KIII network, normal and hypoxia EEGs in this moment can be distinguished remarkably (the mean correction rate is 97%). It provides the possibility to measure the subtle hypoxia quantitatively while other traditional method does not work.

The correction rate at the 16th minute is higher than the one at the 25th minute. It may attribute to adaption of human. Although NE results indicate that the moment, in which the hypoxia pattern comes into being, is the 25th minute, actually, the time is the 16th minute by EEG. Between the 16th and 25th minute, human can adapt to hypoxia, step by step. So, the response to hypoxia at the 16th minute is more intensive than that at the 25th minute. At the 7th minute, the mean correction rate is 51%. The results imply that the time is so early that the hypoxia pattern in EEG has not appeared clearly. Even KIII network, which is sensitive to pattern transition in EEG, can not work well.

The KIII model has good capability for pattern recognition as a form of the biological intelligence. It needs much fewer learning trials when solving problems of pattern recognition. In our study, it is extremely time consuming to use a digital computer to solve the numerous differential equations within KIII model. This problem restricts the application of the KIII network in real time. The implementation of the KIII in analog VLSI [11] is surely a promising research for building more intelligent and powerful artificial neural network.

By providing feature vectors for classification, the EEG might be made to serve as a quantitative indicator of the subtle hypoxia in real time, which might significantly improve the safety of those who work in high altitude.

It is well known that hypoxia disrupts intracellular process and impairs cellular function. Brain cells with a uniquely high oxygen demand are most susceptible to low oxygen tension. Intellectual impairment is currently considered as an early sign of hypoxia, which is particularly dangerous for pilots because the signs and symptoms do not usually cause discomfort or pain to make them recognize their own disability. While numerous physiological indicators, such as neurobehavioral evaluation (NE) used in our research, are available to evaluate hypoxia, the EEG signal is one of the most predictive and reliable method which may assess hypoxia on-line [1].

EEGs are dynamic, stochastic, non-linear and non-stationary and exhibit significant complex behavior [2], [3]. Considering this, traditional methods may not be appropriate approach in characterizing the intrinsic nature of the EEG. According to the hypoxia at the 25th minute, both NE test and EEG give response (T-test on NE results shows $p<0.05$ and the mean correction rate by EEG is 92%). At the 16th minute, NE test makes no response to the hypoxia, However, By KIII network, normal and hypoxia EEGs in this moment can be distinguished remarkably (the mean correction rate is 97%). It provides the possibility to measure the subtle hypoxia quantitatively while other traditional method does not work. According to the hypoxia at the 25th minute, both NE test and EEG give response (T-test on NE results shows $p<0.05$ and the mean correction rate by EEG is 92%). At the 16th minute, NE test makes no response to the hypoxia, However, By KIII network, normal and hypoxia EEGs in this moment can be distinguished remarkably (the mean correction rate is 97%). It provides the possibility to measure the subtle hypoxia quantitatively while other traditional method does not work.

The correction rate at the 16th minute is higher than the one at the 25th minute. It may attribute to adaption of human. Although NE results indicate that the moment, in which the hypoxia pattern comes into being, is the 25th minute, actually, the time is the 16th minute by EEG. Between the 16th and 25th minute, human can adapt to hypoxia, step by step. So, the response to hypoxia at the 16th minute is more intensive than that at the 25th minute. At the 7th minute, the mean correction rate is 51%. The results imply that the time is so early that the hypoxia pattern in EEG has not appeared clearly. Even KIII network, which is sensitive to pattern transition in EEG, can not work well.

The KIII model has good capability for pattern recognition as a form of the biological intelligence. It needs much fewer learning trials when solving problems of pattern recognition. In our study, it is extremely time consuming to use a digital computer to solve the numerous differential equations within KIII model. This problem restricts the application of the KIII network in real time. The implementation of the KIII in analog VLSI [11] is surely a promising research for building more intelligent and powerful artificial neural network.

By providing feature vectors for classification, the EEG might be made to serve as a quantitative indicator of the subtle hypoxia in real time, which might significantly improve the safety of those who work in high altitude.

According to the hypoxia at the 25th minute, both NE test and EEG give response (T-test on NE results shows $p<0.05$ and the mean correction rate by EEG is 92%). At the 16th minute, NE test makes no response to the hypoxia, However, By KIII network, normal and hypoxia EEGs in this moment can be distinguished remarkably (the mean correction rate is 97%). It provides the possibility to measure the subtle hypoxia quantitatively while other traditional method does not work.

The correction rate at the 16th minute is higher than the one at the 25th minute. It may attribute to adaption of human. Although NE results indicate that the moment, in which the hypoxia pattern comes into being, is the 25th minute, actually, the time is the 16th minute by EEG. Between the 16th and 25th minute, human can adapt to hypoxia, step by step. So, the response to hypoxia at the 16th minute is more intensive than that at the 25th minute. At the 7th minute, the mean correction rate is 51%. The results imply that the time is so early that the hypoxia pattern in EEG has not appeared clearly. Even KIII network, which is sensitive to pattern transition in EEG, can not work well.

The KIII model has good capability for pattern recognition as a form of the biological intelligence. It needs much fewer learning trials when solving problems of pattern recognition. In our study, it is extremely time consuming to use a digital computer to solve the numerous differential equations within KIII model. This problem restricts the application of the KIII network in real time. The implementation of the KIII in analog VLSI [11] is surely a promising research for building more intelligent and powerful artificial neural network.

By providing feature vectors for classification, the EEG might be made to serve as a quantitative indicator of the subtle hypoxia in real time, which might significantly improve the safety of those who work in high altitude.

The correction rate at the 16th minute is higher than the one at the 25th minute. It may attribute to adaption of human. Although NE results indicate that the moment, in which the hypoxia pattern comes into being, is the 25th minute, actually, the time is the 16th minute by EEG. Between the 16th and 25th minute, human can adapt to hypoxia, step by step. So, the response to hypoxia at the 16th minute is more intensive than that at the 25th minute. At the 7th minute, the mean correction rate is 51%. The results imply that the time is so early that the hypoxia pattern in EEG has not appeared clearly. Even KIII network, which is sensitive to pattern transition in EEG, can not work well.

The KIII model has good capability for pattern recognition as a form of the biological intelligence. It needs much fewer learning trials when solving problems of pattern recognition. In our study, it is extremely time consuming to use a digital computer to solve the numerous differential equations within KIII model. This problem restricts the application of the KIII network in real time. The implementation of the KIII in analog VLSI [11] is surely a promising research for building more intelligent and powerful artificial neural network.

By providing feature vectors for classification, the EEG might be made to serve as a quantitative indicator of the subtle hypoxia in real time, which might significantly improve the safety of those who work in high altitude.

The architecture of the olfactory system is followed to construct a high dimensional chaotic network, the KIII model, in which the interactions of globally connected nodes are shaped by reinforcement learning to support a global landscape of high dimensional chaotic attractors. Each low-dimensional local basin of attraction corresponds to a learned class of stimulus patterns. Convergence to an attractor constitutes abstraction and generalization from an example to the class. KIII model has performed well on several complex pattern recognition tasks [4], [5], [6]. According to the hypoxia at the 25th minute, both NE test and EEG give response (T-test on NE results shows $p<0.05$ and the mean correction rate by EEG is 92%). At the 16th minute, NE test makes no response to the hypoxia, However, By KIII network, normal and hypoxia EEGs in this moment can be distinguished remarkably (the mean correction rate is 97%). It provides the possibility to measure the subtle hypoxia quantitatively while other traditional method does not work.

The correction rate at the 16th minute is higher than the one at the 25th minute. It may attribute to adaption of human. Although NE results indicate that the moment, in which the hypoxia pattern comes into being, is the 25th minute, actually, the time is the 16th minute by EEG. Between the 16th and 25th minute, human can adapt to hypoxia, step by step. So, the response to hypoxia at the 16th minute is more intensive than that at the 25th minute. At the 7th minute, the mean correction rate is 51%. The results imply that the time is so early that the hypoxia pattern in EEG has not appeared clearly. Even KIII network, which is sensitive to pattern transition in EEG, can not work well.

The KIII model has good capability for pattern recognition as a form of the biological intelligence. It needs much fewer learning trials when solving problems of pattern recognition. In our study, it is extremely time consuming to use a digital computer to solve the numerous differential equations within KIII model. This problem restricts the application of the KIII network in real time. The implementation of the KIII in analog VLSI [11] is surely a promising research for building more intelligent and powerful artificial neural network.

By providing feature vectors for classification, the EEG might be made to serve as a quantitative indicator of the subtle hypoxia in real time, which might significantly improve the safety of those who work in high altitude.

Hypoxic EEG collected after the subjects stayed at environment simulating 3500 m altitude for 25 minutes could be distinguished from normal EEG when the hypoxia It is well known that hypoxia disrupts intracellular process and impairs cellular function. Brain cells with a uniquely high oxygen demand are most susceptible to low oxygen tension. Intellectual impairment is currently considered as an early sign of

hypoxia, which is particularly dangerous for pilots because the signs and symptoms do not usually cause discomfort or pain to make them recognize their own disability. While numerous physiological indicators, such as neurobehavioral evaluation (NE) used in our research, are available to evaluate hypoxia, the EEG signal is one of the most predictive and reliable method which may assess hypoxia on-line [1].

EEGs are dynamic, stochastic, non-linear and non-stationary and exhibit significant complex behavior [2], [3]. Considering this, traditional methods may not be appropriate approach in characterizing the intrinsic nature of the EEG.

The architecture of the olfactory system is followed to construct a high dimensional chaotic network, the KIII model, in which the interactions of globally connected nodes are shaped by reinforcement learning to support a global landscape of high dimensional chaotic attractors. Each low-dimensional local basin of attraction corresponds to a learned class of stimulus patterns. Convergence to an attractor constitutes abstraction and generalization from an example to the class. KIII model has performed well on several complex pattern recognition tasks [4], [5], [6].

Hypoxic EEG collected after the subjects stayed at environment simulating 3500 m altitude for 25 minutes could be distinguished from normal EEG when the hypoxia It is well known that hypoxia disrupts intracellular process and impairs cellular function. Brain cells with a uniquely high oxygen demand are most susceptible to low oxygen tension. Intellectual impairment is currently considered as an early sign of hypoxia, which is particularly dangerous for pilots because the signs and symptoms do not usually cause discomfort or pain to make them recognize their own disability. While numerous physiological indicators, such as neurobehavioral evaluation (NE) used in our research, are available to evaluate hypoxia, the EEG signal is one of the most predictive and reliable method which may assess hypoxia on-line [1].

EEGs are dynamic, stochastic, non-linear and non-stationary and exhibit significant complex behavior [2], [3]. Considering this, traditional methods may not be appropriate approach in characterizing the intrinsic nature of the EEG.

The architecture of the olfactory system is followed to construct a high dimensional chaotic network, the KIII model, in which the interactions of globally connected nodes are shaped by reinforcement learning to support a global landscape of high dimensional chaotic attractors. Each low-dimensional local basin of attraction corresponds to a learned class of stimulus patterns. Convergence to an attractor constitutes abstraction and generalization from an example to the class. KIII model has performed well on several complex pattern recognition tasks [4], [5], [6].

Hypoxic EEG collected after the subjects stayed at environment simulating 3500 m altitude for 25 minutes could be distinguished from normal EEG when the hypoxia It is well known that hypoxia disrupts intracellular process and impairs cellular function. Brain cells with a uniquely high oxygen demand are most susceptible to low oxygen tension. Intellectual impairment is currently considered as an early sign of hypoxia, which is particularly dangerous for pilots because the signs and symptoms do not usually cause discomfort or pain to make them recognize their own disability. While numerous physiological indicators, such as neurobehavioral evaluation (NE) used in our research, are available to evaluate hypoxia, the EEG signal is one of the most predictive and reliable method which may assess hypoxia on-line [1].

EEGs are dynamic, stochastic, non-linear and non-stationary and exhibit significant complex behavior [2], [3]. Considering this, traditional methods may not be appropriate approach in characterizing the intrinsic nature of the EEG.

The architecture of the olfactory system is followed to construct a high dimensional chaotic network, the KIII model, in which the interactions of globally connected nodes are shaped by reinforcement learning to support a global landscape of high dimensional chaotic attractors. Each low-dimensional local basin of attraction corresponds to a learned class of stimulus patterns. Convergence to an attractor constitutes abstraction and generalization from an example to the class. KIII model has performed well on several complex pattern recognition tasks [4], [5], [6].

Hypoxic EEG collected after the subjects stayed at environment simulating 3500 m altitude for 25 minutes could be distinguished from normal EEG when the hypoxia It is well known that hypoxia disrupts intracellular process and impairs cellular function. Brain cells with a uniquely high oxygen demand are most susceptible to low oxygen tension. Intellectual impairment is currently considered as an early sign of hypoxia, which is particularly dangerous for pilots because the signs and symptoms do not usually cause discomfort or pain to make them recognize their own disability. While numerous physiological indicators, such as neurobehavioral evaluation (NE) used in our research, are available to evaluate hypoxia, the EEG signal is one of the most predictive and reliable method which may assess hypoxia on-line [1].

EEGs are dynamic, stochastic, non-linear and non-stationary and exhibit significant complex behavior [2], [3]. Considering this, traditional methods may not be appropriate approach in characterizing the intrinsic nature of the EEG.

The architecture of the olfactory system is followed to construct a high dimensional chaotic network, the KIII model, in which the interactions of globally connected nodes are shaped by reinforcement learning to support a global landscape of high dimensional chaotic attractors. Each low-dimensional local basin of attraction corresponds to a learned class of stimulus patterns. Convergence to an attractor constitutes abstraction and generalization from an example to the class. KIII model has performed well on several complex pattern recognition tasks [4], [5], [6].

Hypoxic EEG collected after the subjects stayed at environment simulating 3500 m altitude for 25 minutes could be distinguished from normal EEG when the hypoxia It is well known that hypoxia disrupts intracellular process and impairs cellular function. Brain cells with a uniquely high oxygen demand are most susceptible to low oxygen tension. Intellectual impairment is currently considered as an early sign of hypoxia, which is particularly dangerous for pilots because the signs and symptoms do not usually cause discomfort or pain to make them recognize their own disability. While numerous physiological indicators, such as neurobehavioral evaluation (NE) used in our research, are available to evaluate hypoxia, the EEG signal is one of the most predictive and reliable method which may assess hypoxia on-line [1].

EEGs are dynamic, stochastic, non-linear and non-stationary and exhibit significant complex behavior [2], [3]. Considering this, traditional methods may not be appropriate approach in characterizing the intrinsic nature of the EEG.

The architecture of the olfactory system is followed to construct a high dimensional chaotic network, the KIII model, in which the interactions of globally connected nodes are shaped by reinforcement learning to support a global landscape of high dimensional chaotic attractors. Each low-dimensional local basin of attraction corresponds to a learned class of stimulus patterns. Convergence to an attractor constitutes abstraction and generalization from an example to the class. KIII model has performed well on several complex pattern recognition tasks [4], [5], [6].

Hypoxic EEG collected after the subjects stayed at environment simulating 3500 m altitude for 25 minutes could be distinguished from normal EEG when the hypoxia It is well known that hypoxia disrupts intracellular process and impairs cellular function. Brain cells with a uniquely high oxygen demand are most susceptible to low oxygen tension. Intellectual impairment is currently considered as an early sign of hypoxia, which is particularly dangerous for pilots because the signs and symptoms do not usually cause discomfort or pain to make them recognize their own disability. While numerous physiological indicators, such as neurobehavioral evaluation (NE) used in our research, are available to evaluate hypoxia, the EEG signal is one of the most predictive and reliable method which may assess hypoxia on-line [1].

EEGs are dynamic, stochastic, non-linear and non-stationary and exhibit significant complex behavior [2], [3]. Considering this, traditional methods may not be appropriate approach in characterizing the intrinsic nature of the EEG.

The architecture of the olfactory system is followed to construct a high dimensional chaotic network, the KIII model, in which the interactions of globally connected nodes are shaped by reinforcement learning to support a global landscape of high dimensional chaotic attractors. Each low-dimensional local basin of attraction corresponds to a learned class of stimulus patterns. Convergence to an attractor constitutes abstraction and generalization from an example to the class. KIII model has performed well on several complex pattern recognition tasks [4], [5], [6].

Hypoxic EEG collected after the subjects stayed at environment simulating 3500 m altitude for 25 minutes could be distinguished from normal EEG when the hypoxia It is well known that hypoxia disrupts intracellular process and impairs cellular function. Brain cells with a uniquely high oxygen demand are most susceptible to low oxygen tension. Intellectual impairment is currently considered as an early sign of hypoxia, which is particularly dangerous for pilots because the signs and symptoms do not usually cause discomfort or pain to make them recognize their own disability. While numerous physiological indicators, such as neurobehavioral evaluation (NE) used in our research, are available to evaluate hypoxia, the EEG signal is one of the most predictive and reliable method which may assess hypoxia on-line [1].

EEGs are dynamic, stochastic, non-linear and non-stationary and exhibit significant complex behavior [2], [3]. Considering this, traditional methods may not be appropriate approach in characterizing the intrinsic nature of the EEG.

The architecture of the olfactory system is followed to construct a high dimensional chaotic network, the KIII model, in which the interactions of globally connected nodes are shaped by reinforcement learning to support a global landscape of high dimensional chaotic attractors. Each low-dimensional local basin of attraction corresponds to a learned class of stimulus patterns. Convergence to an attractor constitutes abstraction and generalization from an example to the class. KIII model has performed well on several complex pattern recognition tasks [4], [5], [6].

Hypoxic EEG collected after the subjects stayed at environment simulating 3500 m altitude for 25 minutes could be distinguished from normal EEG when the hypoxia It is well known that hypoxia disrupts intracellular process and impairs cellular function. Brain cells with a uniquely high oxygen demand are most susceptible to low oxygen tension. Intellectual impairment is currently considered as an early sign of hypoxia, which is particularly dangerous for pilots because the signs and symptoms do not usually cause discomfort or pain to make them recognize their own disability. While numerous physiological indicators, such as neurobehavioral evaluation (NE) used in our research, are available to evaluate hypoxia, the EEG signal is one of the most predictive and reliable method which may assess hypoxia on-line [1].

EEGs are dynamic, stochastic, non-linear and non-stationary and exhibit significant complex behavior [2], [3]. Considering this, traditional methods may not be appropriate approach in characterizing the intrinsic nature of the EEG.

The architecture of the olfactory system is followed to construct a high dimensional chaotic network, the KIII model, in which the interactions of globally connected nodes are shaped by reinforcement learning to support a global landscape of high dimensional chaotic attractors. Each low-dimensional local basin of attraction corresponds to a learned class of stimulus patterns. Convergence to an attractor constitutes abstraction and generalization from an example to the class. KIII model has performed well on several complex pattern recognition tasks [4], [5], [6].

Hypoxic EEG collected after the subjects stayed at environment simulating 3500 m altitude for 25 minutes could be distinguished from normal EEG when the hypoxia It is well known that hypoxia disrupts intracellular process and impairs cellular function. Brain cells with a uniquely high oxygen demand are most susceptible to low oxygen tension. Intellectual impairment is currently considered as an early sign of hypoxia, which is particularly dangerous for pilots because the signs and symptoms do not usually cause discomfort or pain to make them recognize their own disability. While numerous physiological indicators, such as neurobehavioral evaluation (NE) used in our research, are available to evaluate hypoxia, the EEG signal is one of the most predictive and reliable method which may assess hypoxia on-line [1].

EEGs are dynamic, stochastic, non-linear and non-stationary and exhibit significant complex behavior [2], [3]. Considering this, traditional methods may not be appropriate approach in characterizing the intrinsic nature of the EEG.

The architecture of the olfactory system is followed to construct a high dimensional chaotic network, the KIII model, in which the interactions of globally connected nodes are shaped by reinforcement learning to support a global landscape of high dimensional chaotic attractors. Each low-dimensional local basin of attraction corresponds to a learned class of stimulus patterns. Convergence to an attractor constitutes abstraction and generalization from an example to the class. KIII model has performed well on several complex pattern recognition tasks [4], [5], [6].

Hypoxic EEG collected after the subjects stayed at environment simulating 3500 m altitude for 25 minutes could be distinguished from normal EEG when the hypoxia It is well known that hypoxia disrupts intracellular process and impairs cellular function. Brain cells with a uniquely high oxygen demand are most susceptible to low oxygen tension. Intellectual impairment is currently considered as an early sign of

hypoxia, which is particularly dangerous for pilots because the signs and symptoms do not usually cause discomfort or pain to make them recognize their own disability. While numerous physiological indicators, such as neurobehavioral evaluation (NE) used in our research, are available to evaluate hypoxia, the EEG signal is one of the most predictive and reliable method which may assess hypoxia on-line [1].

EEGs are dynamic, stochastic, non-linear and non-stationary and exhibit significant complex behavior [2], [3]. Considering this, traditional methods may not be appropriate approach in characterizing the intrinsic nature of the EEG.

The architecture of the olfactory system is followed to construct a high dimensional chaotic network, the KIII model, in which the interactions of globally connected nodes are shaped by reinforcement learning to support a global landscape of high dimensional chaotic attractors. Each low-dimensional local basin of attraction corresponds to a learned class of stimulus patterns. Convergence to an attractor constitutes abstraction and generalization from an example to the class. KIII model has performed well on several complex pattern recognition tasks [4], [5], [6].

Hypoxic EEG collected after the subjects stayed at environment simulating 3500 m altitude for 25 minutes could be distinguished from normal EEG when the hypoxia It is well known that hypoxia disrupts intracellular process and impairs cellular function. Brain cells with a uniquely high oxygen demand are most susceptible to low oxygen tension. Intellectual impairment is currently considered as an early sign of hypoxia, which is particularly dangerous for pilots because the signs and symptoms do not usually cause discomfort or pain to make them recognize their own disability. While numerous physiological indicators, such as neurobehavioral evaluation (NE) used in our research, are available to evaluate hypoxia, the EEG signal is one of the most predictive and reliable method which may assess hypoxia on-line [1].

EEGs are dynamic, stochastic, non-linear and non-stationary and exhibit significant complex behavior [2], [3]. Considering this, traditional methods may not be appropriate approach in characterizing the intrinsic nature of the EEG.

The architecture of the olfactory system is followed to construct a high dimensional chaotic network, the KIII model, in which the interactions of globally connected nodes are shaped by reinforcement learning to support a global landscape of high dimensional chaotic attractors. Each low-dimensional local basin of attraction corresponds to a learned class of stimulus patterns. Convergence to an attractor constitutes abstraction and generalization from an example to the class. KIII model has performed well on several complex pattern recognition tasks [4], [5], [6].

Hypoxic EEG collected after the subjects stayed at environment simulating 3500 m altitude for 25 minutes could be distinguished from normal EEG when the hypoxia It is well known that hypoxia disrupts intracellular process and impairs cellular function. Brain cells with a uniquely high oxygen demand are most susceptible to low oxygen tension. Intellectual impairment is currently considered as an early sign of hypoxia, which is particularly dangerous for pilots because the signs and symptoms do not usually cause discomfort or pain to make them recognize their own disability. While numerous physiological indicators, such as neurobehavioral evaluation (NE) used in our research, are available to evaluate hypoxia, the EEG signal is one of the most predictive and reliable method which may assess hypoxia on-line [1].

EEGs are dynamic, stochastic, non-linear and non-stationary and exhibit significant complex behavior [2], [3]. Considering this, traditional methods may not be appropriate approach in characterizing the intrinsic nature of the EEG.

The architecture of the olfactory system is followed to construct a high dimensional chaotic network, the KIII model, in which the interactions of globally connected nodes are shaped by reinforcement learning to support a global landscape of high dimensional chaotic attractors. Each low-dimensional local basin of attraction corresponds to a learned class of stimulus patterns. Convergence to an attractor constitutes abstraction and generalization from an example to the class. KIII model has performed well on several complex pattern recognition tasks [4], [5], [6].

Hypoxic EEG collected after the subjects stayed at environment simulating 3500 m altitude for 25 minutes could be distinguished from normal EEG when the hypoxia It is well known that hypoxia disrupts intracellular process and impairs cellular function. Brain cells with a uniquely high oxygen demand are most susceptible to low oxygen tension. Intellectual impairment is currently considered as an early sign of hypoxia, which is particularly dangerous for pilots because the signs and symptoms do not usually cause discomfort or pain to make them recognize their own disability. While numerous physiological indicators, such as neurobehavioral evaluation (NE) used in our research, are available to evaluate hypoxia, the EEG signal is one of the most predictive and reliable method which may assess hypoxia on-line [1].

EEGs are dynamic, stochastic, non-linear and non-stationary and exhibit significant complex behavior [2], [3]. Considering this, traditional methods may not be appropriate approach in characterizing the intrinsic nature of the EEG.

The architecture of the olfactory system is followed to construct a high dimensional chaotic network, the KIII model, in which the interactions of globally connected nodes are shaped by reinforcement learning to support a global landscape of high dimensional chaotic attractors. Each low-dimensional local basin of attraction corresponds to a learned class of stimulus patterns. Convergence to an attractor constitutes abstraction and generalization from an example to the class. KIII model has performed well on several complex pattern recognition tasks [4], [5], [6].

Hypoxic EEG collected after the subjects stayed at environment simulating 3500 m altitude for 25 minutes could be distinguished from normal EEG when the hypoxia It is well known that hypoxia disrupts intracellular process and impairs cellular function. Brain cells with a uniquely high oxygen demand are most susceptible to low oxygen tension. Intellectual impairment is currently considered as an early sign of hypoxia, which is particularly dangerous for pilots because the signs and symptoms do not usually cause discomfort or pain to make them recognize their own disability. While numerous physiological indicators, such as neurobehavioral evaluation (NE) used in our research, are available to evaluate hypoxia, the EEG signal is one of the most predictive and reliable method which may assess hypoxia on-line [1].

EEGs are dynamic, stochastic, non-linear and non-stationary and exhibit significant complex behavior [2], [3]. Considering this, traditional methods may not be appropriate approach in characterizing the intrinsic nature of the EEG.

The architecture of the olfactory system is followed to construct a high dimensional chaotic network, the KIII model, in which the interactions of globally

connected nodes are shaped by reinforcement learning to support a global landscape of high dimensional chaotic attractors. Each low-dimensional local basin of attraction corresponds to a learned class of stimulus patterns. Convergence to an attractor constitutes abstraction and generalization from an example to the class. KIII model has performed well on several complex pattern recognition tasks [4], [5], [6].
Hypoxic EEG collected after the subjects stayed at environment simulating 3500 m altitude for 25 minutes could be distinguished from normal EEG when the hypoxia It is well known that hypoxia disrupts intracellular process and impairs cellular function. Brain cells with a uniquely high oxygen demand are most susceptible to low oxygen tension. Intellectual impairment is currently considered as an early sign of hypoxia, which is particularly dangerous for pilots because the signs and symptoms do not usually cause discomfort or pain to make them recognize their own disability. While numerous physiological indicators, such as neurobehavioral evaluation (NE) used in our research, are available to evaluate hypoxia, the EEG signal is one of the most predictive and reliable method which may assess hypoxia on-line [1].

EEGs are dynamic, stochastic, non-linear and non-stationary and exhibit significant complex behavior [2], [3]. Considering this, traditional methods may not be appropriate approach in characterizing the intrinsic nature of the EEG.

The architecture of the olfactory system is followed to construct a high dimensional chaotic network, the KIII model, in which the interactions of globally connected nodes are shaped by reinforcement learning to support a global landscape of high dimensional chaotic attractors. Each low-dimensional local basin of attraction corresponds to a learned class of stimulus patterns. Convergence to an attractor constitutes abstraction and generalization from an example to the class. KIII model has performed well on several complex pattern recognition tasks [4], [5], [6].

Hypoxic EEG collected after the subjects stayed at environment simulating 3500 m altitude for 25 minutes could be distinguished from normal EEG when the hypoxia It is well known that hypoxia disrupts intracellular process and impairs cellular function. Brain cells with a uniquely high oxygen demand are most susceptible to low oxygen tension. Intellectual impairment is currently considered as an early sign of hypoxia, which is particularly dangerous for pilots because the signs and symptoms do not usually cause discomfort or pain to make them recognize their own disability. While numerous physiological indicators, such as neurobehavioral evaluation (NE) used in our research, are available to evaluate hypoxia, the EEG signal is one of the most predictive and reliable method which may assess hypoxia on-line [1].

EEGs are dynamic, stochastic, non-linear and non-stationary and exhibit significant complex behavior [2], [3]. Considering this, traditional methods may not be appropriate approach in characterizing the intrinsic nature of the EEG.

The architecture of the olfactory system is followed to construct a high dimensional chaotic network, the KIII model, in which the interactions of globally connected nodes are shaped by reinforcement learning to support a global landscape of high dimensional chaotic attractors. Each low-dimensional local basin of attraction corresponds to a learned class of stimulus patterns. Convergence to an attractor constitutes abstraction and generalization from an example to the class. KIII model has performed well on several complex pattern recognition tasks [4], [5], [6].

Hypoxic EEG collected after the subjects stayed at environment simulating 3500 m altitude for 25 minutes could be distinguished from normal EEG when the hypoxia It is well known that hypoxia disrupts intracellular process and impairs cellular function. Brain cells with a uniquely high oxygen demand are most susceptible to low oxygen tension. Intellectual impairment is currently considered as an early sign of hypoxia, which is particularly dangerous for pilots because the signs and symptoms do not usually cause discomfort or pain to make them recognize their own disability. While numerous physiological indicators, such as neurobehavioral evaluation (NE) used in our research, are available to evaluate hypoxia, the EEG signal is one of the most predictive and reliable method which may assess hypoxia on-line [1].

EEGs are dynamic, stochastic, non-linear and non-stationary and exhibit significant complex behavior [2], [3]. Considering this, traditional methods may not be appropriate approach in characterizing the intrinsic nature of the EEG.

The architecture of the olfactory system is followed to construct a high dimensional chaotic network, the KIII model, in which the interactions of globally connected nodes are shaped by reinforcement learning to support a global landscape of high dimensional chaotic attractors. Each low-dimensional local basin of attraction corresponds to a learned class of stimulus patterns. Convergence to an attractor constitutes abstraction and generalization from an example to the class. KIII model has performed well on several complex pattern recognition tasks [4], [5], [6].

Hypoxic EEG collected after the subjects stayed at environment simulating 3500 m altitude for 25 minutes could be distinguished from normal EEG when the hypoxia It is well known that hypoxia disrupts intracellular process and impairs cellular function. Brain cells with a uniquely high oxygen demand are most susceptible to low oxygen tension. Intellectual impairment is currently considered as an early sign of hypoxia, which is particularly dangerous for pilots because the signs and symptoms do not usually cause discomfort or pain to make them recognize their own disability. While numerous physiological indicators, such as neurobehavioral evaluation (NE) used in our research, are available to evaluate hypoxia, the EEG signal is one of the most predictive and reliable method which may assess hypoxia on-line [1].

EEGs are dynamic, stochastic, non-linear and non-stationary and exhibit significant complex behavior [2], [3]. Considering this, traditional methods may not be appropriate approach in characterizing the intrinsic nature of the EEG.

The architecture of the olfactory system is followed to construct a high dimensional chaotic network, the KIII model, in which the interactions of globally connected nodes are shaped by reinforcement learning to support a global landscape of high dimensional chaotic attractors. Each low-dimensional local basin of attraction corresponds to a learned class of stimulus patterns. Convergence to an attractor constitutes abstraction and generalization from an example to the class. KIII model has performed well on several complex pattern recognition tasks [4], [5], [6].

Hypoxic EEG collected after the subjects stayed at environment simulating 3500 m altitude for 25 minutes could be distinguished from normal EEG when the hypoxia It is well known that hypoxia disrupts intracellular process and impairs cellular function. Brain cells with a uniquely high oxygen demand are most susceptible to low oxygen tension. Intellectual impairment is currently considered as an early sign of

hypoxia, which is particularly dangerous for pilots because the signs and symptoms do not usually cause discomfort or pain to make them recognize their own disability. While numerous physiological indicators, such as neurobehavioral evaluation (NE) used in our research, are available to evaluate hypoxia, the EEG signal is one of the most predictive and reliable method which may assess hypoxia on-line [1].

EEGs are dynamic, stochastic, non-linear and non-stationary and exhibit significant complex behavior [2], [3]. Considering this, traditional methods may not be appropriate approach in characterizing the intrinsic nature of the EEG.

The architecture of the olfactory system is followed to construct a high dimensional chaotic network, the KIII model, in which the interactions of globally connected nodes are shaped by reinforcement learning to support a global landscape of high dimensional chaotic attractors. Each low-dimensional local basin of attraction corresponds to a learned class of stimulus patterns. Convergence to an attractor constitutes abstraction and generalization from an example to the class. KIII model has performed well on several complex pattern recognition tasks [4], [5], [6].
Hypoxic EEG collected after the subjects stayed at environment simulating 3500 m altitude for 25 minutes could be distinguished from normal EEG when the hypoxia It is well known that hypoxia disrupts intracellular process and impairs cellular function. Brain cells with a uniquely high oxygen demand are most susceptible to low oxygen tension. Intellectual impairment is currently considered as an early sign of hypoxia, which is particularly dangerous for pilots because the signs and symptoms do not usually cause discomfort or pain to make them recognize their own disability. While numerous physiological indicators, such as neurobehavioral evaluation (NE) used in our research, are available to evaluate hypoxia, the EEG signal is one of the most predictive and reliable method which may assess hypoxia on-line [1].

EEGs are dynamic, stochastic, non-linear and non-stationary and exhibit significant complex behavior [2], [3]. Considering this, traditional methods may not be appropriate approach in characterizing the intrinsic nature of the EEG.

The architecture of the olfactory system is followed to construct a high dimensional chaotic network, the KIII model, in which the interactions of globally connected nodes are shaped by reinforcement learning to support a global landscape of high dimensional chaotic attractors. Each low-dimensional local basin of attraction corresponds to a learned class of stimulus patterns. Convergence to an attractor constitutes abstraction and generalization from an example to the class. KIII model has performed well on several complex pattern recognition tasks [4], [5], [6].
Hypoxic EEG collected after the subjects stayed at environment simulating 3500 m altitude for 25 minutes could be distinguished from normal EEG when the hypoxia It is well known that hypoxia disrupts intracellular process and impairs cellular function. Brain cells with a uniquely high oxygen demand are most susceptible to low oxygen tension. Intellectual impairment is currently considered as an early sign of hypoxia, which is particularly dangerous for pilots because the signs and symptoms do not usually cause discomfort or pain to make them recognize their own disability. While numerous physiological indicators, such as neurobehavioral evaluation (NE) used in our research, are available to evaluate hypoxia, the EEG signal is one of the most predictive and reliable method which may assess hypoxia on-line [1].

EEGs are dynamic, stochastic, non-linear and non-stationary and exhibit significant complex behavior [2], [3]. Considering this, traditional methods may not be appropriate approach in characterizing the intrinsic nature of the EEG.

The architecture of the olfactory system is followed to construct a high dimensional chaotic network, the KIII model, in which the interactions of globally connected nodes are shaped by reinforcement learning to support a global landscape of high dimensional chaotic attractors. Each low-dimensional local basin of attraction corresponds to a learned class of stimulus patterns. Convergence to an attractor constitutes abstraction and generalization from an example to the class. KIII model has performed well on several complex pattern recognition tasks [4], [5], [6].

Hypoxic EEG collected after the subjects stayed at environment simulating 3500 m altitude for 25 minutes could be distinguished from normal EEG when the hypoxia was proved by NE test [7]. However, earlier prediction of hypoxia is valued before the NE decay. In this paper, the KIII model is used as a pattern classifier to diagnose the hypoxia at an early stage before significant NE changes occurred. The features are extracted based on the feature vectors of 30-60 Hz sub-band wavelet packet tree coefficients constructed using wavelet packet decomposition prior to the classification.

2 KIII Model Description

Biologically, the central olfactory neural system is composed of olfactory bulb (OB), anterior nucleus (AON) and prepyriform cortex (PC). In accordance with the anatomic architecture, KIII network is a multi-layer neural network model, which is composed of several K0, KI, KII units [8]. Among the models, every node is described by a second order differential equation. The parameters in the KIII network are optimized to fulfill some criteria that were deduced in electrophysiological experiments [9].

In the KIII network, Gaussian noise is introduced to simulate the peripheral and central biological noise source, respectively; the peripheral noise is rectified to simulate the excitatory action of input axons. The additive noise eliminates numerical instability of the KIII model, and makes the system trajectory stable and robust under statistical measures. Because of this kind of stochastic chaos, the KIII network can approximate the real biological intelligence for pattern recognition [10].

3 Application to Subtle Hypoxic EEG Recognition

3.1 Data Acquisition

A Mixture of nitrogen and oxygen at normal atmosphere pressure, which simulates different altitude atmosphere by adjusting oxygen partial pressure, is provided to subjects via a pilot mask. In the first day, when the subject stays at normal atmosphere, he carries out auditory digit span while his EEG is recorded. In the second day, the sub-ject stays at environment simulating 3500m altitude for 25 minutes. The NE tests were performed at 16th and 25th minute, respectively, while the EEGs were recorded. The experiment is carried out in the same time each day. Five healthy male volunteers around 22 years old are taken as subjects. 1.5 seconds EEGs immediately after neuro-behavioral evaluations are recorded for analysis under both normal oxygen partial pressure and 3500 m altitude.

EEG data were taken from 30 Channels including: FP1, FP2, F7, F3, FZ, F4, F8, FT7, FC3, FCZ, FC4, FT8, T3, C3, CZ, C4, T4, TP7, CP3, CPZ, CP4, TP8, T5, P3, PZ, P4, T6, O1, OZ and O2 (10/20 system). The reference was (A1+A2)/2 (A1 = left mastoid, A2 = right mastoid). The EEG amplifier used was NuAmps Digital Amplifier (Model 7181) purchased from Neuroscan Compumedics Limited, Texas, USA. Sam-pling rate was 250 S/s. All values are in μVolt.

3.2 Evaluation of the Severity of the Effects of Hypoxia by Neurobehavioral Testing

NE is a sensitive and reliable tool for early detection of adverse effects of the environmental hazards on central nervous system. In the normal and simulating 3500m altitude experiments, auditory digit span was utilized to evaluate the degree of hypoxia. Auditory digit span is a common measure of short-term memory, which is the number of digits a person can absorb and recall in correct serial order after hearing them. As is usual in short-term memory tasks, here the person has to remember a small amount of information for a relatively short time, and the order of recall is important.

The result of the test is shown in Table 1. T-tests were performed on the NE under normal and hypoxia conditions. As a result, the NE scores of normal and hypoxia at the 25th minute were different observably ($p<0.05$). Furthermore, the scores under the hypoxia condition were lower distinctly, which means that subjects' behavior capability became weaker under the hypoxia condition. The NE scores at the 16th minute shows that the NE test can not be used to distinguish normal and hypoxia ($p>0.2$).

Table 1. Performance of NES under normal and hypoxia states

Subject	Auditory Digit Span Scores		
	Normal	Hypoxia (16th minute)	Hypoxia (25th minute)
1	30	31	29
2	28	27	24
3	25	27	21
4	32	29	23
5	19	19	9

3.3 Feature Vector Extraction

By wavelet packet decomposition, the original waveform can be reconstructed from a set of analysis coefficients that capture all of the time (or space) and frequency information in the waveform. In our analysis, we use the COIF5 wavelet. The number of levels of decomposition is chosen as two and wavelet packet tree coefficients of a 30-60Hz sub-band are abstracted. The feature vector is a 30-dimensions vector due to 30 EEG channels. For each channel, the square of the wavelet packet tree coefficients are summed up as one dimension of the feature vector. According to the topology of the EEG channel, feature vectors can be transformed as a feature topography. A typical feature topography sample of comparing normal and hypoxic EEGs collected from the same subject is illustrated in Fig. 1 [7].

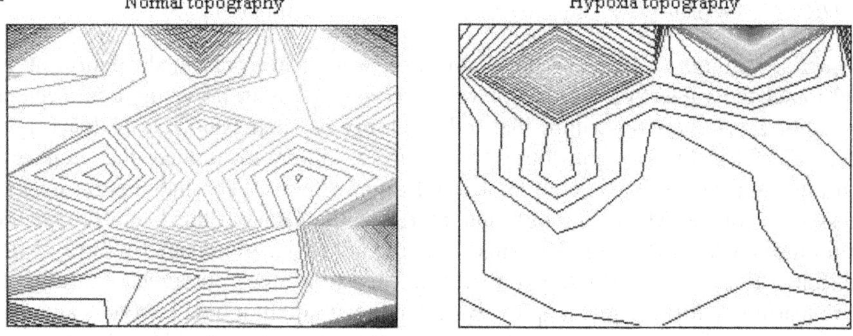

Fig. 1. A feature vector topography of the normal and hypoxia EEG

3.4 Learning Rule

There are two main learning processes: Hebbian associative learning and habituation. Hebbian reinforcement learning is used for establishing the memory basins of certain patterns, while habituation is used to reduce the impact of environment noise or those non-informative signals input to the KIII network.

The output of the KIII network at the mitral level (M) is taken as the activity measure of the system. The activity of the ith channel is represented by SD_{ai}, which is the mean standard deviation of the output of the *i*th mitral node (Mi) over the period of the presentation of input patterns, as Eq.(1). The response period with input patterns is divided into equal segments, and the standard deviation of the *i*th segment is calculated as SD_{aik}, SD_{ai} is the mean value of these *S* segments. SD_a^m is the mean activity measure over the whole OB layer with *n* nodes (Eq.(2)).

$$SD_{ai} = \frac{1}{S}\sum_{k=1}^{s} SD_{aik} \ . \tag{1}$$

$$SD_a^m = \frac{1}{n}\sum_{k=1}^{n} SD_{ai} \ . \tag{2}$$

The modified Hebbian rule holds that each pair of M nodes that are co-activated by the stimulus have their lateral connections $W(mml)_{ij}$ strengthened. Here $W(mml)_{ij}$ stands for the connection weights both from *Mi* to *Mj* and from *Mi* to *Mj*. Those nodes whose activities are larger than the mean activity of the OB layer are considered activated; those whose activity levels are less than the mean are considered not to be activated. Also, to avoid the saturation of the weight space, a bias coefficient K is defined in the modified Hebbian learning rule, as in Eq.(3). $W(mml)_{ij}$ is multiplied by a coefficient r (r>1) to represent the Hebbian reinforcement.

$$\begin{aligned} &IF && SD_{ai} > (1+K)SD_a^m \text{ and } SD_{aj} > (1+K)SD_a^m \\ &THEN && W(mml)_{ij} = W(mml)^{high} \text{ and } W(mml)_{ji} = W(mml)^{high} . \\ &OR && W(mml)_{ij} = r \times W(mml)_{ij} \text{ and } W(mml)_{ji} = r \times W(mml)_{ji} . \end{aligned} \quad (3)$$

Two algorithms to increase the connection weight are presented, algorithm 1 is used to set the value to a fixed high value $W(mml)^{high}$ as in previous references and algorithm 2 is a new algorithm that will multiply an increasing rate to the original value. The habituation constitutes an adaptive filter to reduce the impact of environmental noise that is continuous and uninformative. The habituation exists at the synapse of the M1 nodes on other nodes in the OB and the lateral connection within the M1 layer. It is implemented by incremental weight decay (multiply with a coefficient h_{hab} <1) of all these parameters at each time step continuously through the entire learning period. For example, given that the simulation time is 600ms and h_{hab} = 0.9995, each relevant parameter that is not strengthened by Hebbian learning will reduce to $0.9995^{600} = 0.74$ of its original value [4].

3.5 Recognition of Hypoxia EEG

We use the KIII model to distinguish hypoxic from normal EEGs. The KIII model learns the desired patterns --- the normal and hypoxic EEG patterns for three times in turn. The test data set contains 80 samples of normal and hypoxic EEG for individuals by 5 different subjects. We chose 40 samples in the odd position for training and used all the 80 samples for classification, and then we chose 40 samples in the even position for training and used all the 80 samples for classification. The final correction rate is from the mean of twice correction rate. In this application, a 30-channel KIII net-work is used with system parameters as the reference [9].

First, normal and hypoxia at the 25th minute EEGs are classified by KIII network since NE results in this moment have already shown that subjects' behavior capability became weaker under the hypoxia condition as Table 1. The experimental results are shown in Fig. 2. Effectively, the mean of classification rate for test data set is equal to 92%. Hypoxic EEGs can be distinguished from normal EEG by the KIII network. The conclusion of EEG classification is consonant with NE results.

Secondly, when hypoxia is at a subtle state, for example the 16th minute, the NE test can not reflect the degree of hypoxia. However, we apply KIII network to classify normal and hypoxia at the 16th minute EEGs. The experimental results are shown in Fig. 3. The

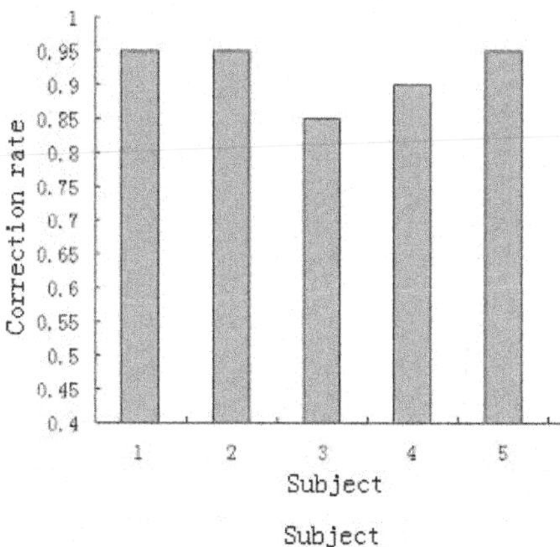

Fig. 2. Rate of correct classification of normal and hypoxic EEGs by the KIII network

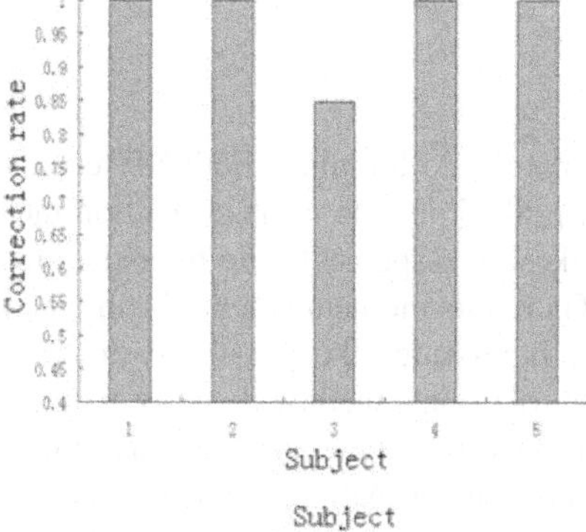

Fig. 3. Rate of correct classification of normal and hypoxic EEGs at the 16th minute by the KIII network

mean of classification rate for test data set is equal to 97%. In other words, a new pattern in EEG induced by hypoxia has come into being at the 16th minute. The new pattern, which can not be detected by NE test, is recognized by KIII network, effectively.

Finally, normal and hypoxia at the earlier state (the 7th minute) EEGs are classified by KIII network. The correction rates of classification of normal and hypoxia at the different minute EEGs are displayed in Table 2. The mean correction rates are illustrated in Fig. 4 to show the correction rate trend according to time.

Table 2. Performance of KIII network classifying normal and hypoxia EEGs

Subject	Correction rate of classification of normal and hypoxia EEGs (%)		
	7th minute	16th minute	25th minute
1	65	100	95
2	50	100	95
3	50	85	85
4	50	100	90
5	40	100	95

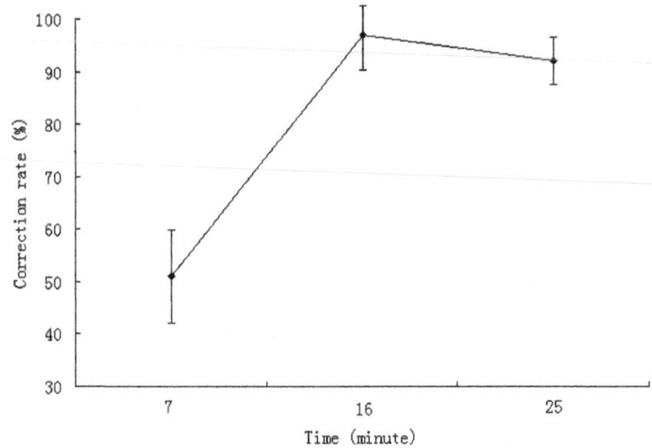

Fig. 4. correction rate trend according to time by the KIII network

4 Discussion

According to the hypoxia at the 25th minute, both NE test and EEG give response (T-test on NE results shows $p<0.05$ and the mean correction rate by EEG is 92%). At the 16th minute, NE test makes no response to the hypoxia, However, By KIII network, normal and hypoxia EEGs in this moment can be distinguished remarkably (the mean correction rate is 97%). It provides the possibility to measure the subtle hypoxia quantitatively while other traditional method does not work.

The correction rate at the 16th minute is higher than the one at the 25th minute. It may attribute to adaption of human. Although NE results indicate that the moment, in which the hypoxia pattern comes into being, is the 25th minute, actually, the time is the 16th minute by EEG. Between the 16th and 25th minute, human can adapt to hypoxia, step by step. So, the response to hypoxia at the 16th minute is more intensive than that at the 25th minute. At the 7th minute, the mean correction rate is 51%. The results imply that the time is so early that the hypoxia pattern in EEG has not appeared clearly. Even KIII network, which is sensitive to pattern transition in EEG, can not work well.

The KIII model has good capability for pattern recognition as a form of the biological intelligence. It needs much fewer learning trials when solving problems of pattern recognition. In our study, it is extremely time consuming to use a digital computer to solve the numerous differential equations within KIII model. This problem restricts the application of the KIII network in real time. The implementation of the KIII in analog VLSI [11] is surely a promising research for building more intelligent and powerful artificial neural network.

By providing feature vectors for classification, the EEG might be made to serve as a quantitative indicator of the subtle hypoxia in real time, which might significantly improve the safety of those who work in high altitude. According to the hypoxia at the 25th minute, both NE test and EEG give response (T-test on NE results shows $p<0.05$ and the mean correction rate by EEG is 92%). At the 16th minute, NE test makes no response to the hypoxia, However, By KIII network, normal and hypoxia

EEGs in this moment can be distinguished remarkably (the mean correction rate is 97%). It provides the possibility to measure the subtle hypoxia quantitatively while other traditional method does not work.

The correction rate at the 16th minute is higher than the one at the 25th minute. It may attribute to adaption of human. Although NE results indicate that the moment, in which the hypoxia pattern comes into being, is the 25th minute, actually, the time is the 16th minute by EEG. Between the 16th and 25th minute, human can adapt to hypoxia, step by step. So, the response to hypoxia at the 16th minute is more intensive than that at the 25th minute. At the 7th minute, the mean correction rate is 51%. The results imply that the time is so early that the hypoxia pattern in EEG has not appeared clearly. Even KIII network, which is sensitive to pattern transition in EEG, can not work well.

The KIII model has good capability for pattern recognition as a form of the biological intelligence. It needs much fewer learning trials when solving problems of pattern recognition. In our study, it is extremely time consuming to use a digital computer to solve the numerous differential equations within KIII model. This problem restricts the application of the KIII network in real time. The implementation of the KIII in analog VLSI [11] is surely a promising research for building more intelligent and powerful artificial neural network.

By providing feature vectors for classification, the EEG might be made to serve as a quantitative indicator of the subtle hypoxia in real time, which might significantly improve the safety of those who work in high altitude.

According to the hypoxia at the 25th minute, both NE test and EEG give response (T-test on NE results shows $p<0.05$ and the mean correction rate by EEG is 92%). At the 16th minute, NE test makes no response to the hypoxia, However, By KIII network, normal and hypoxia EEGs in this moment can be distinguished remarkably (the mean correction rate is 97%). It provides the possibility to measure the subtle hypoxia quantitatively while other traditional method does not work.

The correction rate at the 16th minute is higher than the one at the 25th minute. It may attribute to adaption of human. Although NE results indicate that the moment, in which the hypoxia pattern comes into being, is the 25th minute, actually, the time is the 16th minute by EEG. Between the 16th and 25th minute, human can adapt to hypoxia, step by step. So, the response to hypoxia at the 16th minute is more intensive than that at the 25th minute. At the 7th minute, the mean correction rate is 51%. The results imply that the time is so early that the hypoxia pattern in EEG has not appeared clearly. Even KIII network, which is sensitive to pattern transition in EEG, can not work well.

The KIII model has good capability for pattern recognition as a form of the biological intelligence. It needs much fewer learning trials when solving problems of pattern recognition. In our study, it is extremely time consuming to use a digital computer to solve the numerous differential equations within KIII model. This problem restricts the application of the KIII network in real time. The implementation of the KIII in analog VLSI [11] is surely a promising research for building more intelligent and powerful artificial neural network.

By providing feature vectors for classification, the EEG might be made to serve as a quantitative indicator of the subtle hypoxia in real time, which might significantly improve the safety of those who work in high altitude.
According to the hypoxia at the 25th minute, both NE test and EEG give response (T-test on NE results shows p<0.05 and the mean correction rate by EEG is 92%). At the 16th minute, NE test makes no response to the hypoxia, However, By KIII network, normal and hypoxia EEGs in this moment can be distinguished remarkably (the mean correction rate is 97%). It provides the possibility to measure the subtle hypoxia quantitatively while other traditional method does not work.

The correction rate at the 16th minute is higher than the one at the 25th minute. It may attribute to adaption of human. Although NE results indicate that the moment, in which the hypoxia pattern comes into being, is the 25th minute, actually, the time is the 16th minute by EEG. Between the 16th and 25th minute, human can adapt to hypoxia, step by step. So, the response to hypoxia at the 16th minute is more intensive than that at the 25th minute. At the 7th minute, the mean correction rate is 51%. The results imply that the time is so early that the hypoxia pattern in EEG has not appeared clearly. Even KIII network, which is sensitive to pattern transition in EEG, can not work well.

The KIII model has good capability for pattern recognition as a form of the biological intelligence. It needs much fewer learning trials when solving problems of pattern recognition. In our study, it is extremely time consuming to use a digital computer to solve the numerous differential equations within KIII model. This problem restricts the application of the KIII network in real time. The implementation of the KIII in analog VLSI [11] is surely a promising research for building more intelligent and powerful artificial neural network.

By providing feature vectors for classification, the EEG might be made to serve as a quantitative indicator of the subtle hypoxia in real time, which might significantly improve the safety of those who work in high altitude.
According to the hypoxia at the 25th minute, both NE test and EEG give response (T-test on NE results shows p<0.05 and the mean correction rate by EEG is 92%). At the 16th minute, NE test makes no response to the hypoxia, However, By KIII network, normal and hypoxia EEGs in this moment can be distinguished remarkably (the mean correction rate is 97%). It provides the possibility to measure the subtle hypoxia quantitatively while other traditional method does not work.

The correction rate at the 16th minute is higher than the one at the 25th minute. It may attribute to adaption of human. Although NE results indicate that the moment, in which the hypoxia pattern comes into being, is the 25th minute, actually, the time is the 16th minute by EEG. Between the 16th and 25th minute, human can adapt to hypoxia, step by step. So, the response to hypoxia at the 16th minute is more intensive than that at the 25th minute. At the 7th minute, the mean correction rate is 51%. The results imply that the time is so early that the hypoxia pattern in EEG has not appeared clearly. Even KIII network, which is sensitive to pattern transition in EEG, can not work well.

The KIII model has good capability for pattern recognition as a form of the biological intelligence. It needs much fewer learning trials when solving problems of pattern recognition. In our study, it is extremely time consuming to use a digital computer to solve the numerous differential equations within KIII model. This problem restricts the application of the KIII network in real time. The implementation of the KIII in analog VLSI [11] is surely a promising research for building more intelligent and powerful artificial neural network.

By providing feature vectors for classification, the EEG might be made to serve as a quantitative indicator of the subtle hypoxia in real time, which might significantly improve the safety of those who work in high altitude.

According to the hypoxia at the 25th minute, both NE test and EEG give response (T-test on NE results shows $p<0.05$ and the mean correction rate by EEG is 92%). At the 16th minute, NE test makes no response to the hypoxia, However, By KIII network, normal and hypoxia EEGs in this moment can be distinguished remarkably (the mean correction rate is 97%). It provides the possibility to measure the subtle hypoxia quantitatively while other traditional method does not work.

The correction rate at the 16th minute is higher than the one at the 25th minute. It may attribute to adaption of human. Although NE results indicate that the moment, in which the hypoxia pattern comes into being, is the 25th minute, actually, the time is the 16th minute by EEG. Between the 16th and 25th minute, human can adapt to hypoxia, step by step. So, the response to hypoxia at the 16th minute is more intensive than that at the 25th minute. At the 7th minute, the mean correction rate is 51%. The results imply that the time is so early that the hypoxia pattern in EEG has not appeared clearly. Even KIII network, which is sensitive to pattern transition in EEG, can not work well.

The KIII model has good capability for pattern recognition as a form of the biological intelligence. It needs much fewer learning trials when solving problems of pattern recognition. In our study, it is extremely time consuming to use a digital computer to solve the numerous differential equations within KIII model. This problem restricts the application of the KIII network in real time. The implementation of the KIII in analog VLSI [11] is surely a promising research for building more intelligent and powerful artificial neural network.

By providing feature vectors for classification, the EEG might be made to serve as a quantitative indicator of the subtle hypoxia in real time, which might significantly improve the safety of those who work in high altitude.

Acknowledgments. This research is supported by the National Natural Science Foundation of China (No. 60421002) and the National Basic Research Program of China (973 Program, No. 2004CB720302).

References

1. Saroj, K. L. Lal., Ashley, Craig.: A critical review of the psychophysiology of driver fatigue. Biological Psychology. 55 (2001) 173–194

2. Vuckovic, A., Andrew, R. V., Chen, C. N., Popovic, D.: Automatic recognition of alertness and drowsiness from EEG by an artificial neural network. Medical Engineering & Physics. 24 (2002) 349–360
3. Zhang, X. S., Rob, J.: EEG complexity as a measure of depth of anesthesia for patients. IEEE TRANSACTIONS ON BIOMEDICAL ENGINEERING. 48 (2001) 12
4. Kozma, R., Freeman, W. J.: Chaotic Resonance - Methods and Applications for Robust Classification of Noisy and Variable Patterns. Int. J. Bifurcation and Chaos. 11(6) (2001) 1607–1629
5. Li, G., Lou, Z., Wang, L., Li, X. and Freeman, W. J.: Application of Chaotic Neural Model Based on Olfactory System on Pattern Recognitions. In: Wang, L., Chen, K., Ong Y.S. (eds.): Advances in Natural Computation. Lecture Notes in Computer Science, Vol. 3610. Springer-Verlag, Berlin Heidelberg New York (2005) 378 – 381
6. Quarder, S., Claussnitzer, U., Otto, M.: Using Singular-Value Decompositions to Classify Spatial Patterns Generated by a Nonlinear Dynamic Model of the Olfactory System. Chemometrics and Intelligent Laboratory Systems. 59 (2001) 45–51
7. Hu, M., Li, J. J., Li, G., Tang, X. W. and Freeman, W. J.: Normal and Hypoxia EEG Recog-nition Based on a Chaotic Olfactory Model. In: Wang, J., et al. (eds.): ISNN 2006. Lecture Notes in Computer Science, Vol. 3610. Springer-Verlag, Berlin Heidelberg New York (2006) 554 – 559
8. Chang, H. J., Freeman, W. J.: Optimization of Olfactory Model in Software to Give 1/f Power Spectra Reveals Numerical Instabilities in Solutions Governed by Aperiodic (Chaotic) Attractors. Neural Networks. 11 (1998) 449–466
9. Chang, H. J., Freeman, W. J., Burke, B. C.: Biologically Modeled Noise Stabilizing Neuro-dynamics for Pattern Recognition. Int. J. Bifurcation and Chaos. 8(2) (1998) 321–345
10. Freeman, W. J., Chang, H. J., Burke, B. C., Rose, P. A., Badler, J.: Taming Chaos: Stabilization of Aperiodic Attractors by Noise. IEEE Transactions on Circuits and Systems. 44 (1997) 989–996
11. Principe, J. C., Tavares, V. G., Harris, J. G., Freeman, W. J.: Design and Implementation of a Biologically Realistic Olfactory Cortex in Analog VLSI. Proceedings of the IEEE. 89(7) (2001) 1030–1051

Model-Driven Ontology Engineering

[1]Yue Pan, [1]Guotong Xie, [1]Li Ma,
[1]Yang Yang, [1]ZhaoMing Qiu, and [2]Juhnyoung Lee

[1] IBM China Research Lab
Beijing, China
{panyue, xieguot, malli, yangyy, qiuzhaom}@cn.ibm.com
[2] IBM Watson Research Center
Hawthorne, New York
jyl@us.ibm.com

Abstract. W3C's Semantic Web provides a common framework that allows data to be shared and reused across application and enterprise. As the Semantic Web shapes the future of the Web, it becomes more and more important in software engineering and enterprise application development. While existing *ontology engineering* tools provide a stack of ontology management support and are used successfully in certain domains, there still remains a gap between the ontology engineering tools and the traditional software engineering. For several decades, software engineering has been established on different modeling languages and methodologies such as Unified Modeling Language (UML). The differences in modeling languages and methodologies cause difficulties in enterprise application development involving the Semantic Web technologies. The existing ontology engineering tools provide only an ad hoc approach to bridging this gap with limited functionality and performance. The primary objective of our work is to bridge this gap between two different, but complementary engineering disciplines with a systematic approach. Our approach leverages *Model-Driven Architecture* (MDA) and *Ontology Definition Metamodel* (ODM), which enable model transformation. This approach allows seamlessly supporting existing models in UML and other languages in Semantic Web-based software development. In addition, it allows exploiting the availability and features of UML tools for creation of vocabularies and ontologies. Furthermore, MDA enables code generation and facilitates software tool development. This paper presents an MDA-based system for ontology engineering. In addition, it presents the entire stack of individual components of the developed ontology engineering tool.

Keywords: Semantic Web, ontology engineering, model-driven architecture.

1 Introduction

W3C's Semantic Web [1] provides a common framework that allows data to be shared and reused across application and enterprise. It is based on the Resource Description Framework (RDF), which describes various resources using XML for syntax and URIs for naming [10], and Web Ontology Language (OWL), which provides

S. Spaccapietra (Ed.): Journal on Data Semantics VII, LNCS 4244, pp. 57 – 78, 2006.

modeling constructs for specifying and inferring about knowledge [16]. As the Semantic Web shapes the future of the Web, it becomes more and more important in software engineering and enterprise application development. To meet the needs, a number of tools and systems for ontology development and management such as Protégé [28], Jena [4], Sesame [29], Pellet [26], KAON [15], RStar [14], and SnoBase [12], have been developed.

While these ontology engineering tools provide a relatively complete stack of ontology management support and are used successfully in certain domains, there still remains a gap between the ontology engineering tools and the traditional software engineering. For more than a decade, software engineering has been established on different modeling languages and methodologies such as OMG's Unified Modeling Language (UML). This difference in modeling languages and methodologies causes difficulties in large-scale enterprise application development involving the Semantic Web technologies. The existing ontology engineering tools provide only an ad hoc approach to bridging this gap with limited functionality and performance. The creation of ontologies and their use in software engineering projects is currently cumbersome and not seamless. The transformation of UML models to OWL ontologies and vice versa is conducted only in an ad hoc and incomplete way. Therefore, it is difficult to utilize the vast investment of enterprises in software engineering models, which are often accumulated over a decade, in ontology engineering. For the Semantic Web to have impact on enterprises and their business, and also to be widely accepted as a value-adding technology, bridging this gap in software and ontology engineering is critical.

The primary objective of our work is to bridge this gap between two different, but complementary engineering disciplines with a systematic approach. We leverage OMG's Model-Driven Architecture (MDA) [3] and Ontology Definition Metamodel (ODM) [25] to provide model transformation. This approach allows seamlessly supporting existing models in UML and other languages in Semantic Web-based software development. In addition, it allows exploiting the availability and features of UML tools for creation of vocabularies and ontologies. Furthermore, MDA enables code generation and facilitates tool development. This paper presents a model-driven approach to ontology engineering. It describes the architecture of the ontology engineering system, and mappings between UML and OWL for model transformation. In addition, it presents the entire stack of individual components of the developed ontology engineering tool.

The rest of this paper is structured as follows: In Section 2, we describe a number of existing software tools for ontology development and management. It discusses a gap between these ontology engineering tools and the traditional software engineering tools. Sections 3 and 4 summarize technical background information on the Model-Driven Architecture and Ontology Definition Metamodel, respectively. In Section 5, we explain how EMF-based technologies for MDA and ODM are used to realize the proposed system for ontology engineering. Section 6 presents an implementation of the proposed system with the entire stack of components. Section 7 presents use scenarios illustrating how the features of the developed ontology engineering tool can be utilized in real-world applications. In Section 8, conclusions are drawn and future work is outlined.

2 Traditional Ontology Management Systems

In recent years, there has been a surge of interest in using ontological information for communicating knowledge among software systems. As a result, an increasing range of software systems engage in a variety of ontology management tasks, including the creation, storage, search, query, reuse, maintenance, and integration of ontologies. Recently, there have been efforts to externalize such ontology management burden from individual software systems and put them together in middleware known as an ontology management system. An ontology management system provides a mechanism to deal with ontological information at an appropriate level of abstraction. By using programming interfaces and query languages the ontology management system provides, application programs can manipulate and query ontologies without the need to know their details or to re-implement the semantics of standard ontology languages. Examples of such ontology management systems include Protégé [28], Jena [4], Sesame [29], Pellet [26], KAON [15], Jastor [23], D2RQ [19], RStar [14], and SnoBase [12].

Table 1 summarizes a few ontology management systems. It is important to note that these systems mainly focus on the manipulation of ontologies. The interoperability with other modeling languages and development tools comes as a secondary feature for these systems. That is, they assume separate workspaces for ontology management and software development, and fail to provide a tightly integrated environment for software and ontology engineering.

Table 1. Traditional Ontology Management Systems

Name	Functionalities	Standards	Interoperability
Jena	A program development framework for ontology manipulation and query	RDF, RDFS, OWL, SPARQL	N/A
Sesame	An RDF database allowing ontology manipulation and query	RDF, RDFS, OWL	N/A
Protégé	A graphical ontology editor and knowledge base framework for ontology manipulation and query	RDF, RDFS, OWL	Through plugins (with limited capability); UML → OWL ontology
KOAN	A suite of ontology management tools including ontology creation, ontology manipulation, and inference and query	RDF, RDFS, OWL	RDB schema → RDFS ontology
Jastor	A java code generator for creating Java beans from OWL ontologies	RDF, RDFS, OWL	OWL ontology → Java Beans
D2RQ	A language and a tool for specifying mappings between relational database schema and OWL ontologies	RDF, RDFS, OWL	RDB schema → OWL ontology

While these ontology engineering tools provide a stack of ontology management support, they also show certain limitations in supporting large-scale software engineering projects. Participating in a number of enterprise application development projects by using the SnoBase and RStar Ontology Management System, we learned firsthand that it is critical to provide a comprehensive development environment including supporting tools and facilities for the application developers. A pick-and-choose approach to the best of the breed tools from different environments does not always work well for the majority of the developers and often results in a longer learning curve for the developers. A comprehensive ontology development environment often means a tight integration of tools for software *and* ontology engineering, and model import and transformation, among others.

Semantic markup languages such as W3C's RDF and OWL are based on the work in the logic and Artificial Intelligence communities, such as Description Logic and Knowledge Representation. The syntax of these languages is less intuitive to those trained for object-oriented programming and simple XML-based languages. The lack of a tightly integrated development environment for software and ontology engineering makes the job of subject matter experts and software engineers difficult, and often affects negatively to the adoption of the semantic technology in industry. An effective ontology application development environment should bridge this gap between software engineering and ontology engineering by providing a seamlessly integrated environment.

Another consideration for industry adoption of the semantic Web technology is the interoperability of the semantic markup languages with the well-established and widely-accepted industry standard modeling languages and methodologies such as Entity-Relation (ER) diagrams and Unified Modeling Language (UML). Enterprises developed software models in these languages for more than a decade and invested significantly in building systems around them. Despite all the theoretical advantages the semantic technology brings in, in practice, it is highly unlikely that the enterprises abandon the legacy systems and develop new systems around the semantic Web technology. Instead, users in industry would be interested in the interoperability of the modeling languages, and the reuse of the existing models and data with the semantic Web technology. The traditional ontology management systems currently provide only ad hoc and incomplete methods for the model interoperability. To address the practical requirements of industry, this paper introduces a novel approach to ontology engineering based on the Model Driven Architecture (MDA), which enables software engineers and users to design, build, integrate and manage ontologies and software applications in an integrated development environment.

3 Model-Driven Architecture

Before presenting the model-driven approach to ontology engineering, we summarize the Object Management Group's Model Driven Architecture, which is one of the two pillars of the system's architecture, along with Ontology Definition Metamodel.

In the history of software engineering, there has been a notable increase of the use of models and the level of abstraction in the models. Modeling has become separated from underlying development and deployment platforms, making them more reusable and easier to create and modify by domain experts, and requiring less knowledge of specific deployment systems. This trend places software modeling closer to knowledge engineering. The current stage in this evolution is the *Model Driven Architecture*, which grew out of the standards work conducted in the 1990s for the Unified Modeling Language.

The basic idea of MDA is that the system functionality is defined as a platform-independent model, using an appropriate specification language and then translated to one or more platform-specific models for the actual implementation. To accomplish this goal, the MDA defines an architecture that provides a set of guidelines for structuring specifications expressed as models. The translation between platform-independent model and platform-specific models is normally performed using automated tools. Specifically, MDA defines three levels of abstraction: *Computation Independent Model* (CIM), *Platform Independent Model* (PIM) and *Platform Specific Model* (PSM). CIM is a view of a system that does not show the details of a system structure. In software engineering, it is also known as a *domain model*, which is concerned by domain experts. It is similar to the concept of ontology. PIM is a model that is computation dependent, but it is not aware of specific computer platform details. In other words, it is targeted for a technology-neutral virtual machine. Specification of complete system is completed with PSM. The goal is to move human work from PSM to CIM and PIM, and let the detail implementation for a specific platform be generated as much as possible by automated tools which perform the transformation from PIM to PSM.

MDA comprises of a four-layer metamodel architecture: meta-metamodel (M3) layer, metamodel (M2) layer, model (M1) layer, and instance (M0) layer. Also, it utilizes several complementary standards from OMG including *Meta-Object Facility* (MOF), *Unified Modeling Language* (UML) and *XML Metadata Interchange* (XMI). On the top of the MDA architecture is the meta-metamodel, i.e., MOF. It defines an abstract language and framework for specifying, constructing and managing technology neutral metamodels. It is the foundation for defining any modeling language such as UML or even MOF itself. MOF also defines a framework for implementing repositories that hold metadata (e.g., models) described by metamodels [24]. The main objective of having the four layers with a common meta-metamodel is to support multiple metamodels and models and to enable their extensibility, integration and generic model and metamodel management.

All metamodels, standard or custom, defined by MOF are positioned on the M2 layer. One of these is UML, a graphical modeling language for specifying, visualizing and documenting software systems. With *UML profiles*, basic UML concepts (e.g., class, association, etc.) can be extended with new concepts (*stereotypes*) and adapted to specific modeling needs. The models of the real world, represented by concepts defined in the corresponding metamodel at M2 layer (e.g., UML metamodel) are on M1 layer. Finally, at M0 layer, are things from the real world. Another related standard is XMI. It defines mapping from MOF-defined metamodels to XML documents and schemas. Because of versatile software tool availability for XML, XMI representations of models, metamodels and meta-metamodel facilitate their sharing in software application development.

MOF tools use metamodels to generate code for managing models and metadata. The generated code includes access mechanisms, or application programming interfaces, to read and manipulate, serialize and transform, and abstract the details of various interfaces based on access patterns. *Eclipse Modeling Framework* (EMF) [21] provides a Java implementation of a core subset of the MOF API. EMF started out as an implementation of the MOF specification, and evolved into a generic modeling framework and code generation facility for building tools and other applications based on a structured data model. The MOF-like core metamodel in EMF is called *Ecore*. From a model specification written in XMI, EMF generates tools and runtime support to produce a set of Java classes for the model, a set of adapter classes that enable viewing and command-based editing of the model, and a basic editor. Models can be specified using annotated Java, XML documents, or modeling tools like Rational Rose, then imported into EMF. It is important to note that EMF provides the foundation for interoperability with other EMF-based tools and applications. The proposed MDA-based system leverages EMF for implementing ontology management tools which run on the Eclipse environment, and utilizes its support for model interoperability.

4 Ontology Definition Metamodel

MDA and its four-layer architecture provide a solid basis for defining metamodels of any modeling language, and so provide a foundation for bringing together software engineering and methodologies such as UML with the semantic technology based on W3C's RDF and OWL. Once a semantic markup language such as OWL is defined in MOF, its users can utilize MOF's capabilities for modeling creation, model management, code generation, and interoperability with other MOF-defined metamodels.

Another OMG standard, Ontology Definition Metamodel (ODM) [25] took this approach. To comprehend common ontology concepts, ODM used as a starting point OWL, which is the result of the evolution of existing ontology representation languages. ODM defined individual constructs of OWL in MOF, creating an ODM metamodel. To leverage graphical modeling capabilities of UML in dealing with OWL constructs, ODM also defined an ontology UML profile to support UML notation for ontology definition. This profile enables graphical editing of ontologies in OWL using UML diagrams as well as other benefits of using mature UML CASE tools. Finally, the following bi-directional mappings between metamodels complete the picture:

1. mappings between OWL and ODM,
2. mappings between ODM and the ontology UML profile, and
3. mappings from the ontology UML profile to other UML profiles.

Figure 1 shows a simple example of the bi-directional mappings between metamodels. In practice, both UML and ODM models are serialized in XMI, and OWL model in XML, the two-way mappings can be implemented by XSLT-based transformations [5]. Gasevic et al. summarized existing approaches and tools for transformation

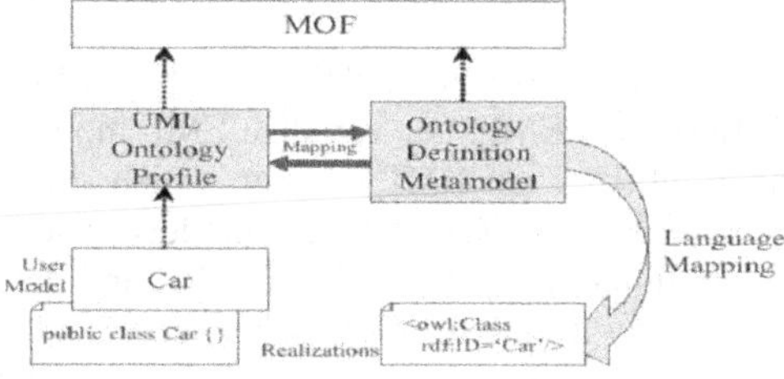

Fig. 1. Bi-directional mapping among metamodels

Fig. 1. Bi-directional mapping among metamodels

based transformations, instead of XSLT, to leverage EMF's generic modeling frame between UML models (or UML profiles) and OWL models in [5, 7], and pointed out that the XSLT-based transformation is widely used in them. Our work utilized EMF-work and code generation facility for building tools and other applications. We implemented *EODM* (EMF-based ODM), which is the underlying object model generated from ODM by using EMF, for model transformations among OWL, UML and other modeling languages. More details will be given in the next section.

Before moving to the main body of this paper, it is useful to briefly mention yet another related effort from W3C, namely, *Ontology Driven Architecture* (ODA) [17]. It combines MDA with the semantic technology differently from the ODM approach. It attempts to augment the MDA standards and methodology stack with the semantic technology to improve the discipline. It aims to enable unambiguous representation of domain terminology, distinct from the rules, enable automated consistency checking and validation of invariant rules, preconditions, and post-conditions, and support knowledge-based terminology mediation and transformation for increased scalability and composition of components. This effort still is in its infancy and at a draft stage.

5 EMF-Based Ontology Engineering System

For realizing the model-driven ontology engineering, we utilized the Eclipse Modeling Framework, which is open source MDA infrastructure for integration of modeling tools [21]. A model specification described in various modeling languages including UML, XML Schema, and annotated Java source can be imported into EMF. Then EMF produces a set of Java classes for the model, a set of adapter classes that enable viewing and editing of the model, and a basic editor. In its current implementation, EMF does not provide formal semantics definitions, inference and the related model specifications. Our work adds this capability to EMF for providing a comprehensive ontology engineering environment and dynamic application integration.

For adding the semantic model transformation capability to EMF, we leverage the specification of Ontology Definition Metamodel. By using EMF and ODM, we generated a foundational memory model, i.e., Java classes, for the constructs of OWL. This foundational memory model is referred to as *EODM* (EMF-based Ontology Definition Metamodel). By adding several necessary helper classes and methods to EODM, we can use it to create, edit, and navigate any models in OWL.

Also, we added an OWL parser to EODM, which can load OWL files into EMF and generate OWL files from EMF, i.e., serialize EMF models to standard OWL files in XML. The parser utilizes an XMI adaptor which enables the transformation between the OWL models and EODM Ecore models. The transformation is made possible by the bi-directional mapping between OWL and the Ecore metamodel. The transformation opens a way to interoperability between OWL models and other EMF supported models, which currently include ones defined in UML, XML Schema, and annotated Java classes. The support of other models such as Entity Relationship models in EMF will be provided in the near future. By leveraging the OWL parser and the bi-directional transformation between the OWL models and the Ecore models, ontology application developers can develop ontologies using their favorite model building tools, import them into EMF, transform their models into OWL ontologies, enrich them with semantics, leverage their inference capability, and utilize the comprehensive development facility of Eclipse and EMF.

To be more specific, the EODM Ecore model is the MOF core model that represents ontologies in memory. It is an intermediate model for imported and transformed legacy models, as well as the generated ontology, Java code, Java editor and Java edit. The development environment allows its users to manipulate EODM Ecore models, enrich it with semantic specification, and generate Java code. A default set of bi-directional mappings between metamodels of legacy models and OWL are developed in EMF. Eclipse plug-in developers can extend the mappings to handle other types of legacy models, or other elements in legacy models specifying semantics. The generated Java editor and Java edit provide ready-to-use visual tools to populate or manipulated instances of OWL models. The visual tools are actually copies of the standard methods of supporting application development in EMF. Figure 2 illustrates the operation of the EMF-based ontology engineering system.

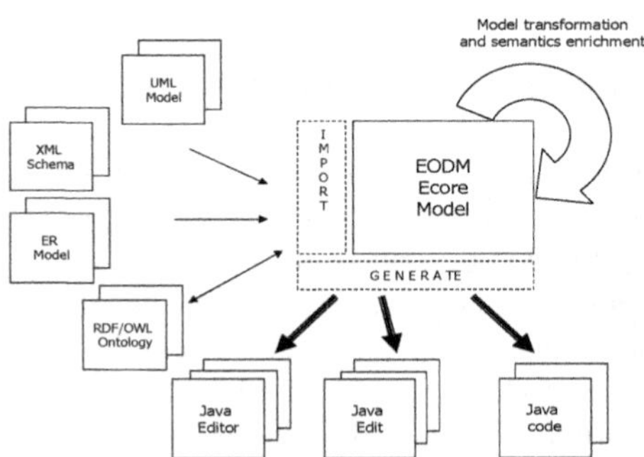

Fig. 2. EMF-based ontology engineering system

6 Components of the EMF-Based Ontology Engineering System

This section presents the entire stack of components of the developed, EMF-based ontology engineering system. We had two primary design objectives for this system: first, support for the entire lifecycle of ontology engineering, and, second, avoiding reinvention of tools and facilities that are already proven to work in software engineering. To achieve these objectives, we designed a software stack which consists of six interdependent layers.

At the core of this EMF-based ontology engineering system is the EODM model, which is derived from the Ontology Definition Metamodel and implemented in Eclipse Modeling Framework. The bottom layer, *EODM core model*, provides the basic Java programming model for OWL ontologies with all the necessary getter and setter functions. It is automatically generated by EMF from the UML models for OWL. To this generated core model implementation, certain *utility classes and methods* are added, to benefit Java programmers. On top of the EODM core model comes the *OWL Parser* which parses OWL ontologies, translates them into EODM models, and serializes EODM models to standard RDF/XML files. EODM core and OWL Parser form the foundation for the entire software stack. The top layer is composed of three relatively independent components that are build on top of this foundation. The first component is the *OWL Inference Engine*. It takes an EODM model as input, and executes user queries, reasoning about instances and relationships among instances and classes. The second component is the *Model Transformation*. It imports existing conceptual models represented in various modeling languages such as UML, ER diagrams, and Java interfaces. Then, it transforms the models into one or more EODM models. Finally, the *OWL Editor* provides a graphical ontology authoring environment where OWL ontologies in graphic notations are serialized to OWL files in a standard XML format. Figure 3 shows the components of the EMF-based ontology engineering system. In the rest of this section, we describe each component in detail.

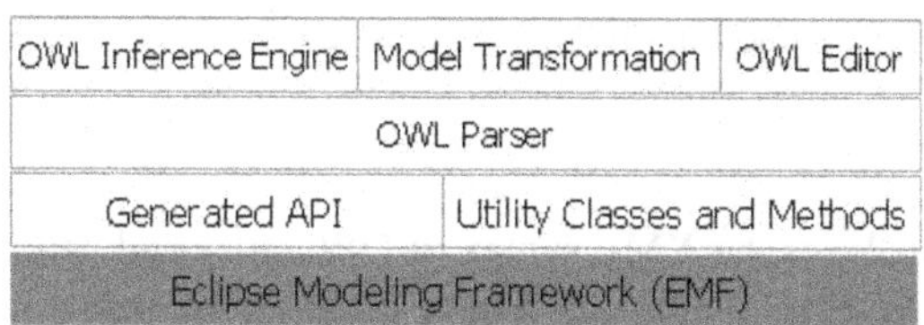

Fig. 3. EMF-based ontology engineering system architecture

6.1 EODM Core Model

The EMF-based ontology engineering system provides tightly integrated environment for software and ontology engineering, providing a stack of useful components. EODM provides the run-time library that allows applications to input and output OWL ontologies, manipulate them by using Java objects, invoke the inference engine and access result sets, and transform among ontologies and other legacy models.

The EODM core model provides useful classes and methods to access OWL ontologies and their instances. Its metamodel is defined in the Ontology Definition Metamodel (ODM) specification [25]. It is an MOF2 compliant metamodel that

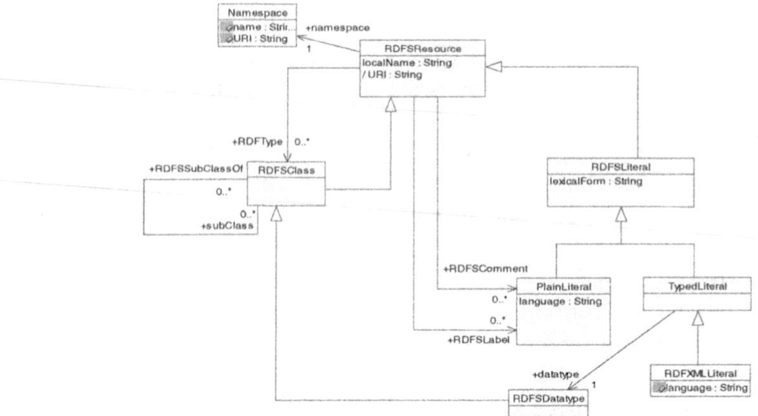

Fig. 4. Class definition in ODM

allows users to define ontologies by using those constructs defined in RDF Schema and extends it. Figure 4 illustrates the class definition of the RDF package. The UML OWL. ODM comprises of two packages that define the metamodels of RDF and OWL, respectively. The OWL package inherits classes from the RDF package, and model of the packages is augmented by a number of bi-directional references to generate APIs that leverage notification and messaging mechanisms in EMF. Also, there are certain design patterns, such as Factory and Singleton, embedded in the code generation engine of EMF. Therefore, the EODM core model automatically complies with the design practices and benefit software engineers.

6.2 OWL Parser

The OWL parser analyzes the XML syntax of OWL files and generates EODM models and a set of RDF triple statements. Figure 5 shows the parser process. The parser utilizes XML SAX API to correctly parse each node and its attributes. Then, the *RDF triple analyzer* assembles the resulting nodes and attributes to generate RDF triples by maintaining a state stack for keeping node and property states. In RDF and OWL, knowledge is simply a collection of statements, each with a subject, verb and object, and nothing else [27]. The RDF triple statements can be directly used by applications. They can be asserted into a working memory of inference engine for reasoning. They also can be stored in a database for triple-based RDF graph retrieval. A model wrapper can envelop RDF triples into an EODM model. Therefore, the OWL parser can create both RDF triple statements and an object-oriented memory model for further manipulation in applications. In addition, we also provide a tool for serializing EODM models into standard OWL files.

The OWL parser is completely compliant with W3C's XML syntax specification and passes all W3C's positive and negative test cases [8]. It utilizes a streaming XML parser, i.e., SAX parser, and once an RDF statement is formed, the parser can

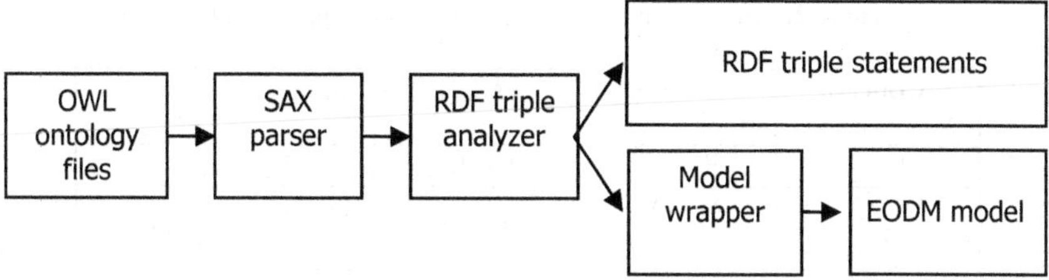

Fig. 5. OWL parser process

immediately export the statement. This property allows the parser to require minimal amount of memory and thus to be scalable in handing large-scale models. Also, it is important to note that the OWL parser can be used independently of other components of the system.

6.3 Inference Engine

The inference engine of the EMF-based ontology engineering system approaches the core inference problem of OWL by a structural subsumption algorithm. The present Description Logic classification algorithm is based on the tableau algorithm [9], which can provide sound and complete reasoning on a very expressive language by satisfaction test. However, this approach focuses on the tractability of a single subsumption test and the worst case computational complexity is NEXP-time [13]. In practical cases, however, an algorithm with high efficiency but less expressiveness would be more useful in supporting large-scale taxonomic classification problems. To achieve a balance between efficiency and expressive power, we leveraged the structural subsumption algorithm, which is known to be an efficient technique but also known to be limited due to its inability to provide complete reasoning for expressive languages. The concepts and axioms supported by this approach is defined as follows:

Concepts: (Cyclic concept definitions are not supported)
$C, D \rightarrow$ A (atomic concept), $\top$ (universal concept), $\bot$ (bottom concept),
$C \sqcap D$ (intersection), $C \sqcup D$ (union), $\exists R.C$ (some value from restriction)
$\forall R.C$ (all value from restriction), $\exists R.\{x\}$ | (hasValue)

Axioms:
Axioms $\rightarrow C \sqsubseteq D$ (concept inclusion), $R \sqsubseteq S$ (role inclusion)

In ontologies without an acyclic definition, every defined concept is treated as a restriction on some properties, and an atom concept is treated as a "special" restriction. For example, $C \equiv A \sqcap B \sqcap \forall R.(\forall S.C)$ is treated as a concept with restriction on R_A, R_B, R, where R_A, R_B is special restriction brought by atom concept A and B. To decide whether two concepts are subsumed by each other, we can recursively compare those restrictions by applying basic comparison rules captured in Table 2. Figure 6 illustrates a simple example of a structural subsumption test by using the comparison rules.

Table 2. Comparison rules for structural subsumption tests

Concept A	Concept B	A ⊑ B Condition
∃R.C	∃S.D	Iff R ≼ S and C⊑D
∀R.C	∀S.D	Iff S ≼ R and C⊑D
⩾nR.C	⩾mS.D	Iff R ≼ S and C⊑D and n⩽m
⩽nR.C	⩽mS.D	Iff S ≼ R and D⊑C and n⩾m

Given A≡∃R1.C⊓∃R2.(∀R4.D)⊓∀R3.E, B≡∃R2.(∀R4.F) ⊓∀R3.G, D⊑F, E⊑G, it can be concluded that A⊑B.

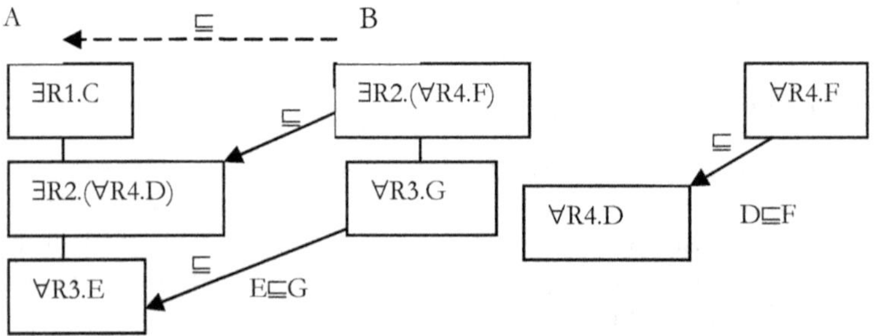

Fig. 6. A simple structural subsumption test example

The main idea of the extended structural subsumption algorithm is to leverage the information of concept definitions by maintaining a classification tree to perform taxonomic classification. The algorithm starts with building the classification tree. Given an axiom C⊑D, the algorithm first recursively classifies C, D and all the sub constitutes until all of them have been correctly linked into the classification tree. Then, it adds the subsumption link between C and D, which will automatically remove all the outdated links. More details of the inference algorithm is a subject of another paper we are preparing. Figure 7 shows an example of classifying a TBox which contains the following definitions:

C ≡ ∃R3.(A⊓B) ⊓ ∃R4.D
F ≡ ∃R1.A ⊓ ∃R2.B
D ⊑ E,
∃R3.A ⊑ ∃R2.B
∃R4.E ⊑ ∃R1.A

6.4 Model Transformation

This layer in the EMF-based ontology engineering system addresses the ontology acquisition and model interoperability issues, as we discussed earlier. Enterprises developed IT models in various modeling languages such as UML and ER diagrams for

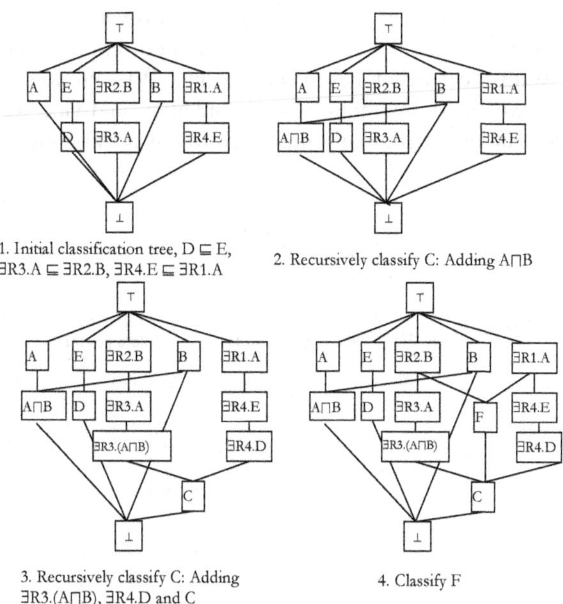

1. Initial classification tree, D ⊑ E, ∃R3.A ⊑ ∃R2.B, ∃R4.E ⊑ ∃R1.A

2. Recursively classify C: Adding A⊓B

3. Recursively classify C: Adding ∃R3.(A⊓B), ∃R4.D and C

4. Classify F

Fig. 7. An example of classifying a TBox

several decades and invested heavily in building systems around them. It is important for the enterprises to protect their investment in the legacy systems. Also, it is important to leverage domain knowledge captured in the existing IT models. Thus, users in industry are interested in the interoperability of the modeling languages and the reuse of the existing models with the semantic Web technology. The interoperability allows exploiting the availability and features of UML tools for creation of vocabularies and ontologies. In addition, it allows augmenting the legacy models with formal semantics, and enabling an inference capability with the models, which can return sound and complete query results.

Figure 8 shows the Ecore metamodel and its role in MDA. Ecore is a java implementation of the MOF model. Therefore, we can utilize Ecore as an intermediate model to support model transformation between OWL and other modeling languages. For example, a UML class diagram can be, first, transformed into an Ecore model by using the mapping between the UML metamodel and the Ecore metamodel, and, then, the resulting Ecore model can be transformed into an EODM model by using the mapping between the ODM metamodel and the Ecore metamodel. This way, it is possible to construct an ontology from legacy models. On the other hand, an OWL ontology can be transformed into a UML diagram. There already exist transformations defined between the Ecore model and other modeling languages such as UML, XSD and Java interfaces. In EODM, a mapping between the Ecore metamodel and the ODM OWL metamodel is defined. Then, we can implement model transformation by leveraging well-developed facilities of EMF as much as possible. XSLT-based approaches are more or less affected by the syntax of OWL and XMI, because the files written in these languages can be represented in different forms, but with the same semantics [5, 7]. Our approach is based on a memory model mapping approach, and, thus, independent of the syntax of OWL and XMI. However, it is fair and important to note that a problem of model transformation is about expressiveness differences between models. With the current Ecore model, an OWL ontology cannot be fully transformed into a UML model without loss of semantics, and vice versa. The expressiveness of the Ecore model is gradually improved to cover more models.

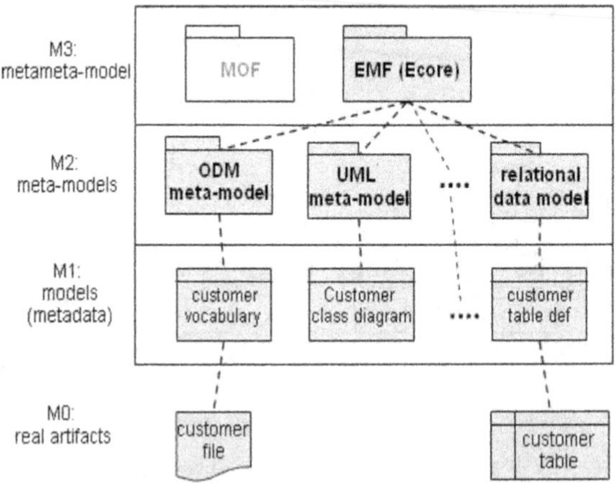

(a) Ecore metamodel as an implementation of MOF

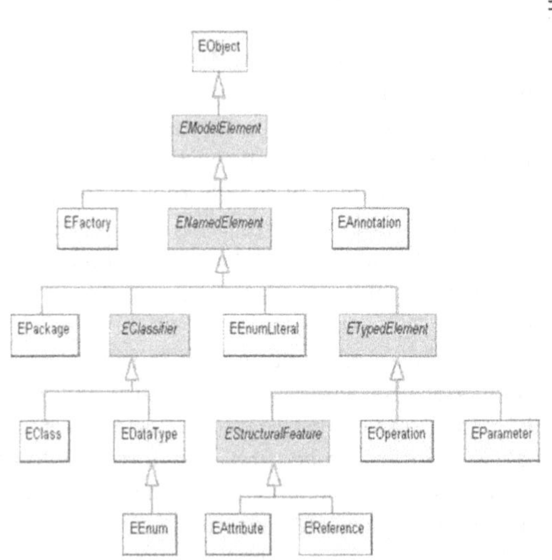

(b) Ecore metamodel structure

Fig. 8. Ecore metamodel and its role in MDA

Figure 9 depicts the bi-directional mappings defined between the Ecore metamodel and the EODM OWL metamodel. An OWL Ontology is transformed to an EPackage and vice versa; an OWL class to an EClass, etc. While the transformation from OWL to Ecore model looks straightforward, there are a few gaps. As in UML, Eclass is a first-class entity in the Ecore model. All other entities such as properties are subordinates to Eclass. In OWL, however, all entities in OWL are equal. Thus, different entities must have different names in OWL. For example, if two properties belonging to two different Eclasses have an identical name, a straightforward transformation will cause a name conflict problem. The EODM Transformation engine renames properties with an identical name to ensure a unique name for every entity. Another gap comes from the difference in expressiveness from different modeling languages. OWL is a formal language which is based on Description Logic. OWL is more expressive than the Ecore model. There are several OWL constructs that the Ecore model does support, e.g., OWL property restrictions used for precise definition of concepts. Therefore, some semantics are lost inevitably when conducting transformation from OWL to Ecore. Also, The Ecore model does not support inference of OWL. Particularly, anonymous classes created by using OWL restrictions make the situation with inference even more difficult. To address these gaps, the EODM Model Transformation engine currently employs the following tactics:

- It appends all unsupported OWL constructs as comments;
- It utilizes the inference engine during transformation to capture all implicit subsumption relationships;
- It only transforms named OWL classes, and discards all anonymous classes; and
- It renames properties with an identical name to ensure a unique name for every entity.

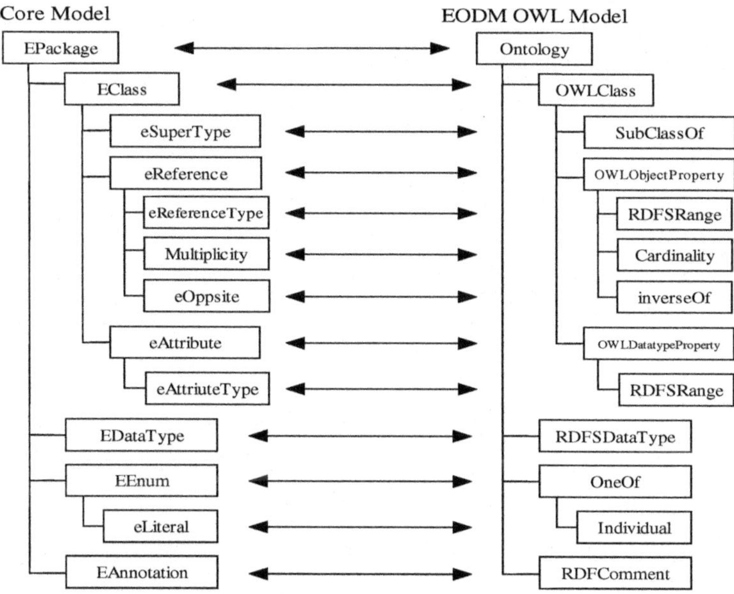

Fig. 9. Transformation between OWL and Ecore

The well-built model mapping realizes model-driven ontology engineering. However, it should be pointed out that the differences between model-driven software engineering and model-driven ontology engineering. The MDA-based approach to software engineering is mostly used to build IT models, automatically transform them into deployable code, and effectively maintain the models and the code. On the other hand, ontology engineering described in this paper aims at creating, representing and maintaining business domain models, which provide rich semantics and are founded on well-formed description logic for knowledge representation. The purpose of the MDA-based ontology engineering is twofold. First, ontology engineering leverages mature technologies and tools developed in software engineering. Second, it is an approach to linking ontologies (business models) and IT models and thus imposing rich semantics to IT models.

6.5 OWL Editor

Finally, the OWL editor provides ontology authors with a GUI which enables them to visually create an ontology file, enrich OWL ontology files transformed from legacy models, and update ontology files. We utilized EMF to automatically generate a tree-based editor in Eclipse, and replaced the default XMI parser in the generated editor with the OWL parser of EODM. The editor framework in EMF follows the Model-Control-View pattern [6] and uses the adaptor pattern [6] to provide a generic content management capability. In addition to the EMF-generated OWL editor, we utilized the Graphic Editing Framework (GEF) [20] to develop a graphic editor referred to as the EODM workbench, to provide the foundation for graphic views of OWL ontologies. GEF also supports drag and drop operations and drawing functions. The EODM

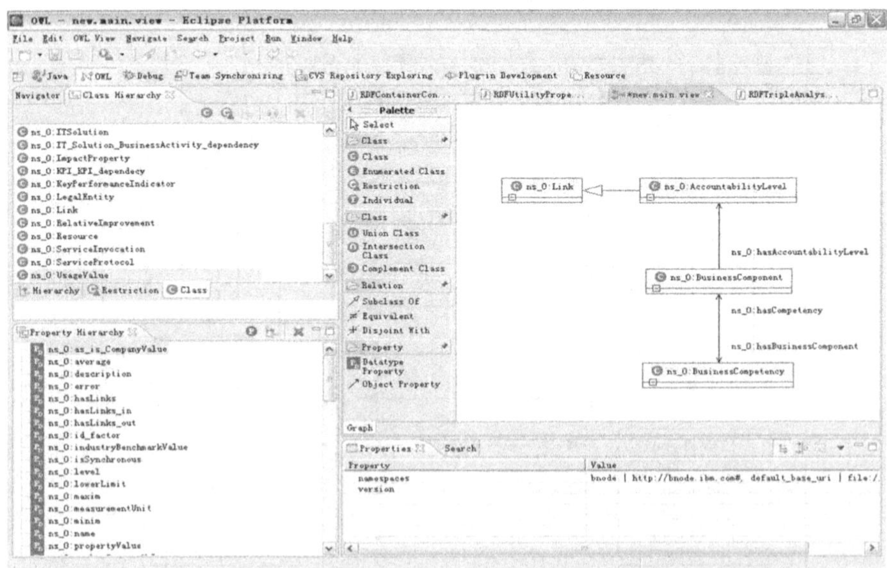

Fig. 10. Screenshot of EODM workbench

workbench provides two hierarchical views; one for OWL classes and restrictions, and the other for OWL objects and datatype properties. Furthermore, it provides multiple views of OWL ontologies and supports different development perspectives. Operations in different views are automatically synchronized in the Eclipse platform. Figure 10 gives a screenshot of the EODM workbench.

In the left hand side of the screen, there are two views of class and property hierarchy, which are constructed based on rdfs:subClassOf and rdfs:subPropertyOf. Users can also add classes and properties such as subClassOf and subPropertyOf in the two trees. In the right hand side, there are a palette, a graphical editor and a property view. Users can drag and drop elements in the palette to the editor. Detailed information about the ontology and its elements that are not showed in the limited space of the editor is viewed and edited in the property view.

7 Use Scenarios

This section presents use scenarios illustrating how the features of the proposed EMF-based ontology engineering tool can be utilized in real-world applications. Our example is the *model-driven business transformation* [11]. Business transformation employs business models such as *component business models* [18] to identify opportunities for reducing costs or improve business processes. The model-driven approach to business transformation requires a model representation of a variety of business entities such as business processes, components, competencies, activities, resources, metrics, KPIs (Key Performance Indicators), etc. and their relations. Semantic models or ontologies provide useful representation of business models because they can effectively represent different types of relations among business entities. Also, the automatic reasoning capability of semantic models provides an effective method for analyzing business models for identifying cost-saving or process improvement opportunities.

For example, business performance metrics are associated with business activities. By using the relations between business activities and metrics, and also the relations between business components and business activities represented in a semantic model, a business analyst can infer relations between business components and metrics. This type of analysis provides business insights into how the corporate can improve its performance metrics by addressing issues with the business components associated with the selected set of metrics. Then, by identifying, again in the semantic model, IT systems associated with the business components, the analyst may be able to suggest recommendations about IT system management to improve performance metrics.

The first step in realizing this model-driven business analysis scenario is the construction of semantic models of various business entities including business processes, components, competencies, activities, resources, operational metrics, KPIs. In many cases in most enterprises, the classes and relations of these business entities are already captured in certain legacy modeling languages such as UML class diagrams, ER diagrams, relational data models, Java interfaces, spreadsheets, or text documents. Therefore, the task of semantic model construction simplifies to transforming the legacy models and merging them into OWL ontologies. The merged OWL ontologies can be enriched with certain semantics such as generalization and specification, and cardinality constraints to enhance the effects of business analysis queries.

To summarize the model transformation process using the EMF-based ontology engineering system, it starts by capturing formal and informal semantics of legacy models. The model transformation engine transforms *formal* semantics of input legacy models into OWL models, by utilizing pre-defined mappings between OWL and the metamodels of the input models. The ontology engineering system allows an expert to look into annotations and code of legacy models, and represent the semantics in OWL models. *Informal* semantics are captured as additional axioms and added to the OWL models by using the OWL editor. Optional functions of the system, such as the source code analysis or natural language processing, facilitate automatically capturing of certain informal semantics and improve the productivity of human experts. The overall process of capturing of formal and informal semantics of legacy models and representing them in OWL models is referred to as *semantics enrichment.*

We have implemented a non-trivial model transformation by using the EODM transformation engine. The source model is the Financial Business Object Model (FS-BOM) from IBM's Information FrameWork (IFW). IFW permits many types of information models required by complex enterprise systems for storing and correlating classes in a consistent manner. FS-BOM is a component of the overall suite of IFW for Financial Services. It was written in UML and provides an enterprise-wide, generic and flexible model for financial services business. It is usually used as a starting point for analysis and design of business systems. Its rich content can be viewed from the fact that it has 582 classes and 5878 attributes and associations. This complicated structure indicates that more knowledge may be buried deep in the FS-BOM. Therefore, an inference-enabled representation, for example, by using OWL, is desirable. This transformation was conducted by using the EODM transformation engine.

For another use scenario, we have practiced model-driven ontology engineering in customer data integration (CDI) by using the Integrated Ontology Development Toolkit (IODT) [22] which includes EODM, the EODM workbench and a persistent ontology repository. IODT is publicly available at IBM's alphaWorks. In the CDI project, we used OWL ontologies to model concepts and properties describing customers, and populated customer data as instance in the OWL ontologies. More precisely, ontologies are adopted to describe and automatically classify customer data, and eventually support semantic queries on the customer data. Figure 11 shows a skeleton model transformation process in CDI. First, there are legacy UML class diagrams representing customer classification hierarchies, for example, (bank subCategoryOf FinancialInstitute). By using the EODM transformation engine, the UML diagrams are transformed into an Ecore model as shown. Next, the Ecore model is transformed into an OWL ontology. In the EODM workbench, the generated ontology is further customized by adding, modifying or deleting classes and properties, as necessary. For instance, an OWL class named "BDWCustomer" is additionally defined as a someValuesFrom restriction on Property "buy" with "BDW" as the range class (BDW means Banking Data Warehouse.). Then, as shown in Figure 12, we deployed the semantically enriched ontologies into IODT's persistent repository and populated customer data as ontology instances. In the ontology repository, customer data is represented and stored as RDF triples. The customer data is classified based on OWL ontology reasoning. For example, the customer "SD Bank" is automatically classified as an

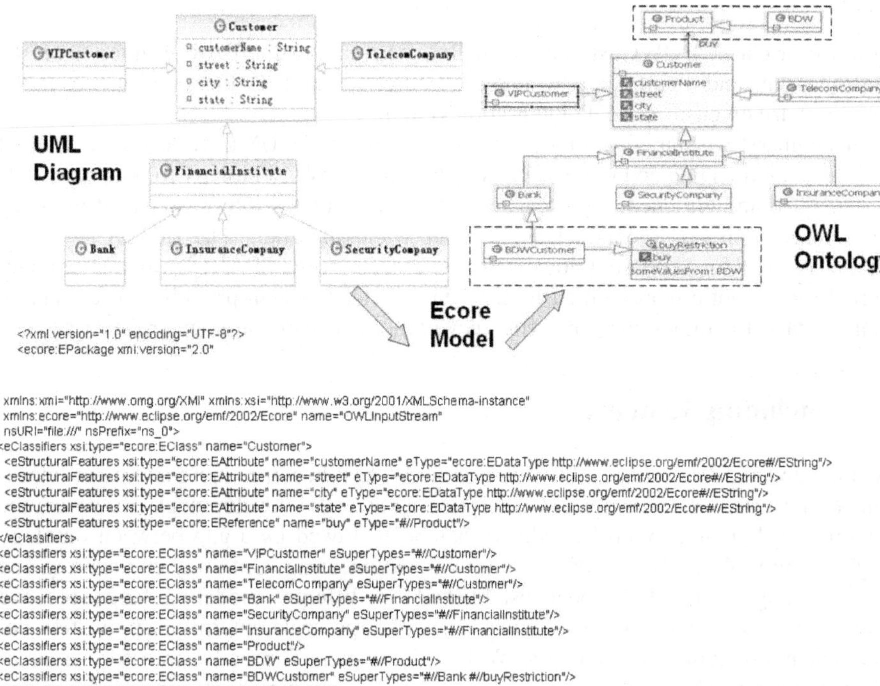

Fig. 11. A model transformation example

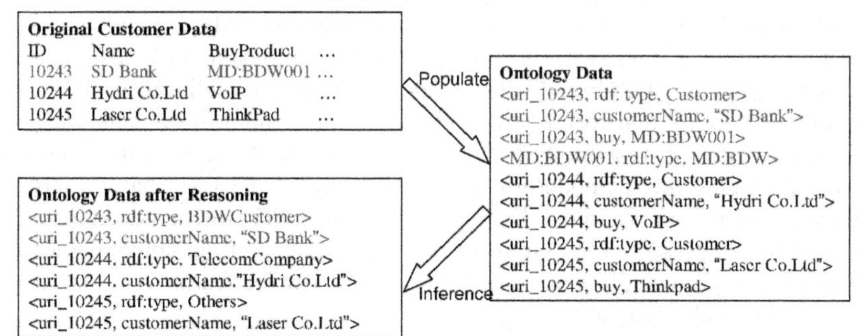

SPARQL Query Example:

```
PREFIX md:<http://ibm.com/CDI>
SELECT?name, ?products
WHERE ( ? customer rdf:type md:Bank ) ( ? customer md:buy ?products )
( ?customer md:customerName ?name )
```

Results:

name	products
SD Bank	MD:BDW001

Fig. 12. Queries in ontology-driven customer data integration

instance of class "BDWCustomer." Finally, users can issue SPARQL queries on the customer data and obtain query results accordingly. Figure 12 illustrates queries in the ontology-driven customer data integration system.

In summary, we started from legacy customer models in UML. By using the EODM transformation engine and the EODM workbench, an OWL ontology for customer data is generated and enriched. After customer data is populated into a persistent ontology repository, inference is conducted for instance classification. The EODM reasoning engine is used for OWL ontology TBox inference. Also, SPARQL queries are supported for semantic search on customer data. The CDI system provides a use scenario that validates the importance and efficiency of model-driven ontology engineering.

8 Concluding Remarks

As the Semantic Web shapes the future of the Web, it becomes more and more important in software engineering and enterprise application development. However, the adoption of Semantic Web by industry has been slowed by a gap between ontology engineering tools and the traditional software engineering. Ontology engineering and software engineering have been established on different modeling languages and methodologies, which has caused difficulties in large-scale enterprise application development involving the Semantic Web technologies. Currently, transformation of UML models to OWL ontologies and vice versa is conducted only in an ad hoc and incomplete way.

This paper presented a novel approach to bridging this gap between two different, but complementary engineering disciplines with a systematic approach. We leveraged OMG's Model-Driven Architecture and Ontology Definition Metamodel to provide model transformation, utilizing underlying standards including MOF-based metamodels, XMI representation, UML extension with profiling, and EMF implementation of MOF. This approach allows seamlessly supporting legacy models in UML and other languages in Semantic Web-based software development. In addition, it allows exploiting the availability and features of UML tools for creation of vocabularies and ontologies. Furthermore, it supports code generation and facilitates tool development. This paper presented the methodology and architecture of the EMF-based ontology engineering system, and mappings between UML and OWL for model transformation. In addition, it presented the entire stack of the developed ontology engineering system. Finally, it presented use scenarios illustrating how the features of this system can be utilized in real-world applications.

This model-driven ontology engineering is still in its infancy. For this approach to meet its promises and scale for industry applications, a number of technical challenges need to be addressed. Some directions for further investigation include:

- Study of the theoretical limitations of the model transformation under the EMF context and a complete definition of bi-directional mappings between the Ecore metamodel and semantic metamodels to support model transformation;
- Support for more legacy modeling languages and methodologies in addition to UML, XSD and Java interfaces which we have addressed in the current system, e.g., relational data models and spreadsheets traditionally popular in the business environment;

- Validation of the proposed advantage of utilizing features of visual UML tools for creating and editing ontologies in real-world applications;
- Evaluation of EMF's capability of code generation for facilitating tool development;
- Augmenting the proposed model transformation method with capabilities for source code analysis and text mining to facilitate acquisition of certain informal semantics of legacy models; and
- Maturation of the holistic EMF-based ontology engineering framework by applying and validating it in real-world business applications.

References

1. T. Berners-Lee, J. Hendler, O. Lassila, "The Semantic WEB," Scientific American, 2001.
2. D. Brickley and R. Guha, "RDF Vocabulary Description Language 1.0: RDF Schema," W3C Recommendation, http://www.w3.org/TR/rdf-schema/, 2004.
3. Brown, "An introduction to Model Driven Architecture – Part I: MDA and today's systems", http://www-106.ibm.com/developerworks/rational/library/3100.html, 2004.
4. J. J. Carroll, I. Dickinson, C. Dollin, D. Reynolds, A. Seaborne, K. Wilkinson, "Jena: Implementing the Semantic Web Recommendations", Proc. of WWW 2004.
5. Djuric, D. Gaševic, and V. Devedžic, "Ontology Modeling and MDA," Journal of Object technology, Vol. 4, No. 1, 2005.
6. Gamma, R. Helm, R. Johnson, J. Vlissides, "Design Patterns: Elements of Reusable Object-Oriented Software," Addison-Wesley Professional; 1st edition, January 15, 1995.
7. D. Gasevic, D. Djuric, V. Devedzic, "Bridging MDA and OWL ontologies," Journal of Web Engineering, Vol.4, No.2, 2005, pp. 119-134.
8. J. Grant and D. Beckett, "RDF Test Cases," http://www.w3.org/TR/rdf-testcases/, 10 Feb. 2004.
9. Hladik, "Implementation and Optimisation of a Tableau Algorithm for the Guarded Fragment," Lecture Notes In Computer Science; Vol. 2381 archive, Proceedings of the International Conference on Automated Reasoning with Analytic Tableaux and Related Methods, Pages: 145 - 159, 2002.
10. G. Klyne and J. Carroll, "Resource Description Framework (RDF): Concepts and Abstract Syntax," W3C Recommendation, http://www.w3.org/TR/rdf-concepts/, 2004.
11. Lee, "Model-Driven Business Transformation and Semantic Web," The Communications of the ACM, Special Issue on Semantic eBusiness Vision, December 2005.
12. J. Lee and R. Goodwin, "Ontology Management for Large-Scale E-Commerce Applications," International Workshop on Data Engineering Issues in E-Commerce, Tokyo, Japan, April 9, 2005.
13. Lutz, "NEXP TIME-Complete Description Logics with Concrete Domains," ACM Transactions on Computational Logic (TOCL) archive, Volume 5, Issue 4, October 2004.
14. L. Ma, Z. Su, Y. Pan, L. Zhang, T. Liu, "RStar: An RDF Storage and Query System for Enterprise Resource Management", Proc. of ACM CIKM, pp. 484-491, 2004.
15. Oberle, R. Volz, B. Motik, S. Staab, "An Extensible Ontology Software Environment," In Steffen Staab and Rudi Studer, Handbook on Ontologies, chapter III, pp. 311-333. Springer, 2004.
16. M. K. Smith, C. Welty, and D. L. McGuinness, "OWL Web Ontology language Guide," http://www.w3.org/TR/owl-guide/, 2004.

17. Tetlow, et al., "Ontology Driven Architectures and Potential Uses of the Semantic Web in Systems and Software Engineering," http://www.w3.org/2001/sw/BestPractices/SE/ODA/, 2005.
18. CBM: Component Business Modeling, http://www-306.ibm.com/e-business/ondemand/us/innovation/ cbm/ cbm_b.shtml.
19. D2RQ V0.4: Treating Non-RDF Databases as Virtual RDF Graphs, http://www.wiwiss.fu-berlin.de/suhl/bizer/d2rq/.
20. GEF (Graphical Editing Framework), http://www.eclipse.org/gef, 2004.
21. EMF (Eclipse Modeling Framework), http://www.eclipse.org/emf, 2004.
22. IBM Integrated Ontology Toolkit, http://www.alphaworks.ibm.com/tech/semanticstk, 2005.
23. Jastor, http://jastor.sourceforge.net/.
24. MOF: Meta-Object Facility, Version 1.4, http://www.omg.org/technology/documents/formal/mof.htm.
25. ODM: Ontology Definition Metamodel, http://www.omg.org/docs/ontology/04-08-01.pdf, 2004.
26. Pellet: an Open-Source Java Based OWL DL Reasoner, http://www.mindswap.org/2003/pellet/index.shtml.
27. Primer: Getting into RDF & Semantic Web using N3, http://www.w3.org/2000/10/swap Primer.html.
28. Protégé, http://protege.stanford.edu/index.html, 2004.
29. Sesame, an Open Source RDF Database with Support for RDF Schema Inferencing and Querying," http://www.openrdf.org/, 2002.

Inheritance in Rule-Based Frame Systems: Semantics and Inference

Guizhen Yang[1] and Michael Kifer[2]

[1] Artificial Intelligence Center
SRI International, Menlo Park, CA 94025, USA
yang@ai.sri.com
[2] Department of Computer Science
State University of New York at Stony Brook
Stony Brook, NY 11794, USA
kifer@cs.stonybrook.edu

Abstract. Knowledge representation languages that combine rules with object-oriented features akin to frame systems have recently attracted a lot of research interest, and F-logic is widely seen as a basis to achieve this integration. In this paper we extend the original F-logic formalism with an array of salient features that are essential for representing and reasoning with commonsense knowledge. In particular, we extend the syntax and semantics of F-logic to incorporate nonmonotonic multiple inheritance of class and instance methods in the presentence of class hierarchies defined via rules. The new semantics is completely model-theoretic and is free of the defects that caused the original F-logic to produce unintuitive results due to the unusual interaction between default inheritance and inference via rules. Moreover, we provide a computational framework for the new F-logic semantics which can be implemented by inference engines using either forward or backward chaining mechanisms.

1 Introduction

With computer systems getting more powerful and once esoteric information management problems becoming commonplace, attention is again shifting to knowledge representation languages that combine rules with object-oriented features akin to frame systems. Recently, W3C created a new working group, which is chartered with producing a recommendation for a standardized rule language that could serve as an interchange format for various rule-based systems [38]. According to the charter, the future language will support features inspired by object-oriented and frame-based languages.

As a prominent formalism in applications where both rules and frame-based representation are highly desired, F-logic has found its success in many areas, including Semantic Web [9,10,3,8], intelligent networking [24], software engineering [17,13], and industrial knowledge management [2,39]. F-logic based systems are available both commercially [33] and from the academia [14,46,40,30]. These systems were built for different purposes and offer different degrees of completeness with respect to the original specification.

S. Spaccapietra (Ed.): Journal on Data Semantics VII, LNCS 4244, pp. 79–135, 2006.

One major technical difficulty in this field is inheritance semantics, especially the issues related to overriding and conflict resolution [22,45]. A recent study [29] shows that inheritance — especially multiple inheritance — permeates RDF schemas developed by various communities over the past few years. Multiple inheritance is therefore likely to arise in Semantic Web applications as they grow in complexity and as rule engines start playing a more prominent role in such applications. However, current Semantic Web standards do not support multiple inheritance. Some of the F-logic based systems mentioned earlier do not support it either. Support provided by other systems is either incomplete or problematic in various ways.

The difficulty in defining a semantics for inheritance is due to the intricate interaction between inference by default inheritance and inference via rules. We illustrate this problem in Section 3. Although this problem was known at the time of the original publication on F-logic [22], no satisfactory solution was found then. Subsequent works either tried to rationalize the original solution or to impose unreasonable restrictions on the language [32,19,31]. We discuss these limitations of the related work in Section 11.

Our earlier work [45] proposed a solution to the above problem by developing a semantics that is both theoretically sound and computationally feasible. However, this semantics (like the one in [22] and most other related works) is restricted to the so called *class methods* [36] (or *static methods* in Java terminology) and to a particular type of inheritance, known as *value inheritance*, which is more common in Artificial Intelligence. The notion of *instance methods* — a much more important object-oriented modeling tool — was not supported in the language or its semantics. In this paper we extend F-logic to include instance methods and a new kind of inheritance, called *code inheritance*, which is analogous to inheritance used in programming languages like C^{++} and Java (and is different from inheritance typically found in AI systems).

Of course, neither instance method nor code inheritance is new by itself. Our contribution is in porting these notions to a logic-based language and the development of a complete model theory and inference procedure for this new class of methods and inheritance. Furthermore, these concepts are defined for vastly more general frameworks than what is found in programming languages or in the literature on logic-based inheritance. This includes systems with class hierarchies defined via rules (*intensional* class hierarchies), multiple inheritance with overriding, deductive systems with inheritance, both instance and class methods, and both value and code inheritance.

This paper is organized as follows. Section 2 introduces the basic F-logic syntax that is used throughout the paper. Section 3 motivates the research problems concerning inheritance and rules by presenting several motivating examples. The new three-valued semantics for F-logic is introduced in Section 4. Section 5 defines inheritance postulates, which bridge the formal semantics and its "real world" interpretation, and Section 6 formalizes the associated notion of object models. The computational framework is presented in Section 7. Section 8 introduces the notion of stable object models. Section 9 further develops the cautious object model semantics and discusses its properties. It is shown that every F-logic knowledge base has a unique cautious object model. Implementation of the cautious object model semantics and its computational complexity is described in Section 10. This implementation can be realized using any deductive engine that supports the well-founded semantics for negation [15] and therefore can be done using either forward or backward chaining mechanisms. Related work is discussed in Section 11 and Section 12 concludes the paper. Since some of the proofs are rather subtle and lengthy, we relegate them to the Appendix in the hope that this will help the reader focus on the main story line. Shorter proofs appear directly in the main text.

2 Preliminaries

F-logic provides frame-based syntax and semantics. It treats instances, classes, properties, and methods as objects in a uniform way. For instance, in one context, the object ostrich can be viewed as a class by itself (with members such as tweety and fred); in a different context, this object can be a member of another class (e.g., species). Whether an object functions as an instance or a class depends on its syntactic position in a logical statement. F-logic does not require instances and classes to be disjoint.[1]

To focus the discussion, we will use a subset of the F-logic syntax and include only three kinds of *atomic* formulas. A formula of the form o : c says that object o is a member of class c; s :: c says that class s is a (not necessarily immediate) subclass of class c; and e[m → v] says that object e has an *inheritable* method, m, whose result is a *set* that contains object v.[2] The symbols o, c, s, e, m, and v here are the usual *first-order* terms.[3]

Traditional object-oriented languages distinguish between two different kinds of methods: *instance methods* and *class methods* (also known as "static" methods in Java). The former apply to all instances of a class while the latter to classes themselves. In object-oriented data modeling, especially in the case of semistructured objects, it is useful to be able to define *object methods*, which are explicitly attached to individual objects. These explicitly attached methods override the methods inherited from superclasses. Object methods are similar to class methods except that they are not intended to be inherited. In F-logic both instance and class/object methods are specified using rules.

Let A be an atom. A literal of the form A is called a *positive* literal and ¬ A is called a *negative* literal. An F-logic *knowledge base* (abbr. KB) is a finite

[1] The same idea is adopted in RDF and OWL-Full.

[2] The syntax for inheritable methods in [22] and in systems like $\mathcal{F}$LORA-2 is e[m ⋆→ v], while atoms of the form e[m → v] are used for *noninheritable* methods. However, noninheritable methods are of no interest here, so we opted for a simpler notation.

[3] Recall that a first-order term is a constant, a variable, or a structure of the form $f(t_1, \ldots, t_n)$, where f is an n-ary function symbol and $t_1, \ldots, t_n$ are first-order terms.

set of rules where all variables are *universally* quantified at the front of a rule. There are two kinds of rules: *regular rules* and *template rules*. Regular rules were introduced in the original F-logic [22] while the concept of template rules is one of the new contributions of this paper. Generally, regular rules define class membership, subclass relationship, and class/object methods. Template rules represent pieces of *code* that define instance methods.

A regular rule has the form $\mathsf{H} :- \mathsf{L}_1, \ldots, \mathsf{L}_n$, where $\mathsf{n} \geq 0$, H is a positive literal, called the rule *head*, and each L_i is either a positive or a negative literal. The conjunction of L_i's is called the rule *body*. A template rule for class c has the form $\mathsf{code(c)}$ @this[m → v] $:- \mathsf{L}_1, \ldots, \mathsf{L}_n$. It is similar to a regular rule except that: (i) it is prefixed with the special notation code(c); (ii) its head must specify a method (i.e., it cannot be o : c or s :: c); and (iii) the object-position in the head literal is occupied by the *template term* @this (which can also appear in other parts of the rule). We will also assume that c is ground (i.e., variable-free) and will say that such a template rule defines instance method m for class c.

In the rest of this paper, we will use uppercase names to denote variables and lowercase names to denote constants. A rule with an empty body is called a *fact*. When a regular rule or a template rule has an empty body, we will call it a *regular fact* or a *template fact*, respectively. For facts, the symbol " :– " will be omitted.

3 Motivating Examples

We will now illustrate some of the problems that arise from unusual interaction among inference via rules, default inheritance, and intensional class hierarchies (i.e., class hierarchies that are defined using rules). In the following examples, a solid arrow from a node x to another node y indicates that x is either an instance or a subclass of y. All examples in this section are discussed informally. The formal treatment is given in Sections 4, 5, 7, and 9.

3.1 Interaction Between Default Inheritance and Rules

Inheritance Triggering Further Inheritance. Consider the KB in Figure 1. Without inheritance, this KB has a unique model, which consists of the first two facts. With inheritance, however, the common intuition tells us that o ought to inherit m → a from c. But if we only add o[m → a], the new set of facts would not be a model, since the last rule is no longer satisfied: with the inherited fact

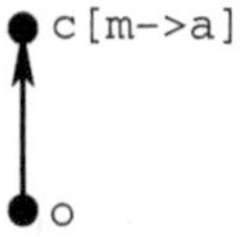

c[m->a]

o

```
o : c.
c[m → a].
c[m → b] :- o[m → a].
```

Fig. 1. Inheritance Leading to More Inheritance

included, the least model must also contain c[m → b]. However, this begs the question as to whether o should inherit m → b from c as well. The intuition suggests that the intended model should be "stable" with respect to not only inference via rules but default inheritance as well. Therefore o[m → b] should also be in that model. This problem was recognized in [22], but the proposed solution was not stable in the above sense — it was based on plausible, ad hoc fixpoint computations rather than semantic principles.

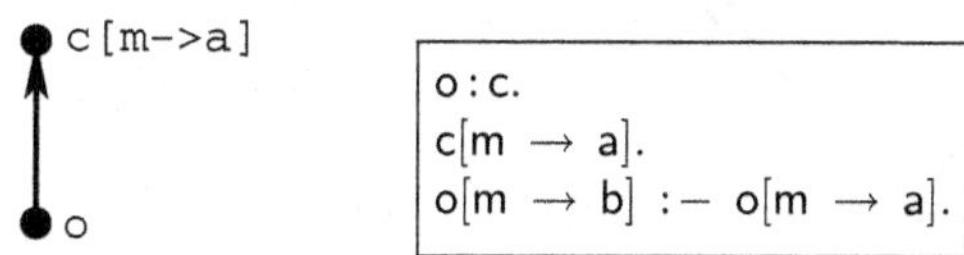

Fig. 2. Interaction between Derived and Inherited Facts

Derived vs. Inherited Information. Now consider Figure 2, which has the same KB as in Figure 1 except for the head of the last rule. Again, the intuition suggests that o[m → a] ought to be inherited, and o[m → b] be derived to make the resulting set of facts into a model in the conventional sense. This, however, leads to the following observation. The method m of o now has one value, a, which is inherited, and another, b, which is derived via a rule. Although the traditional frameworks for inheritance were developed without deduction in mind, it is clear that derived facts like o[m → b] in this example are akin to "explicit" method definitions and should be treated differently. Typically, explicit definitions should override inheritance. Thus our conclusion is that although derivation is done "after" inheritance, this derivation undermines the original reason for inheritance. Again, the framework presented in this paper, which is based on semantic principles, differs from the ad hoc computation in [22] (which keeps both derived and inherited facts).

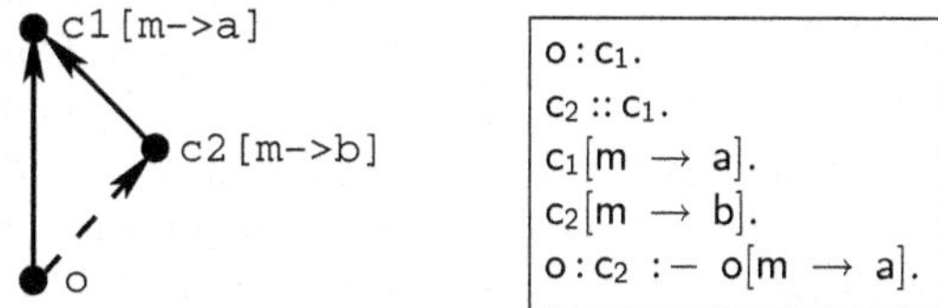

Fig. 3. Inheritance and Intensional Class Hierarchy

Intensionally Defined Class Hierarchy. Figure 3 is an example of an intensional class hierarchy. Initially, o is not known to be an instance of c_1. So, it seems that o can inherit m → a from c_1. However, this makes the fact o[m → a] true, which in turn causes o : c_2 to be derived by the last rule of the KB. Since this makes c_2 a more specific superclass of o than c_1 is, it appears that o ought to inherit $m \rightarrow b$ from c_2 rather than $m \rightarrow a$ from c_1. However, this would make the fact $o : c_2$ unsupported. Either way, the deductive inference enabled by the original inheritance undermines the support for the inheritance itself. Unlike [22], a logically correct solution in this case would be to leave both $o : c_2$ and $o[m \rightarrow a]$ *underdefined.* The dashed arrow from o to c_2 in Figure 3 represents the underdefinedness of $o : c_2$.

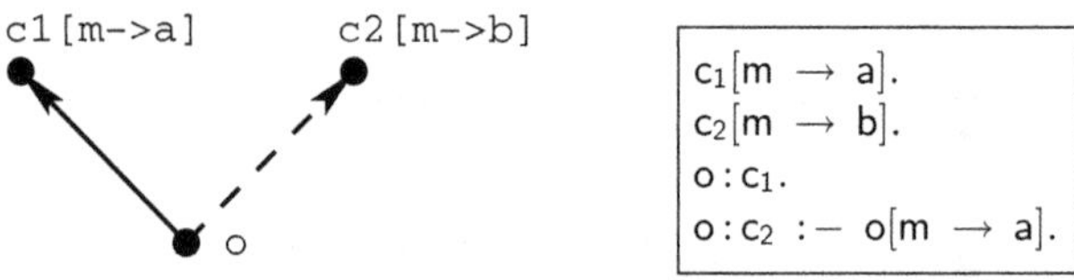

Fig. 4. Derivation Causing Multiple Inheritance Conflicts

Derivation and Multiple Inheritance Conflicts. The example in Figure 4 illustrates a similar problem, but this time it occurs in the context of nonmonotonic multiple inheritance. Initially c_2 is not known to be a superclass of o. So there is no multiple inheritance conflict and the intuition suggests that o should inherit $m \rightarrow a$ from c_1. But then $o : c_2$ has to be added to the model in order to satisfy the last rule. This makes c_2 a superclass of o and introduces a multiple inheritance conflict. As in the previous example, although this conflict became apparent only after inheritance took place, it undermines the original reason for inheritance (which was based on the assumption that $c_1[m \rightarrow a]$ is the only source of inheritance for o). Therefore, both $o[m \rightarrow a]$ and $o : c_2$ should be left underdefined. Again, this conclusion differs from [22].

3.2 Inheritance of Code

The inheritance shown in the previous examples is called *value inheritance.* It is called so because what gets inherited are the individual values that methods have in particular classes rather than the definitions of those methods.

We should note that value inheritance is *data-dependent.* Consider the example in Figure 5. At first glance, it appears that there is a multiple inheritance conflict for object o_2 with respect to method m from class c_1 and c_2. Indeed, in a traditional programming language like C^{++}, the first two rules in Figure 5 would be considered as part of the code that defines method m in class c_1 and c_2, respectively. Since o_2 is an instance of both classes, we have a multiple inheritance conflict. In contrast, value inheritance takes into account what holds in the model of the KB. Clearly, in the example of Figure 5, the premise of the first rule is true whereas the second is false. This means that the model makes $c_1[m \rightarrow a]$ true but $c_2[m \rightarrow b]$ false.[4] Therefore, if we only look at the *values* of method m that actually hold in the model of the KB, then no conflict exists and $m \rightarrow a$ can be readily inherited from c_1 by o_2 (and o_1) through value inheritance.

[4] Our claims here rely on the closed world assumption.

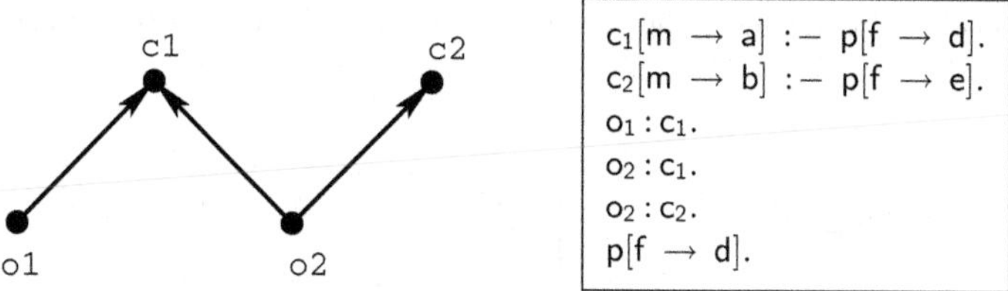

Fig. 5. Value Inheritance vs. Code Inheritance

Code inheritance, in contrast, behaves like in traditional programming languages and the above example would require conflict resolution. In this paper, we resolve multiple inheritance conflicts *cautiously* — whenever a conflict arises, nothing is inherited. To appreciate the difference between value and code inheritance, let us revisit the example of Figure 5 using code inheritance. Now suppose the first two regular rules in Figure 5 are replaced by the following two template rules (introduced in Section 2):

$$\mathsf{code(c_1)}\ @\mathsf{this[m} \rightarrow \mathsf{a]}\ :-\ \mathsf{p[f} \rightarrow \mathsf{d]}.$$
$$\mathsf{code(c_2)}\ @\mathsf{this[m} \rightarrow \mathsf{b]}\ :-\ \mathsf{p[f} \rightarrow \mathsf{e]}.$$

Note that template rules are prefixed with the notation code(c), for some class c, to indicate that they make up the code that defines the instance methods for a particular class.

We call the above rules template rules because they are not the actual rules that we require to hold true in the model of the KB. Instead, once inherited, they will be "instantiated" to the actual regular rules that are required to hold true. In the case of $\mathsf{o_2}$, no code is inherited due to multiple inheritance conflict, as we just explained above. However, $\mathsf{o_1}$ *can* inherit the first template rule from $\mathsf{c_1}$, since there is no conflict. Inheritance of such a template rule is achieved by substituting the template term @this with $\mathsf{o_1}$ in the rule. This results in a *regular rule* of the form $\mathsf{o_1[m} \rightarrow \mathsf{a]}\ :-\ \mathsf{p[f} \rightarrow \mathsf{d]}$. This rule and the fact $\mathsf{p[f} \rightarrow \mathsf{d]}$ together enable the derivation of a new fact, $\mathsf{o_1[m} \rightarrow \mathsf{a]}$.

The above example illustrates the intended use of template rules. The template term in a template rule acts as a *placeholder* for instances of that class. When the rule is inherited by an instance, the template term is replaced by that instance and the result is a regular rule. This is akin to *late binding* in traditional object-oriented languages.

The treatment of template rules should make it clear that the method m in our example above behaves like an instance method in a language like Java: the template rule does not define anything for class $\mathsf{c_1}$ as an object; instead, it defines the method m for all instances of $\mathsf{c_1}$. This is because template rules are not meant to be true in the model of the KB — but those regular rules resulting from code inheritance are.

The above example also alludes to the fact that value inheritance is a more "model-theoretic" notion than code inheritance, and that developing a model theory for code inheritance is not straightforward. We develop a suitable model theory in Section 6.

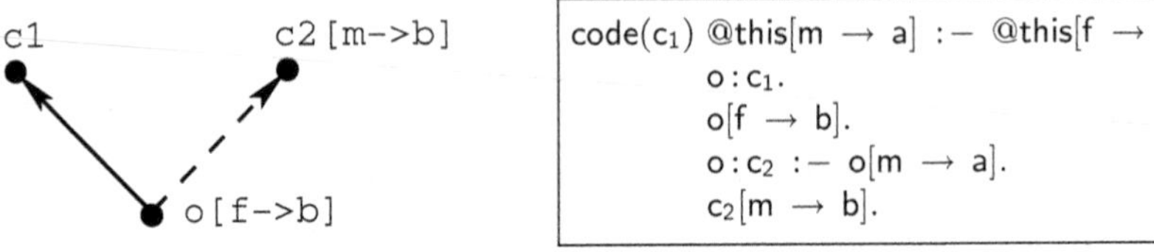

Fig. 6. Interaction between Template Rules and Regular Rules

Subtle interaction may arise between template rules and regular rules. To illustrate the issue, Figure 6 shows a template rule that defines instance method m for class c_1. On the surface, it seems that o should inherit this piece of code from c_1 and thus acquire the regular rule o[m → a] :– o[f → b]. (Recall that the template term in the rule is replaced with the inheriting instance). This inheritance seems to be possible because o is a member of c_1 and at this moment we cannot conclude that o also belongs to c_2.

A more careful look indicates, however, that there is a multiple inheritance conflict. If o inherits the above rule, then we can derive o[m → a]. But then we can also derive o : c_2 using the fourth rule in Figure 6 (which is a regular rule). Now, since c_2[m → b] is also true, we have a multiple inheritance conflict analogous to the example of Figure 4. As in the example of Figure 4, the logically correct solution here is to leave both o[m → a] and o : c_2 underdefined.

We thus see that template rules can interact with regular rules in subtle ways and cause inheritance to be canceled out. In other cases, such interaction might enable more inheritance. For instance, if instead of c_2[m → b] we had c_2[n → b], then inheritance of the template rule by o would *not* be blocked. Furthermore, o would inherit n → b from c_2 by value inheritance.

3.3 Observations

Nonmonotonic Inheritance. Overriding of inheritance leads to nonmonotonic reasoning, since more specific definitions take precedence over more general ones. However, overriding is not the only source of nonmonotonicity here. When an object belongs to multiple incomparable classes, inheritance conflicts can arise and their "canceling" effects can also lead to nonmonotonic inheritance.

Intensional Class Hierarchies. A class hierarchy becomes *intensional* when class membership and/or subclass relationship is defined using rules. In such cases, the inheritance hierarchy can be decided only at runtime, as complex interactions may come into play between inference via default inheritance and inference via rules. In this interaction, an earlier inference by inheritance may trigger a chain of deductions via rules which can result in violation of the assumptions that led to the original inheritance.

Value Inheritance vs. Code Inheritance. Inheritance of values is fundamentally different from inheritance of code. Value inheritance is *data-dependent* — it depends on the set of assertions in the current KB. Code inheritance is not dependent on data. Recall that in the example of Figure 5 we derived the fact $\mathsf{o_2[m \rightarrow a]}$ via value inheritance because the premise of the second rule was false and therefore inheritance was conflict-free from the perspective of value inheritance. If we add the fact $\mathsf{p[f \rightarrow e]}$, then the second rule will derive $\mathsf{c_2[m \rightarrow b]}$ and create a multiple inheritance conflict. In this case, $\mathsf{o_2}$ may inherit nothing.

In contrast, if we turn the rules in Figure 5 into template rules, then a multiple inheritance conflict would always exist regardless of whether the premise of either rule can be satisfied. As a result, $\mathsf{o_2}$ would inherit nothing — whether $\mathsf{p[f \rightarrow d]}$ and $\mathsf{p[f \rightarrow e]}$ hold true or not.

4 Three-Valued Semantics

The examples in Section 3 illustrate the complex interactions between inference via default inheritance and inference via rules. These interactions cause inference to behave nonmonotonically and in many ways like default negation. This suggests that stable models [16] or well-founded models [15] could be adopted as a basis for our semantics. Since default negation is part of our language anyway, adoption of one of these two approaches is fairly natural. In this paper we base the semantics on well-founded models. Since well-founded models are three-valued and the original F-logic models were two-valued [22], we first need to define a suitable three-valued semantics for F-logic KBs. We also need to extend this semantics to accommodate template rules and to make it possible to distinguish facts derived by default inheritance from facts derived via rules.

Let P be an F-logic KB. The *Herbrand universe* of P, denoted $\mathcal{HU}_\mathrm{P}$, consists of all the *ground* (i.e., variable-free) terms constructed using the function symbols and constants found in the KB. The *Herbrand instantiation* of P, denoted *ground*(P), is the set of rules obtained by consistently substituting all the terms in $\mathcal{HU}_\mathrm{P}$ for all variables in every rule of P. The *Herbrand base* of P, denoted $\mathcal{HB}_\mathrm{P}$, consists of the following sorts of atoms: $\mathsf{o:c}$, $\mathsf{s::c}$, $\mathsf{s[m \rightarrow v]_{ex}}$, $\mathsf{o[m \rightarrow v]\,^{c}_{val}}$, and $\mathsf{o[m \rightarrow v]\,^{c}_{code}}$, where o, c, s, m, and v are terms from $\mathcal{HU}_\mathrm{P}$.

An atom of the form $\mathsf{o:c}$ is intended to represent the fact that o is an instance of class c; $\mathsf{s::c}$ states that s is a subclass of c. An atom of the form $\mathsf{s[m \rightarrow v]_{ex}}$ states that $\mathsf{m \rightarrow v}$ is *explicitly defined* at s via a regular rule. Atoms of the forms $\mathsf{o[m \rightarrow v]\,^{c}_{val}}$ and $\mathsf{o[m \rightarrow v]\,^{c}_{code}}$, where $\mathsf{o \neq c}$, imply that object o inherits $\mathsf{m \rightarrow v}$ from class c by value and code inheritance, respectively.

A *three-valued interpretation* $\mathcal{I}$ of an F-logic KB P is a pair $\langle \mathrm{T}; \mathrm{U} \rangle$, where T and U are *disjoint* subsets of $\mathcal{HB}_\mathrm{P}$. The set T contains all atoms that are *true* whereas U contains all atoms that are *underdefined*. Underdefined atoms are called this way because there is insufficient evidence to establish their truth or falsehood. The set F of the *false* atoms in $\mathcal{I}$ is defined as $\mathrm{F} = \mathcal{HB}_\mathrm{P} - (\mathrm{T} \cup \mathrm{U})$. It is easy to see that the usual two-valued interpretations are a special case of three-valued interpretations of the form $\langle \mathrm{T}; \emptyset \rangle$.

Following [34], we will define the truth valuation functions for atoms, literals, and regular rules. The atoms in $\mathcal{HB}_P$ can have one of the following three truth values: **t**, **f**, and **u**. Intuitively, **u** (underdefined) means possibly true or possible false. Underdefined atoms are viewed as being "more true" than false atoms, but "less true" than true atoms. This is captured by the following *truth ordering* among the truth values: $\mathbf{f} < \mathbf{u} < \mathbf{t}$. Given an interpretation $\mathcal{I} = \langle T; U \rangle$ of an F-logic KB P, for any atom A from $\mathcal{HB}_P$ we can define the corresponding truth valuation function $\mathcal{I}$ as follows:

$$\mathcal{I}(\mathsf{A}) = \begin{cases} \mathbf{t}, \text{ if } \mathsf{A} \in T; \\ \mathbf{u}, \text{ if } \mathsf{A} \in U; \\ \mathbf{f}, \text{ otherwise.} \end{cases}$$

Truth valuations are extended to conjunctions of atoms in $\mathcal{HB}_P$ as follows:

$$\mathcal{I}(\mathsf{A}_1 \wedge \ldots \wedge \mathsf{A}_n) = min\{\mathcal{I}(\mathsf{A}_i) | 1 \leq i \leq n\}$$

The intuitive reading of a regular rule is as follows: its rule head acts as an *explicit definition* while its rule body as a *query*. In particular, if $\mathsf{s}[\mathsf{m} \rightarrow \mathsf{v}]$ is in the *head* of a regular rule and the body of this rule is satisfied, then $\mathsf{m} \rightarrow \mathsf{v}$ is *explicitly defined* for s. In the body of a regular rule, the literal $\mathsf{s}[\mathsf{m} \rightarrow \mathsf{v}]$ is true if s has either an explicit definition of $\mathsf{m} \rightarrow \mathsf{v}$, or s inherits $\mathsf{m} \rightarrow \mathsf{v}$ from one of its superclasses by value or code inheritance. Therefore, the truth valuation of a ground F-logic literal depends on whether it appears in a rule head or in a rule body. This is formally defined as follows.

Definition 1 (Truth Valuation of Literals). *Let $\mathcal{I}$ be an interpretation of an F-logic KB* P. *The truth valuation functions, $\mathcal{V}^{\mathbf{h}}_{\mathcal{I}}$ and $\mathcal{V}^{\mathbf{b}}_{\mathcal{I}}$ (**h** and **b** stand for head and body, respectively), on ground F-logic literals are defined as follows:*

$$\mathcal{V}^{\mathbf{h}}_{\mathcal{I}}(\mathsf{o}:\mathsf{c}) = \mathcal{V}^{\mathbf{b}}_{\mathcal{I}}(\mathsf{o}:\mathsf{c}) = \mathcal{I}(\mathsf{o}:\mathsf{c}) \qquad \mathcal{V}^{\mathbf{h}}_{\mathcal{I}}(\mathsf{s}::\mathsf{c}) = \mathcal{V}^{\mathbf{b}}_{\mathcal{I}}(\mathsf{s}::\mathsf{c}) = \mathcal{I}(\mathsf{s}::\mathsf{c})$$

$$\mathcal{V}^{\mathbf{h}}_{\mathcal{I}}(\mathsf{s}[\mathsf{m} \rightarrow \mathsf{v}]) = \mathcal{I}(\mathsf{s}[\mathsf{m} \rightarrow \mathsf{v}]_{\mathrm{ex}})$$

$$\mathcal{V}^{\mathbf{b}}_{\mathcal{I}}(\mathsf{o}[\mathsf{m} \rightarrow \mathsf{v}]) = max_{\mathsf{c} \in \mathcal{HU}_P}\{\mathcal{I}(\mathsf{o}[\mathsf{m} \rightarrow \mathsf{v}]_{\mathrm{ex}}),\ \mathcal{I}(\mathsf{o}[\mathsf{m} \rightarrow \mathsf{v}]^{\mathsf{c}}_{\mathrm{val}}),\ \mathcal{I}(\mathsf{o}[\mathsf{m} \rightarrow \mathsf{v}]^{\mathsf{c}}_{\mathrm{code}})\}$$

Let L *and* L_i $(1 \leq i \leq n)$ *be ground literals. Then:*

$$\mathcal{V}^{\mathbf{b}}_{\mathcal{I}}(\neg\,\mathsf{L}) = \neg\,\mathcal{V}^{\mathbf{b}}_{\mathcal{I}}(\mathsf{L}) \qquad \mathcal{V}^{\mathbf{b}}_{\mathcal{I}}(\mathsf{L}_1 \wedge \ldots \wedge \mathsf{L}_n) = min\{\mathcal{V}^{\mathbf{b}}_{\mathcal{I}}(\mathsf{L}_i) \,|\, 1 \leq i \leq n\}$$

For completeness, we define the negation of a truth value as follows: $\neg\,\mathbf{f} = \mathbf{t}$, $\neg\,\mathbf{t} = \mathbf{f}$, *and* $\neg\,\mathbf{u} = \mathbf{u}$.

The following two lemmas follow directly from the above definitions.

Lemma 1. *Let* $\mathcal{I} = \langle T; U \rangle$ *be an interpretation of an F-logic KB* P, L *a ground literal in ground*(P), $\mathcal{J} = \langle T; \emptyset \rangle$, *and* $\mathcal{K} = \langle T \cup U; \emptyset \rangle$. *Then:*

(1) If L *is a positive literal, then* $\mathcal{V}^{\mathbf{b}}_{\mathcal{I}}(\mathsf{L}) = \mathbf{t}$ *iff* $\mathcal{V}^{\mathbf{b}}_{\mathcal{J}}(\mathsf{L}) = \mathbf{t}$.
(2) If L *is a negative literal, then* $\mathcal{V}^{\mathbf{b}}_{\mathcal{I}}(\mathsf{L}) = \mathbf{t}$ *iff* $\mathcal{V}^{\mathbf{b}}_{\mathcal{K}}(\mathsf{L}) = \mathbf{t}$.

(3) If L *is a positive literal, then* $\mathcal{V}^{\mathbf{b}}_{\mathcal{I}}(\mathsf{L}) \geq \mathbf{u}$ *iff* $\mathcal{V}^{\mathbf{b}}_{\mathcal{K}}(\mathsf{L}) = \mathbf{t}$.
(4) If L *is a negative literal, then* $\mathcal{V}^{\mathbf{b}}_{\mathcal{I}}(\mathsf{L}) \geq \mathbf{u}$ *iff* $\mathcal{V}^{\mathbf{b}}_{\mathcal{J}}(\mathsf{L}) = \mathbf{t}$.

Lemma 2. *Let* $\mathcal{I} = \langle \mathrm{A}; \emptyset \rangle$ *and* $\mathcal{J} = \langle \mathrm{B}; \emptyset \rangle$ *be two-valued interpretations of an F-logic KB* P *such that* $\mathrm{A} \subseteq \mathrm{B}$, *and let* L *be a ground literal in ground*(P). *Then:*

(1) If L *is a positive literal and* $\mathcal{V}^{\mathbf{b}}_{\mathcal{I}}(\mathsf{L}) = \mathbf{t}$, *then* $\mathcal{V}^{\mathbf{b}}_{\mathcal{J}}(\mathsf{L}) = \mathbf{t}$.
(2) If L *is a negative literal and* $\mathcal{V}^{\mathbf{b}}_{\mathcal{J}}(\mathsf{L}) = \mathbf{t}$, *then* $\mathcal{V}^{\mathbf{b}}_{\mathcal{I}}(\mathsf{L}) = \mathbf{t}$.

Having defined the truth valuation functions $\mathcal{V}^{\mathbf{h}}_{\mathcal{I}}$ and $\mathcal{V}^{\mathbf{b}}_{\mathcal{I}}$ for ground literals, we now extend the truth valuation function $\mathcal{I}$ to ground regular rules. Intuitively, a ground regular rule is true if and only if the truth value of its head is at least as high as truth value of the rule body (according to the truth ordering). Note that the truth valuation of either the head or the body is three-valued, but the truth valuation of a rule is always two-valued.

Definition 2 (Truth Valuation of Regular Rules). *Given an interpretation* $\mathcal{I}$ *of an F-logic KB* P, *the truth valuation function* $\mathcal{I}$ *on a ground regular rule,* H :- $\mathsf{B} \in$ *ground*(P), *is defined as follows:*

$$\mathcal{I}(\mathsf{H}\ \text{:-}\ \mathsf{B}) = \begin{cases} \mathbf{t}, & \text{if } \mathcal{V}^{\mathbf{h}}_{\mathcal{I}}(\mathsf{H}) \geq \mathcal{V}^{\mathbf{b}}_{\mathcal{I}}(\mathsf{B}); \\ \mathbf{f}, & \text{otherwise.} \end{cases}$$

Given a ground regular fact, $\mathsf{H} \in$ *ground*(P)*:*

$$\mathcal{I}(\mathsf{H}) = \begin{cases} \mathbf{t}, & \text{if } \mathcal{V}^{\mathbf{h}}_{\mathcal{I}}(\mathsf{H}) = \mathbf{t}; \\ \mathbf{f}, & \text{otherwise.} \end{cases}$$

Satisfaction of nonground regular rules in an interpretation is defined via instantiation, as usual.

Definition 3 (Regular Rule Satisfaction). *A three-valued interpretation* $\mathcal{I}$ *satisfies the regular rules of an F-logic KB* P *if* $\mathcal{I}(\mathsf{R}) = \mathbf{t}$ *for every regular rule* R *in ground*(P).

5 Inheritance Postulates

Even if an interpretation $\mathcal{I}$ satisfies all the regular rules of an F-logic KB P, it does not necessarily mean that $\mathcal{I}$ is an *intended* model of P. An intended model must also include facts that are derived via inheritance and must not include unsupported facts. As we saw in Section 3, defining what should be inherited exactly is a subtle issue. The main purpose of this section is to formalize the common intuition behind default inheritance using what we call *inheritance postulates.*

5.1 Basic Concepts

Intuitively, c[m] is an *inheritance context* for object o, if o is an instance of class c, and either c[m → v] is defined as a regular fact or is derived via a regular rule (in this case we say that m → v is *explicitly defined* at c); or if there is a template rule which specifies the instance method m for class c. Inheritance context is necessary for inheritance to take place, but it is not sufficient: inheritance of m from c might be overridden by a more specific inheritance context that sits below c along the inheritance path. If an inheritance context is not overridden by any other inheritance context, then we call it an *inheritance candidate*. Inheritance candidates represent potential sources for inheritance. But there must be exactly one inheritance candidate for inheritance to take place — having more than one leads to a multiple inheritance conflict, which blocks inheritance.

The concepts to be defined in this section come in two flavors: *strong* or *weak*. The "strong" flavor of a concept requires that all relevant facts be positively established while the "weak" flavor allows some or all facts to be underdefined.

Definition 4 (Explicit Definition). *Let* P *be an F-logic KB and* $\mathcal{I}$ *an interpretation of* P*. We say that* s[m] *has a strong explicit definition in* $\mathcal{I}$*, if* $max\{\mathcal{I}(\mathsf{s}[\mathsf{m} \rightarrow \mathsf{v}]_{ex}) | \mathsf{v} \in \mathcal{HU}_P\} = \mathbf{t}$*. We say that* s[m] *has a weak explicit definition in* $\mathcal{I}$ *if* $max\{\mathcal{I}(\mathsf{s}[\mathsf{m} \rightarrow \mathsf{v}]_{ex}) | \mathsf{v} \in \mathcal{HU}_P\} = \mathbf{u}$*.*

Definition 5 (Value Inheritance Context). *Given an interpretation* $\mathcal{I}$ *of an F-logic KB* P*,* c[m] *is a strong value inheritance context for* o *in* $\mathcal{I}$*, if* $\mathsf{c} \neq \mathsf{o}$ *(i.e.,* c *and* o *are distinct terms) and* $min\{\mathcal{I}(\mathsf{o}:\mathsf{c}), max\{\mathsf{c}[\mathsf{m} \rightarrow \mathsf{v}]_{ex} | \mathsf{v} \in \mathcal{HU}_P\}\} = \mathbf{t}$*. We say that* c[m] *is a weak value inheritance context for* o *in* $\mathcal{I}$*, if* $\mathsf{c} \neq \mathsf{o}$ *and* $min\{\mathcal{I}(\mathsf{o}:\mathsf{c}), max\{\mathsf{c}[\mathsf{m} \rightarrow \mathsf{v}]_{ex} | \mathsf{v} \in \mathcal{HU}_P\}\} = \mathbf{u}$*.*

Definition 6 (Code Inheritance Context). *Given an interpretation* $\mathcal{I}$ *of an F-logic KB* P*,* c[m] *is a strong (respectively, weak) code inheritance context for* o *in* $\mathcal{I}$*, if* $\mathsf{c} \neq \mathsf{o}$*,* $\mathcal{I}(\mathsf{o}:\mathsf{c}) = \mathbf{t}$ *(respectively,* $\mathcal{I}(\mathsf{o}:\mathsf{c}) = \mathbf{u}$*), and there is a template rule in* P *of the form* code(c) @this[m → ...] :− ...*, i.e., there is a template rule that defines instance method* m *for class* c*.*

When the specific type of an inheritance context is immaterial as, for example, in the following definitions, we will use the term *inheritance context* without indicating whether a value or a code inheritance context is meant.

Definition 7 (Overriding). *Let* $\mathcal{I}$ *be an interpretation of an F-logic KB* P*. We will say that class* s *strongly overrides inheritance context* c[m] *for* o*, if* $\mathsf{s} \neq \mathsf{c}$*,* $\mathcal{I}(\mathsf{s} :: \mathsf{c}) = \mathbf{t}$*, and* s[m] *is a strong (value or code) inheritance context for* o*.*

We will say class s *weakly overrides* c[m] *for* o*, if either*

(1) $\mathcal{I}(\mathsf{s} :: \mathsf{c}) = \mathbf{t}$ *and* s[m] *is a weak inheritance context for* o*; or*
(2) $\mathcal{I}(\mathsf{s} :: \mathsf{c}) = \mathbf{u}$ *and* s[m] *is a weak or a strong inheritance context for* o*.*

Definition 8 (Value Inheritance Candidate). *Given an interpretation* $\mathcal{I}$ *of an F-logic KB* P*,* c[m] *is a strong value inheritance candidate for* o*, denoted*

$\mathsf{c[m]} \overset{s.val}{\leadsto}_{\mathcal{I}} \mathsf{o}$, *if* c[m] *is a strong value inheritance context for* o *and there is no class* s *that strongly or weakly overrides* c[m] *for* o.

c[m] *is a weak value inheritance candidate for* o*, denoted* $\mathsf{c[m]} \overset{w.val}{\leadsto}_{\mathcal{I}} \mathsf{o}$, *if the above conditions are relaxed by allowing* c[m] *to be a weak value inheritance context and/or allowing weak overriding. Formally, this means that there is no class* s *that strongly overrides* c[m] *for* o *and either*

(1) c[m] *is a weak value inheritance context for* o*; or*
(2) c[m] *is a strong value inheritance context for* o *and there is some class* s *that weakly overrides* c[m] *for* o.

Definition 9 (Code Inheritance Candidate). *Let $\mathcal{I}$ be an interpretation for an F-logic KB* P. c[m] *is called a strong code inheritance candidate for* o*, denoted* $\mathsf{c[m]} \overset{s.code}{\leadsto}_{\mathcal{I}} \mathsf{o}$, *if* c[m] *is a strong code inheritance context for* o *and there is no* s *that strongly or weakly overrides* c[m] *for* o.

c[m] *is a weak code inheritance candidate for* o*, denoted* $\mathsf{c[m]} \overset{w.code}{\leadsto}_{\mathcal{I}} \mathsf{o}$, *if the above conditions are relaxed by allowing* c[m] *to be a weak code inheritance context and/or allowing weak overriding. Formally, this means that there is no class* s *that strongly overrides* c[m] *for* o *and either*

(1) c[m] *is a weak code inheritance context for* o*; or*
(2) c[m] *is a strong code inheritance context for* o *and there is some class* s *that weakly overrides* c[m] *for* o.

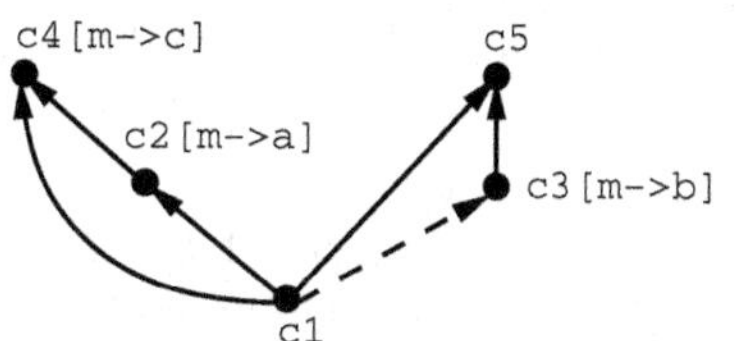

$\mathsf{c_1 : c_2}$.	$\mathsf{c_1 : c_5}$.	
$\mathsf{c_2 :: c_4}$.	$\mathsf{c_3 :: c_5}$.	
$\mathsf{c_2[m \to a]}$.	$\mathsf{c_3[m \to b]}$.	$\mathsf{c_4[m \to c]}$.
$\mathsf{code(c_5)\ @this[m \to v]\ :-\ @this[f \to x]}$.		

Fig. 7. Inheritance Context, Overriding, and Inheritance Candidate

Example 1. Consider an interpretation $\mathcal{I} = \langle \mathrm{T}; \mathrm{U} \rangle$ of an F-logic KB P, where

$$\begin{aligned} \mathrm{T} &= \{\mathsf{c_1 : c_2, c_1 : c_4, c_1 : c_5, c_2 :: c_4, c_3 :: c_5}\} \cup \\ &\quad \{\mathsf{c_2[m \to a]_{ex}, c_3[m \to b]_{ex}, c_4[m \to c]_{ex}}\} \\ \mathrm{U} &= \{\mathsf{c_1 : c_3}\} \end{aligned}$$

$\mathcal{I}$ and P are shown in Figure 7, where solid and dashed arrows represent true and underdefined values, respectively.

In the interpretation $\mathcal{I}$, $\mathsf{c_2[m]}$ and $\mathsf{c_4[m]}$ are strong value inheritance contexts for $\mathsf{c_1}$. $\mathsf{c_5[m]}$ is a strong code inheritance context for $\mathsf{c_1}$. $\mathsf{c_3[m]}$ is a weak value inheritance context for $\mathsf{c_1}$. The class $\mathsf{c_2}$ strongly overrides $\mathsf{c_4[m]}$ for $\mathsf{c_1}$, while $\mathsf{c_3}$ weakly overrides $\mathsf{c_5[m]}$ for $\mathsf{c_1}$. $\mathsf{c_2[m]}$ is a strong value inheritance candidate for $\mathsf{c_1}$. $\mathsf{c_3[m]}$ is a weak value inheritance candidate for $\mathsf{c_1}$. $\mathsf{c_5[m]}$ is a weak code inheritance candidate for $\mathsf{c_1}$. Finally, $\mathsf{c_4[m]}$ is neither a strong nor a weak value inheritance candidate for $\mathsf{c_1}$.

For convenience, we will simply write $\mathsf{c}[\mathsf{m}] \leadsto_{\mathcal{I}} \mathsf{o}$ when it does not matter whether $\mathsf{c}[\mathsf{m}]$ is a strong or a weak value/code inheritance candidate. Now we are ready to introduce the postulates for nonmonotonic multiple value and code inheritance. The inheritance postulates consist of two parts: core inheritance postulates and cautious inheritance postulates. We formalize the core inheritance postulates first.

5.2 Core Inheritance Postulates

The following definition says that class membership and subclass relationship must satisfy the usual transitive closure property.

Definition 10 (Positive ISA Transitivity). *An interpretation $\mathcal{I}$ of an F-logic KB* P *satisfies the positive ISA transitivity constraint if the set of true class membership and subclass relationship atoms is transitively closed. Formally this means that the following two conditions hold:*

(1) *for all* s *and* c*: if there is* x *such that* $\mathcal{I}(\mathsf{s}::\mathsf{x}) = \mathbf{t}$ *and* $\mathcal{I}(\mathsf{x}::\mathsf{c}) = \mathbf{t}$, *then* $\mathcal{I}(\mathsf{s}::\mathsf{c}) = \mathbf{t}$*;*
(2) *for all* o *and* c*: if there is* x *such that* $\mathcal{I}(\mathsf{o}:\mathsf{x}) = \mathbf{t}$ *and* $\mathcal{I}(\mathsf{x}::\mathsf{c}) = \mathbf{t}$, *then* $\mathcal{I}(\mathsf{o}:\mathsf{c}) = \mathbf{t}$.

The context consistency constraint below captures the idea that only explicit definitions are inherited and that explicit definitions override inheritance.

Definition 11 (Context Consistency). *An interpretation $\mathcal{I}$ of an F-logic KB* P *satisfies the context consistency constraint, if the following conditions hold:*

(1) *for all* $\mathsf{o},\mathsf{m},\mathsf{v}$*:* $\mathcal{I}(\mathsf{o}[\mathsf{m} \rightarrow \mathsf{v}]^{\,\mathsf{o}}_{\,\mathrm{val}}) = \mathbf{f}$ *and* $\mathcal{I}(\mathsf{o}[\mathsf{m} \rightarrow \mathsf{v}]^{\,\mathsf{o}}_{\,\mathrm{code}}) = \mathbf{f}$*;*
(2) *for all* $\mathsf{c},\mathsf{m},\mathsf{v}$*: if* $\mathcal{I}(\mathsf{c}[\mathsf{m} \rightarrow \mathsf{v}]_{\mathrm{ex}}) = \mathbf{f}$, *then* $\mathcal{I}(\mathsf{o}[\mathsf{m} \rightarrow \mathsf{v}]^{\,\mathsf{c}}_{\,\mathrm{val}}) = \mathbf{f}$ *for all* o*;*
(3) *for all* c,m*: if ground*(P) *has no template rule that defines instance method* m *for class* c, *then* $\mathcal{I}(\mathsf{o}[\mathsf{m} \rightarrow \mathsf{v}]^{\,\mathsf{c}}_{\,\mathrm{code}}) = \mathbf{f}$ *for all* o,v*;*
(4) *for all* o,m*: if* $\mathsf{o}[\mathsf{m}]$ *has a strong explicit definition, then for all* v, c, $\mathcal{I}(\mathsf{o}[\mathsf{m} \rightarrow \mathsf{v}]^{\,\mathsf{c}}_{\,\mathrm{val}}) = \mathbf{f}$ *and* $\mathcal{I}(\mathsf{o}[\mathsf{m} \rightarrow \mathsf{v}]^{\,\mathsf{c}}_{\,\mathrm{code}}) = \mathbf{f}$.

The first condition in the above definition rules out self inheritance. The second condition states that if $\mathsf{m} \rightarrow \mathsf{v}$ is not explicitly defined at c, then no one can inherit $\mathsf{m} \rightarrow \mathsf{v}$ from c by value inheritance. The third condition says that if a class c does not explicitly specify an instance method m, then no object should inherit $\mathsf{m} \rightarrow \mathsf{v}$ from c by code inheritance, for any v. The fourth condition states that if o has an explicit definition for method m, then this definition should prevent o from inheriting $\mathsf{m} \rightarrow \mathsf{v}$ from any other class for any v (either by value or by code inheritance).

Intuitively, we want our semantics to have the property that if inheritance is allowed, then it should take place from a *unique* source. This is captured by the following definition.

Definition 12 (Unique Source Inheritance). *An interpretation $\mathcal{I}$ of an F-logic KB* P *satisfies the unique source inheritance constraint, if the following three conditions hold:*

(1) *for all* $\mathsf{o}, \mathsf{m}, \mathsf{v}, \mathsf{c}$*: if* $\mathcal{I}(\mathsf{o}[\mathsf{m} \to \mathsf{v}]^{\mathsf{c}}_{\text{val}}) = \mathbf{t}$ *or* $\mathcal{I}(\mathsf{o}[\mathsf{m} \to \mathsf{v}]^{\mathsf{c}}_{\text{code}}) = \mathbf{t}$*, then* $\mathcal{I}(\mathsf{o}[\mathsf{m} \to \mathsf{z}]^{\mathsf{x}}_{\text{val}}) = \mathbf{f}$ *and* $\mathcal{I}(\mathsf{o}[\mathsf{m} \to \mathsf{z}]^{\mathsf{x}}_{\text{code}}) = \mathbf{f}$ *for all* z, x *such that* $\mathsf{x} \neq \mathsf{c}$.

(2) *for all* $\mathsf{c}, \mathsf{m}, \mathsf{o}$*: if* $\mathsf{c}[\mathsf{m}] \overset{s.val}{\leadsto}_{\mathcal{I}} \mathsf{o}$ *or* $\mathsf{c}[\mathsf{m}] \overset{s.code}{\leadsto}_{\mathcal{I}} \mathsf{o}$*, then* $\mathcal{I}(\mathsf{o}[\mathsf{m} \to \mathsf{v}]^{\mathsf{x}}_{\text{val}}) = \mathbf{f}$ *and* $\mathcal{I}(\mathsf{o}[\mathsf{m} \to \mathsf{v}]^{\mathsf{x}}_{\text{code}}) = \mathbf{f}$ *for all* v, x *such that* $\mathsf{x} \neq \mathsf{c}$.

(3) *for all* $\mathsf{o}, \mathsf{m}, \mathsf{v}, \mathsf{c}$*:* $\mathcal{I}(\mathsf{o}[\mathsf{m} \to \mathsf{v}]^{\mathsf{c}}_{\text{val}}) = \mathbf{t}$ *iff*

  (i) $\mathsf{o}[\mathsf{m}]$ *has neither strong nor weak explicit definitions; and*

  (ii) $\mathsf{c}[\mathsf{m}] \overset{s.val}{\leadsto}_{\mathcal{I}} \mathsf{o}$*; and*

  (iii) $\mathcal{I}(\mathsf{c}[\mathsf{m} \to \mathsf{v}]_{\text{ex}}) = \mathbf{t}$*; and*

  (iv) *there is no* x *such that* $\mathsf{x} \neq \mathsf{c}$ *and* $\mathsf{x}[\mathsf{m}] \leadsto_{\mathcal{I}} \mathsf{o}$.

Uniqueness of an inheritance source is captured via three conditions. The first condition above says that an object can inherit from a class only if it does not already inherit from another class. The second condition states that if a strong inheritance candidate, $\mathsf{c}[\mathsf{m}]$, exists, then inheritance of method m cannot take place from any other sources (because there would then be a multiple inheritance conflict). The third condition specifies when value inheritance takes place. An object o inherits $\mathsf{m} \to \mathsf{v}$ from class c by value inheritance iff: (i) o has *no* explicit definition for method m; (ii) $\mathsf{c}[\mathsf{m}]$ is a strong value inheritance candidate for o; (iii) $\mathsf{c}[\mathsf{m} \to \mathsf{v}]$ is explicitly defined; and (iv) there are no other inheritance candidates — weak or strong — from which o could inherit method m.

5.3 Cautious Inheritance Postulates

The core postulates introduced so far impose restrictions only on the part of an interpretation that contains the facts known to be true. For three-valued interpretations, we still need to describe the underdefined part more tightly. Since "underdefined" means possibly true or possibly false, it is natural to expect that the conclusions drawn from underdefined facts remain underdefined. As is typical for three-valued semantics, such as the well-founded semantics, we do not jump to negative conclusions from underdefined facts. This is why we call our semantics "cautious".

Definition 13 (Cautious ISA Transitivity). *We will say that an interpretation* $\mathcal{I}$ *of an F-logic KB* P *satisfies the cautious ISA transitivity constraint if the underdefined part of the class hierarchy is transitively closed; i.e.,*

(1) *for all* s, c*: if there is* x *such that* $\mathcal{I}(\mathsf{s} :: \mathsf{x} \wedge \mathsf{x} :: \mathsf{c}) = \mathbf{u}$ *and* $\mathcal{I}(\mathsf{s} :: \mathsf{c}) \neq \mathbf{t}$*, then* $\mathcal{I}(\mathsf{s} :: \mathsf{c}) = \mathbf{u}$*;*

(2) *for all* o, c*: if there is* x *such that* $\mathcal{I}(\mathsf{o} : \mathsf{x} \wedge \mathsf{x} :: \mathsf{c}) = \mathbf{u}$ *and* $\mathcal{I}(\mathsf{o} : \mathsf{c}) \neq \mathbf{t}$*, then* $\mathcal{I}(\mathsf{o} : \mathsf{c}) = \mathbf{u}$.

Definition 14 (Cautious Inheritance). *We will say that an interpretation* $\mathcal{I}$ *of an F-logic KB* P *satisfies the cautious inheritance constraint, if for all* o, m, v, c*:* $\mathcal{I}(\mathsf{o}[\mathsf{m} \to \mathsf{v}]^{\mathsf{c}}_{\text{val}}) = \mathbf{u}$ *iff*

(1) $\mathsf{o}[\mathsf{m}]$ *does not have a strong explicit definition; and*

(2) $\mathsf{c}[\mathsf{m}] \overset{s.val}{\leadsto}_{\mathcal{I}} \mathsf{o}$ *or* $\mathsf{c}[\mathsf{m}] \overset{w.val}{\leadsto}_{\mathcal{I}} \mathsf{o}$*; and*

(3) $\mathcal{I}(\mathsf{c}[\mathsf{m} \rightarrow \mathsf{v}]_{\text{ex}}) \geq \mathbf{u}$; *and*
(4) *there is no* $\mathsf{x} \neq \mathsf{c}$ *such that* $\mathsf{x}[\mathsf{m}] \overset{s.val}{\leadsto}_{\mathcal{I}} \mathsf{o}$ *or* $\mathsf{x}[\mathsf{m}] \overset{s.code}{\leadsto}_{\mathcal{I}} \mathsf{o}$; *and*
(5) $\mathcal{I}(\mathsf{o}[\mathsf{m} \rightarrow \mathsf{v}]^{\mathsf{c}}_{\text{val}}) \neq \mathbf{t}$.

The cautious inheritance constraint captures the intuition behind multiple inheritance based on underdefined knowledge. The conditions above state when cautious value inheritance takes place. An object o *cautiously* inherits m → v from class c by value inheritance if and only if: (i) there is no strong evidence that method m has an explicitly defined value at o; (ii) c[m] is either a strong or a weak value inheritance candidate for o; (iii) m → v is explicitly defined at c; (iv) there are no other strong inheritance candidates that can block value inheritance from c (by the unique source inheritance constraint); and (v) o does not already inherit m → v from c by value inheritance.

6 Object Models

A model of an F-logic KB should satisfy all the rules in it. In Section 4 we formalized the notion of regular rule satisfaction. Here we will extend this notion to template rules. Recall that when an object inherits a template rule, the rule is evaluated in the context of that object.

Definition 15 (Binding). *Let* R *be the following template rule which defines instance method* m *for class* c*:* code(c) @this[m → v] :– *B. The binding of* R *with respect to object* o*, denoted* $\mathsf{R}_{\|\mathsf{o}}$*, is obtained from* R *by substituting* o *for every occurrence of* @this *in* R*. In general, we will use* $\mathsf{X}_{\|\mathsf{o}}$ *to represent the term that is obtained from* X *by substituting* o *for every occurrence of* @this *in* X.

We call the above process "binding" because it is akin to late binding in traditional programming languages like C^{++}. Recall from Section 3 that template rules are just templates for the regular rules that are obtained via binding when template rules are inherited. Therefore, satisfaction of template rules in a model will have to be defined via satisfaction of their bindings. When an object inherits template rules from a class, the bindings of these template rules with respect to this object should be satisfied similarly to regular rules. However, because only those template rules that are actually inherited need to be satisfied, satisfaction of template rules depends on how they are inherited: strongly or weakly.

Definition 16 (Strong Code Inheritance). *Let* $\mathcal{I}$ *be an interpretation of an F-logic KB* P *and* R≡code(c) @this[m → v] :– B *a template rule in ground*(P). *An object* o *strongly inherits* R, *if the following conditions hold:*

(1) $\mathsf{c}[\mathsf{m}] \overset{s.code}{\leadsto}_{\mathcal{I}} \mathsf{o}$;
(2) o[m] *has neither strong nor weak explicit definitions;*
(3) *there is no* $\mathsf{x} \neq \mathsf{c}$ *such that* $\mathsf{x}[\mathsf{m}] \leadsto_{\mathcal{I}} \mathsf{o}$.

In other words, strong code inheritance happens when there is a strong code inheritance candidate, which is not overwritten and which does not have a rival inheritance candidate of any kind.

Definition 17 (Weak Code Inheritance). *Let $\mathcal{I}$ be an interpretation of an F-logic KB* P *and* $\mathsf{R} \equiv \mathsf{code(c)}$ @$\mathsf{this[m \to v]}$:– B *a template rule in ground*(P). *An object* o *weakly inherits* R, *if all of the following holds:*

(1) $\mathsf{c[m]} \overset{s.code}{\leadsto}_{\mathcal{I}} \mathsf{o}$ *or* $\mathsf{c[m]} \overset{w.code}{\leadsto}_{\mathcal{I}} \mathsf{o}$;
(2) $\mathsf{o[m]}$ *has no strong explicit definitions;*
(3) *there is no* $\mathsf{x} \neq \mathsf{c}$ *such that* $\mathsf{x[m]} \overset{s.val}{\leadsto}_{\mathcal{I}} \mathsf{o}$ *or* $\mathsf{x[m]} \overset{s.code}{\leadsto}_{\mathcal{I}} \mathsf{o}$;
(4) o *does not strongly inherit* R.

In other words, o weakly inherits R, if: $\mathsf{c[m]}$ is a code inheritance candidate for o (strong or weak); $\mathsf{o[m]}$ has no strong explicit definitions; there are no other strong conflicting inheritance candidates; and, of course, o does not strongly inherit R.

For convenience, we define a function, $imode_{\mathcal{I}}$, on the bindings of ground template rules, which returns the "inheritance mode" of a binding:

$$imode_{\mathcal{I}}(\mathsf{R}_{\|\mathsf{o}}) = \begin{cases} \mathbf{t}, \text{ if } \mathsf{o} \text{ strongly inherits } \mathsf{R}; \\ \mathbf{u}, \text{ if } \mathsf{o} \text{ weakly inherits } \mathsf{R}; \\ \mathbf{f}, \text{ otherwise.} \end{cases}$$

When $imode_{\mathcal{I}}(\mathsf{R}_{\|\mathsf{o}}) = \mathbf{t}$, we will say that $\mathsf{R}_{\|\mathsf{o}}$ is in strong code inheritance mode. Similarly, we will say $\mathsf{R}_{\|\mathsf{o}}$ is in weak code inheritance mode if $imode_{\mathcal{I}}(\mathsf{R}_{\|\mathsf{o}}) = \mathbf{u}$. Now we can extend the truth valuation function to template rules as follows.

Definition 18 (Truth Valuation of Template Rules). *Let $\mathcal{I}$ be an interpretation and* $\mathsf{R} \equiv \mathsf{code(c)}$ @$\mathsf{this[m \to v]}$:– B *a ground template rule. The truth valuation function $\mathcal{I}$ on* $\mathsf{R}_{\|\mathsf{o}}$ *is defined as follows:*

$$\mathcal{I}(\mathsf{R}_{\|\mathsf{o}}) = \begin{cases} \mathbf{t}, \textit{ if } imode_{\mathcal{I}}(\mathsf{R}_{\|\mathsf{o}}) \geq \mathbf{u} \textit{ and} \\ \quad \mathcal{I}(\mathsf{o[m \to v]}^{\mathsf{c}}_{\mathsf{code}}) \geq min\{\mathcal{V}^{\mathsf{b}}_{\mathcal{I}}(\mathsf{B}_{\|\mathsf{o}}), imode_{\mathcal{I}}(\mathsf{R}_{\|\mathsf{o}})\}; \\ \mathbf{t}, \textit{ if } imode_{\mathcal{I}}(\mathsf{R}_{\|\mathsf{o}}) = \mathbf{f} \textit{ and } \mathcal{I}(\mathsf{o[m \to v]}^{\mathsf{c}}_{\mathsf{code}}) = \mathbf{f}; \\ \mathbf{f}, \textit{ otherwise.} \end{cases}$$

For ground template facts of the form $\mathsf{F} \equiv \mathsf{code(c)}$ @$\mathsf{this[m \to v]}$, *their truth valuation is defined similarly:*

$$\mathcal{I}(\mathsf{F}_{\|\mathsf{o}}) = \begin{cases} \mathbf{t}, \textit{ if } imode_{\mathcal{I}}(\mathsf{F}_{\|\mathsf{o}}) \geq \mathbf{u} \textit{ and } \mathcal{I}(\mathsf{o[m \to v]}^{\mathsf{c}}_{\mathsf{code}}) \geq imode_{\mathcal{I}}(\mathsf{F}_{\|\mathsf{o}}); \\ \mathbf{t}, \textit{ if } imode_{\mathcal{I}}(\mathsf{F}_{\|\mathsf{o}}) = \mathbf{f} \textit{ and } \mathcal{I}(\mathsf{o[m \to v]}^{\mathsf{c}}_{\mathsf{code}}) = \mathbf{f}; \\ \mathbf{f}, \textit{ otherwise.} \end{cases}$$

Recall that atoms of the form $\mathsf{o[m \to v]}^{\mathsf{c}}_{\mathsf{code}}$ represent those facts that are derived via code inheritance. Note that when $imode_{\mathcal{I}}(\mathsf{R}_{\|\mathsf{o}}) = \mathbf{f}$, i.e., o does not inherit R, it is required that $\mathcal{I}(\mathsf{o[m \to v]}^{\mathsf{c}}_{\mathsf{code}}) = \mathbf{f}$ in order for $\mathsf{R}_{\|\mathsf{o}}$ to be satisfied. This means that if an object, o, does not inherit a template rule, then the binding of that rule with respect to o should not be used to make inference.

Now the idea of template rule satisfaction and the notion of an *object model* can be formalized as follows.

Definition 19 (Template Rule Satisfaction). *An interpretation $\mathcal{I}$ satisfies the template rules of an F-logic KB* P*, if $\mathcal{I}(\mathsf{R}_{\|\mathsf{o}}) = \mathbf{t}$ for all template rule $\mathsf{R} \in ground(\mathrm{P})$ and all $\mathsf{o} \in \mathcal{HU}_{\mathrm{P}}$.*

Observe that in the event of strong code inheritance, $imode_{\mathcal{I}}(\mathsf{R}_{\|\mathsf{o}}) = \mathbf{t}$ and so the truth valuation function on template rules reduces to that on regular rules. Indeed, for template rules, we have from Definition 18 that $\mathcal{I}(\mathsf{R}_{\|\mathsf{o}}) = \mathbf{t}$ iff $\mathcal{I}(\mathsf{o}[\mathsf{m} \rightarrow \mathsf{v}]^{\mathsf{c}}_{\mathsf{code}}) \geq min\{\mathcal{V}^{\mathbf{b}}_{\mathcal{I}}(\mathsf{B}_{\|\mathsf{o}}), imode_{\mathcal{I}}(\mathsf{R}_{\|\mathsf{o}})\} = \mathcal{V}^{\mathbf{b}}_{\mathcal{I}}(\mathsf{B}_{\|\mathsf{o}})$. A similar conclusion can be drawn for template facts.

Definition 20 (Object Model). *An interpretation $\mathcal{I}$ is called an object model of an F-logic KB* P *if $\mathcal{I}$ satisfies:*

- *all the regular rules in* P*,*
- *all the template rules in* P*, and*
- *all the core inheritance postulates (including the positive ISA transitivity constraint, the context consistency constraint, and the unique source inheritance constraint).*

7 Computation

In this section we will define a series of operators, which will form the basis for a bottom-up procedure for computing object models of F-logic KBs.

First we need to extend the definition of an interpretation in Section 4 to include book-keeping information used by the computation. This book-keeping information is cast out at the last stage when the final object model is produced. The *extended Herbrand base* of an F-logic KB P, denoted $\widehat{\mathcal{HB}}_{\mathrm{P}}$, consists of atoms from $\mathcal{HB}_{\mathrm{P}}$ and *auxiliary* atoms of the forms $\mathsf{c}[\mathsf{m}] \overset{val}{\leadsto} \mathsf{o}$ and $\mathsf{c}[\mathsf{m}] \overset{code}{\leadsto} \mathsf{o}$, where c, m, and o are terms from $\mathcal{HU}_{\mathrm{P}}$. During the computation, these auxiliary atoms will be used to approximate value and code inheritance candidates (with which they should not be confused). An *extended atom set* is a subset of $\widehat{\mathcal{HB}}_{\mathrm{P}}$. In the sequel, we will use symbols with a hat (e.g., $\widehat{\mathrm{I}}$) to denote extended atom sets. The *projection* of an extended atom set $\widehat{\mathrm{I}}$, denoted $\pi(\widehat{\mathrm{I}})$, is $\widehat{\mathrm{I}}$ with the auxiliary atoms removed.

We will often need to compare a normal atom set with the projection of an extended atom set. In such cases, when confusion does not arise, we will omit the projection operator π.

It is easy to generalize the definitions of the truth valuation functions in Section 4 to extended atom sets, since the auxiliary atoms do not occur in F-logic KBs. Formally, given an extended atom set $\widehat{\mathrm{I}}$, let $\mathcal{I} = \langle \pi(\widehat{\mathrm{I}}); \emptyset \rangle$. We define: (i) $val^{\mathbf{h}}_{\widehat{\mathrm{I}}}(\mathsf{H}) \overset{\text{def}}{=} \mathcal{V}^{\mathbf{h}}_{\mathcal{I}}(\mathsf{H})$, for a ground rule head H; (ii) $val^{\mathbf{b}}_{\widehat{\mathrm{I}}}(\mathsf{B}) \overset{\text{def}}{=} \mathcal{V}^{\mathbf{b}}_{\mathcal{I}}(\mathsf{B})$, for a ground rule body B; (iii) $val_{\widehat{\mathrm{I}}}(\mathsf{R}) \overset{\text{def}}{=} \mathcal{I}(\mathsf{R})$, for a ground regular rule R; and (iv) $val_{\widehat{\mathrm{I}}}(\mathsf{R}_{\|\mathsf{o}}) \overset{\text{def}}{=} \mathcal{I}(\mathsf{R}_{\|\mathsf{o}})$, for a binding of a ground template rule R.

The computation model for F-logic KBs with regular and template rules was inspired by the alternating fixpoint operator [42] and extends it. The new element here is the book-keeping mechanism, which is necessary for recording inheritance information.

Definition 21. *Given a ground literal* L *of an F-logic KB* P *and an atom* $\mathsf{A} \in \mathcal{HB}_{\mathrm{P}}$, *we say that* L *matches* A, *if one of the following conditions is true: (i)* $\mathsf{L} = \mathsf{o}:\mathsf{c}$ *and* $\mathsf{A} = \mathsf{o}:\mathsf{c}$; *or (ii)* $\mathsf{L} = \mathsf{s}::\mathsf{c}$ *and* $\mathsf{A} = \mathsf{s}::\mathsf{c}$; *or (iii)* $\mathsf{L} = \mathsf{s}[\mathsf{m} \rightarrow \mathsf{v}]$ *and* $\mathsf{A} = \mathsf{s}[\mathsf{m} \rightarrow \mathsf{v}]_{\mathsf{ex}}$.

Definition 22 (Regular Rule Consequence). *The regular rule consequence operator,* $\mathbf{RC}_{\mathrm{P},\widehat{\mathrm{I}}}$, *is defined for an F-logic KB* P *and an extended atom set* $\widehat{\mathrm{I}}$. *It takes as input an extended atom set,* $\widehat{\mathrm{J}}$, *and generates a new extended atom set,* $\mathbf{RC}_{\mathrm{P},\widehat{\mathrm{I}}}(\widehat{\mathrm{J}})$, *as follows:*

$$\left\{ \mathsf{A} \;\middle|\; \begin{array}{l} \textit{ground}(\mathrm{P}) \textit{ has a regular rule, } \mathsf{H} :- \mathsf{L}_1, \ldots, \mathsf{L}_n, \textit{ such that } \mathsf{H} \textit{ matches} \\ \mathsf{A} \textit{ and for every literal } \mathsf{L}_i \;\; (1 \leq i \leq n)\textit{: (i) if } \mathsf{L}_i \textit{ is positive, then} \\ \textit{val}^{\mathbf{b}}_{\widehat{\mathrm{J}}}(\mathsf{L}_i) = \mathbf{t}; \textit{ and (ii) if } \mathsf{L}_i \textit{ is negative, then } \textit{val}^{\mathbf{b}}_{\widehat{\mathrm{I}}}(\mathsf{L}_i) = \mathbf{t}. \end{array} \right\}$$

The regular rule consequence operator is adopted from the usual alternating fixpoint computation. It derives new facts, including class membership, subclass relationship, and explicit method definitions for classes and objects, from the regular rules in an F-logic KB.

Definition 23 (Inheritance Blocking). *The inheritance blocking operator,* $\mathbf{IB}_{\mathrm{P}}$, *is defined for an F-logic KB* P. *It takes as input an extended atom set,* $\widehat{\mathrm{I}}$, *and generates the set,* $\mathbf{IB}_{\mathrm{P}}(\widehat{\mathrm{I}})$, *which is the union of the following sets of atoms.*

Explicit inheritance conflicts:

$$\left\{ \textit{ec}(\mathsf{o},\mathsf{m}) \mid \exists \mathsf{v} \textit{ such that } \mathsf{o}[\mathsf{m} \rightarrow \mathsf{v}]_{\mathsf{ex}} \in \widehat{\mathrm{I}} \right\}$$

Multiple inheritance conflicts:

$$\left\{ \textit{mc}(\mathsf{c},\mathsf{m},\mathsf{o}) \;\middle|\; \exists \mathsf{x} \neq \mathsf{c} \textit{ such that } \mathsf{x}[\mathsf{m}] \overset{\textit{val}}{\rightsquigarrow} \mathsf{o} \in \widehat{\mathrm{I}} \textit{ or } \mathsf{x}[\mathsf{m}] \overset{\textit{code}}{\rightsquigarrow} \mathsf{o} \in \widehat{\mathrm{I}} \right\}$$

Overriding inheritance conflicts:

$$\left\{ \textit{ov}(\mathsf{c},\mathsf{m},\mathsf{o}) \;\middle|\; \begin{array}{l} \exists \mathsf{x} \textit{ such that: (i) } \mathsf{x} \neq \mathsf{c},\ \mathsf{x} \neq \mathsf{o},\ \mathsf{x}::\mathsf{c} \in \widehat{\mathrm{I}}, \\ \mathsf{o}:\mathsf{x} \in \widehat{\mathrm{I}}\textit{; and (ii) } \exists \mathsf{v} \textit{ such that } \mathsf{x}[\mathsf{m} \rightarrow \mathsf{v}]_{\mathsf{ex}} \in \widehat{\mathrm{I}} \\ \textit{or there is a template rule in ground}(\mathrm{P}) \textit{ of the} \\ \textit{form } \mathsf{code}(\mathsf{x})\ \mathsf{@this}[\mathsf{m} \rightarrow \ldots] :- \ldots, \textit{ which} \\ \textit{specifies the instance method } \mathsf{m} \textit{ for class } \mathsf{x}. \end{array} \right\}$$

The inheritance blocking operator is an auxiliary operator used in defining the template rule consequence operator and the inheritance consequence operator below. It returns book-keeping information that is needed to determine inheritance candidates.

Intuitively, $\textit{ec}(\mathsf{o},\mathsf{m})$ means method m is explicitly defined at o; $\textit{mc}(\mathsf{c},\mathsf{m},\mathsf{o})$ means inheritance of method m from c to o is not possible due to a multiple inheritance conflict (because there is a value or a code inheritance candidate other than c); $ov(\mathsf{c},\mathsf{m},\mathsf{o})$ means inheritance of method m from c by o would be overridden by another class that stands between o and c in the class hierarchy. From Definition 23 we can see that a class must have a explicitly defined value for a method or have an instance method definition to be able to override inheritance from its superclasses. The following lemmas follow directly from the above definitions.

Lemma 3. *Given an interpretation* $\mathcal{I} = \langle \mathrm{T};\mathrm{U} \rangle$ *of an F-logic KB* P*:*

(1) *for all* c, m, o*: there is* x *such that* x *strongly overrides* c[m] *for* o *iff* $ov(\mathsf{c},\mathsf{m},\mathsf{o}) \in \mathbf{IB}_{\mathrm{P}}(\mathrm{T})$.
(2) *for all* c, m, o*: there is* x *such that* x *strongly or weakly overrides* c[m] *for* o *iff* $ov(\mathsf{c},\mathsf{m},\mathsf{o}) \in \mathbf{IB}_{\mathrm{P}}(\mathrm{T} \cup \mathrm{U})$.

Lemma 4. *Given an interpretation* $\mathcal{I} = \langle \mathrm{T};\mathrm{U} \rangle$ *of an F-logic KB* P*:*

(1) *for all* c, m, o*:* $\mathsf{c}[\mathsf{m}] \overset{s.val}{\leadsto}_{\mathcal{I}} \mathsf{o}$ *iff* *(i)* $\mathsf{c} \neq \mathsf{o}$, $\mathsf{o}:\mathsf{c} \in \mathrm{T}$*;* *(ii)* $\mathsf{c}[\mathsf{m} \rightarrow \mathsf{v}]_{\mathrm{ex}} \in \mathrm{T}$ *for some* v*;* *and (iii)* $ov(\mathsf{c},\mathsf{m},\mathsf{o}) \notin \mathbf{IB}_{\mathrm{P}}(\mathrm{T} \cup \mathrm{U})$.
(2) *for all* c, m, o*:* $\mathsf{c}[\mathsf{m}] \overset{s.code}{\leadsto}_{\mathcal{I}} \mathsf{o}$ *iff* *(i)* $\mathsf{c} \neq \mathsf{o}$, $\mathsf{o}:\mathsf{c} \in \mathrm{T}$*;* *(ii) there is a template rule in ground*(P) *which specifies the instance method* m *for class* c*;* *and (iii)* $ov(\mathsf{c},\mathsf{m},\mathsf{o}) \notin \mathbf{IB}_{\mathrm{P}}(\mathrm{T} \cup \mathrm{U})$.
(3) *for all* c, m, o*:* $\mathsf{c}[\mathsf{m}] \overset{s.val}{\leadsto}_{\mathcal{I}} \mathsf{o}$ *or* $\mathsf{c}[\mathsf{m}] \overset{w.val}{\leadsto}_{\mathcal{I}} \mathsf{o}$ *iff* *(i)* $\mathsf{c} \neq \mathsf{o}$, $\mathsf{o}:\mathsf{c} \in \mathrm{T} \cup \mathrm{U}$*;* *(ii)* $\mathsf{c}[\mathsf{m} \rightarrow \mathsf{v}]_{\mathrm{ex}} \in \mathrm{T} \cup \mathrm{U}$ *for some* v*;* *and (iii)* $ov(\mathsf{c},\mathsf{m},\mathsf{o}) \notin \mathbf{IB}_{\mathrm{P}}(\mathrm{T})$.
(4) *for all* c, m, o*:* $\mathsf{c}[\mathsf{m}] \overset{s.code}{\leadsto}_{\mathcal{I}} \mathsf{o}$ *or* $\mathsf{c}[\mathsf{m}] \overset{w.code}{\leadsto}_{\mathcal{I}} \mathsf{o}$ *iff* *(i)* $\mathsf{c} \neq \mathsf{o}$, $\mathsf{o}:\mathsf{c} \in \mathrm{T} \cup \mathrm{U}$*;* *(ii) there is a template rule in ground*(P) *which specifies the instance method* m *for class* c*;* *and (iii)* $ov(\mathsf{c},\mathsf{m},\mathsf{o}) \notin \mathbf{IB}_{\mathrm{P}}(\mathrm{T})$.
(5) *for all* c, m, o*:* $\mathsf{c}[\mathsf{m}] \leadsto_{\mathcal{I}} \mathsf{o}$ *iff* *(i)* $\mathsf{c} \neq \mathsf{o}$, $\mathsf{o}:\mathsf{c} \in \mathrm{T} \cup \mathrm{U}$*;* *(ii) there is a template rule in ground*(P) *which specifies the instance method* m *for class* c *or* $\mathsf{c}[\mathsf{m} \rightarrow \mathsf{v}]_{\mathrm{ex}} \in \mathrm{T} \cup \mathrm{U}$ *for some* v*; and (iii)* $ov(\mathsf{c},\mathsf{m},\mathsf{o}) \notin \mathbf{IB}_{\mathrm{P}}(\mathrm{T})$.

Definition 24 (Template Rule Consequence). *The template rule consequence operator,* $\mathbf{TC}_{\mathrm{P},\widehat{\mathrm{I}}}$*, is defined for an F-logic KB* P *and an extended atom set* $\widehat{\mathrm{I}}$*. It takes as input an extended atom set,* $\widehat{\mathrm{J}}$*, and generates a new extended atom set,* $\mathbf{TC}_{\mathrm{P},\widehat{\mathrm{I}}}(\widehat{\mathrm{J}})$*, as follows:*

$$\left\{ \mathsf{o}[\mathsf{m} \rightarrow \mathsf{v}]^{\mathsf{c}}_{\mathsf{code}} \;\middle|\; \begin{array}{l} \mathsf{c}[\mathsf{m}] \overset{code}{\leadsto} \mathsf{o} \in \widehat{\mathrm{J}},\ ec(\mathsf{o},\mathsf{m}) \notin \mathbf{IB}_{\mathrm{P}}(\widehat{\mathrm{I}}),\ mc(\mathsf{c},\mathsf{m},\mathsf{o}) \notin \mathbf{IB}_{\mathrm{P}}(\widehat{\mathrm{I}}); \\ ground(\mathrm{P}) \textit{ has a template rule } \mathsf{code(c)\ @this[m \rightarrow v]\ :-\ B} \\ \textit{and for every literal } \mathsf{L} \in \mathsf{B}_{\|\mathsf{o}}: \\ \qquad (i) \textit{ if } \mathsf{L} \textit{ is positive, then } val^{\mathbf{b}}_{\widehat{\mathrm{J}}}(\mathsf{L}) = \mathbf{t}, \textit{ and} \\ \qquad (ii) \textit{ if } \mathsf{L} \textit{ is negative, then } val^{\mathbf{b}}_{\widehat{\mathrm{I}}}(\mathsf{L}) = \mathbf{t}. \end{array} \right\}$$

The template rule consequence operator is used to derive new facts as a result of code inheritance. It is similar to the regular rule consequence operator except that the regular rule consequence operator is applied to all regular rules whereas the template rule consequence operator is applied only to those selected template rules that could be inherited according to our inheritance semantics.

Given an object o and a template rule, code(c) @this[m $\rightarrow$ v] :– B, which defines instance method m for class c, we first need to decide whether o can inherit this instance method definition from c. If so, then we will bind this instance method definition for o and evaluate it (note that $B_{\|o}$ is obtained from B by substituting o for every occurrence of @this in B). If the rule body is satisfied in the context of o, we will derive $o[m \rightarrow v]^{c}_{code}$ to represent the fact that m $\rightarrow$ v is established for o by inheritance of an instance method definition from c.

We can decide whether object o can inherit the definitions of instance method m from class c by looking up the two sets $\widehat{J}$ and $\mathbf{IB}_P(\widehat{I})$. In particular, such code inheritance can happen only if the following conditions are true: (i) c[m] is a code inheritance candidate for o ($c[m] \overset{code}{\rightsquigarrow} o \in \widehat{J}$); (ii) method m is not explicitly defined at o ($ec(o,m) \notin \mathbf{IB}_P(\widehat{I})$); and (iii) there is no multiple inheritance conflict ($mc(c,m,o) \notin \mathbf{IB}_P(\widehat{I})$).

Definition 25 (Inheritance Consequence). *The inheritance consequence operator,* $\mathbf{IC}_{P,\widehat{I}}$*, where* P *is an F-logic KB and* $\widehat{I}$ *is an extended atom set, takes as input an extended atom set,* $\widehat{J}$*, and generates a new extended atom set as follows:*

$$\mathbf{IC}_{P,\widehat{I}}(\widehat{J}) \overset{\text{def}}{=} \mathbf{IC}^t(\widehat{J}) \cup \mathbf{IC}^c_{P,\widehat{I}}(\widehat{J}) \cup \mathbf{IC}^i_{P,\widehat{I}}(\widehat{J}), \quad \textit{where}$$

$$\mathbf{IC}^t(\widehat{J}) = \left\{ o\!:\!c \;\middle|\; \exists x \textit{ such that } o\!:\!x \in \widehat{J}, x::c \in \widehat{J} \right\} \cup \left\{ s::c \;\middle|\; \exists x \textit{ such that } s::x \in \widehat{J}, x::c \in \widehat{J} \right\}$$

$$\mathbf{IC}^c_{P,\widehat{I}}(\widehat{J}) = \left\{ c[m] \overset{val}{\rightsquigarrow} o \;\middle|\; \begin{array}{l} o\!:\!c \in \widehat{J},\ c \neq o,\ c[m \rightarrow v]_{ex} \in \widehat{J},\ \textit{and} \\ ov(c,m,o) \notin \mathbf{IB}_P(\widehat{I}) \end{array} \right\} \cup \left\{ c[m] \overset{code}{\rightsquigarrow} o \;\middle|\; \begin{array}{l} o\!:\!c \in \widehat{J},\ c \neq o,\ \textit{there is a template rule in} \\ \textit{ground}(P) \textit{ which specifies the instance method } m \\ \textit{for class } c, \textit{ and } ov(c,m,o) \notin \mathbf{IB}_P(\widehat{I}) \end{array} \right\}$$

$$\mathbf{IC}^i_{P,\widehat{I}}(\widehat{J}) = \left\{ o[m \rightarrow v]^{c}_{val} \;\middle|\; \begin{array}{l} c[m] \overset{val}{\rightsquigarrow} o \in \widehat{J},\ c[m \rightarrow v]_{ex} \in \widehat{J}, \\ ec(o,m) \notin \mathbf{IB}_P(\widehat{I}),\ \textit{and } mc(c,m,o) \notin \mathbf{IB}_P(\widehat{I}) \end{array} \right\}$$

The inheritance consequence operator, $\mathbf{IC}_{P,\widehat{I}}$, is the union of three operators: $\mathbf{IC}^t$, $\mathbf{IC}^c_{P,\widehat{I}}$, and $\mathbf{IC}^i_{P,\widehat{I}}$. The operator $\mathbf{IC}^t$ is used to perform transitive closure of the class hierarchy, including class membership and subclass relationship. Value and code inheritance candidates are computed by the operator $\mathbf{IC}^c_{P,\widehat{I}}$, which relies on the overriding information provided by $\mathbf{IB}_P(\widehat{I})$. Finally, the operator $\mathbf{IC}^i_{P,\widehat{I}}$ derives new facts by value inheritance. This operator also relies on the information provided by $\mathbf{IB}_P(\widehat{I})$.

Definition 26 (KB Completion). *The KB completion operator,* $\mathbf{T}_{\mathrm{P},\widehat{\mathrm{I}}}$*, where* P *is an F-logic KB and* $\widehat{\mathrm{I}}$ *an extended atom set, takes as input an extended atom set,* $\widehat{\mathrm{J}}$*, and generates a new extended atom set as follows:*

$$\mathbf{T}_{\mathrm{P},\widehat{\mathrm{I}}}(\widehat{\mathrm{J}}) \stackrel{\mathrm{def}}{=} \mathbf{RC}_{\mathrm{P},\widehat{\mathrm{I}}}(\widehat{\mathrm{J}}) \cup \mathbf{TC}_{\mathrm{P},\widehat{\mathrm{I}}}(\widehat{\mathrm{J}}) \cup \mathbf{IC}_{\mathrm{P},\widehat{\mathrm{I}}}(\widehat{\mathrm{J}})$$

The KB completion operator is the union of the regular rule consequence operator, the template rule consequence operator, and the inheritance consequence operator. It derives new "explicit" method definitions (via regular rules in the KB), new inherited facts (by value and code inheritance), plus inheritance candidacy information that is used to decide which facts to inherit in the future.

We have the following lemma regarding the *monotonicity* property of the operators that we have defined so far.

Lemma 5. *Suppose* P *and* $\widehat{\mathrm{I}}$ *are fixed. Then the following operators are monotonic:* $\mathbf{RC}_{\mathrm{P},\widehat{\mathrm{I}}}$, $\mathbf{IB}_{\mathrm{P}}$, $\mathbf{TC}_{\mathrm{P},\widehat{\mathrm{I}}}$, $\mathbf{IC}^{t}$, $\mathbf{IC}^{c}_{\mathrm{P},\widehat{\mathrm{I}}}$, $\mathbf{IC}^{i}_{\mathrm{P},\widehat{\mathrm{I}}}$, $\mathbf{IC}_{\mathrm{P},\widehat{\mathrm{I}}}$, $\mathbf{T}_{\mathrm{P},\widehat{\mathrm{I}}}$.

Given an F-logic KB P, the set of all subsets of the extended Herbrand base $\widehat{\mathcal{HB}}_{\mathrm{P}}$ constitutes a complete lattice where the partial ordering is defined by set inclusion. Therefore, any monotonic operator, Φ, defined on this lattice has a unique least fixpoint lfp(Φ) [28].

Definition 27 (Alternating Fixpoint). *The alternating fixpoint operator,* Ψ_{P}*, for an F-logic KB* P *takes as input an extended atom set,* $\widehat{\mathrm{I}}$*, and generates a new extended atom set as follows:* $\Psi_{\mathrm{P}}(\widehat{\mathrm{I}}) \stackrel{\mathrm{def}}{=} lfp(\mathbf{T}_{\mathrm{P},\widehat{\mathrm{I}}})$.

Definition 28 (F-logic Fixpoint). *The F-logic fixpoint operator,* $\mathbf{F}_{\mathrm{P}}$*, where* P *is an F-logic KB, takes as input an extended atom set,* $\widehat{\mathrm{I}}$*, and generates a new extended atom set as follows:* $\mathbf{F}_{\mathrm{P}}(\widehat{\mathrm{I}}) \stackrel{\mathrm{def}}{=} \Psi_{\mathrm{P}}(\Psi_{\mathrm{P}}(\widehat{\mathrm{I}}))$.

Lemma 6. *Let* $\widehat{\mathrm{I}}$ *be an extended atom set of an F-logic KB* P, $\widehat{\mathrm{J}} = \Psi_{\mathrm{P}}(\widehat{\mathrm{I}})$. *Then:*

(1) *for all* $\mathsf{c}, \mathsf{m}, \mathsf{o}$*: if* $\mathsf{c}[\mathsf{m}] \overset{val}{\leadsto} \mathsf{o} \in \widehat{\mathrm{J}}$ *then* $\mathsf{c} \neq \mathsf{o}$.

(2) *for all* $\mathsf{c}, \mathsf{m}, \mathsf{o}$*: if* $\mathsf{c}[\mathsf{m}] \overset{code}{\leadsto} \mathsf{o} \in \widehat{\mathrm{J}}$ *then* $\mathsf{c} \neq \mathsf{o}$.

(3) *for all* $\mathsf{o}, \mathsf{m}, \mathsf{v}, \mathsf{c}$*:* $\mathsf{o}[\mathsf{m} \to \mathsf{v}]^{\mathsf{c}}_{\mathsf{val}} \in \widehat{\mathrm{J}}$ *iff* $\mathsf{o}[\mathsf{m} \to \mathsf{v}]^{\mathsf{c}}_{\mathsf{val}} \in \mathbf{IC}^{i}_{\mathrm{P},\widehat{\mathrm{I}}}(\widehat{\mathrm{J}})$.

(4) *for all* $\mathsf{o}, \mathsf{m}, \mathsf{v}, \mathsf{c}$*:* $\mathsf{o}[\mathsf{m} \to \mathsf{v}]^{\mathsf{c}}_{\mathsf{code}} \in \widehat{\mathrm{J}}$ *iff* $\mathsf{o}[\mathsf{m} \to \mathsf{v}]^{\mathsf{c}}_{\mathsf{code}} \in \mathbf{TC}_{\mathrm{P},\widehat{\mathrm{I}}}(\widehat{\mathrm{J}})$.

(5) *for all* $\mathsf{o}, \mathsf{m}, \mathsf{v}, \mathsf{c}$*: if* $\mathsf{o}[\mathsf{m} \to \mathsf{v}]^{\mathsf{c}}_{\mathsf{val}} \in \widehat{\mathrm{J}}$ *then* $\mathsf{c} \neq \mathsf{o}$.

(6) *for all* $\mathsf{o}, \mathsf{m}, \mathsf{v}, \mathsf{c}$*: if* $\mathsf{o}[\mathsf{m} \to \mathsf{v}]^{\mathsf{c}}_{\mathsf{code}} \in \widehat{\mathrm{J}}$ *then* $\mathsf{c} \neq \mathsf{o}$.

Lemma 7. Ψ_{P} *is antimonotonic when* P *is fixed.*

Lemma 8. $\mathbf{F}_{\mathrm{P}}$ *is monotonic when* P *is fixed.*

8 Stable Object Models

Although the inheritance postulates rule out a large number of unintended interpretations of F-logic KBs, they still do not restrict object models tightly enough. There can be *unfounded* object models that do not match the common intuition behind inference. This problem is illustrated with the following example.

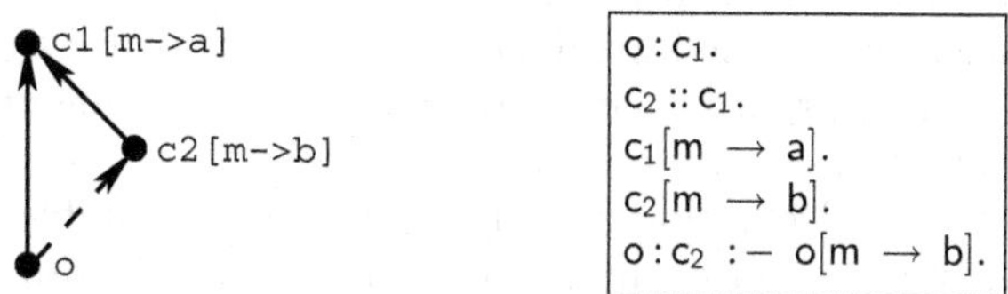

Fig. 8. Unfounded Inference

Example 2. Consider the KB in Figure 8 and the following *two-valued* object model $\mathcal{I} = \langle \mathrm{T}; \emptyset \rangle$, where

$$\mathrm{T} = \{\mathsf{o}:\mathsf{c}_1, \mathsf{c}_2::\mathsf{c}_1, \mathsf{o}:\mathsf{c}_2, \mathsf{c}_1[\mathsf{m} \rightarrow \mathsf{a}]_{\mathrm{ex}}, \mathsf{c}_2[\mathsf{m} \rightarrow \mathsf{b}]_{\mathrm{ex}}, \mathsf{o}[\mathsf{m} \rightarrow \mathsf{b}]^{\mathsf{c}_2}_{\mathrm{val}}\}.$$

Clearly, $\mathcal{I}$ satisfies the regular rules of the KB in Figure 8 and all the inheritance postulates introduced in Section 5. However, we should note that in $\mathcal{I}$ the truth of $\mathsf{o}:\mathsf{c}_2$ and $\mathsf{o}[\mathsf{m} \rightarrow \mathsf{b}]^{\mathsf{c}_2}_{\mathrm{val}}$ is not *well-founded.* Indeed, the truth of $\mathsf{o}:\mathsf{c}_2$ depends on $\mathsf{o}[\mathsf{m} \rightarrow \mathsf{b}]$ being satisfied in the body of the last rule. Since $\mathsf{o}[\mathsf{m} \rightarrow \mathsf{b}]$ does not appear in the head of any rule, there is no way for $\mathsf{m} \rightarrow \mathsf{b}$ to be explicitly defined for o. So the satisfaction of $\mathsf{o}[\mathsf{m} \rightarrow \mathsf{b}]$ depends on o inheriting $\mathsf{m} \rightarrow \mathsf{b}$ from c_2, since c_2 is the only class that has an explicit definition for $\mathsf{m} \rightarrow \mathsf{b}$. However, o can inherit $\mathsf{m} \rightarrow \mathsf{b}$ from c_2 only if the truth of $\mathsf{o}:\mathsf{c}_2$ can be established first. We see that the inferences of $\mathsf{o}:\mathsf{c}_2$ and $\mathsf{o}[\mathsf{m} \rightarrow \mathsf{b}]^{\mathsf{c}_2}_{\mathrm{val}}$ depend on each other like chicken and egg. Therefore, we should not conclude that both $\mathsf{o}:\mathsf{c}_2$ and $\mathsf{o}[\mathsf{m} \rightarrow \mathsf{b}]^{\mathsf{c}_2}_{\mathrm{val}}$ are true as implied by the KB and our semantics for inheritance.

To overcome the problem, we will introduce a special class of *stable* object models, which do not exhibit the aforementioned anomaly.

Definition 29. *Given an interpretation $\mathcal{I} = \langle \mathrm{T}; \mathrm{U} \rangle$ of an F-logic KB* P, *let $\widehat{\mathrm{T}}_{\mathcal{I}}$ be the extended atom set constructed by augmenting* T *with the set of auxiliary atoms corresponding to the strong inheritance candidates in $\mathcal{I}$. Let $\widehat{\mathrm{U}}_{\mathcal{I}}$ be the extended atom set constructed by augmenting* $\mathrm{T} \cup \mathrm{U}$ *with the set of auxiliary atoms corresponding to the strong and weak inheritance candidates in $\mathcal{I}$. More precisely, we define* $\widehat{\mathrm{T}}_{\mathcal{I}} \stackrel{\mathrm{def}}{=} \mathrm{T} \cup \mathrm{A}$, $\widehat{\mathrm{U}}_{\mathcal{I}} \stackrel{\mathrm{def}}{=} \mathrm{T} \cup \mathrm{U} \cup \mathrm{B}$, *where*

$$\mathrm{A} = \{\mathsf{c}[\mathsf{m}] \stackrel{val}{\rightsquigarrow} \mathsf{o} \,|\, \mathsf{c}[\mathsf{m}] \stackrel{s.val}{\rightsquigarrow}_{\mathcal{I}} \mathsf{o}\} \cup \{\mathsf{c}[\mathsf{m}] \stackrel{code}{\rightsquigarrow} \mathsf{o} \,|\, \mathsf{c}[\mathsf{m}] \stackrel{s.code}{\rightsquigarrow}_{\mathcal{I}} \mathsf{o}\}$$

$$\mathrm{B} = \{\mathsf{c}[\mathsf{m}] \stackrel{val}{\rightsquigarrow} \mathsf{o} \,|\, \mathsf{c}[\mathsf{m}] \stackrel{s.val}{\rightsquigarrow}_{\mathcal{I}} \mathsf{o} \textit{ or } \mathsf{c}[\mathsf{m}] \stackrel{w.val}{\rightsquigarrow}_{\mathcal{I}} \mathsf{o}\} \cup$$
$$\{\mathsf{c}[\mathsf{m}] \stackrel{code}{\rightsquigarrow} \mathsf{o} \,|\, \mathsf{c}[\mathsf{m}] \stackrel{s.code}{\rightsquigarrow}_{\mathcal{I}} \mathsf{o} \textit{ or } \mathsf{c}[\mathsf{m}] \stackrel{w.code}{\rightsquigarrow}_{\mathcal{I}} \mathsf{o}\}$$

Definition 30 (Stable Interpretation). *Let $\mathcal{I} = \langle\, \mathrm{T}; \mathrm{U} \,\rangle$ be an interpretation of an F-logic KB* P. *$\mathcal{I}$ is called a stable interpretation of* P, *if $\widehat{\mathrm{T}}_{\mathcal{I}} = \Psi_{\mathrm{P}}(\widehat{\mathrm{U}}_{\mathcal{I}})$ and $\widehat{\mathrm{U}}_{\mathcal{I}} = \Psi_{\mathrm{P}}(\widehat{\mathrm{T}}_{\mathcal{I}})$.*

Our definition of stable interpretations is closely related to that of stable models introduced in [16,35]. The idea is that given an interpretation $\mathcal{I}$ of an F-logic KB P, we first resolve all negative premises using the information in $\mathcal{I}$. The result is a residual positive KB without negation. Then $\mathcal{I}$ is said to be stable if and only if $\mathcal{I}$ can reproduce itself via the least fixpoint computation over the residual KB. This is how stable interpretations can prevent the kind of unfounded inference illustrated in Example 2.

We should note that Definition 30 only requires that a stable interpretation $\mathcal{I} = \langle\, \mathrm{T}; \mathrm{U} \,\rangle$ satisfy a certain computational property with respect to Ψ_{P}, i.e., $\widehat{\mathrm{T}}_{\mathcal{I}} = \Psi_{\mathrm{P}}(\widehat{\mathrm{U}}_{\mathcal{I}})$ and $\widehat{\mathrm{U}}_{\mathcal{I}} = \Psi_{\mathrm{P}}(\widehat{\mathrm{T}}_{\mathcal{I}})$. In fact, it turns out that a stable interpretation of an F-logic KB P satisfies all the regular rules and template rules in P as well as all the core and cautious inheritance postulates.

Theorem 1. *Let $\mathcal{I} = \langle\, \mathrm{T}; \mathrm{U} \,\rangle$ be a stable interpretation of an F-logic KB* P. *Then $\mathcal{I}$ is an object model of* P. *Moreover, $\mathcal{I}$ satisfies the cautious ISA transitivity constraint and the cautious inheritance constraint.*

Proof. By Definition 20, and by Propositions 1, 2, 3, 4, 5, 6, and 7.

Since, by Theorem 1, stable interpretations satisfy all the requirements for object models, we will start referring to stable interpretations as *stable object models*.

There is an interesting correspondence between stable object models and fixpoints of $\mathbf{F}_{\mathrm{P}}$. On one hand, it can be easily seen that stable object models are essentially fixpoints of $\mathbf{F}_{\mathrm{P}}$. Let $\mathcal{I} = \langle\, \mathrm{T}; \mathrm{U} \,\rangle$ be a stable object model of an F-logic KB P. Then $\widehat{\mathrm{T}}_{\mathcal{I}} = \Psi_{\mathrm{P}}(\widehat{\mathrm{U}}_{\mathcal{I}})$ and $\widehat{\mathrm{U}}_{\mathcal{I}} = \Psi_{\mathrm{P}}(\widehat{\mathrm{T}}_{\mathcal{I}})$, by Definition 30. It follows that $\widehat{\mathrm{T}}_{\mathcal{I}} = \Psi_{\mathrm{P}}(\widehat{\mathrm{U}}_{\mathcal{I}}) = \Psi_{\mathrm{P}}(\Psi_{\mathrm{P}}(\widehat{\mathrm{T}}_{\mathcal{I}})) = \mathbf{F}_{\mathrm{P}}(\widehat{\mathrm{T}}_{\mathcal{I}})$ and so $\widehat{\mathrm{T}}_{\mathcal{I}}$ is a fixpoint of $\mathbf{F}_{\mathrm{P}}$. Similarly, $\widehat{\mathrm{U}}_{\mathcal{I}}$ is also a fixpoint of $\mathbf{F}_{\mathrm{P}}$. Moreover, $\widehat{\mathrm{T}}_{\mathcal{I}} \subseteq \widehat{\mathrm{U}}_{\mathcal{I}}$ by Definition 29.

The following theorem shows that stable object models can be constructed using *certain* fixpoints of $\mathbf{F}_{\mathrm{P}}$.

Theorem 2. *Let* P *be an F-logic KB, $\widehat{\mathrm{J}}$ a fixpoint of $\mathbf{F}_{\mathrm{P}}$, $\widehat{\mathrm{K}} = \Psi_{\mathrm{P}}(\widehat{\mathrm{J}})$, and $\widehat{\mathrm{J}} \subseteq \widehat{\mathrm{K}}$. Then $\mathcal{I} = \langle \pi(\widehat{\mathrm{J}}); \pi(\widehat{\mathrm{K}}) - \pi(\widehat{\mathrm{J}}) \rangle$, where π is the projection function defined in Section 7, is a stable object model of* P.

Proof. Let $\mathrm{T} = \pi(\widehat{\mathrm{J}})$ and $\mathrm{U} = \pi(\widehat{\mathrm{K}}) - \pi(\widehat{\mathrm{J}})$. Thus $\mathcal{I} = \langle \mathrm{T}; \mathrm{U} \rangle$. Since $\widehat{\mathrm{J}} \subseteq \widehat{\mathrm{K}}$, it follows that $\pi(\widehat{\mathrm{J}}) \subseteq \pi(\widehat{\mathrm{K}})$, and so $\mathrm{T} \cup \mathrm{U} = \pi(\widehat{\mathrm{K}})$. To show that $\mathcal{I}$ is a stable object model of P, we need to establish that $\widehat{\mathrm{T}}_{\mathcal{I}} = \Psi_{\mathrm{P}}(\widehat{\mathrm{U}}_{\mathcal{I}})$ and $\widehat{\mathrm{U}}_{\mathcal{I}} = \Psi_{\mathrm{P}}(\widehat{\mathrm{T}}_{\mathcal{I}})$. Since $\widehat{\mathrm{J}}$ is a fixpoint of $\mathbf{F}_{\mathrm{P}}$ and $\widehat{\mathrm{K}} = \Psi_{\mathrm{P}}(\widehat{\mathrm{J}})$, it follows that $\widehat{\mathrm{J}} = \Psi_{\mathrm{P}}(\widehat{\mathrm{K}})$, by Definition 28. Therefore, if we can show that $\widehat{\mathrm{T}}_{\mathcal{I}} = \widehat{\mathrm{J}}$ and $\widehat{\mathrm{U}}_{\mathcal{I}} = \widehat{\mathrm{K}}$, then it follows that $\mathcal{I}$ is a stable object model of P.

Since $\widehat{\mathrm{J}} = \Psi_{\mathrm{P}}(\widehat{\mathrm{K}}) = \mathrm{lfp}(\mathbf{T}_{\mathrm{P},\widehat{\mathrm{K}}})$ and $\widehat{\mathrm{K}} = \Psi_{\mathrm{P}}(\widehat{\mathrm{J}}) = \mathrm{lfp}(\mathbf{T}_{\mathrm{P},\widehat{\mathrm{J}}})$, we can derive the following equations, by Definitions 26 and 25:

$$\widehat{\mathrm{J}} = \mathbf{RC}_{\mathrm{P},\widehat{\mathrm{K}}}(\widehat{\mathrm{J}}) \cup \mathbf{TC}_{\mathrm{P},\widehat{\mathrm{K}}}(\widehat{\mathrm{J}}) \cup \mathbf{IC}^{t}(\widehat{\mathrm{J}}) \cup \mathbf{IC}^{c}_{\mathrm{P},\widehat{\mathrm{K}}}(\widehat{\mathrm{J}}) \cup \mathbf{IC}^{i}_{\mathrm{P},\widehat{\mathrm{K}}}(\widehat{\mathrm{J}})$$

$$\widehat{\mathrm{K}} = \mathbf{RC}_{\mathrm{P},\widehat{\mathrm{J}}}(\widehat{\mathrm{K}}) \cup \mathbf{TC}_{\mathrm{P},\widehat{\mathrm{J}}}(\widehat{\mathrm{K}}) \cup \mathbf{IC}^t(\widehat{\mathrm{K}}) \cup \mathbf{IC}^c_{\mathrm{P},\widehat{\mathrm{J}}}(\widehat{\mathrm{K}}) \cup \mathbf{IC}^i_{\mathrm{P},\widehat{\mathrm{J}}}(\widehat{\mathrm{K}})$$

First we will show that for all $\mathsf{c},\mathsf{m},\mathsf{o}$: $\mathsf{c}[\mathsf{m}] \overset{val}{\rightsquigarrow} \mathsf{o} \in \widehat{\mathrm{J}}$ iff $\mathsf{c}[\mathsf{m}] \overset{s.val}{\rightsquigarrow}_{\mathcal{I}} \mathsf{o}$. Indeed, $\mathsf{c}[\mathsf{m}] \overset{val}{\rightsquigarrow} \mathsf{o} \in \widehat{\mathrm{J}}$, iff $\mathsf{c}[\mathsf{m}] \overset{val}{\rightsquigarrow} \mathsf{o} \in \mathbf{IC}^c_{\mathrm{P},\widehat{\mathrm{K}}}(\widehat{\mathrm{J}})$, iff $\mathsf{c} \neq \mathsf{o}$, $\mathsf{o}:\mathsf{c} \in \widehat{\mathrm{J}}$, $\mathsf{c}[\mathsf{m} \rightarrow \mathsf{v}]_{\mathrm{ex}} \in \widehat{\mathrm{J}}$ for some v, and $ov(\mathsf{c},\mathsf{m},\mathsf{o}) \notin \mathbf{IB}_{\mathrm{P}}(\widehat{\mathrm{K}})$, by Definition 25, iff $\mathsf{c} \neq \mathsf{o}$, $\mathsf{o}:\mathsf{c} \in \pi(\widehat{\mathrm{J}})$, $\mathsf{c}[\mathsf{m} \rightarrow \mathsf{v}]_{\mathrm{ex}} \in \pi(\widehat{\mathrm{J}})$ for some v, and $ov(\mathsf{c},\mathsf{m},\mathsf{o}) \notin \mathbf{IB}_{\mathrm{P}}(\pi(\widehat{\mathrm{K}}))$, iff $\mathsf{c} \neq \mathsf{o}$, $\mathsf{o}:\mathsf{c} \in \mathrm{T}$, $\mathsf{c}[\mathsf{m} \rightarrow \mathsf{v}]_{\mathrm{ex}} \in \mathrm{T}$ for some v, and $ov(\mathsf{c},\mathsf{m},\mathsf{o}) \notin \mathbf{IB}_{\mathrm{P}}(\mathrm{T} \cup \mathrm{U})$, iff $\mathsf{c}[\mathsf{m}] \overset{s.val}{\rightsquigarrow}_{\mathcal{I}} \mathsf{o}$, by Lemma 4. Similarly, we can also show that (i) for all $\mathsf{c},\mathsf{m},\mathsf{o}$: $\mathsf{c}[\mathsf{m}] \overset{code}{\rightsquigarrow} \mathsf{o} \in \widehat{\mathrm{J}}$ iff $\mathsf{c}[\mathsf{m}] \overset{s.code}{\rightsquigarrow}_{\mathcal{I}} \mathsf{o}$; and (ii) for all $\mathsf{c},\mathsf{m},\mathsf{o}$: $\mathsf{c}[\mathsf{m}] \overset{val}{\rightsquigarrow} \mathsf{o} \in \widehat{\mathrm{K}}$ or $\mathsf{c}[\mathsf{m}] \overset{code}{\rightsquigarrow} \mathsf{o} \in \widehat{\mathrm{K}}$ iff $\mathsf{c}[\mathsf{m}] \rightsquigarrow_{\mathcal{I}} \mathsf{o}$. Therefore, it follows that $\widehat{\mathrm{T}}_{\mathcal{I}} = \widehat{\mathrm{J}}$ and $\widehat{\mathrm{U}}_{\mathcal{I}} = \widehat{\mathrm{K}}$ by Definition 29. This completes the proof.

It is worth pointing out that the condition $\widehat{\mathrm{J}} \subseteq \widehat{\mathrm{K}}$ in Theorem 2 is *not* necessary for constructing a stable object model out of the extended sets $\widehat{\mathrm{J}}$ and $\widehat{\mathrm{K}}$. In fact, the following example shows that there is an F-logic KB P such that $\widehat{\mathrm{J}}$ is a fixpoint of $\mathbf{F}_{\mathrm{P}}$, $\widehat{\mathrm{K}} = \Psi_{\mathrm{P}}(\widehat{\mathrm{J}})$, and $\widehat{\mathrm{J}} \nsubseteq \widehat{\mathrm{K}}$, but $\mathcal{I} = \langle \pi(\widehat{\mathrm{J}}); \pi(\widehat{\mathrm{K}}) - \pi(\widehat{\mathrm{J}}) \rangle$ is a stable object model of P.

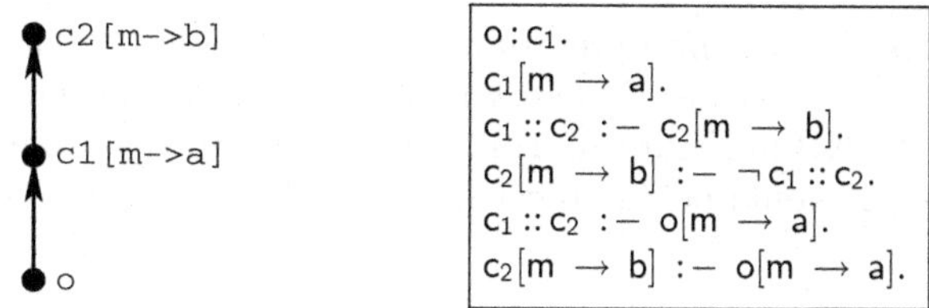

Fig. 9. Constructive Fixpoints

Example 3. Consider the F-logic KB P in Figure 9 and the following two extended sets $\widehat{\mathrm{J}}$ and $\widehat{\mathrm{K}}$:

$$\widehat{\mathrm{J}} = \{\mathsf{o}:\mathsf{c}_1, \mathsf{c}_1[\mathsf{m} \rightarrow \mathsf{a}]_{\mathrm{ex}}, \mathsf{o}[\mathsf{m} \rightarrow \mathsf{a}]^{\mathsf{c}_1}_{\mathrm{val}}, \mathsf{c}_1 :: \mathsf{c}_2, \mathsf{c}_2[\mathsf{m} \rightarrow \mathsf{b}]_{\mathrm{ex}}\} \cup \{\mathsf{c}_1[\mathsf{m}] \overset{val}{\rightsquigarrow} \mathsf{o}, \mathsf{c}_2[\mathsf{m}] \overset{val}{\rightsquigarrow} \mathsf{o}\}$$

$$\widehat{\mathrm{K}} = \{\mathsf{o}:\mathsf{c}_1, \mathsf{c}_1[\mathsf{m} \rightarrow \mathsf{a}]_{\mathrm{ex}}\} \cup \{\mathsf{c}_1[\mathsf{m}] \overset{val}{\rightsquigarrow} \mathsf{o}\}$$

One can verify that $\widehat{\mathrm{J}} = \Psi_{\mathrm{P}}(\widehat{\mathrm{K}})$, $\widehat{\mathrm{K}} = \Psi_{\mathrm{P}}(\widehat{\mathrm{J}})$, and so $\widehat{\mathrm{J}}$ is a fixpoint of Ψ_{P}. Moreover, $\pi(\widehat{\mathrm{J}}) = \{\mathsf{o}:\mathsf{c}_1, \mathsf{c}_1[\mathsf{m} \rightarrow \mathsf{a}]_{\mathrm{ex}}, \mathsf{o}[\mathsf{m} \rightarrow \mathsf{a}]^{\mathsf{c}_1}_{\mathrm{val}}, \mathsf{c}_1 :: \mathsf{c}_2, \mathsf{c}_2[\mathsf{m} \rightarrow \mathsf{b}]_{\mathrm{ex}}\}$, $\pi(\widehat{\mathrm{K}}) - \pi(\widehat{\mathrm{J}}) = \emptyset$. We can also verify that $\mathcal{I} = \langle \pi(\widehat{\mathrm{J}}); \pi(\widehat{\mathrm{K}}) - \pi(\widehat{\mathrm{J}}) \rangle$ is a stable object model of P. But clearly $\widehat{\mathrm{J}} - \widehat{\mathrm{K}} \neq \emptyset$. Thus $\widehat{\mathrm{J}} \nsubseteq \widehat{\mathrm{K}}$.

Another interesting question is whether we can *always* construct stable object models of an F-logic KB P from fixpoints of Ψ_{P}. The answer turns out to be *no*. The following example shows that some F-logic KBs may have fixpoints from which we cannot even construct an object model for that KB.

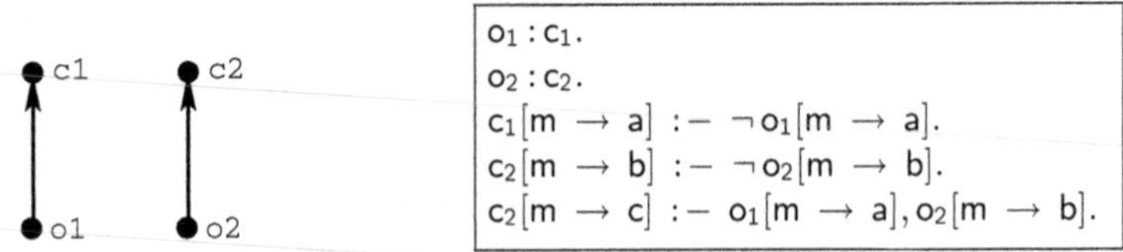

Fig. 10. Nonconstructive Fixpoints

Example 4. Consider the F-logic KB P in Figure 10 and the following two extended sets $\widehat{\mathrm{J}}$ and $\widehat{\mathrm{K}}$:

$$\widehat{\mathrm{J}} = \{\mathsf{o}_1 : \mathsf{c}_1, \mathsf{o}_2 : \mathsf{c}_2, \mathsf{c}_1[\mathsf{m} \to \mathsf{a}]_{\mathrm{ex}}, \mathsf{o}_1[\mathsf{m} \to \mathsf{a}]^{\mathsf{c}_1}_{\mathrm{val}}\} \cup \{\mathsf{c}_1[\mathsf{m}] \overset{val}{\rightsquigarrow} \mathsf{o}_1\}$$
$$\widehat{\mathrm{K}} = \{\mathsf{o}_1 : \mathsf{c}_1, \mathsf{o}_2 : \mathsf{c}_2, \mathsf{c}_2[\mathsf{m} \to \mathsf{b}]_{\mathrm{ex}}, \mathsf{o}_2[\mathsf{m} \to \mathsf{b}]^{\mathsf{c}_2}_{\mathrm{val}}\} \cup \{\mathsf{c}_2[\mathsf{m}] \overset{val}{\rightsquigarrow} \mathsf{o}_2\}$$

One can verify that $\widehat{\mathrm{J}} = \Psi_{\mathrm{P}}(\widehat{\mathrm{K}})$, $\widehat{\mathrm{K}} = \Psi_{\mathrm{P}}(\widehat{\mathrm{J}})$, and so $\widehat{\mathrm{J}}$ is a fixpoint of Ψ_{P}. However,

$$\pi(\widehat{\mathrm{J}}) = \{\mathsf{o}_1 : \mathsf{c}_1, \mathsf{o}_2 : \mathsf{c}_2, \mathsf{c}_1[\mathsf{m} \to \mathsf{a}]_{\mathrm{ex}}, \mathsf{o}_1[\mathsf{m} \to \mathsf{a}]^{\mathsf{c}_1}_{\mathrm{val}}\}$$
$$\pi(\widehat{\mathrm{K}}) - \pi(\widehat{\mathrm{J}}) = \{\mathsf{c}_2[\mathsf{m} \to \mathsf{b}]_{\mathrm{ex}}, \mathsf{o}_2[\mathsf{m} \to \mathsf{b}]^{\mathsf{c}_2}_{\mathrm{val}}\}$$

It is easy to check that the interpretation $\mathcal{I} = \langle\, \pi(\widehat{\mathrm{J}}); \pi(\widehat{\mathrm{K}}) - \pi(\widehat{\mathrm{J}}) \,\rangle$ is not even an object model of P, because $\mathcal{I}$ does not satisfy the KB in Figure 10, namely, the last rule of the KB in Figure 10. But if we remove the last rule from the KB in Figure 10 then $\mathcal{I}$ would be an object model of this new KB, but *not* a stable object model.

9 Cautious Object Models

Here we introduce a special class of stable object models, called *cautious object model.* These models have an important property that every F-logic KB has a unique cautious object model. This notion relates stable object models and the fixpoint computation of $\mathbf{F}_{\mathrm{P}}$. Recall that $\mathbf{F}_{\mathrm{P}} \overset{\mathrm{def}}{=} \Psi_{\mathrm{P}} \cdot \Psi_{\mathrm{P}}$ is monotonic and hence has a unique least fixpoint, denoted lfp($\mathbf{F}_{\mathrm{P}}$).

Definition 31 (Cautious Object Model). *The cautious object model, $\mathcal{M}$, of an F-logic KB* P *is defined as follows:* $\mathcal{M} = \langle\, \mathrm{T}; \mathrm{U} \,\rangle$, *where*

$$\mathrm{T} = \pi(\mathit{lfp}(\mathbf{F}_{\mathrm{P}}))$$
$$\mathrm{U} = \pi(\Psi_{\mathrm{P}}(\mathit{lfp}(\mathbf{F}_{\mathrm{P}}))) - \pi(\mathit{lfp}(\mathbf{F}_{\mathrm{P}}))$$

and π is the projection function defined in Section 7.

Next we will list several important properties of cautious object models. First we need to introduce the notations used for representing the intermediate results of the least fixpoint computation of Ψ_{P} and $\mathbf{F}_{\mathrm{P}}$.

Definition 32. *Let α range over all countable ordinals. We define the following extended atom sets for an F-logic KB* P*:*

$$
\begin{array}{lll}
\widehat{\mathrm{T}}_0 = \emptyset & \widehat{\mathrm{U}}_0 = \Psi_{\mathrm{P}}(\widehat{\mathrm{T}}_0) & \textit{for limit ordinal } 0 \\
\widehat{\mathrm{T}}_\alpha = \Psi_{\mathrm{P}}(\widehat{\mathrm{U}}_{\alpha-1}) & \widehat{\mathrm{U}}_\alpha = \Psi_{\mathrm{P}}(\widehat{\mathrm{T}}_\alpha) & \textit{for successor ordinal } \alpha \\
\widehat{\mathrm{T}}_\alpha = \bigcup_{\beta<\alpha} \widehat{\mathrm{T}}_\beta & \widehat{\mathrm{U}}_\alpha = \Psi_{\mathrm{P}}(\widehat{\mathrm{T}}_\alpha) & \textit{for limit ordinal } \alpha \neq 0 \\
\widehat{\mathrm{T}}_\infty = \bigcup_{\alpha} \widehat{\mathrm{T}}_\alpha & \widehat{\mathrm{U}}_\infty = \Psi_{\mathrm{P}}(\widehat{\mathrm{T}}_\infty) &
\end{array}
$$

Lemma 9. *Let α and β range over all countable ordinals. Then:*

(1) *for all α, β: if $\alpha < \beta$ then $\widehat{\mathrm{T}}_\alpha \subseteq \widehat{\mathrm{T}}_\beta$*
(2) $\widehat{\mathrm{T}}_\infty = \mathit{lfp}(\mathbf{F}_{\mathrm{P}})$
(3) *for all α: $\widehat{\mathrm{T}}_\alpha \subseteq \widehat{\mathrm{T}}_\infty$*
(4) $\widehat{\mathrm{U}}_\infty = \mathit{gfp}(\mathbf{F}_{\mathrm{P}})$
(5) *for all α: $\widehat{\mathrm{U}}_\alpha \supseteq \widehat{\mathrm{U}}_\infty$*
(6) *for all α, β: if $\alpha < \beta$ then $\widehat{\mathrm{U}}_\alpha \supseteq \widehat{\mathrm{U}}_\beta$*
(7) *for all α: $\widehat{\mathrm{T}}_\alpha \subseteq \widehat{\mathrm{U}}_\alpha$*
(8) *for all α, β: $\widehat{\mathrm{T}}_\alpha \subseteq \widehat{\mathrm{U}}_\beta$*

From Definition 31, Lemma 9, and from the definition of the projection function π in Section 7, we obtain a new characterization of the cautious object model.

Lemma 10. *If $\mathcal{M}$ is the cautious object model of an F-logic KB* P *then*

$$\mathcal{M} = \langle\, \pi(\widehat{\mathrm{T}}_\infty); \pi(\widehat{\mathrm{U}}_\infty) - \pi(\widehat{\mathrm{T}}_\infty) \,\rangle = \langle\, \pi(\widehat{\mathrm{T}}_\infty); \pi(\widehat{\mathrm{U}}_\infty - \widehat{\mathrm{T}}_\infty) \,\rangle$$

Let α be a countable ordinal. Given a pair of extended atom sets $\widehat{\mathrm{T}}_\alpha$ and $\widehat{\mathrm{U}}_\alpha$, we know that $\widehat{\mathrm{T}}_\alpha \subseteq \widehat{\mathrm{U}}_\alpha$ and so $\pi(\widehat{\mathrm{T}}_\alpha) \subseteq \pi(\widehat{\mathrm{U}}_\alpha)$ by Lemma 9. We can construct an interpretation $\mathcal{I}_\alpha$ as follows: $\mathcal{I}_\alpha = \langle\, \pi(\widehat{\mathrm{T}}_\alpha); \pi(\widehat{\mathrm{U}}_\alpha) - \pi(\widehat{\mathrm{T}}_\alpha) \,\rangle$. Then the set of atoms $\mathsf{c}[\mathsf{m}] \overset{val}{\leadsto} \mathsf{o}$ ($\mathsf{c}[\mathsf{m}] \overset{code}{\leadsto} \mathsf{o}$) in $\widehat{\mathrm{T}}_\alpha$ constitutes a *subset* of the set of strong value (code) inheritance candidates in $\mathcal{I}_\alpha$, whereas the set of atoms $\mathsf{c}[\mathsf{m}] \overset{val}{\leadsto} \mathsf{o}$ ($\mathsf{c}[\mathsf{m}] \overset{code}{\leadsto} \mathsf{o}$) in $\widehat{\mathrm{U}}_\alpha$ constitutes a *superset* of the set of strong and weak value (code) inheritance candidates in $\mathcal{I}_\alpha$. In other words, $\widehat{\mathrm{T}}_\alpha$ *underestimates* inheritance information whereas $\widehat{\mathrm{U}}_\alpha$ *overestimates* inheritance information. The following lemma illustrates this book-keeping mechanism of the alternating fixpoint computation.

Lemma 11. *Let $\mathcal{I}_\alpha = \langle\, \pi(\widehat{\mathrm{T}}_\alpha); \pi(\widehat{\mathrm{U}}_\alpha) - \pi(\widehat{\mathrm{T}}_\alpha) \,\rangle$ where α ranges over all countable ordinals. Then the following statements are true:*

(1) *for all $\mathsf{c}, \mathsf{m}, \mathsf{o}$: if $\mathsf{c}[\mathsf{m}] \overset{val}{\leadsto} \mathsf{o} \in \widehat{\mathrm{T}}_\alpha$ then $\mathsf{c}[\mathsf{m}] \overset{s.val}{\leadsto}_{\mathcal{I}_\alpha} \mathsf{o}$*
(2) *for all $\mathsf{c}, \mathsf{m}, \mathsf{o}$: if $\mathsf{c}[\mathsf{m}] \overset{code}{\leadsto} \mathsf{o} \in \widehat{\mathrm{T}}_\alpha$ then $\mathsf{c}[\mathsf{m}] \overset{s.code}{\leadsto}_{\mathcal{I}_\alpha} \mathsf{o}$*
(3) *for all $\mathsf{c}, \mathsf{m}, \mathsf{o}$: if $\mathsf{c}[\mathsf{m}] \overset{s.val}{\leadsto}_{\mathcal{I}_\alpha} \mathsf{o}$ or $\mathsf{c}[\mathsf{m}] \overset{w.val}{\leadsto}_{\mathcal{I}_\alpha} \mathsf{o}$ then $\mathsf{c}[\mathsf{m}] \overset{val}{\leadsto} \mathsf{o} \in \widehat{\mathrm{U}}_\alpha$*
(4) *for all $\mathsf{c}, \mathsf{m}, \mathsf{o}$: if $\mathsf{c}[\mathsf{m}] \overset{s.code}{\leadsto}_{\mathcal{I}_\alpha} \mathsf{o}$ or $\mathsf{c}[\mathsf{m}] \overset{w.code}{\leadsto}_{\mathcal{I}_\alpha} \mathsf{o}$ then $\mathsf{c}[\mathsf{m}] \overset{code}{\leadsto} \mathsf{o} \in \widehat{\mathrm{U}}_\alpha$*

Lemma 12. *Let $\mathcal{M}$ be the cautious object model of an F-logic KB* P*. Then the following statements are true:*

(1) *for all* $\mathsf{c}, \mathsf{m}, \mathsf{o}$*:* $\mathsf{c}[\mathsf{m}] \overset{s.val}{\rightsquigarrow}_{\mathcal{M}} \mathsf{o}$ *iff* $\mathsf{c}[\mathsf{m}] \overset{val}{\rightsquigarrow} \mathsf{o} \in \widehat{\mathrm{T}}_{\infty}$

(2) *for all* $\mathsf{c}, \mathsf{m}, \mathsf{o}$*:* $\mathsf{c}[\mathsf{m}] \overset{s.code}{\rightsquigarrow}_{\mathcal{M}} \mathsf{o}$ *iff* $\mathsf{c}[\mathsf{m}] \overset{code}{\rightsquigarrow} \mathsf{o} \in \widehat{\mathrm{T}}_{\infty}$

(3) *for all* $\mathsf{c}, \mathsf{m}, \mathsf{o}$*:* $\mathsf{c}[\mathsf{m}] \overset{s.val}{\rightsquigarrow}_{\mathcal{M}} \mathsf{o}$ *or* $\mathsf{c}[\mathsf{m}] \overset{w.val}{\rightsquigarrow}_{\mathcal{M}} \mathsf{o}$ *iff* $\mathsf{c}[\mathsf{m}] \overset{val}{\rightsquigarrow} \mathsf{o} \in \widehat{\mathrm{U}}_{\infty}$

(4) *for all* $\mathsf{c}, \mathsf{m}, \mathsf{o}$*:* $\mathsf{c}[\mathsf{m}] \overset{s.code}{\rightsquigarrow}_{\mathcal{M}} \mathsf{o}$ *or* $\mathsf{c}[\mathsf{m}] \overset{w.code}{\rightsquigarrow}_{\mathcal{M}} \mathsf{o}$ *iff* $\mathsf{c}[\mathsf{m}] \overset{code}{\rightsquigarrow} \mathsf{o} \in \widehat{\mathrm{U}}_{\infty}$

The lemma above says that $\widehat{\mathrm{T}}_{\infty}$ includes exactly all the strong inheritance candidates while $\widehat{\mathrm{U}}_{\infty}$ includes exactly all the strong and weak inheritance candidates in $\mathcal{M}$. This essentially implies that the cautious object model is indeed a stable object model.

Theorem 3. *The cautious object model* $\mathcal{M}$ *of an F-logic KB* P *is a stable object model of* P.

Proof. Let $\mathcal{M} = \langle\, \mathrm{T}; \mathrm{U} \,\rangle$ be the cautious object model of P. Then $\mathrm{T} = \pi(\widehat{\mathrm{T}}_{\infty})$ and $\mathrm{U} = \pi(\widehat{\mathrm{U}}_{\infty}) - \pi(\widehat{\mathrm{T}}_{\infty})$. So by Definition 29 and Lemma 12, $\widehat{\mathrm{T}}_{\mathcal{M}} = \widehat{\mathrm{T}}_{\infty}$ and $\widehat{\mathrm{U}}_{\mathcal{M}} = \widehat{\mathrm{U}}_{\infty}$. Moreover, $\widehat{\mathrm{U}}_{\infty} = \Psi_{\mathrm{P}}(\widehat{\mathrm{T}}_{\infty})$ and $\widehat{\mathrm{T}}_{\infty} = \Psi_{\mathrm{P}}(\widehat{\mathrm{U}}_{\infty})$ by Definition 32 and Lemma 9. It follows that $\widehat{\mathrm{T}}_{\mathcal{M}} = \Psi_{\mathrm{P}}(\widehat{\mathrm{U}}_{\mathcal{M}})$ and $\widehat{\mathrm{U}}_{\mathcal{M}} = \Psi_{\mathrm{P}}(\widehat{\mathrm{T}}_{\mathcal{M}})$. Therefore, $\mathcal{M}$ is a stable interpretation and thus a stable object model of P.

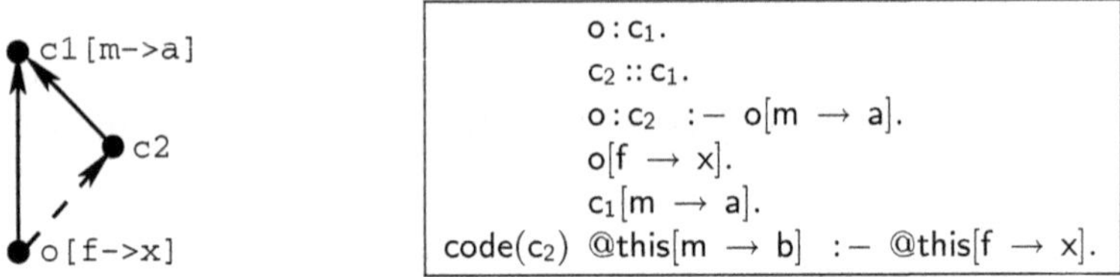

Fig. 11. Computation of Cautious Object Models

Example 5. We illustrate the computation of cautious object models using the F-logic KB P in Figure 11. First let T and U denote the following sets of atoms:

$$\mathrm{T} = \{\mathsf{o} : \mathsf{c}_1, \mathsf{c}_2 :: \mathsf{c}_1, \mathsf{o}[\mathsf{f} \rightarrow \mathsf{x}]_{\mathrm{ex}}, \mathsf{c}_1[\mathsf{m} \rightarrow \mathsf{a}]_{\mathrm{ex}}\}$$
$$\mathrm{U} = \{\mathsf{o} : \mathsf{c}_2, \mathsf{o}[\mathsf{m} \rightarrow \mathsf{a}]^{\mathsf{c}_1}_{\mathrm{val}}, \mathsf{o}[\mathsf{m} \rightarrow \mathsf{b}]^{\mathsf{c}_2}_{\mathrm{code}}\}$$

Then the computation process of Ψ_{P} is as follows:

$$\widehat{\mathrm{T}}_0 = \emptyset$$
$$\widehat{\mathrm{T}}_1 = \Psi_{\mathrm{P}}(\widehat{\mathrm{T}}_0) = \mathrm{T} \cup \mathrm{U} \cup \{\mathsf{c}_1[\mathsf{m}] \overset{val}{\rightsquigarrow} \mathsf{o}, \mathsf{c}_2[\mathsf{m}] \overset{code}{\rightsquigarrow} \mathsf{o}\}$$
$$\widehat{\mathrm{T}}_2 = \Psi_{\mathrm{P}}(\widehat{\mathrm{T}}_1) = \mathrm{T}$$
$$\widehat{\mathrm{T}}_3 = \Psi_{\mathrm{P}}(\widehat{\mathrm{T}}_2) = \widehat{\mathrm{T}}_1$$
$$\widehat{\mathrm{T}}_4 = \Psi_{\mathrm{P}}(\widehat{\mathrm{T}}_3) = \widehat{\mathrm{T}}_2$$

Therefore, $\mathrm{lfp}(\mathbf{F}_{\mathrm{P}}) = \widehat{\mathrm{T}}_2$ and $\Psi_{\mathrm{P}}(\mathrm{lfp}(\mathbf{F}_{\mathrm{P}})) = \widehat{\mathrm{T}}_1$, and so the cautious object model of the KB in Figure 11 is $\langle\, \mathrm{T}; \mathrm{U} \,\rangle$.

Theorem 3 gives a procedural characterization of the cautious object model, i.e., it is essentially defined as the least fixpoint of the extended alternating fixpoint computation. Next we will present two additional characterizations of the cautious object model semantics.

First, by comparing the amount of "definite" information, i.e., truth *and* falsehood, that is contained in different stable object models of an F-logic KB P, we can define a partial order, called *information ordering*, among stable object models.

Definition 33 (Information Ordering). *Let* $\mathcal{I}_1 = \langle \mathrm{P}_1; \mathrm{Q}_1 \rangle$, $\mathcal{I}_2 = \langle \mathrm{P}_2; \mathrm{Q}_2 \rangle$ *be two stable object models of an F-logic KB* P, $\mathrm{R}_1 = \mathcal{HB}_\mathrm{P} - (\mathrm{P}_1 \cup \mathrm{Q}_1)$, $\mathrm{R}_2 = \mathcal{HB}_\mathrm{P} - (\mathrm{P}_2 \cup \mathrm{Q}_2)$. *The information ordering on object models is defined as follows:* $\mathcal{I}_1 \preceq \mathcal{I}_2$ *iff* $\mathrm{P}_1 \subseteq \mathrm{P}_2$ *and* $\mathrm{R}_1 \subseteq \mathrm{R}_2$.

Intuitively, a stable object model is "smaller" in the information ordering, if it contains fewer true facts and fewer false facts. Therefore, the least stable object model contains the smallest set of true atoms and the smallest set of false atoms among all stable object models.

Definition 34 (Least Stable Object Model). *Let* $\mathcal{I}$ *be a stable object model of an F-logic KB* P. $\mathcal{I}$ *is the least stable object model of* P, *if* $\mathcal{I} \preceq \mathcal{J}$ *for any stable object model* $\mathcal{J}$ *of* P.

Theorem 4. *The cautious object model* $\mathcal{M}$ *of an F-logic KB* P *is the least stable object model of* P.

Proof. Let $\mathcal{I} = \langle \mathrm{T}; \mathrm{U} \rangle$ be any stable object model of P. We need to show that $\mathcal{M} \preceq \mathcal{I}$. Recall that $\mathcal{M} = \langle \pi(\widehat{\mathrm{T}}_\infty); \pi(\widehat{\mathrm{U}}_\infty) - \pi(\widehat{\mathrm{T}}_\infty) \rangle$. Therefore, to show that $\mathcal{M} \preceq \mathcal{I}$, it suffices to show that $\pi(\widehat{\mathrm{T}}_\infty) \subseteq \mathrm{T}$ and $\pi(\widehat{\mathrm{U}}_\infty) \supseteq \mathrm{T} \cup \mathrm{U}$. Since $\mathcal{I}$ is a stable object model of P, it follows that $\widehat{\mathrm{T}}_\mathcal{I} = \Psi_\mathrm{P}(\widehat{\mathrm{U}}_\mathcal{I})$ and $\widehat{\mathrm{U}}_\mathcal{I} = \Psi_\mathrm{P}(\widehat{\mathrm{T}}_\mathcal{I})$. Therefore, $\widehat{\mathrm{T}}_\mathcal{I} = \Psi_\mathrm{P}(\widehat{\mathrm{U}}_\mathcal{I}) = \Psi_\mathrm{P}(\Psi_\mathrm{P}(\widehat{\mathrm{T}}_\mathcal{I})) = \mathbf{F}_\mathrm{P}(\widehat{\mathrm{T}}_\mathcal{I})$ and so $\widehat{\mathrm{T}}_\mathcal{I}$ is a fixpoint of $\mathbf{F}_\mathrm{P}$. Similarly, $\widehat{\mathrm{U}}_\mathcal{I}$ is also a fixpoint of $\mathbf{F}_\mathrm{P}$. But $\widehat{\mathrm{T}}_\infty = \mathrm{lfp}(\mathbf{F}_\mathrm{P})$ and $\widehat{\mathrm{U}}_\infty = \mathrm{gfp}(\mathbf{F}_\mathrm{P})$, by Lemma 9. It follows that $\widehat{\mathrm{T}}_\infty \subseteq \widehat{\mathrm{T}}_\mathcal{I}$ and $\widehat{\mathrm{U}}_\infty \supseteq \widehat{\mathrm{U}}_\mathcal{I}$. Thus $\pi(\widehat{\mathrm{T}}_\infty) \subseteq \pi(\widehat{\mathrm{T}}_\mathcal{I})$ and $\pi(\widehat{\mathrm{U}}_\infty) \supseteq \pi(\widehat{\mathrm{U}}_\mathcal{I})$. Moreover, $\pi(\widehat{\mathrm{T}}_\mathcal{I}) = \mathrm{T}$ and $\pi(\widehat{\mathrm{U}}_\mathcal{I}) = \mathrm{T} \cup \mathrm{U}$, by Definition 29. So $\pi(\widehat{\mathrm{T}}_\infty) \subseteq \mathrm{T}$ and $\pi(\widehat{\mathrm{U}}_\infty) \supseteq \mathrm{T} \cup \mathrm{U}$.

Besides comparing different models of a KB with respect to information ordering, it is also common to compare different models based on the amount of "truth" contained in the models. Typically, the true component of a model is minimized and the false component maximized. However, in F-logic we also need to deal with inheritance, which complicates the matters a bit, because some facts may be derived via inheritance. As a consequence, there are object models that look similar but are actually incomparable. This leads to the following definition of truth ordering among object models, which minimizes not only the set of true atoms of an object model, but also the amount of positive inheritance information implied by the object model.

Definition 35 (Truth Ordering). *Let* $\mathcal{I}_1 = \langle\, \mathrm{P}_1; \mathrm{Q}_1 \,\rangle$ *and* $\mathcal{I}_2 = \langle\, \mathrm{P}_2; \mathrm{Q}_2 \,\rangle$ *be two object models of an F-logic KB* P. *We write* $\mathcal{I}_1 \leq \mathcal{I}_2$ *iff*

(1) $\mathrm{P}_1 \subseteq \mathrm{P}_2$; *and*
(2) $\mathrm{P}_1 \cup \mathrm{Q}_1 \subseteq \mathrm{P}_2 \cup \mathrm{Q}_2$; *and*
(3) *for all* $\mathsf{c}, \mathsf{m}, \mathsf{o}$: $\mathsf{c}[\mathsf{m}] \overset{s.val}{\leadsto}_{\mathcal{I}_1} \mathsf{o}$ *implies* $\mathsf{c}[\mathsf{m}] \overset{s.val}{\leadsto}_{\mathcal{I}_2} \mathsf{o}$; *and*
(4) *for all* $\mathsf{c}, \mathsf{m}, \mathsf{o}$: $\mathsf{c}[\mathsf{m}] \overset{s.code}{\leadsto}_{\mathcal{I}_1} \mathsf{o}$ *implies* $\mathsf{c}[\mathsf{m}] \overset{s.code}{\leadsto}_{\mathcal{I}_2} \mathsf{o}$.

Definition 36 (Minimal Object Model). *An object model* $\mathcal{I}$ *is minimal iff there exists no object model* $\mathcal{J}$ *such that* $\mathcal{J} \leq \mathcal{I}$ *and* $\mathcal{J} \neq \mathcal{I}$.

The above definitions minimize the number of strong inheritance candidates implied by an object model *in addition to* the usual minimization of truth and maximization of falsehood. This is needed because increasing the number of false facts might inflate the number of strong inheritance candidates, which in turn might unjustifiably inflate the number of facts that are derived by inheritance.

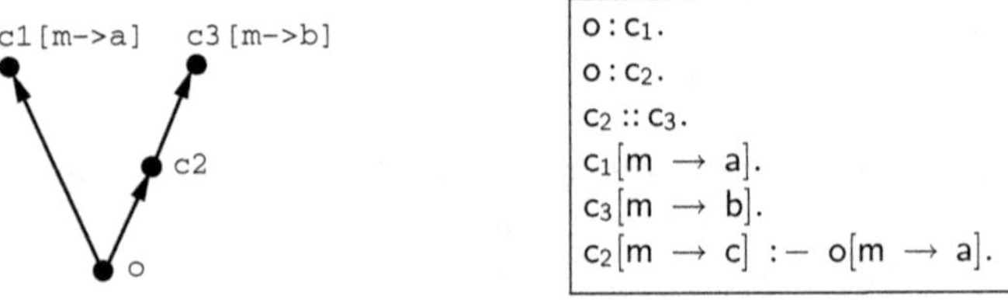

Fig. 12. Minimal Object Model

Example 6. Consider the KB in Figure 12 and the following two object models of the KB: $\mathcal{I}_1 = \langle\, \mathrm{P}_1; \mathrm{Q}_1 \,\rangle$, where

$$\mathrm{P}_1 = \{\mathsf{o}:\mathsf{c}_1, \mathsf{o}:\mathsf{c}_2, \mathsf{c}_2::\mathsf{c}_3, \mathsf{c}_1[\mathsf{m} \rightarrow \mathsf{a}]_{\mathrm{ex}}, \mathsf{c}_3[\mathsf{m} \rightarrow \mathsf{b}]_{\mathrm{ex}}\}$$
$$\mathrm{Q}_1 = \emptyset$$

and $\mathcal{I}_2 = \langle\, \mathrm{P}_2; \mathrm{Q}_2 \,\rangle$, where

$$\mathrm{P}_2 = \mathrm{P}_1$$
$$\mathrm{Q}_2 = \{\mathsf{o}[\mathsf{m} \rightarrow \mathsf{a}]^{\mathsf{c}_1}_{\mathrm{val}}, \mathsf{c}_2[\mathsf{m} \rightarrow \mathsf{c}]_{\mathrm{ex}}\}$$

$\mathcal{I}_1$ and $\mathcal{I}_2$ both agree on the atoms that are true. But in $\mathcal{I}_1$ both $\mathsf{o}[\mathsf{m} \rightarrow \mathsf{a}]^{\mathsf{c}_1}_{\mathrm{val}}$ and $\mathsf{c}_2[\mathsf{m} \rightarrow \mathsf{c}]_{\mathrm{ex}}$ are false, whereas in $\mathcal{I}_2$ they are both underdefined. Clearly, $\mathcal{I}_1$ has more false atoms than $\mathcal{I}_2$ and so with the usual notion of minimality we would say $\mathcal{I}_1 \leq \mathcal{I}_2$. However, $\mathcal{I}_1$ is not as "tight" as it appears, because the additional false atoms in $\mathcal{I}_1$ are not automatically implied by the KB under our cautious object model semantics. Indeed, although $\mathsf{c}_3[\mathsf{m}]$ is a strong value inheritance candidate for o in $\mathcal{I}_1$, it is only a weak value inheritance candidate in $\mathcal{I}_2$. We can see that it is due to this spurious positive information about inheritance candidates that $\mathcal{I}_1$ can have additional false atoms (compared to $\mathcal{I}_2$) while the sets of the true atoms in these interpretations can remain the same. This anomaly is eliminated by the inheritance minimization built into Definition 35, which renders the two models incomparable, i.e., $\mathcal{I}_1 \not\leq \mathcal{I}_2$.

Theorem 5. *The cautious object model $\mathcal{M}$ of an F-logic KB* P *is minimal among those object models of* P *that satisfy the cautious ISA transitivity constraint and the cautious inheritance constraint.*

Proof. This proof is long and is relegated to Section A.2 of the Appendix.

10 Implementation

It turns out that the (unique) cautious object model of an F-logic KB P can be computed as the *well-founded model* of a certain general logic program with negation, which is obtained from P via rewriting. Before describing the rewriting procedure we first define a rewriting function that applies to all regular rules and template rules.

Definition 37. *Given an F-logic KB* P *and a literal* L *in* P, *the functions* ρ^h *and* ρ^b *that rewrite head and body literals in* P *are defined as follows:*

$$\rho^h(\mathsf{L}) = \begin{cases} isa(\mathsf{o},\mathsf{c}), & \textit{if } \mathsf{L} = \mathsf{o}:\mathsf{c} \\ sub(\mathsf{s},\mathsf{c}), & \textit{if } \mathsf{L} = \mathsf{s}::\mathsf{c} \\ exmv(\mathsf{s},\mathsf{m},\mathsf{v}), & \textit{if } \mathsf{L} = \mathsf{s}[\mathsf{m} \to \mathsf{v}] \end{cases} \qquad \rho^b(\mathsf{L}) = \begin{cases} isa(\mathsf{o},\mathsf{c}), & \textit{if } \mathsf{L} = \mathsf{o}:\mathsf{c} \\ sub(\mathsf{s},\mathsf{c}), & \textit{if } \mathsf{L} = \mathsf{s}::\mathsf{c} \\ mv(\mathsf{o},\mathsf{m},\mathsf{v}), & \textit{if } \mathsf{L} = \mathsf{o}[\mathsf{m} \to \mathsf{v}] \\ \neg(\rho^b(\mathrm{G})), & \textit{if } \mathsf{L} = \neg\mathsf{G} \end{cases}$$

The rewriting function ρ *on regular rules and template rules in* P *is defined as follows:*

$$\rho(\mathsf{H}\ :-\ \mathsf{L}_1,\ldots,\mathsf{L}_n) = \rho^h(\mathsf{H})\ :-\ \rho^b(\mathsf{L}_1),\ldots,\rho^b(\mathsf{L}_n)$$
$$\rho(\mathsf{code(c)}\ @\mathsf{this}[\mathsf{m} \to \mathsf{v}]\ :-\ \mathsf{L}_1,\ldots,\mathsf{L}_n) = ins(\mathsf{O},\mathsf{m},\mathsf{v},\mathsf{c})\ :-\ \rho^b(\mathsf{B}_1),\ldots,\rho^b(\mathsf{B}_n)$$

where O *is a new variable that does not appear in* P *and, each* $\mathsf{B}_i = (\mathsf{L}_i)_{\|\mathsf{O}}$, *i.e.,* B_i *is obtained from* L_i *by substituting* O *for all occurrences of the template term* @this. *The predicates, isa, sub, exmv, mv, and ins, are auxiliary predicates introduced by the rewriting.*

Note that since literals in rule heads and bodies have different meanings, they are rewritten differently. Moreover, literals in the heads of regular rules and template rules are also rewritten differently. The rewriting procedure that transforms F-logic KBs into general logic programs is defined next.

Definition 38 (Well-Founded Rewriting). *The well-founded rewriting of an F-logic KB* P, *denoted* P^{wf}, *is a general logic program constructed by the following steps:*

(1) *For every regular rule* R *in* P, *add its rewriting* $\rho(\mathsf{R})$ *into* P^{wf};
(2) *For every template rule* R *in* P, *which specifies an instance method* m *for a class* c, *add its rewriting* $\rho(\mathsf{R})$ *into* P^{wf}. *Moreover, add a fact* $codedef(\mathsf{c},\mathsf{m})$ *into* P^{wf};
(3) *Include the trailer rules shown in Figure 13 to* P^{wf} *(note that uppercase letters denote variables in these trailer rules).*

$$
\begin{array}{rcl}
mv(\mathsf{O},\mathsf{M},\mathsf{V}) & :- & exmv(\mathsf{O},\mathsf{M},\mathsf{V}). \\
mv(\mathsf{O},\mathsf{M},\mathsf{V}) & :- & vamv(\mathsf{O},\mathsf{M},\mathsf{V},\mathsf{C}). \\
mv(\mathsf{O},\mathsf{M},\mathsf{V}) & :- & comv(\mathsf{O},\mathsf{M},\mathsf{V},\mathsf{C}). \\
sub(\mathsf{S},\mathsf{C}) & :- & sub(\mathsf{S},\mathsf{X}),\ sub(\mathsf{X},\mathsf{C}). \\
isa(\mathsf{O},\mathsf{C}) & :- & isa(\mathsf{O},\mathsf{S}),\ sub(\mathsf{S},\mathsf{C}). \\
vamv(\mathsf{O},\mathsf{M},\mathsf{V},\mathsf{C}) & :- & vacan(\mathsf{C},\mathsf{M},\mathsf{O}),\ exmv(\mathsf{C},\mathsf{M},\mathsf{V}),\ \neg\, ex(\mathsf{O},\mathsf{M}),\ \neg\, multi(\mathsf{C},\mathsf{M},\mathsf{O}). \\
comv(\mathsf{O},\mathsf{M},\mathsf{V},\mathsf{C}) & :- & cocan(\mathsf{C},\mathsf{M},\mathsf{O}),\ ins(\mathsf{O},\mathsf{M},\mathsf{V},\mathsf{C}),\ \neg\, ex(\mathsf{O},\mathsf{M}),\ \neg\, multi(\mathsf{C},\mathsf{M},\mathsf{O}). \\
vacan(\mathsf{C},\mathsf{M},\mathsf{O}) & :- & isa(\mathsf{O},\mathsf{C}),\ exmv(\mathsf{C},\mathsf{M},\mathsf{V}),\ \mathsf{C} \neq \mathsf{O},\ \neg\, override(\mathsf{C},\mathsf{M},\mathsf{O}). \\
cocan(\mathsf{C},\mathsf{M},\mathsf{O}) & :- & isa(\mathsf{O},\mathsf{C}),\ codedef(\mathsf{C},\mathsf{M}),\ \mathsf{C} \neq \mathsf{O},\ \neg\, override(\mathsf{C},\mathsf{M},\mathsf{O}). \\
ex(\mathsf{O},\mathsf{M}) & :- & exmv(\mathsf{O},\mathsf{M},\mathsf{V}). \\
multi(\mathsf{C},\mathsf{M},\mathsf{O}) & :- & vacan(\mathsf{X},\mathsf{M},\mathsf{O}),\ \mathsf{X} \neq \mathsf{C}. \\
multi(\mathsf{C},\mathsf{M},\mathsf{O}) & :- & cocan(\mathsf{X},\mathsf{M},\mathsf{O}),\ \mathsf{X} \neq \mathsf{C}. \\
override(\mathsf{C},\mathsf{M},\mathsf{O}) & :- & sub(\mathsf{X},\mathsf{C}),\ isa(\mathsf{O},\mathsf{X}),\ exmv(\mathsf{X},\mathsf{M},\mathsf{V}),\ \mathsf{X} \neq \mathsf{C},\ \mathsf{X} \neq \mathsf{O}. \\
override(\mathsf{C},\mathsf{M},\mathsf{O}) & :- & sub(\mathsf{X},\mathsf{C}),\ isa(\mathsf{O},\mathsf{X}),\ codedef(\mathsf{X},\mathsf{M}),\ \mathsf{X} \neq \mathsf{C},\ \mathsf{X} \neq \mathsf{O}.
\end{array}
$$

Fig. 13. Trailer Rules for Well-Founded Rewriting

Note that while rewriting an F-logic KB into a general logic program, we need to output facts of the form $codedef(\mathsf{c},\mathsf{m})$ to remember that there is a template rule specifying instance method m for class c. Such facts are used to derive overriding and code inheritance candidacy information.

There is a unique well-founded model for any general logic program [15]. Next we will present a characterization of well-founded models based on the alternating fixpoint computation introduced in [42]. Given any general logic program P, we will use $\mathcal{HB}_P$ to denote the Herbrand base of P, which consists of all possible atoms constructed using the predicate symbols and function symbols in P.

Definition 39. *Let* P *be a general logic program and* I *a subset of* $\mathcal{HB}_P$. *The operator* $\mathbf{C}_{P,I}$ *takes as input a set of atoms,* J, *and generates another set of atoms,* $\mathbf{C}_{P,I}(J) \subseteq \mathcal{HB}_P$, *as follows:*

$$
\left\{ \mathsf{H} \;\middle|\; \begin{array}{l} \textit{There is } \mathsf{H} :- \mathsf{A}_1,\ldots,\mathsf{A}_\mathsf{m},\neg\,\mathsf{B}_1,\ldots,\neg\,\mathsf{B}_\mathsf{n} \in ground(\mathrm{P}),\ \ \mathsf{m} \geq 0, \\ \mathsf{n} \geq 0,\ \mathsf{A}_\mathsf{i}\ (1 \leq \mathsf{i} \leq \mathsf{m}) \textit{ and } \mathsf{B}_\mathsf{j}\ (1 \leq \mathsf{j} \leq \mathsf{n}) \textit{ are positive literals, and} \\ \mathsf{A}_\mathsf{i} \in \mathrm{J} \textit{ for all } 1 \leq \mathsf{i} \leq \mathsf{m},\ \mathsf{B}_\mathsf{j} \notin \mathrm{I} \textit{ for all } 1 \leq \mathsf{j} \leq \mathsf{n}. \end{array} \right\}
$$

Lemma 13. $\mathbf{C}_{P,I}$ *is monotonic when* P *and* I *are fixed.*

It follows that $\mathbf{C}_{P,I}$ has a unique least fixpoint. Having defined $\mathbf{C}_{P,I}$ we can introduce two more operators, $\mathbf{S}_P$ and $\mathbf{A}_P$, as follows.

Definition 40. *Let* P *be a general logic program and* I *be a subset of* $\mathcal{HB}_P$. *Then:* $\mathbf{S}_P(I) \stackrel{\text{def}}{=} \mathit{lfp}(\mathbf{C}_{P,I})$, $\mathbf{A}_P(I) \stackrel{\text{def}}{=} \mathbf{S}_P(\mathbf{S}_P(I))$.

Lemma 14. $\mathbf{S}_P$ *is antimonotonic and* $\mathbf{A}_P$ *is monotonic when* P *is fixed.*

It follows that $\mathbf{A}_P$ has a unique least fixpoint, denoted $\mathrm{lfp}(\mathbf{A}_P)$. The following lemma from [42] explains how well-founded models can be defined in terms of alternating fixpoints.

Lemma 15. *The well-founded model, $\langle \mathrm{T}; \mathrm{U} \rangle$, of a general logic program* P*, where* T *is the set of atoms that are true and* U *is the set of atoms that are underdefined, can be computed as follows:* $\mathrm{T} = lfp(\mathbf{A}_\mathrm{P})$, $\mathrm{U} = \mathbf{S}_\mathrm{P}(lfp(\mathbf{A}_\mathrm{P})) - lfp(\mathbf{A}_\mathrm{P})$.

Given the well-founded rewriting, P^{wf}, of an F-logic KB P, the Herbrand base of P^{wf}, denoted $\mathcal{HB}_{\mathrm{P}^{wf}}$, consists of atoms of the following forms: $isa/2$, $sub/2$, $exmv/3$, $vamv/4$, $ins/4$, $codedef/2$, $comv/4$, $mv/3$, $vacan/3$, $cocan/3$, $ex/2$, $multi/3$, and $override/3$. We can establish an isomorphism between interpretations of P^{wf} and P as follows.

Definition 41 (Isomorphism). *Let* P^{wf} *be the well-founded rewriting of an F-logic KB* P, $\mathcal{HB}_{\mathrm{P}^{wf}}$ *the Herbrand base of* P^{wf}, $\widehat{\mathcal{HB}}_\mathrm{P}$ *the extended Herbrand base of* P, I^{wf} *a subset of* $\mathcal{HB}_{\mathrm{P}^{wf}}$, *and* $\widehat{\mathrm{I}}$ *a subset of* $\widehat{\mathcal{HB}}_\mathrm{P}$. *We will say that* I^{wf} *is isomorphic to* $\widehat{\mathrm{I}}$, *if all of the following conditions hold:*

(1) *for all* o, c: $isa(\mathsf{o}, \mathsf{c}) \in \mathrm{I}^{wf}$ *iff* $\mathsf{o}:\mathsf{c} \in \mathrm{I}$
(2) *for all* s, c: $sub(\mathsf{s}, \mathsf{c}) \in \mathrm{I}^{wf}$ *iff* $\mathsf{s}::\mathsf{c} \in \mathrm{I}$
(3) *for all* $\mathsf{s}, \mathsf{m}, \mathsf{v}$: $exmv(\mathsf{s}, \mathsf{m}, \mathsf{v}) \in \mathrm{I}^{wf}$ *iff* $\mathsf{s}[\mathsf{m} \rightarrow \mathsf{v}]_{\mathsf{ex}} \in \mathrm{I}$
(4) *for all* $\mathsf{o}, \mathsf{m}, \mathsf{v}, \mathsf{c}$: $vamv(\mathsf{o}, \mathsf{m}, \mathsf{v}, \mathsf{c}) \in \mathrm{I}^{wf}$ *iff* $\mathsf{o}[\mathsf{m} \rightarrow \mathsf{v}]^{\mathsf{c}}_{\mathsf{val}} \in \mathrm{I}$
(5) *for all* $\mathsf{o}, \mathsf{m}, \mathsf{v}, \mathsf{c}$: $comv(\mathsf{o}, \mathsf{m}, \mathsf{v}, \mathsf{c}) \in \mathrm{I}^{wf}$ *iff* $\mathsf{o}[\mathsf{m} \rightarrow \mathsf{v}]^{\mathsf{c}}_{\mathsf{code}} \in \mathrm{I}$
(6) *for all* $\mathsf{c}, \mathsf{m}, \mathsf{o}$: $vacan(\mathsf{c}, \mathsf{m}, \mathsf{o}) \in \mathrm{I}^{wf}$ *iff* $\mathsf{c}[\mathsf{m}] \overset{val}{\leadsto} \mathsf{o} \in \widehat{\mathrm{I}}$
(7) *for all* $\mathsf{c}, \mathsf{m}, \mathsf{o}$: $cocan(\mathsf{c}, \mathsf{m}, \mathsf{o}) \in \mathrm{I}^{wf}$ *iff* $\mathsf{c}[\mathsf{m}] \overset{code}{\leadsto} \mathsf{o} \in \widehat{\mathrm{I}}$
(8) *for all* o, m: $ex(\mathsf{o}, \mathsf{m}) \in \mathrm{I}^{wf}$ *iff* $ec(\mathsf{o}, \mathsf{m}) \in \mathbf{IB}_\mathrm{P}(\widehat{\mathrm{I}})$
(9) *for all* $\mathsf{c}, \mathsf{m}, \mathsf{o}$: $multi(\mathsf{c}, \mathsf{m}, \mathsf{o}) \in \mathrm{I}^{wf}$ *iff* $mc(\mathsf{c}, \mathsf{m}, \mathsf{o}) \in \mathbf{IB}_\mathrm{P}(\widehat{\mathrm{I}})$
(10) *for all* $\mathsf{c}, \mathsf{m}, \mathsf{o}$: $override(\mathsf{c}, \mathsf{m}, \mathsf{o}) \in \mathrm{I}^{wf}$ *iff* $ov(\mathsf{c}, \mathsf{m}, \mathsf{o}) \in \mathbf{IB}_\mathrm{P}(\widehat{\mathrm{I}})$

Let $\mathcal{M}^{wf}$ *be the well-founded model of* P^{wf} *and* $\mathcal{M}$ *the cautious object model of* P, $\mathcal{M}^{wf} = \langle \mathrm{T}^{wf}; \mathrm{U}^{wf} \rangle$, $\mathcal{M} = \langle \pi(\widehat{\mathrm{T}}_\infty); \pi(\widehat{\mathrm{U}}_\infty - \widehat{\mathrm{T}}_\infty) \rangle$. *We will say that* $\mathcal{M}^{wf}$ *is isomorphic to* $\mathcal{M}$, *if* T^{wf} *and* U^{wf} *are isomorphic to* $\widehat{\mathrm{T}}_\infty$ *and* $\widehat{\mathrm{U}}_\infty - \widehat{\mathrm{T}}_\infty$, *respectively.*

Note that the definition above includes atoms which are not in any interpretation of an F-logic KB P. However, if we can show that the well-founded model of P^{wf} is isomorphic (according to the above definition) to the cautious object model $\mathcal{M}$ of P, we can then establish a one-to-one correspondence between $isa(\mathsf{o}, \mathsf{c}) \in \mathcal{M}^{wf}$ and $\mathsf{o}:\mathsf{c} \in \mathcal{M}$, between $sub(\mathsf{s}, \mathsf{c}) \in \mathcal{M}^{wf}$ and $\mathsf{s}::\mathsf{c} \in \mathcal{M}$, between $exmv(\mathsf{s}, \mathsf{m}, \mathsf{v}) \in \mathcal{M}^{wf}$ and $\mathsf{s}[\mathsf{m} \rightarrow \mathsf{v}]_{\mathsf{ex}} \in \mathcal{M}$, between $comv(\mathsf{o}, \mathsf{m}, \mathsf{v}, \mathsf{c}) \in \mathcal{M}^{wf}$ and $\mathsf{o}[\mathsf{m} \rightarrow \mathsf{v}]^{\mathsf{c}}_{\mathsf{code}} \in \mathcal{M}$, and between $vamv(\mathsf{o}, \mathsf{m}, \mathsf{v}, \mathsf{c}) \in \mathcal{M}^{wf}$ and $\mathsf{o}[\mathsf{m} \rightarrow \mathsf{v}]^{\mathsf{c}}_{\mathsf{val}} \in \mathcal{M}$, taking into account the truth values of atoms. Thus the cautious object model of P can be effectively computed by the well-founded model of P^{wf}.

Definition 42. *Let* P^{wf} *be the well-founded rewriting of an F-logic KB* P *and* I^{wf} *a subset of* $\mathcal{HB}_{\mathrm{P}^{wf}}$. *We will say that* I^{wf} *is in normal form, if for all* $\mathsf{o}, \mathsf{m}, \mathsf{v}$: $mv(\mathsf{o}, \mathsf{m}, \mathsf{v}) \in \mathrm{I}^{wf}$ *iff* $exmv(\mathsf{o}, \mathsf{m}, \mathsf{v}) \in \mathrm{I}^{wf}$, *or there is some class* c *such that* $vamv(\mathsf{o}, \mathsf{m}, \mathsf{v}, \mathsf{c}) \in \mathrm{I}^{wf}$ *or* $comv(\mathsf{o}, \mathsf{m}, \mathsf{v}, \mathsf{c}) \in \mathrm{I}^{wf}$.

In the following we introduce notations to represent the intermediate results during the computation of the well-founded model of a general logic program. These notations are used in the proof of the main theorem of this section.

Definition 43. *Let* P^{wf} *be the well-founded rewriting of an F-logic KB* P*. Define:*

$$
\begin{array}{lll}
\mathrm{T}_0^{wf} = \emptyset & \mathrm{U}_0^{wf} = \mathbf{S}_{\mathrm{P}^{wf}}(\mathrm{T}_0^{wf}) & \textit{for limit ordinal } 0 \\
\mathrm{T}_\alpha^{wf} = \mathbf{S}_{\mathrm{P}^{wf}}(\mathrm{U}_{\alpha-1}^{wf}) & \mathrm{U}_\alpha^{wf} = \mathbf{S}_{\mathrm{P}^{wf}}(\mathrm{T}_\alpha^{wf}) & \textit{for successor ordinal } \alpha \\
\mathrm{T}_\alpha^{wf} = \bigcup_{\beta<\alpha} \mathrm{T}_\beta^{wf} & \mathrm{U}_\alpha^{wf} = \mathbf{S}_{\mathrm{P}^{wf}}(\mathrm{T}_\alpha^{wf}) & \textit{for limit ordinal } \alpha \neq 0 \\
\mathrm{T}_\infty^{wf} = \bigcup_{\alpha} \mathrm{T}_\alpha^{wf} & \mathrm{U}_\infty^{wf} = \mathbf{S}_{\mathrm{P}^{wf}}(\mathrm{T}_\infty^{wf}) &
\end{array}
$$

Now we are ready to present the main theorem of this section. This theorem relies on a number of lemmas and propositions whose proofs are quite long; they can be found in Section A.3 of the Appendix.

Theorem 6. *Given the well-founded rewriting* P^{wf} *of an F-logic KB* P*, the well-founded model of* P^{wf} *is isomorphic to the cautious object model of* P*.*

Proof. Let $\mathcal{M}^{wf} = \langle \mathrm{T}^{wf}; \mathrm{U}^{wf} \rangle$ be the well-founded model of P^{wf}. Then by Lemma 15, $\mathrm{T}^{wf} = \mathrm{T}_\infty^{wf}$ and $\mathrm{U}^{wf} = \mathrm{U}_\infty^{wf} - \mathrm{T}_\infty^{wf}$. Let $\mathcal{M} = \langle \mathrm{T}; \mathrm{U} \rangle$ be the cautious object model of P. Then by Lemma 10, $\mathrm{T} = \pi(\widehat{\mathrm{T}}_\infty)$ and $\mathrm{U} = \pi(\widehat{\mathrm{U}}_\infty - \widehat{\mathrm{T}}_\infty)$. Therefore, by Definition 41, to show that $\mathcal{M}^{wf}$ is isomorphic to $\mathcal{M}$, it suffices to show that T_∞^{wf} is isomorphic to $\widehat{\mathrm{T}}_\infty$ and U_∞^{wf} is isomorphic to $\widehat{\mathrm{U}}_\infty$.

First note that T_α^{wf} and U_α^{wf} are in normal form for any ordinal α, by Proposition 9. Now we will prove by transfinite induction that T_α^{wf} is isomorphic to $\widehat{\mathrm{T}}_\alpha$ and U_α^{wf} is isomorphic to $\widehat{\mathrm{U}}_\alpha$, for any ordinal α. There are three cases to consider:

(1) $\alpha = 0$.
The claim is vacuously true for T_0^{wf} and $\widehat{\mathrm{T}}_0$. $\mathrm{U}_0^{wf} = \mathbf{S}_{\mathrm{P}^{wf}}(\mathrm{T}_0^{wf}) = \mathrm{lfp}(\mathbf{C}_{\mathrm{P}^{wf},\mathrm{T}_0^{wf}})$, by Definitions 43 and 40, and $\widehat{\mathrm{U}}_0 = \Psi_{\mathrm{P}}(\widehat{\mathrm{T}}_0) = \mathrm{lfp}(\mathbf{T}_{\mathrm{P},\widehat{\mathrm{T}}_0})$, by Definitions 32 and 27. It follows that U_0^{wf} is isomorphic to $\widehat{\mathrm{U}}_0$, by Proposition 8.

(2) α is a successor ordinal.
Then $\mathrm{T}_\alpha^{wf} = \mathbf{S}_{\mathrm{P}^{wf}}(\mathrm{U}_{\alpha-1}^{wf}) = \mathrm{lfp}(\mathbf{C}_{\mathrm{P}^{wf},\mathrm{U}_{\alpha-1}^{wf}})$, by Definitions 43 and 40, and $\widehat{\mathrm{T}}_\alpha = \Psi_{\mathrm{P}}(\widehat{\mathrm{U}}_{\alpha-1}) = \mathrm{lfp}(\mathbf{T}_{\mathrm{P},\widehat{\mathrm{U}}_{\alpha-1}})$, by Definitions 32 and 27. Moreover, $\mathrm{U}_{\alpha-1}^{wf}$ is isomorphic to $\widehat{\mathrm{U}}_{\alpha-1}$ by the induction hypothesis. It follows that U_α^{wf} is isomorphic to $\widehat{\mathrm{U}}_\alpha$, by Proposition 8. Similarly to (1), we can also show that U_α^{wf} is isomorphic to $\widehat{\mathrm{U}}_\alpha$.

(3) $\alpha \neq 0$ is a limit ordinal.
Then $\mathrm{T}_\alpha^{wf} = \bigcup_{\beta<\alpha} \mathrm{T}_\beta^{wf}$ and $\widehat{\mathrm{T}}_\alpha = \bigcup_{\beta<\alpha} \widehat{\mathrm{T}}_\beta$. Clearly, T_α^{wf} is isomorphic to $\widehat{\mathrm{T}}_\alpha$, because T_β^{wf} is isomorphic to $\widehat{\mathrm{T}}_\beta$ for all $\beta < \alpha$, by the induction hypothesis. Similarly to (1), we can also show that U_α^{wf} is isomorphic to $\widehat{\mathrm{U}}_\alpha$.

Note that $\mathrm{T}^{wf}_{\infty} = \bigcup_{\alpha} \mathrm{T}^{wf}_{\alpha}$ and $\widehat{\mathrm{T}}_{\infty} = \bigcup_{\alpha} \widehat{\mathrm{T}}_{\alpha}$. Therefore, it follows that T^{wf}_{∞} is isomorphic to $\widehat{\mathrm{T}}_{\infty}$, because T^{wf}_{α} is isomorphic to $\widehat{\mathrm{T}}_{\alpha}$, for any ordinal α. Moreover, $\mathrm{U}^{wf}_{\infty} = \mathbf{S}_{\mathrm{P}^{wf}}(\mathrm{T}^{wf}_{\infty}) = \mathrm{lfp}(\mathbf{C}_{\mathrm{P}^{wf},\mathrm{T}^{wf}_{\infty}})$, by Definitions 43 and 40, and $\widehat{\mathrm{U}}_{\infty} = \Psi_{\mathrm{P}}(\widehat{\mathrm{T}}_{\infty}) = \mathrm{lfp}(\mathbf{T}_{\mathrm{P},\widehat{\mathrm{T}}_{\infty}})$, by Definitions 32 and 27. Thus U^{wf}_{∞} is isomorphic to $\widehat{\mathrm{U}}_{\infty}$, by Proposition 8.

It is easy to see that P^{wf} can be computed in time linear in the size of the original F-logic KB P. Also, the trailer rules in Figure 13 are fixed and do not depend on P. Therefore, the size of P^{wf} is also linear relative to the size of the original F-logic KB P. This observation, combined with Theorem 6, leads to the following claim about the data complexity [43] of our inheritance semantics.

Theorem 7. *The data complexity of the cautious object model semantics for function-free F-logic KBs is polynomial-time.*

11 Related Work

Inheritance is one of the key aspects in frame-based knowledge representation. This problem has been studied quite extensively in the AI and database literature. To make our comparison with the related work concrete, we first list the main features of inheritance that we view should be supported by a general frame-based knowledge system:

- Inference by default inheritance and inference via rules.
- Intentional class hierarchies, *i.e.*, the ability to define both class membership and subclass relationship via rules.
- Data-dependent and data-independent inheritance. As we have shown, value inheritance is data-dependent, and this is the type of inheritance generally considered in AI. Code inheritance is data-independent and is of the kind that is common in imperative programming languages like C^{++} and Java.
- Overriding of inheritance from more general classes by more specific classes. Note that this also needs to take into account the interactions between data-dependent and data-independent inheritance.
- Nonmonotonic inheritance from multiple superclasses. Some proposals avoid this problem by imposing syntactic restrictions on rules. To this end, these proposals do not support nonmonotonic multiple inheritance.
- Introspection, by which variables can range over both class and method names.
- Late binding. This feature is common in imperative object-oriented languages such as C^{++} and Java. Supporting late binding requires resolving method names at runtime, when the class from which the instance method definitions are inherited is decided.

There is a large body of work based on Touretzky's framework of Inheritance Nets [41]. On one hand, the overriding mechanism in this framework is more sophisticated than what is typically considered in the knowledge base context. On the other hand, this framework supports neither deductive inference via rules nor intensional class hierarchies, which makes it too weak for many applications of knowledge bases. A survey on several different approaches to computing inheritance semantics based on Inheritance Nets can be found in [26].

There is also vast literature on extending traditional relational database systems with object-oriented features. However, these proposals do not support deduction via inference rules, which makes them mostly orthogonal to the problems addressed in this paper. For a comprehensive survey on this subject we refer the readers to [23].

The original F-logic [21,22] resolved many semantic and proof-theoretic issues in rule-based frame systems. However, the original semantics for inheritance in F-logic was problematic. It was defined through a nondeterministic inflationary fixpoint and was not backed by a corresponding model theory. This semantics was known to produce questionable results (cf. Section 3) when default inheritance and inference via rules interact. In addition, only value inheritance was considered in the original F-logic.

Ordered Logic [25] incorporates some aspects of the object-oriented paradigm. In this framework, both positive and negative literals are allowed in rule heads, and inference rules are grouped into a set of modules that collectively form a static class hierarchy. Although Ordered Logic supports overriding and propagation of rules among different modules, the idea of late binding is not built into the logic. Since it is primarily committed to resolving inconsistency between positive and negative literals, its semantics has a strong value-based value inheritance flavor. Furthermore, this approach permits only fixed class hierarchies and it does not support introspection.

Abiteboul et al. proposed a framework for implementing inheritance that is based on program rewriting using Datalog with negation [1]. Our implementation of the new F-logic semantics is close in spirit to their approach. However, their proposal is not backed by an independent model-theoretic formalization. Their framework further excludes nonmonotonic multiple inheritance and makes a very strong assumption that the rewritten knowledge base must have a total (two-valued) well-founded model. This latter assumption does not generally hold without strong syntactic restrictions that force stratification of the knowledge base. The framework is also limited to value inheritance.

In [12], Dobbie and Topor developed a model theory for *monotonic* code inheritance in their object-oriented deductive language Gulog. A special feature of their language is that all the variables in a rule must be explicitly typed according to a separate signature declaration. However, this language does not support any kind of nonmonotonic, data-dependent, or multiple inheritance. In [11], Dobbie further extends this approach to allow nonmonotonic inheritance. However, even this extension disallows interaction between inheritance and deduction and does not support multiple inheritance (the user must disambiguate inheritance conflicts manually).

Liu et. al. [27] modified the original F-logic to support code inheritance. However, to achieve that they had to throw out data-dependent inheritance, much of introspection, and intensional class hierarchies.

Bugliesi and Jamil proposed a model-theoretic semantics for value and code inheritance with overriding [5], which bears close resemblance to two-valued stable models [16]. However, their semantics applies only to negation-free knowledge bases (a severe limitation) and does not handle multiple inheritance conflicts. Instead, it makes multiple inheritance behave additively. (Such behavior can be easily simulated via rules.) In addition, their framework does not support data-dependent value inheritance, intensional class hierarchies, and more importantly, it does not provide an algorithm to compute a canonical model under their semantics.

May et al. [32] applied the ideas behind the well-founded semantics to F-logic. However, inheritance is still dealt with in the same way as in the original F-logic. Deduction and inheritance are computed in two separate stages and so the computation process has an inflationary fixpoint flavor. As mentioned in Section 3, this semantics is known to produce counter-intuitive results when intensional class hierarchies interact with overriding and multiple inheritance. Code inheritance is also not handled by this semantics.

In [19,20], Jamil introduced a series of techniques to tackle the inheritance problem. Among these, the ideas of *locality* and *context*, which were proposed to resolve code inheritance and encapsulation in the language Datalog^{++}, have influenced our approach the most. However, this work does not come with a model-theoretic inheritance semantics and supports neither intensional class hierarchies nor introspection. The inheritance semantics in [19] is defined by program rewriting while in [20] the approach is proof-theoretic.

Finally, May and Kandzia [31] showed that the original F-logic semantics can be described using the *inflationary* extension of Reiter's Default Logic [37]. In their framework, inheritance semantics is encoded using *defaults*. However, their inheritance strategy is inflationary — once a fact is derived through inheritance, it is never undone. Therefore, a later inference might invalidate the original conditions (encoded as justifications of defaults) for inheritance (cf. Section 3). Moreover, nonmonotonic multiple inheritance is handled in such a way that when multiple incomparable inheritance sources exist, one of them is randomly selected for inheritance instead of none (as in our framework). Code inheritance is not considered in [31].

12 Conclusion and Future Work

We have developed a novel model theory and a computational framework for nonmonotonic multiple inheritance of value and code in rule-based frame systems. We have shown that this semantics is implementable using a deductive engine, such as XSB [7], that supports well-founded semantics [15]. The value inheritance part of this semantics has been implemented in $\mathcal{F}$LORA-2 [44,46], a knowledge representation system, which is built around F-logic, HiLog [6], and

Transaction Logic [4].[5] Adding code inheritance to $\mathcal{F}$LORA-2 is planned for the near future.

The semantics proposed in this paper can be extended — without adding to the syntax — to allow a new kind of inheritable methods in addition to the traditional instance methods. The idea is to allow the template term @this in a template rule to be instantiated not only with instances of the class for which the template rule is defined, but also with that class itself and its subclasses as well. Effectively this turns template rules into pieces of code that also define class methods and that are inheritable by subclasses. For instance, with such a modification, the template rule

$$\mathsf{code(employee)\ @this[avgSalary} \rightarrow \mathsf{A]}\ :-\ \mathsf{A} = avg\{\mathsf{S|E:@this, E[salary} \rightarrow \mathsf{S]}\}.$$

where $avg\{...\}$ is the averaging aggregate function, could be instantiated with class employee itself to

$$\mathsf{employee[avgSalary} \rightarrow \mathsf{A]}\ :-\ \mathsf{A} = avg\{\mathsf{S|E:employee, E[salary} \rightarrow \mathsf{S]}\}.$$

and instantiated with one of employee's subclasses, secretary, to

$$\mathsf{secretary[avgSalary} \rightarrow \mathsf{A]}\ :-\ \mathsf{A} = avg\{\mathsf{S|E:secretary, E[salary} \rightarrow \mathsf{S]}\}.$$

Similar rules could be obtained for other subclasses of employee, such as engineer and faculty. The last two rules above define the class method, avgSalary, for classes employee and secretary. It returns the average salary of an employee and a secretary, respectively. This kind of methods is not possible using the earlier machinery of class and instance methods.

Our model-theoretic approach points to several future research directions. First, the proposed semantics for inheritance here can be viewed as *source-based*. This means that in determining whether a multiple inheritance conflict exists the semantics takes into account only whether the same method is *defined* at different inheritance sources. A conflict is declared even if they all return exactly the same set of values. A *content-based* inheritance policy would not view this as a conflict. Such content-based inheritance seems harder computationally, but is worth further investigation. Second, it has been observed that inheritance-like phenomena arise in many domains, such as discretionary access control and trust management [18], but they cannot be formalized using a single semantics. We are considering extensions to our framework to allow users to specify their own *ad hoc* inheritance policies in a programmable, yet declarative, way.

Acknowledgment

This work was supported in part by NSF grants IIS-0072927 and CCR-0311512. The authors would like to thank the anonymous referees for their helpful comments and suggestions.

[5] $\mathcal{F}$LORA-2 is freely available from http://flora.sourceforge.net

References

1. S. Abiteboul, G. Lausen, H. Uphoff, and E. Waller. Methods and rules. In *ACM International Conference on Management of Data (SIGMOD)*, 1993.
2. J. Angele, E. Mönch, H. Oppermann, S. Staab, and D. Wenke. Ontology-based query and answering in chemistry: OntoNova @ Project Halo. In *International Semantic Web Conference (ISWC)*, pages 913–928, 2003.
3. D. Berardi, H. Boley, B. Grosof, M. Gruninger, R. Hull, M. Kifer, D. Martin, S. McIlraith, J. Su, and S. Tabet. SWSL: Semantic Web Services Language. Technical report, Semantic Web Services Initiative, April 2005. http://www.w3.org/Submission/SWSF-SWSL/.
4. A. J. Bonner and M. Kifer. An overview of transaction logic. *Theoretical Computer Science*, 133(2):205–265, 1994.
5. M. Bugliesi and H. M. Jamil. A stable model semantics for behavioral inheritance in deductive object oriented languages. In *International Conference on Database Theory (ICDT)*, pages 222–237, 1995.
6. W. Chen, M. Kifer, and D. S. Warren. HiLog: A foundation for higher-order logic programming. *Journal of Logic Programming (JLP)*, 15(3):187–230, 1993.
7. W. Chen and D. S. Warren. Tabled evaluation with delaying for general logic programs. *Journal of the ACM (JACM)*, 43(1):20–74, 1996.
8. J. de Bruijn, H. Lausen, R. Krummenacher, A. Polleres, L. Predoiu, and D. Fensel. The WSML family of representation languages. Technical report, DERI, March 2005. http://www.w3.org/Submission/WSML/.
9. S. Decker, D. Brickley, J. Saarela, and J. Angele. A query and inference service for RDF. In *QL'98 - The Query Languages Workshop*, December 1998.
10. S. Decker, M. Erdmann, D. Fensel, and R. Studer. Ontobroker: Ontology based access to distributed and semi-structured information. In R. Meersman, editor, *Database Semantics, Semantic Issues in Multimedia Systems*, pages 351–369. Kluwer Academic Publisher, Boston, 1999.
11. G. Dobbie. Foundations of deductive object-oriented database systems. Technical Report CS-TR-96/13, Department of Computer Science, Victoria University, 1996. http://citeseer.ist.psu.edu/dobbie96foundations.html.
12. G. Dobbie and R. Topor. Resolving ambiguities caused by multiple inheritance. In *International Conference on Deductive and Object-Oriented Databases (DOOD)*, pages 265–280, 1995.
13. DSTC, IBM, and CBOP. MOF Query/Views/Transformations. Technical report, Object Management Group (OMG), 2003. http://www.dstc.edu.au/Research/Projects/Pegamento/publications/ad-03-08-03.pdf.
14. J. Frohn, R. Himmeröder, G. Lausen, W. May, and C. Schlepphorst. Managing semistructured data with FLORID: A deductive object-oriented perspective. *Information Systems*, 23(8):589–613, 1998.
15. A. V. Gelder, K. Ross, and J. S. Schlipf. The well-founded semantics for general logic programs. *Journal of the ACM (JACM)*, 38(3):620–650, 1991.
16. M. Gelfond and V. Lifschitz. The stable model semantics for logic programming. In *International Conference on Logic Programming (ICLP)*, 1988.
17. A. Gerber, M. Lawley, K. Raymond, J. Steel, and A. Wood. Transformation: The missing link of MDA. In *Graph Transformation: First International Conference (ICGT)*, volume 2505 of *Lecture Notes in Computer Science*, pages 90–105. Springer Verlag, October 2002.

18. S. Jajodia, P. Samarati, M. L. Sapino, and V. S. Subrahmanian. Flexible support for multiple access control policies. *ACM Transactions on Database Systems (TODS)*, 26(2):214–260, June 2001.
19. H. M. Jamil. Implementing abstract objects with inheritance in Datalog^{neg}. In *International Conference on Very Large Data Bases (VLDB)*, pages 46–65. Morgan Kaufmann, 1997.
20. H. M. Jamil. A logic-based language for parametric inheritance. In *International Conference on Principles of Knowledge Representation and Reasoning (KR)*, 2000.
21. M. Kifer and G. Lausen. F-Logic: A higher-order language for reasoning about objects, inheritance and schema. In *ACM International Conference on Management of Data (SIGMOD)*, pages 134–146, New York, 1989. ACM.
22. M. Kifer, G. Lausen, and J. Wu. Logical foundations of object-oriented and frame-based languages. *Journal of the ACM (JACM)*, 42(4):741–843, 1995.
23. W. Kim and F. H. Lochovsky, editors. *Object-Oriented Concepts, Databases, and Applications*. ACM Press and Addison-Wesley, 1989.
24. R. Krishnan. Disruption tolerant networking: SPINDLE project. Technical report, The Internet Engineering Task Force, 2006.
25. E. Laenens and D. Vermeir. A fixpoint semantics for Ordered Logic. *Journal of Logic and Computation*, 1(2):159–185, 1990.
26. L. V. S. Lakshmanan and K. Thirunarayan. Declarative frameworks for inheritance. In J. Chomicki and G. Saake, editors, *Logics for Databases and Information Systems*, pages 357–388. Kluwer Academic Publishers, 1998.
27. M. Liu, G. Dobbie, and T. Ling. A logical foundation for deductive object-oriented databases. *ACM Transactions on Database Systems (TODS)*, 27(1):117–151, 2002.
28. J. W. Lloyd. *Foundations of Logic Programming*. Springer Verlag, 1984.
29. A. Magkanaraki, S. Alexaki, V. Christophides, and D. Plexousakis. Benchmarking RDF Schemas for the Semantic Web. In *International Semantic Web Conference (ISWC)*, pages 132–146, London, UK, 2002. Springer Verlag.
30. W. May. A rule-based querying and updating language for XML. In *International Workshop on Database Programming Languages (DBPL)*, Lecture Notes in Computer Science, pages 165–181. Springer Verlag, 2001.
31. W. May and P.-T. Kandzia. Nonmonotonic inheritance in object-oriented deductive database languages. *Journal of Logic and Computation*, 11(4):499–525, 2001.
32. W. May, B. Ludäscher, and G. Lausen. Well-founded semantics for deductive object-oriented database languages. In *International Conference on Deductive and Object-Oriented Databases (DOOD)*, Lecture Notes in Computer Science, pages 320–336. Springer Verlag, 1997.
33. Ontoprise, GmbH. Ontobroker. http://www.ontoprise.com/.
34. T. C. Przymusinski. Every logic program has a natural stratification and an iterated least fixed point model. In *ACM International Symposium on Principles of Database Systems (PODS)*, pages 11–21, New York, 1989. ACM.
35. T. C. Przymusinski. The well-founded semantics coincides with the three-valued stable semantics. *Fundamenta Informaticae*, 13(4):445–464, 1990.
36. F. Rabitti, E. Bertino, W. Kim, and D. Woelk. A model of authorization for next-generation database systems. *ACM Transactions on Database Systems (TODS)*, 16(1):88–131, 1991.
37. R. Reiter. A logic for default reasoning. *Artificial Intelligence*, 13(1–2):81–132, 1980.
38. Rule Interchange Format. W3C Working Group, 2005. http://www.w3.org/2005/rules/wg.html.

39. H.-P. Schnurr and J. Angele. Do not use this gear with a switching lever! Automotive industry experience with Semantic Guides. In *International Semantic Web Conference (ISWC)*, pages 1029–1040, 2005.
40. M. Sintek and S. Decker. TRIPLE – A query, inference, and transformation language for the semantic Web. In *International Semantic Web Conference (ISWC)*, pages 364–378. Springer Verlag, 2002.
41. D. S. Touretzky. *The Mathematics of Inheritance.* Morgan-Kaufmann, 1986.
42. A. Van Gelder. The alternating fixpoint of logic programs with negation. *Journal of Computer and System Sciences*, 47(1):185–221, 1993.
43. M. Vardi. The complexity of relational query languages. In *ACM Symposium on Theory of Computing (STOC)*, pages 137–146, New York, 1982. ACM.
44. G. Yang and M. Kifer. Implementing an efficient DOOD system using a tabling logic engine. In *First International Conference on Computational Logic, DOOD'2000 Stream*, volume 1861 of *Lecture Notes in Artificial Intelligence*, pages 1078–1083. Springer Verlag, 2000.
45. G. Yang and M. Kifer. Well-founded optimism: Inheritance in frame-based knowledge bases. In *International Conference on Ontologies, Databases, and Applications of Semantics (ODBASE)*, pages 1013–1032. Springer Verlag, 2002.
46. G. Yang, M. Kifer, and C. Zhao. Flora-2: User's Manual. http://flora.sourceforge.net/, June 2005.

A Appendix: Proofs

This appendix includes the proofs of all the main theorems, their supporting lemmas, and propositions found in the main body of the paper.

A.1 Lemmas and Propositions Supporting Theorem 1 in Section 8

Lemma 16. *Let* P *be an F-logic KB and* $\mathcal{I} = \langle \mathrm{T}; \mathrm{U} \rangle$ *a stable interpretation of* P*, then:*

$$\widehat{\mathrm{T}}_{\mathcal{I}} = \mathbf{RC}_{\mathrm{P},\widehat{\mathrm{U}}_{\mathcal{I}}}(\widehat{\mathrm{T}}_{\mathcal{I}}) \cup \mathbf{TC}_{\mathrm{P},\widehat{\mathrm{U}}_{\mathcal{I}}}(\widehat{\mathrm{T}}_{\mathcal{I}}) \cup \mathbf{IC}^{t}(\widehat{\mathrm{T}}_{\mathcal{I}}) \cup \mathbf{IC}^{c}_{\mathrm{P},\widehat{\mathrm{U}}_{\mathcal{I}}}(\widehat{\mathrm{T}}_{\mathcal{I}}) \cup \mathbf{IC}^{i}_{\mathrm{P},\widehat{\mathrm{U}}_{\mathcal{I}}}(\widehat{\mathrm{T}}_{\mathcal{I}})$$
$$\widehat{\mathrm{U}}_{\mathcal{I}} = \mathbf{RC}_{\mathrm{P},\widehat{\mathrm{T}}_{\mathcal{I}}}(\widehat{\mathrm{U}}_{\mathcal{I}}) \cup \mathbf{TC}_{\mathrm{P},\widehat{\mathrm{T}}_{\mathcal{I}}}(\widehat{\mathrm{U}}_{\mathcal{I}}) \cup \mathbf{IC}^{t}(\widehat{\mathrm{U}}_{\mathcal{I}}) \cup \mathbf{IC}^{c}_{\mathrm{P},\widehat{\mathrm{T}}_{\mathcal{I}}}(\widehat{\mathrm{U}}_{\mathcal{I}}) \cup \mathbf{IC}^{i}_{\mathrm{P},\widehat{\mathrm{T}}_{\mathcal{I}}}(\widehat{\mathrm{U}}_{\mathcal{I}})$$

Proposition 1. *Let* $\mathcal{I} = \langle \mathrm{T}; \mathrm{U} \rangle$ *be a stable interpretation of an F-logic KB* P*. Then* $\mathcal{I}$ *satisfies the regular rules of* P.

Proof. By contradiction.

Suppose, to the contrary, that $\mathcal{I}$ does not satisfy the regular rules of P. Then by Definitions 3 and 2, there is a ground regular rule, $\mathsf{H} :- \mathsf{L}_1, \ldots, \mathsf{L}_n$, in *ground*(P), such that $\mathcal{V}^{\mathbf{h}}_{\mathcal{I}}(\mathsf{H}) < \mathcal{V}^{\mathbf{b}}_{\mathcal{I}}(\mathsf{L}_1 \wedge \ldots \wedge \mathsf{L}_n)$. Thus it must be the case that $\mathcal{V}^{\mathbf{b}}_{\mathcal{I}}(\mathsf{L}_1 \wedge \ldots \wedge \mathsf{L}_n) = \mathbf{t}$ and $\mathcal{V}^{\mathbf{h}}_{\mathcal{I}}(\mathsf{H}) \neq \mathbf{t}$, or $\mathcal{V}^{\mathbf{b}}_{\mathcal{I}}(\mathsf{L}_1 \wedge \ldots \wedge \mathsf{L}_n) = \mathbf{u}$ and $\mathcal{V}^{\mathbf{h}}_{\mathcal{I}}(\mathsf{H}) = \mathbf{f}$.

(1) $\mathcal{V}^{\mathbf{b}}_{\mathcal{I}}(\mathsf{L}_1 \wedge \ldots \wedge \mathsf{L}_n) = \mathbf{t}$ and $\mathcal{V}^{\mathbf{h}}_{\mathcal{I}}(\mathsf{H}) \neq \mathbf{t}$
It follows that $\mathcal{V}^{\mathbf{b}}_{\mathcal{I}}(\mathsf{L}_i) = \mathbf{t}$ for all $\mathsf{L}_i, 1 \leq \mathsf{i} \leq \mathsf{n}$, by Definition 1. So by Lemma 1: (i) if L_i is a positive literal then $val^{\mathbf{b}}_{\widehat{\mathrm{T}}_{\mathcal{I}}}(\mathsf{L}_i) = \mathbf{t}$; and (ii) if L_i is a negative literal

then $val^{\mathbf{b}}_{\widehat{\mathrm{U}}_{\mathcal{I}}}(\mathsf{L_i}) = \mathbf{t}$. Therefore, for the atom $\mathsf{A} \in \mathcal{HB}_{\mathrm{P}}$ such that H matches A, it follows that $\mathsf{A} \in \mathbf{RC}_{\mathrm{P},\widehat{\mathrm{U}}_{\mathcal{I}}}(\widehat{\mathrm{T}}_{\mathcal{I}}) \subseteq \widehat{\mathrm{T}}_{\mathcal{I}}$, by Definition 22 and Lemma 16. Thus $\mathcal{I}(\mathsf{A}) = \mathbf{t}$, and so $\mathcal{V}^{\mathbf{h}}_{\mathcal{I}}(\mathsf{H}) = \mathcal{I}(\mathsf{A}) = \mathbf{t}$ by Definitions 21 and 1, a contradiction.

(2) $\mathcal{V}^{\mathbf{b}}_{\mathcal{I}}(\mathsf{L_1} \wedge \ \ldots \ \wedge \mathsf{L_n}) = \mathbf{u}$ and $\mathcal{V}^{\mathbf{h}}_{\mathcal{I}}(\mathsf{H}) = \mathbf{f}$
It follows that $\mathcal{V}^{\mathbf{b}}_{\mathcal{I}}(\mathsf{L_i}) \geq \mathbf{u}$ for all $\mathsf{L_i}, 1 \leq \mathsf{i} \leq \mathsf{n}$, by Definition 1. So by Lemma 1: (i) if $\mathsf{L_i}$ is a positive literal then $val^{\mathbf{b}}_{\widehat{\mathrm{U}}_{\mathcal{I}}}(\mathsf{L_i}) = \mathbf{t}$; and (2) if $\mathsf{L_i}$ is a negative literal then $val^{\mathbf{b}}_{\widehat{\mathrm{T}}_{\mathcal{I}}}(\mathsf{L_i}) = \mathbf{t}$. Therefore, for the atom $\mathsf{A} \in \mathcal{HB}_{\mathrm{P}}$ such that H matches A, it follows that $\mathsf{A} \in \mathbf{RC}_{\mathrm{P},\widehat{\mathrm{T}}_{\mathcal{I}}}(\widehat{\mathrm{U}}_{\mathcal{I}}) \subseteq \widehat{\mathrm{U}}_{\mathcal{I}}$, by Definition 22 and Lemma 16. Thus $\mathcal{I}(\mathsf{A}) \geq \mathbf{u}$, and so $\mathcal{V}^{\mathbf{h}}_{\mathcal{I}}(\mathsf{H}) = \mathcal{I}(\mathsf{A}) \geq \mathbf{u}$ by Definitions 21 and 1, a contradiction.

Proposition 2. *Let $\mathcal{I} = \langle\, \mathrm{T}; \mathrm{U} \,\rangle$ be a stable interpretation of an F-logic KB* P. *Then $\mathcal{I}$ satisfies the positive ISA transitivity constraint.*

Proof. By Definition 10, we need to show that the following conditions hold:

(1) for all s, c: if there is x such that $\mathcal{I}(\mathsf{s} :: \mathsf{x}) = \mathbf{t}$ and $\mathcal{I}(\mathsf{x} :: \mathsf{c}) = \mathbf{t}$, then $\mathcal{I}(\mathsf{s} :: \mathsf{c}) = \mathbf{t}$;

(2) for all o, c: if there is x such that $\mathcal{I}(\mathsf{o} : \mathsf{x}) = \mathbf{t}$ and $\mathcal{I}(\mathsf{x} :: \mathsf{c}) = \mathbf{t}$, then $\mathcal{I}(\mathsf{o} : \mathsf{c}) = \mathbf{t}$.

Note that for all s, c: $\mathcal{I}(\mathsf{s} :: \mathsf{c}) = \mathbf{t}$ iff $\mathsf{s} :: \mathsf{c} \in \mathrm{T} \subseteq \widehat{\mathrm{T}}_{\mathcal{I}}$ and, for all o, c: $\mathcal{I}(\mathsf{o} : \mathsf{c}) = \mathbf{t}$ iff $\mathsf{o} : \mathsf{c} \in \mathrm{T} \subseteq \widehat{\mathrm{T}}_{\mathcal{I}}$. Let $\mathsf{s} :: \mathsf{x} \in \mathrm{T} \subseteq \widehat{\mathrm{T}}_{\mathcal{I}}$ and $\mathsf{x} :: \mathsf{c} \in \mathrm{T} \subseteq \widehat{\mathrm{T}}_{\mathcal{I}}$. Then $\mathsf{s} :: \mathsf{c} \in \mathbf{IC}^t(\widehat{\mathrm{T}}_{\mathcal{I}})$ by Definition 25. It follows that $\mathsf{s} :: \mathsf{c} \in \mathbf{IC}^t(\widehat{\mathrm{T}}_{\mathcal{I}}) \subseteq \widehat{\mathrm{T}}_{\mathcal{I}}$, by Lemma 16. Similarly, if $\mathsf{o} : \mathsf{x} \in \widehat{\mathrm{T}}_{\mathcal{I}}$ and $\mathsf{x} :: \mathsf{c} \in \widehat{\mathrm{T}}_{\mathcal{I}}$, then $\mathsf{o} : \mathsf{c} \in \mathbf{IC}^t(\widehat{\mathrm{T}}_{\mathcal{I}}) \subseteq \widehat{\mathrm{T}}_{\mathcal{I}}$.

Proposition 3. *Let $\mathcal{I} = \langle\, \mathrm{T}; \mathrm{U} \,\rangle$ be a stable interpretation of an F-logic KB* P. *Then $\mathcal{I}$ satisfies the context consistency constraint.*

Proof. By Definition 11, we need to show that the following conditions hold:

(1) for all o, m, v: $\mathcal{I}(\mathsf{o}[\mathsf{m} \rightarrow \mathsf{v}]^{\mathsf{o}}_{\mathrm{val}}) = \mathbf{f}$ and $\mathcal{I}(\mathsf{o}[\mathsf{m} \rightarrow \mathsf{v}]^{\mathsf{o}}_{\mathrm{code}}) = \mathbf{f}$.
Note that $\mathcal{I}(\mathsf{o}[\mathsf{m} \rightarrow \mathsf{v}]^{\mathsf{o}}_{\mathrm{val}}) = \mathbf{f}$ iff $\mathsf{o}[\mathsf{m} \rightarrow \mathsf{v}]^{\mathsf{o}}_{\mathrm{val}} \notin \mathrm{T} \cup \mathrm{U}$ iff $\mathsf{o}[\mathsf{m} \rightarrow \mathsf{v}]^{\mathsf{o}}_{\mathrm{val}} \notin \widehat{\mathrm{U}}_{\mathcal{I}}$ by Definition 29. Similarly, $\mathcal{I}(\mathsf{o}[\mathsf{m} \rightarrow \mathsf{v}]^{\mathsf{o}}_{\mathrm{code}}) = \mathbf{f}$ iff $\mathsf{o}[\mathsf{m} \rightarrow \mathsf{v}]^{\mathsf{o}}_{\mathrm{code}} \notin \widehat{\mathrm{U}}_{\mathcal{I}}$. Since $\mathcal{I}$ is a stable interpretation of P, we have $\widehat{\mathrm{U}}_{\mathcal{I}} = \Psi_{\mathrm{P}}(\widehat{\mathrm{T}}_{\mathcal{I}})$, by Definition 30. It then follows from Lemma 6 that $\mathsf{o}[\mathsf{m} \rightarrow \mathsf{v}]^{\mathsf{o}}_{\mathrm{val}} \notin \widehat{\mathrm{U}}_{\mathcal{I}}$ and $\mathsf{o}[\mathsf{m} \rightarrow \mathsf{v}]^{\mathsf{o}}_{\mathrm{code}} \notin \widehat{\mathrm{U}}_{\mathcal{I}}$, for all $\mathsf{o}, \mathsf{m}, \mathsf{v}$.

(2) for all c, m, v: if $\mathcal{I}(\mathsf{c}[\mathsf{m} \rightarrow \mathsf{v}]_{\mathrm{ex}}) = \mathbf{f}$, then $\mathcal{I}(\mathsf{o}[\mathsf{m} \rightarrow \mathsf{v}]^{\mathsf{c}}_{\mathrm{val}}) = \mathbf{f}$ for all o.
Let $\mathcal{I}(\mathsf{c}[\mathsf{m} \rightarrow \mathsf{v}]_{\mathrm{ex}}) = \mathbf{f}$. It follows that $\mathsf{c}[\mathsf{m} \rightarrow \mathsf{v}]_{\mathrm{ex}} \notin \widehat{\mathrm{U}}_{\mathcal{I}}$. We need to show that $\mathsf{o}[\mathsf{m} \rightarrow \mathsf{v}]^{\mathsf{c}}_{\mathrm{val}} \notin \widehat{\mathrm{U}}_{\mathcal{I}}$ for all o. Suppose, to the contrary, that there exists o such that $\mathsf{o}[\mathsf{m} \rightarrow \mathsf{v}]^{\mathsf{c}}_{\mathrm{val}} \in \widehat{\mathrm{U}}_{\mathcal{I}}$. Because $\mathcal{I}$ is a stable interpretation of P, $\widehat{\mathrm{U}}_{\mathcal{I}} = \Psi_{\mathrm{P}}(\widehat{\mathrm{T}}_{\mathcal{I}})$. It follows that $\mathsf{o}[\mathsf{m} \rightarrow \mathsf{v}]^{\mathsf{c}}_{\mathrm{val}} \in \mathbf{IC}^{i}_{\mathrm{P},\widehat{\mathrm{T}}_{\mathcal{I}}}(\widehat{\mathrm{U}}_{\mathcal{I}})$ by Lemma 6. So $\mathsf{c}[\mathsf{m}] \overset{val}{\leadsto} \mathsf{o} \in \widehat{\mathrm{U}}_{\mathcal{I}}$, by Definition 25. Thus $\mathsf{c}[\mathsf{m}] \overset{val}{\leadsto} \mathsf{o} \in \mathbf{IC}^{c}_{\mathrm{P},\widehat{\mathrm{T}}_{\mathcal{I}}}(\widehat{\mathrm{U}}_{\mathcal{I}})$ by Lemma 16. It follows that $\mathsf{c}[\mathsf{m} \rightarrow \mathsf{v}]_{\mathrm{ex}} \in \widehat{\mathrm{U}}_{\mathcal{I}}$ by Definition 25, which contradicts the premise.

(3) for all c, m: if there is no template rule in *ground*(P) which specifies the instance method m for class c, then $\mathcal{I}(\mathsf{o}[\mathsf{m} \rightarrow \mathsf{v}]^{\mathsf{c}}_{\mathsf{code}}) = \mathbf{f}$ for all o, v.

Suppose, to the contrary, that there exist o, v such that $\mathcal{I}(\mathsf{o}[\mathsf{m} \rightarrow \mathsf{v}]^{\mathsf{c}}_{\mathsf{code}}) \neq \mathbf{f}$. Then $\mathsf{o}[\mathsf{m} \rightarrow \mathsf{v}]^{\mathsf{c}}_{\mathsf{code}} \in \mathrm{T} \cup \mathrm{U} \subseteq \widehat{\mathrm{U}}_{\mathcal{I}}$. It follows that $\mathsf{o}[\mathsf{m} \rightarrow \mathsf{v}]^{\mathsf{c}}_{\mathsf{code}} \in \mathbf{IC}^{i}_{\mathrm{P},\widehat{\mathrm{T}}_{\mathcal{I}}}(\widehat{\mathrm{U}}_{\mathcal{I}})$ by Lemma 6. Thus $\mathsf{c}[\mathsf{m}] \overset{code}{\leadsto} \mathsf{o} \in \widehat{\mathrm{U}}_{\mathcal{I}}$ by Definition 25 and so $\mathsf{c}[\mathsf{m}] \overset{code}{\leadsto} \mathsf{o} \in \mathbf{IC}^{c}_{\mathrm{P},\widehat{\mathrm{T}}_{\mathcal{I}}}(\widehat{\mathrm{U}}_{\mathcal{I}})$ by Lemma 16. Hence, by Definition 25, there must exist a template rule in *ground*(P) which specifies the instance method m for the class c, a contradiction.

(4) for all o, m: if $\mathsf{o}[\mathsf{m}]$ is a strong explicit definition, then $\mathcal{I}(\mathsf{o}[\mathsf{m} \rightarrow \mathsf{v}]^{\mathsf{c}}_{\mathsf{val}}) = \mathbf{f}$ and $\mathcal{I}(\mathsf{o}[\mathsf{m} \rightarrow \mathsf{v}]^{\mathsf{c}}_{\mathsf{code}}) = \mathbf{f}$ for all v, c.

Let $\mathsf{o}[\mathsf{m}]$ be a strong explicit definition. Then there must exist v such that $\mathsf{o}[\mathsf{m} \rightarrow \mathsf{v}]_{\mathsf{ex}} \in \mathrm{T} \subseteq \widehat{\mathrm{T}}_{\mathcal{I}}$ by Definition 4. So $ec(\mathsf{o}, \mathsf{m}) \in \mathbf{IB}_{\mathrm{P}}(\widehat{\mathrm{T}}_{\mathcal{I}})$ by Definition 23. Suppose, to the contrary, that there exist v, c such that $\mathcal{I}(\mathsf{o}[\mathsf{m} \rightarrow \mathsf{v}]^{\mathsf{c}}_{\mathsf{val}}) \neq \mathbf{f}$. Then $\mathsf{o}[\mathsf{m} \rightarrow \mathsf{v}]^{\mathsf{c}}_{\mathsf{val}} \in \mathrm{T} \cup \mathrm{U} \subseteq \widehat{\mathrm{U}}_{\mathcal{I}}$. It follows that $\mathsf{o}[\mathsf{m} \rightarrow \mathsf{v}]^{\mathsf{c}}_{\mathsf{val}} \in \mathbf{IC}^{i}_{\mathrm{P},\widehat{\mathrm{T}}_{\mathcal{I}}}(\widehat{\mathrm{U}}_{\mathcal{I}})$ by Lemma 6. Thus $ec(\mathsf{o}, \mathsf{m}) \notin \mathbf{IB}_{\mathrm{P}}(\widehat{\mathrm{T}}_{\mathcal{I}})$ by Definition 25, a contradiction. Similarly, we can show that $\mathcal{I}(\mathsf{o}[\mathsf{m} \rightarrow \mathsf{v}]^{\mathsf{c}}_{\mathsf{code}}) = \mathbf{f}$ for all v, c.

Proposition 4. *Let $\mathcal{I} = \langle \mathrm{T}; \mathrm{U} \rangle$ be a stable interpretation of an F-logic KB* P. *Then $\mathcal{I}$ satisfies the unique source inheritance constraint.*

Proof. By Definition 12, we need to show that the following conditions hold:

(1) for all $\mathsf{o}, \mathsf{m}, \mathsf{v}, \mathsf{c}$: if $\mathcal{I}(\mathsf{o}[\mathsf{m} \rightarrow \mathsf{v}]^{\mathsf{c}}_{\mathsf{val}}) = \mathbf{t}$ or $\mathcal{I}(\mathsf{o}[\mathsf{m} \rightarrow \mathsf{v}]^{\mathsf{c}}_{\mathsf{code}}) = \mathbf{t}$, then for all z, x such that $\mathsf{x} \neq \mathsf{c}$, $\mathcal{I}(\mathsf{o}[\mathsf{m} \rightarrow \mathsf{z}]^{\mathsf{x}}_{\mathsf{val}}) = \mathbf{f}$ and $\mathcal{I}(\mathsf{o}[\mathsf{m} \rightarrow \mathsf{z}]^{\mathsf{x}}_{\mathsf{code}}) = \mathbf{f}$.

Because $\mathcal{I}$ is a stable interpretation of P, $\widehat{\mathrm{T}}_{\mathcal{I}} = \Psi_{\mathrm{P}}(\widehat{\mathrm{U}}_{\mathcal{I}})$ and $\widehat{\mathrm{U}}_{\mathcal{I}} = \Psi_{\mathrm{P}}(\widehat{\mathrm{T}}_{\mathcal{I}})$, by Definition 30. If $\mathcal{I}(\mathsf{o}[\mathsf{m} \rightarrow \mathsf{v}]^{\mathsf{c}}_{\mathsf{val}}) = \mathbf{t}$, then $\mathsf{o}[\mathsf{m} \rightarrow \mathsf{v}]^{\mathsf{c}}_{\mathsf{val}} \in \mathrm{T} \subseteq \widehat{\mathrm{T}}_{\mathcal{I}}$ by Definition 29. So $\mathsf{o}[\mathsf{m} \rightarrow \mathsf{v}]^{\mathsf{c}}_{\mathsf{val}} \in \mathbf{IC}^{i}_{\mathrm{P},\widehat{\mathrm{U}}_{\mathcal{I}}}(\widehat{\mathrm{T}}_{\mathcal{I}})$ by Lemma 6. It follows that $\mathsf{c}[\mathsf{m}] \overset{val}{\leadsto} \mathsf{o} \in \widehat{\mathrm{T}}_{\mathcal{I}}$ by Definition 25. On the other hand, if $\mathcal{I}(\mathsf{o}[\mathsf{m} \rightarrow \mathsf{v}]^{\mathsf{c}}_{\mathsf{code}}) = \mathbf{t}$, then $\mathsf{o}[\mathsf{m} \rightarrow \mathsf{v}]^{\mathsf{c}}_{\mathsf{code}} \in \mathrm{T} \subseteq \widehat{\mathrm{T}}_{\mathcal{I}}$ by Definition 29. So $\mathsf{o}[\mathsf{m} \rightarrow \mathsf{v}]^{\mathsf{c}}_{\mathsf{code}} \in \mathbf{TC}_{\mathrm{P},\widehat{\mathrm{U}}_{\mathcal{I}}}(\widehat{\mathrm{T}}_{\mathcal{I}})$ by Lemma 6. Thus $\mathsf{c}[\mathsf{m}] \overset{code}{\leadsto} \mathsf{o} \in \widehat{\mathrm{T}}_{\mathcal{I}}$ by Definition 25. Therefore, $\mathsf{c}[\mathsf{m}] \overset{val}{\leadsto} \mathsf{o} \in \widehat{\mathrm{T}}_{\mathcal{I}}$ or $\mathsf{c}[\mathsf{m}] \overset{code}{\leadsto} \mathsf{o} \in \widehat{\mathrm{T}}_{\mathcal{I}}$.

Suppose, to the contrary, that there are z, x such that $\mathsf{x} \neq \mathsf{c}$, $\mathcal{I}(\mathsf{o}[\mathsf{m} \rightarrow \mathsf{z}]^{\mathsf{x}}_{\mathsf{val}}) \geq \mathbf{u}$. Then $\mathsf{o}[\mathsf{m} \rightarrow \mathsf{z}]^{\mathsf{x}}_{\mathsf{val}} \in \mathrm{T} \cup \mathrm{U} \subseteq \widehat{\mathrm{U}}_{\mathcal{I}}$ by Definition 29. So $\mathsf{o}[\mathsf{m} \rightarrow \mathsf{v}]^{\mathsf{x}}_{\mathsf{val}} \in \mathbf{IC}^{i}_{\mathrm{P},\widehat{\mathrm{T}}_{\mathcal{I}}}(\widehat{\mathrm{U}}_{\mathcal{I}})$ by Lemma 6. Therefore, $mc(\mathsf{x}, \mathsf{m}, \mathsf{o}) \notin \mathbf{IB}_{\mathrm{P}}(\widehat{\mathrm{T}}_{\mathcal{I}})$ by Definition 25. Since $\mathsf{x} \neq \mathsf{c}$, it follows that $\mathsf{c}[\mathsf{m}] \overset{val}{\leadsto} \mathsf{o} \notin \widehat{\mathrm{T}}_{\mathcal{I}}$ by Definition 23, which is a contradiction. Therefore, $\mathcal{I}(\mathsf{o}[\mathsf{m} \rightarrow \mathsf{z}]^{\mathsf{x}}_{\mathsf{val}}) = \mathbf{f}$ for all z, x such that $\mathsf{x} \neq \mathsf{c}$. Similarly, we can also show that $\mathcal{I}(\mathsf{o}[\mathsf{m} \rightarrow \mathsf{z}]^{\mathsf{x}}_{\mathsf{code}}) = \mathbf{f}$ for all z, x such that $\mathsf{x} \neq \mathsf{c}$.

(2) for all c, m, o: if $\mathsf{c}[\mathsf{m}] \overset{s.val}{\leadsto}_{\mathcal{I}} \mathsf{o}$ or $\mathsf{c}[\mathsf{m}] \overset{s.code}{\leadsto}_{\mathcal{I}} \mathsf{o}$, then $\mathcal{I}(\mathsf{o}[\mathsf{m} \rightarrow \mathsf{v}]^{\mathsf{x}}_{\mathsf{val}}) = \mathbf{f}$ and $\mathcal{I}(\mathsf{o}[\mathsf{m} \rightarrow \mathsf{v}]^{\mathsf{x}}_{\mathsf{code}}) = \mathbf{f}$, for all v, x such that $\mathsf{x} \neq \mathsf{c}$.

Let $\mathsf{c}[\mathsf{m}] \overset{s.val}{\leadsto}_{\mathcal{I}} \mathsf{o}$ or $\mathsf{c}[\mathsf{m}] \overset{s.code}{\leadsto}_{\mathcal{I}} \mathsf{o}$. Suppose, to the contrary, that there exist v, x such that $\mathsf{x} \neq \mathsf{c}$, $\mathsf{o}[\mathsf{m} \rightarrow \mathsf{v}]^{\mathsf{x}}_{\mathsf{val}} \neq \mathbf{f}$. Then $\mathsf{o}[\mathsf{m} \rightarrow \mathsf{v}]^{\mathsf{x}}_{\mathsf{val}} \in \mathrm{T} \cup \mathrm{U} \subseteq \widehat{\mathrm{U}}_{\mathcal{I}}$ by Definition 29. Because $\mathcal{I}$ is a stable interpretation of P, therefore $\widehat{\mathrm{U}}_{\mathcal{I}} = \Psi_{\mathrm{P}}(\widehat{\mathrm{T}}_{\mathcal{I}})$ by Definition 30. Thus $\mathsf{o}[\mathsf{m} \rightarrow \mathsf{v}]^{\mathsf{x}}_{\mathsf{val}} \in \mathbf{IC}^{i}_{\mathrm{P},\widehat{\mathrm{T}}_{\mathcal{I}}}(\widehat{\mathrm{U}}_{\mathcal{I}})$ by Lemma 6 and so $mc(\mathsf{x}, \mathsf{m}, \mathsf{o}) \notin \mathbf{IB}_{\mathrm{P}}(\widehat{\mathrm{T}}_{\mathcal{I}})$

by Definition 25. However, by Definition 29, $\mathsf{c}[\mathsf{m}] \overset{val}{\leadsto} \mathsf{o} \in \widehat{\mathrm{T}}_{\mathcal{I}}$ or $\mathsf{c}[\mathsf{m}] \overset{code}{\leadsto} \mathsf{o} \in \widehat{\mathrm{T}}_{\mathcal{I}}$. Note that $\mathsf{x} \neq \mathsf{c}$. It follows that $mc(\mathsf{x},\mathsf{m},\mathsf{o}) \in \mathbf{IB}_{\mathrm{P}}(\widehat{\mathrm{T}}_{\mathcal{I}})$ by Definition 23, which is a contradiction. Therefore, $\mathcal{I}(\mathsf{o}[\mathsf{m} \to \mathsf{v}]^{\mathsf{x}}_{\mathsf{val}}) = \mathbf{f}$ for all v,x such that $\mathsf{x} \neq \mathsf{c}$. Similarly, we can also show that $\mathcal{I}(\mathsf{o}[\mathsf{m} \to \mathsf{v}]^{\mathsf{x}}_{\mathsf{code}}) = \mathbf{f}$ for all v,x such that $\mathsf{x} \neq \mathsf{c}$.

(3) for all o, m, v, c: $\mathcal{I}(\mathsf{o}[\mathsf{m} \to \mathsf{v}]^{\mathsf{c}}_{\mathsf{val}}) = \mathbf{t}$ iff
- (i) $\mathsf{o}[\mathsf{m}]$ is neither a strong nor a weak explicit definition; and
- (ii) $\mathsf{c}[\mathsf{m}] \overset{s.val}{\leadsto}_{\mathcal{I}} \mathsf{o}$; and
- (iii) $\mathcal{I}(\mathsf{c}[\mathsf{m} \to \mathsf{v}]_{\mathsf{ex}}) = \mathbf{t}$; and
- (iv) there is no x such that $\mathsf{x} \neq \mathsf{c}$ and $\mathsf{x}[\mathsf{m}] \leadsto_{\mathcal{I}} \mathsf{o}$.

"$\Longrightarrow$". Since $\mathcal{I}$ is a stable interpretation of P, $\widehat{\mathrm{T}}_{\mathcal{I}} = \Psi_{\mathrm{P}}(\widehat{\mathrm{U}}_{\mathcal{I}})$ by Definition 30. Because $\mathcal{I}(\mathsf{o}[\mathsf{m} \to \mathsf{v}]^{\mathsf{c}}_{\mathsf{val}}) = \mathbf{t}$, $\mathsf{o}[\mathsf{m} \to \mathsf{v}]^{\mathsf{c}}_{\mathsf{val}} \in \mathrm{T} \subseteq \widehat{\mathrm{T}}_{\mathcal{I}}$ by Definition 29. Thus $\mathsf{o}[\mathsf{m} \to \mathsf{v}]^{\mathsf{c}}_{\mathsf{val}} \in \mathbf{IC}^{i}_{\mathrm{P},\widehat{\mathrm{U}}_{\mathcal{I}}}(\widehat{\mathrm{T}}_{\mathcal{I}})$ by Lemma 6, and $\mathsf{c}[\mathsf{m}] \overset{val}{\leadsto} \mathsf{o} \in \widehat{\mathrm{T}}_{\mathcal{I}}$, $\mathsf{c}[\mathsf{m} \to \mathsf{v}]_{\mathsf{ex}} \in \widehat{\mathrm{T}}_{\mathcal{I}}$, $ec(\mathsf{o},\mathsf{m}) \notin \mathbf{IB}_{\mathrm{P}}(\widehat{\mathrm{U}}_{\mathcal{I}})$, and $mc(\mathsf{c},\mathsf{m},\mathsf{o}) \notin \mathbf{IB}_{\mathrm{P}}(\widehat{\mathrm{U}}_{\mathcal{I}})$, by Definition 25. Note that $ec(\mathsf{o},\mathsf{m}) \notin \mathbf{IB}_{\mathrm{P}}(\widehat{\mathrm{U}}_{\mathcal{I}})$. It follows that $\mathsf{o}[\mathsf{m} \to \mathsf{x}]_{\mathsf{ex}} \notin \widehat{\mathrm{U}}_{\mathcal{I}}$ for all x, by Definition 23. Thus $\mathcal{I}(\mathsf{o}[\mathsf{m} \to \mathsf{x}]_{\mathsf{ex}}) = \mathbf{f}$ for all x and so $\mathsf{o}[\mathsf{m}]$ is neither a strong nor a weak explicit definition, by Definition 4. Note that $\mathsf{c}[\mathsf{m}] \overset{val}{\leadsto} \mathsf{o} \in \widehat{\mathrm{T}}_{\mathcal{I}}$. It follows that $\mathsf{c}[\mathsf{m}] \overset{s.val}{\leadsto}_{\mathcal{I}} \mathsf{o}$ by Definition 29. $\mathsf{c}[\mathsf{m} \to \mathsf{v}]_{\mathsf{ex}} \in \widehat{\mathrm{T}}_{\mathcal{I}}$ implies $\mathcal{I}(\mathsf{c}[\mathsf{m} \to \mathsf{v}]_{\mathsf{ex}}) = \mathbf{t}$. Because $mc(\mathsf{c},\mathsf{m},\mathsf{o}) \notin \mathbf{IB}_{\mathrm{P}}(\widehat{\mathrm{U}}_{\mathcal{I}})$, therefore there is no $\mathsf{x} \neq \mathsf{c}$ such that $\mathsf{x}[\mathsf{m}] \overset{val}{\leadsto} \mathsf{o} \in \widehat{\mathrm{U}}_{\mathcal{I}}$ or $\mathsf{x}[\mathsf{m}] \overset{code}{\leadsto} \mathsf{o} \in \widehat{\mathrm{U}}_{\mathcal{I}}$, by Definition 23. So there is no x such that $\mathsf{x} \neq \mathsf{c}$ and $\mathsf{x}[\mathsf{m}] \leadsto_{\mathcal{I}} \mathsf{o}$, by Definition 29.

"$\Longleftarrow$". Since $\mathsf{o}[\mathsf{m}]$ is neither a strong nor a weak explicit definition, it follows that $\mathcal{I}(\mathsf{o}[\mathsf{m} \to \mathsf{x}]_{\mathsf{ex}}) = \mathbf{f}$ for all x, by Definition 4. So $\mathsf{o}[\mathsf{m} \to \mathsf{x}]_{\mathsf{ex}} \notin \mathrm{T} \cup \mathrm{U}$ for all x, and $ec(\mathsf{o},\mathsf{m}) \notin \mathbf{IB}_{\mathrm{P}}(\widehat{\mathrm{U}}_{\mathcal{I}})$, by Definitions 29 and 23. Because $\mathsf{c}[\mathsf{m}] \overset{s.val}{\leadsto}_{\mathcal{I}} \mathsf{o}$, therefore $\mathsf{c}[\mathsf{m}] \overset{val}{\leadsto} \mathsf{o} \in \widehat{\mathrm{T}}_{\mathcal{I}}$ by Definition 29. Since $\mathcal{I}(\mathsf{c}[\mathsf{m} \to \mathsf{v}]_{\mathsf{ex}}) = \mathbf{t}$, it follows that $\mathsf{c}[\mathsf{m} \to \mathsf{v}]_{\mathsf{ex}} \in \mathrm{T} \subseteq \widehat{\mathrm{T}}_{\mathcal{I}}$. Because $\mathcal{I}$ is a stable interpretation of P, therefore $\widehat{\mathrm{T}}_{\mathcal{I}} = \Psi_{\mathrm{P}}(\widehat{\mathrm{U}}_{\mathcal{I}})$, by Definition 30. So if we can show that $mc(\mathsf{c},\mathsf{m},\mathsf{o}) \notin \mathbf{IB}_{\mathrm{P}}(\widehat{\mathrm{U}}_{\mathcal{I}})$, then it follows that $\mathsf{o}[\mathsf{m} \to \mathsf{v}]^{\mathsf{c}}_{\mathsf{val}} \in \mathbf{IC}^{i}_{\mathrm{P},\widehat{\mathrm{U}}_{\mathcal{I}}}(\widehat{\mathrm{T}}_{\mathcal{I}}) \subseteq \widehat{\mathrm{T}}_{\mathcal{I}}$, by Definition 25 and Lemma 16. Suppose, to the contrary, that $mc(\mathsf{c},\mathsf{m},\mathsf{o}) \in \mathbf{IB}_{\mathrm{P}}(\widehat{\mathrm{U}}_{\mathcal{I}})$. Then, by Definition 23, there is $\mathsf{x} \neq \mathsf{c}$ such that $\mathsf{x}[\mathsf{m}] \overset{val}{\leadsto} \mathsf{o} \in \widehat{\mathrm{U}}_{\mathcal{I}}$ or $\mathsf{x}[\mathsf{m}] \overset{code}{\leadsto} \mathsf{o} \in \widehat{\mathrm{U}}_{\mathcal{I}}$. It follows that $\mathsf{x}[\mathsf{m}] \leadsto_{\mathcal{I}} \mathsf{o}$ by Definition 29, which contradicts the premise. Therefore, $mc(\mathsf{c},\mathsf{m},\mathsf{o}) \notin \mathbf{IB}_{\mathrm{P}}(\widehat{\mathrm{U}}_{\mathcal{I}})$, and so $\mathsf{o}[\mathsf{m} \to \mathsf{v}]^{\mathsf{c}}_{\mathsf{val}} \in \widehat{\mathrm{T}}_{\mathcal{I}}$, $\mathcal{I}(\mathsf{o}[\mathsf{m} \to \mathsf{v}]^{\mathsf{c}}_{\mathsf{val}}) = \mathbf{t}$.

Proposition 5. *Let $\mathcal{I} = \langle \mathrm{T};\mathrm{U} \rangle$ be a stable interpretation of an F-logic KB* P. *Then $\mathcal{I}$ satisfies the template rules of* P.

Proof. By contradiction. Because $\mathcal{I}$ is a stable interpretation of P, $\widehat{\mathrm{T}}_{\mathcal{I}} = \Psi_{\mathrm{P}}(\widehat{\mathrm{U}}_{\mathcal{I}})$ and $\widehat{\mathrm{U}}_{\mathcal{I}} = \Psi_{\mathrm{P}}(\widehat{\mathrm{T}}_{\mathcal{I}})$ by Definition 30. Suppose, to the contrary, that $\mathcal{I}$ does not satisfy the template rules of P. Then, by Definition 19, *ground*(P) has an object $\mathsf{o} \in \mathcal{HU}_{\mathrm{P}}$ and a template rule R either of the form $\mathsf{code(c)\ @this[m \to v]\ :-\ B}$ or of the form $\mathsf{code(c)\ @this[m \to v]}$, such that $\mathcal{I}(\mathsf{R}_{\|\mathsf{o}}) = \mathbf{f}$. Let us assume that $\mathsf{R} \equiv \mathsf{code(c)\ @this[m \to v]\ :-\ B}$ (the case in which $\mathsf{R} \equiv \mathsf{code(c)\ @this[m \to v]}$ is similar). By Definition 18, there are three possible cases to consider:

(1) $imode_{\mathcal{I}}(\mathsf{R}_{\|\mathsf{o}}) = \mathbf{t}$ and $\mathcal{I}(\mathsf{o}[\mathsf{m} \rightarrow \mathsf{v}]^{\mathsf{c}}_{\text{code}}) < \mathcal{V}^{\mathbf{b}}_{\mathcal{I}}(\mathsf{B}_{\|\mathsf{o}})$
Because $imode_{\mathcal{I}}(\mathsf{R}_{\|\mathsf{o}}) = \mathbf{t}$, therefore by Definition 16: (i) $\mathsf{c}[\mathsf{m}] \overset{s.code}{\leadsto}_{\mathcal{I}} \mathsf{o}$ and so $\mathsf{c}[\mathsf{m}] \overset{code}{\leadsto} \mathsf{o} \in \widehat{\mathrm{T}}_{\mathcal{I}}$ by Definition 29; (ii) $ec(\mathsf{o},\mathsf{m})$ is neither a strong nor a weak explicit definition. So $ec(\mathsf{o},\mathsf{m}) \notin \mathbf{IB}_{\mathrm{P}}(\widehat{\mathrm{U}}_{\mathcal{I}})$ by Definitions 23 and 4; and (iii) there is no $\mathsf{x} \neq \mathsf{c}$ such that $\mathsf{x}[\mathsf{m}] \leadsto_{\mathcal{I}} \mathsf{o}$. It follows that there is no $\mathsf{x} \neq \mathsf{c}$ such that $\mathsf{x}[\mathsf{m}] \overset{val}{\leadsto} \mathsf{o} \in \widehat{\mathrm{U}}_{\mathcal{I}}$ or $\mathsf{x}[\mathsf{m}] \overset{code}{\leadsto} \mathsf{o} \in \widehat{\mathrm{U}}_{\mathcal{I}}$ by Definition 29. Thus $mc(\mathsf{c},\mathsf{m},\mathsf{o}) \notin \mathbf{IB}_{\mathrm{P}}(\widehat{\mathrm{U}}_{\mathcal{I}})$. Since $\widehat{\mathrm{T}}_{\mathcal{I}} \subseteq \widehat{\mathrm{U}}_{\mathcal{I}}$, it also follows that $\mathsf{c}[\mathsf{m}] \overset{code}{\leadsto} \mathsf{o} \in \widehat{\mathrm{U}}_{\mathcal{I}}$, $ec(\mathsf{o},\mathsf{m}) \notin \mathbf{IB}_{\mathrm{P}}(\widehat{\mathrm{T}}_{\mathcal{I}})$, and $mc(\mathsf{c},\mathsf{m},\mathsf{o}) \notin \mathbf{IB}_{\mathrm{P}}(\widehat{\mathrm{T}}_{\mathcal{I}})$, by the monotonicity of $\mathbf{IB}_{\mathrm{P}}$.

First let us assume $\mathcal{V}^{\mathbf{b}}_{\mathcal{I}}(\mathsf{B}_{\|\mathsf{o}}) = \mathbf{t}$. It follows that $\mathcal{I}(\mathsf{o}[\mathsf{m} \rightarrow \mathsf{v}]^{\mathsf{c}}_{\text{code}}) \neq \mathbf{t}$. Since $\mathcal{V}^{\mathbf{b}}_{\mathcal{I}}(\mathsf{B}_{\|\mathsf{o}}) = \mathbf{t}$, it follows that $\mathcal{V}^{\mathbf{b}}_{\mathcal{I}}(\mathsf{L}) = \mathbf{t}$ for all $\mathsf{L} \in \mathsf{B}_{\|\mathsf{o}}$, by Definition 1. So by Lemma 1: (i) if L is a positive literal then $val^{\mathbf{b}}_{\widehat{\mathrm{T}}_{\mathcal{I}}}(\mathsf{L}) = \mathbf{t}$; and (ii) if L is a negative literal then $val^{\mathbf{b}}_{\widehat{\mathrm{U}}_{\mathcal{I}}}(\mathsf{L}) = \mathbf{t}$. Therefore, $\mathsf{o}[\mathsf{m} \rightarrow \mathsf{v}]^{\mathsf{c}}_{\text{code}} \in \mathbf{TC}_{\mathrm{P},\widehat{\mathrm{U}}_{\mathcal{I}}}(\widehat{\mathrm{T}}_{\mathcal{I}}) \subseteq \widehat{\mathrm{T}}_{\mathcal{I}}$, by Definition 24 and Lemma 16. Thus $\mathcal{I}(\mathsf{o}[\mathsf{m} \rightarrow \mathsf{v}]^{\mathsf{c}}_{\text{code}}) = \mathbf{t}$, a contradiction. On the other hand, if $\mathcal{V}^{\mathbf{b}}_{\mathcal{I}}(\mathsf{B}_{\|\mathsf{o}}) = \mathbf{u}$, then $\mathcal{I}(\mathsf{o}[\mathsf{m} \rightarrow \mathsf{v}]^{\mathsf{c}}_{\text{code}}) = \mathbf{f}$. Since $\mathcal{V}^{\mathbf{b}}_{\mathcal{I}}(\mathsf{B}_{\|\mathsf{o}}) = \mathbf{u}$, it follows that $\mathcal{V}^{\mathbf{b}}_{\mathcal{I}}(\mathsf{L}) \geq \mathbf{u}$ for all $\mathsf{L} \in \mathsf{B}_{\|\mathsf{o}}$, by Definition 1. So by Lemma 1: (i) if L is a positive literal then $val^{\mathbf{b}}_{\widehat{\mathrm{U}}_{\mathcal{I}}}(\mathsf{L}) = \mathbf{t}$; and (2) if L is a negative literal then $val^{\mathbf{b}}_{\widehat{\mathrm{T}}_{\mathcal{I}}}(\mathsf{L}) = \mathbf{t}$. Therefore, $\mathsf{o}[\mathsf{m} \rightarrow \mathsf{v}]^{\mathsf{c}}_{\text{code}} \in \mathbf{TC}_{\mathrm{P},\widehat{\mathrm{T}}_{\mathcal{I}}}(\widehat{\mathrm{U}}_{\mathcal{I}}) \subseteq \widehat{\mathrm{U}}_{\mathcal{I}}$, by Definition 22 and Lemma 16. Thus $\mathcal{I}(\mathsf{o}[\mathsf{m} \rightarrow \mathsf{v}]^{\mathsf{c}}_{\text{code}}) \geq \mathbf{u}$, a contradiction.

(2) $imode_{\mathcal{I}}(\mathsf{R}_{\|\mathsf{o}}) = \mathbf{u}$, $\mathcal{I}(\mathsf{o}[\mathsf{m} \rightarrow \mathsf{v}]^{\mathsf{c}}_{\text{code}}) = \mathbf{f}$, and $\mathcal{V}^{\mathbf{b}}_{\mathcal{I}}(\mathsf{B}_{\|\mathsf{o}}) \geq \mathbf{u}$
Because $imode_{\mathcal{I}}(\mathsf{R}_{\|\mathsf{o}}) = \mathbf{u}$, by Definition 17: (i) $\mathsf{c}[\mathsf{m}] \overset{s.code}{\leadsto}_{\mathcal{I}} \mathsf{o}$ or $\mathsf{c}[\mathsf{m}] \overset{w.code}{\leadsto}_{\mathcal{I}} \mathsf{o}$, and so $\mathsf{c}[\mathsf{m}] \overset{code}{\leadsto} \mathsf{o} \in \widehat{\mathrm{U}}_{\mathcal{I}}$ by Definition 29; (ii) $ec(\mathsf{o},\mathsf{m})$ is not a strong explicit definition and so $ec(\mathsf{o},\mathsf{m}) \notin \mathbf{IB}_{\mathrm{P}}(\widehat{\mathrm{T}}_{\mathcal{I}})$ by Definitions 23 and 4; and (iii) there is no $\mathsf{x} \neq \mathsf{c}$ such that $\mathsf{x}[\mathsf{m}] \overset{s.val}{\leadsto}_{\mathcal{I}} \mathsf{o}$ or $\mathsf{x}[\mathsf{m}] \overset{s.code}{\leadsto}_{\mathcal{I}} \mathsf{o}$. It follows that there is no $\mathsf{x} \neq \mathsf{c}$ such that $\mathsf{x}[\mathsf{m}] \overset{val}{\leadsto} \mathsf{o} \in \widehat{\mathrm{T}}_{\mathcal{I}}$ or $\mathsf{x}[\mathsf{m}] \overset{code}{\leadsto} \mathsf{o} \in \widehat{\mathrm{T}}_{\mathcal{I}}$ by Definition 29. Thus $mc(\mathsf{c},\mathsf{m},\mathsf{o}) \notin \mathbf{IB}_{\mathrm{P}}(\widehat{\mathrm{T}}_{\mathcal{I}})$. Since $\mathcal{V}^{\mathbf{b}}_{\mathcal{I}}(\mathsf{B}_{\|\mathsf{o}}) \geq \mathbf{u}$, it follows that $\mathcal{V}^{\mathbf{b}}_{\mathcal{I}}(\mathsf{L}) \geq \mathbf{u}$ for all $\mathsf{L} \in \mathsf{B}_{\|\mathsf{o}}$, by Definition 1. So by Lemma 1: (i) if L is a positive literal then $val^{\mathbf{b}}_{\widehat{\mathrm{U}}_{\mathcal{I}}}(\mathsf{L}) = \mathbf{t}$; and (2) if L is a negative literal then $val^{\mathbf{b}}_{\widehat{\mathrm{T}}_{\mathcal{I}}}(\mathsf{L}) = \mathbf{t}$. Thus $\mathsf{o}[\mathsf{m} \rightarrow \mathsf{v}]^{\mathsf{c}}_{\text{code}} \in \mathbf{TC}_{\mathrm{P},\widehat{\mathrm{T}}_{\mathcal{I}}}(\widehat{\mathrm{U}}_{\mathcal{I}}) \subseteq \widehat{\mathrm{U}}_{\mathcal{I}}$, by Definition 22 and Lemma 16. So, $\mathcal{I}(\mathsf{o}[\mathsf{m} \rightarrow \mathsf{v}]^{\mathsf{c}}_{\text{code}}) \geq \mathbf{u}$, a contradiction.

(3) $imode_{\mathcal{I}}(\mathsf{R}_{\|\mathsf{o}}) = \mathbf{f}$ and $\mathcal{I}(\mathsf{o}[\mathsf{m} \rightarrow \mathsf{v}]^{\mathsf{c}}_{\text{code}}) \geq \mathbf{u}$
Because $\mathcal{I}(\mathsf{o}[\mathsf{m} \rightarrow \mathsf{v}]^{\mathsf{c}}_{\text{code}}) \geq \mathbf{u}$, so $\mathsf{o}[\mathsf{m} \rightarrow \mathsf{v}]^{\mathsf{c}}_{\text{code}} \in \mathrm{U} \subseteq \widehat{\mathrm{U}}_{\mathcal{I}}$. It follows that $\mathsf{o}[\mathsf{m} \rightarrow \mathsf{v}]^{\mathsf{c}}_{\text{code}} \in \mathbf{TC}_{\mathrm{P},\widehat{\mathrm{T}}_{\mathcal{I}}}(\widehat{\mathrm{U}}_{\mathcal{I}})$ by Lemma 6. So by Definition 24, $\mathsf{c}[\mathsf{m}] \overset{code}{\leadsto} \mathsf{o} \in \widehat{\mathrm{U}}_{\mathcal{I}}$, $ec(\mathsf{o},\mathsf{m}) \notin \mathbf{IB}_{\mathrm{P}}(\widehat{\mathrm{T}}_{\mathcal{I}})$, and $mc(\mathsf{c},\mathsf{m},\mathsf{o}) \notin \mathbf{IB}_{\mathrm{P}}(\widehat{\mathrm{T}}_{\mathcal{I}})$. Because $\mathsf{c}[\mathsf{m}] \overset{code}{\leadsto} \mathsf{o} \in \widehat{\mathrm{U}}_{\mathcal{I}}$, so $\mathsf{c}[\mathsf{m}] \overset{s.code}{\leadsto}_{\mathcal{I}} \mathsf{o}$ or $\mathsf{c}[\mathsf{m}] \overset{w.code}{\leadsto}_{\mathcal{I}} \mathsf{o}$, by Definition 29. Since $ec(\mathsf{o},\mathsf{m}) \notin \mathbf{IB}_{\mathrm{P}}(\widehat{\mathrm{T}}_{\mathcal{I}})$, therefore $ec(\mathsf{o},\mathsf{m})$ is not a strong explicit definition, by Definitions 23 and 4. Because $mc(\mathsf{c},\mathsf{m},\mathsf{o}) \notin \mathbf{IB}_{\mathrm{P}}(\widehat{\mathrm{T}}_{\mathcal{I}})$, so there is no $\mathsf{x} \neq \mathsf{c}$ such that $\mathsf{x}[\mathsf{m}] \overset{val}{\leadsto} \mathsf{o} \in \widehat{\mathrm{T}}_{\mathcal{I}}$ or $\mathsf{x}[\mathsf{m}] \overset{val}{\leadsto} \mathsf{o} \in \widehat{\mathrm{T}}_{\mathcal{I}}$. It follows that there is no $\mathsf{x} \neq \mathsf{c}$ such that $\mathsf{x}[\mathsf{m}] \overset{s.val}{\leadsto}_{\mathcal{I}} \mathsf{o}$ or $\mathsf{x}[\mathsf{m}] \overset{s.code}{\leadsto}_{\mathcal{I}} \mathsf{o}$, by Definition 29. Thus o must either weakly or strongly inherit R, by Definitions 17 and 16. Therefore, $imode_{\mathcal{I}}(\mathsf{R}_{\|\mathsf{o}}) \geq \mathbf{u}$, a contradiction.

Proposition 6. *Let $\mathcal{I} = \langle \mathrm{T}; \mathrm{U} \rangle$ be a stable interpretation of an F-logic KB* P. *Then $\mathcal{I}$ satisfies the cautious ISA transitivity constraint.*

Proof. By Definition 13, we need to show that the following conditions hold:

(1) for all s, c: if there is x such that $\mathcal{I}(\mathsf{s} :: \mathsf{x} \wedge \mathsf{x} :: \mathsf{c}) = \mathbf{u}$ and $\mathcal{I}(\mathsf{s} :: \mathsf{c}) \neq \mathbf{t}$, then $\mathcal{I}(\mathsf{s} :: \mathsf{c}) = \mathbf{u}$;

(2) for all o, c: if there is x such that $\mathcal{I}(\mathsf{o} : \mathsf{x} \wedge \mathsf{x} :: \mathsf{c}) = \mathbf{u}$ and $\mathcal{I}(\mathsf{o} : \mathsf{c}) \neq \mathbf{t}$, then $\mathcal{I}(\mathsf{o} : \mathsf{c}) = \mathbf{u}$.

Suppose $\mathcal{I}(\mathsf{s} :: \mathsf{x} \wedge \mathsf{x} :: \mathsf{c}) = \mathbf{u}$. Then $\mathsf{s} :: \mathsf{x} \in \mathrm{T} \cup \mathrm{U}$ and $\mathsf{x} :: \mathsf{c} \in \mathrm{T} \cup \mathrm{U}$. It follows that $\mathsf{s} :: \mathsf{x} \in \widehat{\mathrm{U}}_{\mathcal{I}}$ and $\mathsf{x} :: \mathsf{c} \in \widehat{\mathrm{U}}_{\mathcal{I}}$, by Definition 29. So $\mathsf{s} :: \mathsf{c} \in \mathbf{IC}^t(\widehat{\mathrm{U}}_{\mathcal{I}})$ by Definition 25. Since $\widehat{\mathrm{U}}_{\mathcal{I}} = \Psi_{\mathrm{P}}(\widehat{\mathrm{T}}_{\mathcal{I}})$ by Definition 30, it follows that $\mathsf{s} :: \mathsf{c} \in \mathbf{IC}^t(\widehat{\mathrm{U}}_{\mathcal{I}}) \subseteq \widehat{\mathrm{U}}_{\mathcal{I}}$, by Lemma 16. Thus $\mathcal{I}(\mathsf{s} :: \mathsf{c}) \geq \mathbf{u}$. But $\mathcal{I}(\mathsf{s} :: \mathsf{c}) \neq \mathbf{t}$. It follows that $\mathcal{I}(\mathsf{s} :: \mathsf{c}) = \mathbf{u}$. Similarly, if $\mathcal{I}(\mathsf{o} : \mathsf{x} \wedge \mathsf{x} :: \mathsf{c}) = \mathbf{u}$ and $\mathcal{I}(\mathsf{o} : \mathsf{c}) \neq \mathbf{t}$, then $\mathcal{I}(\mathsf{o} : \mathsf{c}) = \mathbf{u}$.

Proposition 7. *Let $\mathcal{I} = \langle \mathrm{T}; \mathrm{U} \rangle$ be a stable interpretation of an F-logic KB P. Then $\mathcal{I}$ satisfies the cautious inheritance constraint.*

Proof. By Definition 14, we need to show for all o, m, v, c: $\mathcal{I}(\mathsf{o}[\mathsf{m} \rightarrow \mathsf{v}]^{\mathsf{c}}_{\mathsf{val}}) = \mathbf{u}$ iff the following conditions hold:

(i) $\mathsf{o}[\mathsf{m}]$ is not a strong explicit definition;

(ii) $\mathsf{c}[\mathsf{m}] \overset{s.val}{\rightsquigarrow}_{\mathcal{I}} \mathsf{o}$ or $\mathsf{c}[\mathsf{m}] \overset{w.val}{\rightsquigarrow}_{\mathcal{I}} \mathsf{o}$;

(iii) $\mathcal{I}(\mathsf{c}[\mathsf{m} \rightarrow \mathsf{v}]_{\mathsf{ex}}) \geq \mathbf{u}$;

(iv) there is no $\mathsf{x} \neq$ such that $\mathsf{x}[\mathsf{m}] \overset{s.val}{\rightsquigarrow}_{\mathcal{I}} \mathsf{o}$ or $\mathsf{x}[\mathsf{m}] \overset{s.code}{\rightsquigarrow}_{\mathcal{I}} \mathsf{o}$;

(v) $\mathcal{I}(\mathsf{o}[\mathsf{m} \rightarrow \mathsf{v}]^{\mathsf{c}}_{\mathsf{val}}) \neq \mathbf{t}$.

"$\Longrightarrow$". Because $\mathcal{I}$ is a stable interpretation of P, therefore $\widehat{\mathrm{U}}_{\mathcal{I}} = \Psi_{\mathrm{P}}(\widehat{\mathrm{T}}_{\mathcal{I}})$ by Definition 30. Because $\mathsf{o}[\mathsf{m} \rightarrow \mathsf{v}]^{\mathsf{c}}_{\mathsf{val}} = \mathbf{u}$, therefore $\mathsf{o}[\mathsf{m} \rightarrow \mathsf{v}]^{\mathsf{c}}_{\mathsf{val}} \in \mathrm{T} \cup \mathrm{U} \subseteq \widehat{\mathrm{U}}_{\mathcal{I}}$ by Definition 29. Thus $\mathsf{o}[\mathsf{m} \rightarrow \mathsf{v}]^{\mathsf{c}}_{\mathsf{val}} \in \mathbf{IC}^i_{\mathrm{P},\widehat{\mathrm{T}}_{\mathcal{I}}}(\widehat{\mathrm{U}}_{\mathcal{I}})$, by Lemma 6. So $\mathsf{c}[\mathsf{m}] \overset{val}{\rightsquigarrow} \mathsf{o} \in \widehat{\mathrm{U}}_{\mathcal{I}}$, $\mathsf{c}[\mathsf{m} \rightarrow \mathsf{v}]_{\mathsf{ex}} \in \widehat{\mathrm{U}}_{\mathcal{I}}$, $ec(\mathsf{o}, \mathsf{m}) \notin \mathbf{IB}_{\mathrm{P}}(\widehat{\mathrm{T}}_{\mathcal{I}})$, and $mc(\mathsf{c}, \mathsf{m}, \mathsf{o}) \notin \mathbf{IB}_{\mathrm{P}}(\widehat{\mathrm{T}}_{\mathcal{I}})$, according to Definition 25. Because $ec(\mathsf{o}, \mathsf{m}) \notin \mathbf{IB}_{\mathrm{P}}(\widehat{\mathrm{T}}_{\mathcal{I}})$, it follows that $\mathsf{o}[\mathsf{m} \rightarrow \mathsf{x}]_{\mathsf{ex}} \notin \widehat{\mathrm{T}}_{\mathcal{I}}$ for all x, by Definition 23. So $\mathcal{I}(\mathsf{o}[\mathsf{m} \rightarrow \mathsf{x}]_{\mathsf{ex}}) \neq \mathbf{t}$ for all x. Thus $\mathsf{o}[\mathsf{m}]$ is not a strong explicit definition by Definition 4. Because $\mathsf{c}[\mathsf{m}] \overset{val}{\rightsquigarrow} \mathsf{o} \in \widehat{\mathrm{U}}_{\mathcal{I}}$, it follows that $\mathsf{c}[\mathsf{m}] \overset{s.val}{\rightsquigarrow}_{\mathcal{I}} \mathsf{o}$ or $\mathsf{c}[\mathsf{m}] \overset{w.val}{\rightsquigarrow}_{\mathcal{I}} \mathsf{o}$, by Definition 29. $\mathsf{c}[\mathsf{m} \rightarrow \mathsf{v}]_{\mathsf{ex}} \in \widehat{\mathrm{U}}_{\mathcal{I}}$ implies $\mathcal{I}(\mathsf{c}[\mathsf{m} \rightarrow \mathsf{v}]_{\mathsf{ex}}) \geq \mathbf{u}$. Because $mc(\mathsf{c}, \mathsf{m}, \mathsf{o}) \notin \mathbf{IB}_{\mathrm{P}}(\widehat{\mathrm{T}}_{\mathcal{I}})$, it follows that there is no $\mathsf{x} \neq \mathsf{c}$ such that $\mathsf{c}[\mathsf{m}] \overset{val}{\rightsquigarrow} \mathsf{o} \in \widehat{\mathrm{T}}_{\mathcal{I}}$ or $\mathsf{c}[\mathsf{m}] \overset{code}{\rightsquigarrow} \mathsf{o} \in \widehat{\mathrm{T}}_{\mathcal{I}}$. So there is no $\mathsf{x} \neq \mathsf{c}$ such that $\mathsf{c}[\mathsf{m}] \overset{s.val}{\rightsquigarrow}_{\mathcal{I}} \mathsf{o}$ or $\mathsf{c}[\mathsf{m}] \overset{s.code}{\rightsquigarrow}_{\mathcal{I}} \mathsf{o}$, by Definition 29.

"$\Longleftarrow$". Because $\mathsf{o}[\mathsf{m}]$ is not a strong explicit definition, $\mathcal{I}(\mathsf{o}[\mathsf{m} \rightarrow \mathsf{x}]_{\mathsf{ex}}) \neq \mathbf{t}$ for all x, by Definition 4. It follows that $\mathsf{o}[\mathsf{m} \rightarrow \mathsf{x}]_{\mathsf{ex}} \notin \mathrm{T}$ for all x, and so $ec(\mathsf{o}, \mathsf{m}) \notin \mathbf{IB}_{\mathrm{P}}(\widehat{\mathrm{T}}_{\mathcal{I}})$, by Definitions 29 and 23. Because $\mathsf{c}[\mathsf{m}] \overset{s.val}{\rightsquigarrow}_{\mathcal{I}} \mathsf{o}$ or $\mathsf{c}[\mathsf{m}] \overset{w.val}{\rightsquigarrow}_{\mathcal{I}} \mathsf{o}$, therefore $\mathsf{c}[\mathsf{m}] \overset{val}{\rightsquigarrow} \mathsf{o} \in \widehat{\mathrm{U}}_{\mathcal{I}}$ by Definition 29. Since $\mathcal{I}(\mathsf{c}[\mathsf{m} \rightarrow \mathsf{v}]_{\mathsf{ex}}) \geq \mathbf{u}$, it follows that $\mathsf{c}[\mathsf{m} \rightarrow \mathsf{v}]_{\mathsf{ex}} \in \mathrm{T} \cup \mathrm{U} \subseteq \widehat{\mathrm{U}}_{\mathcal{I}}$. Because $\mathcal{I}$ is a stable interpretation of P, therefore $\widehat{\mathrm{U}}_{\mathcal{I}} = \Psi_{\mathrm{P}}(\widehat{\mathrm{T}}_{\mathcal{I}})$, by Definition 30. So if we can show $mc(\mathsf{c}, \mathsf{m}, \mathsf{o}) \notin \mathbf{IB}_{\mathrm{P}}(\widehat{\mathrm{T}}_{\mathcal{I}})$, then it follows that $\mathsf{o}[\mathsf{m} \rightarrow \mathsf{v}]^{\mathsf{c}}_{\mathsf{val}} \in \mathbf{IC}^i_{\mathrm{P},\widehat{\mathrm{T}}_{\mathcal{I}}}(\widehat{\mathrm{U}}_{\mathcal{I}}) \subseteq \widehat{\mathrm{U}}_{\mathcal{I}}$, by Definition 25 and Lemma 16. Suppose, to the contrary, that $mc(\mathsf{c}, \mathsf{m}, \mathsf{o}) \in \mathbf{IB}_{\mathrm{P}}(\widehat{\mathrm{T}}_{\mathcal{I}})$. Then there is $\mathsf{x} \neq \mathsf{c}$ such that $\mathsf{x}[\mathsf{m}] \overset{val}{\rightsquigarrow} \mathsf{o} \in \widehat{\mathrm{T}}_{\mathcal{I}}$ or $\mathsf{x}[\mathsf{m}] \overset{code}{\rightsquigarrow} \mathsf{o} \in \widehat{\mathrm{T}}_{\mathcal{I}}$ by Definition 23. It follows that $\mathsf{x}[\mathsf{m}] \overset{s.val}{\rightsquigarrow}_{\mathcal{I}} \mathsf{o}$ or $\mathsf{x}[\mathsf{m}] \overset{s.code}{\rightsquigarrow}_{\mathcal{I}} \mathsf{o}$, by Definition 29, which contradicts the premise. Therefore,

$mc(\mathsf{c},\mathsf{m},\mathsf{o}) \notin \mathbf{IB}_{\mathrm{P}}(\widehat{\mathrm{T}}_{\mathcal{I}})$, and so $\mathsf{o}[\mathsf{m} \to \mathsf{v}]^{\mathsf{c}}_{\mathrm{val}} \in \widehat{\mathrm{U}}_{\mathcal{I}}$, $\mathcal{I}(\mathsf{o}[\mathsf{m} \to \mathsf{v}]^{\mathsf{c}}_{\mathrm{val}}) \geq \mathbf{u}$. But $\mathcal{I}(\mathsf{o}[\mathsf{m} \to \mathsf{v}]^{\mathsf{c}}_{\mathrm{val}}) \neq \mathbf{t}$. So $\mathcal{I}(\mathsf{o}[\mathsf{m} \to \mathsf{v}]^{\mathsf{c}}_{\mathrm{val}}) = \mathbf{u}$.

A.2 Proof of Theorem 5 in Section 9

Theorem 5. *The cautious object model $\mathcal{M}$ of an F-logic KB* P *is minimal among those object models of* P *that satisfy the cautious ISA transitivity constraint and the cautious inheritance constraint.*

Proof. Recall that $\mathcal{M} = \langle\, \pi(\widehat{\mathrm{T}}_\infty); \pi(\widehat{\mathrm{U}}_\infty) - \pi(\widehat{\mathrm{T}}_\infty)\,\rangle$. Let $\mathcal{I} = \langle\, \mathrm{T}; \mathrm{U}\,\rangle$ be an object model of P that satisfies the cautious ISA transitivity constraint and the cautious inheritance constraint. Moreover, $\mathcal{I} \leq \mathcal{M}$. To show that $\mathcal{M}$ is minimal, it suffices to show that $\mathrm{T} = \widehat{\mathrm{T}}_\infty$ and $\mathrm{T} \cup \mathrm{U} = \widehat{\mathrm{U}}_\infty$. By Definition 35: (i) $\mathrm{T} \subseteq \widehat{\mathrm{T}}_\infty$; (ii) $\mathrm{T} \cup \mathrm{U} \subseteq \widehat{\mathrm{U}}_\infty$; (iii) for all $\mathsf{c},\mathsf{m},\mathsf{o}$: $\mathsf{c}[\mathsf{m}] \overset{s.val}{\rightsquigarrow}_{\mathcal{I}} \mathsf{o}$ implies $\mathsf{c}[\mathsf{m}] \overset{s.val}{\rightsquigarrow}_{\mathcal{M}} \mathsf{o}$; and (iv) for all $\mathsf{c},\mathsf{m},\mathsf{o}$: $\mathsf{c}[\mathsf{m}] \overset{s.code}{\rightsquigarrow}_{\mathcal{I}} \mathsf{o}$ implies $\mathsf{c}[\mathsf{m}] \overset{s.code}{\rightsquigarrow}_{\mathcal{M}} \mathsf{o}$. Let $\mathcal{J} = \langle\, \mathrm{T}; \emptyset\,\rangle$ and $\mathcal{K} = \langle\, \mathrm{T} \cup \mathrm{U}; \emptyset\,\rangle$.

Suppose, to the contrary, that $\mathrm{T} \subset \widehat{\mathrm{T}}_\infty$. Since $\widehat{\mathrm{T}}_\infty = \bigcup_\gamma \widehat{\mathrm{T}}_\gamma$ by Definition 32 and $\{\widehat{\mathrm{T}}_\gamma\}$ is an increasing sequence by Lemma 9, let α be the first ordinal such that $\mathrm{T} \subset \widehat{\mathrm{T}}_\alpha$ and $\mathrm{T} \supseteq \widehat{\mathrm{T}}_\gamma$ for all $\gamma < \alpha$. Clearly, α must be a successor ordinal. Thus $\widehat{\mathrm{T}}_\alpha = \mathrm{lfp}(\mathbf{T}_{\mathrm{P},\widehat{\mathrm{U}}_{\alpha-1}})$, by Definitions 32 and 27. Since $\mathbf{T}_{\mathrm{P},\widehat{\mathrm{U}}_{\alpha-1}}$ is monotonic by Lemma 5, it follows that the ordinal powers of $\mathbf{T}_{\mathrm{P},\widehat{\mathrm{U}}_{\alpha-1}}$ is an increasing sequence. Denote $\widehat{\mathrm{J}}_\gamma = \mathbf{T}^{\gamma}_{\mathrm{P},\widehat{\mathrm{U}}_{\alpha-1}}$ for all ordinal γ. Let β be the first ordinal such that $\mathrm{T} \subset \widehat{\mathrm{J}}_\beta$ and $\mathrm{T} \supseteq \widehat{\mathrm{J}}_\gamma$ for all $\gamma < \beta$. Clearly, β must be a successor ordinal. Let A be any atom in $\mathcal{HB}_{\mathrm{P}}$ such that $\mathsf{A} \notin \mathrm{T}$ and $\mathsf{A} \in \widehat{\mathrm{J}}_\beta$. By Definitions 26 and 25, we have:

$$\begin{aligned}\widehat{\mathrm{J}}_\beta = {} & \mathbf{RC}_{\mathrm{P},\widehat{\mathrm{U}}_{\alpha-1}}(\widehat{\mathrm{J}}_{\beta-1}) \cup \mathbf{TC}_{\mathrm{P},\widehat{\mathrm{U}}_{\alpha-1}}(\widehat{\mathrm{J}}_{\beta-1}) \cup \\ & \mathbf{IC}^{t}(\widehat{\mathrm{J}}_{\beta-1}) \cup \mathbf{IC}^{c}_{\mathrm{P},\widehat{\mathrm{U}}_{\alpha-1}}(\widehat{\mathrm{J}}_{\beta-1}) \cup \mathbf{IC}^{i}_{\mathrm{P},\widehat{\mathrm{U}}_{\alpha-1}}(\widehat{\mathrm{J}}_{\beta-1})\end{aligned}$$

There are four cases to consider:

(1) $\mathsf{A} \in \mathbf{RC}_{\mathrm{P},\widehat{\mathrm{U}}_{\alpha-1}}(\widehat{\mathrm{J}}_{\beta-1})$
By Definition 22, there must exist a regular rule, $\mathsf{H} :- \mathsf{L}_1, \ldots, \mathsf{L}_n$, in *ground*(P), such that H matches A, and for all $\mathsf{L}_i, 1 \leq i \leq n$: (i) if L_i is a positive literal, then $val^{\mathbf{b}}_{\widehat{\mathrm{J}}_{\beta-1}}(\mathsf{L}_i) = \mathbf{t}$; and (ii) if L_i is a negative literal, then $val^{\mathbf{b}}_{\widehat{\mathrm{U}}_{\alpha-1}}(\mathsf{L}_i) = \mathbf{t}$. Next we show that for all $\mathsf{L}_i, 1 \leq i \leq n$, $\mathcal{V}^{\mathbf{b}}_{\mathcal{I}}(\mathsf{L}_i) = \mathbf{t}$. If L_i is a positive literal, since $\widehat{\mathrm{J}}_{\beta-1} \subseteq \mathrm{T}$ and $val^{\mathbf{b}}_{\widehat{\mathrm{J}}_{\beta-1}}(\mathsf{L}_i) = \mathbf{t}$, then it follows that $\mathcal{V}^{\mathbf{b}}_{\mathcal{J}}(\mathsf{L}_i) = \mathbf{t}$, by Lemma 2. Thus $\mathcal{V}^{\mathbf{b}}_{\mathcal{I}}(\mathsf{L}_i) = \mathbf{t}$ by Lemma 1. Note that $\widehat{\mathrm{U}}_\infty \subseteq \widehat{\mathrm{U}}_{\alpha-1}$ by Lemma 9. It follows that $\mathrm{T} \cup \mathrm{U} \subseteq \widehat{\mathrm{U}}_\infty \subseteq \widehat{\mathrm{U}}_{\alpha-1}$. Therefore, if L_i is a negative literal, since $val^{\mathbf{b}}_{\widehat{\mathrm{U}}_{\alpha-1}}(\mathsf{L}_i) = \mathbf{t}$, then it follows that $\mathcal{V}^{\mathbf{b}}_{\mathcal{K}}(\mathsf{L}_i) = \mathbf{t}$, by Lemma 2. Thus $\mathcal{V}^{\mathbf{b}}_{\mathcal{I}}(\mathsf{L}_i) = \mathbf{t}$ by Lemma 1. Because $\mathcal{I}$ satisfies P, it follows that $\mathcal{I}(\mathsf{A}) = \mathcal{V}^{\mathbf{h}}_{\mathcal{I}}(\mathsf{H}) = \mathbf{t}$. Thus $\mathsf{A} \in \mathrm{T}$, a contradiction.

(2) $\mathsf{A} \in \mathbf{TC}_{\mathrm{P},\widehat{\mathrm{U}}_{\alpha-1}}(\widehat{\mathrm{J}}_{\beta-1})$
It must be true that $\mathsf{A} = \mathsf{o}[\mathsf{m} \to \mathsf{v}]^{\mathsf{c}}_{\mathsf{code}}$. So, by Definition 24, $\mathsf{c}[\mathsf{m}] \overset{code}{\rightsquigarrow} \mathsf{o} \in \widehat{\mathrm{J}}_{\beta-1}$, $ec(\mathsf{o},\mathsf{m}) \notin \mathbf{IB}_{\mathrm{P}}(\widehat{\mathrm{U}}_{\alpha-1})$, $mc(\mathsf{c},\mathsf{m},\mathsf{o}) \notin \mathbf{IB}_{\mathrm{P}}(\widehat{\mathrm{U}}_{\alpha-1})$, and there is a template rule, $\mathsf{R} \equiv \mathsf{code(c)}\ \mathsf{@this}[\mathsf{m} \to \mathsf{v}]\ :-\ \mathsf{B}$, in *ground*(P) such that for every literal $\mathsf{L} \in \mathsf{B}_{\|\mathsf{o}}$: (i) if L is a positive literal then $val^{\mathbf{b}}_{\widehat{\mathrm{J}}_{\beta-1}}(\mathsf{L}) = \mathbf{t}$; and (ii) if L is a negative literal then $val^{\mathbf{b}}_{\widehat{\mathrm{U}}_{\alpha-1}}(\mathsf{L}) = \mathbf{t}$.

Because $\mathsf{c}[\mathsf{m}] \overset{code}{\rightsquigarrow} \mathsf{o} \in \widehat{\mathrm{J}}_{\beta-1}$, there must exist a successor ordinal $\rho \leq \beta-1 < \beta$, such that $\mathsf{c}[\mathsf{m}] \overset{code}{\rightsquigarrow} \mathsf{o} \in \widehat{\mathrm{J}}_{\rho}$. It follows that $\mathsf{c}[\mathsf{m}] \overset{code}{\rightsquigarrow} \mathsf{o} \in \mathbf{IC}^{c}_{\mathrm{P},\widehat{\mathrm{U}}_{\alpha-1}}(\widehat{\mathrm{J}}_{\rho-1})$. Thus $\mathsf{c} \neq \mathsf{o}$, $\mathsf{o}:\mathsf{c} \in \widehat{\mathrm{J}}_{\rho-1}$, and $ov(\mathsf{c},\mathsf{m},\mathsf{o}) \notin \mathbf{IB}_{\mathrm{P}}(\widehat{\mathrm{U}}_{\alpha-1})$, by Definition 25. Note that $\widehat{\mathrm{J}}_{\rho-1} \subseteq \mathrm{T}$ and $\mathrm{T} \cup \mathrm{U} \subseteq \widehat{\mathrm{U}}_{\infty} \subseteq \widehat{\mathrm{U}}_{\alpha-1}$. So, $\mathsf{o}:\mathsf{c} \in \mathrm{T}$ and $ov(\mathsf{c},\mathsf{m},\mathsf{o}) \notin \mathbf{IB}_{\mathrm{P}}(\mathrm{T} \cup \mathrm{U})$. Thus $\mathsf{c}[\mathsf{m}] \overset{s.code}{\rightsquigarrow}_{\mathcal{I}} \mathsf{o}$ by Lemma 4. Because $ec(\mathsf{o},\mathsf{m}) \notin \mathbf{IB}_{\mathrm{P}}(\widehat{\mathrm{U}}_{\alpha-1})$, it follows that $ec(\mathsf{o},\mathsf{m}) \notin \mathbf{IB}_{\mathrm{P}}(\mathrm{T} \cup \mathrm{U})$ by the monotonicity of $\mathbf{IB}_{\mathrm{P}}$. It follows that $\mathsf{o}[\mathsf{m}]$ is neither a strong nor a weak explicit definition in $\mathcal{I}$, by Definitions 23 and 4.
Next we show that there is no x such that $\mathsf{x} \neq \mathsf{c}$, $\mathsf{x}[\mathsf{m}] \rightsquigarrow_{\mathcal{I}} \mathsf{o}$. Suppose, to the contrary, that there is $\mathsf{x} \neq \mathsf{c}$ such that $\mathsf{x}[\mathsf{m}] \rightsquigarrow_{\mathcal{I}} \mathsf{o}$. Then $\mathsf{x} \neq \mathsf{o}$, $\mathsf{o}:\mathsf{x} \in \mathrm{T} \cup \mathrm{U}$, $\mathsf{x}[\mathsf{m} \to \mathsf{y}]_{\mathsf{ex}} \in \mathrm{T} \cup \mathrm{U}$ for some y or there is a template rule in *ground*(P) that specifies the instance method m for class c, and $ov(\mathsf{x},\mathsf{m},\mathsf{o}) \notin \mathbf{IB}_{\mathrm{P}}(\mathrm{T})$, by Lemma 4. Since $\mathrm{T} \cup \mathrm{U} \subseteq \widehat{\mathrm{U}}_{\infty} \subseteq \widehat{\mathrm{U}}_{\alpha-1}$ and $\mathrm{T} \supseteq \widehat{\mathrm{T}}_{\alpha-1}$, so $\mathsf{o}:\mathsf{x} \in \widehat{\mathrm{U}}_{\alpha-1}$, $\mathsf{x}[\mathsf{m} \to \mathsf{y}]_{\mathsf{ex}} \in \widehat{\mathrm{U}}_{\alpha-1}$ for some y or there is a template rule that specifies the instance method m for class c, and $ov(\mathsf{x},\mathsf{m},\mathsf{o}) \notin \mathbf{IB}_{\mathrm{P}}(\widehat{\mathrm{T}}_{\alpha-1})$. It follows that $\mathsf{x}[\mathsf{m}] \overset{val}{\rightsquigarrow} \mathsf{o} \in \mathbf{IC}^{c}_{\mathrm{P},\widehat{\mathrm{T}}_{\alpha-1}}(\widehat{\mathrm{U}}_{\alpha-1})$ or $\mathsf{x}[\mathsf{m}] \overset{code}{\rightsquigarrow} \mathsf{o} \in \mathbf{IC}^{c}_{\mathrm{P},\widehat{\mathrm{T}}_{\alpha-1}}(\widehat{\mathrm{U}}_{\alpha-1})$, by Definition 25. Thus $mc(\mathsf{c},\mathsf{m},\mathsf{o}) \in \mathbf{IB}_{\mathrm{P}}(\widehat{\mathrm{U}}_{\alpha-1})$, by Definition 23, which contradicts the fact that $mc(\mathsf{c},\mathsf{m},\mathsf{o}) \notin \mathbf{IB}_{\mathrm{P}}(\widehat{\mathrm{U}}_{\alpha-1})$.

So far we have shown that $\mathsf{o}[\mathsf{m}]$ is neither a strong nor a weak explicit definition in $\mathcal{I}$, $\mathsf{c}[\mathsf{m}] \overset{s.code}{\rightsquigarrow}_{\mathcal{I}} \mathsf{o}$, and there is no x such that $\mathsf{x} \neq \mathsf{c}$ and $\mathsf{x}[\mathsf{m}] \rightsquigarrow_{\mathcal{I}} \mathsf{o}$. Therefore, o strongly inherits R in $\mathcal{I}$, by Definition 16. So $imode_{\mathcal{I}}(\mathsf{R}_{\|\mathsf{o}}) = \mathbf{t}$. We already know that for every literal $\mathsf{L} \in \mathsf{B}_{\|\mathsf{o}}$: (i) if L is positive then $val^{\mathbf{b}}_{\widehat{\mathrm{J}}_{\beta-1}}(\mathsf{L}) = \mathbf{t}$; and (ii) if L is negative then $val^{\mathbf{b}}_{\widehat{\mathrm{U}}_{\alpha-1}}(\mathsf{L}) = \mathbf{t}$. Now we will show that for all $\mathsf{L} \in \mathsf{B}_{\|\mathsf{o}}$, $\mathcal{V}^{\mathbf{b}}_{\mathcal{I}}(\mathsf{L}) = \mathbf{t}$. If L is a positive literal, since $\widehat{\mathrm{J}}_{\beta-1} \subseteq \mathrm{T}$ and $val^{\mathbf{b}}_{\widehat{\mathrm{J}}_{\beta-1}}(\mathsf{L}) = \mathbf{t}$, then it follows that $\mathcal{V}^{\mathbf{b}}_{\mathcal{J}}(\mathsf{L}) = \mathbf{t}$, by Lemma 2. Thus $\mathcal{V}^{\mathbf{b}}_{\mathcal{I}}(\mathsf{L}) = \mathbf{t}$ by Lemma 1. Note that $\widehat{\mathrm{U}}_{\infty} \subseteq \widehat{\mathrm{U}}_{\alpha-1}$ by Lemma 9. It follows that $\mathrm{T} \cup \mathrm{U} \subseteq \widehat{\mathrm{U}}_{\infty} \subseteq \widehat{\mathrm{U}}_{\alpha-1}$. Therefore, if L is a negative literal, since $val^{\mathbf{b}}_{\widehat{\mathrm{U}}_{\alpha-1}}(\mathsf{L}) = \mathbf{t}$, then it follows that $\mathcal{V}^{\mathbf{b}}_{\mathcal{K}}(\mathsf{L}) = \mathbf{t}$, by Lemma 2. Thus $\mathcal{V}^{\mathbf{b}}_{\mathcal{I}}(\mathsf{L}) = \mathbf{t}$ by Lemma 1.

Therefore, $\mathcal{V}^{\mathbf{b}}_{\mathcal{I}}(\mathsf{L}) = \mathbf{t}$ for every literal $\mathsf{L} \in \mathsf{B}_{\|\mathsf{o}}$. It follows that $\mathcal{V}^{\mathbf{b}}_{\mathcal{I}}(\mathsf{B}_{\|\mathsf{o}}) = \mathbf{t}$. In the above we have shown that $imode_{\mathcal{I}}(\mathsf{R}_{\|\mathsf{o}}) = \mathbf{t}$. Since $\mathcal{I}$ is an object model of P, so $\mathcal{I}$ should satisfy $\mathsf{R}_{\|\mathsf{o}}$. Thus $\mathcal{I}(\mathsf{o}[\mathsf{m} \to \mathsf{v}]^{\mathsf{c}}_{\mathsf{code}}) = \mathbf{t}$, by Definition 18. It follows that $\mathsf{o}[\mathsf{m} \to \mathsf{v}]^{\mathsf{c}}_{\mathsf{code}} \in \mathrm{T}$, a contradiction.

(3) $\mathsf{A} \in \mathbf{IC}^{t}(\widehat{\mathrm{J}}_{\beta-1})$
If $\mathsf{A} = \mathsf{o}:\mathsf{c}$, then there exists x, such that $\mathsf{o}:\mathsf{x} \in \widehat{\mathrm{J}}_{\beta-1}$ and $\mathsf{x}::\mathsf{c} \in \widehat{\mathrm{J}}_{\beta-1}$, by Definition 25. Since $\widehat{\mathrm{J}}_{\beta-1} \subseteq \mathrm{T}$, it follows that $\mathsf{o}:\mathsf{x} \in \mathrm{T}$ and $\mathsf{x}::\mathsf{c} \in \mathrm{T}$. So $\mathcal{I}(\mathsf{o}:\mathsf{x}) = \mathbf{t}$ and $\mathcal{I}(\mathsf{x}::\mathsf{c}) = \mathbf{t}$. Because $\mathcal{I}$ is an object model of P and so satisfies

the positive ISA transitivity constraint, therefore $\mathcal{I}(\mathsf{o}:\mathsf{c}) = \mathbf{t}$ by Definition 10. It follows that $\mathsf{o}:\mathsf{c} \in \mathrm{T}$, a contradiction. Similarly, if $\mathsf{A} = \mathsf{s}::\mathsf{c}$, then we can also show that $\mathsf{s}::\mathsf{c} \in \mathrm{T}$, which is a contradiction.

(4) $\mathsf{A} \in \mathbf{IC}^{i}_{\mathrm{P},\widehat{\mathrm{U}}_{\alpha-1}}(\widehat{\mathrm{J}}_{\beta-1})$

It must be the case $\mathsf{A} = \mathsf{o}[\mathsf{m} \rightarrow \mathsf{v}]^{\mathsf{c}}_{\mathsf{val}}$. Thus, by Definition 25, $\mathsf{c}[\mathsf{m}] \overset{val}{\rightsquigarrow} \mathsf{o} \in \widehat{\mathrm{J}}_{\beta-1}$, $\mathsf{c}[\mathsf{m} \rightarrow \mathsf{v}]_{\mathsf{ex}} \in \widehat{\mathrm{J}}_{\beta-1}$, $ec(\mathsf{o},\mathsf{m}) \notin \mathbf{IB}_{\mathrm{P}}(\widehat{\mathrm{U}}_{\alpha-1})$, and $mc(\mathsf{c},\mathsf{m},\mathsf{o}) \notin \mathbf{IB}_{\mathrm{P}}(\widehat{\mathrm{U}}_{\alpha-1})$. Because $\mathsf{c}[\mathsf{m}] \overset{val}{\rightsquigarrow} \mathsf{o} \in \widehat{\mathrm{J}}_{\beta-1}$, there must exist a successor ordinal $\rho \leq \beta - 1 < \beta$, such that $\mathsf{c}[\mathsf{m}] \overset{val}{\rightsquigarrow} \mathsf{o} \in \widehat{\mathrm{J}}_{\rho}$. It follows that $\mathsf{c}[\mathsf{m}] \overset{val}{\rightsquigarrow} \mathsf{o} \in \mathbf{IC}^{c}_{\mathrm{P},\widehat{\mathrm{U}}_{\alpha-1}}(\widehat{\mathrm{J}}_{\rho-1})$. So, $\mathsf{c} \neq \mathsf{o}$, $\mathsf{o}:\mathsf{c} \in \widehat{\mathrm{J}}_{\rho-1}$, $\mathsf{c}[\mathsf{m} \rightarrow \mathsf{z}]_{\mathsf{ex}} \in \widehat{\mathrm{J}}_{\rho-1}$ for some z, and $ov(\mathsf{c},\mathsf{m},\mathsf{o}) \notin \mathbf{IB}_{\mathrm{P}}(\widehat{\mathrm{U}}_{\alpha-1})$, by Definition 25. Since $\widehat{\mathrm{J}}_{\rho-1} \subseteq \widehat{\mathrm{J}}_{\beta-1} \subseteq \mathrm{T}$ and $\mathrm{T} \cup \mathrm{U} \subseteq \widehat{\mathrm{U}}_{\infty} \subseteq \widehat{\mathrm{U}}_{\alpha-1}$, it follows that $\mathsf{o}:\mathsf{c} \in \mathrm{T}$, $\mathsf{c}[\mathsf{m} \rightarrow \mathsf{v}]_{\mathsf{ex}} \in \mathrm{T}$, and $ov(\mathsf{c},\mathsf{m},\mathsf{o}) \notin \mathbf{IB}_{\mathrm{P}}(\mathrm{T} \cup \mathrm{U})$. Thus $\mathsf{c}[\mathsf{m}] \overset{s.val}{\rightsquigarrow}_{\mathcal{I}} \mathsf{o}$ by Lemma 4. Because $ec(\mathsf{o},\mathsf{m}) \notin \mathbf{IB}_{\mathrm{P}}(\widehat{\mathrm{U}}_{\alpha-1})$, so $ec(\mathsf{o},\mathsf{m}) \notin \mathbf{IB}_{\mathrm{P}}(\mathrm{T} \cup \mathrm{U})$ by the monotonicity of $\mathbf{IB}_{\mathrm{P}}$. It follows that $\mathsf{o}[\mathsf{m}]$ is neither a strong nor a weak explicit definition in $\mathcal{I}$, by Definitions 23 and 4.

Next we show that there is no x such that $\mathsf{x} \neq \mathsf{c}$, $\mathsf{x}[\mathsf{m}] \rightsquigarrow_{\mathcal{I}} \mathsf{o}$. Suppose, to the contrary, that there is $\mathsf{x} \neq \mathsf{c}$ such that $\mathsf{x}[\mathsf{m}] \rightsquigarrow_{\mathcal{I}} \mathsf{o}$. Then $\mathsf{x} \neq \mathsf{o}$, $\mathsf{o}:\mathsf{x} \in \mathrm{T} \cup \mathrm{U}$, $\mathsf{x}[\mathsf{m} \rightarrow \mathsf{y}]_{\mathsf{ex}} \in \mathrm{T} \cup \mathrm{U}$ for some y or there is a template rule in $ground(\mathrm{P})$ which specifies the instance method m for class c, and $ov(\mathsf{x},\mathsf{m},\mathsf{o}) \notin \mathbf{IB}_{\mathrm{P}}(\mathrm{T})$, by Lemma 4. Since $\mathrm{T} \cup \mathrm{U} \subseteq \widehat{\mathrm{U}}_{\infty} \subseteq \widehat{\mathrm{U}}_{\alpha-1}$ and $\mathrm{T} \supseteq \widehat{\mathrm{T}}_{\alpha-1}$, it follows that $\mathsf{o}:\mathsf{x} \in \widehat{\mathrm{U}}_{\alpha-1}$, $\mathsf{x}[\mathsf{m} \rightarrow \mathsf{y}]_{\mathsf{ex}} \in \widehat{\mathrm{U}}_{\alpha-1}$ for some y or there is a template rule that specifies the instance method m for class c, and $ov(\mathsf{x},\mathsf{m},\mathsf{o}) \notin \mathbf{IB}_{\mathrm{P}}(\widehat{\mathrm{T}}_{\alpha-1})$. It follows that $\mathsf{x}[\mathsf{m}] \overset{val}{\rightsquigarrow} \mathsf{o} \in \mathbf{IC}^{c}_{\mathrm{P},\widehat{\mathrm{T}}_{\alpha-1}}(\widehat{\mathrm{U}}_{\alpha-1})$ or $\mathsf{x}[\mathsf{m}] \overset{code}{\rightsquigarrow} \mathsf{o} \in \mathbf{IC}^{c}_{\mathrm{P},\widehat{\mathrm{T}}_{\alpha-1}}(\widehat{\mathrm{U}}_{\alpha-1})$, by Definition 25. Therefore, $mc(\mathsf{c},\mathsf{m},\mathsf{o}) \in \mathbf{IB}_{\mathrm{P}}(\widehat{\mathrm{U}}_{\alpha-1})$, by Definition 23, which contradicts the fact that $mc(\mathsf{c},\mathsf{m},\mathsf{o}) \notin \mathbf{IB}_{\mathrm{P}}(\widehat{\mathrm{U}}_{\alpha-1})$.

So far we have shown that $\mathsf{o}[\mathsf{m}]$ is neither a strong nor a weak explicit definition in $\mathcal{I}$, $\mathsf{c}[\mathsf{m}] \overset{s.val}{\rightsquigarrow}_{\mathcal{I}} \mathsf{o}$, $\mathcal{I}(\mathsf{c}[\mathsf{m} \rightarrow \mathsf{v}]_{\mathsf{ex}}) = \mathbf{t}$, and there is no x such that $\mathsf{x} \neq \mathsf{c}$ and $\mathsf{x}[\mathsf{m}] \rightsquigarrow_{\mathcal{I}} \mathsf{o}$. Because $\mathcal{I}$ is an object model of P and so satisfies the unique source inheritance constraint, therefore $\mathsf{o}[\mathsf{m} \rightarrow \mathsf{v}]^{\mathsf{c}}_{\mathsf{val}} \in \mathrm{T}$ by Definition 12, a contradiction.

Therefore, if $\mathrm{T} \subset \widehat{\mathrm{T}}_{\infty}$, then we can derive a contradiction in all four possible cases. So it must be true that $\mathrm{T} = \widehat{\mathrm{T}}_{\infty}$. It remains to show that $\mathrm{T} \cup \mathrm{U} = \widehat{\mathrm{U}}_{\infty}$. We know that $\mathrm{T} \cup \mathrm{U} \subseteq \widehat{\mathrm{U}}_{\infty}$, because $\mathcal{I} \leq \mathcal{M}$. Therefore, if we can show that $\mathrm{T} \cup \mathrm{U} \supseteq \widehat{\mathrm{U}}_{\infty}$, then $\mathrm{T} \cup \mathrm{U} = \widehat{\mathrm{U}}_{\infty}$. By Definitions 32 and 27, $\widehat{\mathrm{U}}_{\infty} = \mathrm{lfp}(\mathbf{T}_{\mathrm{P},\widehat{\mathrm{T}}_{\infty}})$. Since $\mathbf{T}_{\mathrm{P},\widehat{\mathrm{T}}_{\infty}}$ is monotonic, the ordinal powers of $\mathbf{T}_{\mathrm{P},\widehat{\mathrm{T}}_{\infty}}$ is an increasing sequence. Denote $\widehat{\mathrm{K}}_{\gamma} = \mathbf{T}^{\gamma}_{\mathrm{P},\widehat{\mathrm{T}}_{\infty}}$ for all ordinal γ. We will prove by transfinite induction that $\mathrm{T} \cup \mathrm{U} \supseteq \widehat{\mathrm{K}}_{\alpha}$ for all ordinal α, thus complete the proof.

The case for a limit ordinal α is trivial. If $\alpha = 0$, then $\widehat{\mathrm{K}}_{0} = \emptyset \subseteq \mathrm{T} \cup \mathrm{U}$. If $\alpha \neq 0$, then $\widehat{\mathrm{K}}_{\alpha} = \bigcup_{\beta<\alpha} \widehat{\mathrm{K}}_{\beta}$. By the induction hypothesis we know that $\mathrm{T} \cup \mathrm{U} \supseteq \widehat{\mathrm{K}}_{\beta}$ for all $\beta < \alpha$. So $\mathrm{T} \cup \mathrm{U} \supseteq \widehat{\mathrm{K}}_{\alpha}$.

Let α be a successor ordinal and A any atom in $\mathcal{HB}_{\mathrm{P}}$ such that $\mathsf{A} \in \widehat{\mathrm{K}}_\alpha$. We will show $\mathsf{A} \in \mathrm{T} \cup \mathrm{U}$. By Definitions 26 and 25, we have:

$$\begin{aligned}\widehat{\mathrm{K}}_\alpha &= \mathbf{RC}_{\mathrm{P},\widehat{\mathrm{T}}_\infty}(\widehat{\mathrm{K}}_{\alpha-1}) \cup \mathbf{TC}_{\mathrm{P},\widehat{\mathrm{T}}_\infty}(\widehat{\mathrm{K}}_{\alpha-1}) \cup \\ &\quad \mathbf{IC}^t(\widehat{\mathrm{K}}_{\alpha-1}) \cup \mathbf{IC}^c_{\mathrm{P},\widehat{\mathrm{T}}_\infty}(\widehat{\mathrm{K}}_{\alpha-1}) \cup \mathbf{IC}^i_{\mathrm{P},\widehat{\mathrm{T}}_\infty}(\widehat{\mathrm{K}}_{\alpha-1})\end{aligned}$$

There are four cases to consider:

(1) $\mathsf{A} \in \mathbf{RC}_{\mathrm{P},\widehat{\mathrm{T}}_\infty}(\widehat{\mathrm{K}}_{\alpha-1})$
By Definition 22, there must exist a regular rule, $\mathsf{H} \text{ :- } \mathsf{L}_1, \ldots, \mathsf{L}_n$, in *ground*(P), such that H matches A, and for all $\mathsf{L}_i, 1 \leq i \leq n$: (i) if L_i is a positive literal, then $val^{\mathbf{b}}_{\widehat{\mathrm{K}}_{\alpha-1}}(\mathsf{L}_i) = \mathbf{t}$; and (ii) if L_i is a negative literal, then $val^{\mathbf{b}}_{\widehat{\mathrm{T}}_\infty}(\mathsf{L}_i) = \mathbf{t}$. Next we show that for all $\mathsf{L}_i, 1 \leq i \leq n$, $\mathcal{V}^{\mathbf{b}}_{\mathcal{I}}(\mathsf{L}_i) \geq \mathbf{u}$. If L_i is a positive literal, since $\widehat{\mathrm{K}}_{\alpha-1} \subseteq \mathrm{T} \cup \mathrm{U}$ by the induction hypothesis and $val^{\mathbf{b}}_{\widehat{\mathrm{K}}_{\alpha-1}}(\mathsf{L}_i) = \mathbf{t}$, then it follows that $\mathcal{V}^{\mathbf{b}}_{\mathcal{K}}(\mathsf{L}_i) = \mathbf{t}$, by Lemma 2. Thus $\mathcal{V}^{\mathbf{b}}_{\mathcal{I}}(\mathsf{L}_i) \geq \mathbf{u}$ by Lemma 1. We have proved that $\mathrm{T} = \widehat{\mathrm{T}}_\infty$. Therefore, if L_i is a negative literal, then $\mathcal{V}^{\mathbf{b}}_{\mathcal{J}}(\mathsf{L}_i) = \mathcal{V}^{\mathbf{b}}_{\widehat{\mathrm{T}}_\infty}(\mathsf{L}_i) = \mathbf{t}$. Thus $\mathcal{V}^{\mathbf{b}}_{\mathcal{I}}(\mathsf{L}_i) \geq \mathbf{u}$ by Lemma 1. Because $\mathcal{I}$ satisfies P, so $\mathcal{I}(\mathsf{A}) = \mathcal{V}^{\mathbf{h}}_{\mathcal{I}}(\mathsf{H}) \geq \mathbf{u}$. Thus $\mathsf{A} \in \mathrm{T} \cup \mathrm{U}$.

(2) $\mathsf{A} \in \mathbf{TC}_{\mathrm{P},\widehat{\mathrm{T}}_\infty}(\widehat{\mathrm{K}}_{\alpha-1})$
It must be true that $\mathsf{A} = \mathsf{o}[\mathsf{m} \to \mathsf{v}]^{\mathsf{c}}_{\mathsf{code}}$. So, by Definition 24, $\mathsf{c}[\mathsf{m}] \overset{code}{\leadsto} \mathsf{o} \in \widehat{\mathrm{K}}_{\alpha-1}$, $ec(\mathsf{o},\mathsf{m}) \notin \mathbf{IB}_{\mathrm{P}}(\widehat{\mathrm{T}}_\infty)$, $mc(\mathsf{c},\mathsf{m},\mathsf{o}) \notin \mathbf{IB}_{\mathrm{P}}(\widehat{\mathrm{T}}_\infty)$, and *ground*(P) has a template rule, $\mathsf{R} \equiv \mathsf{code(c)}\ \mathsf{@this}[\mathsf{m} \to \mathsf{v}] \text{ :- } \mathsf{B}$, such that for every literal $\mathsf{L} \in \mathsf{B}_{\|\mathsf{o}}$: (i) if L is a positive literal then $val^{\mathbf{b}}_{\widehat{\mathrm{K}}_{\alpha-1}}(\mathsf{L}) = \mathbf{t}$; and (ii) if L is a negative literal then $val^{\mathbf{b}}_{\widehat{\mathrm{T}}_\infty}(\mathsf{L}) = \mathbf{t}$.

Because $\mathsf{c}[\mathsf{m}] \overset{val}{\leadsto} \mathsf{o} \in \widehat{\mathrm{K}}_{\alpha-1}$, there must exist a successor ordinal $\rho \leq \alpha - 1 < \alpha$, such that $\mathsf{c}[\mathsf{m}] \overset{val}{\leadsto} \mathsf{o} \in \widehat{\mathrm{K}}_\rho$. It follows that $\mathsf{c}[\mathsf{m}] \overset{val}{\leadsto} \mathsf{o} \in \mathbf{IC}^c_{\mathrm{P},\widehat{\mathrm{T}}_\infty}(\widehat{\mathrm{K}}_{\rho-1})$. Therefore, $\mathsf{c} \neq \mathsf{o}$, $\mathsf{o}:\mathsf{c} \in \widehat{\mathrm{K}}_{\rho-1}$, and $ov(\mathsf{c},\mathsf{m},\mathsf{o}) \notin \mathbf{IB}_{\mathrm{P}}(\widehat{\mathrm{T}}_\infty)$, by Definition 25. Note that $\widehat{\mathrm{K}}_{\rho-1} \subseteq \mathrm{T} \cup \mathrm{U}$, by the induction hypothesis. We have proved that $\mathrm{T} = \widehat{\mathrm{T}}_\infty$. It follows that $\mathsf{o}:\mathsf{c} \in \mathrm{T} \cup \mathrm{U}$ and $ov(\mathsf{c},\mathsf{m},\mathsf{o}) \notin \mathbf{IB}_{\mathrm{P}}(\mathrm{T})$. Therefore $\mathsf{c}[\mathsf{m}] \overset{s.code}{\leadsto}_{\mathcal{I}} \mathsf{o}$ or $\mathsf{c}[\mathsf{m}] \overset{w.code}{\leadsto}_{\mathcal{I}} \mathsf{o}$, by Lemma 4. Because $ec(\mathsf{o},\mathsf{m}) \notin \mathbf{IB}_{\mathrm{P}}(\widehat{\mathrm{T}}_\infty)$, so $ec(\mathsf{o},\mathsf{m}) \notin \mathbf{IB}_{\mathrm{P}}(\mathrm{T})$. Thus $\mathsf{o}[\mathsf{m}]$ is not a strong explicit definition, by Definitions 23 and 4. Because $\mathsf{c}[\mathsf{m} \to \mathsf{v}]_{\mathsf{ex}} \in \widehat{\mathrm{K}}_{\alpha-1} \subseteq \mathrm{T} \cup \mathrm{U}$, it follows that $\mathcal{I}(\mathsf{c}[\mathsf{m} \to \mathsf{v}]_{\mathsf{ex}}) \geq \mathbf{u}$.

Next we show that there is no $\mathsf{x} \neq \mathsf{c}$ such that $\mathsf{x}[\mathsf{m}] \overset{s.val}{\leadsto}_{\mathcal{I}} \mathsf{o}$ or $\mathsf{x}[\mathsf{m}] \overset{s.code}{\leadsto}_{\mathcal{I}} \mathsf{o}$. Suppose, to the contrary, that there exists $\mathsf{x} \neq \mathsf{c}$ such that $\mathsf{x}[\mathsf{m}] \overset{s.val}{\leadsto}_{\mathcal{I}} \mathsf{o}$ or $\mathsf{x}[\mathsf{m}] \overset{s.code}{\leadsto}_{\mathcal{I}} \mathsf{o}$. Then $\mathsf{x}[\mathsf{m}] \overset{s.val}{\leadsto}_{\mathcal{M}} \mathsf{o}$ or $\mathsf{x}[\mathsf{m}] \overset{s.code}{\leadsto}_{\mathcal{M}} \mathsf{o}$, because $\mathcal{I} \leq \mathcal{M}$. Thus $\mathsf{x}[\mathsf{m}] \overset{val}{\leadsto} \mathsf{o} \in \widehat{\mathrm{T}}_\infty$ or $\mathsf{x}[\mathsf{m}] \overset{code}{\leadsto} \mathsf{o} \in \widehat{\mathrm{T}}_\infty$, by Lemma 12. Thus $mc(\mathsf{c},\mathsf{m},\mathsf{o}) \in \mathbf{IB}_{\mathrm{P}}(\widehat{\mathrm{T}}_\infty)$ by Definition 23, which contradicts the fact that $mc(\mathsf{c},\mathsf{m},\mathsf{o}) \notin \mathbf{IB}_{\mathrm{P}}(\widehat{\mathrm{T}}_\infty)$.

So far we have shown that $\mathsf{c}[\mathsf{m}] \overset{s.code}{\leadsto}_{\mathcal{I}} \mathsf{o}$ or $\mathsf{c}[\mathsf{m}] \overset{w.code}{\leadsto}_{\mathcal{I}} \mathsf{o}$, $\mathsf{o}[\mathsf{m}]$ is not a strong explicit definition, and there is no $\mathsf{x} \neq \mathsf{c}$ such that $\mathsf{x}[\mathsf{m}] \overset{s.val}{\leadsto}_{\mathcal{I}} \mathsf{o}$ or $\mathsf{x}[\mathsf{m}] \overset{s.code}{\leadsto}_{\mathcal{I}} \mathsf{o}$. Therefore, o must either strongly or weakly inherit R in $\mathcal{I}$, by Definitions 16 and 16. So $imode_{\mathcal{I}}(\mathsf{R}_{\|\mathsf{o}}) \geq \mathbf{u}$. We already know that for every literal $\mathsf{L} \in \mathsf{B}_{\|\mathsf{o}}$:

(i) if L is a positive literal then $val^{\mathbf{b}}_{\widehat{\mathrm{K}}_{\alpha-1}}(\mathsf{L}) = \mathbf{t}$; and (ii) if L is a negative literal then $val^{\mathbf{b}}_{\widehat{\mathrm{T}}_\infty}(\mathsf{L}) = \mathbf{t}$. Now we show that for all $\mathsf{L}_i, 1 \le i \le n, \mathcal{V}^{\mathbf{b}}_{\mathcal{I}}(\mathsf{L}_i) \ge \mathbf{u}$. If L_i is a positive literal, since $\widehat{\mathrm{K}}_{\alpha-1} \subseteq \mathrm{T} \cup \mathrm{U}$ by the induction hypothesis and $val^{\mathbf{b}}_{\widehat{\mathrm{K}}_{\alpha-1}}(\mathsf{L}_i) = \mathbf{t}$, then it follows that $\mathcal{V}^{\mathbf{b}}_{\mathcal{K}}(\mathsf{L}_i) = \mathbf{t}$, by Lemma 2. Thus $\mathcal{V}^{\mathbf{b}}_{\mathcal{I}}(\mathsf{L}_i) \ge \mathbf{u}$ by Lemma 1. Note that $\mathrm{T} = \widehat{\mathrm{T}}_\infty$. Therefore, if L_i is a negative literal, then $\mathcal{V}^{\mathbf{b}}_{\mathcal{J}}(\mathsf{L}_i) = \mathcal{V}^{\mathbf{b}}_{\widehat{\mathrm{T}}_\infty}(\mathsf{L}_i) = \mathbf{t}$. Thus $\mathcal{V}^{\mathbf{b}}_{\mathcal{I}}(\mathsf{L}_i) \ge \mathbf{u}$ by Lemma 1. Therefore, $\mathcal{V}^{\mathbf{b}}_{\mathcal{I}}(\mathsf{L}) \ge \mathbf{u}$ for every literal $\mathsf{L} \in \mathsf{B}_{\|\mathsf{o}}$. It follows that $\mathcal{V}^{\mathbf{b}}_{\mathcal{I}}(\mathsf{B}_{\|\mathsf{o}}) \ge \mathbf{u}$. Moreover, $imode_{\mathcal{I}}(\mathsf{R}_{\|\mathsf{o}}) \ge \mathbf{u}$. Because $\mathcal{I}$ is an object model of P, so $\mathcal{I}$ should satisfy $\mathsf{R}_{\|\mathsf{o}}$. It follows that $\mathcal{I}(\mathsf{o}[\mathsf{m} \to \mathsf{v}]^{\mathsf{c}}_{\mathrm{code}}) \ge \mathbf{u}$, by Definition 18. Thus $\mathsf{o}[\mathsf{m} \to \mathsf{v}]^{\mathsf{c}}_{\mathrm{code}} \in \mathrm{T} \cup \mathrm{U}$.

(3) $\mathsf{A} \in \mathbf{IC}^t(\widehat{\mathrm{K}}_{\alpha-1})$

If $\mathsf{A} = \mathsf{o}:\mathsf{c}$, then there exists x such that $\mathsf{o}:\mathsf{x} \in \widehat{\mathrm{K}}_{\alpha-1}$ and $\mathsf{x}::\mathsf{c} \in \widehat{\mathrm{K}}_{\alpha-1}$, by Definition 25. Since $\widehat{\mathrm{K}}_{\alpha-1} \subseteq \mathrm{T} \cup \mathrm{U}$ by the induction hypothesis, it follows that $\mathsf{o}:\mathsf{x} \in \mathrm{T}\cup\mathrm{U}$ and $\mathsf{x}::\mathsf{c} \in \mathrm{T}\cup\mathrm{U}$. So $\mathcal{I}(\mathsf{o}:\mathsf{x}) \ge \mathbf{u}$ and $\mathcal{I}(\mathsf{x}::\mathsf{c}) \ge \mathbf{u}$. Because $\mathcal{I}$ satisfies the cautious ISA transitivity constraint, therefore $\mathcal{I}(\mathsf{o}:\mathsf{c}) \ge \mathbf{u}$ by Definitions 13 and 10. It follows that $\mathsf{o}:\mathsf{c} \in \mathrm{T}\cup\mathrm{U}$. Similarly, if $\mathsf{A} = \mathsf{s}::\mathsf{c}$, then we can also show that $\mathsf{s}::\mathsf{c} \in \mathrm{T}\cup\mathrm{U}$.

(4) $\mathsf{A} \in \mathbf{IC}^i_{\mathrm{P},\widehat{\mathrm{T}}_\infty}(\widehat{\mathrm{K}}_{\alpha-1})$

It must be the case that $\mathsf{A} = \mathsf{o}[\mathsf{m} \to \mathsf{v}]^{\mathsf{c}}_{\mathrm{val}}$. It follows that $\mathsf{c}[\mathsf{m}] \overset{val}{\leadsto} \mathsf{o} \in \widehat{\mathrm{K}}_{\alpha-1}$, $\mathsf{c}[\mathsf{m} \to \mathsf{v}]_{\mathrm{ex}} \in \widehat{\mathrm{K}}_{\alpha-1}$, $ec(\mathsf{o},\mathsf{m}) \notin \mathbf{IB}_{\mathrm{P}}(\widehat{\mathrm{T}}_\infty)$, and $mc(\mathsf{c},\mathsf{m},\mathsf{o}) \notin \mathbf{IB}_{\mathrm{P}}(\widehat{\mathrm{T}}_\infty)$, by Definition 25. Because $\mathsf{c}[\mathsf{m}] \overset{val}{\leadsto} \mathsf{o} \in \widehat{\mathrm{K}}_{\alpha-1}$, so there must exist a successor ordinal $\rho \le \alpha - 1 < \alpha$, such that $\mathsf{c}[\mathsf{m}] \overset{val}{\leadsto} \mathsf{o} \in \widehat{\mathrm{K}}_\rho$. Thus $\mathsf{c}[\mathsf{m}] \overset{val}{\leadsto} \mathsf{o} \in \mathbf{IC}^c_{\mathrm{P},\widehat{\mathrm{T}}_\infty}(\widehat{\mathrm{K}}_{\rho-1})$. Therefore, by Definition 25, $\mathsf{c} \ne \mathsf{o}$, $\mathsf{o}:\mathsf{c} \in \widehat{\mathrm{K}}_{\rho-1}$, $\mathsf{c}[\mathsf{m} \to \mathsf{z}]_{\mathrm{ex}} \in \widehat{\mathrm{K}}_{\rho-1}$ for some z, and $ov(\mathsf{c},\mathsf{m},\mathsf{o}) \notin \mathbf{IB}_{\mathrm{P}}(\widehat{\mathrm{T}}_\infty)$. Since $\widehat{\mathrm{K}}_{\rho-1} \subseteq \widehat{\mathrm{K}}_{\alpha-1} \subseteq \mathrm{T}\cup\mathrm{U}$ by the induction hypothesis and $\mathrm{T} = \widehat{\mathrm{T}}_\infty$, it follows that $\mathsf{o}:\mathsf{c} \in \mathrm{T}\cup\mathrm{U}$, $\mathsf{c}[\mathsf{m} \to \mathsf{v}]_{\mathrm{ex}} \in \mathrm{T}\cup\mathrm{U}$, and $ov(\mathsf{c},\mathsf{m},\mathsf{o}) \notin \mathbf{IB}_{\mathrm{P}}(\mathrm{T})$. Thus $\mathsf{c}[\mathsf{m}] \overset{s.val}{\leadsto}_{\mathcal{I}} \mathsf{o}$ or $\mathsf{c}[\mathsf{m}] \overset{w.val}{\leadsto}_{\mathcal{I}} \mathsf{o}$ by Lemma 4. Because $ec(\mathsf{o},\mathsf{m}) \notin \mathbf{IB}_{\mathrm{P}}(\widehat{\mathrm{T}}_\infty)$, it follows that $ec(\mathsf{o},\mathsf{m}) \notin \mathbf{IB}_{\mathrm{P}}(\mathrm{T})$, and so $\mathsf{o}[\mathsf{m}]$ is not a strong explicit definition, by Definitions 23 and 4. Because $\mathsf{c}[\mathsf{m} \to \mathsf{v}]_{\mathrm{ex}} \in \mathrm{T}\cup\mathrm{U}$, it follows that $\mathcal{I}(\mathsf{c}[\mathsf{m} \to \mathsf{v}]_{\mathrm{ex}}) \ge \mathbf{u}$.

Now we show that there is no $\mathsf{x} \ne \mathsf{c}$ such that $\mathsf{x}[\mathsf{m}] \overset{s.val}{\leadsto}_{\mathcal{I}} \mathsf{o}$ or $\mathsf{x}[\mathsf{m}] \overset{s.code}{\leadsto}_{\mathcal{I}} \mathsf{o}$. Suppose, to the contrary, that there exists $\mathsf{x} \ne \mathsf{c}$ such that $\mathsf{x}[\mathsf{m}] \overset{s.val}{\leadsto}_{\mathcal{I}} \mathsf{o}$ or $\mathsf{x}[\mathsf{m}] \overset{s.code}{\leadsto}_{\mathcal{I}} \mathsf{o}$. Then $\mathsf{x}[\mathsf{m}] \overset{s.val}{\leadsto}_{\mathcal{M}} \mathsf{o}$ or $\mathsf{x}[\mathsf{m}] \overset{s.code}{\leadsto}_{\mathcal{M}} \mathsf{o}$, because $\mathcal{I} \le \mathcal{M}$. It follows that $\mathsf{x}[\mathsf{m}] \overset{val}{\leadsto} \mathsf{o} \in \widehat{\mathrm{T}}_\infty$ or $\mathsf{x}[\mathsf{m}] \overset{code}{\leadsto} \mathsf{o} \in \widehat{\mathrm{T}}_\infty$, by Lemma 12. Thus $mc(\mathsf{c},\mathsf{m},\mathsf{o}) \in \mathbf{IB}_{\mathrm{P}}(\widehat{\mathrm{T}}_\infty)$ by Definition 23, which contradicts the fact that $mc(\mathsf{c},\mathsf{m},\mathsf{o}) \notin \mathbf{IB}_{\mathrm{P}}(\widehat{\mathrm{T}}_\infty)$.

So far we have shown that $\mathsf{o}[\mathsf{m}]$ is not a strong explicit definition, $\mathsf{c}[\mathsf{m}] \overset{s.val}{\leadsto}_{\mathcal{I}} \mathsf{o}$ or $\mathsf{c}[\mathsf{m}] \overset{w.val}{\leadsto}_{\mathcal{I}} \mathsf{o}$, $\mathcal{I}(\mathsf{c}[\mathsf{m} \to \mathsf{v}]_{\mathrm{ex}}) \ge \mathbf{u}$, and there is no $\mathsf{x} \ne \mathsf{c}$ such that $\mathsf{x}[\mathsf{m}] \overset{s.val}{\leadsto}_{\mathcal{I}} \mathsf{o}$ or $\mathsf{x}[\mathsf{m}] \overset{s.code}{\leadsto}_{\mathcal{I}} \mathsf{o}$. Because $\mathcal{I}$ satisfies the cautious inheritance constraint, therefore $\mathcal{I}(\mathsf{o}[\mathsf{m} \to \mathsf{v}]^{\mathsf{c}}_{\mathrm{val}}) \ge \mathbf{u}$, by Definition 14. So $\mathsf{o}[\mathsf{m} \to \mathsf{v}]^{\mathsf{c}}_{\mathrm{val}} \in \mathrm{T}\cup\mathrm{U}$.

We have shown that in all four possible cases, if $\mathsf{A} \in \widehat{\mathrm{K}}_\alpha$, then $\mathsf{A} \in \mathrm{T}\cup\mathrm{U}$. It follows that $\mathrm{T}\cup\mathrm{U} \supseteq \widehat{\mathrm{K}}_\alpha$. This completes the induction step.

A.3 Lemmas and Propositions Supporting Theorem 6 in Section 10

Lemma 17. *Let* P^{wf} *be the well-founded rewriting of an F-logic KB* P *and* I^{wf} *be a subset of* $\mathcal{HB}_{\mathrm{P}^{wf}}$. *Then* $lfp(\mathbf{C}_{\mathrm{P}^{wf},\mathrm{I}^{wf}})$ *is in normal form.*

Lemma 18. *Let* P^{wf} *be the well-founded rewriting of an F-logic KB* P, $\widehat{\mathrm{I}}$ *a subset of* $\widehat{\mathcal{HB}}_{\mathrm{P}}$, I^{wf} *a subset of* $\mathcal{HB}_{\mathrm{P}^{wf}}$ *which is isomorphic to* $\widehat{\mathrm{I}}$ *and is in normal form, and* G *a ground positive literal. Then* $val^{\mathbf{b}}_{\widehat{\mathrm{I}}}(\neg\,\mathsf{G}) = \mathbf{t}$ *iff* $\rho^b(\mathsf{G}) \notin \mathrm{I}^{wf}$.

Proposition 8. *Let* P^{wf} *be the well-founded rewriting of an F-logic KB* P, I^{wf} *a subset of* $\mathcal{HB}_{\mathrm{P}^{wf}}$ *which is in normal form, and* $\widehat{\mathrm{I}}$ *a subset of* $\widehat{\mathcal{HB}}_{\mathrm{P}}$. *If* I^{wf} *is isomorphic to* $\widehat{\mathrm{I}}$, *then* $lfp(\mathbf{C}_{\mathrm{P}^{wf},\mathrm{I}^{wf}})$ *is isomorphic to* $lfp(\mathbf{T}_{\mathrm{P},\widehat{\mathrm{I}}})$.

Proof. Let $\mathrm{J}^{wf} = \mathrm{lfp}(\mathbf{C}_{\mathrm{P}^{wf},\mathrm{I}^{wf}})$ and $\widehat{\mathrm{J}} = \mathrm{lfp}(\mathbf{T}_{\mathrm{P},\widehat{\mathrm{I}}})$. First we will show that all of the following conditions are true:

(1) for all o,c: $isa(\mathsf{o},\mathsf{c}) \in \mathrm{J}^{wf}$ iff $\mathsf{o}\!:\!\mathsf{c} \in \widehat{\mathrm{J}}$
(2) for all s,c: $sub(\mathsf{s},\mathsf{c}) \in \mathrm{J}^{wf}$ iff $\mathsf{s}::\mathsf{c} \in \widehat{\mathrm{J}}$
(3) for all $\mathsf{s},\mathsf{m},\mathsf{v}$: $exmv(\mathsf{s},\mathsf{m},\mathsf{v}) \in \mathrm{J}^{wf}$ iff $\mathsf{s}[\mathsf{m} \to \mathsf{v}]_{\mathsf{ex}} \in \widehat{\mathrm{J}}$
(4) for all $\mathsf{o},\mathsf{m},\mathsf{v},\mathsf{c}$: $vamv(\mathsf{o},\mathsf{m},\mathsf{v},\mathsf{c}) \in \mathrm{J}^{wf}$ iff $\mathsf{o}[\mathsf{m} \to \mathsf{v}]^{\mathsf{c}}_{\mathsf{val}} \in \widehat{\mathrm{J}}$
(5) for all $\mathsf{o},\mathsf{m},\mathsf{v},\mathsf{c}$: $comv(\mathsf{o},\mathsf{m},\mathsf{v},\mathsf{c}) \in \mathrm{J}^{wf}$ iff $\mathsf{o}[\mathsf{m} \to \mathsf{v}]^{\mathsf{c}}_{\mathsf{code}} \in \widehat{\mathrm{J}}$
(6) for all $\mathsf{c},\mathsf{m},\mathsf{o}$: $vacan(\mathsf{c},\mathsf{m},\mathsf{o}) \in \mathrm{J}^{wf}$ iff $\mathsf{c}[\mathsf{m}] \overset{val}{\leadsto} \mathsf{o} \in \widehat{\mathrm{J}}$
(7) for all $\mathsf{c},\mathsf{m},\mathsf{o}$: $cocan(\mathsf{c},\mathsf{m},\mathsf{o}) \in \mathrm{J}^{wf}$ iff $\mathsf{c}[\mathsf{m}] \overset{code}{\leadsto} \mathsf{o} \in \widehat{\mathrm{J}}$

I. $\Rightarrow$

Let us define:

$\mathrm{S}^{wf}_0 = \emptyset$	$\widehat{\mathrm{S}}_0 = \emptyset$	for limit ordinal 0
$\mathrm{S}^{wf}_\alpha = \mathbf{C}_{\mathrm{P}^{wf},\mathrm{I}^{wf}}(\mathrm{S}^{wf}_{\alpha-1})$	$\widehat{\mathrm{S}}_\alpha = \mathbf{T}_{\mathrm{P},\widehat{\mathrm{I}}}(\widehat{\mathrm{S}}_{\alpha-1})$	for successor ordinal α
$\mathrm{S}^{wf}_\alpha = \bigcup_{\beta<\alpha} \mathrm{S}^{wf}_\beta$	$\widehat{\mathrm{S}}_\alpha = \bigcup_{\beta<\alpha} \widehat{\mathrm{S}}_\beta$	for limit ordinal $\alpha \neq 0$
$\mathrm{S}^{wf}_\infty = \bigcup_{\alpha} \mathrm{S}^{wf}_\alpha$	$\widehat{\mathrm{S}}_\infty = \bigcup_{\alpha} \widehat{\mathrm{S}}_\alpha$	

Then $\mathrm{S}^{wf}_\infty = \mathrm{lfp}(\mathbf{C}_{\mathrm{P}^{wf},\mathrm{I}^{wf}})$ and $\widehat{\mathrm{S}}_\infty = \mathrm{lfp}(\mathbf{T}_{\mathrm{P},\widehat{\mathrm{I}}})$. We will prove by transfinite induction that for any ordinal α and for all $\mathsf{o},\mathsf{s},\mathsf{c},\mathsf{m},\mathsf{v}$, the following conditions are true:

(1) if $isa(\mathsf{o},\mathsf{c}) \in \mathrm{S}^{wf}_\alpha$ then $\mathsf{o}\!:\!\mathsf{c} \in \widehat{\mathrm{S}}_\alpha$
(2) if $sub(\mathsf{s},\mathsf{c}) \in \mathrm{S}^{wf}_\alpha$ then $\mathsf{s}::\mathsf{c} \in \widehat{\mathrm{S}}_\alpha$
(3) if $exmv(\mathsf{s},\mathsf{m},\mathsf{v}) \in \mathrm{S}^{wf}_\alpha$ then $\mathsf{s}[\mathsf{m} \to \mathsf{v}]_{\mathsf{ex}} \in \widehat{\mathrm{S}}_\alpha$
(4) if $vamv(\mathsf{o},\mathsf{m},\mathsf{v},\mathsf{c}) \in \mathrm{S}^{wf}_\alpha$ then $\mathsf{o}[\mathsf{m} \to \mathsf{v}]^{\mathsf{c}}_{\mathsf{val}} \in \widehat{\mathrm{S}}_\alpha$
(5) if $comv(\mathsf{o},\mathsf{m},\mathsf{v},\mathsf{c}) \in \mathrm{S}^{wf}_\alpha$ then $\mathsf{o}[\mathsf{m} \to \mathsf{v}]^{\mathsf{c}}_{\mathsf{code}} \in \widehat{\mathrm{S}}_\alpha$
(6) if $vacan(\mathsf{c},\mathsf{m},\mathsf{o}) \in \mathrm{S}^{wf}_\alpha$ then $\mathsf{c}[\mathsf{m}] \overset{val}{\leadsto} \mathsf{o} \in \widehat{\mathrm{S}}_\alpha$
(7) if $cocan(\mathsf{c},\mathsf{m},\mathsf{o}) \in \mathrm{S}^{wf}_\alpha$ then $\mathsf{c}[\mathsf{m}] \overset{code}{\leadsto} \mathsf{o} \in \widehat{\mathrm{S}}_\alpha$

The case for a limit ordinal α is trivial. Now let α be a successor ordinal. So $S^{wf}_{\alpha} = \mathbf{C}_{P^{wf},I^{wf}}(S^{wf}_{\alpha-1})$. First we show that for any ground positive literal L, if $\rho^b(\mathsf{L}) \in S^{wf}_{\alpha-1}$, then $val^{\mathbf{b}}_{\widehat{S}_{\alpha-1}}(\mathsf{L}) = \mathbf{t}$: (i) If $\mathsf{L} = \mathsf{o}:\mathsf{c}$, then $\rho^b(\mathsf{L}) = isa(\mathsf{o},\mathsf{c})$. It follows that $\mathsf{o}:\mathsf{c} \in \widehat{S}_{\alpha-1}$ by the induction hypothesis. Thus $val^{\mathbf{b}}_{\widehat{S}_{\alpha-1}}(\mathsf{o}:\mathsf{c}) = \mathbf{t}$; (ii) Similarly, we can show if $\rho^b(\mathsf{L}) = sub(\mathsf{s},\mathsf{c}) \in S^{wf}_{\alpha-1}$, then $val^{\mathbf{b}}_{\widehat{S}_{\alpha-1}}(\mathsf{s}::\mathsf{c}) = \mathbf{t}$; (iii) If $\mathsf{L} = \mathsf{o}[\mathsf{m} \rightarrow \mathsf{v}]$, then $\rho^b(\mathsf{L}) = mv(\mathsf{o},\mathsf{m},\mathsf{v})$. Note that $S^{wf}_{\gamma} \subseteq S^{wf}_{\alpha-1}$ for all $\gamma \leq \alpha - 1$. Therefore, there must exist a successor ordinal $\rho \leq \alpha - 1$ such that $mv(\mathsf{s},\mathsf{m},\mathsf{v}) \in S^{wf}_{\rho} = \mathbf{C}_{P^{wf},I^{wf}}(S^{wf}_{\rho-1})$. It follows that $exmv(\mathsf{o},\mathsf{m},\mathsf{v}) \in S^{wf}_{\rho-1}$, or there is c such that $vamv(\mathsf{o},\mathsf{m},\mathsf{v},\mathsf{c}) \in S^{wf}_{\rho-1}$ or $comv(\mathsf{o},\mathsf{m},\mathsf{v},\mathsf{c}) \in S^{wf}_{\rho-1}$, according to the trailer rules in Definition 38. Thus $\mathsf{o}[\mathsf{m} \rightarrow \mathsf{v}]_{\mathsf{ex}} \in \widehat{S}_{\rho-1}$, or there is c such that $\mathsf{o}[\mathsf{m} \rightarrow \mathsf{v}]^{\mathsf{c}}_{\mathsf{val}} \in \widehat{S}_{\rho-1}$ or $\mathsf{o}[\mathsf{m} \rightarrow \mathsf{v}]^{\mathsf{c}}_{\mathsf{code}} \in \widehat{S}_{\rho-1}$, by the induction hypothesis. Clearly, $\widehat{S}_{\rho-1} \subseteq \widehat{S}_{\alpha-1}$. Thus $val^{\mathbf{b}}_{\widehat{S}_{\alpha-1}}(\mathsf{o}[\mathsf{m} \rightarrow \mathsf{v}]) = \mathbf{t}$.

Now consider the following cases:

(1) $isa(\mathsf{o},\mathsf{c}) \in S^{wf}_{\alpha}$ and $isa(\mathsf{o},\mathsf{c})$ is derived via a rule $\mathsf{R}^{wf} \in ground(P^{wf})$ which is rewritten from a regular rule $\mathsf{R} \in ground(P)$.
Then $\mathsf{R}^{wf} \equiv isa(\mathsf{o},\mathsf{c}) :- \rho^b(\mathsf{C}_1),\ldots,\rho^b(\mathsf{C}_m),\neg\rho^b(\mathsf{G}_1),\ldots,\neg\rho^b(\mathsf{G}_n)$ must be the rewriting of $\mathsf{R} \equiv \mathsf{o}:\mathsf{c} :- \mathsf{C}_1,\ldots,\mathsf{C}_m,\neg\mathsf{G}_1,\ldots,\neg\mathsf{G}_n$, where C_i, $1 \leq i \leq m$, and G_j, $1 \leq j \leq n$, are positive literals. By Definition 39, each $\rho^b(\mathsf{C}_i) \in S^{wf}_{\alpha-1}$ and each $\rho^b(\mathsf{G}_j) \notin I^{wf}$. Following the above claim, $val^{\mathbf{b}}_{\widehat{S}_{\alpha-1}}(\mathsf{C}_i) = \mathbf{t}$ for all $1 \leq i \leq m$. Moreover, I^{wf} is isomorphic to $\widehat{I}$ and is in normal form, therefore $val^{\mathbf{b}}_{\widehat{I}}(\neg\mathsf{G}_j) = \mathbf{t}$ for all $1 \leq j \leq n$, by Lemma 18. So $\mathsf{o}:\mathsf{c} \in \mathbf{RC}_{P,\widehat{I}}(\widehat{S}_{\alpha-1}) \subseteq \mathbf{T}_{P,\widehat{I}}(\widehat{S}_{\alpha-1}) = \widehat{S}_{\alpha}$, by Definitions 22 and 26.

(2) $isa(\mathsf{o},\mathsf{c}) \in S^{wf}_{\alpha}$ and $isa(\mathsf{o},\mathsf{c})$ is derived via a trailer rule R^{wf} in $ground(P^{wf})$. Then there exists s such that $\mathsf{R}^{wf} = isa(\mathsf{o},\mathsf{c}) :- isa(\mathsf{o},\mathsf{s}), sub(\mathsf{s},\mathsf{c})$. It follows that $isa(\mathsf{o},\mathsf{s}) \in S^{wf}_{\alpha-1}$ and $sub(\mathsf{s},\mathsf{c}) \in S^{wf}_{\alpha-1}$. Thus $\mathsf{o}:\mathsf{s} \in \widehat{S}_{\alpha-1}$ and $\mathsf{s}::\mathsf{c} \in \widehat{S}_{\alpha-1}$ by the induction hypothesis. So $\mathsf{o}:\mathsf{c} \in \mathbf{IC}^t(\widehat{S}_{\alpha-1}) \subseteq \mathbf{T}_{P,\widehat{I}}(\widehat{S}_{\alpha-1}) = \widehat{S}_{\alpha}$, by Definitions 25 and 26.

(3) $sub(\mathsf{s},\mathsf{c}) \in S^{wf}_{\alpha}$ and $sub(\mathsf{s},\mathsf{c})$ is derived via a rule $\mathsf{R}^{wf} \in ground(P^{wf})$ which is rewritten from a regular rule $\mathsf{R} \in ground(P)$.
Similarly to (1), we can show that $\mathsf{s}::\mathsf{c} \in \widehat{S}_{\alpha}$.

(4) $sub(\mathsf{s},\mathsf{c}) \in S^{wf}_{\alpha}$ and $sub(\mathsf{s},\mathsf{c})$ is derived via a trailer rule R^{wf} in $ground(P^{wf})$. Similarly to (2), we can show that $\mathsf{s}::\mathsf{c} \in \widehat{S}_{\alpha}$.

(5) $exmv(\mathsf{s},\mathsf{m},\mathsf{v}) \in S^{wf}_{\alpha}$
Then $exmv(\mathsf{s},\mathsf{m},\mathsf{v})$ must be derived via a rule $\mathsf{R}^{wf} \in ground(P^{wf})$ which is rewritten from a regular rule $\mathsf{R} \in ground(P)$. Similarly to (1), we can also show that $\mathsf{s}[\mathsf{m} \rightarrow \mathsf{v}]_{\mathsf{ex}} \in \widehat{S}_{\alpha}$.

(6) $vamv(\mathsf{o},\mathsf{m},\mathsf{v},\mathsf{c}) \in S^{wf}_{\alpha}$
By Definition 38, $vamv(\mathsf{o},\mathsf{m},\mathsf{v},\mathsf{c})$ should be derived via a trailer rule from $ground(P^{wf})$. So $vacan(\mathsf{c},\mathsf{m},\mathsf{o}) \in S^{wf}_{\alpha-1}$, $exmv(\mathsf{c},\mathsf{m},\mathsf{v}) \in S^{wf}_{\alpha-1}$, $ex(\mathsf{o},\mathsf{m}) \notin I^{wf}$,

and $multi(\mathsf{c},\mathsf{m},\mathsf{o}) \notin \mathrm{I}^{wf}$. Thus $\mathsf{c}[\mathsf{m}] \overset{val}{\leadsto} \mathsf{o} \in \widehat{\mathrm{S}}_{\alpha-1}$ and $\mathsf{c}[\mathsf{m} \to \mathsf{v}]_{\mathsf{ex}} \in \widehat{\mathrm{S}}_{\alpha-1}$, by the induction hypothesis. Since I^{wf} is isomorphic to $\widehat{\mathrm{I}}$, $ec(\mathsf{o},\mathsf{m}) \notin \mathbf{IB}_{\mathrm{P}}(\widehat{\mathrm{I}})$ and $mc(\mathsf{c},\mathsf{m},\mathsf{o}) \notin \mathbf{IB}_{\mathrm{P}}(\widehat{\mathrm{I}})$. Thus $\mathsf{o}[\mathsf{m} \to \mathsf{v}]^{\mathsf{c}}_{\mathsf{val}} \in \mathbf{IC}^{i}_{\mathrm{P},\widehat{\mathrm{I}}}(\widehat{\mathrm{S}}_{\alpha-1}) \subseteq \mathbf{T}_{\mathrm{P},\widehat{\mathrm{I}}}(\widehat{\mathrm{S}}_{\alpha-1}) = \widehat{\mathrm{S}}_{\alpha}$, by Definitions 25 and 26.

(7) $comv(\mathsf{o},\mathsf{m},\mathsf{v},\mathsf{c}) \in \mathrm{S}^{wf}_{\alpha}$
Then $comv(\mathsf{o},\mathsf{m},\mathsf{v},\mathsf{c})$ must be derived via a trailer rule. So $cocan(\mathsf{c},\mathsf{m},\mathsf{o}) \in \mathrm{S}^{wf}_{\alpha-1}$, $ins(\mathsf{o},\mathsf{m},\mathsf{v},\mathsf{c}) \in \mathrm{S}^{wf}_{\alpha-1}$, $ex(\mathsf{o},\mathsf{m}) \notin \mathrm{I}^{wf}$, and $multi(\mathsf{c},\mathsf{m},\mathsf{o}) \notin \mathrm{I}^{wf}$. By the induction hypothesis, $\mathsf{c}[\mathsf{m}] \overset{code}{\leadsto} \mathsf{o} \in \widehat{\mathrm{S}}_{\alpha-1}$. Since I^{wf} is isomorphic to $\widehat{\mathrm{I}}$, it follows that $ec(\mathsf{o},\mathsf{m}) \notin \mathbf{IB}_{\mathrm{P}}(\widehat{\mathrm{I}})$, $mc(\mathsf{c},\mathsf{m},\mathsf{o}) \notin \mathbf{IB}_{\mathrm{P}}(\widehat{\mathrm{I}})$. Clearly, $ins(\mathsf{o},\mathsf{m},\mathsf{v},\mathsf{c})$ must be derived via a rule $\mathsf{R}^{wf} \equiv ins(\mathsf{o},\mathsf{m},\mathsf{v},\mathsf{c}) \text{ :- } \rho^{b}(\mathsf{C}_1),\ldots,\rho^{b}(\mathsf{C}_\mathsf{m}),\neg\,\rho^{b}(\mathsf{G}_1),\ldots,\neg\,\rho^{b}(\mathsf{G}_\mathsf{n})$, in $ground(\mathrm{P}^{wf})$, which is rewritten from the following template rule in $ground(\mathrm{P})$, $\mathsf{R} \equiv \mathsf{code(c)\ @this[m \to v]} \text{ :- } \mathsf{B}_1,\ldots,\mathsf{B}_\mathsf{m},\neg\,\mathsf{F}_1,\ldots,\neg\,\mathsf{F}_\mathsf{n}$, where B_i and F_j are positive literals, $\mathsf{C}_\mathsf{i} = (\mathsf{B}_\mathsf{i})_{\|\mathsf{o}}$ and $\mathsf{G}_\mathsf{j} = (\mathsf{F}_\mathsf{j})_{\|\mathsf{o}}$, for all $1 \leq \mathsf{i} \leq \mathsf{m}$ and $1 \leq \mathsf{j} \leq \mathsf{n}$. Similarly to (1), we can show that $val^{\mathbf{b}}_{\widehat{\mathrm{S}}_{\alpha-1}}((\mathsf{B}_\mathsf{i})_{\|\mathsf{o}}) = \mathbf{t}$ for all $1 \leq \mathsf{i} \leq \mathsf{m}$ and $val^{\mathbf{b}}_{\widehat{\mathrm{I}}}(\neg\,(\mathsf{F}_\mathsf{j})_{\|\mathsf{o}}) = \mathbf{t}$ for all $1 \leq \mathsf{j} \leq \mathsf{n}$. It follows that by Definitions 24 and 26, $\mathsf{o}[\mathsf{m} \to \mathsf{v}]^{\mathsf{c}}_{\mathsf{val}} \in \mathbf{TC}_{\mathrm{P},\widehat{\mathrm{I}}}(\widehat{\mathrm{S}}_{\alpha-1}) \subseteq \mathbf{T}_{\mathrm{P},\widehat{\mathrm{I}}}(\widehat{\mathrm{S}}_{\alpha-1}) = \widehat{\mathrm{S}}_{\alpha}$.

(8) $vacan(\mathsf{c},\mathsf{m},\mathsf{o}) \in \mathrm{S}^{wf}_{\alpha}$
Then $vacan(\mathsf{c},\mathsf{m},\mathsf{o})$ must be derived via a trailer rule in $ground(\mathrm{P}^{wf})$. It follows that $isa(\mathsf{o},\mathsf{c}) \in \mathrm{S}^{wf}_{\alpha-1}$, $exmv(\mathsf{c},\mathsf{m},\mathsf{v}) \in \mathrm{S}^{wf}_{\alpha-1}$, $\mathsf{c} \neq \mathsf{o}$, and $override(\mathsf{c},\mathsf{m},\mathsf{o}) \notin \mathrm{I}^{wf}$, by Definition 38. So $\mathsf{o}\!:\!\mathsf{c} \in \widehat{\mathrm{S}}_{\alpha-1}$ and $\mathsf{c}[\mathsf{m} \to \mathsf{v}]_{\mathsf{ex}} \in \widehat{\mathrm{S}}_{\alpha-1}$, by the induction hypothesis. Moreover, $ov(\mathsf{c},\mathsf{m},\mathsf{o}) \notin \mathbf{IB}_{\mathrm{P}}(\widehat{\mathrm{I}})$, since I^{wf} is isomorphic to $\widehat{\mathrm{I}}$. Thus $\mathsf{c}[\mathsf{m}] \overset{val}{\leadsto} \mathsf{o} \in \mathbf{IC}^{c}_{\mathrm{P},\widehat{\mathrm{I}}}(\widehat{\mathrm{S}}_{\alpha-1}) \subseteq \mathbf{T}_{\mathrm{P},\widehat{\mathrm{I}}}(\widehat{\mathrm{S}}_{\alpha-1}) = \widehat{\mathrm{S}}_{\alpha}$, by Definitions 25 and 26.

(9) $cocan(\mathsf{c},\mathsf{m},\mathsf{o}) \in \mathrm{S}^{wf}_{\alpha}$
Then $cocan(\mathsf{c},\mathsf{m},\mathsf{o})$ must be derived via a trailer rule in $ground(\mathrm{P}^{wf})$. It follows that $isa(\mathsf{o},\mathsf{c}) \in \mathrm{S}^{wf}_{\alpha-1}$, $codedef(\mathsf{c},\mathsf{m}) \in \mathrm{S}^{wf}_{\alpha-1}$, $\mathsf{c} \neq \mathsf{o}$, and $override(\mathsf{c},\mathsf{m},\mathsf{o}) \notin \mathrm{I}^{wf}$, by Definition 38. Note that $\mathsf{o}\!:\!\mathsf{c} \in \widehat{\mathrm{S}}_{\alpha-1}$, by the induction hypothesis, and $ov(\mathsf{c},\mathsf{m},\mathsf{o}) \notin \mathbf{IB}_{\mathrm{P}}(\widehat{\mathrm{I}})$, because I^{wf} is isomorphic to $\widehat{\mathrm{I}}$. Since $codedef(\mathsf{c},\mathsf{m}) \in \mathrm{S}^{wf}_{\alpha-1}$, there is a template rule in P which specifies the instance method m for class c, by Definition 38. It follows that $\mathsf{c}[\mathsf{m}] \overset{code}{\leadsto} \mathsf{o} \in \mathbf{IC}^{c}_{\mathrm{P},\widehat{\mathrm{I}}}(\widehat{\mathrm{S}}_{\alpha-1}) \subseteq \mathbf{T}_{\mathrm{P},\widehat{\mathrm{I}}}(\widehat{\mathrm{S}}_{\alpha-1}) = \widehat{\mathrm{S}}_{\alpha}$, by Definitions 25 and 26.

II. $\Leftarrow$

Let us construct an extended atom set $\widehat{\mathrm{K}}$ from J^{wf} as follows: generate one $\mathsf{o}\!:\!\mathsf{c}$ in $\widehat{\mathrm{K}}$ for every $isa(\mathsf{o},\mathsf{c})$ in J^{wf}, one $\mathsf{s}::\mathsf{c}$ in $\widehat{\mathrm{K}}$ for every $sub(\mathsf{s},\mathsf{c})$ in J^{wf}, one $\mathsf{s}[\mathsf{m} \to \mathsf{v}]_{\mathsf{ex}}$ in $\widehat{\mathrm{K}}$ for every $exmv(\mathsf{s},\mathsf{m},\mathsf{v})$ in J^{wf}, one $\mathsf{o}[\mathsf{m} \to \mathsf{v}]^{\mathsf{c}}_{\mathsf{val}}$ in $\widehat{\mathrm{K}}$ for every $vamv(\mathsf{o},\mathsf{m},\mathsf{v},\mathsf{c})$ in J^{wf}, one $\mathsf{o}[\mathsf{m} \to \mathsf{v}]^{\mathsf{c}}_{\mathsf{code}}$ in $\widehat{\mathrm{K}}$ for every $comv(\mathsf{o},\mathsf{m},\mathsf{v},\mathsf{c})$ in J^{wf}, one $\mathsf{c}[\mathsf{m}] \overset{val}{\leadsto} \mathsf{o}$ in $\widehat{\mathrm{K}}$ for every $vacan(\mathsf{c},\mathsf{m},\mathsf{o})$ in J^{wf}, and one $\mathsf{c}[\mathsf{m}] \overset{code}{\leadsto} \mathsf{o}$ in $\widehat{\mathrm{K}}$ for every $cocan(\mathsf{c},\mathsf{m},\mathsf{o})$ in J^{wf}. Clearly, to prove that the conditions are true, it suffices to show that $\widehat{\mathrm{K}} \supseteq \widehat{\mathrm{J}}$.

Because $\widehat{\mathrm{J}} = \mathrm{lfp}(\mathbf{T}_{\mathrm{P},\widehat{\mathrm{I}}})$, therefore, to show that $\widehat{\mathrm{K}} \supseteq \widehat{\mathrm{J}}$, it suffices to show that $\mathbf{T}_{\mathrm{P},\widehat{\mathrm{I}}}(\widehat{\mathrm{K}}) \subseteq \widehat{\mathrm{K}}$ according to the conventional fixpoint theory [28]. Recall that by Definitions 26 and 25,

$$\mathbf{T}_{P,\widehat{I}}(\widehat{K}) = \mathbf{RC}_{P,\widehat{I}}(\widehat{K}) \cup \mathbf{TC}_{P,\widehat{I}}(\widehat{K}) \cup \mathbf{IC}^t(\widehat{K}) \cup \mathbf{IC}^c_{P,\widehat{I}}(\widehat{K}) \cup \mathbf{IC}^i_{P,\widehat{I}}(\widehat{K})$$

Let A be any atom in $\mathbf{T}_{P,\widehat{I}}(\widehat{K})$. There are five possible cases to consider:

(1) $\mathsf{A} \in \mathbf{RC}_{P,\widehat{I}}(\widehat{K})$
Then there is a regular rule $\mathsf{R} \equiv \mathsf{H} :- \mathsf{C}_1, \ldots, \mathsf{C}_m, \neg \mathsf{G}_1, \ldots, \neg \mathsf{G}_n$ in *ground*(P), such that H matches A, C_i $(1 \le i \le m)$ and G_j $(1 \le j \le n)$ are positive literals, $val^{\mathbf{b}}_{\widehat{K}}(\mathsf{C}_i) = \mathbf{t}$ for all $1 \le i \le m$ and $val^{\mathbf{b}}_{\widehat{I}}(\neg \mathsf{G}_j) = \mathbf{t}$ for all $1 \le j \le n$. Consider the rewriting R^{wf} of R, $\rho^h(\mathsf{H}) :- \rho^b(\mathsf{C}_1), \ldots, \rho^b(\mathsf{C}_m), \neg \rho^b(\mathsf{G}_1), \ldots, \neg \rho^b(\mathsf{G}_n)$. First we show $\rho^b(\mathsf{C}_i) \in \mathrm{J}^{wf}$ for all $1 \le i \le m$: (i) If $\mathsf{C}_i = \mathsf{o}:\mathsf{c}$, then $\rho^b(\mathsf{C}_i) = isa(\mathsf{o},\mathsf{c})$. Since $val^{\mathbf{b}}_{\widehat{K}}(\mathsf{o}:\mathsf{c}) = \mathbf{t}$, it follows that $\mathsf{o}:\mathsf{c} \in \widehat{K}$ by Definition 1. Therefore, $isa(\mathsf{o},\mathsf{c}) \in \mathrm{J}^{wf}$, by the construction of $\widehat{K}$; (ii) Similarly, we can show if $\mathsf{C}_i = \mathsf{s}::\mathsf{c}$, then $\rho^b(\mathsf{C}_i) = sub(\mathsf{s},\mathsf{c}) \in \mathrm{J}^{wf}$; (iii) If $\mathsf{C}_i = \mathsf{s}[\mathsf{m} \to \mathsf{v}]$, then $\rho^b(\mathsf{C}_i) = mv(\mathsf{s},\mathsf{m},\mathsf{v})$. Since $val^{\mathbf{b}}_{\widehat{K}}(\mathsf{s}[\mathsf{m} \to \mathsf{v}]) = \mathbf{t}$, so $\mathsf{s}[\mathsf{m} \to \mathsf{v}]_{\mathsf{ex}} \in \widehat{K}$, or there exists c such that $\mathsf{s}[\mathsf{m} \to \mathsf{v}]^{\mathsf{c}}_{\mathrm{val}} \in \widehat{K}$ or $\mathsf{s}[\mathsf{m} \to \mathsf{v}]^{\mathsf{c}}_{\mathrm{code}} \in \widehat{K}$. So $exmv(\mathsf{s},\mathsf{m},\mathsf{v}) \in \mathrm{J}^{wf}$, or there exists c such that $vamv(\mathsf{s},\mathsf{m},\mathsf{v},\mathsf{c}) \in \mathrm{J}^{wf}$ or $comv(\mathsf{s},\mathsf{m},\mathsf{v},\mathsf{c}) \in \mathrm{J}^{wf}$, by the construction of $\widehat{K}$. Because $\mathrm{J}^{wf} = \mathbf{C}_{\mathrm{P}^{wf},\mathrm{I}^{wf}}(\mathrm{J}^{wf})$, therefore $mv(\mathsf{s},\mathsf{m},\mathsf{v}) \in \mathrm{J}^{wf}$, according to the trailer rules in Definition 38. By Lemma 18, $\rho^b(\mathsf{G}_j) \notin \mathrm{I}^{wf}$ for all $1 \le j \le n$. So $\rho^h(\mathsf{H}) \in \mathbf{C}_{\mathrm{P}^{wf},\mathrm{I}^{wf}}(\mathrm{J}^{wf}) = \mathrm{J}^{wf}$, by Definition 39. It follows that: (i) If $\mathsf{A} = \mathsf{o}:\mathsf{c}$, then $\mathsf{H} = \mathsf{o}:\mathsf{c}$. So $\rho^h(\mathsf{H}) = isa(\mathsf{o},\mathsf{c}) \in \mathrm{J}^{wf}$, thus $\mathsf{o}:\mathsf{c} \in \widehat{K}$; (ii) Similarly, if $\mathsf{A} = \mathsf{s}::\mathsf{c}$, then $\mathsf{s}::\mathsf{c} \in \widehat{K}$; (iii) If $\mathsf{A} = \mathsf{s}[\mathsf{m} \to \mathsf{v}]_{\mathsf{ex}}$, then $\mathsf{H} = \mathsf{s}[\mathsf{m} \to \mathsf{v}]$. So $\rho^h(\mathsf{H}) = exmv(\mathsf{s},\mathsf{m},\mathsf{v}) \in \mathrm{J}^{wf}$, thus $\mathsf{s}[\mathsf{m} \to \mathsf{v}]_{\mathsf{ex}} \in \widehat{K}$.

(2) $\mathsf{A} \in \mathbf{TC}_{P,\widehat{I}}(\widehat{K})$
It must be the case that $\mathsf{A} = \mathsf{o}[\mathsf{m} \to \mathsf{v}]^{\mathsf{c}}_{\mathrm{code}}$. It follows that $mc(\mathsf{c},\mathsf{m},\mathsf{o}) \notin \mathbf{IB}_{\mathrm{P}}(\widehat{I})$, $ec(\mathsf{o},\mathsf{c}) \notin \mathbf{IB}_{\mathrm{P}}(\widehat{I})$, $\mathsf{c}[\mathsf{m}] \overset{code}{\leadsto} \mathsf{o} \in \widehat{K}$, and *ground*(P) has a template rule, R, of the form $\mathsf{code(c)\ @this[m} \to \mathsf{v]} :- \mathsf{C}_1, \ldots, \mathsf{C}_m, \neg \mathsf{G}_1, \ldots, \neg \mathsf{G}_n$, where C_i $(1 \le i \le m)$ and G_j $(1 \le j \le n)$ are positive literals, $val^{\mathbf{b}}_{\widehat{K}}((\mathsf{C}_i)_{\|\mathsf{o}}) = \mathbf{t}$ for all $1 \le i \le m$ and $val^{\mathbf{b}}_{\widehat{I}}(\neg (\mathsf{G}_j)_{\|\mathsf{o}}) = \mathbf{t}$ for all $1 \le j \le n$. Consider the rewriting R^{wf} of R, such that $\mathsf{R}^{wf} \equiv ins(\mathsf{o},\mathsf{m},\mathsf{v},\mathsf{c}) :- \rho^b(\mathsf{B}_1), \ldots, \rho^b(\mathsf{B}_m), \neg \rho^b(\mathsf{F}_1), \ldots, \neg \rho^b(\mathsf{F}_n)$, where $\mathsf{B}_i = (\mathsf{C}_i)_{\|\mathsf{o}}$ for all $1 \le i \le m$ and $\mathsf{F}_j = (\mathsf{G}_j)_{\|\mathsf{o}}$ for all $1 \le j \le n$. Similarly to (1), we can also show that $\rho^b(\mathsf{B}_i) \in \mathrm{J}^{wf}$ for all $1 \le i \le m$. By Lemma 18, $\rho^b(\mathsf{F}_j) \notin \mathrm{I}^{wf}$ for all $1 \le j \le n$. So $ins(\mathsf{o},\mathsf{m},\mathsf{v},\mathsf{c}) \in \mathbf{C}_{\mathrm{P}^{wf},\mathrm{I}^{wf}}(\mathrm{J}^{wf}) = \mathrm{J}^{wf}$, by Definition 39. Because $\mathsf{c}[\mathsf{m}] \overset{code}{\leadsto} \mathsf{o} \in \widehat{K}$, therefore $cocan(\mathsf{c},\mathsf{m},\mathsf{o}) \in \mathrm{J}^{wf}$, by the construction of $\widehat{K}$. Note that $ec(\mathsf{o},\mathsf{c}) \notin \mathbf{IB}_{\mathrm{P}}(\widehat{I})$ and $mc(\mathsf{c},\mathsf{m},\mathsf{o}) \notin \mathbf{IB}_{\mathrm{P}}(\widehat{I})$. Since I^{wf} is isomorphic to $\widehat{I}$, it follows that $ex(\mathsf{o},\mathsf{c}) \notin \mathrm{I}^{wf}$ and $multi(\mathsf{c},\mathsf{m},\mathsf{o}) \notin \mathrm{I}^{wf}$. So $comv(\mathsf{o},\mathsf{m},\mathsf{v},\mathsf{c}) \in \mathbf{C}_{\mathrm{P}^{wf},\mathrm{I}^{wf}}(\mathrm{J}^{wf}) = \mathrm{J}^{wf}$, according to the trailer rules of P^{wf} and Definition 39. It follows that $\mathsf{o}[\mathsf{m} \to \mathsf{v}]^{\mathsf{c}}_{\mathrm{code}} \in \widehat{K}$.

(3) $\mathsf{A} \in \mathbf{IC}^t(\widehat{K})$
If $\mathsf{A} = \mathsf{o}:\mathsf{c}$, then there is x such that $\mathsf{o}:\mathsf{x} \in \widehat{K}$, $\mathsf{x}::\mathsf{c} \in \widehat{K}$. So $isa(\mathsf{o},\mathsf{x}) \in \mathrm{J}^{wf}$ and $sub(\mathsf{x},\mathsf{c}) \in \mathrm{J}^{wf}$, by the construction of $\widehat{K}$. Thus $isa(\mathsf{o},\mathsf{c}) \in \mathbf{C}_{\mathrm{P}^{wf},\mathrm{I}^{wf}}(\mathrm{J}^{wf}) = \mathrm{J}^{wf}$,

by Definition 39 and the trailer rules of P^{wf}. Thus $o:c \in \widehat{K}$. Similarly, we can show that if $A = s::c$, then $s::c \in \widehat{K}$.

(4) $A \in \mathbf{IC}^{c}_{P,\widehat{I}}(\widehat{K})$
If $A = c[m] \overset{val}{\leadsto} o$, then $o:c \in \widehat{K}$, $c \neq o$, $c[m \rightarrow v]_{ex} \in \widehat{K}$, and $ov(c,m,o) \notin \widehat{I}$, by Definition 25. Because $\widehat{K}$ is constructed from J^{wf} and I^{wf} is isomorphic to $\widehat{I}$, it follows that $isa(o,c) \in J^{wf}$, $exmv(c,m,v) \in J^{wf}$, and $override(c,m,o) \notin I^{wf}$. So $vacan(c,m,o) \in \mathbf{C}_{P^{wf},I^{wf}}(J^{wf}) = J^{wf}$, by Definition 39 and the trailer rules of P^{wf}. Thus $c[m] \overset{val}{\leadsto} o \in \widehat{K}$. Similarly, if $A = c[m] \overset{code}{\leadsto} o$, we can also show that $c[m] \overset{code}{\leadsto} o \in \widehat{K}$.

(5) $A \in \mathbf{IC}^{i}_{P,\widehat{I}}(\widehat{K})$
Then $A = o[m \rightarrow v]^{c}_{val}$, and $c[m] \overset{val}{\leadsto} o \in \widehat{K}$, $c[m \rightarrow v]_{ex} \in \widehat{K}$, $ec(o,m) \notin \widehat{I}$, $mc(c,m,o) \notin \widehat{I}$, by Definition 25. Because $\widehat{K}$ is constructed from J^{wf}, and I^{wf} is isomorphic to $\widehat{I}$, it follows that $vacan(c,m,o) \in J^{wf}$, $exmv(c,m,v) \in J^{wf}$, $ex(o,m) \notin I^{wf}$, $multi(c,m,o) \notin I^{wf}$. So by Definition 39 and the trailer rules of P^{wf}, $vamv(o,m,v,c) \in \mathbf{C}_{P^{wf},I^{wf}}(J^{wf}) = J^{wf}$. Thus $o[m \rightarrow v]^{c}_{val} \in \widehat{K}$.

Finally, to finish the proof for the claim that J^{wf} is isomorphic to $\widehat{J}$, we still need to show that the following conditions are true:

(1) for all o, m: $ex(o,m) \in J^{wf}$ iff $ec(o,m) \in \mathbf{IB}_P(\widehat{J})$
(2) for all c, m, o: $multi(c,m,o) \in J^{wf}$ iff $mc(c,m,o) \in \mathbf{IB}_P(\widehat{J})$
(3) for all c, m, o: $override(c,m,o) \in J^{wf}$ iff $ov(c,m,o) \in \mathbf{IB}_P(\widehat{J})$

Note that $ex/2$, $multi/3$, and $override/3$ can only be derived via the trailer rules as defined in Definition 38. Moreover, $J^{wf} = \mathbf{C}_{P^{wf},I^{wf}}(J^{wf})$. It follows that:

(1) $ex(o,m) \in J^{wf}$, iff there exists v such that $exmv(o,m,v) \in J^{wf}$, iff there exits v such that $o[m \rightarrow v]_{ex} \in \widehat{J}$, iff $ec(o,m) \in \mathbf{IB}_P(\widehat{J})$.

(2) $multi(c,m,o) \in J^{wf}$, iff there exists $x \neq c$ such that $vacan(x,m,o) \in J^{wf}$ or $cocan(x,m,o) \in J^{wf}$, iff there is $x \neq c$ such that $x[m] \overset{val}{\leadsto} o \in \widehat{J}$ or $x[m] \overset{code}{\leadsto} o \in \widehat{J}$, iff $mc(c,m,o) \in \mathbf{IB}_P(\widehat{J})$.

(3) $override(c,m,o) \in J^{wf}$, iff there exists some x, such that $x \neq c$, $x \neq o$, $sub(x,c) \in J^{wf}$, $isa(o,x) \in J^{wf}$, and there is v such that $exmv(x,m,v) \in J^{wf}$ or $codedef(x,m) \in J^{wf}$, iff there is x such that $x \neq c$, $x \neq o$, $x::c \in \widehat{J}$, $o:x \in \widehat{J}$, and there is v such that $x[m \rightarrow v]_{ex} \in \widehat{J}$ or there is a template rule in P which specifies the instance method m for class c, iff $ov(c,m,o) \in \mathbf{IB}_P(\widehat{J})$.

Proposition 9. *Let α range over all ordinals, then T^{wf}_{α}, T^{wf}_{∞}, U^{wf}_{α}, and U^{wf}_{∞} are all in normal form. (The notations used here are from Definition 43.)*

Proof. First we show by transfinite induction that T^{wf}_{α} is in normal form for any ordinal α. The case is trivial for limit ordinal 0. If α is a successor ordinal, then $T^{wf}_{\alpha} = \mathbf{S}_{P^{wf}}(U^{wf}_{\alpha-1}) = \mathrm{lfp}(\mathbf{C}_{P^{wf},U^{wf}_{\alpha-1}})$. It follows that T^{wf}_{α} is in normal form, by Lemma 17. Now suppose $\alpha \neq 0$ is a limit ordinal, $T^{wf}_{\alpha} = \bigcup_{\beta<\alpha} T^{wf}_{\beta}$. According to Definition 42, we need to show for all o, m, v: $mv(o,m,v) \in T^{wf}_{\alpha}$

iff $exmv(\mathsf{o},\mathsf{m},\mathsf{v}) \in \mathrm{T}_{\alpha}^{wf}$, or there is c such that $vamv(\mathsf{o},\mathsf{m},\mathsf{v},\mathsf{c}) \in \mathrm{T}_{\alpha}^{wf}$ or $comv(\mathsf{o},\mathsf{m},\mathsf{v},\mathsf{c}) \in \mathrm{T}_{\alpha}^{wf}$.

(1) $\Rightarrow$
If $mv(\mathsf{o},\mathsf{m},\mathsf{v}) \in \mathrm{T}_{\alpha}^{wf}$, then there is $\beta < \alpha$ such that $mv(\mathsf{o},\mathsf{m},\mathsf{v}) \in \mathrm{T}_{\beta}^{wf}$. By the induction hypothesis, $\mathrm{T}_{\beta}^{wf} \subseteq \mathrm{T}_{\alpha}^{wf}$ is in normal form. Thus $exmv(\mathsf{o},\mathsf{m},\mathsf{v}) \in \mathrm{T}_{\beta}^{wf}$, or there is c such that $vamv(\mathsf{o},\mathsf{m},\mathsf{v},\mathsf{c}) \in \mathrm{T}_{\beta}^{wf}$ or $comv(\mathsf{o},\mathsf{m},\mathsf{v},\mathsf{c}) \in \mathrm{T}_{\beta}^{wf}$.

(2) $\Leftarrow$
If $exmv(\mathsf{o},\mathsf{m},\mathsf{v}) \in \mathrm{T}_{\alpha}^{wf}$, then there is $\beta < \alpha$ such that $exmv(\mathsf{o},\mathsf{m},\mathsf{v}) \in \mathrm{T}_{\beta}^{wf}$. It follows that $mv(\mathsf{o},\mathsf{m},\mathsf{v}) \in \mathrm{T}_{\beta}^{wf} \subseteq \mathrm{T}_{\alpha}^{wf}$, since T_{β}^{wf} is in normal form by the induction hypothesis. On the other hand, if there exists c such that $vamv(\mathsf{o},\mathsf{m},\mathsf{v},\mathsf{c}) \in \mathrm{T}_{\alpha}^{wf}$ or $vamv(\mathsf{o},\mathsf{m},\mathsf{v},\mathsf{c}) \in \mathrm{T}_{\alpha}^{wf}$, then there is $\gamma < \alpha$ such that $vamv(\mathsf{o},\mathsf{m},\mathsf{v},\mathsf{c}) \in \mathrm{T}_{\gamma}^{wf}$ or $comv(\mathsf{o},\mathsf{m},\mathsf{v},\mathsf{c}) \in \mathrm{T}_{\gamma}^{wf}$. It follows that $mv(\mathsf{o},\mathsf{m},\mathsf{v},\mathsf{c}) \in \mathrm{T}_{\gamma}^{wf} \subseteq \mathrm{T}_{\alpha}^{wf}$, since T_{γ}^{wf} is in normal form by the induction hypothesis.

Similarly, we can also prove that T_{∞}^{wf} is in normal form. Moreover, for any ordinal α, $\mathrm{U}_{\alpha}^{wf} = \mathbf{S}_{\mathrm{P}^{wf}}(\mathrm{T}_{\alpha}^{wf}) = \mathrm{lfp}(\mathbf{C}_{\mathrm{P}^{wf},\mathrm{T}_{\alpha}^{wf}})$. It follows that U_{α}^{wf} is in normal form, by Lemma 17. Similarly, we can show that U_{∞}^{wf} is in the normal form.

Unsupervised Duplicate Detection Using Sample Non-duplicates

Patrick Lehti and Peter Fankhauser

Fraunhofer IPSI
Dolivostr. 15
Darmstadt
Germany
{Patrick.Lehti, Peter.Fankhauser}@ipsi.fraunhofer.de

Abstract. The problem of identifying objects in databases that refer to the same real world entity, is known, among others, as duplicate detection or record linkage. Objects may be duplicates, even though they are not identical due to errors and missing data. Typical current methods require deep understanding of the application domain or a good representative training set, which entails significant costs. In this paper we present an unsupervised, domain independent approach to duplicate detection that starts with a broad alignment of potential duplicates, and analyses the distribution of observed similarity values among these potential duplicates and among representative sample non-duplicates to improve the initial alignment. Additionally, the presented approach is not only able to align flat records, but makes also use of related objects, which may significantly increase the alignment accuracy. Evaluations show that our approach supersedes other unsupervised approaches and reaches almost the same accuracy as even fully supervised, domain dependent approaches.

1 Introduction

The goal of data integration is to provide uniform, non-redundant access to a set of typically heterogeneous data sources. If the sources contain overlapping data, not only their schemas need to be integrated, but also their instances, i.e., duplicate instances that refer to the same real world object need to be to detected and merged.

Traditional scenarios for duplicate detection are data warehouses, which are populated by several data sources. Analyses on the data warehouse influences business decisions, therefore a high data quality resulting from the populating is of high importance. This is in general done by what is known as data cleansing process, which also detects and removes duplicates. Reaching a high data quality with a data cleansing process is currently very costly.

More recently duplicate detection is also arising in ad-hoc integration over the internet, e.g., in P2P, web service or grid settings, where datasets and services are virtually integrated for temporary applications. In such scenarios no long

S. Spaccapietra (Ed.): Journal on Data Semantics VII, LNCS 4244, pp. 136–164, 2006.

and expensive data cleansing process can be carried out, but good duplicate estimations must be available directly.

This paper describes a method for unsupervised duplicate detection by using a representative set of sample non-duplicates. These sample non-duplicates can be obtained under the assumption that individual data sources are duplicate free. The approach starts with a set of potential duplicates and a set of representative sample non-duplicates identified in a preprocessing phase and iteratively determines the matching probability of the potential duplicates by analyzing the distribution of observed similarities among the potential duplicates and among the non-duplicates. The approach can be alternatively used with either a refinement of the Fellegi-Sunter model for record linkage [1], which is able to use continuous similarity measures and takes attribute dependencies into account, or it can be used with machine learning techniques like Support Vector Machines (SVM) [2]. Further the method can be simply extended to be used with not only flat records, but on graph data models consisting of interrelated objects. It is shown that such an extension also increases the accuracy of the duplicate detection process.

In more detail, the contributions of this paper are the following:

- a method for unsupervised detection of duplicates between two data sources
- a way to automatically infer a representative sample of non-duplicates that can be used by a duplicate decision model to increase the decision accuracy
- the usage of the Fellegi-Sunter model for record linkage [1] with such sample non-duplicates
- the usage of Support Vector Machines with such sample non-duplicates
- extensions to the classic Fellegi-Sunter model for determining the parameters without the independence assumption and using continuous similarity values; a probabilistic model that simplifies finding a good threshold on the result; the handling of null values and multi-valued attributes
- an extension to detect duplicates not only on flat records, but on interrelated objects

The remainder of this paper is organized as follows. Section 1.1 gives a more formal definition of the problem of duplicate detection. Section 2 summarizes related work and and briefly introduces into the Fellegi-Sunter model. Section 3 gives an overview of the architecture and explains how the representative sample non-duplicates can be obtained. Section 4 presents the extensions to the Fellegi-Sunter model and shows how it can make use of the sample non-duplicates. Section 5 presents the results of the evaluation of our approach compared to other approaches. Finally Section 6 concludes and shows potentials for future work.

1.1 Problem Definition

The problem of detecting duplicates can be defined as follows: Given two sets of objects A and B divide the set of all object-pairs $(a, b) \in A \times B$ into a set of matching object-pairs M and unmatching object-pairs U. Sets are denoted by upper-case letters, individual instances by lower-case letters. An object is basically a vector of attributes (also called fields, properties or features), thus, an object-pair is a vector of attribute-pairs.

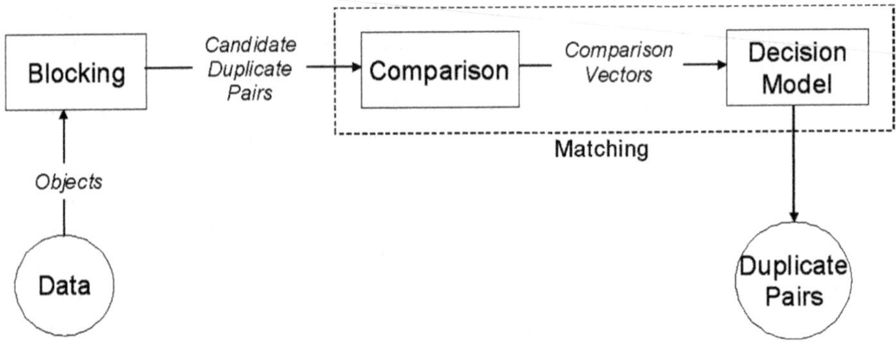

Fig. 1. General architecture of a duplicate detection system

In general the overall duplicate detection process consists of several phases as illustrated in Figure 1. The first phase, often called blocking, tries to efficiently find a candidate set of duplicates, then a second phase, sometimes called matching, performs the actual duplicate decision. The matching phase in general involves an in-depth comparison of the candidate duplicate pairs, i.e., comparing the individual attribute-pairs, which results in what is called a comparison vector $\gamma[a, b]$ for every candidate pair. The individual components of the comparison vector ($\gamma_i[a, b]$) represent the comparison results between the individual attribute-pairs. These individual comparison results can be boolean (attribute matches or does not match), discrete (e.g., matches, possibly matches or does not match) or continuous (e.g., attribute values have a similarity of 0.2).

The task for the matching algorithm is then to classify such a given comparison vector $\gamma[a, b]$ into the sets M or U by some kind of decision model. Therefore the components of the comparison vector must be combined to an overall result. It can be easily seen that the individual attributes do not have the same relevance for this overall result. E.g., a matching "person name" is a much stronger indication for a duplicate record than a matching "year of birth", because of the higher *uniqueness* of "person name" in contrast to "year of birth". However, a non-matching "year of birth" is a strong indication for a non-duplicate, may be even higher as a slightly different "person name", under the assumption of a high *reliability* for "year of birth".

2 Related Work

Methods from the Database Community In the database community a few knowledge-intensive approaches have been developed. Hernandez and Stolfo [3]

present a two phase data cleansing approach based on key expressions for blocking and logic rules for the matching phase. The selection of appropriate keys as well as the logic rules are both very knowledge-intensive tasks. Galhardas et al. [4] present a framework for data cleansing based on a set of rules. This framework is very flexible, but requires intensive human interaction and knowledge in order to provide good rules. Monge and Elkan [5] compare instances based on a concatenation of all attributes with the help of distance functions and present a blocking algorithm. A concatenation of all attributes only produces reasonable results if all data sources are complete, i.e., have no null values for attributes and all attributes show the same relevance for duplicate detection. In our evaluation one baseline experiment also concatenates all attribute values and uses the string distance between these concatenated strings as overall result.

The Fellegi-Sunter Model for Record Linkage Based on the initial ideas and problem description of Newcombe [6], Fellegi and Sunter [1] defined a theory for record linkage including relevance for individual attributes. To this end, they define the following probabilities on the comparison vector $\gamma[a,b]$ for an object pair (a,b):

$$m(\gamma[a,b]) = P(\gamma[a,b] \mid (a,b) \in M) \tag{1}$$

$$u(\gamma[a,b]) = P(\gamma[a,b] \mid (a,b) \in U) \tag{2}$$

Here $m(\gamma[a,b])$ is the conditional probability of $\gamma[a,b]$, given that (a,b) is an element of M and $u(\gamma[a,b])$ is the conditional probability of $\gamma[a,b]$, given that (a,b) is an element of U. They have shown that the ratio $w(\gamma[a,b]) = m(\gamma[a,b])/u(\gamma[a,b])$ can then be used to decide for a duplicate, non-duplicate or potential duplicate. To this end they define how to set the appropriate thresholds on $w(\gamma[a,b])$ given acceptable error rates for false misses and false matches.

In order to determine the parameters $u(\gamma[a,b])$ and $m(\gamma[a,b])$ often a conditional independence assumption between the individual components of the comparison vector is made. Under this assumption the parameters $u(\gamma[a,b])$ and $m(\gamma[a,b])$ can be computed using m_i and u_i for the individual probabilities for the comparison vector component $\gamma_i[a,b]$:

$$m(\gamma[a,b]) = m_1(\gamma_1[a,b]) * m_2(\gamma_2[a,b]) ... m_k(\gamma_k[a,b]) \tag{3}$$

$$u(\gamma[a,b]) = u_1(\gamma_1[a,b]) * u_2(\gamma_2[a,b]) ... u_k(\gamma_k[a,b]) \tag{4}$$

This simplification only produces good results if the conditional independence assumption really holds, which is often not the case for real data. E.g. in the address domain the attributes street and city are not independent, as a particular street is only present in one or a few cities.

Fellegi and Sunter propose two methods for determining the individual values $m_i(\gamma_i[a,b])$, one relies on additional knowledge of error rates in the values, the second is limited on comparison vectors of size 3. Winkler [7] showed that the EM algorithm (Expectation-Maximization) [8] can be used for unsupervised learning of the $m(\gamma[a,b])$ and $u(\gamma[a,b])$ parameters under the independence assumption.

Using the independence assumption is the second baseline experiment for our approach.

Several approaches, e.g., from Winkler [9] and Larsen and Rubin [10] tried to determine the $m(\gamma[a,b])$ and $u(\gamma[a,b])$ values in cases where conditional independence does not hold. All these approaches try to explicitly model the dependencies and only works for boolean variables.

Ravikumar and Cohen [11] present an unsupervised learning approach based on the Fellegi-Sunter model that takes attribute dependencies into account and uses continuous similarity measures. They use a hierarchical latent variable graphical model to model dependencies between the individual attributes with continuous values. They showed that their approach helps reducing overfitting of dependency models. Their model is used as third baseline in our experiments.

Machine Learning Methods. Elfeky et al. [12] claim that probabilistic record linkage models always have the disadvantage to handle only boolean or categorical values and require a training set.[1] Therefore they propose to use continuous values with machine learning techniques either based on supervised training of a classifier (e.g. some kind of decision model) or using unsupervised clustering methods like k-means. However, building an appropriate training set is a manual and knowledge-intensive task and simple clustering methods like k-means are only able to identify clusters that are linear separable, which is in general not the case for real world data.

The AI community has proposed various other approaches using supervised learning. Cohen and Richman [13] learn to combine multiple similarity metrics to identify duplicates. Bilenko and Mooney [14] learn in a first step distance metrics for individual fields, and in a second step they learn a combining metric for similarity between records using Support Vector Machines (SVM). Their results are compared to ours in section 5. Tejada et al. [15] use a supervised learning method that generates rules that describe which combination of thresholds on the individual attributes are necessary to declare a pair as duplicate. Sarawagi and Bhamidipaty [16] present an approach of active learning that reduces the user-overhead for selecting an appropriate learning set.

A few more recent approaches try to take similarities between related objects in a graph data model into account, which is orthogonal to our approach. Ananthakrishna et al. [17] use a co-occurrence similarity in addition to a simple concatenation based string similarity. This co-occurrence similarity checks for co-occurrences in the sets of related entities. Their approach is restricted to hierarchical relationships. Domingos [18] take similarities between related objects into account by setting up a network with a node for each record pair. This allows to propagate duplicate detection results to related objects. Similarly Dong et al. [19] build up a graph and propagate duplicate information to related objects. Such naive propagation may also lead to significantly reduced precision, if an errorneous duplicate detection is propagated through the graph. Bhattacharya and Getoor [20] introduce new distance measures that take entity relationships

[1] Our approach shows otherwise.

into account. They have shown that this can be used for the duplicate detection task. Pasula et al. [21] introduce a generative probability model for the related problem of "identity uncertainty" based on probabilistic relational networks.

3 Extending the Fellegi-Sunter Model

The Fellegi-Sunter model uses the ratio $w(\gamma[a,b]) = m(\gamma[a,b])/u(\gamma[a,b])$ as decision function. The problems using this function are in general the following: 1. how to find a threshold on $w(\gamma[a,b])$; 2. how to determine the parameters $m(\gamma[a,b])$ and $u(\gamma[a,b])$, when using continous similarity measures and taking dependencies into account.

3.1 A Probability Interpretation for the Fellegi-Sunter Model

In order to intuitivly define an appropriate threshold that is independent of the concrete application and data, a probability interpretation for the Fellegi-Sunter model is defined as the conditional probability of a and b being duplicates (element of M), given the comparison vector $\gamma[a,b]$. This conditional probability can be calculated as follows:

$$P((a,b) \in M \mid \gamma[a,b]) = \frac{m(\gamma[a,b]) * P(M)}{m(\gamma[a,b]) * P(M) + u(\gamma[a,b]) * P(U)} \quad (5)$$

This formula follows directly from the Bayes rule [2] and the total probability theorem:

$$P((a,b) \in M \mid \gamma[a,b]) = \frac{m(\gamma[a,b]) * P(M)}{P(\gamma[a,b])} \quad (6)$$

$$P(\gamma[a,b]) = m(\gamma[a,b]) * P(M) + u(\gamma[a,b]) * P(U) \quad (7)$$

The probability $P(M)$ is the general probability that two records are duplicates and is defined as the ratio between the set of duplicates and the set of all pairs:

$$P(M) = \frac{|M|}{|M| + |U|} \quad (8)$$

$P(U)$ is simply the complement of $P(M)$; $P(U) = 1 - P(M)$. It can be easily seen that $P(M)$ is always very small and $P(U)$ always nearly 1. In particular for duplicate free individual data sets (A and B), P(M) is between 0 (no overlap) and $\frac{min(|A|,|B|)}{|M|+|U|}$ (one data set is a subset of the other).

The main difference to the original Fellegi-Sunter ratio is that now the value range is {0,1}, whereas in Fellegi-Sunter it is {0,infinite}. This allows to use a fixed threshold for duplicate decision, instead of the problem to find an appropriate threshold for every duplicate detection application, e.g., if the probability is greater than 50% (> 0.5) than they are declared as duplicates. Additionally our ratio introduces the term $P(M)$. If there are only few duplicates expected,

$P(M)$ will be very small and accordingly the matching probability for potential duplicates will be small as well.

However, the order based on the original Fellegi-Sunter ratio and the order based on the Bayes formula 5, is always identical. This can be easily shown, because the inequation based on Bayes (9) telling that the probability for the comparison vector $\gamma[a,b]$ belonging to a duplicate is less than the probability for the comparison vector $\gamma[x,y]$ can be transformed by simple inequality transformations into the equal inequation based on the original Fellegi-Sunter ratio (10):

$$\frac{m(\gamma[a,b]) * P(M)}{m(\gamma[a,b]) * P(M) + u(\gamma[a,b]) * P(U)} < \frac{m(\gamma[x,y]) * P(M)}{m(\gamma[x,y]) * P(M) + u(\gamma[x,y]) * P(U)} \tag{9}$$

$$\frac{m(\gamma[a,b])}{u(\gamma[a,b])} < \frac{m(\gamma[x,y])}{m(\gamma[x,y])} \tag{10}$$

3.2 Definition of the $m(\gamma[a,b])$ Parameter

In the most easiest case assuming independence between the attributes and mapping the continuous similarity values of the comparison vector to boolean values using some threshold, the probability $m_i(\gamma_i[a,b])$ is the ratio between the number of all pairs in M that match with this $\gamma_i[a,b]$ to the size of M. Without the independence assumption between the attributes, the probability $m(\gamma)$ can be defined as the ratio between the number of all pairs in M, where all individual components of γ match, to the size of M.

$$m_i(\gamma_i[a,b]) = \frac{|\{(x,y) \in M \mid \gamma_i[x,y] = \gamma_i[a,b]\}|}{|M|} \tag{11}$$

$$m(\gamma[a,b]) = \frac{|\{(x,y) \in M \mid \forall \gamma_i[x,y] = \gamma_i[a,b]\}|}{|M|} \tag{12}$$

In the case when the continuous similarity values should not be mapped to boolean values the definition for $m(\gamma[a,b])$ is not so obvious. But using continuous values is definitely preferrable, because value-pairs are not always clearly categorizable as definite match or not match, but there is a whole range of similarity, which makes it hard to define a good threshold.

In order to define the probability $m(\gamma[a,b])$ for the continuous case, the following assumption is made:

Assumption 1. *The probability* $m(\gamma[a,b])$ *is monotonically* increasing *with the* increase *of the similarity between value-pairs, i.e., if the similarity measures in a* $\gamma[a,b]$ *are greater than the similarity measures in* $\gamma[x,y]$, $m(\gamma[a,b])$ *is greater than* $m(\gamma[x,y])$.

Using this assumption the independent probability $m_i(\gamma_i[a,b])$ can be defined to be the ratio between the number of all pairs in M whose $\gamma_i[a,b]$ is less than or equal to $\gamma_i[a,b]$, to the number of all pairs in M. Without the independence assumption this corresponds to the number of all pairs in M whose comparison vector is absolutely less than $\gamma[a,b]$ to the number of all pairs in M.

$$m_i(\gamma_i[a,b]) = \frac{|\{(x,y) \in M \mid \gamma_i[x,y] <= \gamma_i[a,b]\}|}{|M|} \tag{13}$$

$$m(\gamma[a,b]) = \frac{|\{(x,y) \in M \mid \forall \gamma_i[x,y] <= \gamma_i[a,b]\}|}{|M|} \tag{14}$$

3.3 Definition of the $u(\gamma[a,b])$ Parameter

$u(\gamma[a,b])$ is analogous to the definition for $m(\gamma[a,b])$. Equation (15) defines $u_i(\gamma_i[a,b])$ when assuming independence and using boolean values. Equation (16) defines $u(\gamma[a,b])$ without the independence assumption.

$$u_i(\gamma_i[a,b]) = \frac{|\{(x,y) \in U \mid \gamma_i[x,y] = \gamma_i[a,b]\}|}{|U|} \tag{15}$$

$$u(\gamma[a,b]) = \frac{|\{(x,y) \in U \mid \forall \gamma_i[x,y] = \gamma_i[a,b]\}|}{|U|} \tag{16}$$

In order to define the probability $u(\gamma[a,b])$ for the continuous case, the following assumption is made:

Assumption 2. *The probability $u(\gamma[a,b])$ is monotonically* increasing *with the* decrease *of the similarity between value-pairs, i.e., if the similarity measures in a $\gamma[a,b]$ are less than the similarity measures in $\gamma[x,y]$, $u(\gamma[a,b])$ is greater than $u(\gamma[x,y])$.*

Using this assumption Equation (17) defines $u_i(\gamma_i[a,b])$ for continuous values and assuming independence. Equation (18) defines $u(\gamma[a,b])$ for continuous values without the independence assumption.

$$u_i(\gamma_i[a,b]) = \frac{|\{(x,y) \in U \mid \gamma_i[x,y] >= \gamma_i[a,b]\}|}{|U|} \tag{17}$$

$$u(\gamma[a,b]) = \frac{|\{(x,y) \in U \mid \forall \gamma_i[x,y] >= \gamma_i[a,b]\}|}{|U|} \tag{18}$$

4 Unsupervised Matching

This section presents the developed approach for the matching phase. The first section explains the basic architecture, the following sections then present the methods and algorithms of the individual modules in detail.

4.1 Overview

The architecture consists of the usual two phases that are blocking, which generates a set of potential duplicates, and matching, which compares the potential duplicates in detail and finally decides for being an actual duplicate or not. However, the matching phase in the approach takes not only a set of potential duplicates (M') as input, but additionally a set of non-duplicates (U'). This additional input should enable the matching algorithm to work completely unsupervised.

The idea is that the matching algorithm is able to remove the non-duplicates from M' given the set of sample true non-duplicates of U'. Therefore these sample non-duplicates must be representative for the non-duplicates in M', which are some kind of similar object-pairs, as otherwise they would not have been declared as potential duplicates.

For a large family of applications this set of representative non-duplicates can be generated in an unsupervised way. These applications are characterized by the following properties:

- only duplicates between different data sources need to be detected
- these individual data sources themselves are more or less duplicate free

These high quality data sources typically occur in commercial settings like webshops or product catalogs or other manually maintained data sources, e.g., the publication data bases DBLP [22] and CompuScience [23].

When these properties hold for the given application and data sources, the following sets can be defined; Ω defines the set of all pairs within and between the individual data sources:

$$\Omega = A \times A \cup B \times B \cup A \times B \tag{19}$$

The set of duplicates M is a subset of the pairs only between the data sources:

$$M \subset A \times B \tag{20}$$

The set of non-duplicates U is the union of all pairs within the data sources and the pairs between the data sources without M.

$$U = \Omega \setminus M \tag{21}$$

The set of potential duplicates M' is generated as usual by a blocking method on the set of object-pairs between the data sources ($A \times B$). It is therefore a subset of all object-pairs between the data sources and also a superset of the true M:

$$M' \subset A \times B \tag{22}$$

$$M' \supseteq M \tag{23}$$

A representative set U' can now be generated by applying the same blocking algorithm to the sets of object-pairs within the individual data sources

$(A \times A \cup B \times B)$. This set is a subset of U and shows the same kind of similarity as the non-duplicates in M', because they were generated using the same algorithm.

$$U' \subset A \times A \cup B \times B \tag{24}$$

$$U' \subset U \tag{25}$$

This architecture is shown in Figure 2.

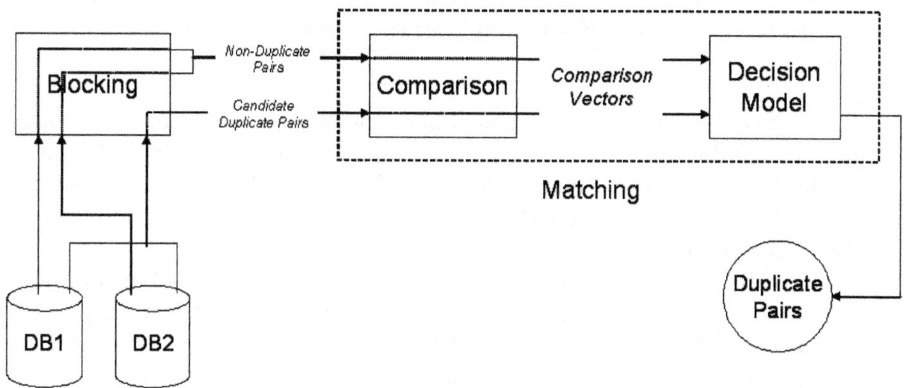

Fig. 2. Architecture of the duplicate detection system

If the properties do not hold for the given application, because duplicates within a single data source should be detected or the individual data sources contain too many duplicates, the set of non-duplicates U' must be generated differently, e.g., by manually selecting such pairs. In the following, it is assumed that these properties hold.

After the sets M' and U' are generated by the blocking module, a comparison module compares the given object-pairs in detail and produces comparison vectors for all pairs in M' and U'. Given these comparison vectors as input, the decision module tries to identify actual non-duplicates in M' based on the samples from U' and finally generates a set of duplicate pairs. This remaining set of duplicates should be ranked by some kind of confidence into this decision.

The decision module is herein faced with the problem to find a way to seperate the data points represented by their comparison vectors into the two classes duplicates and non-duplicates.

4.2 The Comparison Module

The comparison module compares object-pairs in detail and creates a comparison vector γ for every such object-pair. An individual component of this comparison vector is a similarity measure for an individual attribute-pair. Such a similarity measure is defined to be greater if more similarity is detected, the range for such a similarity value can be {-infinite,infinite}. Although one typical kind of similarity measures are distance functions, which are dissimilarity measures with a range of {0,1}, where 0 means identical and 1 stands for maximal distance. These distances values are translated to a similarity measure by simply taking the complement of it.

The influence on the overall matching performance of such similarity measures can be enormous, i.e., a decision module has only a chance if the distribution of the similarity values between the duplicates and the non-duplicates are significantly different. But the selection of an appropriate similarity measure is difficult, as the cause for differences between actually equivalent values can be manifold:

- *Typos:* The easiest case are typos, where the same string contains wrong, missing, additional or interchanged characters or tokens. Similarity measures for this kind of errors are numerous and well studied [24]. They are in general called distance functions, which are dissimilarity measures - the complement of a similarity measure.
- *Datatype Dependency:* If a value is not a simple string, but some kind of primitive datatype, simple string-based similarity measures often work poorly. E.g. a year value of "2000" and "1999" do not have a single character in common and would therefore be judged as very different by a string-based similarity measure, in this case a simple arithmetic difference based similarity measure would be much more effective. However, for the same datatype year the values "2001" and "2010" would be better judged by the string-based similarity, as a simple typo is possible.
- *Domain Dependency:* The most difficult case is, where an equivalence between values can only be recognized if additional domain knowledge is available. E.g. in the publication domain the two values for the conference event "VLDB-95" and "Int. Conference on Very Large Data Bases, 1995" look very different and can only be recognized as equivalent, when knowing that "VLDB" is a common abbreviation for "Int. Conference on Very Large Data Bases".

Therefore the comparison module allows to use several similarity measures for the same attribute-pair, like a string-edit-distance and an arithmetic difference for a "year" attribute, and stores the individual similarity values in individual comparison vector components. That means the length of a comparison vector may not be identical with the number of attribute-pairs.

Null Values. Datasets often contain optional attributes, i.e., attributes may contain null values. E.g., in the person domain, the middle name of a person often does either not exist or is not available. In general such null values cannot be used by similarity functions.

Therefore the comparison module allows a comparison vector component to be either a continuous similarity value, or "null", indicating that this similarity function was not able to calculate a similarity score for this attribute-pair. How a null value is treated for the duplicate decision is the task of the decision module.

Multi-valued Attributes. So far only flat records are handled with the approach. In order to extend it to multi-valued attributes, i.e., attributes that contain an arbitrary number of individual values, e.g., the list of authors of a publication, the approach must be slightly modified.

Comparing multi-valued attributes requires comparing all corresponding individual values and results in a sequence of similarity values, i.e., a comparison vector itself. If one multi-valued attribute contains less individual values than the other, this is seen as missing values, i.e., containing null values. The way of finding the corresponding value depends on whether the values are ordered or not. If the multi-valued attributes are ordered, e.g., the author names of a publication, simply the values at the same position are compared. Unordered multi-valued attributes require some form of set comparison, selecting the comparison vector with the shortest length.

Using a comparison vector with arbitrary length n_i directly as value within the comparison vector (γ) of the object-pair to be examined, would result in independent distributions for every occuring length of this multi-valued attribute. Therefore it is preferable to collapse the comparison vector of the multi-valued attribute to a single similarity measure.

In order to collapse such a comparison vector, the following assumptions are made:

- the relevance of every individual value is the same, i.e., the similarity of every individual value contributes the same amount to the overall similarity of the set.
- the similarities between the individual values are independent, i.e., there is no dependency between the individual values.

Under these assumptions the individual similarity values γ_{ik} can be collapsed to a single similarity value by simply using the arithmetic mean of the individual similarity values. If several similarity functions were used for the comparison of the attribute-pairs, the mean of every such similarity function must be calculated.

$$\gamma_i = \frac{\sum_k^{n_i} \gamma_{ik}}{n_i} \tag{26}$$

Relationships. Beside multi-valued attributes in many data models also relationships to other objects are possible. An example of such a relationship is the *conference paper* to its *conference.* When supporting relationships in the approach, it is necessary to compare the related objects. This is done in an independent duplicate detection process, which needs its own sets of potential duplicates ($M^{1\prime}$) and representative non-duplicates ($U^{1\prime}$). In order to obtain these input sets, a blocking phase is not necessary, but these sets can be obtained from the initial potential duplicates M' and non-duplicates U'. To this end, all distinct pairs of related objects from M' form $M^{1'}$ and all distinct pairs of related objects from U' form $U^{1'}$. This initial set $U^{1'}$ may still contain duplicates, because although U' only contains clear non-duplicates, the related objects may even so be duplicates, e.g., non-duplicates conference papers may still be published at the same conference. However, because U' contains only pairs from the same source, duplicate related objects must be identical and therefore directly identifiable as such. That means $U^{1'}$ can be easily filtered to contain only non-duplicates.

Using these sets $M^{1'}$ and $U^{1'}$ as input for a separate duplicate decision, all related object-pairs get some kind of duplicate estimation score, which can then be used as similarity value in the comparison vector for the initial duplicate detection process.

However, relationships offer additional information that can be used for their duplicate estimation. This is the number how often two related objects occur together within potential duplicates. If this number is significantly higher than they should be randomly, this strongly indicates duplicate related objects even if their similarity score calculated by convential methods is low. Therefore an additional kind of similarity measures is suggested in the case of relationships using this information. Such similarity measures are known as association measures [25]. The most commonly used association measures in information theory are the *mutual information score* [26] and the *t-score* [27].

It should be noted that not only explictly modeled relationships with objects each consisting of several attributes can profit from such measures, but also single attributes in flat record lists, which occur regurlarly and therefore can be seen as unnormalized relations.

If relationships are cyclic then following such a relationship recursivly would result in an infinite loop. Therefore relationships that refer to objects that are currently estimated are ignored.

4.3 The Extended Fellegi-Sunter Model as Decision Model

The extended Fellegi-Sunter model as described in Section 3 can be used as decision model given only the input sets M' and U'. In this case only an approximation for $P((a,b) \in M \mid \gamma[a,b])$ can be calculated that is called P' based on approximations of $m'(\gamma[a,b])$ and $u'(\gamma[a,b])$, which are introduced below:

$$P'((a,b) \in M \mid \gamma[a,b]) = \frac{m'(\gamma[a,b]) * P'(M)}{m'(\gamma[a,b]) * P'(M) + u'(\gamma[a,b]) * P'(U)} \tag{27}$$

This P' is used to identify actual non-duplicates in M' and new revised sets M'_1 and U'_1 are constructed. To this end all object-pairs in M', whose probability P' is below some threshold Θ, are moved to U'_1. This threshold can be naturally set to 50%, which corresponds to an equal probability for being a duplicate or a non-duplicate. This is iteratively done until no more non-duplicates are identified in M'_t.

$$M'_{t+1} = \{(a,b) \in M'_t \mid P'_t((a,b) \in M \mid \gamma[a,b]) >= \Theta\} \tag{28}$$

$$U'_{t+1} = U'_t \cup \{(a,b) \in M'_t \mid P'_t((a,b) \in M \mid \gamma[a,b]) < \Theta\} \tag{29}$$

This iteration always converges, because $U'_{t+1} \supseteq U'_t$ and $M'_{t+1} \subseteq M'_t$. However, in order that no true duplicates are moved into U'_t, it is important that the following condition holds:

Condition 1. *The estimated probability* $P'_t((a,b) \in M \mid \gamma[a,b])$ *is never less than the true probability for being a duplicate* $P((a,b) \in M \mid \gamma[a,b])$.

$$P_t((a,b) \in M \mid \gamma[a,b]) >= P((a,b) \in M \mid \gamma[a,b]) \tag{30}$$

The difference between $P'_t((a,b) \in M \mid \gamma[a,b])$ and the true $P((a,b) \in M \mid \gamma[a,b])$ result from the fact that the parameters $m'_t(\gamma[a,b])$, $u'_t(\gamma)[a,b]$ and $P'_t(M)$ can only be calculated from the given input sets M'_t and U'_t, which are not identical with M and U. Condition 1 can be broken down to the following sufficient conditions:

Condition 2. $m'_t(\gamma[a,b])$ *must always be greater or equal to the true* $m(\gamma[a,b])$.

$$m'_t(\gamma[a,b]) >= m(\gamma[a,b]) \tag{31}$$

Condition 3. $u'_t(\gamma[a,b])$ *must always be less or equal to the true* $u(\gamma[a,b])$.

$$u'_t(\gamma[a,b]) <= u(\gamma[a,b]) \tag{32}$$

Condition 4. $P'_t(M)$ *must always be greater or equal to the true* $P(M)$.

$$P'_t(M) >= P(M) \tag{33}$$

Determination of P'_t. $P'_t(M)$ is defined as the ratio between the size of M'_t to the number of all possible pairs, which is definitely greater than the true $P(M)$ as M'_t being a superset of M, therefore this definition meets Condition 4:

$$P'_t(M) = \frac{|M'_t|}{|\Omega|} \tag{34}$$

Determination of $m'_t(\gamma[a,b])$. The parameter $m'_t(\gamma[a,b])$ for continuous values in $\gamma[a,b]$ and taking dependencies into account, is defined as the ratio of the number of all pairs in M'_t whose comparison vector is absolutely less than $\gamma[a,b]$ to the number of all pairs in M'_t.

$$m'_t(\gamma[a,b]) = \frac{|\{(x,y) \in M'_t \mid \forall \gamma_i[x,y] <= \gamma_i[a,b]\}|}{|M'_t|} \tag{35}$$

Although the nominator of this definition will always be greater than the true value, it does not guarantee Condition 2, because the denominator will also be greater as it is calculated on a superset of M. In order to fulfil the condition, an upper bound for $m'_t(\gamma[a,b])$ is required that is guaranteed to be greater than $m(\gamma[a,b])$. Therefore statistic confidence intervals are used that allow to specify upper and lower bounds for the occurence of an event given the number of observations of such an event within a sample.

The ratio $\pi = x/n$ between the number of all occurrences of such an event (x) to the number of all observations (n) corresponds to the probability $m'_t(\gamma[a,b])$. The lower bound π_l and the upper bound π_u for the ratio π are given in statistics literature [28] via the following formulas:

$$\pi_l = \frac{x}{x + (n - x + 1) * F_l} \tag{36}$$

$$\pi_u = \frac{(x + 1) * F_u}{n - x + (x + 1) * F_u} \tag{37}$$

with:

$$F_{l\{df_1=2*(n-x+1), df_2=2*x\}}(\lambda/2) \tag{38}$$

$$F_{u\{df_1=2*(x+1), df_2=2*(n-x)\}}(\lambda/2) \tag{39}$$

Where F denotes the F-distribution, df_1 and df_2 denote the two degrees of freedom for the F-distribution and λ is the probability of error for these bounds, e.g. for a 95% confidence interval λ is 5%.

This upper bound on $m'_t(\gamma[a,b])$ is used during iteration to guarantee the overestimation of $P'_t((a,b) \in M \mid \gamma[a,b])$. However, for the final matching estimation of a pair always the truly observed $m'_t(\gamma[a,b])$ is used.

For boolean values in $\gamma[a,b]$ or under the independence assumption the definition is analoguous to the definition in Section 3.2.

Determination of $u'_t(\gamma[a,b])$. The parameter $u'_t(\gamma[a,b])$ for continuous values in $\gamma[a,b]$ and taking dependencies into account, is defined as the ratio of the number of all pairs in U'_t whose comparison vector is absolutely greater than $\gamma[a,b]$ to the number of all pairs Ω.

$$u'_t(\gamma[a,b]) = \frac{|\{(x,y) \in U'_t \mid \forall \gamma_i[x,y] >= \gamma_i[a,b]\}|}{|\Omega|} \tag{40}$$

This definition does guarantee Condition 3 as the numerator is always less than or equal to the true value as being calculated on a subset of U and the denominator is always greater than the true value as being calculated on a superset of U. Therefore $u'(\gamma[a,b])$ is always an underestimation of $u(\gamma[a,b])$. For boolean values in $\gamma[a,b]$ or under the independence assumption the definition is analoguous to the definition in Section 3.3.

Based on the fact that U'_t is only a subset of U it may happen that a rarely occurring $\gamma[a,b]$ can not be observed. This results in $u'_t(\gamma[a,b])$ to be 0 and $P'_t((a,b) \in M \mid \gamma[a,b])$ to be 1 independent of the value of $m'_t(\gamma[a,b])$. This problem is addressed by approximation, i.e. observing this case an approximation for $u'_t(\gamma[a,b])$ is needed, which is slightly higher than 0.

The approximation that shows the best results is simply the fallback to the independence assumption. Approximations like multi-dimensional linear interpolation are computationally very expensive and requires to find the nearest larger and nearest smaller available points in every dimension, i.e. 2^k points.

Using the mean between a statistic upper bound for this γ occurence and 0 performed poorer as it is independent of the concrete values of the comparison vector components, i.e. the 0 vector would get the same probability as a vector, where only one component is very untypically.

However, this approximation is only used for the final estimation of the duplicate probability. For constructing the revised sets M'_t and U'_t the observed probability of 0 for $u'_t(\gamma[a,b])$ is used, as otherwise Condition 3 could not be guaranteed anymore.

4.4 Handling Null Values

The problem of handling null values occurs for the determination of $u'_t(\gamma[a,b])$ and $m'_t(\gamma[a,b])$, when one $\gamma_i[a,b]$ component is a null value and the other is a continuous similarity value. There are several ways to decide, if such components match or not:

- A null value never matches a distance value. This basically means that comparison vectors with null values can only be compared with other comparison vectors that also contain null values for exactly the same component, i.e., the sets U' and M' are split into subsets, one for each null value combination. These subsets might be very small depending on the input sets and this would result in poor accuracy/confidence for the probabilities.
- A null value matches every distance value. This basically means that this comparison vector component is ignored and has no further influence on the resulting probabilities.
- The null value is replaced with a similarity value. This similariy value can be the most probable value for this comparison vector component, which is e.g. the mean value of all non-null similarity values for this component.

4.5 Machine Learning Methods as Decision Model

For machine learning methods the problem can be seen as classification problem, where the unlabeled data points in M' should be classified into the two distinct classes of duplicates M and non-duplicates U. In general, machine learning methods can be distinguished in supervised and unsupervised methods. Supervised methods use a set of labeled examples to train a classification function, which is then used to classify the unlabeled data points. State of the art for supervised classification are Support Vector Machines (SVM) [2]. Unsupervised methods are in general clustering algorithms, which try to separate the unlabeled data points into two clusters of data points that seem to belong together based on some distance between the data points. Examples for such clustering algorithms are KMeans [29] and spectral clustering [30].

However, the problem at hand does have additional labeled data points for only one class, which are the data points in U'. Therefore these methods can not be used in their usual way. Two state of the art machine learning methods are tried as decision models in the approach; the simple KMeans clustering and the SVM classification algorithm.

Null values are handled by replacing them with the most probable similarity value for this component, which is the mean of all non-null similarity values.

Simple KMeans. The KMeans algorithm tries to find two cluster centroids, such that all data points in this cluster are nearer to their centroid than to the other. To this end KMeans starts with initial centroids, assigns all data points to the centroid that is nearest to them and afterwards calculates new centroids for the identified clusters. This is done iteratively until the centroids stay fixed. As the distances to the centroid are in general calculated by a simple euclidean distance, the assumed cluster shape is spherical.

This is the main disadvantage of KMeans: it fails, if the cluster shape strongly differs from a spherical shape. The features of the comparison vector in duplicate detection usally show very different distributions (based on the uniqueness and reliability of the attribute) and they may also depend on each other, which may result in non-spherical cluster shapes.

In order to use KMeans, one has to specify the initial cluster centroids. In the given scenario this can be achieved by calculating the centroid for the non-duplicates out of U' and setting the centroid of the duplicates to 0.

Experiments using KMeans did either perform very poor (lower accuracy than a baseline) or did fail completely (identifying random clusters). All this can be explained with the distribution of the clusters is neither spherically shaped nor linearly separable and therefore KMeans is not well suited for this scenario.

Iterative Support Vector Machines. Support Vector Machines try to find a hyperplane between the two classes, such that the margin between the hyperplane and the data points of both classes is maximized. SVMs use kernel functions that are able to separate many kinds of cluster shapes. SVMs need to be trained with data points of both classes. Here the same trick as for the Fellegi-Sunter model can be used, the set M' is assumed to contain only duplicates and is used to train the SVM together with the clear non-duplicate data points from U'. This SVM is then used to classify M' and altough these data points were all used as duplicate examples, the SVM will classify some as non-duplicates. In another iteration these detected non-duplicates can then be used as additional non-duplicate examples and a cleaner M'_1 is used as better examples for the duplicates. This is done iteratively as no further non-duplicates are detected in M'_t.

SVMs are parameterized and these parameters must in general be learned from the training set. However, as no clean training sets exist, default parameter settings are used in this approach and still show very good results.

5 Evaluation

This section shows the results of the evaluation of the matching method. In detail the following objectives are met by the evaluation:

– All presented decision models outperform a simple baseline method that simply decides on the basis of an unweighted arithmetic mean of the distance values.
– The presented extensions for the Fellegi-Sunter model for continuous distance values and taking dependencies into account outperform the classic approaches.
– The SVM and Fellegi-Sunter based decision models outperform other state of the art unsupervised models and are even nearly as good as fully supervised methods.
– The used distance measure has an enormous impact on the results of the decision module.

5.1 Datasets

For an evaluation a *Restaurant* and a *Census* data set are chosen, which were previously used as benchmarks for duplicate detection, e.g. in [14,11]. The restaurant dataset contains 864 restaurant names and addresses with 112 duplicates, composed of 533 and 331 restaurants assembled from Fodor's and Zagat's restaurant guides. These individual datasets are duplicate free. The attributes being restaurant name, street address, city and cuisine. Table 1 shows a sample duplicate record from this dataset.

Table 1. Sample duplicate records from the *Restaurant* data set

name	address	city	cuisine
uncle nick's	747 ninth ave.	new york city	greek
uncle nick's	747 9th ave. between 50th and 51st sts.	new york	mediterranean

The census data set is a synthetic dataset containing 824 census-like records with 327 duplicates, composed of two duplicate free sets with 449 and 375 records. The attributes being last name, first name, house number and street. Table 2 shows a sample duplicate record from this data set.

Table 2. Sample duplicate records from the *Census* data set

last name	first name	house number	street
JIMENCZ	WILLPAMINA	S 214	BANK
JIMENEZ	WILHEMENIA	214	BANKS

5.2 Experimental Methodology

For the blocking phase the multi-pass algorithm as described in [31] is used with a window distance size of 0.25. On the restaurant dataset the blocking was done on the name and address attribute resulting in 251 potential duplicate pairs for the set M', which corresponds to 100% recall and 45% precision, and 188 non-duplicate pairs for the set U'. On the census dataset the blocking was done on the last name and first name attribute resulting in 1524 potential duplicate pairs for the set M', which corresponds to 90% recall and 19% precision, and 1607 non-duplicate pairs for the set U'.

For comparison of the experimental results precision, recall and F-measures. are calculated. These are defined as usual in information retrieval [32]:

$$Precision = \frac{|CorrectlyIdentifiedDuplicates|}{|IdentifiedDuplicates|}$$

$$Recall = \frac{|CorrectlyIdentifiedDuplicates|}{|TrueDuplicates|}$$

$$F\text{-}measure = \frac{2 * Precision * Recall}{Precision + Recall}$$

The precision-recall curves in the figures use interpolated precision values at 20 standard recall levels following the traditional procedure in information retrieval [32]. However, the figures show only the interesting area between the recall levels 0.6 and 1.

5.3 The Fellegi-Sunter Model as Decision Model

For the evaluation of the approach using the Fellegi-Sunter model as decision model, a threshold of 50% is used, i.e. all pairs that have a matching probability of less than 50% are removed from M'_t.

Dependencies. A first experiment compares the precision and recall of the Fellegi-Sunter model under and without the independence assumption. This is done using continuous values and in the described unsupervised way as well as a supervised way, which calculates the $m(\gamma[a,b])$ and $u(\gamma[a,b])$ values on the true sets M and U. Furthermore the results are also compared against a simple baseline, which simply concatenates the string values of the individual attributes and takes the string similarity between these concatenated strings as overall result - ignoring attribute relevance.

The maximum F-measures of these methods on both data sets are shown in Table 3. Figure 3 shows the precision and recall curves for the restaurant dataset, Figure 4 the curves for the census dataset.

These results show that the Fellegi-Sunter model taking dependencies into account always reaches one of the highest accuracies. Even under the independence assumption it performs significantly better than the baseline. However, the effect of taking dependencies into account depends on the dataset, which can be explained that in the restaurant dataset, there exist less dependencies between the attributes.

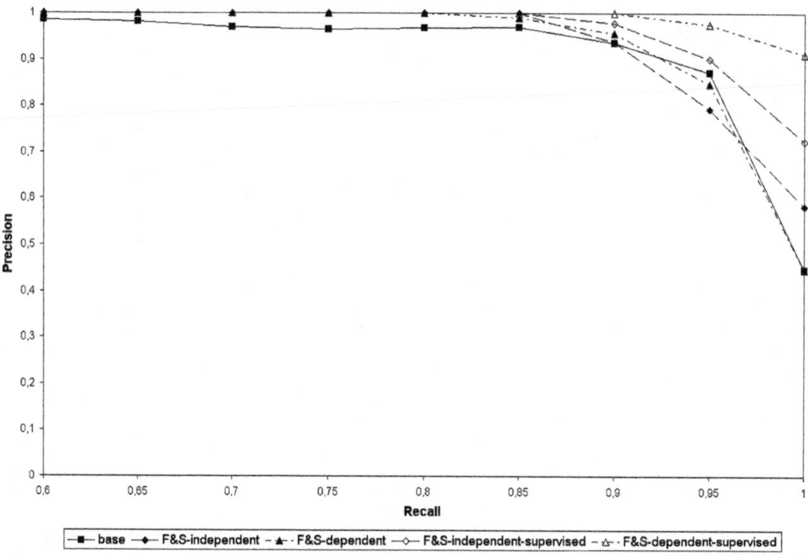

Fig. 3. Precision-Recall for the restaurant dataset

Table 3. Maximum F-measures using the Fellegi-Sunter model as decision model

Method	Restaurant	Census
Baseline	0.916	0.725
unsupervised		
F&S independent	0.943	0.855
F&S dependent	0.940	0.875
supervised		
F&S independent	0.953	0.834
F&S dependent	0.973	0.909

Continuous Values. The previous experiment has already used the extension for continuous distances measures. In order to show the impact of these continuous values in contrast to thresholded boolean "match" - "not match" values is shown in the following experiments. The results of the Fellegi-Sunter model with continuous values and taking dependency into account is compared to the results using thresholded boolean values, with thresholds of 0.1, 0.2, 0.3 and 0.4. The maximum F-measures of these methods on both data sets are shown in table 4. Figure 5 shows the precision and recall curves for the restaurant dataset, Figure 6 the curves for the census dataset.

These results show that boolean values can reach results nearly as good as continuous values under the condition that they are well calibrated. Poorly calibrated thresholds for the boolean values can result in very poor results, like the results for the thresholds 0.1 or 0.4. Therefore the use of continuous distance

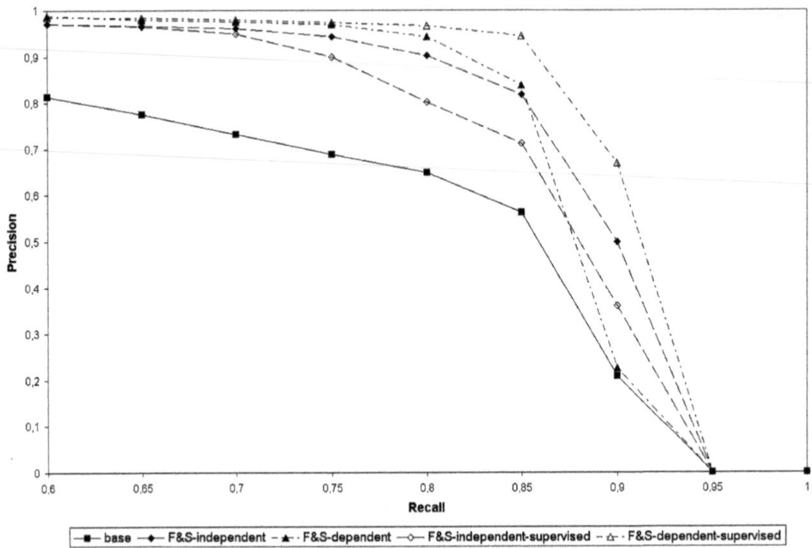

Fig. 4. Precision-Recall for the census dataset

Table 4. Maximum F-measures for boolean variables

Method	Restaurant	Census
F&S continuous	0.940	0.875
boolean - 0.1	0.845	0.649
boolean - 0.2	0.915	0.834
boolean - 0.3	0.930	0.874
boolean - 0.4	0.902	0.803

measures for the comparison vector is not only highly accurate, but also requires much less user-interaction than using boolean values and is therefore preferable.

5.4 Support Vector Machines as Decision Model

The next experiment uses the support vector machines in the way as described in Section 4.5, i.e., the svm is trained with U' as negative examples and with M' as positive examples. To this end the libsvm library was used as provided by [33], taking c-svcs, with a radial basis kernel and setting the gamma and cost parameter to 1. This results in maximum f-measures for the restaurant data set of 0.949 and for the census data set of 0.908. The precision and recall curves are shown in comparison to other approaches in the following section.

These results are very convincing, but it is interesting to note that when changing the parameters gamma and cost the results may vary dramatically and particularly different for the two data sets, i.e., the best parameter settings depend on the data and the default settings that worked for both data sets may not work for others!

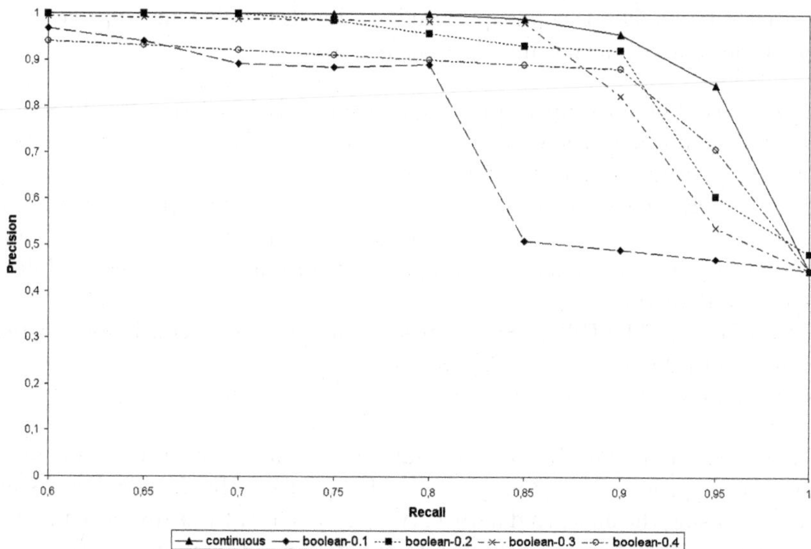

Fig. 5. Precision-Recall for boolean variables on the restaurant dataset

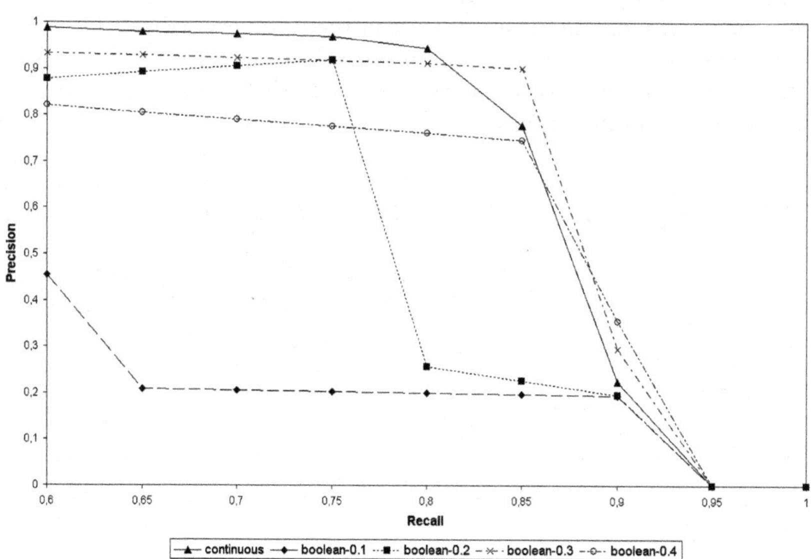

Fig. 6. Precision-Recall for boolean variables on the census dataset

5.5 Comparison of the Approaches

This section compares the Fellgi-Sunter based and SVM based approaches with other state of the art methods. This is done for the unsupervised and the supervised setting. For the unsupervised setting the following approaches are compared on the restaurant and the census data set:

- Base: this baseline simply concatenates the individual string values of the attributes and takes the string similarity between these concatenated strings as overall result - ignoring attribute relevance.
- HGM (Hierarchical Graphical Model): this is the unsupervised approach presented in [11] that uses the same datasets for their evaluation. Their results are simply copied for comparison, although they used a different blocking algorithm.
- Fellegi-Sunter: The Fellegi-Sunter based approach using continuous distance values and taking dependencies into account.
- SVM: The SVM based approach.

It must be noted that the Jaro distance is used as distance function for the experiments as provided by [34], whereas [11] was using the SoftTFIDF distance and [14] was using the Jaccard distance. A comparison of these distance functions is presented in [24]. The impact of different distance functions is evaluated in Section 5.6.

The maximum F-measures of these methods on both data sets are shown in table 5. Figure 7 shows the precision and recall curves for the restaurant dataset, Figure 8 the curves for the census dataset in the unsupervised setting.

These results clearly show that the proposed unsupervised methods significantly outperform other exisiting unsupervised methods and they are even not far away from the results of fully supervised methods.

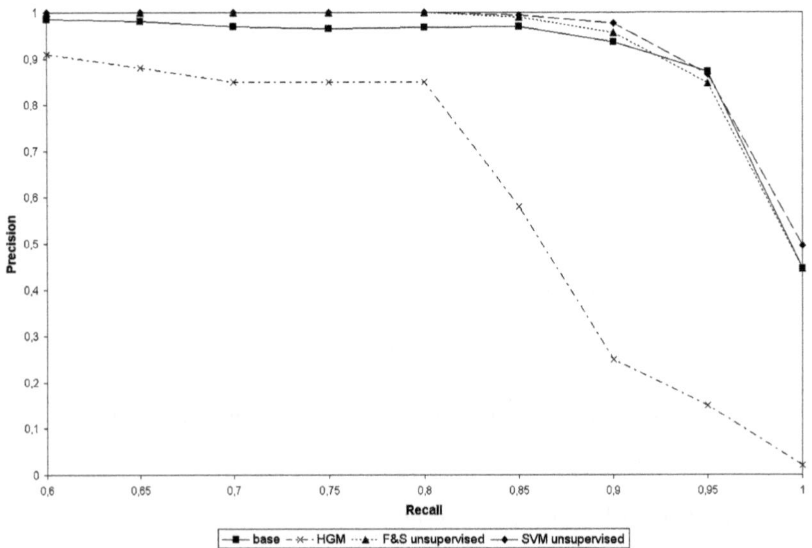

Fig. 7. Precision-Recall for the restaurant dataset

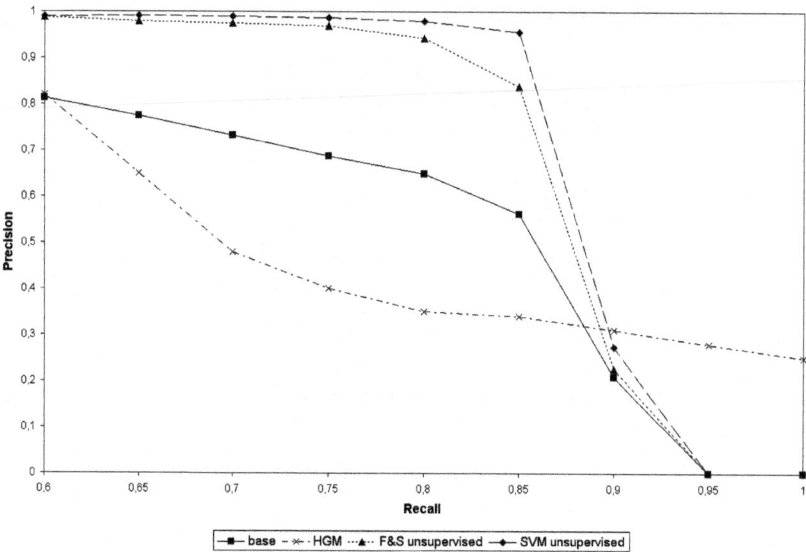

Fig. 8. Precision-Recall for the census dataset

Table 5. Maximum F-measures for detecting duplicates

Method	Restaurant	Census
Base	0.916	0.725
HGM (SoftTFIDF)	0.844	0.759
F&S unsupervised	0.940	0.875
SVM unsupervised	0.949	0.908
SVM B&M (Jaccard)	0.971	-

The higher precision of the HGM method for the census dataset at the 100% recall level is caused by the different blocking algorithm. Ours reaches here around 90% recall, therefore the precision for the 95% and 100% recall levels are 0.

5.6 Impact of Distance Functions

The previous experiments used the Jaro distance for comparison. In order to assess the impact of different similarity functions, the experiments using the Fellegi-Sunter model and the SVM are also carried out with a simple Levenshtein distance [35] and a TFIDF (term frequency/inverse document frequency) distance as often used in information retrieval. Additionally on the restaurant data set a combination of the Jaro and the TFIDF similarity is tested. The maximum F-measures can be found in Table 6 the precision-recall curves for the restaurant data set can be found in Figure 9 and Figure 10. The curves for the census data set are left out for space reasons.

Table 6. Maximum F-measures using different distance measures

Method	Restaurant	Census
F&S levenshtein	0.914	0.851
F&S jaro	0.940	0.875
F&S tfidf	0.964	0.546
F&S tfidf+jaro	0.965	
SVM levenshtein	0.735	0.489
SVM jaro	0.949	0.908
SVM tfidf	0.898	0.600
SVM tfidf+jaro	0.974	

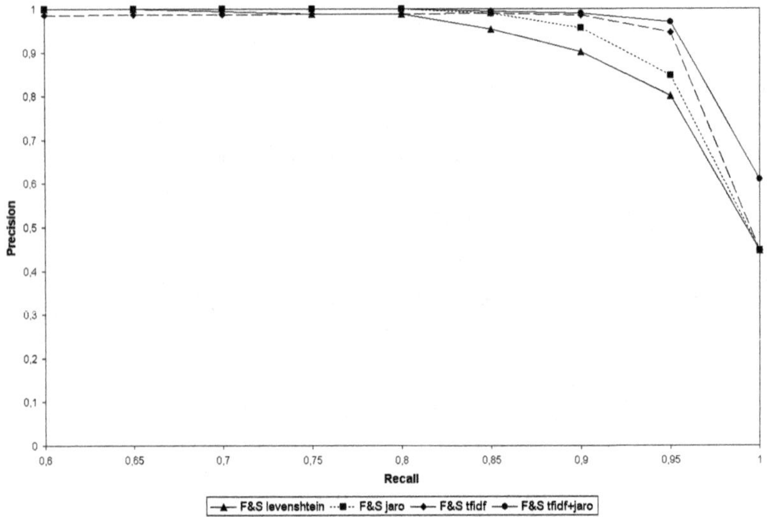

Fig. 9. Precision-Recall for the restaurant dataset using the Fellegi&Sunter model with different similarity measures

The experiment shows that the selection of a good similarity function is of great importance. It shows that the effectiveness of a similarity function depends on the data, in particular the TFIDF similarity function performs much better on the restaurant data set than on the census data. The results further show that the SVM approach is much more sensible to a good similarity function, both alternative similarity functions result in a much worse accuracy. The combination of several similarity measures significantly outperforms those with just one, this can be explained by that a single similarity function in general only detects one kind of error, if several kinds of error might occur, like in the restaurant data set, several similarity measures should be used together for maximum accuracy. These results demand for further work in unsupervised finding ideal similarity functions.

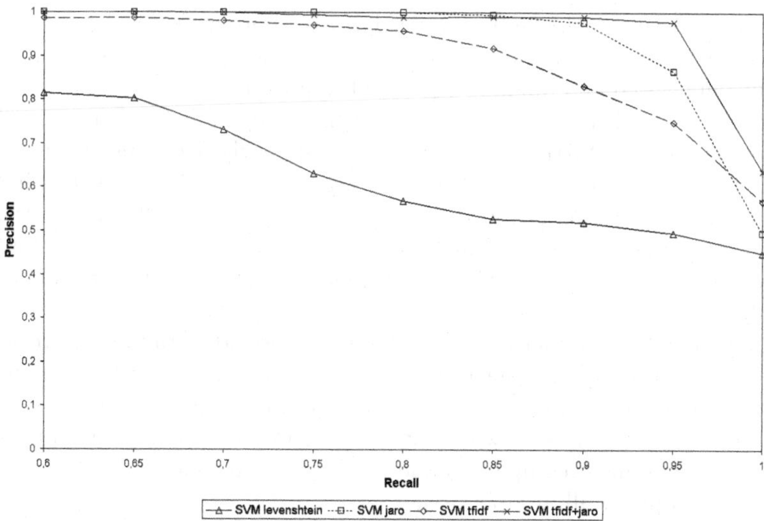

Fig. 10. Precision-Recall for the restaurant dataset using the SVM model with different similarity measures

Relationships. In order to evaluate the approach for taking relationships into account, the "cuisine" attribute of the restaurant data set can be seen as related object, because it realizes a $n : 1$ relationship. The similarity of these attribute values were also difficult to measure with string similarity measures as can be easily seen for examples like "greek-mediterranean" or "asian-chinese". Therefore the *jaro* measure was replaced with the *mutual information score*, which is basically the ratio between the true number of cooccurences of a value-pair to the expected statistical random number of cooccurences.

Using this measure for the "cuisine" attribute and the *jaro* measure for all others, yields a maximum F-measure of 0.955 (vs. 0.940) for the Fellegi-Sunter based model and 0.973 (vs. 0.949) for the SVM based model. This clearly shows the potential of this method, although further experiments with other data sets are required. We expect a much more significant gain in accuracy for more relevant attributes/relationships in other domains.

6 Conclusion and Future Work

This paper has presented an unsupervised approach for duplicate detection, which incorporates sample non-duplicates into the duplicate decision process. This is used either with a refinement of the classic Fellegi-Sunter model for record linkage, which allows determining appropriate parameter values using continuous similarity measures and taking attribute dependencies into account or by using Support Vector Machines. The proposed approach is based on unsupervised learning and domain independence, which makes it completely free from user interaction, i.e., removing the main reason, why classical approaches are very expensive. The evaluations on two test datasets showed that the approach reaches very high accuracy, outperforms existing unsupervised approaches and is nearly competitive with fully supervised and domain dependent approaches.

It has been shown that the importance of the used similarity function is high, therefore we want to further investigate in unsupervised finding ideal (combinations of) similarity functions. Also the usage of association measures like the mutual information score has been shown to be a simple but effective method to incorporate interrelated objects into the duplicate detection process. However, other data sets that are expected to profit more of this method need to be found and evaluated.

Ongoing scalability experiments on large real world data sets, have shown that the naive training of Fellegi-Sunter distributions and SVMs with the full M' and U' sets result in quadratic behavior. The simple optimization, restricting the size of these training sets with a fixed threshold has shown very promising results and allows linear complexity and for this reason good scalability. Finding an ideal threshold is still an open issue.

References

1. Fellegi, I.P., Sunter, A.B.: A theory for record linkage. Journal of the American Statistical Association **64** (1969) 1183–1210
2. Russell, S., Norvig, P.: Artificial Intelligence: A Modern Approach. Prentice Hall (2002)
3. Hernandez, M.A., Stolfo, S.J.: Real-world data is dirty: Data cleansing and the merge/purge problem. Data Mining and Knowledge Discovery **2** (1998) 9–37
4. Galhardas, H., Florescu, D., Shasha, D., Simon, E.: An extensible framework for data cleaning. In: Proceddings of the 16th International Conference on Data Engineering (ICDE '00). (2000) 312
5. Monge, A., Elkan, C.: An efficient domain independent algorithm for detecting approximately duplicate database records. In: In Proceedings of the SIGMOD Workshop on Data Mining and Knowledge Discovery. (1997)
6. Newcombe, H.B., Kennedy, J.M., Axford, S.J., James, A.P.: Automatic linkage of vital records. Science **130** (1959) 954–959
7. Winkler, W.E.: Using the em algorithm for weight computation in the fellegi-sunter model of record linkage. In: Proceedings of the Section on Survey Research Methods, American Statistical Association. (1988) 667–671
8. Dempster, A.P., Laird, N.M., Rubin, D.B.: Maximum likelihood from incomplete data via the em algorithm. Journal of the Royal Statistical Society, Series B **34** (1977) 1–38
9. Winkler, W.E.: Improved decision rules in the fellegi-sunter model of record linkage. In: Proceedings of the Section on Survey Research Methods, American Statistical Association. (1993) 274–279
10. Larsen, M.D., Rubin, D.B.: Alternative automated record linkage using mixture models. Journal of the American Statistical Association **79** (2001) 32–41
11. Ravikumar, P., Cohen, W.W.: A hierarchical graphical model for record linkage. In: AUAI '04: Proceedings of the 20th conference on Uncertainty in artificial intelligence, AUAI Press (2004) 454–461

12. Elfeky, M.G., Verykios, V.S., Elmargarid, A.K.: Tailor: A record linkage toolbox. In: Proceedings of the 18th International Conference on Data Engineering (ICDE'02), Washington, DC, USA, IEEE Computer Society (2002) 17
13. Cohen, W.W., Richman, J.: Learning to match and cluster large high-dimensional data sets for data integration. In: Proceedings of the Eighth ACM SIGKDD International Conference on Knowledge Discovery and Data Mining (KDD-2002), Edmonton, Alberta (2002)
14. Bilenko, M., Mooney, R.J.: Learning to combine trained distance metrics for duplicate detection in databases. Technical Report AI 02-296, Artificial Intelligence Laboratory, University of Texas at Austin, Austin, TX (2002)
15. Tejada, S., Knoblock, C.A., Minton, S.: Learning object identification rules for information integration. Information Systems Journal **26** (2001) 635–656
16. Sarawagi, S., Bhamidipaty, A.: Interactive deduplication using active learning. In: Proceedings of the Eighth ACM SIGKDD International Conference on Knowledge Discovery and Data Mining (KDD-2002), Edmonton, Alberta (2002)
17. Ananthakrishna, R., Chaudhuri, S., Ganti, V.: Eliminating fuzzy duplicates in data warehouses. In: Proceedings of the 28th International Conference on Very Large Data Bases(VLDB '02). (2002)
18. Parag, Domingos, P.: Multi-relational record linkage. In: Proceedings of the KDD-2004 Workshop on Multi-Relational Data Mining. (2004) 31–48
19. Dong, X., Halevy, A.Y., Madhavan, J.: Reference reconciliation in complex information spaces. In: SIGMOD Conference. (2005) 85–96
20. Bhattacharya, I., Getoor, L.: Deduplication and group detection using links. In: Proceedings of the KDD-2004 Workshop on Link Analysis and Group Detection. (2004)
21. Pasula, H., Marthi, B., Milch, B., Russell, S., Shpitser, I.: Identity uncertainty and citation matching. In: Advances in Neural Information Processing Systems 15, MIT Press (2003)
22. Ley, M.: DBLP computer science bibliography. (http://dblp.uni-trier.de/)
23. Fachinformationszentrum-Karlsruhe: CompuScience. (http://www.zblmath.fiz-karlsruhe.de/cs/)
24. Cohen, W.W., Ravikumar, P., Fienberg, S.E.: A comparison of string metrics for matching names and records. In: Proceedings of the KDD-2003 Workshop on Data Cleaning, Record Linkage, and Object Consolidation, Washington, DC (2003) 13–18
25. Evert, S.: Computational approaches to collocations. (http://www.collocations.de/)
26. Church, K.W., Hanks, P.: Word association norms, mutual information and lexicography. Computational Linguistics **16** (1990) 22–29
27. Church, K.W., Gale, W., Hanks, P., Hindle, D.: Using statistics in lexical analysis. Lexical Acquisition: Using On-line Recources to Build a Lexicon (1991) 115–164
28. Sachs, L. In: Angewandte Statistik. Springer, Berlin (2004) 434–435
29. MacQueen, J.: Some methods for classification and analysis of multivariate observations. In: Proceedings of the Fifth Berkeley Symposium on Math., Stat. and Prob. (1967) 281–296
30. Shi, J., Malik, J.: Normalized cuts and image segmentation. IEEE Trans. CAD-Integrated Circuits and Systems **13** (2000) 888–905
31. Lehti, P., Fankhauser, P.: A precise blocking method for record linkage. In: Proceedings of the 7th International Conference on Data Warehousing and Knowledge Discovery (DaWaK'05). (2005)

32. Baeza-Yates, R., Ribiero-Neto, B. In: Modern Information Retrieval. Addison Wesley (1999) 74–79
33. Chang, C.C., Lin, C.J.: Libsvm - a library for support vector machines. (http:// www.csie.ntu.edu.tw/ cjlin/libsvm/)
34. Cohen, W.W., Ravikumar, P., Fienberg, S.: Secondstring - an open-source java-based package of approximate string-matching techniques. (http:// secondstring.sourceforge.net/)
35. Levenshtein, V.I.: Binary codes capable of correcting insertions and reversals. Soviet Physics Doklady **10** (1966) 707–710

Towards Algebraic Query Optimisation for XQuery*

Markus Kirchberg, Faizal Riaz-ud-Din,
Klaus-Dieter Schewe, and Alexei Tretiakov

Massey University, Department of Information Systems and
Information Science Research Centre
Private Bag 11 222, Palmerston North, New Zealand
{m.kirchberg, f.din, k.d.schewe, a.tretiakov}@massey.ac.nz

Abstract. XML-based databases have become a major area of interest in database research. Abstractly speaking they can be considered as a resurrection of complex-value databases using constructors for records, lists, unions plus optionality and references. XQuery has become the standard query language for XML. As XQuery is a declarative query language, the problem of query optimisation arises. In this paper an algebraic approach to query optimisation is introduced. This is based on a translation of XQuery into a query algebra for rational tree types. The algebra uses simple operations on types and structural recursion for lists. The translation exploits linguistic reflection for the type-safe expansion of path expressions. The availability of an algebraic representation of queries permits query rewriting, which in combination with cost heuristics permits queries to be rewritten and thus optimised.

1 Introduction

Though XML is more than a database language [26], it has become a major area of interest in database research. XML can be considered as a complex-value data model using constructors for records, lists, unions plus optionality and references [1,36].

Using XML for databases requires schema definition, query and update languages. By now, XML Schema [46] has become the W3C standard for defining schemata, while XQuery [16,47] is the recommended standard for querying XML documents. For updates only little work has been done so far, e.g. [42,22].

In fact, XML Schema supports almost directly the definition of tree types using the mentioned constructors. XQuery combines ideas from various predecessor proposals for XML query languages [4,6,12]. Most importantly, queries are composed of a matching part that binds variables to values according to a given XML document, and a construction part that creates new XML documents from these variables.

* The work reported in this paper was supported by FRST/NERF grant MAUX0025 "DIMO – Distributed Multi-Level Object Bases".

S. Spaccapietra (Ed.): Journal on Data Semantics VII, LNCS 4244, pp. 165–195, 2006.

As XQuery is a declarative query language with XPath [14] as its core, the problem of query optimisation arises. This problem is directly related to the implementation of XQuery, for which there are two major lines of research. The first one, e.g. [11], attempts a translation to SQL based on a reification of XML via relational database technology. The drawback of this approach is that semantics may be lost in the translation from trees to relations. The alternative is to approach a direct implementation of XQuery, e.g. [28].

In this paper we take a different approach, which is closer to the corresponding relational theory. Considering XML as a complex value data model, each XML document can be represented by a rational tree, i.e. a (possibly infinite) tree with only finitely many different subtrees. In fact, rational trees represent possibly infinite data structures that still can be finitely represented. The seminal work in [10] contains the mathematical theory of rational trees. In [3,32] it was shown that rational trees capture indeed the gist of the structural notion of "object" in object oriented databases. In [30] this was extended to show that in fact each reasonable data model can be represented using rational trees. In fact, the finite representation of a rational tree results from breaking cycles and introducing identifiers. Conversely, a collection of objects with identifiers and references based on these identifiers can be expanded into rational trees, provided a condition known as "value representability" is satisfied [31,32]. Value representability and thus the representation by rational trees is also known as a necessary and sufficient condition for the unique identification of objects and the existence of schema-defined generic update operations [32].

Our idea is to exploit a query algebra for rational trees and to use algebraic query rewriting in combination with query costs heuristics for query optimisation. This idea requires a translation of XQuery into a rational tree query algebra. In [30] it has been shown how the gist of query algebras can be expressed in a generic rational tree algebra. In fact, only operations defined for the constructors of a type system plus a single generalised join-operation are needed. In [19] this has been extended by showing that indeed all query algebras that were developed together with object oriented databases, e.g. RELOOP [8], ENCORE [33], AQUA [24], QAL [29], HERM-algebra [43] and GOMext [9,17], can be expressed in a generic rational tree algebra. Though that is has not yet been formally proven, the same presumably holds for algebras proposed for XML such as XAlgebra [13] and TAX [15].

For short let RTA denote the query algebra for rational trees from [30]. RTA uses operators for the type system, i.e. for the abstract system of types as defined in [16]. In particular, it exploits structural recursion [25,41,44] for lists. More generally, structural recursion was developed for all kinds of bulk types such as lists, sets, multisets (aka bags), binary trees, etc. [5,41,44], but the primary interest was on finite sets [40,41,45]. Structural recursion was thoroughly investigated throughout the nineties. The fundamental idea of structural recursion on such bulk types is simple and powerful at the same time exploiting the simple fact that non-empty lists can be constructed by using singleton lists and list concatenation, so three constructors – the third one producing the empty list – are sufficient for the representation of lists. Consequently, operations on lists are sufficiently determined by their effects on the empty list, singleton lists, which can be defined by an operation on the list element, and lists that are the concatenation of two sublists. Similarly, constructors for the empty set, singleton sets and set union will give us all finite sets with elements of a particular type. Koch in [23] has used a similar approach based on list comprehensions. However, his work is placed in a complexity-theoretic setting.

As shown in [20] the translation of XQuery to RTA works best, if schema information is available, in particular for the path expressions. This reflects the fact that the major difficulty in implementing XQuery results from path expressions [14,27], i.e. from the fragment of the language that subsumes XPath [7]. Then it is a natural idea to exploit type-safe linguistic reflection [38,37] to deal with this problem. The basic idea of linguistic reflection consists of providing macros in a language that will be expanded during compilation or execution. In the case of XQuery these macros will be parts of FLWOR- and in particular path expressions. The macro expansion requires some complex computation, during which the information about the schema will be needed. In order to do this, the expression at hand will be treated as a value of some type, such that a predefined process can take this value as its input and produce another value representing the expanded macro as its output. This output value has to be treated again as part of the code to be compiled or executed. Linguistic reflection is as old as the roots of functional programming, but due to the work of mainly Stemple and Sheard [39,35,34] it has been shifted from a run-time to a compile-time approach and in addition has been extended to guarantee type-safety. The work in [18] contains an implementation of linguistic reflection in the context of persistent programming languages.

Using this idea of linguistic reflection is what we do in our approach, i.e. we present a translation from essential parts of XQuery to RTA and show how this translation benefits from linguistic reflection. In case there is no schema information, it must be derived from a given document, but we will not explore this direction in this paper.

Besides algebraic query optimisation, the expected benefits of the translation to a query algebra are the easy implementation of the operations and the integration with programming languages, e.g. using the physical architecture from [21], and the easy extension to other constructors such as sets and multisets in case the order that comes with the list constructor is considered unnecessary or even undesired.

We first introduce an abstract model of XML, XQuery and RTA in Sections 2 and 3, respectively. In Section 4 we then outline the translation from XQuery to RTA. We focus on structural recursion and show that some of the functions used as parameters are complicated, as they refer to path finding. We show how linguistic reflection can be used to expand these functions. In particular, the complexity arising from the paths will be taken up by the translation. Section 5 is then devoted to algebraic query optimisation. For this we explore cost heuristics for the various operators of RTA, which directly lead to query rewriting rules. We conclude with a brief summary.

2 Abstract Model of XML and XQuery

In this section we describe some basics of XML and XQuery. Of course, as both of these are complex languages, we cannot describe all details and therefore take a more abstract view focusing more on the semantics than on the syntax.

2.1 XML Documents as Trees

Start with a type system that supports records, lists and unions. Using abstract syntax this type system can be described by

$$t = b \mid (t_1, \dots, t_n) \mid [t] \mid t_1 \oplus \cdots \oplus t_n.$$

Here b represents a (not further specified) collection of base types, e.g. the base types supported by XML such as *String*, *Integer*, *Double*, *ID*, etc. For reasons that will become clear, when we add references, we only use a single type *ID* for identifiers. Furthermore, assume that one of the base types is *Empty* with only one possible value. This type can be used to support optionality.

We use $(t_1, \dots, t_n)$ to denote an ordered record type with component types t_i, the type $[t]$ is used for finite lists, and $t_1 \oplus \cdots \oplus t_n$ is used for a (disjoint) union type with components t_i.

Each type t denotes a set of values called its *domain* $dom(t)$. Formally, we obtain these domains as follows:

- $dom(b_i) = V_i$, i.e. for each base type b_i we assume some set V_i of values of that type, e.g. $dom(EMPTY) = \{\perp\}$.
- $dom((t_1, \dots, t_n)) = dom(t_1) \times \cdots \times dom(t_n)$.
- $dom([t]) = \{[v_1, \dots, v_k] \mid k \in \mathbb{N}, v_i \in dom(t)\}$.
- $dom(t_1 \oplus \cdots \oplus t_n) = \{(i, v_i) \mid 1 \leq i \leq n, v_i \in dom(t_i)\}$.

Then an XML document can be represented by a value of some type t, which in turn is representable as a tree, provided the document does not contain references. In particular, we can treat attributes in the same way as subelements – which is no loss of generality for databases, whereas for text markup it may make a significant difference.

In order to also capture references, we extend the type system to

$$t = b \mid \ell \mid (t_1, \dots, t_n) \mid [t] \mid t_1 \oplus \cdots \oplus t_n \mid \ell : t,$$

where ℓ represents reference labels. The domains are simply $dom(\ell) = dom(ID)$ and $dom(\ell : t) = \{(i, v) \mid i \in dom(\ell), v \in dom(t)\}$. Following [1] each occurrence of a value i of type *ID* in some complex value v that corresponds to a labelled type $\ell : t$ *defines* a reference, whereas each occurrence of a value i of type *ID* in

v that corresponds to a label ℓ *uses* the reference. In XML Schema the usage of references corresponds to the type *IDREF*, whereas the definition of references corresponds to the type *ID*. Furthermore, *IDREFS* corresponds to a list type $[\ell]$ – in fact, here we would prefer to use a set type, but for simplicity and orthogonality of the constructors let us use only one bulk type constructor.

Example 2.1. Let us look at the following schema definition in XML Schema:

```
<xs:schema xmlns:xs="http://www.w3.org/2001/XMLSchema">
  <xs:element name="coffee-shop">
    <xs:complexType>
      <xs:sequence>
        <xs:element ref="coffees"/>
        <xs:element ref="growers"/>
        <xs:element ref="regions"/>
      </xs:sequence>
    </xs:complexType>
  </xs:element>
  <xs:element name="coffees">
    <xs:complexType>
      <xs:sequence>
        <xs:element ref="coffee" minOccurs="0" maxOccurs="unbounded"/>
      </xs:sequence>
    </xs:complexType>
  </xs:element>
  <xs:element name="growers">
    <xs:complexType>
      <xs:sequence>
        <xs:element ref="grower" minOccurs="0" maxOccurs="unbounded"/>
      </xs:sequence>
    </xs:complexType>
  </xs:element>
  <xs:element name="regions">
    <xs:complexType>
      <xs:sequence>
        <xs:element ref="region" minOccurs="0" maxOccurs="unbounded"/>
      </xs:sequence>
    </xs:complexType>
  </xs:element>
  <xs:element name="coffee">
    <xs:complexType>
      <xs:sequence>
        <xs:element name="name" type="xs:string"/>
        <xs:element name="body" type="xs:string" minOccurs="0"/>
        <xs:element ref="blend" maxOccurs="unbounded"/>
        <xs:element name="price" type="xs:decimal"/>
      </xs:sequence>
      <xs:attribute name="c-id" type="xs:ID" use="required"/>
      <xs:attribute name="producer" type="xs:IDREF" use="required"/>
    </xs:complexType>
```

```
  </xs:element>
  <xs:element name="blend">
    <xs:complexType>
      <xs:sequence>
        <xs:element name="bean" type="xs:string"/>
        <xs:element name="percentage" type="xs:integer"/>
      </xs:sequence>
    </xs:complexType>
  </xs:element>
  <xs:element name="grower">
    <xs:complexType>
      <xs:sequence>
        <xs:element name="name" type="xs:string"/>
        <xs:element name="owner" type="xs:string" maxOccurs="unbounded"/>
        <xs:element name="area" type="xs:string" minOccurs="0"/>
        <xs:element name="established" type="xs:date" minOccurs="0"/>
      </xs:sequence>
      <xs:attribute name="g-id" type="xs:ID" use="required"/>
      <xs:attribute name="in-region" type="xs:IDREF" use="required"/>
    </xs:complexType>
  </xs:element>
  <xs:element name="region">
    <xs:complexType>
      <xs:sequence>
        <xs:element name="name" type="xs:string"/>
      </xs:sequence>
      <xs:attribute name="r-id" type="xs:ID" use="required"/>
      <xs:attribute name="famous-coffees" type="xs:IDREFS"
       use="required"/>
    </xs:complexType>
  </xs:element>
</xs:schema>
```

That is, a coffee-shop contains a list of coffees, growers and regions. A coffee is described by a name, a body (optional) and a blend, which is a sequence of beans together with their percentages. A grower is described by a name, a list of owners, an area (optional) and an establishment date (optional). A region just has a name. Furthermore, there are references from a coffee to the grower that produces it, from a grower to the region it is located in, and from a region to all its famous coffees.

Using our type system, we obtain the following complex type definitions for representing this schema:

coffee-shop = (coffees, growers, regions)
coffees = [c-id : coffee]
growers = [g-id : grower]
regions = [r-id : region]
coffee = (c-name, body $\oplus$ *Empty*, [blend], price, producer)
c-name = *String*

body = *String*
price = *Decimal*
producer = g-id
blend = (bean, percentage)
bean = *String*
percentage = *Integer*
grower = (g-name, [owner], area ⊕ *Empty*, established ⊕ *Empty*, in-region)
g-name = *String*
owner = *String*
area = *String*
established = *Date*
in-region = r-id
region = (r-name, famous-coffees)
r-name = *String*
famous-coffees = [c-id]

Here c-id, g-id and r-id are labels.

Example 2.2. Consider the following XML document that is in accordance with the schema defined in Example 2.1:

```
<coffee-shop
  xmlns:xsi="http://www.w3.org/2001/XMLSchema-instance"
  xsi:noNamespaceSchemaLocation="coffee.xsd">
  <coffees>
    <coffee c-id="o11" producer="o1">
      <name>Java</name>
      <body>full</body>
      <blend>
        <bean>Arabica</bean>
        <percentage>100</percentage>
      </blend>
      <price>31.95</price>
    </coffee>
    <coffee c-id="o12" producer="o1">
      <name>Sumatra</name>
      <body>very full</body>
      <blend>
        <bean>Robusta</bean>
        <percentage>100</percentage>
      </blend>
      <price>34.95</price>
    </coffee>
    <coffee c-id="o13" producer="o1">
      <name>New Guinea</name>
      <blend>
        <bean>Arabica Old</bean>
        <percentage>65</percentage>
```

```
      </blend>
      <blend>
        <bean>Robusta Old</bean>
        <percentage>35</percentage>
      </blend>
      <price>29.95</price>
    </coffee>
  </coffees>
  <growers>
    <grower g-id="o1" in-region="o2">
      <name>Fine Blend</name>
      <owner>Mr Bean</owner>
      <owner>Mrs Bean</owner>
      <area>231 ha</area>
      <established>1987-01-01</established>
    </grower>
  </growers>
  <regions>
    <region r-id="o2" famous-coffees="o11 o12">
      <name>Asia</name>
    </region>
  </regions>
</coffee-shop>
```

This XML document can be represented by the following complex value:

$$
\begin{array}{l}
(\; [\; (\&o_{11}, (\text{Java}, (1, \text{full}), [(\text{Arabica}, 100)], 31.95, \&o_1)), \\
\quad (\&o_{12}, (\text{Sumatra}, (1, \text{very full}), [(\text{Robusta}, 100)], 34.95, \&o_1)), \\
\quad (\&o_{13}, (\text{New Guinea}, (2, \perp), \\
\qquad [(\text{Arabica Old}, 65), (\text{Robusta Old}, 35)], 29.95, \&o_1))], \\
\; [\; (\&o_1, (\text{Fine Blend}, [\text{Mr Bean}, \text{Mrs Bean}], \\
\qquad (1, 231 \text{ ha}), (1, 1987\text{-}01\text{-}01), \&o_2))], \\
\; [\; (\&o_2, (\text{Asia}, [\&o_{11}, \&o_{12}]))])
\end{array}
$$

2.2 XQuery in a Nutshell

XQuery is a query language allowing to extract sequences of subtrees and base type values from any number of XML document trees, and to combine them to construct a sequence of trees and basic values (the so-called **items**) forming the result of the query. In practice, most often the result of the query is a sequence consisting of a single tree.

In XQuery, the XML documents serving as input are identified by using the so-called input functions, of which the most commonly used one is doc, which accepts a URL corresponding to the location of an XML document as a parameter. For example, `doc("coffee-shop.xml")` would retrieve the `coffee-shop.xml` document from the current directory.

Sequences of subtrees are retrieved by using the so-called path expressions, consisting of one or more **steps** separated by a slash, `/`, or double slash, `//`. Each step acts on the sequence of items created by the previous step to form a further sequence, which either forms the output of the path expression (if the step is the last one), or serves as input for further steps. The following query, formed by combining an input function with a path expression, will result in a sequence of `name` elements representing coffee names (assuming `coffee-shop.xml` is the XML document introduced in the previous section): `doc("coffee-shop.xml")/coffee-shop/coffees/coffee/name`.

`doc("coffee-shop.xml")/coffee-shop` results in a sequence consisting of a single `coffee-shop` element, `doc("coffee-shop.xml")/coffee-shop/coffees` results in a sequence consisting of a single `coffees` element (a sub-element of the `coffee-shop` element obtained in the previous step), `doc("coffee-shop.xml")/coffee-shop/coffees/coffee` will result in a sequence of all `coffee` elements from `coffees` and so on. Filtering can be applied to restrict which of the items are to be included in a given step. While `/` retrieves child items (branches immediately connected to the root), `//` forms a sequence consisting of all matching subtrees, at all depths. `/` and `//` are illustrated in examples 2.3 and 2.4, respectively.

As XQuery is a functional language, an XQuery program can be regarded as an expression formed by subexpressions which, at execution time, are evaluated in the order of precedence. The most commonly used type of expressions in XQuery are the so-called FLWOR (`for`, `let`, `where`, `order by`, `return`) expressions. In a FLWOR expression, a `for` clause binds each item of a sequence to a variable, and evaluates the rest of the expression with that binding, resulting in as many evaluations as there are items in the sequence. The `for` clause is illustrated in Example 2.4 below.

A `let` clause binds the whole sequence to a variable, and evaluates the rest of the expression just once, with that binding. The `let` clause is illustrated in Examples 2.5, 2.6, and 2.7.

The `where` clause serves as a filter: the rest of the FLWOR expression is executed only if the boolean expression associated with the `where` clause evaluates to true. This is illustrated in Example 2.5, 2.6, and 2.7.

The `order by` clause is used for sorting (we do not discuss it here any further).

Finally, the `return` clause is a constructor, instantiating an item that is to be included as the result of the query. By using `return`, items retrieved from different parts of the same document, or from different documents, can be combined together, resulting in sophisticated joins. As shown in Example 2.7, the constructor formed by using the `return` clause can include subqueries, whose output is incorporated into the sequence created by the constructor.

XML Query can make use of type information from XML Schema documents associated with XML documents inputted by the query by explicitly specifying the type of items to be included in sequences or to be constructed. In addition, parsers are able to analyse and to reject a query based on schema information only, if the query is found to construct items that do not match the declared types for constructor output.

Example 2.3. Assume the document in Example 2.2 is stored in coffee-shop.xml. Then

```
<coffees>
  {
    doc("coffee-shop.xml")/coffee-shop/coffees/coffee/name
  }
</coffees>
```

is a simple query that will select the names of coffees. For our example document the result would be

```
<coffees>
   <name>Java</name>
   <name>Sumatra</name>
   <name>New Guinea</name>
</coffees>
```

Example 2.4. The query

```
<coffee-makers>
  {
    for $N in doc("coffee-shop.xml")//owner
    return <name>{ $N/text() }</name>
  }
</coffee-makers>
```

returns the names of coffee owners.

Example 2.5. The following is a query with a more interesting `where`-clause, which returns the names of Arabica coffees:

```
<Arabicas>
  {
    for $W in doc("coffee-shop.xml")/coffee-shop/coffees/coffee
    let $N := $W/name, $B := $W/blend
    where $B/bean/text() = "Arabica" and $B/percentage/text() = 100
    return <name>{ $N/text() }</name>
  }
</Arabicas>
```

Example 2.6. The following query, which contains selection conditions on the paths, will produce a list of coffees with their producers:

```
<coffees>
  {
    let $db := doc("coffee-shop.xml")
    for $W in $db//coffee, $V in $db//grower
    let $P := $W/@producer, $N := $W/name, $M := $V/name,
        $I := $V/@g-id
    where $I = $P
```

```
      return
        <coffee>
          <product>{ $N/text() }</product>
          <producer>{ $M/text() }</producer>
        </coffee>
    }
  </coffees>
```

Example 2.7. The following is an example of a nested query:

```
  <coffees>
    {
      let $db := doc("coffee-shop.xml")
      for $N in $db//coffee/name
      return
        <coffee>
          { $N }
          {
            for $W in $db//coffee
            where $W/name = $N
            return $W/body
          }
        </coffee>
    }
  </coffees>
```

The query lists the names of all coffees, adding to each name the corresponding body, when such information is available.

3 RTA: A Rational Tree Query Algebra

Following a basic idea in [30] we use a query algebra with operations "induced" from the type system plus a join-operation. For our purposes here it is more convenient to consider products instead of joins.

In doing so, let $\mathbb{1}$ denote a trivial type with only one value in its domain. We use a unique "forget"-operation $\mathtt{triv} : t \to \mathbb{1}$ for each type t. Assume further a boolean type $BOOL$ with constant values $\mathbf{T}$ and $\mathbf{F}$. Thus, we may consider the operations $\wedge : BOOL \times BOOL \to BOOL$ (conjunction), $\neg : BOOL \to BOOL$ (negation) and $\Rightarrow: BOOL \times BOOL \to BOOL$ (implication).

We also use a polymorphic equality function $\mathtt{eq} : t \times t \to BOOL$ for any type t. Obviously, $\mathtt{eq}(x, y) = \mathbf{T}$ iff $x = y$ holds.

For record types we consider *projection* $\pi_i : (t_1, \dots, t_n) \to t_i$ and *product* $o_1 \times \cdots \times o_n : t \to (t_1, \dots, t_n)$ for given operations $o_i : t \to t_i$. Obviously, we have $\pi_i(x_1, \dots, x_n) = x_i$ and $(o_1 \times \cdots \times o_n)(x) = (o_1(x), \dots, o_n(x))$. As usual, we write $\pi_{i_1,\dots,i_k}$ as a shortcut for $\pi_{i_1} \times \cdots \times \pi_{i_k}$.

For union types we use the canonical embeddings $\iota_i : t_i \to t_1 \oplus \cdots \oplus t_n$ with $\iota_i(x) = (i, x)$. Other operations on union types take the form $o_1 + \cdots + o_n$:

$t_1 \oplus \cdots \oplus t_n \to t$ for given operations $o_i : t_i \to t$, so we have $(o_1 + \cdots + o_n)(i, x) = o_i(x)$.

For list types we may consider $\frown$ (concatenation), the constant $\mathtt{empty} : \mathbb{1} \to [t]$ and the *singleton* operation $\mathtt{single} : t \to [t]$ with well known semantics.

It should be noted here that document order is preserved through the use of lists. The ordering of the elements in the lists conforms to the ordering of the elements in the queried XML document (or conforms to specific re-ordering in the query itself) throughout the execution process.

3.1 Structural Recursion

In addition, we consider structural recursion $\mathtt{src}[e, g, \sqcup] : [t] \to t'$ with a value e of type t', an operation $g : t \to t'$ and an operation $\sqcup : (t', t') \to t'$, which is defined as follows:

$$\begin{aligned} \mathtt{src}[e, g, \sqcup]([]) &= e \\ \mathtt{src}[e, g, \sqcup]([x]) &= g(x) \\ \mathtt{src}[e, g, \sqcup](X \frown Y) &= \mathtt{src}[e, g, \sqcup](X) \sqcup \mathtt{src}[e, g, \sqcup](Y) \end{aligned}$$

In order to be well-defined $\sqcup$ must be associative with e as neutral element, i.e. $(x \sqcup y) \sqcup z = x \sqcup (y \sqcup z)$ and $x \sqcup e = e \sqcup x = x$ hold for all $x, y, z \in dom(t')$.

Let us illustrate structural recursion by some more or less standard examples. First assume that t is a "number type", on which addition $+ : t \times t \to t$ is defined. Then $\mathtt{src}[0, id, +]$ with the identity function id on t defines the sum of the elements in a set. In this way all the known aggregate functions of SQL and more can be defined by structural recursion.

Now consider an operation $f : t \to t'$. We want to raise f to an operation $\mathtt{map}(f) : [t] \to [t']$ by applying f to each element of a list. Obviously, we have $\mathtt{map}(f) = \mathtt{src}[[], \mathtt{single} \circ f, \frown]$.

Next consider an operation $\varphi : t \to BOOL$, i.e. a predicate. We want to define an operation $\mathtt{filter}(\varphi) : [t] \to [t]$, which maps a given list to the sublist of all elements satisfying the predicate φ. For this we may write $\mathtt{filter}(\varphi) =$

$$\mathtt{src}[[], \mathtt{if\_else} \circ (\varphi \times \mathtt{single} \times (\mathtt{empty} \circ \mathtt{triv})), \frown]$$

with the operation $\mathtt{if\_else} : (BOOL, t, t) \to t$ with $(\mathbf{T}, x, y) \mapsto x$ and $(\mathbf{F}, x, y) \mapsto y$.

As a third example assume that t is a type, on which addition $+ : (t, t) \to t$ is defined. Then $\mathtt{src}[0, id, +]$ with the identity id on t defines the sum of the elements in a list.

3.2 Querying XML with RTA

Let us simply illustrate now how RTA can be applied to query XML. We will use the queries from the previous section and write equivalent queries in RTA.

Example 3.1. Let us consider first the query in Example 2.3. In this case we basically have to analyse a path expression. For this assume that v_{in} is the complex value in Example 2.2, i.e. it represents the corresponding XML document coffee-shop.xml.

The construct doc(coffee-shop.xml)/coffee-shop creates a list with the whole document as its only entry, which corresponds to applying the RTA-operation `single` to v_{in}. Then /coffees selects the first successor of the root. As v_{in} is a triple, this corresponds to applying $\mathtt{map}(\pi_1)$ to $[v_{\text{in}}]$. This gives

$$\begin{aligned}\mathtt{map}(\pi_1)([v_{\text{in}}]) &= \mathtt{src}[[], \mathtt{single} \circ \pi_1, \frown]([v_{\text{in}}]) \\ &= \mathtt{single} \circ \pi_1(v_{\text{in}}) \\ &= [\pi_1(v_{\text{in}})]\end{aligned}$$

The effect of /coffee in the XQuery path expression is to produce only the list of coffees, i.e. $\pi_1(v_{\text{in}})$. This can be achieved by another application of structural recursion, in this case $\mathtt{src}[[], \mathtt{id}, \frown]$. This gives

$$\mathtt{src}[[], \mathtt{id}, \frown]([\pi_1(v_{\text{in}})]) = \pi_1(v_{\text{in}})$$

as desired. Finally, the effect of /name in the XQuery path expression is first to throw away the identifiers for coffees, which can be achieved by applying π_2, then taking the first component, i.e. to apply π_1. Thus, the last step is the application of $\mathtt{map}(\pi_1 \circ \pi_2)$.

In summary, the query in Example 2.3 corresponds to the query

$$\mathtt{map}(\pi_1 \circ \pi_2) \circ \mathtt{src}[[], \mathtt{id}, \frown] \circ \mathtt{map}(\pi_1) \circ \mathtt{single}.$$

Applied to v_{in} we obtain the list value [Java, Sumatra, New Guinea] as desired.

Example 3.1 already gives valuable hints, how a translation of XQuery into RTA might work. Basically, we follow the execution model for XQuery, which works on lists and applies operations to the elements of the list. So, basically each step corresponds to some structural recursion operation.

Example 3.1 also indicates the expected advantage from the translation into RTA, as we were able to simplify the algebraic query. This is a first step towards query "optimisation".

However, in Example 3.1 we used only explicit path expressions. The next example handles a query, in which we have to search for the path. We will see that this constitutes a much more complicated application of structural recursion.

Example 3.2. Let us now consider the query in Example 2.4. As in the previous example we first have to apply `single` to v_{in} to achieve the same effect as doc(coffee-shop.xml) in the XQuery path expression. However, the follow-on RTA-operation has to capture the effect of //owner, which can be done by structural recursion. That is, we apply $\mathtt{src}[[], h, \frown]$ to $[v_{\text{in}}]$ with an operation h that searches for successors with the name owner.

The application of this operation h to some x can be defined recursively as follows:

```
if type(x) = owner
then [x]
else
  if type(x) = (t_1, ..., t_n)
  then h(π_1(x))⌢ ... ⌢h(π_n(x))
  else
    if type(x) = [t]
    then src[[], h, ⌢](x)
    else
      if type(x) = t_1 ⊕ ··· ⊕ t_n
      then h(π_2(x))
      else []
      endif
    endif
  endif
endif
```

Finally, we can neglect the return-clause, as it is just a renaming of tags, which do not appear in our anonymised complex values.

In summary, the corresponding RTA-query is $\mathtt{src}[[], h, \frown] \circ \mathtt{single}$ with

$$\begin{aligned} h &= \mathtt{if\_then} \circ (\varphi_1 \times \mathtt{single} \times h_1) \\ h_1 &= \mathtt{if\_then} \circ (\varphi_2 \times (\frown \circ (h \circ \pi_1 \times \frown \circ (\ldots (h \circ \pi_{n-1} \times h \circ \pi_n) \ldots))) \times h_2) \\ h_2 &= \mathtt{if\_then} \circ (\varphi_3 \times \mathtt{src}[[], h, \frown] \times h_3) \\ h_3 &= \mathtt{if\_then} \circ (\varphi_4 \times h \circ \pi_2 \times \mathtt{empty}) \end{aligned}$$

and the obvious Boolean operations

$$\begin{aligned} \varphi_1(x) &\equiv \text{type}(x) = \text{owner} \\ \varphi_2(x) &\equiv \text{type}(x) = (t_1, \ldots, t_n) \\ \varphi_3(x) &\equiv \text{type}(x) = [t] \\ \varphi_4(x) &\equiv \text{type}(x) = t_1 \oplus \cdots \oplus t_n \end{aligned}$$

Example 3.2 shows that some of the operations used within RTA-queries require complex definitions. It is not difficult to see that the other examples of queries from the previous section require analogous techniques. We will present a general solution for the translation in Section 4.

3.3 Multi-dimensional Extension

Let us finally mention a "multi-dimensional" extension of structural recursion, but let us restrict for simplicity to the binary case. That is, we define an operation $src2[f, g, h] : ([t_1], [t_2]) \rightarrow t$ with parameters $f : [t_2] \rightarrow t$, $g : (t_1, [t_2]) \rightarrow t$, and $h : (t, t) \rightarrow t$. Similarly to the "one-dimensional" case we define

$$\begin{aligned}\texttt{src2}[f,g,h]([],L_2) &= f(L_2)\\ \texttt{src2}[f,g,h]([x],L_2) &= g(x,L_2)\\ \texttt{src2}[f,g,h](X\frown Y,L_2) &= h(\texttt{src2}[f,g,h](X,L_2),\texttt{src2}[f,g,h](Y,L_2))\end{aligned}$$

This can be used to define the product of lists (both of type $[t]$) as

$$L_1 \times L_2 = \texttt{src2}[[],g,\frown](L_1,L_2),$$

where $[]$ is treated as a constant function, and g is defined by

$$g(x,L_2) = \texttt{src}[[],\texttt{single}\circ(x\times\texttt{id}),\frown](L_2).$$

4 Linguistic Reflection in Translating XQuery to RTA

Our goal is to translate XQuery into RTA. For this recall that XQuery is basically a functional language, so each query corresponds to a sequence of function calls. For instance, for the simple query in Example 2.3 we would first evaluate ⟨coffees⟩ by simply printing it, then evaluate the expression { doc(coffee-shop.xml)/... }, finally evaluate ⟨/coffees⟩, which again amounts only to a simple print. Therefore, we concentrate on expressions of the form { ... } with the dots standing for a FLWOR-expression.

4.1 The Basic Translation Model

XQuery works on lists, and each part of a query corresponds to some function that is executed on all elements of the list. As we assume to be given a FLWOR-expression, we first look at the `for`-construct. In its simple form it has the form

`for` $\$X$ `in` ⟨path-expression⟩,

so we have to evaluate the path expression first:

- If doc(xxx.xml) appears in the path expression, then xxx.xml is some input document, which is represented by some complex value, say v_{in}. As we have already seen in Examples 3.1 and 3.2, the input-function doc simply corresponds to the RTA-operation `single`.
- If p/name appears in the path expression, we first translate p, say the result is trans(p). Then /name gives rise to an application of structural recursion, say $\texttt{src}[[],g_{/\text{name}},\frown]$. Thus, the translation of p/name is

  $$\text{trans}(p/\text{name}) = \texttt{src}[[],g_{/\text{name}},\frown](\text{trans}(p)).$$

  The difficult part is then to determine the operation $g_{/\text{name}}$. Note that all applications of structural recursion in Example 3.1 refer to this step.
- If p//name appears in the path expression, we proceed analogously. That is, //name gives rise to an application of structural recursion $\texttt{src}[[],g_{//\text{name}},\frown]$, and the translation of p//name is

  $$\text{trans}(p//\text{name}) = \texttt{src}[[],g_{//\text{name}},\frown](\text{trans}(p)).$$

Note that the structural recursion in Example 3.2 refers to this step. It also indicates how to define $g = g_{//\text{name}}$ in general:

$$\begin{aligned} g &= \texttt{if\_then} \circ (\varphi_1 \times \texttt{single} \times h_1) \\ h_1 &= \texttt{if\_then} \circ (\varphi_2 \times (\frown \circ (g \circ \pi_1 \times \frown \circ (\dots \\ &\qquad (g \circ \pi_{n-1} \times g \circ \pi_n) \dots))) \times h_2) \\ h_2 &= \texttt{if\_then} \circ (\varphi_3 \times \texttt{src}[[], g, \frown] \times h_3) \\ h_3 &= \texttt{if\_then} \circ (\varphi_4 \times g \circ \pi_2 \times \texttt{empty}) \end{aligned}$$

with the Boolean operations

$$\begin{aligned} \varphi_1(x) &\equiv \text{type}(x) = \text{name} \\ \varphi_2(x) &\equiv \text{type}(x) = (t_1, \dots, t_n) \\ \varphi_3(x) &\equiv \text{type}(x) = [t] \\ \varphi_4(x) &\equiv \text{type}(x) = t_1 \oplus \dots \oplus t_n \end{aligned}$$

The crucial remaining part is to take care of the Boolean operations, as these require type-checks.

- If p[test] appears in the path expression, we first translate p. Furthermore, test will be translated into a Boolean condition ψ, and we can combine both using structural recursion, in this case a `filter`-operation, i.e.

$$\text{trans}(p[\text{test}]) = \texttt{filter}(\psi)(\text{trans}(p)).$$

If there is more than one condition in the `for`-clause, say

`for` $\$X_1$ `in` ⟨path-expression$_1$⟩ ,. . . , $\$X_n$ `in` ⟨path-expression$_n$⟩,

each path expression will be translated separately resulting in RTA-operations $o_1, \dots, o_n$, each producing some list, say L_i. Then we have to combine these lists into one list containing all tuple combinations, i.e. we obtain $L_1 \times \dots \times L_n$.

The following `let`-clause simply binds further variables depending on the list resulting from evaluating the `for`-clause. As this may again require evaluating a path expression, we proceed analogously to translating the `for`-clause.

Example 4.1. Look at the query in Example 2.5. Analogous to Example 3.1 the `for`-clause will be translated to the operation

$$\texttt{src}[[], \texttt{id}, \frown] \circ \texttt{map}(\pi_1) \circ \texttt{single},$$

which will be applied to v_{in}. Now the first part of the `let`-clause corresponds to `map`$(\pi_1 \circ \pi_2)$ as already seen in Example 3.1. Similarly, the second part of the `let`-clause corresponds to `map`$(\texttt{first} \circ \pi_3 \circ \pi_2)$ with an operation `first` that selects the first element of a list.

However, we do not want to replace the $\$W$-values by the $\$N$-values or the $\$B$-values, but keep all three, so the `let`-clause defines the operation

$$\texttt{map}(\texttt{id} \times (\pi_1 \circ \pi_2) \times (\texttt{first} \circ \pi_3 \circ \pi_2)).$$

The remaining clauses in FLWOR expressions are easy to handle. A `where`-clause defines a `filter`-operation. The greatest difficulty is to determine the Boolean operation, which may again involve the translation of a path expression. An `order`-clause corresponds to applying a sorting-operation, which can be expressed by structural recursion. Finally, the `return`-clause only constructs a value, so the only difficulty that may occur is that this construction involves evaluating another query.

Example 4.2. Let us continue our previous example, as Example 2.5 contains a `where`-clause. The list resulting from the application of the operation in Example 4.1, which represents the combination of the `for`- and `let`-clause, contains triples, where the first component corresponds to a coffee, the second one to its name and the third one to the first-listed component of its blend. Thus, applying $\pi_1 \circ \pi_3$ to such a triple gives the requested name of the first bean, while the application of $\pi_2 \circ \pi_3$ results in the corresponding percentage.

Thus, the first condition in the `where`-clause corresponds to the Boolean operation $\mathtt{eq} \circ ((\pi_1 \circ \pi_3) \times \text{Arabica})$, in which Arabica is treated as a constant operation. Similarly, the second condition gives the Boolean operation $\mathtt{eq} \circ ((\pi_2 \circ \pi_3) \times 100)$, and thus, the whole `where`-clause corresponds to the RTA-operation $\mathtt{filter}(\varphi)$, where φ is defined by the Boolean operation

$$\wedge \circ ((\mathtt{eq} \circ ((\pi_1 \circ \pi_3) \times \text{Arabica})) \times (\mathtt{eq} \circ ((\pi_2 \circ \pi_3) \times 100))).$$

Finally, let us complete the translation of the query in Example 2.5. Taking all the parts together, we obtain the RTA-operation

$$\mathtt{map}(\pi_2) \circ \mathtt{filter}(\varphi) \circ \mathtt{map}((\mathtt{id} \times \pi_1 \times (\mathtt{first} \circ \pi_3)) \circ \pi_2) \circ \\ \mathtt{src}[[], \mathtt{id}, \frown] \circ \mathtt{map}(\pi_1) \circ \mathtt{single}$$

4.2 Type-Safe Linguistic Reflection

In the previous subsection we have seen that the translation of XQuery can be done by parsing through FLWOR expressions and translating them step-by-step into RTA-operations, most of which happen to be special cases of structural recursion. More than this, all applications of structural recursion have the form $\mathtt{src}[[], g, \frown]$ and the real difficulty is to determine the functions g. For this we identify two cases:

- We obtain a highly recursive operation g that searches through the whole document. Example 3.2 is a prototype for this case.
- We obtain an operation that is determined by the schema. Example 3.1 is a prototype for this case.

As the chances for query optimisation are much higher in the second case – as already seen in Example 3.1 – it will be advantageous to apply this case, wherever it is possible. However, this means to explore the schema. As shown in [37] a type-safe way of doing this is to apply linguistic reflection.

Linguistic reflection is the ability of a system to observe and manipulate its own components. This is done by extending the system with extra modules which are created, compiled and linked in by the system itself, either during execution or at compile-time. The language in which the system has been written would, of course, need to provide the ability for the system to behave in this manner.

The general idea is to consider constructs in a query that are used for defining an operation, such as /name for $g_{/\text{name}}$ in the previous subsection, as macros that have to be expanded. In the case of XQuery these macros will be parts of FLWOR- and in particular path expressions. The macro expansion requires some complex computation, during which the information about the schema will be needed. This can be done by ignoring that they represent query code, thus *drop* this meaning, and treat them as values of some type. The expansion function will then take this value plus the schema, which is represented as a value of some other type, and create a new value. This new value will finally be *raised* back to an executable operation. This is illustrated by Figure 1.

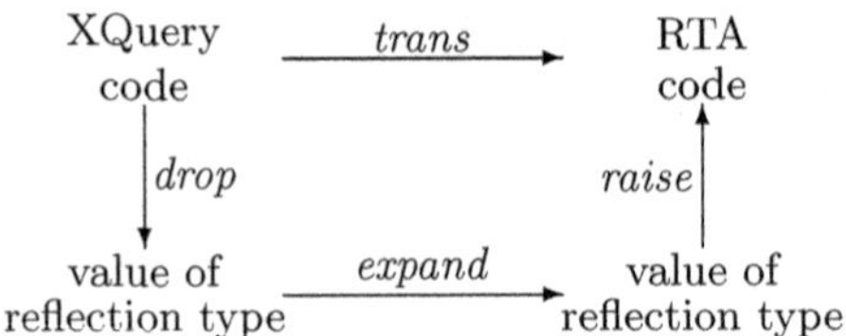

Fig. 1. Linguistic Reflection

Therefore, we will define reflection types in the next subsection, and finally illustrate, how the expansion procedure for paths works.

4.3 Reflection Types

In order to represent XSchema schemata we need at least reflection types for types, elements, attributes, and schemata. So we get the reflection type $\text{type}_{\text{rep}} = \text{Xtype}_{\text{rep}} \oplus \text{RTtype}_{\text{rep}}$ indicating that we are using types within XSchema and the rational tree types. For the types that are used to describe XSchema types we then get the following definitions:

$$\text{Xtype}_{\text{rep}} = \text{xs\_complex\_type}_{\text{rep}} \oplus \text{xs\_simple\_type}_{\text{rep}}$$
$$\text{xs\_simple\_type}_{\text{rep}} = \mathit{String}$$
$$\text{xs\_complex\_type}_{\text{rep}} = \text{xs\_sequence}_{\text{rep}} \oplus \text{xs\_choice}_{\text{rep}}$$
$$\text{xs\_sequence}_{\text{rep}} = [(\text{name}_{\text{rep}} \oplus \text{xs\_element}_{\text{rep}}, \text{min}, \text{max} \oplus \mathit{Empty})]$$
$$\text{xs\_choice}_{\text{rep}} = [(\text{name}_{\text{rep}} \oplus \text{xs\_element}_{\text{rep}}, \text{min}, \text{max} \oplus \mathit{Empty})]$$
$$\text{min} = \mathit{Integer}$$
$$\text{max} = \mathit{Integer}$$
$$\text{name}_{\text{rep}} = \mathit{String}$$

$\text{xs\_element}_{\text{rep}} = (\text{name}_{\text{rep}}, \text{Xtype}_{\text{rep}}, [\text{xs\_attribute}_{\text{rep}}])$
$\text{xs\_attribute}_{\text{rep}} = (\text{name}_{\text{rep}}, \text{xs\_simple\_type}_{\text{rep}}, \text{use}_{\text{rep}})$
$\text{use}_{\text{rep}} = \textit{String}$
$\text{XSchema}_{\text{rep}} = (\text{namespace}_{\text{rep}}, \text{name}_{\text{rep}}, [\text{xs\_element}_{\text{rep}}])$
$\text{namespace}_{\text{rep}} = \textit{String}$

Example 4.3. The value (1, (1, (1, [((1, "coffees"), 1, (1, 1)), ((1, "growers"), 1, (1, 1)), ((1, "regions"), 1, (1, 1))]))) of type type_{rep} represents the complex type used for the element "coffee-shop" in Example 2.1. As type_{rep} is a union type, the leading 1 indicates that we deal with a value of type $\text{Xtype}_{\text{rep}}$. Similarly, the next one indicates a complex type, i.e. a value of type $\text{xs\_complex\_type}_{\text{rep}}$, etc. Thus, the leading 1s indicate that it is a value of an XSchema type, a complex type, and a sequence type, respectively. For the sequence type representation we obtain a list of the representations for the elements. The first of these is ((1, "coffees"), 1, (1, 1)), in which the first component states that we have just a name, i.e. "coffees". The following 1 is the default min-value, and the third component contains the default max-value 1.

Analogously, the value (1, (1, (1, [((1, "region"), 0, (2, $\perp$))]))) represents the complex type for the element "regions" in Example 2.1. The schema in Example 2.1 is represented by the value

("http://www.w3.org/2001/XMLSchema", "coffee-shop", [("coffee-shop",
(1, (1, (1, [((1, "coffees"), 1, (1, 1)), ((1, "growers"), 1, (1, 1)),
((1, "regions"), 1, (1, 1))]))), []), ...])

of type $\text{XSchema}_{\text{rep}}$. Here the dots stand for representations of all the elements used in the schema.

The value ("coffee", (1, (1, [((2, ("name", (2, "*String*"), [])), 1, (1, 1)), ((2, ("body", (2, "*String*"), [])), 0, (1, 1)), ((1, "blend"), 1, (2, $\perp$)), ((2, ("price", (2, "*Decimal*"), [])), 1, (1, 1))])), [("c-id", "*ID*", "required"), ("producer", "*IDREF*", "required")]) of type $\text{xs\_element}_{\text{rep}}$ represents the element specification for "coffee" in Example 2.1. It would of course be part of the value representing the schema.

Analogously, for the types used with RTA we obtain the following reflection types:

$\text{RTtype}_{\text{rep}} = (\text{name}_{\text{rep}}, \text{type\_exp}_{\text{rep}})$
$\text{type\_exp}_{\text{rep}} = \text{base\_type}_{\text{rep}} \oplus \text{label}_{\text{rep}} \oplus \text{record\_type}_{\text{rep}} \oplus \text{list\_type}_{\text{rep}}$
$\qquad \oplus \text{union\_type}_{\text{rep}} \oplus \text{labelled\_type}_{\text{rep}} \oplus \text{name}_{\text{rep}}$
$\text{base\_type}_{\text{rep}} = \textit{String}$
$\text{label}_{\text{rep}} = \textit{String}$
$\text{record\_type}_{\text{rep}} = [\text{type\_exp}_{\text{rep}}]$
$\text{list\_type}_{\text{rep}} = \text{type\_exp}_{\text{rep}}$
$\text{union\_type}_{\text{rep}} = [\text{type\_exp}_{\text{rep}}]$
$\text{labelled\_type}_{\text{rep}} = (\text{label}_{\text{rep}}, \text{type\_exp}_{\text{rep}})$

Example 4.4. The type grower from Example 2.1 will be represented by the value

("grower", (3, [(7, "g-name"), (4, (7, "owner")), (5, [(7, "area"), (1, "*Empty*")]), (5, [(7, "established"), (1, "*Empty*")]), (7, "in-region")]))

of type $\text{RTtype}_{\text{rep}}$. Analogous to Example 4.3 it indicates that the name of the type is "grower", and that it has the structure of a record type, which is indicated by the number 3, as $\text{record\_type}_{\text{rep}}$ is the third component of the union type $\text{type\_exp}_{\text{rep}}$. Then the following list represents the components of this record type. The first of these is represented by the value (7, "g-name"), so the 7 indicates that we simply use the name of a type. The second component is represented by (4, (7, "owner")), so due to the 4 we know that it is a list type, the component type of which is again simply given by a name "owner".

Similarly, the type in-region is represented by ("in-region", (2, "r-id")), and the type growers is represented by the value ("growers", (4, (6, ("c-id", (7, "coffee"))))).

Finally, we also need representation types for the RTA-operations. For this, the following is sufficient:

$$\begin{aligned}
\text{Operation}_{\text{rep}} &= \text{base_op}_{\text{rep}} \oplus \text{projection}_{\text{rep}} \oplus \text{product}_{\text{rep}} \\
&\quad \oplus \text{embedding}_{\text{rep}} \oplus \text{sum}_{\text{rep}} \oplus \text{src}_{\text{rep}} \oplus \text{composition}_{\text{rep}} \\
\text{base_op}_{\text{rep}} &= \mathit{String} \\
\text{projection}_{\text{rep}} &= \mathit{Integer} \\
\text{product}_{\text{rep}} &= [\text{Operation}_{\text{rep}}] \\
\text{embedding}_{\text{rep}} &= \mathit{Integer} \\
\text{sum}_{\text{rep}} &= [\text{Operation}_{\text{rep}}] \\
\text{src}_{\text{rep}} &= \text{Operation}_{\text{rep}} \times \text{Operation}_{\text{rep}} \times \text{Operation}_{\text{rep}} \\
\text{composition}_{\text{rep}} &= [\text{Operation}_{\text{rep}}]
\end{aligned}$$

Example 4.5. The values (1, "single") and (1, "concat") represent the operations `single` and concatenation $\frown$ on lists, respectively. The value (6, ((1, "empty"), (2, 3), (1, "concat"))) represents the operation $\texttt{src}[[], \pi_3, \frown]$. The value (7, [(2, 2), (2, 1), (1, "single")]) represents the operation $\pi_2 \circ \pi_1 \circ \texttt{single}$.

4.4 The Expansion Procedure for Paths

Let us now look at the problem of expanding paths, as this turned out to be the core of the translation problem. We have seen above that /name gives rise to a structural recursion operation $\texttt{src}[[], g_{/\text{name}}, \frown]$, so we have to determine a representation of $g_{/\text{name}}$. In order to do so, we first determine the RT type that corresponds to an element in the schema using an operation

$$\text{expand\_elt\_type} : (\mathit{String}, \text{XSchema}_{\text{rep}}) \to \text{RTtype}_{\text{rep}},$$

i.e. we associate with an element name and a representation of a schema a rational tree type. This can be achieved by parsing through the schema representation and then applying the rules for type transformation that we used in Section 2. In particular, we blur the differences between subelements and attributes, and we replace references by occurrences of the base type *ID*:

```
expand_elt_type(n, S) = expand_elt_type'(n, search(n, π3(S)), S)
search(n, S) =
    if π1(first(S)) = n
    then (π2 × π3)(first(S))
    else search(n, rest(S))
    endif
expand_elt_type'(n, (e, L), S) =
    case π1(π2(e)) = 2
      then (n, (1, π2(π2(e))))
    case π1(π2(π2(e))) = 1
      then (n, (3, check_ID(parse_seq(π2(π2(π2(e)))⌢L, S))))
    case π1(π2(π2(e))) = 2
      then (n, (5, check_ID(parse_seq(π2(π2(π2(e)))⌢L, S))))
    endcase
parse_seq(L, S) =
    if L = []
    then []
    elsif first(L) = ((1, n'), m, M)
    then if m = 1 ∧ M = (1, 1)
          then [π2(expand_elt_type(n', S))]⌢parse_seq(rest(L), S)
          elsif m = 0 ∧ M = (1, 1)
          then [(5, [π2(expand_elt_type(n', S)), (1, "Empty")])]⌢
                parse_seq(rest(L), S)
          else [(4, π2(expand_elt_type(n', S)))]⌢parse_seq(rest(L), S)
          endif
    elsif first(L) = ((2, e), m, M)
    then if m = 1 ∧ M = (1, 1)
          then [π2(expand_elt_type'(π1(e), (π2(e), π3(e)), S))]⌢
                parse_seq(rest(L), S)
          elsif m = 0 ∧ M = (1, 1)
          then [(5, [π2(expand_elt_type'(π1(e), (π2(e), π3(e)), S)),
                (1, "Empty")])]⌢parse_seq(rest(L), S)
          else [(4, π2(expand_elt_type'(π1(e), (π2(e), π3(e)), S)))]⌢
                parse_seq(rest(L), S)
          endif
    elsif first(L) = (n', t, u)
    then if t ≠ "IDREFS"
          then [(1, t)]⌢parse_seq(rest(L), S)
          else [(4, (1, "ID"))]⌢parse_seq(rest(L), S)
          endif
    endif
```

```
check_ID(L) =
    if L = []
    then []
    elsif π1(first(L)) = 1 ∧ π2(first(L)) = "ID"
    then (3, [first(L), (3, rest(L))])
    elsif first(check_ID(rest(L))) = (1, "ID")
    then (3, [(1, "ID"), (3, [first(L)]⌢π2(first(rest(check_ID(rest(L))))))])
    else L
    endif
```

Example 4.6. If S represents the schema from Example 2.1, we obtain

```
expand_elt_type("coffee", S) =
    ("coffee", (3, [(1, "ID"), (3, [(1, "String"),
        (5, [(1, "String"), (1, "Empty")]),
        (4, (3, [(1, "String"), (1, "Integer")])),
        (1, "Decimal"), (1, "ID")])]))
```

and expand_elt_type("name", S) = ("c-name", (1, "*String*")) assuming in the latter case that we add some renaming to avoid name-conflicts.

Now that we got the transformation of types, we can define the expansion of paths, i.e. we get an operation

$$\text{expand\_elt} : (\mathit{String}, \text{XSchema}_{\text{rep}}) \to \text{Operation}_{\text{rep}}$$

such that expand_elt(n, S) will be a representation of the operation $g_{/n}$. In order to define the expansion we need both the types for the element n and its parent, and the position at which the type of n appears inside the type of its parent. We then parse through the parent type and determine the operation $g_{/n}$ according to the given position:

```
expand_elt(n, s) =
    parse_type(π2(expand_elt_type(n, S)), π2(first(parents(n, π3(S)))),
        π2(expand_elt_type(π1(first(parents(n, π3(S)))), S)))
parents(n, L) =
    if L = []
    then []
    else list_match(n, π1(first(L)), π2(π2(π2(first(L)))), 1)⌢
      parents(n, rest(L))
    endif
list_match(n, n', L, i) =
    if L = []
    then []
    else match(n, n', π1(first(L)), i)⌢list_match(n, n', rest(L), i + 1)
    endif
```

```
match(n, n', e, i) =
    if π1(e) = 1 ∧ π2(e) = n
    then [(n', i)]
    elsif π1(e) = 2 ∧ π1(π2(e)) = n
    then [(n', i)]
    else []
    endif

parse_type(t, i, t') =
    if π1(t') = 3 ∧ first(π2(t')) = (1, "ID")
    then (7, [parse_type(t, i, first(rest(π2(t')))), (2, 2)])
    else case t = t'
           then (1, "id")
         case π1(t') = 3
           then (2, i)
         case π1(t') = 4
           then (1, "id")
         case π1(t') = 5
           then (7, [(1, "if_else"), (3, [(7, [(1, "eq"), (3, [(2, 1), (1, i)])]),
             (1, "single"), (7, [(1, "empty"), (1, "triv")])])])
         endcase
    endif
```

Example 4.7. For the S in Example 2.1 we obtain expand_elt("coffee", S) = (1, "id"), and expand_elt("name", S) = $(7, [(2, 1), (2, 2)])$.

Similarly, we get an operation expand_att such that expand_att(n, S) will be a representation of the operation $g_{/@n}$. We omit the details.

Finally, let us look at the expansion of paths containing some //name. In this case we get an operation

$$\text{expand\_elt}^* : (\mathit{String}, \text{XSchema}_{\text{rep}}) \rightarrow \text{Operation}_{\text{rep}}$$

such that expand_elt$^*(n, S)$ will be a representation of the operation $g_{//n}$. We already saw the general structure of this operation, when we discussed the basic model of the translation into RTA, so let us now concentrate on the Boolean operations only. The only condition that involves the element name n is φ_1. So, let

$$\text{expand\_bool1} : (\mathit{String}, \text{XSchema}_{\text{rep}}) \rightarrow \text{Operation}_{\text{rep}}$$

be such that expand_bool1(n, S) will be a representation of the operation φ_1 associated with n. Thus, we get:

$$\text{expand\_bool1}(n, S) = (7, [(1, \text{“eq”}), (3, [(1, \text{“type”}), (7, [(1, \text{expand\_elt\_type}(n, S)), (1, \text{“triv”})])])])$$

The other operations can be obtained analogously.

5 Algebraic Query Optimisation

While the translation to a query algebra that we described in the previous section has its merits in its own right with respect to type-safe implementation as discussed in [20], let us now address the presumably largest advantage of this approach exploiting it for (heuristic) algebraic query optimisation. For this we consider again the basic translation model for FLWOR-expressions, which result in a sequence of structural recursion operations.

5.1 The For-Clauses

Let us start looking at a single for-clause, which gives rise to a sequence

$$f_n \circ \cdots \circ f_1 \circ \mathtt{single}(v_{\text{in}}),$$

in which each f_i has the form $\mathtt{src}[[], g_i, \frown]$. Furthermore, each g_i has a signature $g_i : t_i \to [t_{i+1}]$, i.e. the application of g_i results in a list.

We investigate $f_{i+1} \circ f_i$ looking first at the possible cases for g_i. As the application of g_i results in a list, we must have one of the following three cases:

1. In case $g_i = \mathtt{single} \circ h_i$ holds, i.e. $f_i = \mathtt{map}(h_i)$, we obtain $f_{i+1} \circ f_i = \mathtt{src}[[], g_{i+1} \circ h_i, \frown]$. As it is presumably more efficient both in terms of query processing time and storage needed for the intermediate result to execute just one structural recursion operation instead of two, we can use this equation as an optimisation rule:

   Rule 1. Replace $\mathtt{src}[[], g, \frown] \circ \mathtt{map}(h)$ by $\mathtt{src}[[], g \circ h, \frown]$.

2. In case $g_i = \mathtt{empty} \circ \mathtt{triv}$ holds, $f_{i+1} \circ f_i$ degenerates to a trivial function $\mathtt{empty} \circ \mathtt{triv}$, i.e. the result is always the empty list. This gives rise to a second optimisation rule:

   Rule 2. Replace $\mathtt{src}[[], g, \frown] \circ \mathtt{src}[[], \mathtt{empty} \circ \mathtt{triv}, \frown]$ by $\mathtt{empty} \circ \mathtt{triv}$.

3. In case g_i is itself defined by structural recursion, say $g_i = \mathtt{src}[e, k_i, \sqcup] \circ h_i$, nothing can be derived in particular, unless k_i is a trivial constant $e \circ \mathtt{triv}$, in which case we obtain $g_i = e \circ \mathtt{triv}$, which gives another optimisation rule:

   Rule 3. Replace $\mathtt{src}[[], \mathtt{src}[e, e \circ \mathtt{triv}, \sqcup] \circ h, \frown]$ by $\mathtt{src}[[], e \circ \mathtt{triv}, \frown]$.

Example 5.1. Let us look at the sequence of structural recursion from Example 3.1 which results from the translation of the for-clause in Example 2.3. Applying rule 1 we can rewrite the query as follows:

$$\begin{aligned}
&\mathtt{src}[[], \mathtt{single} \circ \pi_1 \circ \pi_2, \frown] \circ \mathtt{src}[[], \mathtt{id}, \frown] \circ \mathtt{src}[[], \mathtt{single} \circ \pi_1, \frown] \circ \mathtt{single} \\
&= \mathtt{src}[[], \mathtt{single} \circ \pi_1 \circ \pi_2, \frown] \circ \mathtt{src}[[], \pi_1, \frown] \circ \mathtt{single} \\
&= \mathtt{src}[[], \mathtt{single} \circ \pi_1 \circ \pi_2, \frown] \circ \pi_1
\end{aligned}$$

This is exactly what we already observed in Example 3.1.

So far we only considered the cases for f_i. Let us now take a closer look at f_{i+1}, in particular, if this is defined by a `filter` or a `map` operation. If

$$f_{i+1} = \mathtt{filter}(\varphi) = \mathtt{src}[[], \mathtt{if\_else} \circ (\varphi \times \mathtt{single} \times (\mathtt{empty} \circ \mathtt{triv})), \frown],$$

we may reconsider the three cases above.

1. In case $g_i = \mathtt{single} \circ h_i$ holds, we obtain

$$\begin{aligned} &\mathtt{if\_else} \circ (\varphi \times \mathtt{single} \times (\mathtt{empty} \circ \mathtt{triv})) \circ h_i \\ = &\mathtt{if\_else} \circ ((\varphi \circ h_i) \times (\mathtt{single} \circ h_i) \times (\mathtt{empty} \circ \mathtt{triv})), \end{aligned}$$

   which gives rise to $f_{i+1} \circ f_i = \mathtt{map}(h_i) \circ \mathtt{filter}(\varphi \circ h_i)$, which is almost swapping the order of a `filter` and a `map` operation. As a `filter` operation presumably reduces the size of the argument, whereas we do not know such a property for the `map` operation, we may use this to define another heuristic optimisation rule:

   Rule 4. Replace $\mathtt{filter}(\varphi) \circ \mathtt{map}(h)$ by $\mathtt{map}(h) \circ \mathtt{filter}(\varphi \circ h)$.

2. In case $g_i = \mathtt{empty} \circ \mathtt{triv}$ holds, there is nothing to be added to rule 2, as the application of this rule already eliminates the `filter` operation f_{i+1} completely.
3. In case the first two cases do not apply to g_i, we still know that $f_i([x_1, \ldots, x_k] = g_i(x_1)\frown \ldots \frown g_i(x_k)$, which implies

$$\begin{aligned} &\mathtt{filter}(\varphi)(f_i([x_1, \ldots, x_k])) = \\ &\qquad (\mathtt{filter}(\varphi) \circ g_i)(x_1)\frown \ldots \frown(\mathtt{filter}(\varphi) \circ g_i)(x_k), \end{aligned}$$

   which gives rise to $f_{i+1} \circ f_i = \mathtt{src}[[], \mathtt{filter}(\varphi) \circ g_i, \frown]$. That is, we may shift the `filter` operation inside the structural recursion, which presumably leads to smaller intermediate results. Therefore, we obtain the following heuristic optimisation rule:

   Rule 5. Replace $\mathtt{filter}(\varphi) \circ \mathtt{src}[[], g, \frown]$ by $\mathtt{src}[[], \mathtt{filter}(\varphi) \circ g, \frown]$.

Example 5.2. Let us look at optimising the result from Example 4.2, which was a translation of the XQuery query shown in Example 2.5. Applying rules 4 and 5 we can rewrite the query as follows:

$$\begin{aligned} &\mathtt{map}(\pi_2) \circ \mathtt{filter}(\varphi) \circ \mathtt{map}((\mathtt{id} \times \pi_1 \times (\mathtt{first} \circ \pi_3)) \circ \pi_2) \circ \mathtt{src}[[], \mathtt{id}, \frown] \circ \\ &\mathtt{map}(\pi_1) \circ \mathtt{single} = \\ &\mathtt{map}(\pi_2) \circ \mathtt{map}((\mathtt{id} \times \pi_1 \times (\mathtt{first} \circ \pi_3)) \circ \pi_2) \circ \\ &\mathtt{filter}(\varphi \circ \mathtt{map}((\mathtt{id} \times \pi_1 \times (\mathtt{first} \circ \pi_3)) \circ \pi_2)) \circ \mathtt{src}[[], \mathtt{id}, \frown] \circ \mathtt{map}(\pi_1) \circ \\ &\mathtt{single} = \\ &\mathtt{map}(\pi_2) \circ \mathtt{map}((\mathtt{id} \times \pi_1 \times (\mathtt{first} \circ \pi_3)) \circ \pi_2) \circ \\ &\mathtt{src}[[], \mathtt{filter}(\varphi \circ \mathtt{map}((\mathtt{id} \times \pi_1 \times (\mathtt{first} \circ \pi_3)) \circ \pi_2)) \circ \mathtt{id}, \frown] \circ \mathtt{map}(\pi_1) \circ \\ &\mathtt{single} \end{aligned}$$

Next consider the case $f_{i+1} = \mathtt{map}(h_{i+1})$. As before, we do not have to reconsider the second case above, as we cannot obtain more than rule 2, but we may look at the other two cases again.

1. In case $g_i = \mathtt{single} \circ h_i$ holds, we obtain

$$f_{i+1} \circ f_i = \mathtt{src}[[], \mathtt{single} \circ h_{i+1} \circ h_i, \frown] = \mathtt{map}(h_{i+1} \circ h_i).$$

   So we may combine two consecutive `map` operations into one using the following rule:

   Rule 6. Replace $\mathtt{map}(h) \circ \mathtt{map}(g)$ by $\mathtt{map}(h \circ g)$.

2. In the general case we have $f_i([x_1, \dots, x_k]) = g_i(x_1)^\frown \dots ^\frown g_i(x_k)$, which implies

$$\mathtt{map}(h_{i+1})(f_i([x_1, \dots, x_k])) = (\mathtt{map}(h_{i+1}) \circ g_i)(x_1)^\frown \dots ^\frown(\mathtt{map}(h_{i+1}) \circ g_i)(x_k),$$

   which further leads to $f_{i+1} \circ f_i = \mathtt{src}[[], f_{i+1} \circ g_i, \frown]$. That is, we may shift the `map` operation inside the structural recursion, which defines the following heuristic optimisation rule:

   Rule 7. Replace $\mathtt{map}(h) \circ \mathtt{src}[[], g, \frown]$ by $\mathtt{src}[[], \mathtt{map}(h) \circ g, \frown]$.

Example 5.3. Carrying on from Example 5.2 above, we can now apply rules 6 and 7 to perform further optimisations as follows:

$$\begin{aligned}
&\mathtt{map}(\pi_2) \circ \mathtt{map}((\mathtt{id} \times \pi_1 \times (\mathtt{first} \circ \pi_3)) \circ \pi_2) \circ \\
&\mathtt{src}[[], \mathtt{filter}(\varphi \circ \mathtt{map}((\mathtt{id} \times \pi_1 \times (\mathtt{first} \circ \pi_3)) \circ \pi_2)) \circ \mathtt{id}, \frown] \circ \mathtt{map}(\pi_1) \circ \\
&\mathtt{single} = \\
&\mathtt{map}(\pi_2 \circ (\mathtt{id} \times \pi_1 \times (\mathtt{first} \circ \pi_3)) \circ \pi_2) \circ \\
&\mathtt{src}[[], \mathtt{filter}(\varphi \circ \mathtt{map}((\mathtt{id} \times \pi_1 \times (\mathtt{first} \circ \pi_3)) \circ \pi_2)) \circ \mathtt{id}, \frown] \circ \mathtt{map}(\pi_1) \circ \\
&\mathtt{single} = \\
&\mathtt{src}[[], \mathtt{map}(\pi_2 \circ (\mathtt{id} \times \pi_1 \times (\mathtt{first} \circ \pi_3)) \circ \pi_2) \circ \mathtt{filter}(\varphi \circ \\
&\mathtt{map}((\mathtt{id} \times \pi_1 \times (\mathtt{first} \circ \pi_3)) \circ \pi_2)) \circ \mathtt{id}, \frown] \circ \mathtt{map}(\pi_1) \circ \mathtt{single}
\end{aligned}$$

Finally, consider several `for`-clauses producing lists $L_1, \dots, L_n$, which are then combined into

$$\begin{aligned}
L_1 \times \dots \times L_n &= \mathtt{src2}[[], g, \frown](L_1, L_2 \times \dots \times L_n) \\
&= \mathtt{src2}[[], g, \frown](L_1, \\
&\qquad \mathtt{src2}[[], g, \frown](L_2, \\
&\qquad\qquad \dots \\
&\qquad\qquad\qquad \mathtt{src2}[[], g, \frown](L_{n-1}, L_n) \dots))
\end{aligned}$$

with $g(x, L) = \mathtt{src}[[], \mathtt{single} \circ (x \times \mathtt{id}), \frown](L)$. So basically we have to consider $\mathtt{src2}[[], g, \frown](L_1, L_2)$ with $L_1 = \mathtt{src}[[], g_1, \frown](L_1')$. However, even, if we consider the case $g_1 = \mathtt{single} \circ h_1$, this does not give rise to meaningful equations that could be used to define further optimisation rules. It may, however, be the case that structural recursion applied to the result of this product can lead to further optimisation rules. We will explore this in the remaining subsection.

5.2 The LWOR Clauses

As shown in the previous section, each `let`-clause gives rise to a `map` operation. However, as there may be more than one `for`-clause, we have to take into account that the result of processing the `for`-clauses leads to a list of tuples. Let ℓ be the number of `for`-clauses, and let m be the number of `let`-clauses. Then we obtain

$$\mathtt{map}(\pi_1 \times \cdots \times \pi_\ell \times k_1 \times \cdots \times k_m)(L_1 \times \cdots \times L_\ell)$$

as the subquery resulting from the `for`- and the `let`-clauses. As for the product we cannot derive anything meaningful in addition to the already discovered optimisation rules.

So let us address the `where`-clause, which gives rise to another `filter` operation, say $\mathtt{filter}(\varphi)$. As this operation is applied to a list of $(\ell + m)$-tuples, we may rewrite φ as a conjunction $\varphi_0 \wedge \varphi_1 \wedge \cdots \wedge \varphi_{\ell+m}$ such that φ_i for $i > 0$ only depends on the i'th component. Then we obtain

$$\begin{aligned}
&\mathtt{filter}(\varphi)(\mathtt{map}(\pi_1 \times \cdots \times \pi_\ell \times k_1 \times \cdots \times k_m)(L_1 \times \cdots \times L_\ell)) = \\
&\mathtt{filter}(\varphi_0)(\mathtt{src}[[], (\mathtt{single} \circ \pi_1) \times \cdots \times (\mathtt{single} \circ \pi_\ell) \times \\
&(\mathtt{if_else} \circ ((\varphi_{\ell+1} \circ k_1) \times (\mathtt{single} \circ k_1)) \times (\mathtt{empty} \circ \mathtt{triv})) \\
&\times \cdots \times \\
&(\mathtt{if_else} \circ ((\varphi_{\ell+m} \circ k_m) \times (\mathtt{single} \circ k_m) \times (\mathtt{empty} \circ \mathtt{triv}))), \frown] \\
&(\mathtt{filter}(\varphi_1)(L_1) \times \cdots \times \mathtt{filter}(\varphi_\ell)(L_\ell))
\end{aligned}$$

As we can assume that an early application of a `filter` operation will be advantageous in terms of obtaining a smaller intermediate result, we can formulate the following two heuristic optimisation rules, which would produce the result above:

Rule 8. Replace $\mathtt{filter}(\varphi \wedge \psi)$ by $\mathtt{filter}(\varphi) \circ \mathtt{filter}(\psi)$.

Rule 9. Replace $\mathtt{filter}(\varphi)$ by $\mathtt{filter}(\varphi \circ \pi_i)$, if the operation is to be applied to a list of k-tuples, and φ only depends on the i'th component.

Example 5.4. Continuing from Example 5.3 above, we can now apply rule 9 to optimise the filter operation as follows:

$$\begin{aligned}
&\mathtt{src}[[], \mathtt{map}(\pi_2 \circ (\mathtt{id} \times \pi_1 \times (\mathtt{first} \circ \pi_3)) \circ \pi_2) \circ \mathtt{filter}(\varphi \circ \\
&\mathtt{map}((\mathtt{id} \times \pi_1 \times (\mathtt{first} \circ \pi_3)) \circ \pi_2)) \circ \mathtt{id}, \frown] \circ \mathtt{map}(\pi_1) \circ \mathtt{single} = \\
&\mathtt{src}[[], \mathtt{map}(\pi_2 \circ (\mathtt{id} \times \pi_1 \times (\mathtt{first} \circ \pi_3)) \circ \pi_2) \circ \mathtt{filter}(\varphi \circ \pi_3 \circ \\
&\mathtt{map}((\mathtt{id} \times \pi_1 \times (\mathtt{first} \circ \pi_3)) \circ \pi_2)) \circ \mathtt{id}, \frown] \circ \mathtt{map}(\pi_1) \circ \mathtt{single}
\end{aligned}$$

Additionally, the corresponding Boolean operation φ in `filter` would be rewritten from

$$\wedge \circ ((\mathsf{eq} \circ ((\pi_1 \circ \pi_3) \times \mathrm{Arabica})) \times (\mathsf{eq} \circ ((\pi_2 \circ \pi_3) \times 100)))$$

to

$$\wedge \circ ((\mathsf{eq} \circ (\pi_1 \times \mathrm{Arabica})) \times (\mathsf{eq} \circ (\pi_2 \times 100))).$$

6 Conclusion

In this paper we addressed the algebraic optimisation of XQuery based on a translation to a rational tree query algebra. The model underlying this algebra is based on a type system that supports constructors for records, lists and unions as well as optionality and references. The query algebra uses operations defined on this type system, in particular structural recursion for lists.

We demonstrated that the basic execution model of XQuery easily gives rise to nested structural recursion. However, the function parameters involved in these operations require complex definitions resulting from information about the schema. These functions can be generated using compile-time linguistic reflection.

An obvious advantage of this approach is that it shifts part of the intrinsic complexity of XQuery to the query compilation avoiding unnecessary path search during query execution. Of course, this benefit cannot be claimed for ad-hoc queries, in which case the overhead resulting from the translation may bite off the performance gain resulting from the optimised query. A careful investigation of what might still be gained for ad-hoc queries was so far beyond the scope of our research, but will be addressed in future work.

The representation of XQuery by a query algebra gives rise to equivalences that are the basis for query rewriting, which is performed in a way that will always result in queries with presumably lower costs. It may further be used for the generalisation of other query optimisation techniques such as join reordering, tableau optimisation, and selection-projection optimisation [2, chapter 6]. These extensions to query optimisation will be addressed in future work. We also plan to support the algebraic approach to query optimisation by rigorous case-based comparison with other approaches to XQuery implementation and optimisation.

An obvious further advantage of the use of a query algebra is type safety as emphasised in [20]. Furthermore, a translation to a simple query algebra enables the easy implementation of the operations and thus the integration with programming languages, and the easy extension to other constructors such as sets and multisets in case the order that comes with the list constructor is considered unnecessary or even undesired. These two expected benefits, however, still have to be explored in more detail in our future work. In particular, much of the complexity resulting from path expressions is captured in the translation process.

References

1. Abiteboul, S., Buneman, P., and Suciu, D. *Data on the Web: From Relations to Semistructured Data and XML.* Morgan Kaufmann Publishers, 2000.
2. Abiteboul, S., Hull, R., and Vianu, V. *Foundations of Databases.* Addison-Wesley, 1995.
3. Abiteboul, S., and Kanellakis, P. C. Object identity as a query language primitive. In *Building an Object-Oriented Database System, The Story of O2*, F. Bancilhon, C. Delobel, and P. C. Kanellakis, Eds. Morgan Kaufmann, 1992, pp. 97–127.

4. Abiteboul, S., Quass, D., McHugh, J., Widom, J., and Wiener, J. The LOREL query language for semi-structured data. *International Journal on Digital Libraries 1*, 1 (1997), 68–88.
5. Beeri, C., and Ta-Shma, P. Bulk data types, a theoretical approach. In *Database Programming Languages (DBPL-4)* (1993), Workshops in Computing, Springer-Verlag, pp. 80–96.
6. Buneman, P., Davidson, S., Hillebrand, G., and Suciu, D. A query language and optimization techniques for unstructured data. In *Proceedings of the International Conference on Management of Data* (1996), ACM, pp. 505–516.
7. Chen, Y., Davidson, S. B., and Zheng, Y. BLAS: An efficient XPath processing system. In *Proceedings of the Symposium on Principles of Database Systems* (2004), G. Weikum, A. C. König, and S. Deßloch, Eds., ACM, pp. 47–58.
8. Cluet, S., Delobel, C., Lécluse, C., and Richard, P. RELOOP: An algebra-based query language for O_2. In *Building an Object-Oriented Database System – The Story of O_2*, F. Bancilhon, C. Delobel, and P. Kanellakis, Eds. Morgan Kaufmann, 1992.
9. Cluet, S., and Moerkotte, G. Nested queries in object bases. In *Database Programming Languages (DBPL-4)* (1993), C. Beeri, A. Ohori, and D. Shasha, Eds., Workshops in Computing, Springer-Verlag, pp. 226–242.
10. Courcelle, B. Fundamental properties of infinite trees. *Theoretical Computer Science 25* (1983), 95–169.
11. DeHaan, D., Toman, D., Consens, M. P., and Özsu, M. T. A comprehensive XQuery to SQL translation using dynamic interval encoding. In *Proceedings of the Symposium on Principles of Database Systems* (2003), A. Y. Halevy, Z. G. Ives, and A. Doan, Eds., ACM, pp. 623–634.
12. Deutsch, A., Fernandez, M., Florescu, D., Levy, A., and Suciu, D. A query language for XML. *Computer Networks 31*, 11–16 (1999), 1155–1169.
13. Fernandez, M. F., Siméon, J., and Wadler, P. An algebra for XML query. In *Proceedings of the 20th Conference on Foundations of Software Technology and Theoretical Computer Science* (2000), Springer-Verlag, pp. 11–45.
14. Gottlob, G., Koch, C., and Pichler, R. The complexity XPath query evaluation. In *Proceedings of the 22nd Symposium on Principles of Database Systems* (2003), ACM, pp. 179–190.
15. Jagadish, H. V., Lakshmanan, L. V. S., Srivastava, D., and Thompson, K. TAX: A tree algebra for XML. In *Revised Papers from the 8th International Workshop on Database Programming Languages* (2002), Springer-Verlag, pp. 149–164.
16. Katz, H., Ed. *XQuery from the Experts – A Guide to the W3C XML Query Language*. Addison-Wesley, 2003.
17. Kemper, A., and Moerkotte, G. Query optimization in object bases: Exploiting relational techniques. In *Proceedings of the Dagstuhl Workshop on Query Optimization* (1993), J.-C. Freytag, D. Maier, and G. Vossen, Eds., Morgan Kaufmann.
18. Kirby, G. N. C., Connor, R. C. H., and Morrison, R. START: A linguistic reflection tool using hyper-program technology. In *Proceedings of the Sixth International Workshop on Persistent Object Systems* (1994), M. P. Atkinson, D. Maier, and V. Benzaken, Eds., Workshops in Computing, Springer-Verlag, pp. 355–373.
19. Kirchberg, M., Ma, H., ud Din, F. R., and Schewe, K.-D. A unified approach to object algebras. unpublished, available from the authors, 2003.
20. Kirchberg, M., Riaz-ud-Din, F., Schewe, K.-D., and Tretiakov, A. Using reflection for querying XML documents. In *Database Technologies 2006. Proceedings of the 17th Australasian Database Conference (ADC)*, J. Bailey and G. Dobbie, Eds., vol. 49 of *CRPIT*. Australian Computer Society, 2006, pp. 119–128.

21. Kirchberg, M., Schewe, K.-D., and Tretiakov, A. A multi-level architecture for distributed object bases. In *Proceedings of the 5th International Conference on Enterprise Information Systems (ICEIS)* (2003), O. Camp, J. Filipe, S. Hammoudi, and M. Piattini, Eds., vol. 1, ICEIS Press, pp. 63–70.
22. Kirchberg, M., Schewe, K.-D., and Tretiakov, A. Using XML to support media types. In *Information Systems Technology and its Applications, 4th International Conference*, R. Kaschek, H. C. Mayr, and S. W. Liddle, Eds., vol. 63 of *LNI*. GI, 2005, pp. 101–113.
23. Koch, C. On the complexity of nonrecursive XQuery and functional query languages on complex values. In *Principles of Database Systems* (2005), ACM.
24. Leung, T. W., Mitchell, G., Subramanian, B., Vance, B., Vandenberg, S. L., and Zdonik, S. B. The AQUA data model and algebra. In *Database Programming Languages (DBPL-4)* (1993), C. Beeri, A. Ohori, and D. Shasha, Eds., Workshops in Computing, Springer-Verlag, pp. 157–175.
25. Libkin, L., and Wong, L. New techniques for studying set languages, bag languages and aggregate functions. In *Principles of Database Systems (PODS)* (1994), ACM, pp. 155–166.
26. Lobin, H. *Informationsmodellierung in XML und SGML*. Springer-Verlag, 2001.
27. Marx, M. Conditional XPath, the first order complete XPath dialect. In *Proceedings of the 23rd Symposium on Principles of Database Systems (PoDS)* (2004), ACM, pp. 13–22.
28. Paparizos, S., Wu, Y., Lakshmanan, L. V. S., and Jagadish, H. V. Tree logical classes for efficient evaluation of XQuery. In *Proceedings of the Symposium on Principles of Database Systems (SIGMOD)* (2004), G. Weikum, A. C. König, and S. Deßloch, Eds., ACM, pp. 71–82.
29. Savnik, I., Tari, Z., and Mohoric, T. QAL: A query algebra of complex objects. *Data and Knowledge Engineering 30*, 1 (1999), 57–94.
30. Schewe, K.-D. On the unification of query algebras and their extension to rational tree structures. In *Database Technologies – Proceedings of the 12th Australasian Database Conference (ADC)* (2001), M. E. Orlowska and J. F. Roddick, Eds., IEEE Computer Society, pp. 52–59.
31. Schewe, K.-D., Schmidt, J. W., and Wetzel, I. Identification, genericity and consistency in object-oriented databases. In *Proceedings of the 4th International Conference on Database Theory (ICDT)* (1992), J. Biskup and R. Hull, Eds., vol. 646 of *Lecture Notes in Computer Science*, Springer-Verlag, pp. 341–356.
32. Schewe, K.-D., and Thalheim, B. Fundamental concepts of object oriented databases. *Acta Cybernetica 11*, 4 (1993), 49–84.
33. Shaw, G. M., and Zdonik, S. B. An object-oriented query algebra. In *Proceedings of the Second International Workshop on Database Programming Languages* (1989), R. Hull, R. Morrison, and D. W. Stemple, Eds., Morgan Kaufmann, pp. 103–112.
34. Sheard, T., and Fegaras, L. A fold for all seasons. In *Conference on Functional Programming Languages and Computer Architecture* (1993), ACM, pp. 233–242.
35. Sheard, T., and Stemple, D. W. Automatic verification of database transaction safety. *ACM Transactions on Database Systems 14*, 3 (1989), 322–368.
36. Siméon, J., and Wadler, P. The essence of XML. In *Proceedings of the 30th Symposium on Principles of Programming Languages (POPL)*. ACM, 2003.
37. Stemple, D. W., Fegaras, L., Sheard, T., and Socorro, A. Exceeding the limits of polymorphism in database programming languages. In *Advances in Database Technology (EDBT)* (1990), F. Bancilhon, C. Thanos, and D. Tsichritzis, Eds., vol. 416 of *LNCS*, Springer-Verlag, pp. 269–285.

38. Stemple, D. W., Morrison, R., and Atkinson, M. P. Type-safe linguistic reflection. In *Database Programming Languages: Bulk Types and Persistent Data* (1991), P. C. Kanellakis and J. W. Schmidt, Eds., Morgan Kaufmann, pp. 357–360.
39. Stemple, D. W., and Sheard, T. A recursive base for database programming primitives. In *Next Generation Information System Technology – East/West Database Workshop* (1990), J. W. Schmidt and A. A. Stogny, Eds., vol. 504 of *Lecture Notes in Computer Science*, Springer-Verlag, pp. 311–332.
40. Suciu, D., and Wong, L. On two forms of structural recursion. In *Proceedings of the International Conference on Database Theory (ICDT)* (1995), vol. 893 of *Lecture Notes in Computer Science*, Springer-Verlag, pp. 111–124.
41. Tannen, V., Buneman, P., and Wong, L. Naturally embedded query languages. In *Proceedings of the International Conference on Database Theory (ICDT)*, J. Biskup and R. Hull, Eds., vol. 646 of *LNCS*. Springer-Verlag, 1992, pp. 140–154.
42. Tatarinov, I., Ives, Z., Halevy, A., and Weld, D. Updating XML. In *Proceedings of the International Conference on Management of Data* (2001), ACM, pp. 413–424.
43. Thalheim, B. *Entity-Relationship Modeling: Foundations of Database Technology*. Springer-Verlag, 2000.
44. Wadler, P. Comprehending monads. *Mathematical Structures in Computer Science 2*, 4 (1992), 461–493.
45. Wong, L. Normal forms and conservative properties for query languages over collection types. In *Principles of Database Systems (PODS)* (1993), ACM, pp. 26–36.
46. World Wide Web Consortium (W3C). XML Schema. `http://www.w3c.org/TR/xmlschema-0`, `http://www.w3c.org/TR/xmlschema-1`, `http://www.w3c.org/TR/xmlschema-2`, 2001.
47. World Wide Web Consortium (W3C). XQuery. `http://www.w3c.org/TR/xquery`, 2004.

Automatic Image Description Based on Textual Data

Youakim Badr[1] and Richard Chbeir[2]

[1] PRISMa – INSA de Lyon,
20 Av. Einstein F-69621 VILLEURBANNE - France
Phone: (+33) 4 72 43 63 52, Fax: (+33) 4 72 43 85 18
youakim.badr@insa-lyon.fr
[2] LE2I – Bourgogne University
BP 47870 21078 DIJON CEDEX - France
Phone: (+33) 3 80 39 36 55, Fax: (+33) 3 80 39 68 69
richard.chbeir@u-bourgogne.fr

Abstract. In the last two decades, images are quite produced in increasing amounts in several application domains. In medicine, for instance, a large number of images of various imaging modalities (e.g. computer tomography, magnetic resonance, nuclear imaging, etc.) are produced daily to support clinical decision-making. Thereby, a fully functional Image Management System becomes a requirement to the end-users. In spite of current researches, the practice has proved that the problem of image management is highly related to image representation. This paper contribution is twofold in facilitating the representation of images and the extraction of its content and context descriptors. In fact, we introduce an expressiveness and extendable XML-based meta-model able to capture the metadata and content-based of images. We also propose an information extraction approach to provide automatic description of image content using related metadata. It automatically generates XML instances, which mark up metadata and salient objects matched by extraction patterns. In this paper, we illustrate our proposal by using the medical domain of lungs x-rays and we show our first experimental results.

Keywords: Image Representation, Indexing Method, Information Extraction, Electronic Dictionaries, Specification Language.

1 Introduction

The problem of image management is a subject of extensive research in pattern recognition, information retrieval, and databases communities [1, 2]. The need of efficient image management systems has several reasons to rapidly grow further and to play a very important role in the society. In medicine, for example, a large number of images of various imaging modalities (e.g. computer tomography, magnetic resonance, nuclear imaging, etc.) are produced daily to support clinical decision-making. A lot of work has been done in order to integrate image data in the standard data processing environments of different applications [3, 6, 10, 13].

In essence, the problem of image management is highly related to image representation. In the literature, two complimentary approaches are used for image representation:

S. Spaccapietra (Ed.): Journal on Data Semantics VII, LNCS 4244, pp. 196–218, 2006.

- *The content-based approach*: Issued from computer vision and pattern recognition community, the content-based approach uses the low-level features of images such as colors, textures, and shapes obtained through automatic extraction algorithms [1, 2, 16]. Thus, image retrieval is done automatically by similarity matching methods. However good the content-based approach is, practice has shown that the use of complementary metadata description is essential.
- *The metadata-based approach*: Issued from information retrieval and databases communities, the metadata-based approach consists of using alphanumeric attributes to describe the context and/or the content of an image. Thus, metadata-based image retrieval follows the traditional techniques (keywords, phrases, etc.) [14, 19]. However in several application domains, it is mostly difficult or not possible to fully or adequately describe an image using metadata representation [6, 12, 16, 25]. Due to problems of subjectivity and high-expressive representations. Furthermore, image description is usually done with human assistance, which is time-consuming when having huge amount of data.

The current trend is then towards a system that uses both metadata and content-based image description [4, 23, 24]. A mixed use of both approaches, results to means of image management that can satisfy many application areas. However, the proposals so far lack to address issues of:

- Extensible and high expressive image and salient objects description using both metadata and content-based representations,
- Automatic extraction methods of both (low-level and metadata) features,

In this paper, we present a novel image representation meta-model based on XML format. The key feature of the meta-model is that it captures in a single modeling meta-concept the low-level features, the structural and semantic properties, as well as the relationship descriptions of both multimedia object and meta-object. The image description meta-model proposed here considers the main features of a still image suggested in MPEG-7 standard [41]. On the other hand, we propose an information extraction approach to provide automatic description of images using related metadata. The main idea is to process some image related data, which are usually paragraphs of free natural text, in order to extract metadata and semantic features automatically. The extraction approach relies on extraction patterns that describe the context of relevant data and on a light parsing to recognize these data and to match them against extraction patterns. Once the matching holds successfully, the relevant metadata and features are tagged into a new XML document, which conforms to our XML-based meta-model. Hence, a repository of XML documents is built on the fly. Further documentary or database management systems can easily manipulate the image data model and formulate XQL or SQL queries. We complete the scheme of our work with a study case in medical x-rays imaging domain.

The paper is organized as follows. Section 2 presents a motivation example to be used throughout the paper. Related works are summarized in section 3. In section 4, we present our XML-based image data meta-model and illustrate it through a study case in the medical domain. In section 5, we present a high-level specification language to design extraction patterns; as well necessary dictionaries for lung x-ray are built and applied to extract relevant metadata and salient objects. Conclusions and future directions are given in section 6.

2 Motivation Example

The aim of this work is to facilitate the image retrieval by providing multi-dimensional representation. In this paper, we use the domain of lungs x-rays to illustrate our approach where each medical image (or a set of) is associated to a diagnosis written by the physician in a natural way as free text paragraphs. Through the paper, we use the following study case to illustrate how to present the entire required image information of both metadata and content-based using the meta-model, and how to define extraction patterns to extract relevant image information from diagnosis in order to fill in the meta-model. Fig. 1 shows both the image and the associated diagnosis, and the required extraction result which identifies salient objects, corresponding states and inter-relations, as well as other important metadata.

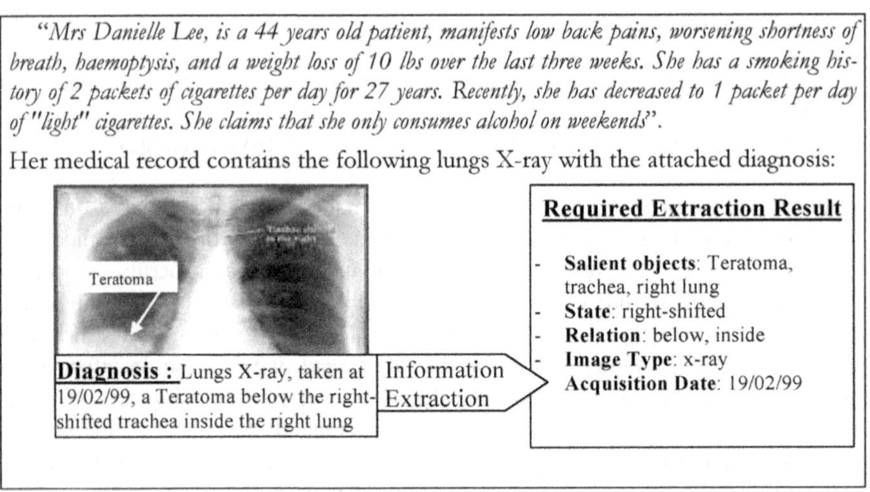

"Mrs Danielle Lee, is a 44 years old patient, manifests low back pains, worsening shortness of breath, haemoptysis, and a weight loss of 10 lbs over the last three weeks. She has a smoking history of 2 packets of cigarettes per day for 27 years. Recently, she has decreased to 1 packet per day of "light" cigarettes. She claims that she only consumes alcohol on weekends".
Her medical record contains the following lungs X-ray with the attached diagnosis:
Teratoma
Diagnosis : Lungs X-ray, taken at 19/02/99, a Teratoma below the right-shifted trachea inside the right lung
Information Extraction
Required Extraction Result
- Salient objects: Teratoma, trachea, right lung
- State: right-shifted
- Relation: below, inside
- Image Type: x-ray
Acquisition Date: 19/02/99

Fig. 1. The study case: An example of a diagnosis and the required extraction result

3 Related Work

In the literature, image representation and retrieval follow two directions: the meta-data oriented and the content-based oriented. For more than two decades, the work on content-based image analysis, representation and retrieval have known a big success among researchers. As a result, several applications based on automatic low-level features of color, texture, shape, etc. have been implemented [6, 10, 12]. Photobook, Netra, QBIC, Surfimage, VisualSeek, CAFIIR, etc. are some of the many content-based image retrieval systems [1, 3, 6, 12, 16]. However, these systems mainly focus on retrieval by low-level features and give emphasis (only keywords) or no emphasis to the role of metadata-based image retrieval.

The image management by metadata approach has been practiced in different fields of applications such as medicine, GIS, the Web, etc. Keywords are an example of meta-data widely used in image description. It goes without saying that there is a great waste of data when replacing an image by a set of metadata descriptors. Since subjectivity, ambiguity and imprecision are usually associated to the context and the semantic content of images, metadata descriptions are mostly incomplete [14]. This is why, some meta-data approaches suggested image description on the basis of salient objects position and relationships [42, 43, 44, 45, 46]. However, they are found to be imperfect at retrieval process in several application domains where translation, scaling, perfect and multiple rotations, or any arbitrary combination of transformations is applied. For instance, the spatial content in terms of relationships in surgical or radiation therapy of brain tumors is decisive because the location of a tumor has profound implications on a therapeutic decision [22].

In the literature, several hybrid image data models have been proposed [11, 22, 24] attempting to mix low-level feature with meta-data in order to provide multi-criteria queries. However, these models lack an appropriate representation of all necessary image related data for different applications. In [11] for example, the authors do not consider content and semantic representations of salient object related data and the relationship between salient objects. The approaches provided in [22, 24] do not allow the integration of several types of low-level features. This is why, a new standard has emerged called MPEG-7 for providing description of multimedia data content [41]. It offers a set of Descriptors and Description Schemes aiming to enable common access (search, filtering and browsing) to multimedia content. However, MPEG-7 suffers from its inability to taxonomically hierarchize the descriptors and thus its inability to express their semantics. This is due to the XML Schema in MPEG-7 DDL (Definition Description Language). Other drawbacks are MPEG-7 non-modularity and non-extensibility — or rather MPEG-7 inability to validate extensions of its description schemes.

As mentioned earlier, several automatic low-level features extraction algorithms are provided in the literature [6, 10, 12]. However, only rare approaches conceive an automatic extraction of metadata values. Primitive meta-data extraction approaches provided writing customized programs in programming languages such as Perl [30]. This is impractical because the programs are too hard to maintain. Some other approaches defined specialized languages to create kind of Information Extraction Systems and Wrappers [31, 32, 33]. These languages are expressiveness, but mastering them still requires computer expertise and skillful programmers. Most of the extraction approaches [33, 34, 35], however, fail to extract properly relevant data, although the text appears to be structured in a highly regular fashion. The main reason, that makes an extraction fails to find metadata values, is the nature of the relevant data structure, which is irregular e.g. missing or multiple metadata values in a text or even a permutation of their order.

The growth in the amount of textual data that are available in electronic documents makes humans incapable of reading and synthesizing such a wealth of data. Information Extraction (IE) is concerned with the extraction of relevant data from a collection of documents. In the literature [59], there are two main approaches for designing IE systems: the knowledge engineering approach and the empirical or corpus-based approach [60, 61]. In the first approach, the IE system is built manually by users and by using knowledge of the application domain. In the second approach, there is no similar need for expertise when customizing the system for a new domain. Instead, it requires the annotation of the training corpus of documents to mark relevant data. A training algorithm 'learns' from the corpus how to extract relevant data from novel texts [62]. This approach is faster than the knowledge engineering approach, but requires sufficient volume of training documents.

Most of the techniques used for the empirical Natural Language Processing employ (and exclusively) statistical techniques (i.e., as n-gram models and Hidden Markov Models [63]), neural network [64], symbolic learning (i.e., transformation rules [65], decision trees [66] and symbolic methods [67]), relational learning and/or Inductive Logic Programming [68]. An intensive research has been found in the literature [20, 69] to apply learning methods to the construction of IE systems.

To our knowledge, the survey of the literature points out the beginning of the academic prototypes, which deal with the information extraction. These approaches have evolved over the last decades but in some ways their behavior is not intuitive for non expert users and at times they do not behave the way the novice users may expect them to. However, the development process can be very laborious and requires expertise in natural language processing and information extraction approaches.

An approach of information extraction for users, who they are professional in a domain of interest (i.e. medical domain) and not expert in linguistic or programming languages, becomes interesting to match relevant data. An appropriate approach may stress on what a user wants to extract based on his/her knowledge of the domain rather than how to extract. The information extraction approach may also propose expressiveness and easy extraction patterns to deal with irregular structure of data that describes, for examples, images.

4 Modeling Images

We propose here an original image meta-model able to integrate the metadata and the content features related to the whole image and/or to its salient objects. Fig. 2 shows our model in the standard DTD format. We intentionally decided to use this format to provide generic description and domain independent approach. We note that DTD format can be easily converted into other semantic formats (such as XML schema, RDF, etc.) using current XML tools (XML spy, Stylus Studio, etc.). Our meta-model associates an abstraction level to both the metadata and the salient objects. The abstraction level notion is very important in our model and allows easy identifying of:

1. The impact of the metadata on the image description.
2. The granularity of content features.

Furthermore, our meta-model takes into consideration several types of relations (temporal, spatial, semantic, etc.) between image and its salient objects, and between salient objects. In the following, we detail each component and we illustrate this in our case study.

```
<!ELEMENT ImageModel (MetaDataBased*, ContentBased*)>
<!ELEMENT MetaDataBased (AbstractionLevel, MetaData*)>
<!ELEMENT ContentBased (AbstractionLevel, SalientObject*)>
<!ELEMENT AbstractionLevel (LevelName?, LevelDesription?)>
<!ELEMENT MetaData (MetaName, MetaType, MetaValue)>
<!ELEMENT SalientObject (Feature*, Relation*)>
<!ATTLIST SalientObject SOI CDATA #REQUIRED >
<!ELEMENT Relation (RelationType, RelationValue, Relationmember)>
<!ELEMENT Relationmember EMPTY>
<!ATTLIST Relationmember soi CDATA #REQUIRED >
<!ELEMENT Feature (FeatureName?, Descriptor*)>
<!ELEMENT Descriptor (DescriptorName, DescriptorValue, RepresentationFormatName)>
<!ELEMENT DescriptorName (#PCDATA)>
<!ELEMENT DescriptorValue (#PCDATA)>
<!ELEMENT RepresentationFormatName (#PCDATA)>
<!ELEMENT LevelDesription (#PCDATA)>
<!ELEMENT LevelName (#PCDATA)>
<!ELEMENT FeatureName (#PCDATA)>
<!ELEMENT MetaName (#PCDATA)>
<!ELEMENT MetaType (#PCDATA)>
<!ELEMENT MetaValue (#PCDATA)>
<!ELEMENT RelationType (#PCDATA)>
<!ELEMENT RelationValue (#PCDATA)>
```

Fig. 2. Our image meta-model in DTD format

4.1 The MetaData-Based Level

The metadata-based level captures the general data, which are *external* to the image content. In [22], three metadata sublevels are distinguished in the medical domain. This distinction is related to the data impact on image description:

- The context-oriented sublevel: contains application-oriented data that are completely independent of the image content and have no impact on the image description. For example, it contains data such as the hospital name, the physician identity, the patient name, gender, etc.
- The domain-oriented sublevel: includes data that are indirectly related to the image but strictly related to the application domain. For instance in the medical application, it includes the medical doctor's general observations, previous associated diseases, etc. This sublevel is very important because it allows one to highlight several associated issues (particularly when identifying associated medical anomalies).
- The image-oriented sublevel: corresponds to the data that are directly associated to the image. For example, the image compression type, the format of image creation (X-ray, scanner, MRI, etc.), the incidence (sagittal, coronal, axial, etc.), the scene, the study (thoracic traumatism due to a cyclist accident), the series, image acquisition date, etc. These data can significantly help the image content description.

Fig. 3 shows an example of the metadata-based content level.

```
<MetaDataBased>
   <AbstractionLevel>
        <LevelName> Domain_Oriented </LevelName>
        <LevelDesription> consists of the data that are directly or indirectly
            related to the image </LevelDesription>
      </AbstractionLevel>
   <MetaData>
        <MetaName>Patient Gender</MetaName>
        <MetaType>String</MetaType>
        <MetaValue>Woman</MetaValue>
     </MetaData>
   <MetaData>
        <MetaName>Patient Age</MetaName>
        <MetaType>Integer</MetaType>
        <MetaValue>44</MetaValue>
      </MetaData>
    <MetaData>
        <MetaName>Disease History</MetaName>
        <MetaType>Long</MetaType>
        <MetaValue>low back pains, worsening shortness of breath, haemoptysis,
            and a weight loss of 10 lbs over the last three weeks. She has a
            smoking history of 2 packets of cigarettes per day for 27 years.
            Recently, she has decreased to 1 packet per day of "light" ciga-
            rettes. She claims that she only consumes alcohol on week-
            ends"</MetaValue>
  </MetaData>
</MetaDataBased>
<MetaDataBased>
   <AbstractionLevel>
        <LevelName>Image_Oriented</LevelName>
        <LevelDesription> corresponds to the information that is directly asso-
            ciated to the image creation, storage, and type
            </LevelDesription>
     </AbstractionLevel>
   <MetaData>
        <MetaName>Imaging Technique</MetaName>
        <MetaType>String</MetaType>
        <MetaValue>X-rays</MetaValue>
     </MetaData>
   <MetaData>
        <MetaName>Compression</MetaName>
        <MetaType>String</MetaType>
        <MetaValue>None</MetaValue>
     </MetaData>
   <MetaData>
        <MetaName>Acquisition Date</MetaName>
        <MetaType>Date</MetaType>
        <MetaValue>19/02/99</MetaValue>
  </MetaData>
</MetaDataBased>
```

Fig. 3. Example of MetaData-Based content

4.2 The Content-Based Level

The content-based level describes the content of the image using several features detected throughout an abstraction level. The image description meta-model proposed here is designed in a manner that considers the common features of a still image suggested in MPEG-7 standard. In our meta-model, content features can be assigned to the whole image and/or to its salient objects. Furthermore, the content-based level maintains relations of different types between either the salient objects, or the salient objects and the image. In the literature, physical, spatial and semantic features are commonly used and briefly described here below:

The Physical Feature: describes the image (or the salient object) using its low-level features such as color, texture, etc. The color feature, for instance, can be described by our meta-model *via* several descriptors (such as color distribution, histograms, dominant color, etc.) where each descriptor is obtained by assembling a set of values in respect to a color space model. Fig. 4 shows an example of several physical features represented within our meta-model. The use of physical features allows answering non-traditional queries such as: "Find lung x-rays where they contain objects that are similar (using colors) to a given salient object SO_2".

```
<ContentBased>
  <AbstractionLevel>
      <LevelName>Physical Level</LevelName>
      <LevelDesription>
        describes the image (or  the salient object) using its low-level  features
        </LevelDesription>
  </AbstractionLevel>
  <SalientObject SOI="Image">
      <Feature>
          <FeatureName>Color</FeatureName>
          <Descriptor>
              <DescriptorName>Dominant Color      </DescriptorName>
              <DescriptorValue>(162, 158, 168)      </DescriptorValue>
              <RepresentationFormatName>  RGB Format  </RepresentationFormatName>
          </Descriptor>
      </Feature>
  </SalientObject>
  <SalientObject SOI="SO_2">
      <Feature>
          <FeatureName>Texture</FeatureName>
          <Descriptor>
          <DescriptorName> Histogram    </DescriptorName>
           <DescriptorValue>   (53, 54, 68, 14, 165, 152, 165) </DescriptorValue>
              <RepresentationFormatName> CMY Format </RepresentationFormatName>
          </Descriptor>
      </Feature>
  </SalientObject>
.......
```

Fig. 4. Example of content-based data applied on physical features description using our meta-model

The Spatial Feature: is an intermediate (middle-level) feature that concerns geometric aspects of either images or salient objects such as shape and position. Each spatial feature can have several descriptors such as: MBR (Minimum Bounding Rectangle), bounding circle, surface, volume, etc. Using our meta-model, each descriptor may have a set of values (Fig. 5). The use of spatial features allows replying to queries in medical systems such as: "Find lung x-rays where left lung surface is bigger than a given object SO_1".

```
<ContentBased>
<AbstractionLevel>
    <LevelName> Spatial Level </LevelName>
    <LevelDesription>is an intermediate (middlelevel) feature that concerns
geometric aspects of images (or salient objects)
    </LevelDesription>
</AbstractionLevel>
<SalientObject SOI="SO_1">
    <Feature>
        <FeatureName>Position</FeatureName>
        <Descriptor>
          <DescriptorName> Barycenter </DescriptorName>
          <DescriptorValue>(120, 154) </DescriptorValue>
          <RepresentationFormatName>2D Format </RepresentationFormatName>
        </Descriptor>
</Feature>
<Relation>
    <RelationType>Directional</RelationType>
    <RelationValue>Aboveright</RelationValue>
    <Relationmember soi="SO_2" />
</Relation>
<Relation>
    <RelationType>Directional</RelationType>
    <RelationValue>Left</RelationValue>
    <Relationmember soi="SO_3" />
</Relation>
<Relation>
    <RelationType>Topological</RelationType>
    <RelationValue>Disjoint</RelationValue>
    <Relationmember soi="SO_2" />
</Relation>
<Relation>
    <RelationType>Topological</RelationType>
    <RelationValue>Touch</RelationValue>
    <Relationmember soi="SO_3" />
</Relation>
</SalientObject>
 ...
```

Fig. 5. Example of content-based data applied on spatial features description using our meta-model

The Semantic Feature: integrates high-level descriptions of image and salient-objects using application domain keywords. In the medical domain, for example, terms such as name (lungs, trachea, tumor, etc.), states (inflated, exhausted, dangerous, etc.) are commonly used to describe medical image content (Fig. 6). The aim of the semantic feature is to increase the expression power of users in a manner that usual domain terms can be used to describe and retrieve the image. The use of semantic features is important to answer for traditional queries in medical systems such as: “Find lung x-rays where hypervascularized tumor is invading the left lung”.

4.3 The Relation

Our meta-model allows also representing several useful types of relations between salient objects (spatial, semantic, temporal, etc.).

Spatial relations may exist either between two salient objects or a salient object and the image. Three types of spatial relations are considered in the literature [48]:

- Metric relations: measure the distance between salient objects [47]. For instance, the metric relation “far” between two objects A and B indicates that each pair of points A_i and B_j has a distance grater than a threshold δ.

- Directional relations: describe the order between two salient objects according to a direction, or the localization of salient object inside the image [46]. In the literature, fourteen directional relations are considered:
    - Strict: north, south, east, and west.
    - Mixed: north-east, north-west, south-east, and south-west.
    - Positional: left, right, up, down, front and behind.

```
<ContentBased>
   <AbstractionLevel>
         <LevelName> Semantic Level </LevelName>
        <LevelDesription> integrates high-level descriptions of image (or sa-
         lient-objects) with the use of an application domain oriented key-
         words </LevelDesription>
   </AbstractionLevel>
   <SalientObject SOI="Image">
     <Feature>
       <FeatureName />
       <Descriptor>
          <DescriptorName> Diagnosis </DescriptorName>
           <DescriptorValue> taken at 19/02/99, a tumor below the right-
           shifted trachea (in the inferior part of the right lung)
           </DescriptorValue>
          <RepresentationFormatName />
       </Descriptor>
       <Descriptor>
          <DescriptorName> Keywords </DescriptorName>
          <DescriptorValue> Lungs, Trachea, Tumor </DescriptorValue>
          <RepresentationFormatName />
       </Descriptor>
      </Feature>
    </SalientObject>
   <SalientObject SOI="SO_1">
     <Feature>
        <FeatureName />
       <Descriptor>
          <DescriptoName> Identification </DescriptorName>
          <DescriptorValue> Trachea </DescriptorValue>
          <RepresentationFormatName />
       </Descriptor>
       <Descriptor>
          <DescriptorName> State </DescriptorName>
          <DescriptorValue> Right-shifted </DescriptorValue>
          <RepresentationFormatName />
       </Descriptor>
      </Feature>
    </SalientObject>
```

Fig. 6. Description of the semantic features using our meta-model

Furthermore, directional relations do not exist in several configurations.

- Topological relations: describe the intersection and the incidence between objects [45]. Egenhofer [45, 48] has identified six basic relations: *Disjoint, Meet,*

Overlap, Cover, Contain, and Equal. Topological relations present several characteristics:

- they are *exclusive* to two objects: there is one and only one topological relation between two objects,
- they have *absolute* value because of their constant existence between objects,
- they are transformation, translation, scaling, and zooming *invariant.*

With our model, temporal or spatio-temporal relations can also be captured [21]. This type of relations is very useful to describe the evolution of image objects between two periods. In the medical domain, this kind of relation can be very helpful for users to study the impact of treatments (the evolution of tumor, the displacement of a fibrinocruorique clot through a deep vein of the lower limb, etc.).

Furthermore, semantic relations are of high importance and can be considered in our meta-model as well. In several domains such as medicine, users need to search images using familiar terms like invading, attacking, shifting, etc.

In this manner, the user will have access to a comprehensive and intelligent description of image and its related data. Relevant descriptions of an image can then be used to provide multi-criteria retrieval.

5 Information Extraction

We restrict our work in Information Extraction (IE) to the knowledge engineering approach. We have studied the potential of regular expressions in extracting information. We have tracked several works similar to information extraction based on regular expressions and used in medical domains. These works are most commonly used as a means to identify biological terms [52], protein names [53] or as a way to extract relevant data based on ontology [54, 55].

In our context, applying information extraction to medical diagnosis aims to facilitate image description and retrieval processes. It allows extracting two types of data: metadata related to the image-oriented level, and semantic data related to the whole image and its salient objects such as the identification of objects, their states and relations. In the following paragraphs, we present the high-level specification language for information extraction applied to medical diagnosis and introduce the overall data extraction process.

5.1 High-Level Specification Language

Regular expressions are concise and expressiveness notation [28]. They are good rival for manual pattern recognition. Many people routinely use regular expressions to specify searches in text editors and with standalone tools such as the Unix grep utility [29]. Relevant data can be well located by describing their context and their characteristics. Informally, characteristics such as multiple values, missing value and permutations can be easily simulated by using basic operators in regular expressions like Kleene (*), optional (?), union (|) and concatenation (white-space). Complex regular expressions can be built up from simpler ones by means of regular expressions operators and parenthesis. Because regular languages are closed under concatenation and union, the basic operators can be combined with any kind of regular expressions.

Using regular expressions in information extraction from natural language corpus stipulates long expressions with increasing complexity to deal with most of possible cases. Clearly, long regular expressions with multiple nesting levels and operators become unreadable and hard to maintain. Another drawback is encountered with regular expression engines [39, 40], which are defined on a finite set of letters. In such a way, each single word is composed of the underlying letters.

To overcome major drawbacks and restraints of regular expressions, we extended the syntax of regular expressions by words and meta-words over the alphabet of any natural language such as the English's. Meta-words denote semantic categories of related words usually defined in dictionaries. Yet, another simple but powerful solution to resolve the visibility of long expressions is to provide layer-oriented approach to build regular expressions. Three layers can be introduced to decompose a long regular expression into modular pattern (called extraction pattern): **term layer, expression layer and slot layer**. Slot layer is made of expression layers including term layers. Such convenient extensions and hierarchy allow a concise and expressiveness abstraction for casual users to compose extraction patterns by a means of words, meta-words and layers. In this manner, one builds its dictionary of extraction patterns and assigns a set of extraction patterns to image description.

The ***term layer*** consists of a finite set of *terms*. A term represents an abstraction of linguistic information in the text. A term *t* is either:

- A word: denotes a sequence of letters delimited by simple quotes such as 'tumor', 'artery', 'near', 'in contact with', 'on the left', and so on.
- A meta-word denoting
  - Generic entities delimited by open and close angles such as numbers (e.g. <NB>), any word (e.g. <W>), empty word (e.g. <E>),
  - Classes of words such as general classes (e.g. <body>), specialized classes (e.g. <bodybones>),
  - Classes of expressions e.g. <metric> to denote metric expressions (ml, mol/mm, m^2, etc.), <spatial> to denote directional or topological expressions (right, left, under, overlap, converge, join etc.), or <temporal> to denote time dimension (second, minute, hour, etc.).

The ***expression layer*** contains a finite set of expressions. We denote by an expression a concatenation of terms by a means of separate operator (white-space, tabulation, new-line). We say that an expression holds if a sequence of words in the text matches the expression. For example, the expression *<body> 'x-ray' <show> <symptom> 'on' 'the' <body>* recognizes all sequences of any body part followed by the term 'x-ray', followed by the verb 'show', followed by any symptom, followed by the term 'on', and the term 'the', and finally by any body part.

A ***slot layer*** is a set of alternates of expressions. We denote the alternate operator as | (pipe symbol), and we say that a slot holds if one of its expressions holds. For example, the following slot of four date expressions:

<NB> <month> <NB> | *<NB> '/' <NB> '/' <NB>* | *<day> ',' <month> <NB> ',' <NB>* | *<month> <NB> ',' <NB>*

can locate a date of the format *02 February 1969* or *Sunday, February 02, 2003* and so on.

Unary operators could be applied on expressions in slots such as kleene (*), optional (?), and one or more (+). We note that priority order can be changed by parenthesis. For example, the expression *('phone' ':'? <NB> ('-' <NB>)+)** keeps the usual interpretation as in regular expression syntax.

An ***extraction pattern*** P is a finite and unordered set of slots/features. |P| denotes the cardinality of P (number of slots). Furthermore, an extraction pattern of cardinality n has n! possible combinations.

Since the extraction patterns are slightly regular expressions, it is convenient to mark up relevant metadata once the regular expression holds. To deal with this issue, a key idea is to delimit relevant metadata by XML tags, and then to produce for each image and for its salient objects an XML document describing its representation in terms of content features and metadata attributes.

In the extraction pattern, the tag name is specified by an *identifier* of the format *TagName*[*term*] or *TagName*[*expression*], where the *TagName* encloses the *term* or *expression* in the output when entirely the extraction pattern holds. Hence, the *TagName*[*term*] in extraction pattern is equivalently mapped to *<TagName> term </TagName>* in XML format and respectively to *<TagName> expression </TagName>* in the case of expression.

Roughly speaking, the notation specification of terms, expressions, slots, and extraction patterns is implemented as a formal syntax similar to procedural programming languages, where identifiers of expressions, slots and patterns are declared and defined within the scope of a dictionary of extraction patterns. The formal syntax is illustrated in Fig. 7. We observe that, at the expression level, the keyword *expression* declares an expression identifier, and the concatenation operator between sequence of terms and tagged terms defines its value. In similar way, the keyword *slot* declares a slot identifier at the slot level, and the identifier value is defined by the disjunction operator over a list of expression identifiers. Finally, a pattern identifier is declared by the *pattern* keyword. The definition of a pattern identifier is an unordered list of slot identifiers separated by a comma. However, identifiers of slot, respectively identifiers of expression, can be re-used in different patterns and respectively in different slots. All declarations and definitions are going inside the scope of a named dictionary, which is introduced after the keyword *dictionary*.

```
dictionary dictionary_name:

expression   expression_identifier =  concatenation of terms or tagged
terms ;

slot slot_identifier =  disjunction of  expression_identifiers ;

pattern pattern_identifier = unordered list of slot_identifiers separated
by comma ;
```

Fig. 7. Formal syntax for declarations and definitions of extraction patterns

5.2 Dictionaries for Image Description

For a given domain of interest, such as lungs x-rays', it is easy to elaborate dictionaries for describing frequent words in the image description. A dictionary is a flat file of entries where each entry defines a *lemma* followed by its *canonical form* and a list of *categories* to which the lemma belongs. For example, the following entries:

axes, axe: <position>, <topology>.
axe, axe: < position>, <topology>.

denote the lemmas axe and its inflected plural noun axes. We also notice that position and topology stand for categories, which referred to by <position> and <topology> in extraction pattern. Often, it is as well useful to define compound words as lemma entry in dictionaries (e.g. hypervascular tumor), and to associate it with a category for high level of abstraction (e.g. tumor).

In the discourse universe of a particular application, we distinguish two sets of dictionaries: dictionaries of the current natural language e.g. English, and dictionaries of the current domain of interest i.e. the lungs x-ray domain. In spite of the large spectrum of frequent words, we build many dictionaries to cover the lungs x-ray domain such as anatomy of body parts, diseases, disorders, symptoms, sign, x-ray, etc. Furthermore, special dictionaries related to pathology are also built to describe different exams like echo-doppler, radioisotopic, and irrigraphy. We completed our dictionary family with a list of spatial terms and rules. In fact, small dictionaries of special terms (e.g. above, under, near, etc) are enumerated to capture and deduce relationships between salient objects. It is interesting to notice that dictionaries are re-usable components and they can be exchange across multiple application domains.

The definitions of the natural language dictionaries and their entry structures are simply inherited from the electronic dictionaries of simple and compound words [49, 50], which have been developed at the Laboratory of Automatic Documentation and Linguistics (LADL - University of Paris 7). In reality, the dictionaries of simple words (DELAS) and compound words (DELAC) contain more than 430 000 canonical entries, which cover most of the words that annotate paragraphs. The dictionaries of a domain of interest can be easily viewed as subsets of linguistic dictionaries and thus can be built using tools such as INTEXT [51].

5.3 Application on Diagnosis

Let us consider now the motivation example previously mentioned. The diagnosis related to the medical image mentions the existence of a teratoma below the right-shifted trachea inside the right lung. Without any treatment, this information is used as a descriptor of the semantic level of the default salient object, which denotes the whole image (see Fig. 8). In background, the extraction mechanism is intended to identify the content of the semantic level in terms of salient objects and relations, like teratoma, trachea and right lung, as well as the metadata like the acquisition date of the image. Salient objects and metadata have to be structured.

```
<SalientObject SO_Id="Image">
  .........
   <Descriptor>
     <DescriptorName> Diagnosis<DescriptorName/>
     <Value> Lungs X-ray, taken at 19/02/99, a teratoma below the
     right-shifted trachea inside the right lung </Value>
     <RepresentationFormatName/>
   </Descriptor>
  .........
</SalientObject>
```

Fig. 8. A salient object and its diagnosis descriptor of an x-ray image

By XML format conforming to the DTD of the meta-model, we emphasize the metadata-based level by looking for metadata features in the image-oriented sublevel. We consider the acquisition date, for example, with four possible expressions to recognize variant date formats. Then, a slot of date is defined as alternation of these expressions as follows:

```
expression AcquisitionDate1 = DATE[ <NB> <month> <NB> ];
expression AcquisitionDate2 = DATE[ <NB> '/' <NB> '/' <NB> ];
expression AcquisitionDate3 = DATE[ <day> ',' <month> <NB> ',' <NB> ];
expression AcquisitionDate4 = DATE[ <month> <NB> ',' <NB> ];
slot Acquisition_date = AcquisitionDate1 | AcquisitionDate2 | AcquisitionDate3 | Acquisi-
 tionDate4 ;
```

When applying the date slot to the diagnosis, the second expression will recognize the date '19/02/99' and produce a date in the metadata image-oriented sublevel as illustrated in Fig. 9.

As we mentioned previously in semantic sublevel, we are interested in capturing salient objects features and different types of relations between salient objects. For that, several dictionaries, such as lung anatomy and pathology types are necessarily to refer to their contents by means of categories in extraction patterns.

```
<AbstractionLevel>
        <LevelName>Image_Oriented</LevelName>
         </LevelDesription/>
</AbstractionLevel>
<MetaData>
        <MetaName>Acquisition_Date</MetaName>
        <MetaType>Date</MetaType>
        <MetaValue>19/02/99</MetaValue>
</MetaData>
```

Fig. 9. Output of the slot Acquisition date

In our context, body parts and diseases identify convenient salient objects. In similar way, directional, metric and topological relations can be described by spatial relation dictionary.

Fig. 10 snapshots a subset of our dictionaries used in metadata and semantic extraction process. Each entry in the lung anatomy is classified under multi-axial taxonomy, which means that a term can be referred to by several categories or meta-words (e.g. the term *posterior basal* is referred by *bronchial* and *lung* categories). In

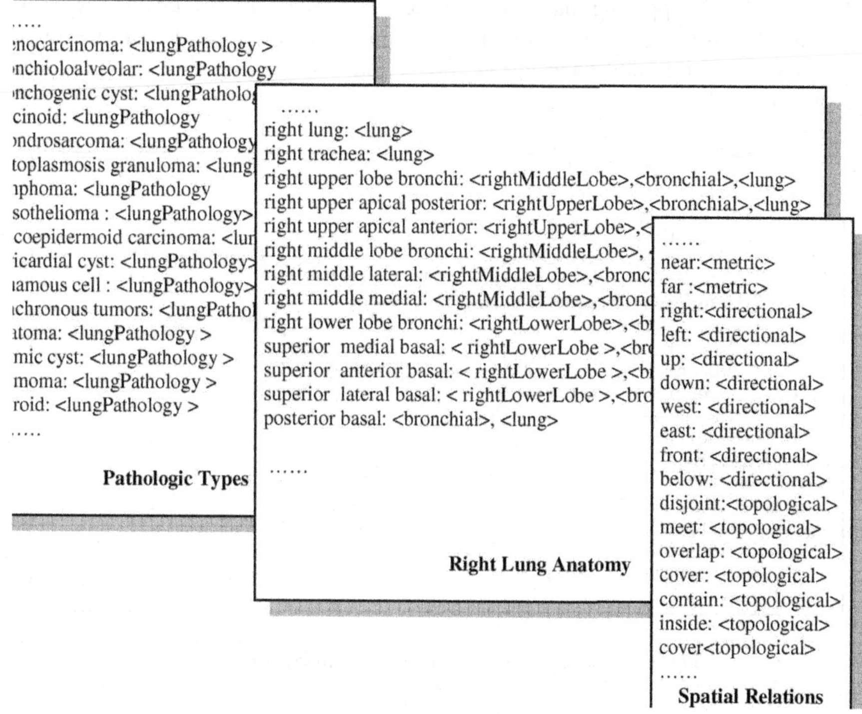

.....
:nocarcinoma: <lungPathology >
nchioloalveolar: <lungPathology
nchogenic cyst: <lungPatholo
cinoid: <lungPathology
ondrosarcoma: <lungPathology
toplasmosis granuloma: <lung
nphoma: <lungPathology
sothelioma : <lungPathology>
coepidermoid carcinoma: <lu
icardial cyst: <lungPathology>
iamous cell : <lungPathology>
ichronous tumors: <lungPatho
itoma: <lungPathology >
mic cyst: <lungPathology >
moma: <lungPathology >
roid: <lungPathology >
.....
Pathologic Types
......
right lung: <lung>
right trachea: <lung>
right upper lobe bronchi: <rightMiddleLobe>,<bronchial>,<lung>
right upper apical posterior: <rightUpperLobe>,<bronchial>,<lung>
right upper apical anterior: <rightUpperLobe>,<
right middle lobe bronchi: <rightMiddleLobe>,
right middle lateral: <rightMiddleLobe>,<bronc
right middle medial: <rightMiddleLobe>,<bronc
right lower lobe bronchi: <rightLowerLobe>,<b
superior medial basal: < rightLowerLobe >,<br
superior anterior basal: < rightLowerLobe >,<b
superior lateral basal: < rightLowerLobe >,<br
posterior basal: <bronchial>, <lung>
......
Right Lung Anatomy
......
near:<metric>
far :<metric>
right:<directional>
left: <directional>
up: <directional>
down: <directional>
west: <directional>
east: <directional>
front: <directional>
below: <directional>
disjoint:<topological>
meet: <topological>
overlap: <topological>
cover: <topological>
contain: <topological>
inside: <topological>
cover<topological>
......
Spatial Relations

Fig. 10. Snapshots of lung pathology, anatomy of the right lung bronchial and relations

contrast, entries in pathology and spatial relation dictionaries are classified under single category.

Based on dictionary categories, we propose some of possible expressions allowing capturing salient objects, their states, and relations in diagnosis text. Of course, other expressions can be figured out to cover large number of possible cases. Finally, a diagnosis slot as an alternation of all possible expressions is built.

```
expression  diagnosis1  =  SO_x[<lung>]  <W>*  REL1[<relation>]  <W>*
SO_y[<lungPathology>] ;
expression  diagnosis2  =  SO_x[<lung>]  <W>*  REL1[<relation>]  <W>*
SO_y[<lungPathology>] <W>*  REL2[<relation>] <W>* SO_z[<lung>];
expression diagnosis3 = SO_x[<lung>] <W>* REL1[<relation>] STATE1[<W> '-' <W>
'ed'] <W>*  SO_y[<lungPathology>] <W>* REL2[<relation>] <W>* SO_z[<lung>] ;
slot diagnosis = diagnosis1 | diagnosis2 | diagnosis3 ;
```

Clearly, the first diagnosis is looking for a lung body part by using the <lung> category as a salient object SO_x, and lung disease by referring to <lungPathology> category as salient object SO_y. A relation REL1 separates SO_x and SO_y preceded and followed by many words as indicating by <W>*. The comprehension of the remaining diagnosis expressions are defined similarly.

The resulting of applying diagnosis slot identifies *teratoma*, *trachea* and *right lung* as salient objects, *below* and *inside* as directional and topological relations respectively, and at last right-shifted as a state. Fig. 11 shows the extraction result on the salient object SO_1.

```
<SalientObject SOI="SO_1">
   <Feature>
      <FeatureName/>
      <Descriptor>
         <DescriptorName>Identification </DescriptorName>
         <DescriptorValue>Trachea</DescriptorValue>
         <RepresentationFormatName/>
      </Descriptor>
      <Descriptor>
         <DescriptorName>State</DescriptorName>
         <DescriptorValue>Right-shifted</DescriptorValue>
         <RepresentationFormatName/>
      </Descriptor>
   </Feature>
</SalientObject>
   <Relation>
      <RelationType>Directional</RelationType>
      <RelationValue>below</RelationValue>
      <Relationmember soi="SO_2"/>
   </Relation>
```

Fig. 11. Trachea salient object and its directional relation

By using previous expression identifiers, date and diagnosis, we construct an extraction pattern and we associate it to the original diagnosis descriptor. The resulting is an extraction of the following format:

Pattern LungDiagnosis = date, diagnosis+ ;

In order to validate our approach of information extraction, we have developed a wrapper, called Xtractor [15], to implement the specification language of extraction patterns. The Xtractor relies on linguistic parsing of paragraphs. It applies natural language dictionaries as well as dictionaries related to a specific domain such as the lung diagnosis. More details about Xtractor are provided in [15].

6 Experimental Results

To validate our approach, we have selected a corpus of 105 patient records provided by the Rouen Hospital throughout the TIPHAD project [56]. We have focused on extracting relevant data such as salient objects, relations between salient objects, acquisition date, image-type, states and symptoms from patient records paragraphs of lung diagnosis to in order to annotate the images. The first experimental results aimed at validating the precision of our approach but time-based performance was out of scope of tests. For our experiments, we have chosen 45 records for the tuning set and 60 records for the test set. We used the tuning set to write the extraction patterns. Moreover, we generalize the extraction patterns through a process of successive refinement. Beside the linguistic dictionaries of the French language provided by the INTEX [57] community, we built medical dictionaries describing the lung x-rays domain. In order to run the experimental tests, we built the following dictionaries:

- medicament.dic: containing 3693 medical entries,
- lungPathologie.dic: with 728 entries to describe the lung anatomy and the related organisms,
- maladie.dic: including 69 diseases,
- symptomes.dic: involving 33 symptoms,
- relation.dic: containing 53 spatial and directional relations,
- glossaire.dic: having 2638 medical terms.

A dictionary of 60 extraction patterns has been used to extract relevant data from x-lungs diagnosis records. The compilation of these extractions generated 463 elementary regular expressions for all the expressions and the slots.

According to the information retrieval, we define a *fact* as a particular attribute-value pair such a salient object (Salient_Object, *trachea*), a relation (Relation, *inside*) or a metadata (Acquisition_date, 2/2/2006). If N is the number of facts in the corpus, C is the number of facts declared correctly, and I is the number declared incorrectly, the recall ratio is $\frac{C}{N}$, and the precision ratio is $\frac{C}{C+I}$.

In experiments we conducted, the Xtractor applies extraction patterns against the pre-processed paragraphs in order to locate relevant data. As illustrated in Table 1, we were able to achieve recall and precision ratios of 0.91% and 0.97%. The measurement of precision and recall shows precisely the correctness of the system based on the small corpus. These high numbers are typical of the traditional information extraction for small corpus and well hand written patterns.

Table 1. Recall and precision results

	N	***C***	***I***	***recall***	***precision***
Salient Object_1	60	57	2	0.95	0.96
Special Relation	60	60	1	1.00	0.98
Salient Object_2	60	56	2	0.93	0.96
State	49	44	1	0.89	0.97
Acquisition date	60	58	0	0.96	1.00
Image type	51	51	0	1.00	1.00
Symptoms	83	62	5	0.74	0.92
All attributes	**423**	**388**	**11**	**0.91**	**0.97**

7 Conclusion

In this paper, we presented an original image XML-based meta-model able to describe the image content and all related metadata. Built on several abstraction levels, our meta-model provides the possibility to be adaptable to the domain and the user needs (in respect to all current standards). We are convinced that our multi-spaced image meta-model brings new trends and provides all requirements for main efficient image operations (in particular indexing and retrieval operations.

On the other hand, we observed that image diagnosis could be used to extract some meaningful data. The relevant data exhibits some regularity that can be processed efficiently by regular expressions. We extended the notation of regular expressions by providing meta-words and a mutli-layer approach to define a high specification language for extraction patterns. The notations of the specification language render long and complex regular expressions to be concise, expressiveness and easy to maintain by casual users. The extraction patterns are mainly based on different metadata permutations, expression disjunction and on the context to identify salient objects. Along the paper, we showed how applying extraction patterns over image descriptions produce XML instances conforming to the DTD of our meta-model. We validate the feasibility of our information extraction approach to annotate images with the Xtractor prototype. In fact, the high specification language and the extraction wrapper (Xtractor) are implemented; a lexical and syntax analyzer is developed by JavaCC [37] to recognize extraction patterns and to generate regular expressions. The resulting regular expressions [38] are then used by the Xtractor wrapper to match relevant metadata. The initial experiment results show satisfactory performance near 0.91% recall and 0.97% precision on test data.

We are currently building and updating the electronic dictionaries for a large cover of x-lung images. Furthermore, a large corpus of image descriptions and domain-specific dictionaries are compulsory to improve the precision and recall ratio and to test the complexity and the performance of our application. Future work will also address the integration of low-level features algorithms to provide fully-automated description process and multi-criteria queries possibilities.

References

1. J.K.Wu and A.D. Narasimhalu and B.M. Mehtre and C.P. Lam and Y.J. Gao, CORE: A Content-Based Retrieval Engine for Multimedia Information Systems, Multimedia Systems, 1995, Vol. 3, pp. 25-41.
2. S. Berchtold, C. Boehm, B. Braunmueller, et.al.: Fast Parallel Similarity Search in Multimedia Databases, SIGMOD Conference, AZ, USA, 1997, pp. 1-12.
3. A. Yoshitaka and T. Ichikawa: A Survey on Content-Based Retrieval for Multimedia Databases, IEEE Transactions on Knowledge and Data Engineering, Vol. 11, No. 1, 1999, pp.81-93.
4. V.Oria, M.T. Özsu, L. Liu, et.al.: Modeling Images for Content-Based Queries: The DISMA Approach, VIS'97, San Diago, 1997, pp.339-346.
5. J.K. Wu: Content-Based Indexing of Multimedia Databases, IEEE TKDE, 1997, Vol. 9, No. 6, pp.978-989.
6. Y. Rui, T.S. Huang, S.F. Chang: Image Retrieval: Past, Present, and Future, Journal of Visual Communication and Image Representation, 1999, Vol. 10, pp.1-23.
7. M. Stonebraker, and P. Brown: Object-Relational DBMSs, Mogan Kaufmann Pub. Inc, 1999, San. Francisco, ISBN 1-55860-452-9.

8. Excalibur Image Datablade Module User's Guide, Informix Press, March, 1999, Ver. 1.2, P. No. 000-5356.
9. Oracle8i, Visual Information Retrieval Users Guide & Reference, Oracle Press, 1999, Release 8.1.5, A67293-01.
10. W.I. Grosky: Managing Multimedia Information in Database Systems, Communications of the ACM, 1997, Vol. 40, No. 12, pp. 72-80.
11. W.I. Grosky, and P.L. Stanchev: An Image Data Model, Advances in Visual Information Systems, Visual-2000, 4th International Conference, LNCS 1929, Springer Verlag Lyon, France, 2000, pp. 14-25.
12. J.P. Eakins, and M.E. Graham: Content-Based Image Retrieval: A Report to the JISC Technology Applications Programme, January, 1999, Inst. for Image Data Research, Univ. of Northumbria at Newcastle.
13. A.W.M. Smeulders, T. Gevers, and M.L. Kersten: Crossing the Divide Between Computer Vision and Databases in Search of Image Databases, Visual Database Systems Conf., Italy, 1998, pp. 223-239.
14. A. Sheth, and W. Klas: Multimedia Data Management: Using Metadata to Integrate and Apply Digital Media, McGraw-Hill, 1998, San Francisco.
15. Badr Y. "Xtractor: A Light Wrapper For XML Paragraph-Centric Documents", in Proceedings of the 2005 International Conference on Signal-Image Technology & Internet - Based Systems (IEEE - SITIS'05), Yaoundé Cameroon, 2005, p. 150-155.
16. R.C. Veltkamp, and M. Tanase: Content-Based Image Retrieval Systems: A Survey, October, 2000, Technical Report UU-cs-2000-34, Department of Computer Science, Utrecht University.
17. V. Oria, M.T. Özsu, P. Iglinski, et.al.: DISMA: An Object Oriented Approach to Developing an Image Database System, ICDE 2000, February, 2000, 16th Int. Conf. on Data Engineering, San Diego, California.
18. V. Oria, M.T. Özsu, P. Iglinski, et.al.: DISMA: A Distributed and Interoperable Image Database System, SIGMOD 2000, May, 2000, In Proc. of ACM SIGMOD Int. Conf. on Management of Data, Dallas, Texas.
19. J.S. Duncan, and N. Ayache: Medical Image Analysis: Progress over Two Decades and the Challenges Ahead; IEEE Transactions on Pattern Analysis and Machine Intelligence, Vol. 22, No. 1, January 2000.
20. Soderland S., Fisher D., Aseltine J., and al. "Issues in inductive learning of domain-specic text extraction rules". In Learning for Natural Language Processing. Berlin: Springer, 1996, p. 290-301.
21. Allen, J.E., Maintaining Knowledge about Temporal Intervals, Communications of ACM, Volume 26, November 1983, pp. 832-843.
22. R. Chbeir, F. Favetta: A Global Description of Medical Image with a High Precision; in IEEE International Symposium on Bio-Informatics and Biomedical Engineering IEEE-BIBE'2000, IEEE Computer Society, Washington D.C., USA, (2000) November 8th-10th, pp. 289-296.
23. W.W. Chu, ,C.C. Hsu, A.F. Cárdenas, et al.: Knowledge-Based Image Retrieval with Spatial and Temporal Constraints, IEEE Transactions on Knowledge and Data Engineering, Vol. 10, No. 6, November/December 1998, pp. 872-888.
24. M. Mechkour: EMIR2. An Extended Model for Image Representation and Retrieval, Database and EXpert system Applications (DEXA), Sep. 1995, pp. 395-404.
25. G. Trayser: Interactive System for Image Selection, Digital Imaging Unit Center of Medical Informatics University Hospital of Geneva, http://www.expasy.ch/UIN/html1/ projects/isis/isis.html

26. A.D. Narasimhalu: Multimedia Databases, Multimedia Systems, Springer-Verlag, 1996, vol. 4, pp.226-249.
27. G. Lu: Multimedia Database Management Systems, 1999, Artech House Computing library, ISBN 0-089006-342-7
28. J.E. Hopcroft, and J.D. Ullman: Introduction to automata theory languages, and computation. Addison-Wesley Publishing Co., Reading, M.A., 1979.
29. A. Hume: A tale of two greps. Software Practice and Experience, volume 18, number 11, November 1988, pp. 1063-1072.
30. L. Wall, T. Christensen, and R.L. Schwartz: Programming Perl. O'Reilly & Associates, Inc., second edition, September 1996.
31. D.J. Smith, and M Lopez: Information extraction for semi-structured documents, Proc. Workshop on Management of Semi-structured Data, May 1997
32. J. Hammer, H. Garcia-Molina, J. Cho, et al.: Extracting Semi structured Information from the Web. In Proceedings of the Workshop on Management of Semistructured Data. Tucson, Arizona, May 1997
33. C.N. Hsu, and M.T. Dung: Generating finite-state transducers for semistructured data extraction from the web. Information Systems, 23(8):521-538, Special Issue on Semistructured Data, 1998.
34. N. Ashish, and C. Knoblock: Wrapper Generation for Semi-structured Internet Sources. ACM SIGMOD Workshop on Management of Semi-structured Data, 1997, Tucson , Arizona
35. S. Kuhlins, R. Tredwell: Toolkits for Generating Wrappers: A survey, In Net.ObjectDays, Erfurt, Germany, September, 2002.
36. S. Sankar, S. Viswanadha, and R. Duncan: Java Compiler Compiler (JavaCC)
37. The Java Parser Generator. Located at \http://www.suntest.com/JavaCC/".
38. D.F. Savarese: OROmatcher - Regular Expressions for Java, http://www.savarese.org/
39. L. Karttunen, J-P. Chanod, G. Grefenstette, A. Schiller: Regular expressions for language engineering, Journal of national language engineering 2(4): 305-328, 1996.
40. G.V. Noord, and D. Gerdemann: An extendible regular expression compiler for finite approaches in natural language processing. In O. Boldt, H Juergensen, and L. Robbonss, editors, Workshop on Implementing Automata; WIA99 Pre-Proceedings, Ptsdam Germany 1999.
41. MPEG-7 Overview, http://www.chiariglione.org/MPEG/standards/mpeg-7/mpeg-7.htm, (visited at 26/02/2006).
42. Chang S.K., Shi Q.Y., Yan C.W., "Iconic Indexing by 2-D Strings", IEEE-Transactions-on-Pattern-Analysis-and-Machine-Intelligence, 1987, Vol. PAMI-9, N° 3, P. 413-428.
43. Chang S.K., Jungert E., "Human- and System-Directed Fusion of Multimedia and Multimodal Information using the Sigma-Tree Data Model", Proceedings of the 2nd International Conference on Visual Information Systems, 1997, San Diego, P. 21-28.
44. Huang P.W. and Jean Y.R., "Using 2D C+-Strings as spatial knowledge representation for image database management systems", Pattern Recognition, 1994, Vol. 27, N° 9, P. 1249-1257.
45. Egenhofer M., "Query Processing in Spatial Query By Sketch", Journal of Visual Language and Computing, Vol 8 (4), 1997, P. 403-424.
46. El-kwae M.A. and Kabuka M.R., "A robust framework for Content-Based Retrieval by Spatial Similarity in Image Databases", ACM Transactions on Information Systems, vol. 17, N° 2, avril 1999, P. 174-198.
47. Peuquet D. J., "The use of spatial relationships to aid spatial database retrieval", Proc. Second Int. Symp. on Spatial Data Handling, Seattle, 1986, P. 459 – 471.

48. Egenhofer M., Frank A., and Jackson J., "A Topological Data Model for Spatial Databases", Symposium on the Design and Implementation of Large Spatial Databases, Santa Barbara, CA, Lecture Notes in Computer Science, Vol. 409, P. 271-286. , July 1989
49. Gross M. "The Use of Finite Automata in the Lexical Representation of Natural Language". In Electronic Dictionaries and Automata in Computational Linguistics. Berlin: Springer-Verlag, 1989, vol 377, p.34-50.
50. Courtois B. "Le dictionnaire electronique des mots simples". In Les dctionnaires electroniques. Langue francaise no 87. Larousse, Paris.1990.
51. Max Silberztein "INTEX: a Finite State Transducer toolbox", in Theoretical Computer Science #231:1, Elsevier Science, 1999.
52. Information Extraction from Biomedical Literature: Methodology, Evaluation and an Application. L. Venkata Subramaniam, Sougata Mukherjea, Pankaj Kankar, Biplav Srivastava, Vishal S. Batra, Pasumarti V. Kamesam, Ravi Kothari IBM India Research Lab, New Delhi, India
53. K. Fukuda, T. Tsunoda, A. Tamura, and T. Takagi, "Toward Information Extraction: Identifying Protein Names from Biological Papers," Proceedings of the Pacific Symposium on Biocomputing, Hawaii, 1998, pp. 707–718.
54. Daniel Q. and Hesham A. Ontology Specific Data Mining Based on Dynamic Grammars, Bioinformatics conference, Stanford, CA. August 16-19, 2004.
55. Embley D.W., Campbell D.M., and Smith R.D., Ontology-Based Extraction and Structuring of Information from Data-Rich Unstructured Documents, *CIKM'98* Proceedings, Bethesda, Maryland, 1998.
56. Bricon-Souf N., Beuscart-Zéphir M.C., Watbled L., Laforest F., Karadimas H., Anceaux F., Flory A., Lepage E., Beuscart R. Technologies de l'Information Pour l'Hospitalisation A Domicile : le projet TIPHAD, Télémédecine et e-Santé, Springer- Verlag, Collection Informatique et Santé N° 13, Paris, 2002.
57. Unitex Home page [online]. Available at: http://www-igm.univ-mlv.fr/~unitex/ (last visited march 12th 2006)
58. W.B. Frakes and R. Baeza-Yates. Information Retrieval: Data Structures & Algorithms. Prentice Hall, Englewood Cliffs, New Jersey, 1992.
59. Appelt D. E., Israel D. J. "Introduction to Information Extraction Technology". Tutorial for IJCAI-99, 1999, Stockholm.
60. Charniak E. "Statistical Language Learning". MIT Press, 1994, 192 p. ISBN 0262032163.
61. Brill E., Church K. "Proceedings of the Conference on Empirical Methods in Natural Language Processing". University of Pennsylvania. Philadelphia, PA, 1996.
62. Marcus M., Santorini B. Marcinkiewicz M. "Building a large annotated corpus of English". Computational Linguistics. 1993, vol 19, n°2, p.313-330.
63. Freitag D., McCallum A. "Information extraction with HMMs and shrinkage". Proceedings of the AAAI-99 Workshopon Machine Learning for Information Extraction. 1999, p.31-36.
64. Miikkulainen R. "Subsymbolic Natural Language Processing: An Integrated Model of Scripts, Lexicon, and Memory". MIT Press. Cambridge, MA, 1993.
65. Brill E. "Transformation-based error-driven learning and natural language processing: A case study in part-of-speech tagging". Computational Linguistics. 1995, vol 21, n°4, p.543-565.
66. Magerman D.M. "Statistical decision-tree models for parsing". Proceedings of the 33rd Annual Meeting of the Association for Computational Lenguistics, 1995, Cambridge, p.276-283.

67. Wermter S., Rilo E., Scheler G. "Connectionist, Statistical, and Symbolic Approaches to Learning for Natural Language Processing". Berlin: Springer Verlag, 1996, p. 315-328
68. Lavrac, N., & Dzeroski, S. Inductive Logic Programming: Techniques and Applications. Ellis Horwood, 1994.
69. Huffman S. "Learning information extraction patterns from examples". In Learning for Natural Language Processing. Canada: IJCAI-95 Workshop on, 1995, p. 246-260.

Reasoning About ORA-SS Data Models Using the Semantic Web

Yuan Fang Li[1], Jing Sun[2], Gillian Dobbie[2], Hai H. Wang[3], and Jun Sun[1]

[1] School of Computing, National University of Singapore, Republic of Singapore
{liyf, sunj}@comp.nus.edu.sg
[2] Department of Computer Science, The University of Auckland, New Zealand
{j.sun, gill}@cs.auckland.ac.nz
[3] Department of Computer Science, The University of Manchester, United Kingdom
hwang@cs.manchester.ac.uk

Abstract. There has been a rapid growth in the use of semistructured data in both web applications and database systems. Consequently, the design of a good semistructured data model is essential. In the relational database community, algorithms have been defined to transform a relational schema from one normal form to a more suitable normal form. These algorithms have been shown to preserve certain semantics during the transformation. The work presented in this paper is the first step towards representing such algorithms for semistructured data, namely formally defining the semantics necessary for achieving this goal. Formal semantics and automated reasoning tools enable us to reveal the inconsistencies in a semistructured data model and its instances. The Object Relationship Attribute model for Semistructured data (ORA-SS) is a graphical notation for designing and representing semistructured data. This paper presents a methodology of encoding the semantics of the ORA-SS notation into the Web Ontology Language (OWL) and automatically verifying the semistructured data design using the OWL reasoning tools. Our methodology provides automated consistency checking of an ORA-SS data model at both the schema and instance levels.

Keywords: Semistructured Data, Semantic Web, Ontology Web Language, ORA-SS, Formal Verification.

1 Introduction

Semistructured data has become prevalent in both web applications and database systems. With the growth in its usage, questions have arisen about the effective storage and management of semistructured data. In the relational database community, algorithms have been defined to transform a relational schema from one norm form to a more suitable normal form. These algorithms have been shown to preserve certain semantics during the transformation. In order to verify the correctness of the similar transformations for semistructured data, we need to have a standard representation of schemas and the transformation operators that are used to transform schemas. This process can be achieved by describing a formal model for semistructured data schemas and verifying that instances of schemas conform to the schema model. Then the basic transformation operators can be formally defined on this schema model. In this paper we undertake the first step of the process defined above.

S. Spaccapietra (Ed.): Journal on Data Semantics VII, LNCS 4244, pp. 219–241, 2006.

Many data modeling languages [1–4] for semistructured data have been introduced to capture more detailed semantic information. The Object Relationship Attribute model for Semistructured data (ORA-SS) [5, 6] is a semantically enriched graphical notation for designing and representing semistructured data [6–9]. The ORA-SS data model not only reflects the nested structure of semistructured data, but also distinguishes between object classes, relationship types and attributes. The main advantages of ORA-SS over other data models are its ability to express the semantics that are necessary for designing effective storage and management algorithms, such as the degree of an n-ary relationship type, and distinguish between the attributes of relationship types and the attributes of object classes. This semantic information is essential, even crucial for semistructured data representation and management, but it is lacking in other existing semistructured data modeling notations.

Semistructured data also acts as a hinge technology between the data exchanged on the web and the data represented in a database system. Recent research on the World Wide Web has extended to the semantics of web content. More meaningful information is embedded into the web content, which makes it possible for intelligent agent programs to retrieve relevant semantic as well as structural information based on their requirements. The Semantic Web [10] approach proposed by the World Wide Web Consortium (W3C) attracts the most attention. It is regarded as the next generation of the web. The Web Ontology Language (OWL) [11] is an ontology language for the Semantic Web. It consists of three increasingly expressive sub-languages: OWL Lite, DL and Full. OWL can provide not only the structural information of the web content but also meaningful semantics for the information presented. The aim of this paper is to encode the semantics of the ORA-SS notation into the Web Ontology Language (OWL) and automatically verify the semistructured data design using the OWL reasoning tool RACER [12].

The reason that we chose the OWL ontology language is because of the strong relationship between semistructured data and web technologies. Semistructured data is typically represented using eXtensible Markup Language (XML). XML is a commonly used exchange format in many web and database applications. The introduction of the Semantic Web is to overcome the structure-only information of XML, and to provide deeper semantic meaning to the data on the web. The ORA-SS language is a semantically enriched data modeling notation for describing semistructured data. From the point of capturing more semantic information in content representation, OWL and ORA-SS are two approaches that fulfil the same goal, where the former is rooted in the web community and the latter has its basis in the database community. Thus it is natural to explore the synergy of the two approaches. We believe that semantic web and its reasoning tools can contribute greatly to the design and verification phases of ORA-SS data models.

In this paper, we propose a methodology to verify ORA-SS data design using OWL and its reasoner RACER. Fig. 1 shows the overall process of our approach. Firstly, we define an ontology model of the ORA-SS data modeling language in OWL. It provides a rigorous semantic basis for the ORA-SS graphical notation and enables us to represent customized ORA-SS data models and their instances in OWL. Secondly, ORA-SS schema and instance models are translated into their corresponding OWL ontologies. Finally, RACER is used to perform the automated verification of the ORA-SS ontologies.

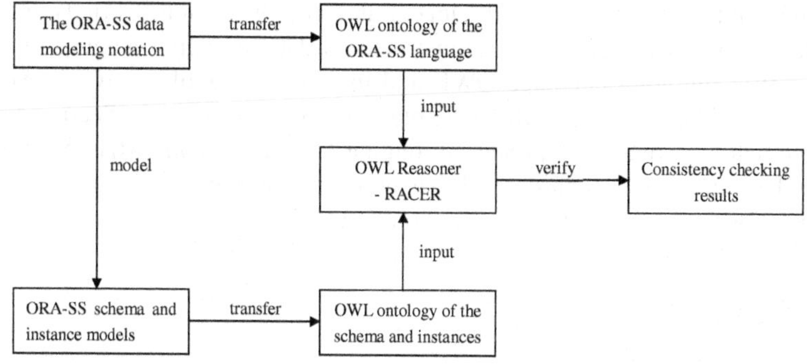

Fig. 1. The overall approach to verify ORA-SS data models using OWL

Our approach is able to provide automatic consistency checking on large ORA-SS data models and their instances. Examples are given through out the paper to illustrate the reasoning process.

A major concern in designing a good semistructured data model using ORA-SS for a particular application is to reveal any possible inconsistencies at both the schema and instance levels. Inconsistencies at the schema level arise if a customized ORA-SS schema model does not conform to the ORA-SS semantics. Inconsistencies at the instance level arise if an ORA-SS instance model is not consistent with its ORA-SS schema definition. For example, an inconsistency that might arise at the schema level is the specification of a ternary relationship between only two object classes. An inconsistency that might arise at the instance level is a many to many relationship between objects when a one to many relationship is specified in the schema. These two aspects of validation are essential in the semistructured data design process. Thus, the provision of formal semantics and automated reasoning support for verifying ORA-SS semistructured data modeling is very beneficial.

There has been other research that provides a formal semantics for semistructured data. For example, the formalization of DTD (Document Type Definition) and XML declarative description documents using expressive description logic has been presented by Calvanese et al. [13]. Anutariya et al. presented the same formalization using a theoretical framework developed using declarative description theory [14]. Also spatial tree logics has been used to formalize semistructured data by Conforti and Ghelli [15]. More recently, hybrid multimodal logic was used to formalize semistructured data by Bidoit et al. [16]. We also applied a similar approach to formalize ORA-SS data models using Z/EVES [17]. While this work has helped us develop a better understanding of the semantics of semistructured data, it does not provide automated verification. In another research we presented a formalization of the ORA-SS notation in the Alloy [18] language. Although the automated verification was available using the Alloy Analyzer, it had a scalability problem, making the verification of large sets of semistructured data impossible. In addition, there were also research for providing better validation support of semistructured data, such as algorithms on incremental validation of XML documents [19, 20]. However, these approaches still focused on the syntax-only checking of semistructured data instances.

The remainder of the paper is organized as follows. Section 2 briefly introduces the background knowledge for the semistructured data modeling language ORA-SS, Semantic Web ontology language OWL and its reasoning tool - RACER. Section 3 presents OWL semantics of the ORA-SS notation and its data models. Section 4 demonstrates the ontology reasoning process through a *Course-Student* ORA-SS data model example. Examples of both class-level reasoning and instance-level reasoning are presented. Section 5 concludes the paper and outlines the future work.

2 Background

2.1 The ORA-SS Data Modeling Language

The Object-Relationship-Attribute model for Semistructured data (ORA-SS) is a semantically enriched data modeling language for semistrctured data design [5, 6]. It has been used in many XML related database applications [8, 9]. The ORA-SS notation consists of four basic concepts: object class, relationship type, attribute and reference. A full description of the ORA-SS data modeling language can be found in [5, 6].

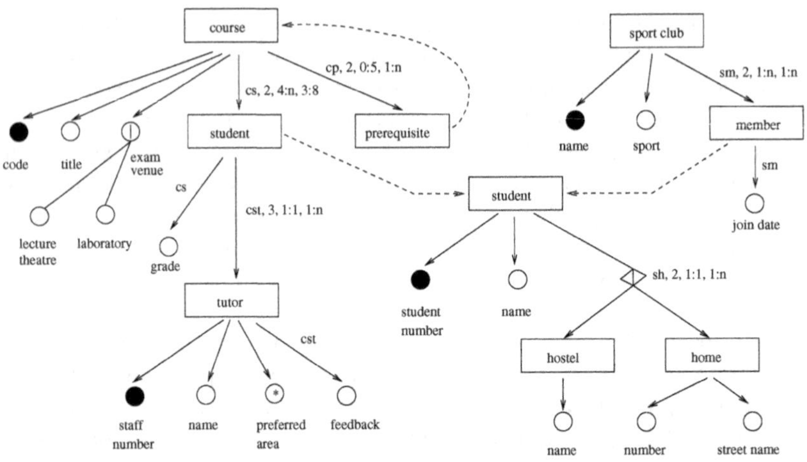

Fig. 2. The ORA-SS schema diagram of a *Course-Student* data model

- An object class is like an entity type in an ER diagram, a class in an object-oriented diagram or an element in an XML document. The object classes are represented as labeled rectangles in an ORA-SS diagram.
- A relationship type represents a nesting relationship among object classes. It is described as a labeled edge by a tuple (`name`, `n`, `p`, `c`), where the `name` denotes the name of relationship type, integer `n` indicates degree of relationship type, `p` represents participation constraint of parent object class in relationship type and `c` represents participation constraint of child object class in relationship type.

- Attributes represent properties and are denoted by labeled circle. An attribute can be a key attribute which has a unique value and is represented as a filled circle. Other types of attributes include single valued attribute, multi-valued attribute, required attribute, composite attribute, etc. An attribute can be a property of an object class or a property of a relationship type.
- An object class can reference another object class to model recursive and symmetric relationships, or to reduce redundancy especially for many-to-many relationships. It is represented by a labeled dashed edge.

For the design of semistructured data, an ORA-SS schema diagram represents the constraints on relationships, participations and cardinalities among the instances of the object classes in a semistructured data model. For example, Fig. 2 represents an ORA-SS schema diagram of a `Course-Student` data model. In the diagram, each `course` has `code`, `title`, and `exam venue` as its attributes. A relationship type `cs`, which indicates the relationship between a `course` object class and a `student` object class is binary, and each course consists of 4 to many students and each student can select 3 to 8 courses. The `student` object class in the `cs` relationship type has a reference pointing to its complete definition. The `grade` attribute is an attribute belonging to the `cs` relationship type. Based on the above schema definition, two levels of validation can be carried out. Firstly, consistency checking can be performed to determine whether the defined schema model is correct with respect to the ORA-SS language. Secondly, consistency checking can be performed to determine whether a particular instance of semistructured data satisfies the defined ORA-SS schema model. This checking could be done manually only if it is a relatively small sized model. However, examining complicated and large ORA-SS data models for semistructured data is almost manually impossible. Furthermore, manual diagrammatic checking does not guarantee the consistency of the schema since it is likely that inconsistencies are not revealed when the schema is large and complicated. Therefore, automated verification support based on the formal specification of ORA-SS semantics is highly desirable.

2.2 Semantic Web – OWL and RACER

Description logics [21] are logical formalisms for representing information about knowledge in a particular domain. It is a subset of first-order predicate logic and is well-known for the trade-off between expressivity and decidability. Based on RDF Schema [22] and DAML+OIL [23], the Web Ontology Language (OWL) [11] is the de facto ontology language for the Semantic Web. It consists of three increasingly expressive sub-languages: OWL Lite, DL and Full. OWL DL is very expressive yet decidable. As a result, core inference problems, namely concept subsumption, consistency and instantiation, can be performed automatically.

In OWL, conceptual entities are organized as classes in hierarchies. Individual entities are grouped under classes and are called instances of the classes. Classes and individuals can be related by properties. Table 1 summarizes the ‘DL syntax’ used in the following sections. Interested readers may refer to [11] for full details.

RACER, the **R**enamed **A**Box and **C**oncept **E**xpression **R**easoner [12], is a reasoning engine for ontology languages DAML+OIL and OWL. It implements a TBox and ABox

Table 1. Summary of OWL syntax used in the paper

Notation	Explanation
$\top / \bot$	Super class/sub class of every class
$N_1 \sqsubseteq N_2$	N_1 is a sub class/property of N_2
$C_1 = C_2$	Class equivalence
$C_1 \sqcap / \sqcup C_2$	Class intersection/union
$\geq 1\, P \sqsubseteq C$	Domain of property P is class C
$\top \sqsubseteq \forall P.C$	Range of P is C
$\top \sqsubseteq \leq 1\, P$	Property P is functional
$P_2 = (^- P_1)$	Property P_2 is inverse of P_1
$\forall / \exists P.C$	allValuesFrom/someValuesFrom restriction, giving the class that for every instance of this class that has instances of property P, the values of the property are all/some members of the class C
$= / \leq / \geq n\, P$	Cardinality restriction, the class each of whose instances mapped by property P forms a set whose cardinality must be exactly/less than/greater than n

reasoner for the description logic $\mathcal{ALCQHI}_{\mathcal{R}^+}(\mathcal{D})^-$ [12]. It is automated for reasoning over OWL Lite and DL ontologies.

3 Modeling the ORA-SS Data Model in OWL

In this section, we present the modeling of ORA-SS schema and instance diagram as OWL ontologies in three steps. Firstly, we define the ORA-SS ontology, which contains the OWL definitions of essential ORA-SS concepts, such as object class, relationship type, etc. Secondly, we show how individual ORA-SS schema diagram ontologies can be constructed based on the ORA-SS ontology together with a case tool for achieving this. Finally, in Section 3.6, we show how ORA-SS instance diagrams can be represented in OWL. To effectively illustrate the modeling approach, the schema diagram in Fig. 2 is used as a running example.

3.1 The ORA-SS Ontology

The ORA-SS ontology [1] contains the OWL definitions for ORA-SS concepts such as object class, relationship type, attribute, etc. We model these definitions as OWL classes. The basic assumption here is that all named OWL classes are by default mutually disjoint, which is implied in the ORA-SS diagrams. Essential properties are also defined in the ontology. This ontology, with a namespace of `ora-ss`, can be used later to define ontologies for ORA-SS schema diagrams.

Entities – As each object class and relationship type can be associated with attributes and other object classes or relationship types, we define an OWL class *ENTITY* to

[1] Due to the space limit, only part of the ORA-SS OWL semantics are presented in the paper. A complete ORA-SS ontology can be found at `http://www.comp.nus.edu.sg/~liyf/ora-ss/ora-ss.owl`.

represent the super class of both object class and relationship type. The OWL class structure is shown as follows.

$$ENTITY \sqsubseteq \top \qquad ATTRIBUTE \sqsubseteq \top$$
$$OBJECT \sqsubseteq ENTITY \qquad ENTITY \sqcap ATTRIBUTE = \bot$$
$$RELATIONSHIP \sqsubseteq ENTITY \qquad OBJECT \sqcap RELATIONSHIP = \bot$$

It may not seem very intuitive to define relationship types as OWL classes. In ORA-SS, relationship types are used to relate various object classes and relationship types, it might seem more natural to model relationship types as OWL properties. However, there are two reasons that we decide to model relationship types as OWL classes. Firstly, the domain of ORA-SS relationship types can be relationship types themselves, when describing the relationships of ternary and more. Secondly, classes and properties in OWL DL are disjoint. In our model, an OWL relationship type consists of instances which are actually pointers to the pairs of object classes or relationship types that this relationship relates.

As ORA-SS is a modeling notation for semistructured data, we need to cater for unstructured data. We define a subclass of *ATTRIBUTE* called *ANY* as a place holder to denote any unstructured data appearing in a model. In ORA-SS, a composite attribute is an attribute composed of other attributes. We also define it as a subclass of *ATTRIBUTE*.

$$ANY \sqsubseteq ATTRIBUTE \qquad CompositeAttribute \sqsubseteq ATTRIBUTE$$
$$ANY \sqcap CompositeAttribute = \bot$$

Properties – A number of essential properties are defined in the `ora-ss` ontology.

1. **Properties among entities**
   In ORA-SS, object classes and relationship types are inter-related to form new relationship types. As mentioned above, since we model relationship types as OWL classes, we need additional properties to connect various object classes and relationship types.
   Firstly, this is accomplished by introducing two object-properties, *parent* and *child*, which map a *RELATIONSHIP* to its domain and range *ENTITY*s. The following statements define the domain and range of *parent* and *child*. As in ORA-SS, the domain of a relationship (*parent*) can be either an object class or another relationship type, i.e., an *ENTITY*. The range (*child*) must be an *OBJECT*. These two properties are functional as one relationship type has exactly one domain and one range node. Moreover, we assert that only relationship types can have parents and child but object classes cannot.

$$\geq 1\, parent \sqsubseteq RELATIONSHIP \qquad \geq 1\, child \sqsubseteq RELATIONSHIP$$
$$\top \sqsubseteq \forall parent.ENTITY \qquad \top \sqsubseteq \forall child.OBJECT$$
$$\top \sqsubseteq \leq 1\, parent \qquad \top \sqsubseteq \leq 1\, child$$

$$OBJECT \sqsubseteq \neg\, \exists parent.\top \qquad RELATIONSHIP \sqsubseteq \forall parent.ENTITY$$
$$OBJECT \sqsubseteq \neg\, \exists child.\top \qquad RELATIONSHIP \sqsubseteq \forall child.OBJECT$$

   Secondly, we define two more object-properties: *p-ENTITY-OBJECT* and *p-OBJECT-ENTITY*. These two properties are the inverse of each other and they serve

as the super properties of the properties that are to be defined in later ontologies of ORA-SS schema diagrams. Those properties will model the restrictions imposed on the relationship types.
The domain and range of *p-ENTITY-OBJECT* are *ENTITY* and *OBJECT*, respectively. Since the two properties are inverses, the domain and range of *p-OBJECT-ENTITY* can be deduced.

$p\text{-}OBJECT\text{-}ENTITY = (^{-}p\text{-}ENTITY\text{-}OBJECT)$
$\geq 1\ p\text{-}ENTITY\text{-}OBJECT \sqsubseteq ENTITY$ $\quad$ $\geq 1\ p\text{-}OBJECT\text{-}ENTITY \sqsubseteq OBJECT$
$\top \sqsubseteq \forall p\text{-}ENTITY\text{-}OBJECT.OBJECT$ $\quad$ $\top \sqsubseteq \forall p\text{-}OBJECT\text{-}ENTITY.ENTITY$

$ENTITY \sqsubseteq \forall p\text{-}ENTITY\text{-}OBJECT.OBJECT$ $\quad$ $OBJECT \sqsubseteq \forall p\text{-}OBJECT\text{-}ENTITY.ENTITY$

2. **Properties between entities and attributes**
First of all, we define an object-property *has-ATTRIBUTE*, whose domain is *ENTITY* and range is *ATTRIBUTE*. Every *ENTITY* must have *ATTRIBUTE* as the range of *has-ATTRIBUTE*.

$\geq 1\ has\text{-}ATTRIBUTE \sqsubseteq ENTITY$ $\quad$ $ENTITY \sqsubseteq \forall\ has\text{-}ATTRIBUTE.ATTRIBUTE$
$\top \sqsubseteq \forall .has\text{-}ATTRIBUTE.ATTRIBUTE$

For modeling the ORA-SS candidate and primary keys, we define two new object properties that are sub-properties of *has-ATTRIBUTE*. We also make the property *has-primary-key* inverse functional and state that each *ENTITY* must have at most one primary key. Moreover, we restrict the range of *has-candidate-key* to be *ATTRIBUTE*.

$has\text{-}candidate\text{-}key \sqsubseteq has\text{-}ATTRIBUTE$ $\quad$ $has\text{-}primary\text{-}key \sqsubseteq has\text{-}candidate\text{-}key$
$\top \sqsubseteq \forall\ has\text{-}candidate\text{-}key.ATTRIBUTE$ $\quad$ $\top \sqsubseteq\leq 1\ has\text{-}primary\text{-}key^{-}$

$ENTITY \sqsubseteq\leq 1\ has\text{-}primary\text{-}key$

3.2 Object Classes

In this subsection, we present how ORA-SS object classes in a schema diagram are represented in OWL. Moreover, we will discuss how object class referencing is modeled.

Example 1. The schema diagram in Fig. 2 contains a number of object classes [2].

$course \sqsubseteq OBJECT$ $\quad$ $tutor \sqsubseteq OBJECT$
$student \sqsubseteq OBJECT$ $\quad$ $sport\_club \sqsubseteq OBJECT$
$hostel \sqsubseteq OBJECT$ $\quad$ $home \sqsubseteq OBJECT$
... $\quad$ ...

Referencing – In ORA-SS, an object class can reference another object class to refer to its definition. We say that a *reference* object class references a *referenced* object class. In our model, we model the *reference* object class as a sub-class of the *referenced* object class. If the two object classes have the same name, the reference object class is renamed. By doing so, we ensure that all the attributes and relationship types of the referenced object classes are reachable (meaningful). Note that there are no disjointness axioms among the reference and referenced object classes.

[2] For brevity reasons, the class disjointness statements are not shown from here onwards.

Example 2. In Fig. 2, the object class student is referenced by object classes student and member. Hence, we rename the reference student to *student_1* and add the following axioms in to the model.

$student \sqsubseteq OBJECT \qquad student\_1 \sqsubseteq student \qquad member \sqsubseteq student$

3.3 Relationship Types

In this subsection, we present the details of how ORA-SS relationship types are modeled in OWL. Various kinds of relationship types, such as disjunctive relationship types and recursive relationship types are also modeled. We begin with an example to show the basic modeling of relationship types.

Example 3. Fig. 2 contains 5 relationship types.

$$cs \sqsubseteq RELATIONSHIP \qquad sm \sqsubseteq RELATIONSHIP \qquad cst \sqsubseteq RELATIONSHIP$$
$$sh \sqsubseteq RELATIONSHIP \qquad cp \sqsubseteq RELATIONSHIP$$

The relationship type *cs* is bound by the *parent/child* properties as follows. We use both *allValuesFrom* and *someValuesFrom* restriction to make sure that only the intended class can be the parent/child class of *cs*.

$$cs \sqsubseteq \forall parent.course \qquad cs \sqsubseteq \forall child.student\_1$$
$$cs \sqsubseteq \exists parent.course \qquad cs \sqsubseteq \exists child.student\_1$$

Auxiliary Properties – As discussed in Section 3.1, for each ORA-SS relationship type we define two object-properties that are the inverse of each other.

Example 4. Take *cs* as an example, we construct two object-properties: *p-course-student* and *p-student-course*. Their domain and range are also defined.

$$p\text{-}student\text{-}course = (^{-}p\text{-}course\text{-}student)$$
$$p\text{-}student\text{-}course \sqsubseteq p\text{-}ENTITY\text{-}OBJECT$$
$$p\text{-}student\text{-}course \sqsubseteq p\text{-}OBJECT\text{-}ENTITY$$

$$\geq 1\, p\text{-}course\text{-}student \sqsubseteq course \qquad \geq 1\, p\text{-}student\text{-}course \sqsubseteq student\_1$$
$$\top \sqsubseteq \forall p\text{-}course\text{-}student.student\_1 \qquad \top \sqsubseteq \forall p\text{-}student\text{-}course.course$$

Participation Constraints – One of the important advantages that ORA-SS has over XML Schema language is the ability to express participation constraints for parent/child nodes of a relationship type. This ability expresses the cardinality restrictions that must be satisfied by ORA-SS instances.

Using the terminology defined previously, ORA-SS parent participation constraints are expressed using cardinality restrictions in OWL on a sub-property of *p-ENTITY-OBJECT* to restrict the parent class *Prt*. Child participation constraints can be similarly modeled, using a sub property of *p-OBJECT-ENTITY*.

Example 5. In Fig. 2, the constraints captured by the relationship type `cs` state that a `course` must have at least 4 students; and a `student` must take at least 3 and at most

8 courses. The following axioms are added to the ontology. The two object-properties defined above capture the relationship type between `course` and `student`.

$course \sqsubseteq$
$\quad \forall\, p\text{-}course\text{-}student.student\_1$
$course \sqsubseteq \geq 4\; p\text{-}course\text{-}student$

$student\_1 \sqsubseteq \forall\, p\text{-}student\text{-}course.course$
$student\_1 \sqsubseteq \geq 3\; p\text{-}student\text{-}course$
$student\_1 \sqsubseteq \leq 8\; p\text{-}student\text{-}course$

Disjunctive Relationship Types – In ORA-SS, a disjunctive relationship type is used to represent relationship consists of disjunctive object classes, where only one object can be selected to the relationship instance from the set of disjunctive object classes. To model this in OWL, we will create a dummy class as the *union* of the disjoint classes and use it as the range of the object-property representing the relationship type. Together with the cardinality constraint that exactly one individual of the range can be selected, the disjunctive relationship type can be precisely modeled.

Example 6. In Fig. 2, *sh* is a disjunctive relationship type where a student must live in exactly one hostel or one home, but not both. We use the following OWL statements to model this situation. Note that *p-student-sh* is an object-property that maps *student* to its range class *home_hostel*, which is the union of *hostel* and *home*.

$hostel \sqsubseteq OBJECT$ $\quad home \sqsubseteq OBJECT$ $\quad hostel \sqcap home = \bot$
$home\_hostel \sqsubseteq OBJECT$ $\quad home\_hostel = hostel \sqcup home$
$\geq 1\; p\text{-}student\text{-}sh \sqsubseteq student$ $\quad \top \sqsubseteq \forall\, p\text{-}student\text{-}sh.hostel\_home$

Given the above definitions, the disjunctive relationship type *sh* in the schema diagram can be modeled as follows.

$student \sqsubseteq \forall\, p\text{-}student\text{-}sh.hostel\_home$ $\quad student \sqsubseteq = 1\; p\text{-}student\text{-}sh$

Recursive Relationship Types – Recursive relationship types in ORA-SS are modeled using referencing. In our model, by defining the reference object class as a sub class of the referenced object class, recursive relationship types can be modeled as a regular relationship type.

Example 7. Fig. 2 depicts such a recursive relationship type where a *course* object class has at most 5 *prerequisite* objects, whereas a *prerequisite* must have at least one *course*. This can be modeled as follows.

$course \sqsubseteq \top$ $\quad prerequisite \sqsubseteq course$
$\geq 1\; p\text{-}course\text{-}prerequisite \sqsubseteq course$ $\quad \top \sqsubseteq \forall\, p\text{-}course\text{-}prerequisite.prerequisite$
$p\text{-}prerequisite\text{-}course = (^{-}p\text{-}course\text{-}prerequisite)$

$course \sqsubseteq$
$\quad \forall\, p\text{-}course\text{-}prerequisite.prerequisite$
$course \sqsubseteq \leq 5\; p\text{-}course\text{-}prerequisite$

$prerequisite \sqsubseteq$
$\quad \forall\, p\text{-}prerequisite\text{-}course.course$
$prerequisite \sqsubseteq \geq 1\; p\text{-}prerequisite\text{-}course$

3.4 Attributes

The semantically rich ORA-SS model notation defines many kinds of attributes for object classes and relationship types. These include candidate and primary keys, single-valued and multi-valued attributes, required and optional attributes, etc. In this subsection, we will discuss how these attributes can be modeled.

Example 8. The schema diagram in Fig. 2 generates the following OWL classes for attributes.

$code \sqsubseteq ATTRIBUTE$ $\quad$ $grade \sqsubseteq ATTRIBUTE$
$title \sqsubseteq ATTRIBUTE$ $\quad$ $student\_number \sqsubseteq ATTRIBUTE$
$exam\_venue \sqsubseteq ATTRIBUTE$ $\quad$ $sport \sqsubseteq ATTRIBUTE$
...

Modeling Various Definitions – As OWL adopts the Open World Assumption [11] and an ORA-SS model is closed, we need to find ways to make the OWL model capture the intended meaning of the original diagram. The following are some modeling *conventions*.

- For each *ENTITY*, we use an *allValuesFrom* restriction on *has-ATTRIBUTE* over the union of all its *ATTRIBUTE* classes. This denotes the complete set of attributes that the *ENTITY* holds.

  Example 9. In the running example, the object class *student* has student number and name as its attributes.

  $$student \sqsubseteq \forall has\text{-}ATTRIBUTE.(student\_number \sqcup name)$$

- Each entity (object class or relationship type) can have a number of attributes. For each of the entity-attribute pairs in an ORA-SS schema diagram, we define an object-property, whose domain is the entity and range is the attribute. For an entity *Ent* and its attribute *Att*, we have the following definitions.

  $has\text{-}Ent\text{-}Att \sqsubseteq has\text{-}ATTRIBUTE$ $\quad$ $\top \sqsubseteq \forall has\text{-}Ent\text{-}Att.Att$
  $\geq 1\ has\text{-}Ent\text{-}Att \sqsubseteq Ent$

  Example 10. In Fig. 2, the object class *sport club* has an attribute name. It can be modeled as follows.

  $\geq 1\ has\text{-}sport\_club\text{-}name \sqsubseteq sport\_club$ $\quad$ $has\text{-}sport\_club\text{-}name \sqsubseteq has\text{-}ATTRIBUTE$
  $\top \sqsubseteq \forall has\text{-}sport\_club\text{-}name.name$ $\quad$ $sport\_club \sqsubseteq \forall has\text{-}sport\_club\text{-}name.name$

Required and Optional Attributes – We use cardinality restrictions of respective object-properties on the owning *ENTITY* to model the attribute cardinality constraints in the ORA-SS model. The default is (0:1). We use a cardinality ≥ 1 restriction to state a required attribute.

Example 11. Take sport club as an example again, it can have 0 or 1 sport.

$$sport\_club \sqsubseteq \leq 1\ has\text{-}sport\_club\text{-}sport$$

Single-Valued vs. Multi-valued Attributes – Single-valued attributes can be modeled by specifying the respective object-property as functional. Multi-valued attributes, on the contrary, are not functional. An attribute is by default single valued.

Example 12. In Fig. 2, object tutor has a single-valued attribute name. This can be modeled as follow.

$\geq 1\ has\text{-}tutor\text{-}name \sqsubseteq tutor$ $\quad$ $has\text{-}tutor\text{-}name.name \sqsubseteq has\text{-}ATTRIBUTE$
$\top \sqsubseteq \forall has\text{-}tutor\text{-}name.name$ $\quad$ $\top \sqsubseteq \leq 1\ has\text{-}tutor\text{-}name$

Primary Key Attributes – For an entity with a primary key attribute, we use an *allValuesFrom* restriction on the property *has-primary-key* to constrain it. Since we have specified that *has-primary-key* is inverse functional, this suffices to show that two different objects will have different primary keys. Moreover, for every attribute that is the primary key attribute, we assert that the corresponding object property is a sub property of *has-primary-key*.

Example 13. In Fig. 2, object class *course* has an attribute *code* as its primary key and this is modeled as follows. The `hasValuesFrom` restriction enforces that each individual must have some *code* value as its primary key.

$$course \sqsubseteq \forall\, has\text{-}primary\text{-}key.code \qquad course \sqsubseteq \exists\, has\text{-}primary\text{-}key.code$$

Disjunctive Attributes – Similar to the treatment of disjunctive relationship types, we create a class as the *union* of a set of disjunctive attribute classes. Together with the cardinality ≤ 1 restriction, disjunctive attributes can be represented in OWL.

Example 14. In Fig. 2, *course* has a disjunctive attribute exam venue, which is either lecture theater or laboratory. It can be modeled as follows.

$$lecture\_theatre \sqsubseteq ATTRIBUTE \qquad lecture\_theatre \sqcap laboratory = \bot$$
$$laboratory \sqsubseteq ATTRIBUTE \qquad exam\_venue = lecture\_theatre \sqcup laboratory$$
$$exam\_venue \sqsubseteq ATTRIBUTE$$

$$course \sqsubseteq \forall\, \text{has-course-exam\_venue}.exam\_venue$$
$$course \sqsubseteq \leq 1\ \text{has-course-exam\_venue}$$

Fixed-Value Attributes – A fixed-value attribute is one whose value is the same for every instance and cannot be changed. To model this, we define the attribute to be an OWL class that has only one instance. Suppose that the object *obj* has a fixed-value attribute *attr*, whose value is *attr_val*. The OWL ontology will then contain the following statements.

$$obj \sqsubseteq OBJECT \qquad has\text{-}obj\text{-}attr \sqsubseteq has\text{-}ATTRIBUTE$$
$$attr \sqsubseteq ATTRIBUTE \qquad \geq 1\ has\text{-}obj\text{-}attr \sqsubseteq obj$$
$$attr\_val \in attr \qquad \top \sqsubseteq \forall\, has\text{-}obj\text{-}attr.attr$$
$$attr = \{attr\_val\}$$

3.5 Presenting and Transforming ORA-SS Diagrams in OWL

In the previous subsections, we presented some of the formal definitions of the ORA-SS language constructs in OWL. Part of the ontology (in OWL XML syntax) of the ORA-SS schema diagram in Fig. 2 is shown below.

```
<owl:Class rdf:about="#student">
  <rdfs:subClassOf>
    <owl:Restriction>
      <owl:onProperty rdf:resource="http://www.comp.nus.edu.sg/
                          ~liyf/ora-ss/ora-ss.owl#has-primary-key"/>
```

```
      <owl:someValuesFrom rdf:resource="#student_number"/>
    </owl:Restriction>
  </rdfs:subClassOf>
  <rdfs:subClassOf>
    <owl:Restriction>
      <owl:maxCardinality rdf:datatype=
                        "http://www.w3.org/2001/XMLSchema#int">1
      </owl:maxCardinality>
      <owl:onProperty>
        <owl:FunctionalProperty rdf:ID=
                        "has-student-student_number"/>
      </owl:onProperty>
    </owl:Restriction>
  </rdfs:subClassOf>
```

Note that because OWL has XML syntax as its presentation form, further automated transformation tools can be easily developed to assist the translation from ORA-SS data models into their corresponding OWL representations. We are in the process of developing a visual case tool which provides a high-level and intuitive environment for constructing ORA-SS data models in OWL. Our ORA-SS modeling tool was built based on the meta-tool Pounamu [24]. Pounamu is a meta-case tool for developing multi-view visual environments. Fig. 3 shows the *Course-Student* schema example in section 2.1 defined by the tool. From the diagram, we can see that the customized schema model

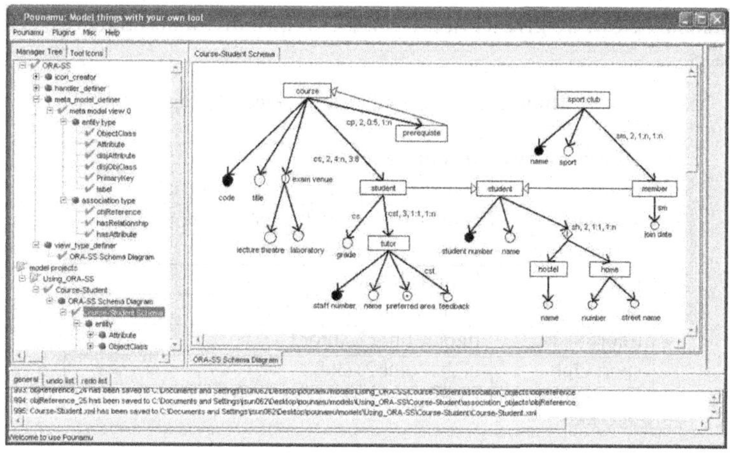

Fig. 3. A case tool for ORA-SS data modeling

can be defined easily by creating instances of the pre-defined model entities and associations. By triggering the defined event handler menu item in the tool, it transforms all the default XML format of each entity in the diagram into a single OWL representation of the ORA-SS schmea model and saves it for later reasoning purpose. One ongoing development is to develop our tool as a plugin within the overall Protégé plug-and-play framework.

In the next section, we show how to model ORA-SS instance diagrams using OWL individuals based on the classes, properties defined in the OWL schema ontology.

3.6 Instance Diagrams in OWL

The representation of ORA-SS instance diagrams [3] in OWL is a straightforward task. As the name suggests, instance diagrams are semistructured data instances of a particular ORA-SS schema diagram. The translation of an instance diagram to an OWL ontology is described by the following 3 steps:

1. Defining individuals and stating the membership of these individuals, by declaring them as instances of the respective OWL classes of object classes, relationship types and attributes defined in the schema diagram ontology.
2. For each OWL class, we state that all its instances are different from each other.
3. By making use of the object-properties defined in the schema diagram ontology, we state the relationships among the individuals.

This is best illustrated with an example. We create an instance ontology for the schema ontology defined in Fig. 2. In this paper, we use a table form to illustrate the ORA-SS OWL instances. This is just for the sake of easy representation. Actual ORA-SS instances are defined in the ORA-SS instance diagrams and transformed into their corresponding OWL representations in XML.

– In Table 2 below, we give a brief overview of the individuals under respective object classes [4].

Table 2. Instances of various objects of Fig. 2

Object classes	Instances
course	course1, course2, course3, course4
student	student1, student 2, ..., student8
prerequisite	course1, course2, course3, course4
home	home1, home2
hostel	hostel1, hostel2, hostel3
tutor	tutor1, tutor2, tutor3
sport club	club1, club2, club3
member	student1, ..., student6

– Next, we define the instances of various attributes of Fig. 2 in Table 3 listed in the appendix.
– Having defined all the instances of objects and attributes, the next step is to relate them. We proceed by populating various memberships. In Table 4 listed in the appendix, we show the pairs of instances related by each relationship type in Fig. 2. It is worthwhile pointing out that ternary or higher-degree relationships are viewed

[3] In this paper, we present the schema instances in a table format rather than in a proper ORA-SS instance diagram. This is just for the sack of presentation purpose only.

[4] Due to the space limit, not all the OWL individuals of the schema diagram in Fig. 2 are shown.

as pairs of pairs. Also note that for brevity reasons, we will refer to the members of relationships such as *cs*, *cst* and *sm* as *cs1,.., cs24*, *cst1,.. cst24* and *sm1, .. sm6* respectively.

- The last task in modeling this instance diagram in OWL is to associate object classes and relationship types to the attributes. We show the instances of object classes and relationship types of Fig. 2 in Table 5 listed in the appendix. Note that attributes whose names are in italic and bold fonts are primary key attributes.

By following the above steps, we can easily represent an ORA-SS instance diagram in OWL [5]. Similarly, an OWL instance diagram generation functionality is under development in the ORA-SS case tool presented earlier. In addition, direct transformation from an XML document into its ORA-SS OWL instance can also be implemented. With the constraints defined in the OWL schema ontology, we are able to perform automated reasoning over these instances (OWL individuals), as detailed in the next section.

4 Reasoning About ORA-SS Data Models

In this section, we demonstrate the validation of ORA-SS schema and instance diagrams using OWL and RACER. We will again use Fig. 2 as the running example.

4.1 Verification of Schema Diagram Ontologies

In order to ensure the correctness of an ORA-SS schema diagram, a number of properties have to be checked, such as:

- The parent of a relationship type should be either a relationship type or an object class, where the child should only be an object class.
- The parent of a higher-degree relationship type (higher than 2) must be a relationship type.
- The child participants of a disjunctive relationship type or attribute must be a set of disjunctive object classes or attributes.
- A composite attribute or disjunctive attribute has an attribute that is related to two or more sub-attributes.
- A candidate (primary) key attribute of an object class must be selected from the set of attributes of the object class.
- A composite key is selected from 2 or more attributes of an object class.
- An object class or relationship type can have at most one primary key, which must be part of the candidate keys.
- Relationship attributes have to relate to an existing relationship type.
- An object class can reference one object class only, but an object class can be referenced by multiple object classes.

[5] The complete OWL representation of the *Course-Student* instance example can be found athttp://www.comp.nus.edu.sg/~liyf/ora-ss/case_instance.owl.

The above are some of the criteria for validating a schema diagram against the ORA-SS notation. To manually check the validity of a given schema diagram against these constraints is a highly laborious and error-prone task. By following the methodology presented in this section systematically, potential violations of the above constraints can be avoided. This is because the formal semantics of the OWL language allows precise specifications to be expressed.

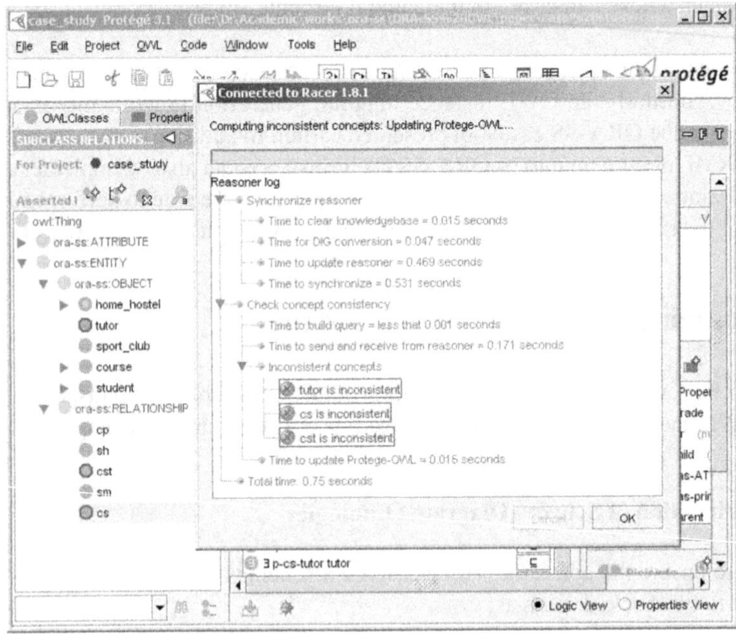

Fig. 4. Schema inconsistency detected by RACER

Moreover, highly efficient OWL reasoners such as RACER can check the consistency of ORA-SS schema diagrams in OWL automatically. For example, suppose that in Fig. 2, the child of relationship type *cs* is mistakenly associated with a relationship type *cst* instead of the reference object class *student_1*. This error can be picked up by RACER automatically, as shown in Fig. 4. Three classes, *cs*, *cst* and *tutor* are highlighted as inconsistent. It is inconsistent because both *cst* and *tutor* are related to *cs* using existential or cardinality restrictions. Other types of checking can be similarly performed.

4.2 Verification of Instance Diagram Ontologies

The ORA-SS instance validation is defined to check whether there are any possible inconsistencies in a semistructured data instance, where an ORA-SS instance should be consistent with regard to the designated ORA-SS schema diagram. Possible guidelines for validating an ORA-SS instance are as follow.

- Relationship instances must conform to the parent participation constraints, e.g., the number of child objects related to a single parent object or relationship instance should be consistent with the parent participation constraints; and the number of parent objects or relationship instances that a single child object relates to should be consistent with the child participation constraints.
- In a disjunctive relationship, only one object class can be selected from the disjunctive object class set and associated to a particular parent instance.
- For a candidate key (single or composite), its value should uniquely identify the object that this key attribute belongs to.
- Each object can have one and only one primary key.
- All attributes have their own cardinality and the number of attributes that belong to an object should be limited by the minimum and maximum cardinality values of the attribute.
- For a set of disjunctive attributes, only one of the attribute choices can be selected and associated to an object instance.

These are some of the criteria of instance level validation. Given an ORA-SS instance, we first transform it into its corresponding OWL instance representation, then verify the consistency of the instance ontology automatically by invoking ontology reasoners capable of ABox reasoning. We will use RACER to demonstrate the checking of the above ontology through a few examples.

- Entity/attribute cardinality constraints
  In the schema ontology, each instance of relationship type *cst* has exactly one *tutor*. Suppose that in the instance ontology, *(course1, student)* has both *tutor1* and *tutor2* as the child for the relationship type *cst*.

  $\langle cs1, tutor1 \rangle \in p\text{-}cs\text{-}tutor \qquad \langle cs1, tutor2 \rangle \in p\text{-}cs\text{-}tutor$

  By using RACER, the instance ontology is detected to be inconsistent.
- Primary key related properties
  Suppose that by accident, two students, *student4* and *student5*, are both assigned to the same student number.

  $\langle student4, student\_number\_4 \rangle \in student\_number \qquad \langle student5, student\_number\_4 \rangle \in student\_number$

  Similarly, RACER instantly detects the inconsistency.

4.3 Debugging ORA-SS OWL Models

The OWL reasoners, such as RACER, can perform efficient reasoning on large ontologies automatically. They can detect whether an OWL ontology is consistent or not *as a whole*. However, it is not capable of locating which individual caused the inconsistency. When checking satisfiability (consistency), the OWL reasoners can only provide a list of unsatisfiable classes and offer no further explanation for their unsatisfiability. It means that the reasoner can only conclude if an ORA-SS data model is consistent and flag the invalid class or individuals. The process of 'debugging' an ORA-SS data model is left for the user. When faced with several unsatisfiable individuals in a moderately large ORA-SS data model, even expert ontology engineers can find it difficult to work out the underlying error. Debugging an ontology has been well recognized as a non-trivial task. To provide some debugging assistance for the inconsistent ORA-SS models, we have built an OWL debugging tool [6] based on the heuristics [25]. Our OWL debugger has been designed to adopt the general OWL DL ontology and it can also be used to explain the errors in the ORA-SS data models as well.

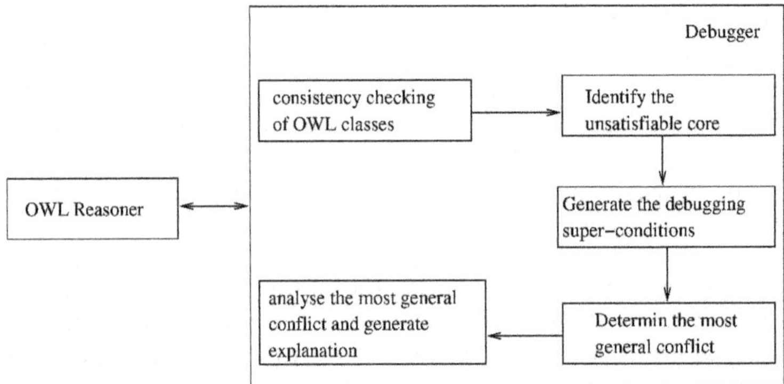

Fig. 5. The debugging process

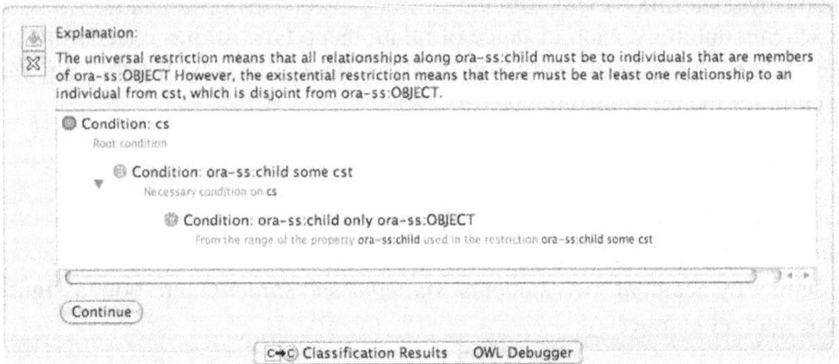

Fig. 6. Debugging the ORA-SS schema model

Figure 5 illustrates the main steps of the debugging process. The user selects an OWL class for debugging, which is checked to ensure it is indeed inconsistent, and that the user is making a valid request to the debugger. The debugger then attempts to identify the *unsatisfiable core* for the input class in order to minimize the search space. The *unsatisfiable core* is the smallest set of local conditions (direct super classes) that

[6] The work is supported in part by the CO-ODE project funded by the UK Joint Information Services Committee and the HyOntUse Project (GR/S44686) funded by the UK Engineering and Physical Science Research Council.

leads to the class in question being inconsistent. Having determined the unsatisfiable core, the debugger attempts to generate the *debugging super conditions*, which are the conditions that are implied by the conditions in the *unsatisfiable core*. The debugger then examines the *debugging super conditions* in order to identify the *most general conflicting* class set, which is analyzed to produce an explanation as to why the class in question is inconsistent.

For example, Figure 6 shows the result of the debugging for the inconsistent example in Section 4.1, where the child of relationship type *cs* is mistakenly associated with another relationship type *cst* instead of the reference object class *student_1*. Previously, three classes, *cs*, *cst* and *tutor* were highlighted as inconsistent by the RACER. With the help of our debugger, it was pinpointed that the *cs* should have an *OBJECT* in its *child* relationship and not an individual from the *cst* relationship type. This is exactly the reason for the inconsistency as found using manual inspection earlier.

5 Conclusion

In this paper, we explored the synergy between the Semantic Web and the database modeling approaches in the context of validating semistructured data design. We demonstrate the approach of using OWL and its reasoning tool for consistency checking of the ORA-SS data models and their instances. The advantages of our approach lie in the following aspects. Firstly, we defined a Semantic Web ontology model for the ORA-SS data modeling language. It not only provides a formal semantic for the ORA-SS graphical notation, but also demonstrates that Semantic Web languages such as OWL can be used to capture deeper semantic information of semistructured data. Furthermore, such semantics can be adopted by many Semantic Web applications that use the ORA-SS semistructured data model. Secondly, an ontology reasoning tool was adopted to perform automated verification of ORA-SS data models. The RACER reasoner was used to check the consistency of an ORA-SS schema model and its instances. We illustrated the various checking tasks through a `Course-Student` example model. In our previous work, we used the Alloy Analyzer for the validation of the ORA-SS data model [18]. The main advantage of our OWL approach over this is that consistency checking on large ORA-SS data models are made feasible. The current OWL reasoner can classify an ontology with 30,000 concepts within 4 seconds [26], which well satisfies the needs for any real-sized ORA-SS schemas and their instances.

In the future, we will further develop the visual case tool for editing and auto-generation of ORA-SS data models into their corresponding OWL representations for machine verification. Furthermore, we plan to extend and concentrate our work on defining the basic transformation operators that are used to transform ORA-SS schemas and providing verification for transformed schemas of semistructured data. By doing so, verifying the results of applications or databases that transforms the schema of semistructured data can be possible. In addition, we plan to extend the semantics of ORA-SS in OWL to investigate normalization issues in semistructured data design. The normal form of the ORA-SS data model for designing semistructured databases has been proposed in [9]. We would like to verify whether the semantics of a normalized schema is the same as its original form, showing whether a normalization algorithm changes the semantics of the schema during the transformation process.

References

1. Apparao, V., Byrne, S., Champion, M., Isaacs, S., Jacobs, I., Hors, A.L., Nicol, G., Robie, J., Sutor, R., Wilson, C., Wood, L.: Document Object Model (DOM) Level 1 Specification (1998) http://www.w3.org/TR/1998/REC-DOM-Level-1-19981001/.
2. Buneman, P., Davidson, S.B., Fernandez, M.F., Suciu, D.: Adding Structure to Unstructured Data. In: ICDT '97: Proceedings of the 6th International Conference on Database Theory, Springer-Verlag (1997) 336–350
3. Goldman, R., Widom, J.: DataGuides: Enabling Query Formulation and Optimization in Semistructured Databases. In Jarke, M., Carey, M.J., Dittrich, K.R., Lochovsky, F.H., Loucopoulos, P., Jeusfeld, M.A., eds.: VLDB'97: Proceedings of 23rd International Conference on Very Large Data Bases, Morgan Kaufmann (1997) 436–445
4. McHugh, J., Abiteboul, S., Goldman, R., Quass, D., Widom, J.: Lore: A Database Management System for Semistructured Data. SIGMOD Record **26**(3) (1997) 54–66
5. Dobbie, G., Wu, X., Ling, T., Lee, M.: ORA-SS: Object-Relationship-Attribute Model for Semistructured Data. Technical Report TR 21/00, School of Computing, National University of Singapore, Singapore (2001)
6. Ling, T.W., Lee, M.L., Dobbie, G.: Semistructured Database Design. Springer (2005)
7. Chen, Y., Ling, T.W., Lee, M.L.: A Case Tool for Designing XML Views. In: DIWeb'02: Proceedings of the 2nd International Workshop on Data Integratino over the Web, Toronto, Canada (2002) 47–57
8. Ling, T., Lee, M., Dobbie, G.: Applications of ORA-SS: An Object-Relationship-Attribute data model for Semistructured data. In: IIWAS '01: Proceedings of 3rd International Conference on Information Integration and Web-based Applications and Serives. (2001)
9. Wu, X., Ling, T.W., Lee, M.L., Dobbie, G.: Designing Semistructured Databases Using the ORA-SS Model. In: WISE '01: Proceedings of 2nd International Conference on Web Information Systems Engineering, Kyoto, Japan, IEEE Computer Society (2001)
10. Berners-Lee, T., Hendler, J., Lassila, O.: The Semantic Web. Scientific American **284**(5) (2001) 35–43
11. Horrocks, I., Patel-Schneider, P.F., van Harmelen, F.: From $\mathcal{SHIQ}$ and RDF to OWL: The making of a web ontology language. J. of Web Semantics **1**(1) (2003) 7–26
12. Haarslev, V., Möller, R.: Practical Reasoning in Racer with a Concrete Domain for Linear Inequations. In Horrocks, I., Tessaris, S., eds.: Proceedings of the International Workshop on Description Logics (DL-2002), Toulouse, France, CEUR-WS (2002)
13. Calvanese, D., Giacomo, G.D., Lenzerini, M.: Representing and Reasoning on XML Documents: A Description Logic Approach. Journal of Logic and Computation **9**(3) (1999) 295–318
14. Anutariya, C., Wuwongse, V., Nantajeewarawat, E., Akama, K.: Towards a Foundation for XML Document Databases. In: EC-Web. (2000) 324–333
15. Conforti, G., Ghelli, G.: Spatial Tree Logics to reason about Semistructured Data. In: SEBD. (2003) 37–48
16. Bidoit, N., Cerrito, S., Thion, V.: A First Step towards Modeling Semistructured Data in Hybrid Multimodal Logic. Journal of Applied Non-Classical Logics **14**(4) (2004) 447–475
17. Lee, S.U., Sun, J., Dobbie, G., Li, Y.F.: A Z Approach in Validating ORA-SS Data Models. In: 3rd International Workshop on Software Verification and Validation, Electronic Notes in Theoretical Computer Science, Volume 157, Issue 1, Manchester, United Kingdom (2005) 95-109
18. Wang, L., Dobbie, G., Sun, J., Groves, L.: Validating ORA-SS Data Models using Alloy. In: The Australian Software Engineering Conference (ASWEC 2006), Sydney, Australia (2006) 231–240

19. Papakonstantinou, Y., Vianu, V.: Incremental validation of XML documents. In: 9th International Conference on Database Theory (ICDT 2003), Siena, Italy, Springer (2003) 47–63
20. Bouchou, B., Alves, M.H.F.: Updates and Incremental Validation of XML Documents. In: Database Programming Languages: 9th International Workshop, DBPL 2003, Potsdam, Germany, Springer (2003) 216–232
21. Nardi, D., Brachman, R.J.: An introduction to description logics. In Baader, F., Calvanese, D., McGuinness, D., Nardi, D., Patel-Schneider, P., eds.: The description logic handbook: theory, implementation, and applications. Cambridge University Press (2003) 1–40
22. D. Brickley and R.V. Guha (editors): Resource description framework (rdf) schema specification 1.0. `http://www.w3.org/TR/rdf-schema/` (2004)
23. Harmelen, F., Patel-Schneider, P.F., (editors), I.H.: Reference description of the DAML+OIL ontology markup language. Contributors: T. Berners-Lee, D. Brickley, D. Connolly, M. Dean, S. Decker, P. Hayes, J. Heflin, J. Hendler, O. Lassila, D. McGuinness, L. A. Stein, et. al. (March, 2001)
24. Zhu, N., Grundy, J., Hosking, J.: Pounamu: a meta-tool for multi-view visual language environment construction. In: Proceedings of the IEEE Symposium on Visual Languages and Human-Centric Computing (VL/HCC'04), Rome, Italy (2004)
25. Wang, H., Horridge, M., Rector, A., Drummond, N., Seidenberg, J.: Debugging OWL-DL Ontologies: A Heuristic Approach. In: Proc. of 4th International Semantic Web Conference (ISWC'05), Galway, Ireland, Springer-Verlag (2005)
26. Tsarkov, D., Horrocks, I.: Optimised Classification for Taxonomic Knowledge Bases. In: Proceedings of the 2005 International Workshop on Description Logics (DL-2005), Edinburgh, United Kingdom (2005)

Appendix

Table 3. Instances of various attributes of the ORA-SS schema diagram in Fig. 2

Attribute	Instances
code	CS1101, CS1301, MA1102, CS2104
title	"Java Programming", "Computer Architecture", "Calculus", "Programming Languages"
lecture threater	LT27, LT34, LT8
laboratory	SR6, PL1, PL2
grade	A, B, C, D, F
student number	stu no 1, stu no2, stu no3, ..., stu no 8
name (student)	Jim, Gill, Mike, Rudy, Martin, Shirley, Tracy, Keith
number (home)	20-22, 6-7
street name (home)	Sunset Avenue, Avenue George V
name (hostel)	KR, SH, KEVII
staff number	stf no 1, stf no 2, stf no 3
name (staff)	J-Sun, G-Dobbie, M-Jacksoon
preferred area	RE, SE, FM, DB, Network, Grid, SW
feedback	positive, negative, neutral
name (sport club)	yachting club, boxing club, tennis club
sport	yachting, boxing, tennis
join date	aug-02-2002, jan-25-2003, may-15-2003, oct-01-2003, dec-31-2004, jul-19-2005

Table 4. Instances of relationship types of the ORA-SS schema diagram in Fig. 2

Relationship types	Members
cs	(course1, student1), (course1, student2), (course1, student3), (course1, student4), (course1, student5), (course1, student6), (course1, student7), (course1, student8), (course2, student5), (course2, student6), (course2, student7), (course2, student8), (course2, student1), (course2, student2), (course2, student3), (course2, student4), (course3, student1), (course3, student3), (course3, student5), (course3, student7), (course4, student2), (course4, student4), (course4, student6), (course4, student8)
cp	(course4, course1)
sh	(student1, home1), (student2, home2), (student3, hostel1), (student4, hostel2), (student5, hostel3), (student6, home1), (student7, hostel), (student8, hostel2)
cst	((course1, student1), tutor1), ((course1, student2), tutor2), ((course1, student3), tutor3), ((course1, student4), tutor1), ((course1, student5), tutor2) ((course1, student6), tutor3), ((course1, student7), tutor1), ((course1, student8), tutor2), ((course2, student5), tutor3), ((course2, student6), tutor1), ((course2, student7), tutor2), ((course2, student8), tutor3), ((course2, student1), tutor1), ((course2, student2), tutor2), ((course2, student3), tutor3), ((course2, student4), tutor1), ((course3, student1), tutor2), ((course3, student3), tutor3), ((course3, student5), tutor1), ((course3, student7), tutor2), ((course4, student2), tutor3), ((course4, student4), tutor1), ((course4, student6), tutor2), ((course4, student8), tutor3)
sm	(club1, student1), (club1, student3), (club2, student2), (club2, student4), (club3, student5), (club3, student6)

Table 5. Attribute values associated with the objects and relationships in Fig. 2

Entity	Attribute association			
course	*instances*	***code***	*title*	*exam venue*
	course1	CS1101	"Java Programming"	LT27
	course2	CS1301	"Computer Architecture"	LT34
	course3	MA1102	"Calculus"	LT8
	course4	CS2104	"Programming Languages"	SR6

Entity	*instances*	*name*	***student number***
student	student1	Jim	stu no1
	student2	Gill	stu no2
	student3	Mike	stu no3
	student4	Rudy	stu no4
	student5	Martin	stu no 5
	student6	Shirley	stu no 6
	student7	Tracy	stu no 7
	student8	Keith	stu no 8

Entity	*instances*	*grade*	*instances*	*grade*	*instances*	*grade*
cs	cs1	A	cs2	B	cs3	B
	cs4	C	cs5	C	cs6	B
	cs7	A	cs8	F	cs9	B
	cs10	D	cs11	C	cs12	B
	cs13	B	cs14	B	cs15	F
	cs16	A	cs17	C	cs18	D
	cs19	C	cs20	D	cs21	A
	cs22	B	cs23	B	cs24	A

Entity	*instances*	*number*	*street name*
home	home1	20-22	Sunset Avenue
	home2	6-7	Avenue George V

Entity	*instances*	*name*
hostel	hostel1	KR
	hostel2	SH
	hostel3	KEVII

Entity	*instances*	***staff number***	*name*	*preferred area*
tutor	tutor1	stf no 1	J-Sun	SE, RE, FM, SW
	tutor2	stf no2	G-Dobbie	SE, DB, Network
	tutor3	stf no 3	M-Jackson	RE, SE, Grid

Entity	*instances*	*feedback*	*instances*	*feedback*	*instances*	*feedback*
cst	cst1	positive	cst2	neutral	cst3	neutral
	cst4	neutral	cst5	neutral	cst6	neutral
	cst7	positive	cst8	negative	cst9	neutral
	cst10	negative	cst11	neutral	cst12	neutral
	cst13	neutral	cst14	neutral	cst15	negative
	cst16	positive	cst17	neutral	cst18	negative
	cst19	neutral	cst20	negative	cst21	positive
	cst22	neutral	cst23	neutral	cst24	positive

Entity	*instances*	***name***	*sport*
sport club	club1	yachting club	yachting
	club2	boxing club	boxing
	club3	tennis club	tennis

Entity	*instances*	*join date*	*instances*	*join date*
sm	sm1	aug-02-2002	sm2	may-15-2003
	sm3	jan-25-2003	sm4	oct-01-2003
	sm5	jul-19-2005	sm6	dec-31-2004

A Pragmatic Approach to Model and Exploit the Semantics of Product Information

Taehee Lee[1], Junho Shim[2,*], Hyunja Lee[2], and Sang-goo Lee[1]

[1] School of Computer Science & Engineering, Seoul National University, Korea
{thlee, sglee}@europa.snu.ac.kr
[2] Department of Computer Science, Sookmyung Women's University, Korea
{jshim, hyunjalee}@sookmyung.ac.kr

Abstract. Recently researchers have tried to apply ontology to the product information domain. From a practical point of view, a key problem to streamline this trend is how to make a product ontology database operational. Technical solutions should consider the characteristics that a pragmatic product ontology database contains; first, the database size is quite huge, and second, ontological manipulation and utilization should be realistically feasible. We recently engaged in a project to build an operational product ontology system. The system is designed to serve as a product ontology knowledge base, not only for the design and construction of product databases but also for the search and discovery of products. From the insights gained through this project, we believe that ontological modeling and its implementation on an operational database, as well as the building applications which exploit ontological benefits, are the most important facets towards the successful deployment of a practical product ontology system. As such, searching techniques should take into account the features of an underlying ontological model especially with product searching being one of the most popular applications within product information systems. In this paper, we present these two issues; product ontology modeling and searching techniques. Although our work presented herein may not be the only way to build an operational product ontology database, it may serve as an important reference model for similar projects in future.

1 Introduction

Product information is an essential component in e-commerce. It contains information such as pricing, features, and terms about the goods and services offered or requested by the trade partners. A base of precisely and clearly defined product information is a necessary foundation for collaborative business processes. In addition, semantically enriched product information may enhance the quality and effectiveness of business transactions and can be used to support production planning and management. These features can be offered by ontology, and the potential benefits of ontology on product information have been introduced by researchers in recent years [8,23,37,17,18].

* Corresponding author.

S. Spaccapietra (Ed.): Journal on Data Semantics VII, LNCS 4244, pp. 242–266, 2006.

Product ontology requires specifying a conceptualization of product information in terms of classes, properties, relationships, and constraints. Although there has been a vast amount of research in ontology, there are still gaps to be filled in actual deployment of the technology/concept in a real-life commercial environment. These gaps are especially prevalent in certain domains such as product information management where mission critical applications need to be 'operational'. We recently participated in a project to build an operational product ontology system for a government procurement service [19]. Herein, by 'operational' we mean that product ontology should run in a large scale database with gigabytes or terabytes size and that applications built on the product ontology database should benefit a proper degree of inference functionalities. This means that we may compensate some degree of ontological beauties such as full-fledged reasoning with the availability, robustness, and performance that operational product ontology should provide.

Two major issues for building an operational ontology not only limited to product but in other domains may include 1) how to model and implement operational ontology and 2) to build an application that runs in large scale and benefits the underlying ontology model. One of the most important and popular applications related to product information system is product searching. Product searching that exploits the ontological benefits may provide users with more a precise and relevant set of products than is possible with conventional IR-based searching. Obviously, searching techniques over product ontology should be different from the techniques of processing queries over conventional document or relational databases, and should take into account of the features of the underlying ontological model.

In this paper, we present these two issues; product ontology modeling and searching techniques. The rest of this paper is structured as follows: Section 2 describes related work and offers a brief introduction of how to build an operational product ontology system. In Sections 3 and 4, we present our modeling methodology for building an operational product ontology database and explain how our model corresponds to OWL representation. In Section 5 we discuss how to design and develop a searching technique over a product ontology model. Conclusions are drawn in Section 6.

2 Related Work

The Web has been extended in a way that information is incorporated into well-defined semantics, better enabling computers and people to work in cooperation. Ontology plays an essential role in realizing the Semantic Web. It is concerned with the taxonomic hierarchies of classes and class definitions, relationships between classes, and knowledge about beings and their world. XML based markup languages such as DAML+OIL [11] and OWL [31] have been developed to represent ontology in the Web, and also have given influence to the Web applications such as e-commerce systems.

Product information has the taxonomic hierarchies and consists of multiple attributes. In addition, exchanging product information among business partners requires it to have well-defined semantics. That makes product information an adequate domain within e-commerce where ontology can play a vital role. In [8] the authors list the difficulties of building, maintaining, and integrating product information, and propose that an ontological approach may be the answer. In [25] the authors propose to use cross industry standard classifications such as UNSPSC[1] and eCl@ss[2] as the upper ontology and industry specific classifications as lower ontology. An upper ontology is about concepts that are generic, abstract and, therefore, are general enough to address (at a high level) a broad range of domain areas, while lower ontology contains domain-specific knowledge [35]. An effort to introduce the ISO standard for product library is presented in [22]. All of these authors' work, however, focuses mainly on classification standards as the shape of ontology for product information. Classification hierarchies are an essential part of product information semantics but make up only one piece of the picture.

The importance of attributes in product information management is well-introduced in [12,17]. In [12], the quality of product classification standards is evaluated by a number of factors including the quality of their attribute lists. In [17], the authors point out that a classification hierarchy is a representation of just one of many views over the set of products, and that a product's identity and property are not decided only by how the product is classified. Product database design issues and guidelines are presented, where the focus is on properties (attributes) rather than on classification hierarchies.

For any semantic modeling to be suitable for its application domain, it is crucial to investigate what semantic concepts and relationships are desirable for the domain and to capture them in a model. More specifically, as mentioned in [8], ontological modeling of e-Catalog requires specifying a conceptualization of e-Catalog in terms of classes, properties, relationships and constraints. Concepts presented in this paper are gleaned through a real project that we participated in [19], and their formal representations are presented using description logics [21]. In this paper, we summarized the types of semantic relationships that need to be identified during product ontology modeling. Furthermore, we showed how to use OWL to formalize the semantics of product data stored in a relational database [20].

[18] is a recent work that points out that building an OWL knowledgebase is not pragmatically adequate for a large-scale ontology. Instead the authors promote a relational database approach in which reasoning is supported by storing facts in tables and representing rules in SQL triggers. However, their work is different from ours in that they focus on providing a programmatic framework rather than on modeling related issues. E-procurement is one of the most suitable domains that can benefit from well-defined product information. The process of registering or searching for a product, adding a new supplier, or placing a purchase order requires accurate product information. We have built an ontology system[3] for the Public Procurement Services of Korea, which is responsible for procurement for government and public agencies. The purpose of the system is to provide a universal ontology repository with browsing and searching capabilities in order to facilitate e-catalog sharing and interoperability [19].

---

1 http://www.unspsc.org

2 http://www.eclass-online.com

3 The system is called KOCIS (Korea Ontology-based e-Catalog Information System), and accessible online at http://www.g2b.go.kr:8100/index.jsp

The system consists of product ontology database and two subsystems; the ontology construction & maintenance system and the ontology search system (Figure 1). The ontology database model uses a meta-modeling approach, and includes the key semantic concepts including products, classification schemes, attribute requirement for each product, and unit of measures and their relationships to each other. We also organized and built a number of TDs (technical dictionary) to view the contents of the database. Further discussion on this is given in Section 3.

Ontology construction and maintenance subsystem populates the product ontology database from an existing product database by transforming (*preprocessor*) and bulk-loading (*loader*) the data periodically (*scheduler*). It also manages updates (*synchronizer* and *logging module*) while maintaining the consistency of the ontology database (*consistency checker*). The ontology search subsystem helps users navigate through or search the domain knowledge stored in the ontology database. Further information on how to develop our ontological product searching is given in Section 5.

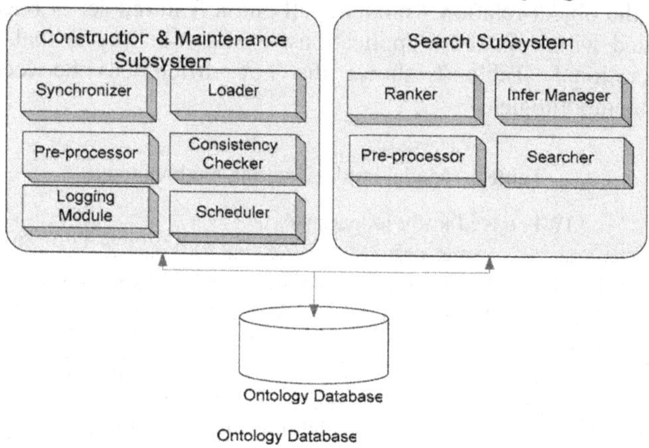

Fig. 1. The product ontology system at KOCIS [19]

3 Modeling for Operational Product Ontology

3.1 Modeling Methodology

Our modeling goal is not only to design a 'conceptual' product ontology model but also to implement it as an operational ontology database. One way to achieve this goal may be through using an ontology language such as OWL and building an OWL knowledgebase that represents the intentional and extensional concepts and relationships for the product ontology. This approach, mainly favored by the research community with extensive computer science backgrounds, may be beneficial for integrating the domain ontology model with an inference engine for the language. However, it is technically too complicated to represent and comprehend the domain for a domain expert who has little knowledge in the formal language. More importantly, from a practical point of view, there is no publicly known robust engine to manage a large knowledgebase with practical performance. For example, our product ontology database contains over five hundred thousands products and more than nine hundred thousands concepts including product classes, attributes and UOMs. Concepts are linked by the semantic relationships, and the total number of the semantic links is more than twenty-one million [19], not to mention that the size of the database keeps growing. In addition, we only needed a rather limited-set of reasoning capabilities such as transitivity and inverse. Naturally, the general purpose reasoning capability of an OWL engine was considered as over-kill. Consequently, we may regard this approach to be of little pragmatic value if used for an operational product ontology.

From a purely pragmatic point of view, an alternative way is to build a product ontology database on commercially operational database systems, i.e., more specifically object-relational DBMSs. It takes advantage of existing standards for data management and the DBMS features that have been optimized over the years in terms of robustness, scalability, or performance. Although it can support a limited set of reasoning by the object-relational model itself and a featured set of reasoning should be implemented within database applications, it is a sure way to make an ontology database operational. Table 1 shows the key differences between these two comparative methodologies.

Table 1. Model implementation methodology

	OWL-based knowledgebase approach	Relational database approach
Theoretical background	OWL, DAML+OIL, Topic Maps, Description Logics, FOL, …	EER, Table, SQL, Relational Algebra & Calculus, …
Pragmatism	Theoretical yet ideal	Operational and practical
Ontology representation	Rich for various semantic constraints	Rather limited for complicated semantic constraints
Ontological Reasoning or inference	Supported by the OWL-reasoning engine. Yet reasoning complexity may be high.	Limited. And featured reasoning capabilities should be coded within applications.
Commercial level	Publicly no engine is available to support a large knowledgebase.	Many DBMSs are commercially available.

In order to moderate between those two extreme methodologies, we need an adaptive approach which is practical in scalability and yet open for future technology. We claim that one way to achieve this is through building a product ontology database on top of an operational database system and yet providing an exporting mechanism from the database to an OWL knowledgebase. In other words, each modeling construct in an object-relational database can be translated into the corresponding OWL representation. Then a set of translated representation may form an OWL knowledgebase, and the ontological reasoning could be exploited by a 'robust' OWL engine should the engine indeed exist.

In fact, within our project we developed a mechanism to translate relational tables representing concepts such as products, classification schemes, attributes and UOMs (unit of measure), and their relationships into OWL representations. In the following subsections we discuss in more detail how we developed an ontological product model and implement it on an object-relational database. In Section 4 we overview the correspondence between our model and the OWL representation.

3.2 Meta Modeling for Product Ontology

Ontological modeling is an inherent process for building an ontology application regardless of the application domain. After the domain analysis, one needs to first conceive the key concepts and their relationships which may best portray the domain. In our product ontology, we regard *products*, *classification scheme*, *attributes* and *UOMs* as the key concepts. The products, the most important concept, are for the goods or services. The classification scheme and the attributes are used for the classifications and descriptions of products respectively. The UOM is associated with the attributes.

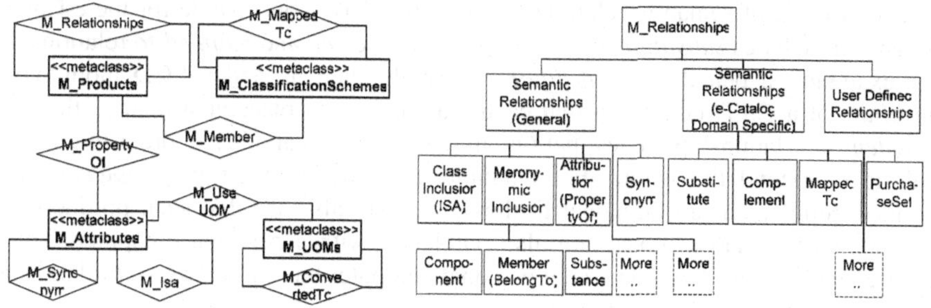

Fig. 2. a) Concepts and relationships in meta-level b) Taxonomy of semantic relationships

Figure 2-a) illustrates our view for product ontology using the meta-model approach. The meta-modeling approach enables a product ontology model to be more extensible and flexible. Our product model follows the basic meta-model which employs three modeling-levels: M0 meta-class level, M1 class level and M2 instance level. Within M0 level, which describes high level conceptual product ontology, we have the aforementioned key concepts as meta-classes. Key concepts are *products*, *classification schemes*, *attributes* and *UOMs* in our model, and they are represented by M_Products, M_ClassificationSchemes, M_Attributes and M_UOMs, respectively. As illustrated in Figure 2, meta-classes may have relationships (meta-relationships) with each other.

Various types of semantic relationships have been researched for a long time in multidiscipline areas such as cognitive science, logics and databases. A classification scheme by [36] presents one of the various viewpoints of classifying the semantic relationships. Based on both their work and our field experience [19], we created a taxonomy of semantic relationships for product information domain as in Figure 2-b), in which top-level relationships include the general domain relationships, e-Catalog domain specific relationships and user-defined relationships. The relationships for general domain include *inclusion*, *attribution*, and *synonym*. As in [34, 36], they are semantically generic to various domains and should be considered as meaningful semantic relationships for the e-Catalog domain as well.

The *inclusion* relationship describes cases in which an entity type contains other entity types, and it can be classified into the *class inclusion* or *meronymic inclusion*. The *class inclusion* represents the standard subtype/supertype relationship. The *meronymic inclusion* between *C* and *D* represents a *part-whole* relationship, i.e., *C* is a part of *D* (*D* is the whole of *C*), or simply *C* has *D*. For example, HDD and CPU are the parts of computer just as a beef-stew has beef, garlic, and onion as its ingredients. There are different semantic interpretations of this part-whole relationship. Similar to [36] we found the part-whole relationships to include *component-of*, *substance-of*, *member-of*, *portion-of*, and *feature-of* relationships. The *attribution* describes situation where an entity type describes properties or characteristics of other entity types. Finally, the *synonym* relationship describes an entity type that contains similar semantics to other entity types. For example, price and weight are attributes of *Laptop*; and *Laptop* is a synonym of *Notebook*.

The next set of semantic relationships is particularly conceivable for the e-Catalog domain. It includes *substitute*, *complement, purchase-set*, and *mapped-to* relationships. For examples, a pencil is a *substitute* of a ballpoint pen, and a LCD monitor is a *substitute* of a CRT monitor in that each may act as a replacement of the other. The *complement* relationship means that one may be added to another in order to complete a thing or extend the whole. For example, an antiglare filter is *complement* to a monitor. Similar but not identical to these, we may also see that such products as a monitor, an OS, and a mouse are also purchased with a personal computer. This is represented as a *purchase-set*, i.e., a personal computer has a *purchase-set* relationship with a monitor, an OS, and a mouse.

While substitute, complement, or purchase-set are relationships among product classes, the *mapped-to* relationship assigns a product into a specific class code within a classification scheme, or maps a class code of a classification scheme into the codes of different classification schemes. For example, a LCD panel product is *mapped to (belongs to)* 43172410 commodity class under a certain standard classification scheme. A product class can then be defined or classified differently depending on classification schemes. For example, the product personal computer is mapped to 43171803 in UNSPSC classification system, and 8471-10 or 8471-41 in HS code system.

Note that in Figure 2, meta-class and meta-relationships are identified by the prefix 'M_' to indicate that they are meta-concepts. M1 class level contains a snapshot or instance of the product ontology model in M0. That is, it illustrates a class schema of a product ontology database. The conceptual class schema may be then translated into its logical schema managed by an operational DBMS. The logical schema in our case is a set of object-relational tables and views. Figure 3 illustrates a part of the class schema of our product ontology database whereas M2 instance level refers to the physical ontology data managed by the system. For example, *notebook* and *LCD panel* products in M1 level are instances of *products* meta-class in M0 level, and there is a *component* relationship between them, i.e., a notebook *contains* a LCD panel and a LCD panel is a *component of* a notebook. Note that *contains* and *component-of* are in an inverse relationship with one another and are the instance relationships of *component* meta-relationships existing between *products* meta-classes. A notebook has attributes (described as *propertyOf* relationship) such as manufacturer, price, weight, and so on. Therefore, an individual notebook product, IBMX306 should appear in M2 level. Readers who are interested in the details of our product ontology model including the types of semantic relationships are referred to [21].

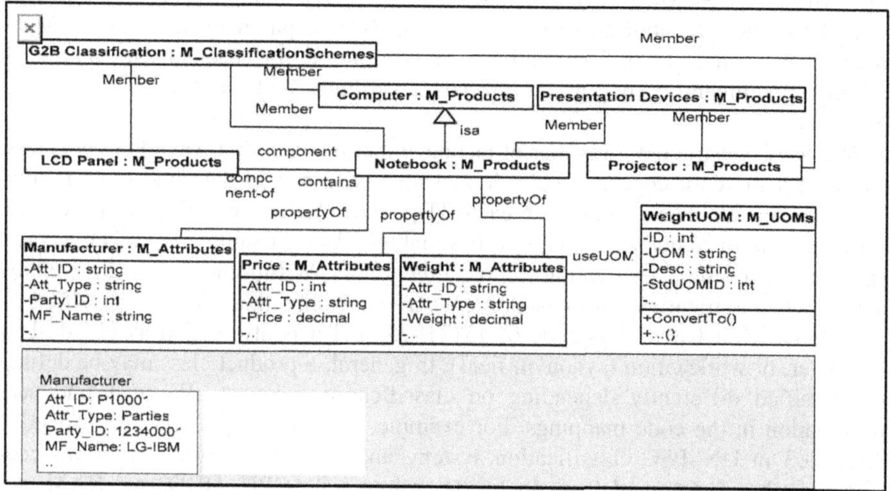

Fig. 3. Product ontology model in conceptual level and an exemplary instance product

The meta-modeling is a modeling methodology which can be generally applied to other domains as well. It should be pointed out that conceptualizing the concepts and relationships within a given domain is subjective and susceptible to various enterprise environments. Thus, the principle at the bottom of ontology modeling is that a model should be flexible enough to adapt to those variations, which is the greatest benefit that the meta-modeling approach may provide [2,29]. For any ontological modeling to be suitable in an application domain, it is crucial to investigate what semantic concepts and relationships are desirable for the domain and to capture them in a model. The main procedure of our meta-modeling consists of conceiving the key meta-concepts and relationships (M0), identifying the instances (individual concepts) of the meta-concepts (M1), and materializing the individuals. For example, in medical (in contexts of anatomy and pathology) ontology, the examples of key meta-concepts and relationships may include Structures (organ structures), Diseases, or Medicine (meta-concepts), and is-a, part-of, has-location, or effective (meta-relationships), respectively [32]. Then, the examples of individual concepts and relationships (M1) may include the following (in the above order): Appendicitis is a enteritis; appendix is an anatomical-part-of the colon; enteritis presents its symptoms in the intestines; and electrolytes may be used to treat enteritis. Individual electrolytes products (made by various medicine manufacturers) can be purchased at pharmacies. Other types of concepts and relationships can be appended without changing the framework.

3.3 Model Implementation and Technical Dictionary

We create an object-relational product ontology database consisting of more than forty base tables to reflect the aforementioned conceptual and class schemas. One novel feature that our ontology database provides is that it organizes and displays the product information in the form of technical dictionaries. Technical dictionaries, (TDs), are used frequently in the e-Catalog domain to describe the products and their properties. Well-known TDs include eOTD, GDD, and RNTD of ECCMA, EAN/UCC, and RosettaNet, respectively [7,9,28]. Compared to these TDs, our TD holds a far richer set of information that is required for machines to operate on products intelligently; such as the product's attributes and its relationship to other products.

We have constructed a number of technical dictionaries, in a way along which we can reflect the core concepts and relationships explained in the conceptual product ontology model. The contents of each TD are extracted and organized from the different sets of underlying ontology base tables. As an example of a TD, Table 2 shows a part of the classification technical dictionary. Within the dictionary, we have a product classification for *personal computers*. Under this specific classification scheme (g2b), it has a class code of 43171825, and it is also called as PC, desktop computer, or workstation (synonym field). In general, a product class may be defined or classified differently depending on classification schemes. We can find such information in the code mappings. For example, *personal computers* are mapped to 43171803 in UNSPSC classification system, and 8471-10 or 8471-41 in HS code system. It has component (contains) relationships with CPU, HDD, and RAM, and substitute relationships with notebook computers. We may also see that such products as a monitor, an OS, and a mouse are also purchased with a personal computer.

Note that each item within the same TD might have different columns to the ones that other items have, in that they can have different classification code mappings and relationships in actual contexts. For example, while the item *personal computer* has

Table 2. An example of a technical dictionary: g2b classification TD

class name	G2B code	description	synonyms	code mappings			relationships			etc
personal computers	43171825	A computer built for use by an individual ...	PC,desktop computers, workstations	UNSPSC	HS	GUNGB	component	substitute	purchase-set	..
				43171803	8471-10, 8471-	7010300	CPU, HDD, RAM,	notebook computers	monitors, OS, mouse,	
LCD monitors	43172410	A low-power flat-panel display used for ...	LCD, liquid crystal displays, flat panel displays	UNSPSC	GUNGB		complement	substitute	purchase-set	..
				43172402, 4317240, 431724	7025366, 7025302		arm stand, antiGlare filter	CRT monitors	personal computers	
...	...	...	...	...			...			..

three columns of code mappings for UNSPSC, HS, and GUNGB, another item such as a *LCD monitor* has just two columns of code mappings for UNSPSC and GUNGB. This means that in the actual product ontology database the item *LCD monitor* does not have any mapping relationship to HS. Similarly, the types of relationships that personal computers and LCD monitors have are different; personal computers have component but no complements while LCD monitors have complement but no component products.

4 Product Ontology Model: OWL Perspectives

4.1 Comprehensive Correspondence

A feature of our modeling approach is that we may represent the product ontology model in a standard ontology language. In this section, we illustrate how the model can be represented in OWL [31,20,10]. An OWL knowledge representation for specific domain may be the best means to utilize the techniques from so-called ontology-engineering [14,32]. For instances, it is beneficial for making a knowledgebase loosely-coupled from the application codes, enabling it to develop knowledge bases independent and interoperable from each other, and automating reasoning facility by OWL inference engines [26]. Recently, in the product ontology domain, there have been efforts by researchers to transform or publish the domain representation into OWL versions as well. Two most important related works are [13,21].

In [13], the authors focus on OWL derivation for industry standard taxonomy, such as UNSPSC and eCl@ss. They classify concepts into three parts; generic concept, annotation concept, and taxonomy concept for capturing the original semantics of existing standards taxonomy. In our preliminary work [21], we introduced a modeling framework which formally represents product ontology in DL(description logics). OWL and DL share a theoretical background. Furthermore, a model in DL may be translated into OWL representation. This requires consideration of the employed OWL language in terms of expressiveness and complexity along with its practical usage in the product information domain.

Figure 4 illustrates a basic mapping from our product meta-model (Figure 2-a) to the OWL representation. Note that we rename Attribution('PropertyOf') relationship between Products and Attributes with 'hasAttribute' to avoid confusion with the property expression in OWL.

Basically, concepts can be represented by *owl:Class*, and relationships by *owl:ObjectProperty* or *owl:DatatypeProperty*, in general. The class inclusion (isa) can be represented by '*rdfs:SubClassOf*'. Datatype property is used for relationships which exist between a class instance and a data value, while object property is used for relationships between class instances. An in and outgoing edge of arcs illustrates the property domain and the range of a property respectively. Note that in OWL, the domain and the range of a property limit the individuals to which the property can be applied and the property it may have as its values respectively. Relationships may have additional property restrictions (*owl:Restrictions*) or property characteristics

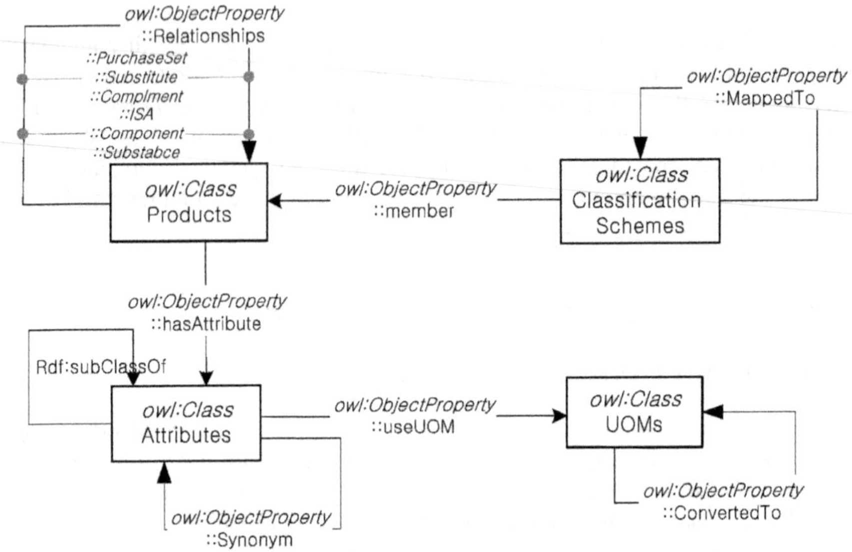

Fig. 4. Basic OWL correspondence in meta-level

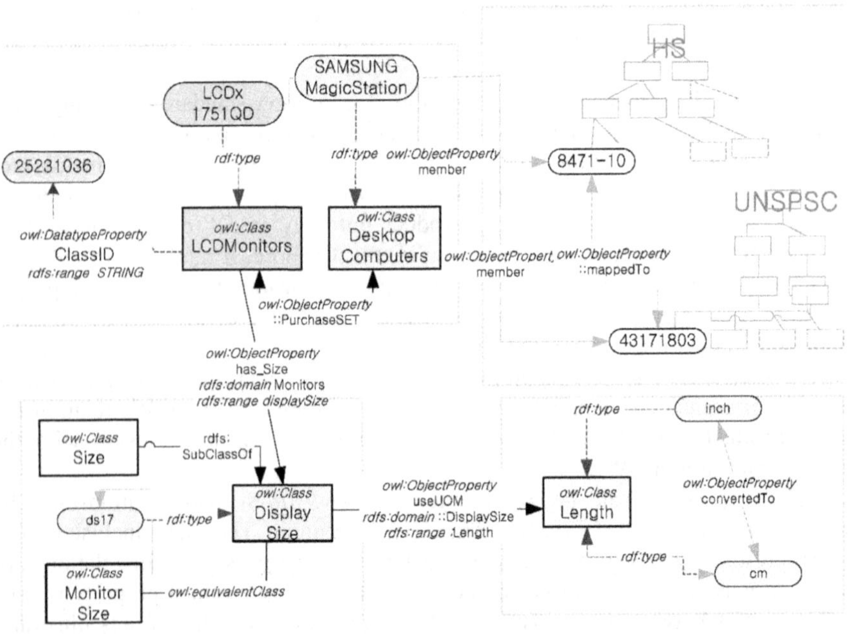

Fig. 5. An exemplary OWL representation for computer-related products

(*owl:TransitiveProperty, owl:SymmetricProperty, owl:inverseOf, or owl:FunctionalProperty*) to convey the proper semantics of the relationship. This can be seen in Figure 5 which is essentially a more detailed illustration of Figure 4.

In Figure 5, desktop computers are members of 8471-10 and of 43171803 commodities in HS and UNSPSC classification systems respectively. The member relationship may be represented by the *owl:ObjectProperty::member* object property with *rdfs:domain::ClassificationScheme* and *rdfs:range::Product* restrictions. The object properties are also used in other places such as purchaseSET between LCD Monitor and Desktop Computer, and has_Size between LCD Monitor products and Displaysize attributes. ClassID is an attribute of LCD Monitors and has a string data type value of '25231036'. This can be represented by *owl:DatatypeProperty* with a restriction of *rdfs:range::STRING.*

Consider that desktop computers and LCD Monitors may be purchased together. This can be represented using *owl:ObjectProperty::purchaseSET* with an additional restriction with *owl:SymmetricProperty* to denote the symmetric property of the purchaseSET property. Additionally, if the domain of purchaseSET is limited to Desktop computers, then the range should be limited by adding the *owl:someValuesFrom* restriction.

The individual products are represented by using *rdf:type*, that ties an individual to a class to which it belongs. For example, LCDx1751QD and SAMSUNG MagicStation are the individuals of LCD Monitors and Desktop computers, respectively, and can be represented by *<LCDMonitors rdf:ID="LCDx1751QD">* and *<DesktopComputer rdf:ID ="SAMSUNGMgicStation">*.

LCD Monitors products have DisplaySize as an attribute. This is represented by *owl:ObjectPropertyOf::hasDisplaySize* of which domain and range are restricted to LCD Monitors and DisplaySize. In attribute classes, DisplaySize is a sub type of Size and also synonym for MonitorSize. This may be represented using *rdfs:SubClassOf* and *owl:EquivalentClass* respectively.

Finally, DisplaySize attribute associated with the Length UOM and the instances of Length UOMS include 'inch' and 'cm'. Similar to the previous examples, these may be represented using *owl:ObjectPropertyOf::useUOM* and *rdf:type*. Note that 'inch' and 'cm' UOMs may be converted, i.e., 1inch = 2.54cm. In our project, each equation is represented as a convertedTo relationship and maintained in a relational table.

4.2 OWL Property Restrictions for Semantic Relationships

As mentioned in the previous section, although relationships may be corresponded to *owl:ObjectProperty*, more restrictions should be selectively added to each object property to convey precise semantics. Those restrictions include *owl:TransitiveProperty, owl:SymmetricProperty, owl:inverseOf, and owl:FunctionalProperty*, and owl:someValuesFrom and owl:allValuesFrom to further constrain the range of a property in specific contexts.

As an example, let us consider that a DC spindle motor is a component (or part) of HDD(hard disk) product which is also a component of computer products (Figure 6). The component relationship, in general, is not always transitive in that it usually contains both aggregational and functional semantics; being a functional part of its whole does not necessarily mean that the part is functional for another object which is composed of the whole [34]. However in practice, people often do not clarify the precise semantics of the component relationship that they use. For example, a query to find all hardware classes which contain DC Spindle as its "component" is not clear whether it is meant to search for any hardware having DC Spindle as its direct part or as its both direct and indirect parts (being contained within another product). In order to handle an indirect part-whole relationship, we need the transitive property, i.e., $x{\cdot}y$ & $y{\cdot}z \Rightarrow x{\cdot}z$. This can be represented in OWL using *owl:TransitiveProperty* . If HDD is a component(part) of Computer, then Computer is the composed(whole) of HDD. This may be represented using *owl:inverseOf*. In addition, the value restriction *owl:someValuesFrom* should be applied to the component property since Computers have not only HDD but also other parts such as CPU, a graphic card, RAM and etc..

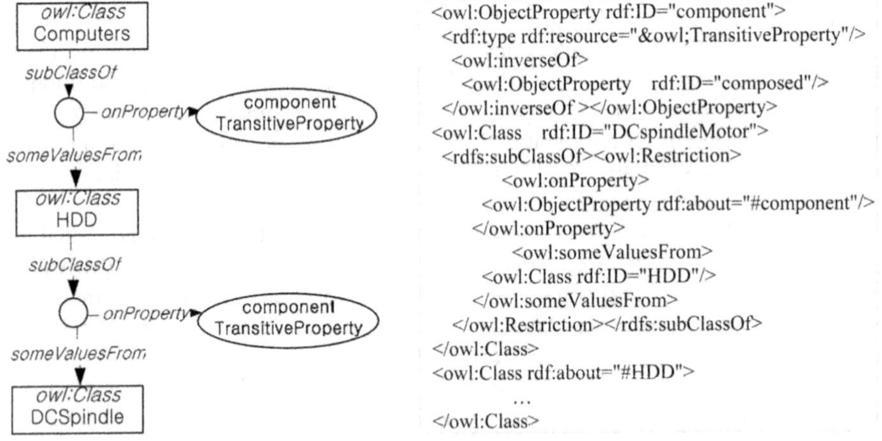

Fig. 6. Restrictions on component relationships

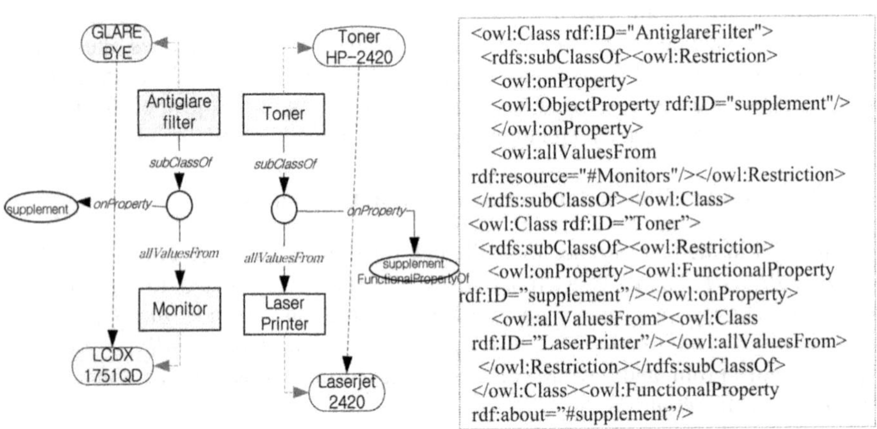

Fig. 7. Restrictions on supplement relationships

Table 3. OWL correspondence to semantic relationships

Semantic relationships	Examples in OWL	Semantic relationships	Examples in OWL
General domain relationships			
Class Inclusion **Restriction for Semantics** SubClass Of	<owl:Class rdf:ID=”DeskTopComputers”> <rdfs:subClassOf rdf:resource=”#Computers”/> <owl:disjointWith rdf:resource=”#NotebookComputers” /> </owl:Class>	**Meronymic Inclusion** **Restriction for Semantics** ObjectProperty InverseProperty TransitiveProperty(optional) SomeValuesFrom	<owl:Class rdf:ID=”HDD”> <rdfs:subClassOf> <owl:Restriction> <owl:someValuesFrom rdf:resource=”#Computers”/> <owl:onProperty> <owl:ObjectProperty rdf:ID=”component”/> </owl:onProperty> </owl:Restriction></rdfs:subClassOf> </owl:Class> <owl:ObjectProperty rdf:about=”# component”><rdf:type rdf:resource=”&owl;TransitiveProperty”/> <owl:inverseOf><owl:ObjectProperty rdf:ID=”compose”/> </owl:inverseOf> </owl:ObjectProperty>
Synonym equivalentClass	<owl:Class rdf:ID=”PersonalComputer”> <equivalentClass rdf:resource=”# PC ”/></owl:Class>		
Attribution **Restriction for Semantics** DatatypeProperty Domain Range	<owl:DatatypeProperty rdf:ID=”ClassID”><rdfs:range rdf:resource=”XMLSchema#string”/> <rdfs:domain><owl:Class rdf:about=”#Product” /> </rdfs:domain> </owl:DatatypeProperty>		
e-Catalog specific relationships			
Substitute **Restriction For Semantics** SymmetricProperty TransitiveProperty AllValuesFrom	<owl:Class rdf:ID=”LCDmonitors”> <rdfs:subClassOf> <owl:Restriction> <owl:allValuesFrom rdf:resource=”#CRTmonitors”/> <owl:onProperty> <owl:SymmetricProperty rdf:ID=”substitute”/> </owl:onProperty> </owl:Restriction> </rdfs:subClassOf></owl:Class> <owl:ObjectProperty rdf:about=”#substitute”> <rdf:type rdf:resource="&owl;TransitiveProperty"/></owl:ObjectProperty>	**Supplement** **Restriction for Semantics** FunctionalProperty (optional) AllValuesFrom	<owl:Class rdf:ID=”Toner”> <rdfs:subClassOf><owl:Restriction> <owl:onProperty> <owl:FunctionalProperty rdf:ID=”supplement”/> </owl:onProperty> <owl:allValuesFrom> <owl:Class rdf:ID=”LaserPrinter”/> </owl:allValuesFrom> </owl:Restriction> </rdfs:subClassOf> </owl:Class> <owl:FunctionalProperty rdf:about=”#supplement”/>
PurchaseSet **Restriction for Semantics** SymmetricProperty SomeValuesFrom	<owl:Class rdf:ID="Computer"> <rdfs:subClassOf> <owl:Restriction> <owl:onProperty> <owl:SymmetricProperty rdf:ID="purchaseSet"> </owl:onProperty> <owl:someValuesFrom> <owl:Class rdf:ID="Monitors"/> </owl:someValuesFrom> </owl:Restriction> </rdfs:subClassOf> </owl:Class>	**MappedTo** **Restriction for Semantics** SymmetricProperty allValuesFrom	<owl:Class rdf:ID=” HS 8471-10”> <rdfs:subClassOf> <owl:Restriction> <owl:allValuesFrom> <owl:Class rdf:ID=”UNSPSC43172402”/> </owl:allValuesFrom> <owl:onProperty> <owl:SymmetricProperty rdf:ID=”MappedTO”/> </owl:onProperty> </owl:Restriction> </rdfs:subClassOf> </owl:Class>

Let us consider that any individual antiglare filter product may serve as a supplement to any monitor product while only a specific type of toner product may serve as a laser printer. For example, TonerHP-2420 works with Laserjet2420, but other toners may work with it as well (Figure 7). In this case, *owl:Objectproperty: supplement* with *owl:allValuesFrom* may be enough to represent the supplement relationship between Antiglare filter and Monitor product classes. Whereas, we should add the *owl:FuctionalProperty* restriction to the supplement relationship between TonerHP-2420 and Laserjet2420.

A substitute relationship means that one may act as a replacement for the other. For example, a pencil is a substitute for a ballpoint pen. A substitute relationship might contain symmetric property, i.e., *x substitute y* ⇒ *y substitute*, which is represented in OWL as *owl:ObjectProperty::substitute* with the restriction of *owl:SymmerticProperty*.

Due to space limitations, we do not provide more details in translation scheme and associated property restrictions for each semantic relationship. Rather, we summarize them in Table 3. Readers who are interested in more details are referred to [20].

5 Building Applications on Product Ontology

5.1 Ontology-Based Searching

A product ontology may contain a large number of concepts and relationships. For naive users to search and navigate the ontology efficiently, good search and visualization functionalities should be provided. In practice, we may not expect ordinary users to have sufficient knowledge of the underlying schema to be able to compose their queries precisely in query languages such as OWL-QL or SQL. We contemplate the problem of ranking keyword search results over product ontology databases. First, we summarize some of the related works.

Traditionally ranking keyword search results have been extensively studied in the context of text. Ever since the big bang of the Internet, it has received more attention in other contexts such as web and xml documents. In the IR (information retrieval) research community, text ranking is typically done using keywords and its occurrence frequencies such as *tf* and *idf* values [30]. In the web environment, PageRank [5] and HITS [16] are the most well-known ranking algorithms. Both algorithms compute the authority of a document by considering hyperlinks. Documents with higher authority are positioned in higher ranks as they are regarded as globally important ones. The database research community has also paid attention to the keyword search problem. For example, [4] presents ObjectRank, which may be regarded as a modification of PageRank for relational databases. All the above works do not exploit ontology in their searching algorithms, which is what distinguishes our work. In [33] the authors propose a context-sensitive searching algorithm to exploit the ontology concept. However, they use ontology only for refining the meaning of search terms while the underlying data is not ontologically modeled but stored in plain HTML or XML format. An abundance of semantic relationships and their characteristics in the context of the Semantic Web are well documented in [1]. In that paper, the authors blended semantics and information-theoretic techniques for their general search model, in which users can vary their search modes to affect the ordering of results depending on whether they need conventional search or investigative search. Other researchers [27, 24] use a similar approach that combines the weight of relationships into their ranking functions. Their algorithms do not consider cases in which a search term may occur in a relationship name but only deal with the occurrence frequencies of relationships associated with each concept.

Processing keyword search queries over product ontology databases are different from processing queries over documents, web, or relational databases. First, searching product ontology should consider relationships between concepts while IR-based searching considers only the term occurrences in product data. Obviously, the ranking function should be altered to properly reflect the product ontology while utilizing IR-style information such as keyword proximity [30] as well. Considering relationships in a ranking function helps to understand the meaning of concepts and improve the recall by retrieving more related concepts. Furthermore, users in the product ontology domain tend to have more definite intention on issuing queries. They are more likely to search for products or product classes, which are represented by nodes in our product ontology graph (see the following subsection). In the semantic web or relational databases, instead, the target of the keyword search is usually a subgraph, rather than nodes. Note that a subgraph represents a relationship (or edge) between concepts or records in the semantic web or relational database respectively.

5.2 Product Searching and Product Ontology Graph

Our searching algorithm employs a graph structure, called a product ontology graph, to represent a snapshot of the underlying product ontology. An example of a product ontology graph appears in Figure 8. There are two types of nodes in a product ontology graph. The first type is a schematic node. The schematic node, represented by a rectangle in the graph, denotes a concept in M1 class-level, such as product class, classification scheme, UOM, and attribute. The second type of node is an instance node. The instance node, represented by an ellipse in the graph, denotes an instance in M2 instance level. Accordingly, every instance node has an associated schematic node. For example, an instance node "*IBM S40*"and "*WD 2120*" denote individual products which are associated with "*Desktop computers*" and "*HDD*" product class respectively. Note the schematic nodes are annotated by the corresponding concepts in M0 meta-level: e.g. *Computers* are annotated by *<<Products>>*.

Example 1. Given a query to find a UNSPSC code for products "IBM P4 3.0GHz", the system should return 48171803 (desktop computers) or 48171801 (notebook computers), or both. Conventional cumulative ranking functions such as PageRank[5] would rank *desktop computers* higher than *notebook computers* simply because they would determine that the global importance of *desktop computers* is greater than that of *notebook computers*, i.e., the number of incoming edges for *desktop computers* is greater. However, from a probabilistic point of view, the keywords "IBM P4 3.0GHz" are likely more relevant for *notebook computers* since every product in *notebook computers* is "IBM P4 3.0GHz" whereas only half of the products in *desktop computers* are "IBM P4 3.0GHz". Note that most of the probabilistic classification algorithm such as Naïve Bayesian Classifier would return *notebook computers* as a result. (See Appendix for an explanation.)

Example 2. Keywords used in a query may be values, attribute names, category names, and even relationship names etc., whereas in a typical keyword search they are confined to attribute values only. As an example, in a query "IBM computer with components of P4 CPU", the keywords "computer", "component", and "CPU" are names of product class, relationship, and attribute class respectively. For this query, both IBM S40 and IBM G41 may be retrieved as results, since *desktop computers* and *notebook computers* are sub-classes of the *computer* class, and both are made by IBM and contain P4 CPUs.

Example 3. Given a query to find an "IBM desktop computer with SG HDD", there is no individual product satisfying the keywords in the *desktop computers'* class. Since a *substitute* relationship between desktop and notebook computers was found in the product ontology graph, an IBM G41 notebook would be returned as a result, more precisely as a substituting product.

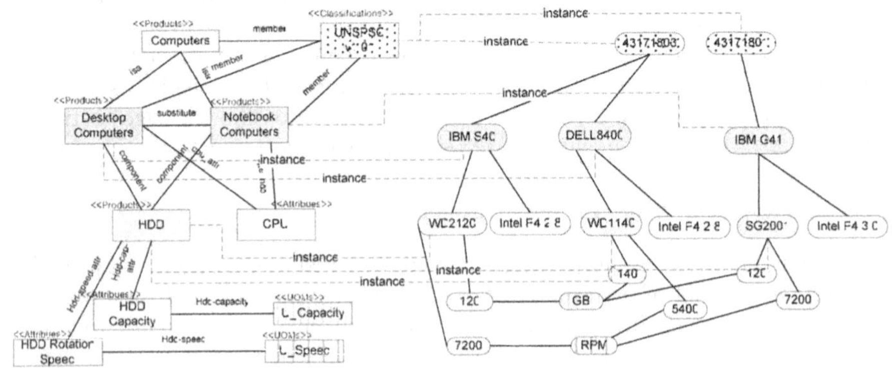

Fig. 8. An example of product ontology graph

As we have shown in the previous examples, there are particular features to notice in product ontology searching. First, the ranking function should consider not only the concepts that contain the keywords but also other context information such as the number of products in the same class and the number of edges (in Example 1). We use a well-known probabilistic model to accurately measure the relevance of query results, while others either use a simple additive function to compute the ranks or never even tried to apply the probabilistic model to product ontology.

Second, the ranking function should consider various kinds of relationships. There exist a large number of relationships which include member, instance, attribute and other relationships between products. As we saw in Example 2, keywords in the query can be attribute or relationship names. If a name of a relationship existing between products is matched with the given keyword, then it would make the incident products relevant with the query. We allow the ranking function to use a different score propagation method for each relationship in order to consider the types and names of relationships.

Third, a relationship, such as *substitute* in Example 3, could be used to offer relevant products to users. Even though the name of the relationship is not mentioned in the query, scores of the relevant nodes are propagated to adjacent nodes in the graph. In our algorithm, the propagated score decreases as the degree of propagation increases. In the following subsection we overview our ranking algorithm which considers the features mentioned above.

Our ranking model is based on the Bayesian Belief Network (BBN) [3]. In our model, every concept and relationship in ontology represents a variable and a conditional dependence on the BBN. As we have seen in previous examples, we assume that the scores of concepts are determined not only by the concepts but also by their associated relationships. Specifically, the scores of concepts are propagated to other concepts through the relationships as PageRank [5] does. But our propagation method is different from PageRank in that the scores of nodes are not equally distributed. In our model, scores are propagated to adjacent nodes by multiplying a propagation ratio which is defined distinctly on each relationship type.

As for an instance edge, we have the propagation ratio defined probabilistically. For example, the propagation ratio of an edge between an instance and a class can be defined as the probability of selecting the instance from the whole instances of the class. Then the propagation ratio of a relationship may be defined as the degree of belief on the relationship type and its value may be given by the administrator. Let us say that the substitute and synonym relationships have 1 while the part-whole relationship has 0.1 as their propagation ratios. That may rank products associated with the substitute or synonyms relationship higher compared to products associated with the part-whole relationships. In the meantime, if a relationship name contains the keywords used in query as in Example 2, the propagation ratio may be determined on the fly while processing the given query. See the Appendix for more details.

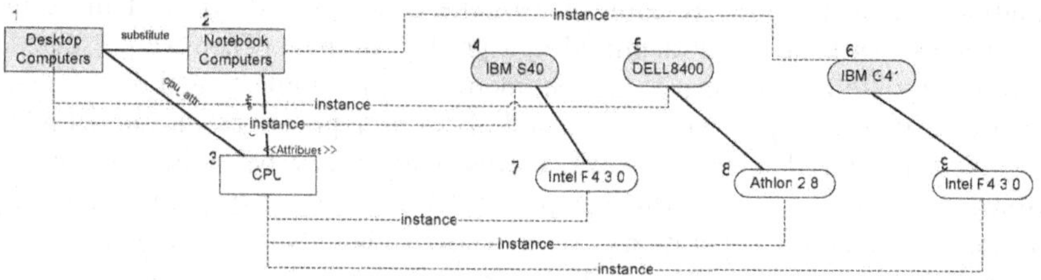

Fig. 9. A product ontology subgraph from Fig 8

Example 4. Consider a product ontology graph as in Figure 9 and a query for "IBM P4 3.0 computers." We can otherwise assume that the scores of nodes containing given keywords are 1 and 0. Arranged according to the subscription above each node, the scores of nodes are <1, 1, 0, 1, 0, 1, 1, 0, 1>. Since the propagation ratio of the instance relationship between node 1 and node 4 (i.e. the probability of selecting node 4 among instances of node 1) is 0.5, the score of node 4 is increased by 0.5 after the score propagation. The score of node 2 is increased by 1 after the score propagation from node 6 since the score propagation ratio of the relationship between node 2 and node 6 is 1.

The idea of the score propagation may be found in previous works such as PageRank and spreading activation [6]. Our contribution is that we developed a framework in which various types of relationships existing in product ontology are exploited for the score propagation. Furthermore, we are able to find not only instances (M2 level) but also classes (M1 level) in the product ontology graph. This is useful especially in product domain where users are interested in finding out not only individual products (instance) but also product classification (class), as shown in Example 1. Score propagation may be computationally expensive since the score of each node is propagated to every connected node in the ontology graph. In the KOCIS system, we limit the number of score propagations to 4 levels in depth, i.e., each node affects the nodes only reachable by equal to or less than 4 links (relationships).

6 Conclusions

Although there has been a vast amount of research in ontology, there are still gaps to be filled in the actual deployment of the technology in a commercial environment. There are numerous problems to overcome especially in those applications that require well-defined semantics in mission critical operations. Our work is based on the observation that the main challenges in building those applications is to maintain a balance between built-in functionality and domain/scenario-specific customization [17,15].

The main purpose of our paper was to present a modeling approach of a product ontology database which can be operational in practice. To achieve this; we identified the fundamental product semantics to describe product ontology. It included the definitions, properties, and relationships of the concepts and types of the semantic relationships that have to be identified in a product domain. Then we presented how the product ontology database can be modeled and implemented in a relational database so that it may be operational and also run applications on top. In addition, since exporting the database in OWL representation may be of benefit for several reasons, we showed how to formalize our model in OWL language. Our approach to make product ontology operational, as a whole rather than in the individual steps contained in the approach, has not been proposed or done before as far as we are aware.

Ontological product searching techniques should be designed in order to benefit the features that the underlying ontological model provides. Our approach enables users to reference product ontology directly through simple keyword search interface, thus opening up the door for people with little knowledge of product ontology systems. Ranking is important in practice in that searching may result in numerous outputs. We have been developing a ranking algorithm based on our product ontology search model and the Bayesian belief network. Our ranking algorithm is intended to be intuitive and also feasible to run on reasonably large ontology databases. However, neither formal description nor the practical performance competency of the algorithm is yet provided but are in progress.

The correctness verification of our product ontology database is another important subject that we continue to work on. It has been conducted in part either by providing various types of pre-processing modules and human experts to complement the quality of raw product data or by checking the consistency of OWL representation for each modeling unit basis. In addition, we are seeking alternative ways to effectively improve the correctness of the entire database.

References

1. B. Aleman-Meza, C. Halaschek, I. B. Arpinar, C. Ramakrishnan, and A. Sheth, “A Flexible approach for analyzing and ranking complex relationships on the semantic web”, IEEE Internet Computing, Special Issue on Information Discovery: Needles and Haystacks, 2005.
2. C. Atkinson and T. Kühne, "The Essence of Multilevel Metamodeling", 4th International Conference on the Unified Modeling Language, Modeling Languages, Concepts, and Tools, Springer-Verlag, 2001.
3. R. Baeza-Yates and B. Ribeiro-Neto, Modern Information Retrieval, Addison-Wesley, 1999.
4. A. Balmin, V. Hristidis, and Y. Papakonstantinou, “ObjectRank : Authority-based keyword search in databases”, VLDB, 2004.
5. S. Brin and L. Page, “The anatomy of a large-scale hyper-textual web search engine”, 7th WWW Conference, 1998.
6. F. Crestani, “Application of Spreading Activation Techniques in Information Retrieval”, Artificial Intelligence Review, Vol. 11, No. 6, Kluwer Academic Publishers, 1997.
7. eOTD, ECCMA Open Technical Dictionary, http://www.eccma.org/eotd/index.html, accessed on Sep, 2005.
8. D. Fensel, Y. Ding, B. Omelayenko, E. Schulten, G. Botquin, M. Brown, and A. Flet, “Product Data Integration in B2B E-Commerce”, IEEE Intelligent Systems, Vol. 16, No. 4, IEEE Society, 2001.
9. GDD, Global Data Dictionary, http://www.ean-ucc.org/global_smp/global_data_ dictionary. htm, accessed on Sep, 2005.
10. V. Haarslev and R. Möller, “Description Logic Systems with Concrete Domains: Applications for the Semantic Web”, 10th International Workshop on Knowledge Representation meets Databases (KRDB 2003), CEUR Workshop Proceedings, 2003.
11. F. van Harmelen, P.F. Patel-Schneider, and I. Horrocks (Eds.), Reference description of the DAML+OIL ontology markup language, http://www.daml.org/2001/03/reference, 2001.
12. M. Hepp, “Measuring the Quality of Descriptive Languages for Products and Services”, in E-Business – Standardisierung und Integration, F.-D. Dorloff, et al(Editors), Tagungsband zur Multikonferenz Wirtschaftsinformatik, 2004.
13. M. Hepp, “A Methodology for Deriving OWL Ontologies from Products and Services Categorization Standards”, 13th European Conference on Information Systems (ECIS), 2005.
14. V. Kashyap and A. Borgida, “Representing the UMLS Semantic Network Using OWL”, International Semantic Web Conference, 2003.
15. D. Kim, S. Lee, J. Shim, J. Chun, Z. Lee, and H. Park, “Practical Ontology Systems for Enterprise Application”, 10th Asian Computing Science Conference Data management on the Web (ASIAN2005), Springer-Verlag, 2005.
16. J. M. Kleinberg, “Authoritative sources in hyperlinked environment”, Journal of the ACM, Vol. 46, No. 5, ACM Press, 1999.

17. S. Lee, "Design & Implementation of an e-Catalog Management System", Tutorial at 9th International Conference on Database Systems for Advances Applications (DASFAA 2004), 2004.
18. J. Lee and R. Goodwin, "SNOBASE, for Semantic Network Ontology Base", http://www.alphaworks.ibm.com/aw.nsf/bios/snobase.
19. I. Lee, S. Lee, T. Lee, S. Lee, D. Kim, J. Chun, H. Lee, and J. Shim, "Practical Issues for Building a Product Ontology System", International Workshop on Data Engineering Issues in E-Commerce (DEEC2005), IEEE Society, 2005.
20. H. Lee and J. Shim, "Product Ontology and OWL Correspondence", IEEE Pacific Rim International Workshop on Electronic Commerce (IEEE-PRIWEC2006), 2006.
21. H. Lee, J. Shim, and D. Kim, "Ontological Modeling of e-Catalogs using EER and Description Logic", International Workshop on Data Engineering Issues in E-Commerce (DEEC2005), IEEE Society, 2005.
22. J. Leukel, "Standardization of Product Ontologies in B2B Relationships – On the Role of ISO 13584", 10th Americas Conference on Information Systems, 2004.
23. J. Leukel, V. Schmitz, and F. Dorloff, "A Modeling Approach for Product Classification Systems", 13th International Conference on Database and Expert Systems Applications (DEXA 2002), Springer-Verlag, 2002.
24. S. Mukherjea and B. Bamba, "BioPatentmINER : An information retrieval system for biomedical patents", VLDB, 2004.
25. L. Obrst, R.E. Wray, and H. Liu, "Ontological Engineering for B2B E-Commerce", International Conference on Formal Ontology in Information Systems (FOIS'01), ACM Press, 2001.
26. J. Pollock, "Using the W3C Standard OWL in Adaptive Business Solutions", WWW2004 Conference, http://www.w3.org/2001/sw/EO/talks, 2004.
27. C. Rocha, D. Schwabe, and M. Aragao, "A hybrid approach for searching in the semantic web", WWW 2004 Conference, 2004.
28. RosettaNet, The RosettaNet Technical Dictionary, http://www.rosettanet.org, accessed on Sep, 2005.
29. J. Shim, S. Lee, and C. Wu, "A Unified Approach for Software Policy Modeling: Incorporating Implementation into a Modeling Methodology", 22nd International Conference on Conceptual Modeling, Springer-Verlag, 2003.
30. A. Singhal, "Modern information retrieval : a brief overview", IEEE Data Engineering Bulletin, Special Issue on Text and Databases, Vol. 24, No. 4, IEEE Society, 2001.
31. M.K. Smith, C. Welty, and D.L. McGuinness, "OWL Web Ontology Language Guide – W3C Recommendation", http://www.w3c.org/TR/owl-guide/, 2004.
32. S. Staab and R. Studer (Eds.), Handbook on Ontologies. International Handbooks on Information Systems, Springer-Verlag, 2004.
33. N. Stojanovic, "On the Query Refinement in the Ontology-Based Searching for Information", 15th International Conference on Advanced Information Systems Engineering, Lecture Notes in Computer Science 2681, Springer-Verlag, 2003.
34. V. C. Storey, "Understanding Semantic Relationships", VLDB Journal, Vol. 2, VLDB Endowment, 1993.
35. SUO, IEEE Standard Upper Ontology Working group, http://suo.ieee.org/, accessed on Mar, 2006.
36. M.E. Winston, R. Chaffin, and D. Herrmann, "A Taxonomy of Part-whole Relations", Cognitive Science, Vol. 11, Cognitive Science Society, 1987.
37. G. Yan, W. K. Ng, and E. Lim, "Product Schema integration for Electronic Commerce - A Synonym Comparison Approach", IEEE Transaction on Knowledge and Data Engineering, Vol. 14, No. 3, IEEE Society, 2002.

Appendix: Ranking by Probabilistic Similarity

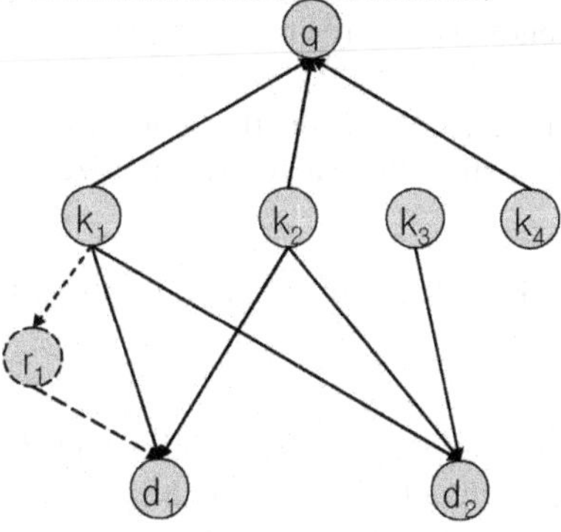

Fig. 10. An example of Bayesian Belief Network

For illustrating our searching and scoring methods, we require the fundamentals of Bayesian belief network. Figure 10 illustrates a simple Bayesian belief network model. In this model, there are nodes k_i ($1 \le i \le 4$), each of which denote the ith index term. The user query q is modeled as a node and linked to the keywords node k_i if the user query contains the ith index term. Nodes in product ontology graph are also modeled as nodes r_1, d_1, d_2, which are pointed to by the keywords nodes if they contain the keywords. In the belief network model, nodes represent random variables, the arcs portray causal relationships between these variables, and the strengths of these causal influences are expressed by conditional probabilities. According to [3], $P(d_j|q)$ is adopted as the similarity of the concept d_j with respect to q, which is computed as

$$P(d_j \mid q) \cong \sum_{\forall k_i \in K} P(d_j \mid k_i) P(q \mid k_i) P(k_i), \text{ where } K \text{ is a set of all keywords} \quad (1)$$

The problem of equation (1) is that it does not consider a related concept, r_1 in Figure 10, in ranking concept d_1. Now we extend equation (1) to incorporate the related concepts in calculating the scores. Let R denotes a set of nodes related to node d_j and containing the given keywords. Considering the score propagation from r to d_j, we can compute $P(d_j \mid q)$ as the following:

$$P(d_j \mid q) \cong \sum_{\forall k_i \in K} P(q \mid k_i) \times \left(P(d_j \mid k_i) + \sum_{\forall r \in R} P(r \mid k_i) \times P(d_j \mid r) \right) \times P(k_i) \quad (2)$$

In equation (2), the score of d_j given query q is determined by not only $P(d_j|k_i)$ – as is in equation (1) - but also $P(d_j|r)$ and $P(r|k_i)$. By $P(d_j|r)$ and $P(r|k_i)$, we denote the causal relationships from r to d_j given keyword k_i. Specifically, the score of r, $P(r|k_i)$, is propagated to d_j by multiplying a propagation ratio $P(d_j|r)$ and added to its original score $P(d_j|k_i)$.

To complete the belief network we need to specify the conditional probabilities, $P(d_j|k_i)$, $P(r|k_i)$, $P(q|k_i)$ and $P(d_j|r)$. Distinct specifications of these probabilities allow the modeling of different ranking strategies. For example, $P(d_j|k_i)$ can be estimated by

$\frac{n_{ij}}{n_i}$, where n_{ij} and n_i denote the number of occurrences of each keyword k_i in d_j and the number of occurrences of k_i in the entire ontology graph, respectively. Alternatively, if we normalize the value by the size of data, $|d_j|$, $P(d_j|k_i)$ can be estimated as $\frac{\frac{n_{ij}}{|d_j|}}{\sum_{d_l \in D} \frac{n_{il}}{|d_l|}}$, where D is the set of concepts in the ontology. $P(r|k_i)$ can be estimated as the same way as $P(d_j|k_i)$ since both r and d_j denote the concepts in the ontology graph. $P(q|k_i)$, on the other hand, can be estimated as *idf* value[3] of term k_i since it denotes the importance of the term in the query.

$P(d_j|r)$ in equation (2) represents the degree of belief on d_j given r. Even though the exact value is not known at the time of ontology construction, it can be estimated by link analysis or can be determined by an administrator. For example, $d_{in,\,r}/r_{out}$, where $d_{in,r}$ is the number of incoming edges of d from r and r_{out} is the number of outgoing edges from r, can be used as such an estimation. This is similar to the PageRank computation in that the amount of score propagation is proportional to the probability of selecting node d from r_{out} related nodes. Note that we can also simulate Naïve Bayesian Classifier if we use $d_{in,\,r}/d_{in}$ instead of $d_{in,\,r}/r_{out}$, where d_{in} is the total number of incoming edges to d. In some cases, $P(d_j|r)$ can be predefined by the administrator depending on the relationship types. For example, we can set the value to 1 for instance relationship from the instance product to the product class and 0 for reverse direction in order to make the relevance of instance products not affected by the keywords of other instances.

```
NaïveAlgorithm(G, k, l, n)
        G : ontology of n instances;
        k : a set of keywords
        l: maximal level of inferences
        n : the number of returned results

        For each node d_j in G, compute P(d_j|k);
        Let S denote the vector : <P(d_1|k), P(d_2|k), ..., P(d_n|k)>;
        Let E denote the n * n vector where each element e_i,j is P(d_i|d_j);
        D=S;
            For i = 1, 2, ..., l
            D= E□D;
            S = S +D;
        End
        Return top-n elements from S
```

Fig. 11. Probabilistic ranking algorithm : NaïveAlgorithm

Given the probabilistic similarity computation defined in equation (2), we need an algorithm that ranks the query results from the ontology databases. We provide a simple ranking algorithm, NaïveAlgorithm, which iteratively approximates the ranks of concepts.

The NaïveAlgorithm is summarized in Figure 11. The algorithm is given as inputs the ontology database *G*, a set of keywords *k*, the number of returned results *n*, and the maximal level of inferences *l*. The maximal level of inferences *l* denotes the degree of inferences (following semantically relevant concepts) that can be applied to each node. Initially, it computes $P(d_j|k)$ for each node d_j ($1 \leq j \leq n$) in the product ontology graph and makes a vector S : $<P(d_1|k), P(d_2|k), \ldots, P(d_n|k)>$. For ease of exposition, we assume $P(d_j|k)$ denotes the result of summing $P(d_j|k_i)$ multiplied by $P(q|k_i)$ for every *i* as equation (1). Then we make a $n \times n$ matrix *E* where each element $e_{i,j}$ is $P(d_i|d_j)$ specified by the administrator or estimated by link analysis (as explained above). By adding $E \times D$ to *S*, we compute the propagated score of nodes denoted in equation (2) after following the semantically relevant concept node. We iterate *E*□*D l* times, where *l* is a user-defined threshold. NaiveAlgorithm is similar to PageRank and HITS in a sense that it iteratively computes instances' score by vector calculation. [16] shows that *S* converges to an equilibrium state, an eigenvector of *E*, when the number of inferences increases arbitrarily. Analogously, our algorithm converges to an equilibrium state, but we limit the maximum number of iterations because it is shown that a relatively small value (about 20) of *l* is sufficient for the vectors to become stable in [16]. Then we can compute the score of every node in a timely manner.

```
NaïveAlgorithm(G, k, l, n)
        G : ontology of n instances;
        k : a set of keywords
        l: maximal level of inferences
        n : the number of returned results

        For each node d_i in G, compute P(d_i|k);
        Let S denote the vector : <P(d_1|k), P(d_2|k), …, P(d_n|k)>;
        Let E denote the n * n vector where each element e_i,j is P(d_i|d_j);
        D=S;
             For i = 1, 2, …, l
             D= E x D;
             S = S +D;
        End
        Return top-n elements from S
```

Fig. 12. Probabilistic ranking algorithm : NaïveAlgorithm

Example 5. Consider a product ontology graph in Figure 9. Given the query "IBM P4 3.0" and *l*=2, let us show how the nodes are ranked by the NaïveAlgorithm algorithm. We set $P(d_i \mid \vec{k})$ to 1 for *d* containing some keywords in *k* and to 0 otherwise. First we sort the nodes according to the subscription above each node and make the score vector *S*. After calculating $P(d_i \mid \vec{k})$ for each node we get <0, 0, 0, 1, 0, 1, 1, 0, 1>. We assume that $P(d_j \mid r, \vec{k}_i)$ is $d_{in,\,r}/d_{in}$ for instance relationships and 1 for the other relationships. Then we make the matrix *E*.

$$E = \begin{bmatrix} 0 & 0 & 0 & 1/2 & 1/2 & 0 & 0 & 0 & 0 \\ 0 & 0 & 0 & 0 & 0 & 1 & 0 & 0 & 0 \\ 0 & 0 & 0 & 0 & 0 & 0 & 1/3 & 1/3 & 1/3 \\ 1 & 0 & 0 & 0 & 0 & 0 & 1 & 0 & 0 \\ 1 & 0 & 0 & 0 & 0 & 0 & 0 & 1 & 0 \\ 0 & 1 & 0 & 0 & 0 & 0 & 0 & 0 & 1 \\ 0 & 0 & 1 & 1 & 0 & 0 & 0 & 0 & 0 \\ 0 & 0 & 1 & 0 & 1 & 0 & 0 & 0 & 0 \\ 0 & 0 & 1 & 0 & 0 & 1 & 0 & 0 & 0 \end{bmatrix}$$

By *E* x *S*, we get *D*,

$$D = \begin{bmatrix} 0 & 0 & 0 & 1/2 & 1/2 & 0 & 0 & 0 & 0 \\ 0 & 0 & 0 & 0 & 0 & 1 & 0 & 0 & 0 \\ 0 & 0 & 0 & 0 & 0 & 0 & 1/3 & 1/3 & 1/3 \\ 1 & 0 & 0 & 0 & 0 & 0 & 1 & 0 & 0 \\ 1 & 0 & 0 & 0 & 0 & 0 & 0 & 1 & 0 \\ 0 & 1 & 0 & 0 & 0 & 0 & 0 & 0 & 1 \\ 0 & 0 & 1 & 1 & 0 & 0 & 0 & 0 & 0 \\ 0 & 0 & 1 & 0 & 1 & 0 & 0 & 0 & 0 \\ 0 & 0 & 1 & 0 & 0 & 1 & 0 & 0 & 0 \end{bmatrix} \times \begin{bmatrix} 0 \\ 0 \\ 0 \\ 1 \\ 0 \\ 1 \\ 1 \\ 0 \\ 1 \end{bmatrix} = \begin{bmatrix} 1/2 \\ 1 \\ 2/3 \\ 1 \\ 0 \\ 1 \\ 1 \\ 0 \\ 1 \end{bmatrix}, \text{ and } S = \begin{bmatrix} 1/2 \\ 1 \\ 2/3 \\ 2 \\ 0 \\ 2 \\ 2 \\ 0 \\ 2 \end{bmatrix}.$$

By *E* x *D* again we get D=[1/2 1 2/3 3/2 1/2 2 5/3 2/3 5/3]^T and S=[1 2 4/3 7/2 1/2 4 11/3 2/3 11/3]^T. Overall ranking should be <6, 7, 9, 4, 2, 3, 1, 8, 5> represented by node numbers. The most relevant product is "IBM G41" represented by node 6. If our intention was to find product classes, the algorithm would return *Notebook Computers* as illustrated in Example 1.

Author Index

Lecture Notes in Computer Science

For information about Vols. 1–4185

please contact your bookseller or Springer

Vol. 4272: P. Havinga, M. Lijding, N. Meratnia, M. Wegdam (Eds.), Smart Sensing and Context. XI, 267 pages. 2006.

Vol. 4270: H. Zha, Z. Pan, H. Thwaites, A.C. Addison, M. Forte (Eds.), Interactive Technologies and Sociotechnical Systems. XVI, 547 pages. 2006.

Vol. 4269: R. State, S. van der Meer, D. O'Sullivan, T. Pfeifer (Eds.), Large Scale Management of Distributed Systems. XIII, 282 pages. 2006.

Vol. 4268: G. Parr, D. Malone, M. Ó Foghlú (Eds.), Autonomic Principles of IP Operations and Management. XIII, 237 pages. 2006.

Vol. 4267: A. Helmy, B. Jennings, L. Murphy, T. Pfeifer (Eds.), Autonomic Management of Mobile Multimedia Services. XIII, 257 pages. 2006.

Vol. 4266: H. Yoshiura, K. Sakurai, K. Rannenberg, Y. Murayama, S. Kawamura (Eds.), Advances in Information and Computer Security. XIII, 438 pages. 2006.

Vol. 4265: N. Lavrač, L. Todorovski, K.P. Jantke (Eds.), Discovery Science. XIV, 384 pages. 2006. (Sublibrary LNAI).

Vol. 4264: J.L. Balcázar, P.M. Long, F. Stephan (Eds.), Algorithmic Learning Theory. XIII, 393 pages. 2006. (Sublibrary LNAI).

Vol. 4263: A. Levi, E. Savas, H. Yenigün, S. Balcisoy, Y. Saygin (Eds.), Computer and Information Sciences – ISCIS 2006. XXIII, 1084 pages. 2006.

Vol. 4260: Z. Liu, J. He (Eds.), Formal Methods and Software Engineering. XII, 778 pages. 2006.

Vol. 4257: I. Richardson, P. Runeson, R. Messnarz (Eds.), Software Process Improvement. XI, 219 pages. 2006.

Vol. 4256: L. Feng, G. Wang, C. Zeng, R. Huang (Eds.), Web Information Systems Engineering – WISE 2006 Workshops. XIV, 320 pages. 2006.

Vol. 4255: K. Aberer, Z. Peng, E.A. Rundensteiner, Y. Zhang, X. Li (Eds.), Web Information Systems Engineering – WISE 2006. XIV, 563 pages. 2006.

Vol. 4254: T. Grust, H. Höpfner, A. Illarramendi, S. Jablonski, M. Mesiti, S. Müller, P.-L. Patranjan, K.-U. Sattler, M. Spiliopoulou (Eds.), Current Trends in Database Technology – EDBT 2006. XXXI, 932 pages. 2006.

Vol. 4253: B. Gabrys, R.J. Howlett, L.C. Jain (Eds.), Knowledge-Based Intelligent Information and Engineering Systems, Part III. XXXII, 1301 pages. 2006. (Sublibrary LNAI).

Vol. 4252: B. Gabrys, R.J. Howlett, L.C. Jain (Eds.), Knowledge-Based Intelligent Information and Engineering Systems, Part II. XXXIII, 1335 pages. 2006. (Sublibrary LNAI).

Vol. 4251: B. Gabrys, R.J. Howlett, L.C. Jain (Eds.), Knowledge-Based Intelligent Information and Engineering Systems, Part I. LXVI, 1297 pages. 2006. (Sublibrary LNAI).

Vol. 4249: L. Goubin, M. Matsui (Eds.), Cryptographic Hardware and Embedded Systems - CHES 2006. XII, 462 pages. 2006.

Vol. 4248: S. Staab, V. Svátek (Eds.), Engineering Knowledge in the Age of the Semantic Web. XIV, 400 pages. 2006. (Sublibrary LNAI).

Vol. 4247: T.-D. Wang, X. Li, S.-H. Chen, X. Wang, H. Abbass, H. Iba, G. Chen, X. Yao (Eds.), Simulated Evolution and Learning. XXI, 940 pages. 2006.

Vol. 4245: A. Kuba, L.G. Nyúl, K. Palágyi (Eds.), Discrete Geometry for Computer Imagery. XIII, 688 pages. 2006.

Vol. 4244: S. Spaccapietra (Ed.), Journal on Data Semantics VII. XI, 267 pages. 2006.

Vol. 4243: T. Yakhno, E.J. Neuhold (Eds.), Advances in Information Systems. XIII, 420 pages. 2006.

Vol. 4241: R.R. Beichel, M. Sonka (Eds.), Computer Vision Approaches to Medical Image Analysis. XI, 262 pages. 2006.

Vol. 4239: H.Y. Youn, M. Kim, H. Morikawa (Eds.), Ubiquitous Computing Systems. XVI, 548 pages. 2006.

Vol. 4238: Y.-T. Kim, M. Takano (Eds.), Management of Convergence Networks and Services. XVIII, 605 pages. 2006.

Vol. 4237: H. Leitold, E. Markatos (Eds.), Communications and Multimedia Security. XII, 253 pages. 2006.

Vol. 4236: L. Breveglieri, I. Koren, D. Naccache, J.-P. Seifert (Eds.), Fault Diagnosis and Tolerance in Cryptography. XIII, 253 pages. 2006.

Vol. 4234: I. King, J. Wang, L. Chan, D. Wang (Eds.), Neural Information Processing, Part III. XXII, 1227 pages. 2006.

Vol. 4233: I. King, J. Wang, L. Chan, D. Wang (Eds.), Neural Information Processing, Part II. XXII, 1203 pages. 2006.

Vol. 4232: I. King, J. Wang, L. Chan, D. Wang (Eds.), Neural Information Processing, Part I. XLVI, 1153 pages. 2006.

Vol. 4229: E. Najm, J.F. Pradat-Peyre, V.V. Donzeau-Gouge (Eds.), Formal Techniques for Networked and Distributed Systems - FORTE 2006. X, 486 pages. 2006.

Vol. 4228: D.E. Lightfoot, C.A. Szyperski (Eds.), Modular Programming Languages. X, 415 pages. 2006.

Vol. 4227: W. Nejdl, K. Tochtermann (Eds.), Innovative Approaches for Learning and Knowledge Sharing. XVII, 721 pages. 2006.

Vol. 4225: J.F. Martínez-Trinidad, J.A. Carrasco Ochoa, J. Kittler (Eds.), Progress in Pattern Recognition, Image Analysis and Applications. XIX, 995 pages. 2006.

Vol. 4224: E. Corchado, H. Yin, V. Botti, C. Fyfe (Eds.), Intelligent Data Engineering and Automated Learning – IDEAL 2006. XXVII, 1447 pages. 2006.

Vol. 4223: L. Wang, L. Jiao, G. Shi, X. Li, J. Liu (Eds.), Fuzzy Systems and Knowledge Discovery. XXVIII, 1335 pages. 2006. (Sublibrary LNAI).

Vol. 4222: L. Jiao, L. Wang, X. Gao, J. Liu, F. Wu (Eds.), Advances in Natural Computation, Part II. XLII, 998 pages. 2006.

Vol. 4221: L. Jiao, L. Wang, X. Gao, J. Liu, F. Wu (Eds.), Advances in Natural Computation, Part I. XLI, 992 pages. 2006.

Vol. 4219: D. Zamboni, C. Kruegel (Eds.), Recent Advances in Intrusion Detection. XII, 331 pages. 2006.

Vol. 4218: S. Graf, W. Zhang (Eds.), Automated Technology for Verification and Analysis. XIV, 540 pages. 2006.

Vol. 4217: P. Cuenca, L. Orozco-Barbosa (Eds.), Personal Wireless Communications. XV, 532 pages. 2006.

Vol. 4216: M.R. Berthold, R. Glen, I. Fischer (Eds.), Computational Life Sciences II. XIII, 269 pages. 2006. (Sublibrary LNBI).

Vol. 4215: D.W. Embley, A. Olivé, S. Ram (Eds.), Conceptual Modeling - ER 2006. XVI, 590 pages. 2006.

Vol. 4213: J. Fürnkranz, T. Scheffer, M. Spiliopoulou (Eds.), Knowledge Discovery in Databases: PKDD 2006. XXII, 660 pages. 2006. (Sublibrary LNAI).

Vol. 4212: J. Fürnkranz, T. Scheffer, M. Spiliopoulou (Eds.), Machine Learning: ECML 2006. XXIII, 851 pages. 2006. (Sublibrary LNAI).

Vol. 4211: P. Vogt, Y. Sugita, E. Tuci, C. Nehaniv (Eds.), Symbol Grounding and Beyond. VIII, 237 pages. 2006. (Sublibrary LNAI).

Vol. 4210: C. Priami (Ed.), Computational Methods in Systems Biology. X, 323 pages. 2006. (Sublibrary LNBI).

Vol. 4209: F. Crestani, P. Ferragina, M. Sanderson (Eds.), String Processing and Information Retrieval. XIV, 367 pages. 2006.

Vol. 4208: M. Gerndt, D. Kranzlmüller (Eds.), High Performance Computing and Communications. XXII, 938 pages. 2006.

Vol. 4207: Z. Ésik (Ed.), Computer Science Logic. XII, 627 pages. 2006.

Vol. 4206: P. Dourish, A. Friday (Eds.), UbiComp 2006: Ubiquitous Computing. XIX, 526 pages. 2006.

Vol. 4205: G. Bourque, N. El-Mabrouk (Eds.), Comparative Genomics. X, 231 pages. 2006. (Sublibrary LNBI).

Vol. 4204: F. Benhamou (Ed.), Principles and Practice of Constraint Programming - CP 2006. XVIII, 774 pages. 2006.

Vol. 4203: F. Esposito, Z.W. Raś, D. Malerba, G. Semeraro (Eds.), Foundations of Intelligent Systems. XVIII, 767 pages. 2006. (Sublibrary LNAI).

Vol. 4202: E. Asarin, P. Bouyer (Eds.), Formal Modeling and Analysis of Timed Systems. XI, 369 pages. 2006.

Vol. 4201: Y. Sakakibara, S. Kobayashi, K. Sato, T. Nishino, E. Tomita (Eds.), Grammatical Inference: Algorithms and Applications. XII, 359 pages. 2006. (Sublibrary LNAI).

Vol. 4200: I.F.C. Smith (Ed.), Intelligent Computing in Engineering and Architecture. XIII, 692 pages. 2006. (Sublibrary LNAI).

Vol. 4199: O. Nierstrasz, J. Whittle, D. Harel, G. Reggio (Eds.), Model Driven Engineering Languages and Systems. XVI, 798 pages. 2006.

Vol. 4198: O. Nasraoui, O. Zaiane, M. Spiliopoulou, B. Mobasher, B. Masand, P. Yu (Eds.), Advances in Web Minding and Web Usage Analysis. IX, 177 pages. 2006. (Sublibrary LNAI).

Vol. 4197: M. Raubal, H.J. Miller, A.U. Frank, M.F. Goodchild (Eds.), Geographic, Information Science. XIII, 419 pages. 2006.

Vol. 4196: K. Fischer, I.J. Timm, E. André, N. Zhong (Eds.), Multiagent System Technologies. X, 185 pages. 2006. (Sublibrary LNAI).

Vol. 4195: D. Gaiti, G. Pujolle, E. Al-Shaer, K. Calvert, S. Dobson, G. Leduc, O. Martikainen (Eds.), Autonomic Networking. IX, 316 pages. 2006.

Vol. 4194: V.G. Ganzha, E.W. Mayr, E.V. Vorozhtsov (Eds.), Computer Algebra in Scientific Computing. XI, 313 pages. 2006.

Vol. 4193: T.P. Runarsson, H.-G. Beyer, E. Burke, J.J. Merelo-Guervós, L.D. Whitley, X. Yao (Eds.), Parallel Problem Solving from Nature - PPSN IX. XIX, 1061 pages. 2006.

Vol. 4192: B. Mohr, J.L. Träff, J. Worringen, J. Dongarra (Eds.), Recent Advances in Parallel Virtual Machine and Message Passing Interface. XVI, 414 pages. 2006.

Vol. 4191: R. Larsen, M. Nielsen, J. Sporring (Eds.), Medical Image Computing and Computer-Assisted Intervention – MICCAI 2006, Part II. XXXVIII, 981 pages. 2006.

Vol. 4190: R. Larsen, M. Nielsen, J. Sporring (Eds.), Medical Image Computing and Computer-Assisted Intervention – MICCAI 2006, Part I. XXXVVIII, 949 pages. 2006.

Vol. 4189: D. Gollmann, J. Meier, A. Sabelfeld (Eds.), Computer Security – ESORICS 2006. XI, 548 pages. 2006.

Vol. 4188: P. Sojka, I. Kopeček, K. Pala (Eds.), Text, Speech and Dialogue. XV, 721 pages. 2006. (Sublibrary LNAI).

Vol. 4187: J.J. Alferes, J. Bailey, W. May, U. Schwertel (Eds.), Principles and Practice of Semantic Web Reasoning. XI, 277 pages. 2006.

Vol. 4186: C. Jesshope, C. Egan (Eds.), Advances in Computer Systems Architecture. XIV, 605 pages. 2006.